PERSPECTIVES ON THE FAMILY:
History, Class, and Feminism

PERSPECTIVES ON THE FAMILY
History, Class, and Feminism

Christopher Carlson
Cornell College

Wadsworth Publishing Company
Belmont, California
A Division of Wadsworth, Inc.

Sociology Editor: Serina Beauparlant
Editorial Assistant: Marla Nowick
Production: Sara Hunsaker, ExLibris
Print Buyer: Martha Branch
Designer: Gary Head, adapted by Sara Hunsaker
Copy Editor: Pam Howell Fischer
Compositor: Carlisle Communications
Cover: Vargas/Williams/Design

Printed in the United States of America

1 2 3 4 5 6 7 8 9 10 — 94 93 92 91 90

Library of Congress Cataloging-in-Publication Data

Perspectives on the family: history, class, and feminism /
    Christopher Carlson, [editor].
        p.   cm.
    ISBN 0-534-12576-X
    1. Family—United States. I. Carlson, Christopher Dean.

HQ536.P48 1989
306.85′0973—dc20   89–16604
                        CIP

For Jane Risé

Preface

The 1970s and 1980s were remarkably productive and exciting years for those interested in the sociology of the family. During this time, scholars explored new areas of inquiry, asked new questions about subjects of continuing interest, and reexamined the research findings of previous decades. Research on the family in the 1990s promises to be no less provocative or plentiful.

For those of us teaching the sociology of the family, incorporating the results of this new scholarship into our courses is a continuing and challenging endeavor. In this collection of readings, I have attempted to make a contribution to this integrative task. I have done so by focusing on three diverse but interrelated perspectives represented in current research on the family. These perspectives are: history, class, and feminism. Each chapter includes readings representative of these three perspectives.

Briefly, the readings representing the perspective of history reflect the recognition that the family is not an unchanging entity in either its form or function, and they examine the development of specific family patterns over time. The readings representing the perspective of social class focus on variations in family patterns associated with socioeconomic status. Finally, the readings representing the perspective of feminism examine the impact of gender as a socially constructed category on the organization and experience of family life.

The book begins with a general introductory chapter that describes the three perspectives in greater detail and explains their relevance to the study of the family. This introduction is followed by seven chapters, each focusing on a substantive area in the study of the family. I have not attempted to be exhaustive in the substantive areas that I have chosen to include or in the coverage of specific topics within each chapter. The study of the family now includes so many subfields covering such a vast array of topics that an attempt to be comprehensive would necessarily have been unsuccessful. I have chosen instead to include chapters on substantive areas that are likely to be central to any course on the family. I selected the readings for each chapter to illustrate the importance of the three perspectives in the study of specific topics.

Each chapter includes an introduction that discusses some important research findings and issues in the area covered. In these introductions, I have attempted to provide students with information that will help them place the reading selections in the chapters in broader context. For example, the introduction to Chapter Three, Dating and Mate Choice, discusses the history of courtship, theories of mate selection, and homogamy in mate choice. The introduction to Chapter Four, Love, Marriage, and Intimate Relationships, discusses the concept of marital adjustment and the issue of power in intimate relationships. Each introduction ends with a discussion of how the readings included in the chapter are related to these and other research findings and issues.

The selections included in this reader come from a variety of sources. Most are from professional research journals such as *Social Problems, Journal of Marriage and the Family, Signs, Sex Roles,* and *Journal of Family History,* to name a few. There are also several selections from books, such as Lillian Rubin's *Worlds of Pain* and Susan Strasser's *Never Done.* I have attempted to include readings that students will find both challenging and interesting. I have assumed that students in upper-level sociology courses have had sufficient introduction to research methods to allow them to manage readings with data analysis. Although students may require guidance in reading some of the selections, they should not be overwhelmed by any of them.

This book can be used in several ways in courses on the sociology of the family. For those who use textbooks, the selections in each chapter will provide students with examples of research in areas covered by text chapters or will allow students to investigate topics omitted or covered only briefly in their texts. The selections may also illustrate viewpoints on specific topics not found in a particular text. In addition, the selections lend themselves to provoking class discussions and developing paper and research topics. For those who use a set of monographs as an alternative to a textbook, the book can serve similar purposes. However, it can also serve a more integral function by filling in the gaps often left by a particular set of monographs. In this case, the book can link the various parts of the course together and provide a foundation on which to build the course. I hope that the introductions to each chapter will make this book particularly useful for those who do not use textbooks.

Although the organization of the book is similar to the organization of many textbooks, instructors can easily recombine the selections to suit their own needs. For example, several of the selections on the history of the family could be added to the selections in Chapter Two to form an expanded section on the emergence of the modern family. "Selling Mrs. Consumer" by Susan Strasser and "Marriage" by Robert and Helen Lynd could be used in this way. As another example, several selections on class differences in family life could be combined to complement a text chapter on this topic. Lillian Rubin's "Marriage: The

Dream and the Reality—The Middle Years" and Melvin Kohn's "The Effects of Social Class on Parental Values and Practices" would be useful for this purpose. Certainly, many other combinations are possible.

Many people have made contributions to this book, and I would like to express my appreciation to them. At Wadsworth, sociology editor Sheryl Fullerton helped me develop my initial ideas for the book and urged me to pursue them. Serina Beauparlant took over the book when Sheryl moved on to become executive editor for Wadsworth and saw the project through to its completion. I thank both of them for their skillful guidance and words of encouragement. Sara Hunsaker was in charge of production and competently steered the book through the final stages to publication. I enjoyed working with her and appreciated her politely but firmly established deadlines. Pam Fischer did the copyediting. It was a pleasure to observe the results her fine hand, and this book is much improved because of her efforts. My appreciation also goes to those who reviewed the manuscript for Wadsworth: Kathleen Blee, University of Kentucky; Pamela Hewitt, University of Northern Colorado; Rachel Kahn-Hut, San Francisco State University; David Klein, University of Notre Dame; Ross Klein, Memorial University; David Lee, California State University, Sacramento; Gary R. Lee, University of Florida; Boyd Rollins, University of Utah; Ruth Sidel, Hunter College. Although I was unable to incorporate all of their many excellent suggestions for improvement, I am sure that the book is much better because of the careful and critical examination they gave it.

I would also like to thank Dennis Damon Moore, Dean of Cornell College, for his generous support at a very crucial time in my work on this book. He made a very difficult year a little easier. Finally, I wish to extend special thanks to Richard Peterson and Charlotte Vaughan of the sociology department at Cornell. They have been an unfailing source of encouragement and counsel throughout my work on this book and my career at Cornell. I am fortunate indeed to have them as colleagues and as friends.

Contents

Chapter 4   Love, Marriage, and Intimate Relationships   133

Chapter 5   Paid Work and Family Work   231

Chapter 6   Fertility and Childbirth   295

Chapter 7   Child Rearing and Parenthood   365

1

Three Perspectives on the Family

In 1949, anthropologist George Murdock defined the family as "a group characterized by common residence, economic cooperation, and reproduction." He went on to suggest that the family "includes adults of both sexes, at least two of whom maintain a socially approved sexual relationship, with one or more children, own or adopted, of the sexually cohabiting pair." In the 1950s, this definition did not generate much controversy. The media were filled with images of happily married suburban couples and their children, and many American families conformed or aspired to this ideal. However, in the following decades, sociologists began to recognize the diversity among American families, calling into question the usefulness of Murdock's definition. Contributing to this recognition were a series of important changes in the family. For example, in the 1960s the percentages of single-parent families, couples choosing to remain childless, and unmarried couples living together all began to increase substantially. The divorce rate also began to rise, and the marriage rate began to decline. Some individuals began to experiment with communal forms of family life, and the gay and lesbian movements called attention to the fact that not all couples were heterosexual.

Most families continue to conform to many or all of the characteristics included in Murdock's definition. By present estimates, for example, approximately 90 percent of American men and women will marry at some point in their lifetimes, and only about 10 percent of American women will remain childless. Nevertheless, defining the family as a "fixed, unchanging, and singular entity" is clearly inadequate for capturing the variety manifested in the American family (Glenn, 1987:349). Instead, it is necessary to conceptualize the family more broadly, and it has become the task of the sociology of the family to explore the multiple and changing ways in which people arrange their sexual, reproductive, emotional, and domestic lives. As a result, the "family" has become a sensitizing concept, directing our attention to the study of specific phenomena, rather than a precise term telling us in advance what we will find.

Three perspectives have proven useful as sociologists have begun to explore diversity and change in American family life. These are the perspectives of history, class, and feminism. Each is an alternative way of examining the family and calls attention to aspects that escape the view of other perspectives. Just as viewing an object from a new angle calls attention to features that have gone unnoticed or unseen, the perspectives of history, class, and feminism provide different angles from which to view the family. Together they contribute to a comprehensive understanding of contemporary family patterns. This chapter describes the three perspectives and explains their relevance to the study of the family. Subsequent chapters illustrate the utility of the three perspectives in understanding various facets of family life.

History

The rapid changes in the family since the 1950s have contributed to a widespread belief that the family is in the process of dramatic transformation. However, as profound as these changes are, they are not without precedent. A series of changes in the structure, functions, demographic characteristics, and internal dynamics of the American family have taken place in the past three centuries (Mintz and Kellog, 1988:xiv). Contemporary changes in the family must be placed in this historical context if we are to appreciate their magnitude and understand their significance.

Prior to the 1970s the American family was virtually ignored as a subject of historical inquiry. With the exceptions of Arthur Calhoun's (1917) *A Social History of the American Family* and Edmund Morgan's (1966) *The Puritan Family,* those seeking the history of the American family would have found the record virtually bare. However, beginning with some notable studies of the family in colonial New England (Demos, 1970; Greven, 1970), interest in and research on the family among historians grew rapidly (Gordon, 1978:5). Consequently, family history is now a recognized and thriving field of study.

Several factors help explain the explosion of interest in the history of the family. First, the dramatic changes in the family itself drew the attention of scholars to the process of family change and demonstrated that the family is as much a part of the historical process as are other institutions (Mintz and Kellog, 1988:xiv). Second, the growth of the field of social history in the 1960s focused attention on the lives of common people rather than on the lives of those playing key roles in great events (Gordon, 1978:1). Social historians seek to discover the meaning of societal changes for ordinary individuals, as well as the role of ordinary individuals in the process of social change. This emphasis led to research in such areas as labor movements, migration, social mobility, slavery, and eventually the family. A third reason for the increase in research in family history was the development of some innovative methodological techniques (Gordon,

1978:3). In the absence of traditional sources, social historians have found it necessary to exploit new types of data to illuminate the lives of people for whom few written records exist. For example, the use of birth, death, and marriage records has allowed historians to reconstruct the typical life course for individuals at different times. Similarly, census data have allowed historians to examine the composition of households in communities in various historical periods. In many cases, the computer has expedited the analysis of these new data sources.

Early studies of the history of the family promptly discredited many preconceptions concerning the family in past times. According to the "traditional view," industrialization and urbanization in the nineteenth and early twentieth centuries were responsible for a number of drastic changes in the family (Seward, 1978:27). For example, many scholars maintained that households in preindustrial America often included extended kin and that industrialization was responsible for a decline in the importance of kinship ties. However, research shows conclusively that extended family households were no more common in the past than they are today. In fact, historians have discovered a remarkable stability in household structure over time. As another example, we now know that the average age at marriage actually declined throughout most of the twentieth century rather than rising as many believed. In fact, teenage brides and grooms were probably more common in 1960 than in either 1860 or 1760. Other changes, such as the increasing importance of romantic love as a basis for marriage and declines in fertility rates, actually preceded industrialization.

As a result of these and many other discoveries, we have begun to develop an understanding of the complexity of the process of social change in the American family. It is now clear that change in the family is a continuous process and that no single development such as industrialization can account for the multitude of changes that have taken place. Although economic changes associated with industrialization were a potent force in bringing about alterations in family patterns, many other developments have contributed to family change. Some scholars have broadened their focus to examine the impact of modernization on the family (e.g., Hareven, 1976; Shorter, 1975; Wells, 1978)—a process more encompassing than industrialization. Modernization refers to a set of societal changes occurring over several centuries in Western Europe and North America, including the development of market economies, the emergence of political democracies, and an increasing pace of technological and scientific change. These societal changes were associated with an emphasis on the values of personal freedom and autonomy. According to advocates of modernization theory, these developments help explain changes in the family that occurred well before industrialization. Other scholars have narrowed their focus to the impact of limited factors or short-range changes such as economic fluctuations, the availability of land, and death rates (e.g., Elder, 1974; Greven, 1970; Uhlenberg, 1980).

Recent research has also demonstrated that family change does not take place evenly. Some groups adopt new patterns long before others, so at any one time a society will be composed of a diversity of families rather than a single family type. Similarly, some groups may change in one aspect of their family behavior but remain unchanged in other aspects, so families will contain a mix of old and new characteristics. It is also clear that many developments have different effects on some groups than on others. For example, the separation of some productive labor from the home in the nineteenth century affected both middle- and working-class families, but in different ways. Therefore, we now understand that the pathways of family change are diverse and that multiple and even contradictory directions of change characterize the history of the American family (Elder, 1981:499).

When historians suggest that one reason to study the past is to better understand the present, they mean that we can appreciate the distinguishing features of our own times only by contrasting them with the characteristics of the past (Demos, 1986:x). In the process of discovering the differences and similarities between our own lives and the lives of men and women of past times, we gain an increased understanding of what is unique about our own experience. The importance of placing the present in historical context is well illustrated in the study of the family. Precisely because current patterns of family life are so familiar, viewing them from the perspective of history helps us appreciate their distinctiveness.

Class

Even the most casual observer of American life is aware of the inequalities existing between individuals in our society. The gulf that divides the bottom fifth of the population, which receives less than 5 percent of the total of all income and wages, and the top fifth, which receives nearly 45 percent, is a tremendous one. Even between these two extremes, however, Americans are divided into groups whose life conditions vary substantially. These differences extend beyond income to include access to many other resources and benefits, such as health care, education, and housing.

Although inequality is an important feature of American society, the study of inequality does not have a long history in American sociology. Some sociologists did recognize the importance of this topic earlier in the century, but the first textbook dealing with the subject did not appear until the 1950s. According to Lucille Duberman (1976:3), several factors accounted for the failure of sociologists to address this topic. First, the United States was a land of expanding opportunities with a steadily increasing standard of living. Second, most people believed that these opportunities were available to everyone. Third, many Americans were reluctant to admit that their society contained the same inequalities that pervaded other societies. Although the Depression of the 1930s temporarily made many people aware of the existence of inequality, the immediate postwar years witnessed the return of prosperity. The percentage of the American population with a middle-class standard of living doubled between the late 1920s and the early 1950s, rising from 30 to 60 percent (Skolnick, 1987:154). As a result, concern with inequality again became less prevalent.

However, in the 1960s public attention began to focus on the continuing disparities of wealth in the United States. In *The Other America* (1963), Michael

Harrington estimated that between thirty and forty million people were living in poverty, and he examined the factors responsible for the existence of this deprivation amidst general prosperity. Other authors began to call attention to the continuing divisions between middle- and working-class Americans (e.g., Berger, 1960; Lemasters, 1975; Rubin, 1976). More recently, the disturbing trend toward increasing inequality has been noted (Skolnick, 1987:155). Since the late 1970s the distribution of income has begun to resemble an hourglass, with a shrinking middle and expanding upper and lower section, rather than a diamond, with a large and expanding middle group. Debate exists about the sources and eventual outcome of this development, but clearly disparities in wealth are at least temporarily increasing.

A central concept in the study of inequality is social class. Although sociologists disagree about the precise definition of social class, generally it refers to the hierarchical division of societies into groups sharing similar life conditions. Sociologists have focused on three interdependent dimensions of inequality in their discussions of social class—economic, prestige, and power (Vanfossen, 1979:13–15). The economic dimension of inequality refers to the distribution of wealth and income as a result of the roles of groups in the economic system. For many sociologists, economic inequality is the most important component of social class. The prestige dimension refers to the respect which groups are granted by others. Prestige has many sources, including occupation, lifestyle, and group affiliations. The power dimension refers to the ability of a group to achieve its goals despite opposition from other groups. The examination of inequalities of power focuses on access to the political decision-making process and the distribution of authority in the workplace and community.

Groups that share benefits (or lack benefits) across these dimensions compose social classes (Rossides, 1976:23). Sociologists commonly distinguish five social classes in the United States (Robertson, 1987:271). At the top is a small upper class, perhaps 2 to 3 percent of the population, composed of individuals of great wealth. These are the owners and executives of large businesses and corporations. Below this elite group is the upper-middle class, comprising 10 to 15 percent of the population, made up of professionals, such as doctors and lawyers, upper-level managers, and high government officials. The lower-middle class is composed of lower-level professionals, such as teachers and nurses, office workers, farmers, and small business owners. This group comprises 30 to 35 percent of the population. The largest group is the working class, 40 to 45 percent of the population, composed of factory workers, skilled craftspeople, and service workers. At the bottom is a lower class composed of the unemployed and very poorly paid workers, such as domestic, restaurant, and hospital workers. Twenty to twenty-five percent of the population is in this group.

In general, movement from one of these five social classes to another involves simultaneous movement on the three dimensions of inequality. However, the lines between social classes are blurred because a segment of a social class may be higher on one dimension of inequality than a segment of the class immediately above it. For example, many members of the working class have higher annual incomes than members of the lower-middle class, although their occupations do not carry the same degree of prestige as do middle-class occupations. Variations on these dimensions also create differences within social classes. For example, among the upper class, the newly rich do not have the same prestige as do those with inherited wealth.

Although the lines between social classes are not hard and fast, important differences do exist between groups variously placed in the stratification system. Groups with similar occupations, education levels, and incomes develop distinctive attitudes, values, and lifestyles (Duberman, 1976:116). Collectively, these characteristics define class cultures that divide Americans into distinctive subgroups (Collins, 1988:39). Class cultures are evident in the realm of the family. Research has shown class differences in virtually all areas of family life, including child-rearing patterns, husband/wife relationships, and relationships with extended kin, to name just a few. As a result, Americans experience the family in different ways, depending on their location in the class structure.

The study of the impact of social class on the family has been complicated in recent years by the increase in the percentage of women working outside the home. The increase has been most dramatic for married women, more than half of whom are now employed. In the past, studies of social class have ignored the occupations of married women, focusing instead on the class position of husbands. However, subsuming the class position of women under that of their husbands is inadequate, particularly when the occupations of husbands and wives differ significantly in prestige and pay. Research suggests, for example, that when one spouse holds a working-class job and the other holds a middle-class job, couples frequently disagree on the identification of their class position (Hiller and Philliber, 1986). Other research suggests that husbands and wives in mixed-class marriages have conflicts over the values and norms of family life (Lemasters, 1975; Halle, 1984). Although sociologists are just beginning to take these issues into account, the differing class positions of husbands and wives are likely to become of increasing importance in the future. As Randall Collins (1988:29) asserts, "it is foolish to assume males are directly affected by class conditions where they work, but women are affected only indirectly through their male relatives." Therefore, social class will continue to be an important, although increasingly complex, perspective on the family.

Feminism

The feminist movement in the United States had its beginning in the social-reform movements of the nineteenth century. American women played active, although often subordinate, roles in the campaign to abolish slavery, the temperance movement, and many other crusades to improve the lot of the exploited and downtrodden. Galvanized by their participation in these movements, women started to organize to improve their own status, beginning with the Seneca Falls Declaration of Rights of Women in 1848, which called for a comprehensive extension of equal economic, legal, and political rights to women (Degler, 1980:190). However, the early feminist movement was consumed with a prolonged and exhausting campaign for women's suffrage. The right to vote was finally won in 1920 after seven decades of struggle against intense opposition.

Although feminism certainly did not disappear following the suffrage victory, the organized feminist movement temporarily collapsed after the ratification of the Nineteenth Amendment. Several factors explain this collapse, among them the length of the struggle for the vote itself and the fragility of the coalition that eventually secured the victory. Another important factor was the high hopes that supporters of suffrage held for change once the vote was won. Many expected dramatic improvements in the status of women, seeing suffrage as the means to political power women had lacked. In fact, few advances in the status of women occurred in the 1920s, and then the Depression and World War II drew attention away from the continuing subordination of women.

The reemergence of the feminist movement followed in the wake of the civil rights movement and student protests of the 1960s. Like their sisters in the nineteenth century, women again played important roles in these liberation movements, and in the process they began to rediscover the injustice of their own situation (Skolnick, 1987:403). The second stage of feminism did not concentrate its energies on a single issue but instead began a wide-ranging struggle against women's subordination in all phases of contemporary life. Occupational segregation, wage discrimination, reproductive rights, violence against women, sexual harassment, pornography, and discriminatory marriage and divorce laws were all subjects of attention and action in the 1970s and 1980s. The vigorous, although unsuccessful, struggle for the passage of the Equal Rights Amendment, which would have eliminated all laws that discriminated on the basis of sex, symbolized the broad scope of contemporary feminism.

The resurgence of feminism has also had an impact on all academic disciplines, from political science to physics, from literature to sociology. Encouraged by the rapidly expanding women's movement, scholars began to search their disciplines for answers to questions about the status and experiences of women. In doing so, they discovered that women had been all but invisible in the academic world, both as producers of knowledge and as subjects of study. In fact, most knowledge has been produced by men, who have dominated most fields of intellectual endeavor. Because the experiences of men and women differ, it is not surprising that men have asked questions that reflect their own concerns and points of view. As a result scholarship in all disciplines produced knowledge that was incomplete because it omitted the interests of women and examined the experiences of women from the vantage point of men (Spender, 1981:15).

Feminist scholarship seeks to bring what women know and what women are into all forms of intellectual inquiry (Gould, 1980:459). One result of this inclusion has been attention to many neglected aspects of women's experience and the gradual filling in of the huge gaps in our knowledge created by the myopia of the past. Another result has been the demonstration of the importance of "gender" as a category of analysis. *Gender* does not refer to the biological differences between males and females but to the differences between men and women created and sustained by the organization of particular societies (Gould, 1980:462; Stacey and Thorne, 1985:307). Feminist scholars have begun to explore the fundamental ways in which gender, as a socially constructed category, shapes our experience and behavior.

The reorienting effect of feminism is perhaps nowhere better illustrated than in the sociology of the family. Feminist scholars have asked new questions, opened up new areas of inquiry, and developed new ways of thinking about family experience. Unlike many other fields, family sociology has in the past given considerable attention to the lives of women. In fact, women became so closely identified with the family that the study of women was basically contained within this subfield of the discipline. However, as Evelyn Glenn (1987:349) points out, equating women and the family is quite different from making women's experience a central focus in the analysis of the family or from understanding how gender organizes family experience. According to Glenn, the sociological study of the family traditionally defined as inevitable and immutable, the position of women as housewives and mothers, the outcome of both biological characteristics and unchanging social needs. Further, in this view, the family was not a collection of individuals with different experiences, resources, and needs, but a group based on unitary interests and consensus. As a result, women's roles were not analyzed as outcomes of specific historical developments and social arrangements, and women's experience of these roles was not deemed worthy of analysis.

In contrast, a feminist perspective requires that women's (and men's) position in the family and the impact of specific family arrangements on the lives of women and men be made the focus of analysis. This approach has many and far-reaching consequences. For example, conceptualizing men's and women's roles in the family as the product of specific social arrangements allows one to discover the diversity of family forms and opens the way for including cohabiting couples, childlessness, and single-parent households in the study of the family. This approach also allows one to see the roles of men and women in the family as social constructions rather than as unchanging or natural and opens the way to an examination of variation in these roles. Similarly, focusing on family members as individuals allows one to discover the different ways in which men and women have experienced the family and allows one to consider such previously ignored topics as housework, widowhood, and power and inequality in family relationships (Komarovsky, 1988:590; Glenn, 1987:362)

An extended example may help clarify the reorienting effect of feminist scholarship on the study of the family. Prior to the 1960s, many sociologists considered the division of labor in the family between men as breadwinners and women as child rearers and homemakers to be ideally suited for a society in which paid work and the family had become largely differentiated. Although some gave passing recognition to the strains created for women by a division of labor that isolated them from the occupational world, the experiences of women in the family were basically ignored because of the presumed functionality of these gender roles (Komarovsky, 1988:586). However, when feminist scholars began to examine the lives of women as wives and mothers, many important discoveries resulted. For example, in *The Future of Marriage* (1982), Jessie Bernard compared the scores of married men and married women on various measures of mental and physical well-being. These measures suggested that married men were better off than married women. After analyzing the source of these differences, Bernard concluded that isolation in the home as housewives was quite harmful to many women. This conclusion led her to state that "there are two marriages, then, in every marital union. And. . . his is better than hers" (p. 14).

Therefore, the feminist perspective has changed the way sociologists approach the family and has opened a vast array of new and important topics for investigation. Although relatively new, it has generated a great deal of research and invigorated the study of the family. By placing women at the center of analysis, this new perspective has added an important new dimension to our understanding of the family.

Readings

The sociology of the family includes a large number of subfields, and research in each of these many areas is voluminous. This book does not attempt to be exhaustive, either in the range of the topics it covers or in its presentation of research findings. Instead, it aims to provide an introduction to several key areas in the sociology of the family, while incorporating the three perspectives of history, class, and feminism. The book begins with an examination of some changes that took place in the nineteenth and early twentieth centuries that were crucial in shaping contemporary family life. Subsequent chapters examine dating and mate choice, marriage and intimate relationships, the division of paid work and family work, fertility and childbirth, child rearing and parenthood, and divorce.

Each chapter consists of an introduction and several readings drawn from a variety of research journals and monographs. The introductions provide a brief overview of some important issues and research findings in the area and describe the readings that follow. The readings either explore the issues raised in the introductions or pursue some related lines of inquiry. In most cases, the readings report the results of recent research in an area. Although some of the selections presenting historical perspectives are less recent, all are enduring contributions to the sociology of the family.

The readings in each chapter include the three perspectives of history, class, and feminism. However, it is important to recognize at the outset that these perspectives are not mutually exclusive. Instead, they are complementary and often combine in various ways. For example, an historical approach may focus on class differences among families. Similarly, a feminist approach may focus on the historical experience of women or be attentive to the differences in women's experiences by class (or both). Therefore, although some readings may more clearly represent one of the perspectives than another, many other readings include more than a single perspective. In fact, it is the importance of incorporating all three of these perspectives in the study of the family that each chapter of this book demonstrates. Together, the three perspectives allow us to understand the diverse and changing relationships of individuals in families.

References

Berger, Bennett. 1960. *Working-Class Suburb*. Berkeley: University of California Press.

Bernard, Jessie. 1982. *The Future of Marriage*. 1982 Edition. New Haven, Conn.: Yale University Press.

Calhoun, Arthur Wallace. 1917. *A Social History of the American Family*. Cleveland: Arthur H. Clark.

Collins, Randall. 1988. "Women and Men in the Class Structure." *Journal of Family Issues* 9:27–50.

Degler, Carl. 1980. *At Odds: Women and the Family in America from the Revolution to the Present*. New York: Oxford University Press.

Demos, John. 1970. *A Little Commonwealth: Family Life in Plymouth Colony*. New York: Oxford University Press.

Demos, John. 1986. *Past, Present, and Personal: The Family and the Life Course in American History*. New York: Oxford University Press.

Duberman, Lucille. 1976. *Social Inequality: Caste and Class in America*. Philadelphia: Lippincott.

Elder, Glen H., Jr. 1974. *Children of the Great Depression*. Chicago: University of Chicago Press.

————. 1981. "History and the Family: The Discovery of Complexity." *Journal of Marriage and the Family* 43:489–518.

Glenn, Evelyn Nakano. 1987. "Gender and the Family." In *Analyzing Gender: A Handbook of Social Science Research,* edited by Beth B. Hess and Myra Marx Ferree, 348–80. Newbury Park, Calif.: Sage.

Gordon, Michael. 1978. "Introduction." In *The American Family in Social-Historical Perspective,* 2d ed., edited by Michael Gordon, 1–15. New York: St. Martin's Press.

Gould, Meredith. 1980. "The New Sociology." *Signs* 5:459–67.

Greven, Phillip J., Jr. 1970. *Four Generations: Population, Land, and the Family in Colonial Andover*. Ithaca, N.Y.: Cornell University Press.

Halle, David. 1984. *America's Working Man: Work, Home, and Politics among Blue-Collar Property Owners*. Chicago: University of Chicago Press.

Hareven, Tamara K. 1976. "Modernization and Family History." *Signs* 2:190–206.

Harrington, Michael. 1963. *The Other America: Poverty in the United States*. Baltimore: Penguin.

Hiller, Dana V., and William W. Philliber. 1986. "Determinants of Social Class Identification for Dual-Earner Couples." *Journal of Marriage and the Family* 43:583–87.

Komarovsky, Mirra. 1988. "The New Feminist Scholarship: Some Precursors and Polemics." *Journal of Marriage and the Family* 50:585–93.

Lemasters, Edgar. 1975. *Blue-Collar Aristocrats: Life-Styles in a Working-Class Tavern*. Madison: University of Wisconsin Press.

Mintz, Steven, and Susan Kellog. 1988. *Domestic Revolutions: A Social History of American Family Life*. New York: Free Press.

Morgan, Edmund. 1966. *The Puritan Family: Religion and Domestic Relations in Seventeenth-Century New England*. New York: Harper & Row.

Murdock, George. 1949. *Social Structure*. New York: Macmillan.

Robertson, Ian. 1987. *Sociology*. 3d ed. New York: Worth.

Rossides, Daniel W. 1976. *The American Class System: An Introduction to Social Stratification*. Boston: Houghton Mifflin.

Rubin, Lillian. 1976. *Worlds of Pain*. New York: Basic Books.

Seward, Rudy Ray. 1978. *The American Family: A Demographic History*. Newbury Park, Calif.: Sage.

Shorter, Edward. 1975. *The Making of the Modern Family*. New York: Basic Books.

Skolnick, Arlene. 1987. *The Intimate Environment: Exploring Marriage and the Family*, 4th ed. Boston: Little, Brown.

Spender, Dale. 1981. "Introduction." In *Men's Studies Modified: The Impact of Feminism on the Academic Disciplines*, edited by Dale Spender, 1–9. Oxford: Pergamon Press.

Stacey, Judith, and Barrie Thorne. 1985. "The Missing Feminist Revolution in Sociology." *Social Problems* 32:301–16.

Uhlenberg, Peter. 1980. "Death and the Family." *Journal of Family History* 5:313–30.

Vanfossen, Beth Ensminger. 1979. *The Structure of Social Inequality*. Boston: Little, Brown.

Wells, Robert. 1978. "Family History and Demographic Transition." In *The American Family in Social-Historical Perspective*, 2d ed., edited by Michael Gordon, 516–32. New York: St. Martin's Press.

2

The American Family in History

Perceptions of American family life today are governed by commonly held myths about American family life in the past. Such myths maintain that there was once a golden age of family relations, when three generations lived together happily in the same household. This belief in a lost golden age has led people to depict the present as a period of decline and family breakdown. . . . In order to come to grips with the problems of the present, it is essential to examine changes in family life over the last two centuries [*Hareven, 1982:447*].

In 1963, the sociologist William Goode suggested that a stereotype, which he labeled "the classical family of western nostalgia," governed our perceptions of family life in the past. According to this stereotype, families of past times were composed of a husband, wife, and their children along with assorted kinfolk living together in a large house in a rural setting. Family members labored long hours, producing goods for sale and consumption, and spent what leisure time they had together. Men and women married in their teens, and old people lived out their years being cared for in the homes of their sons or daughters. Divorce, premarital sex, and parent/child conflicts were rare, if not totally absent. Like many stereotypes, this view of the large, cooperating, and harmonious family of yesteryear contains elements of truth. However, it probably tells us more about our concerns in the present than it does about families in the past.

Since the 1960s, social historians have created a rich, although far from complete, record of the history of the American family, allowing the development of a more accurate view than we once had of the family's history. Subsequent chapters of this book examine specific parts of this fascinating historical record. This chapter examines changes in some basic characteristics of family life that occurred in the nineteenth and twentieth centuries, as the United

States evolved from an agricultural to an urban/industrial society. However, in order to place these changes in context, we must consider what historians have discovered about the preindustrial family.

The Family in the Preindustrial United States

From its earliest settlement by Europeans in the 1600s until well into the nineteenth century, the United States was primarily a rural society. Throughout this period, most white Americans lived and worked on small family-operated farms. Even individuals who earned their livelihood as independent artisans or shopkeepers often engaged in farming also. American farmers produced goods for home consumption, for barter with other members of their communities, and for sale in both domestic and foreign markets. The type of agricultural production varied greatly from region to region and by size of landholding. For example, a study of eighteenth-century Pennsylvania found that farmers with holdings over 125 acres sometimes marketed as much as 40 percent of their produce (Lemon, 1972). Southern plantations also relied heavily on cash crops for export prior to the Revolution. However, farmers in the Appalachian Mountains of West Virginia were primarily subsistence farmers until the coming of the coal companies in the twentieth century.

Although region, local economic conditions, and increasing ethnic diversity all had an impact on family life in early American communities, it is possible to specify some general characteristics of the preindustrial family among those of European descent. Early studies of the preindustrial family focused on household membership. These studies have destroyed the myth of the large, extended family of the past (Hareven, 1976:194). Most preindustrial households in the United States contained only nuclear family members, and most families apparently preferred to establish separate households for newly married couples (what anthropologists term *neolocal residence patterns*). For example, Phillip Greven's (1970) study of families over four generations in colonial Andover, Massachusetts, demonstrated that parents made great efforts to acquire sufficient land to establish their children in independent households. Because young men and women did not marry until they had the wherewithal to establish a household and, therefore, a means of livelihood, many postponed marriage until their late twenties and even early thirties.

Households were certainly larger in the preindustrial United States than they are today. For example, John Demos (1970) discovered an average household size of 6.0 in Bristol, Rhode Island, in 1688. In 1790, the year of the first federal census, the average household size in the United States was 5.8. However, the large size of preindustrial households was due, for the most part, to the presence of many children. In colonial Bristol, the average household contained three children and over a sixth of all households contained six or more children. In the seventeenth century, American women bore an average of eight children in their lifetimes. As birthrates fell in the nineteenth century, so too did the average household size. By 1920, when the average woman bore two or three children, the average household size was 4.3.

Studies of preindustrial households are not without their critics. For example, Lutz Berkner (1975) points out that studies of household membership, which are based on listings of the inhabitants of a community at one time, obscure the extent to which extended family households were a common phase in the life cycle of preindustrial families. For example, households may have expanded to include extended kin when the demand for labor was high, only to contract again when demand declined. It may also have been common for the elderly to live briefly with a married son or daughter prior to their deaths. The discovery of these variations in household membership requires tracing households of the past through time, an extremely difficult task. Berkner's own study of eighteenth-century Austria (1972) demonstrates that elderly parents often did live with a married son or daughter. This living arrangement probably occurred frequently in the preindustrial United States as well among those whose parents survived to advanced ages (Seward, 1978:86).

Berkner also argues that household membership is only one aspect of kinship ties and that the existence of a large proportion of nuclear households does not mean that extended kin did not have extensive social and economic contact. Unfortunately, studies of kin contact beyond the household must rely on personal documents, such as diaries, letters, and wills. These documents are rare and exist primarily for middle- and upper-class families. As a result, we know little about social contact and patterns of economic aid between kin in preindustrial communities. Although it is difficult to imagine that such contacts did not exist, studies have shown that extensive interaction between kin also exists in contemporary urban/industrial communities, particularly among the working class (Young and Willmott, 1957; Adams, 1968). Therefore, the extent of change in the frequency of extended-kin contacts is difficult to determine.

Despite their drawbacks, studies of household membership have revealed a distinctive feature of families of the past. Although preindustrial households did not often include extended kin, they frequently included individuals unrelated to nuclear family members. Nonkin were present in preindustrial households as apprentices, servants, hired hands, orphans, and other dependent members of the community, and as boarders (Hareven, 1976:194). Unrelated individuals have, for the most part, disappeared from households. However, many upper-class households contained servants throughout the nineteenth century, and boarders remained common in working- and middle-class homes in the early twentieth century (Modell and Hareven, 1973).

Although the early American family did not differ significantly from the contemporary family in form, major differences existed in its function and in the beliefs held about the place of the family in the broader community. The preindustrial family was the locus of daily activities. Among its primary functions was economic production, and all but the youngest family members took part in the daily activities of the family enterprise. Furthermore, work often took place in the same spaces where families came together to eat, sleep, and spend their leisure time.

Demos's (1970) description of houses in Plymouth colony gives an idea of how dramatically the texture of family life must have differed when the household was also a workshop. The first permanent structures in Plymouth often consisted of a single main-floor room called the "hall," normally between fifteen and twenty feet square, with a loft above. These houses were small by contemporary standards in the United States and would have seemed even more so because they had few windows. (For residents of colonial New England, keeping out the elements was more important than having views of the surrounding countryside.) The hall was a central site of family activities. At one end was a fireplace, a massive affair surrounded by cumbersome iron cookware. The hall also contained chairs, benches, tables, bedsteads, and storage chests. Other items necessary for home production, such as spinning wheels, butter churns, and candle-making equipment, were probably brought into the hall as occasion required. All this furniture and equipment was pushed out of the way or stored elsewhere until needed. Nevertheless, the average house must have been very cluttered as individuals went about their assorted tasks.

Because children participated in family labor as they became physically able to do so, the family also served as a vocational school. In colonial America, the practice of "putting out" one's own children to live and work in other households was common. Parents placed their children in service to learn a specific trade or simply to serve as general laborers. Prior to the advent of formal schooling, parents who placed their children into service sometimes expected them to be taught to read and write. Records show some children living away from their parents as servants as early as age seven.

The reasons parents put their children out probably varied by social class. As one might expect, poor parents bound out their children to contribute to the family income or to assure that their children learned a trade or to read and write. Nevertheless, many wealthy families also put their children out when no obvious reason existed for them to do so. Edmund Morgan (1966) suggests that Puritan parents were afraid of spoiling their children and put them out so they would be raised with the necessary discipline. However, an alternative explanation may be that the labor requirements of households differed over a family's life cycle. At certain times households may have had "spare" children and at others a deficit. Swedish historian Brengt Ankarloo (1979) suggests this situation may have given rise to a "cyclical redistribution of labor" in which households exchanged children as their labor requirements varied.

Prior to the development of asylums, jails, and poorhouses in the nineteenth century, the family also served important social-control and welfare functions. Community authorities sometimes placed individuals who were incapable of providing for themselves or who violated community norms in households where they would be under the "good government" of a family. Taking in errant members of the community may have been an inexpensive source of labor for some families, but handicapped and ill individuals were maintained at community expense. So central was the family in everyday life that some communities in colonial America even prohibited individuals from living alone. However, such prohibitions must rarely have required enforcement because the family provided so many services that living alone was probably inconceivable for most people.

The conception of the family that preindustrial people shared reflected its centrality. Demos (1982:45) has labeled this conception "family as community." In one sense, the family was a community for the individual because much of what an individual did contributed to the well-being of the other members of his or her family. The family was a corporate body in which individuals often made choices about marriage and occupation with the benefit of the entire group in mind (Hareven, 1976:202). The family also was a community in another sense because the boundaries between it and the outside world were not firmly drawn. For one thing, as we have seen, members of the outside community were often present in households as full-fledged members. For another, individuals often participated in other institutions as families or as representatives of families. In politics, economics, and religion the primary unit of preindustrial society was the family. To be sure, not all members of the family were equal participants in other institutions, but the family did frame everyday experience so that family and community were not separate spheres but continuous and inseparable worlds of experience. Finally, because the family was an important unit, the community freely intervened to assure its smooth functioning. Court records are replete with evidence of the attempts of community authorities to improve husband/wife and parent/child relationships (Demos, 1982:48).

Because of the mutual interpenetration of family and community, participation in the family and in broader community affairs was thought to be governed by the same behavioral principles, the family being simply a smaller version of more-encompassing institutions such as church and state. In the words of one preacher, the family prepared individuals for "greater matters in church or commonwealth" (William Gouge cited in Demos,1970). Demos (1982:47) suggests that people were able to move back and forth between the two realms without a sense of discontinuity. As we will discover, the connections and sense of continuity between the family and other institutions began to change radically in the nineteenth century. This change would have a significant impact on the family, particularly on women.

Nearly all women in the preindustrial United States lived and worked within the boundaries of the family as wives, daughters, or servants. Women performed a critical role in the preindustrial system of home-based production. Although women's labor was concentrated in and around the household, the tasks that fell to them were formidable. Women were responsible for the cultivation and preparation of much of the food for family consumption, as well as for the manufacture of clothing, soap, candles, medicine, and other necessities (Ryan, 1979:10). Because of the gender-based division of labor in the preindustrial economy, women probably had substantial autonomy in making decisions about the organization and goals of their labor. And because married women often directed the work of their daughters and servants, they probably had substantial authority in their own households as well.

The views of women expressed by men reflected the importance of women in preindustrial families. For example, the Puritan preacher John Cotton wrote: "Women are creatures without which there would be no comfortable living for man: it is true of them what is wont to be said of governments, that bad ones are better than none: They are a sort of blasphemer then who despise them and call them a necessary evil for they are a necessary good, such as it is not good that men should be without" (quoted in Morgan, 1966:29). Men did not consider women their equals, as Cotton's statement and the common early American designation for women, "Adam's rib," suggest. However, men did understand the reciprocity inherent in the roles of men and women in the family and their corresponding dependence on women.

We know little about women's view of their own role in preindustrial society because women did not leave written records as frequently as did men. However, historians Barbara Ehrenreich and Deirdre English (1978) suggest that the place of women in the preindustrial world was perhaps more secure than in the early stages of industrialization, when the sphere of their activities was restricted. Women's skills and knowledge were indispensable, and women must have understood the importance of their place. The tangible contributions they made to the survival of their families also made it unlikely that they felt alienated from their own labor (Ryan, 1979:12).

One must be cautious, however, about overestimating the impact of the importance of women's family roles on their relative status in past times. Despite the central contributions women made to the home economy and the recognition they received for it, the preindustrial world was patriarchal. Under the common law doctrine of coverture, a married woman's legal identity was subsumed under her husband's. Although conditions varied somewhat from colony to colony and began to change after the Revolution, a married woman's personal property and the control of her real property (land and other means of production) went to her husband at marriage. Of course, women did not usually own real property when they married, and once married they could not acquire property, enter into contracts, or sue or be sued in their own name (Basch, 1986:99). Women could acquire property when their husbands died. In most colonies and states, laws required husbands to leave at least one-third of their estates to their widows. Demos (1970:85) suggests that these laws reflected a recognition of the contributions women made to their families and a belief that a portion of the property was their due. However, women inherited property only as proxies for their dead husbands. They controlled the property and retained it if they remarried. Nevertheless, when widows died, the property reverted to their husbands' heirs (Ryan, 1979:7). Therefore, women were denied control of the most fundamental source of power in the preindustrial world, the land.

In addition to occupying a subordinate place in the family, women were virtually excluded from positions of influence beyond the family. Women did not participate in the political process except as they could influence individual men, did not hold positions of authority in the church, did not have equal access to educational institutions, and only rarely participated independently in the economy. Some women occasionally broke the barriers that kept them from the public sphere, and women sometimes protested the restrictions on their activities. Nevertheless, most early American women spent their lives in the family, perhaps secure in their place and often exercising substantial autonomy but only within the context of a patriarchal world.

This portrait of the preindustrial family requires substantial modification for the half million Africans who came to this country in bondage and their descendants. In 1790, the year of the first federal census, approximately 750,000 blacks were held in servitude in the United States, about one-fifth of the population. Roughly three male slaves were brought to this country for every two female slaves. At first, this imbalance between the sexes, along with the dispersal of slaves among many small farms, made a viable family life extremely difficult. However, as natural increase brought the sex ratio into balance and as a plantation system developed where large numbers of slaves labored together, vital family and kinship patterns evolved (Mintz and Kellog, 1988:32–35).

Although slave marriages were not legally recognized, enslaved men and women established long-lasting relationships. Research indicates that most slaves married and that most couples remained together throughout their lifetimes. In addition, most children lived with both their parents (Gutman, 1976:3–44). However, it would be a mistake to conclude from this evidence that slaves were able to maintain stable families. Marriages were frequently cut short by death because of the high mortality rates among slaves. Just as tragically, slave families were subject to forced disruption because of the sale of their members. Slaveholders may have been reluctant to break up slave marriages because it was in their interest to increase the number of slaves they owned. Nevertheless, many slave marriages ended as a result of the sale of one partner (Staples, 1988:305). The sale of children away from their parents was probably even more frequent. The strength of the bonds between the members of slave families is demonstrated by the attempts slaves made to stay in contact with kin who had been forcibly taken from them. For example, many slaves who fled their masters did so in attempts to locate a spouse or a child, and, after emancipation, freed men and women from all over the South made efforts to find kinfolk with whom they had lost contact (Mintz and Kellog, 1988:69)

The family assumed vital importance to slaves because it helped them endure the harsh conditions under which they lived and labored. Family members provided each other with love, companionship, and empathy, and helped each other learn the strategies for survival under chattel slavery (Staples, 1988:305). The conditions of slavery encouraged ties between extended kin on and between plantations. Kinspeople cooperated in supplementing the meager diets provided by their owners and in providing other types of material assistance. When sale divided parents and children, extended kin stepped in to shoulder the responsibilities of the absent parents (Mintz and Kellog, 1988:69). Genealogical studies show that slaves developed elaborate kin groups over time. They did so, in part, by prohibiting first-cousin marriages, a prohibition apparently not shared by white plantation owners. The practice of naming offspring after members of blood-kin groups shows the importance attached to relationships with these extended kin (Gutman, 1976:45–100). Therefore, despite inimical circumstances, black Americans developed a strong, although not necessarily "stable," family life under slavery.

Industrialization and the Family

In the nineteenth century, two related developments were underway that would eventually transform American society and have a dramatic impact on the family. These developments were urbanization and industrialization. Although each of these developments had its origins in the previous century, the pace of change accelerated in the nineteenth century. By 1900, the United States was well on its way to becoming an urban nation with the largest industrial output in the world.

From 1800 until after the Civil War, the United States remained a predominantly rural society. In 1800, only 5 percent of the population lived in villages or cities that had populations over 2,500 and that were classified as urban by the Bureau of the Census. The largest city in 1800 was Philadelphia, with a population of approximately 70,000. By 1860, the urban population had increased to approximately 20 percent of the total, and by 1900 it had risen to about 40 percent. In 1800, no Americans lived in cities with populations of over 100,000. By 1900, well over forty million Americans did so. The rapid rate of urban growth in the United States in the nineteenth century is perhaps best epitomized by Chicago, which grew from a town of about 5,000 in 1840 to a city of over 1,000,000 in 1880.

Urbanization was integrally related to the industrial growth that began with the opening of the first textile mills in the late eighteenth century. Between 1820 and 1860, cotton production grew at an annual rate of 15 percent, and in 1860 textile production was the largest industry in the United States. However, not until after the Civil War and the expansion of steel, electrical, chemical, and other new industries did manufacturing overtake agricultural production. In 1859, agriculture accounted for over 50 percent of commodity output, while manufactured goods ranked second with 32 percent (followed by construction and mining.) By 1899, manufacturing accounted for 53 percent of commodity output and agriculture 33 percent.

Changes in occupational distribution reflected the urban and industrial growth of the nineteenth century. As late as 1860, agricultural workers outnumbered all those employed in construction, manufacturing, mining, transportation, trade, and finance combined. However, by 1900 the number of agricultural workers had fallen below the totals in these occupations, and by 1930 those employed in manufacturing alone outnumbered agricultural workers. According to census estimates, approximately 70 percent of those gainfully employed worked on farms in 1820. In 1860, the proportion of agricultural workers had fallen to 60 percent, and in 1900 it was approximately 40 percent.

Equally important were changes in the ways individuals took part in the production process. Early in the nineteenth century, the United States was a society of small property owners and their families. These small property owners were primarily farmers, but their numbers also included independent artisans and shopkeepers. In the early nineteenth century, 80 percent of the adult white population was self-employed. However, by 1880 only 40 percent was self-employed, and by 1940 the percentage had fallen to 16. Independent producers were replaced by industrial workers and a propertyless middle class. By 1870, the industrial workers who tended the nation's assembly lines made up nearly 30 percent of the work force. This percentage remained constant for the next century. Salaried workers made up only 7 percent of the work force in 1870. However, the increasing scale of production required managers, engineers, technicians, secretaries, and other white–collar workers, and this group made up 25 percent of the labor force by 1940.

   The developments of the nineteenth century had a dramatic impact on the family as rural-born Americans and European immigrants found themselves in growing industrial cities. In these unfamiliar surroundings, routines that had guided behavior for centuries were disrupted, and new ways of relating to one's family and the surrounding community were fashioned. Change in the family occurred gradually, and some members were more affected by change than others. For example, the family did not lose its productive function entirely in urban America. Many families continued to raise and process much of their own food, occasionally even keeping livestock in the city. In addition, only some of the work of the family moved to other locales. Much of the work of women remained in the home, a subject we will examine in detail in a later chapter. Nevertheless, in the city family members participated in the productive process primarily as paid laborers. Furthermore, the family did not frame daily experience as it had in preindustrial communities. For men, and many women, work no longer took place in the intimate and familiar environment of the home but in increasingly mechanized and impersonal factories and offices.

Readings

The articles in this chapter examine some of the changes that occurred in American families as they moved from farm to city in the nineteenth and twentieth centuries, and they raise important issues concerning the place of the family in contemporary society. In "The Family as Utopian Retreat from the City," Kirk Jeffrey describes the new beliefs about the family that began to take shape in the mid-nineteenth century. Jeffrey bases his description on the fictional and hortatory writing of the period. This literature was written by and for the middle class. As Jeffrey's title implies, middle-class Americans in the nineteenth century were encouraged to entertain extravagant hopes about the perfectibility of family life. Although they perceived the city as a hostile and even uncontrollable environment, they viewed the family as a place that offered the possibility of harmony and tranquility. The perception of a radical discontinuity between the family and society contrasts sharply with ideas about the family attributed by historians to preindustrial Americans.

   Although Jeffrey only briefly considers the developments giving rise to these new beliefs about the family, he examines the implications of these new ideas for men and women in detail. Here again, a sharp contrast is evident with the preindustrial family. Emerging conceptions of the family assigned women responsibility as guardians of the home and charged men with the task of venturing into the outside world. The gulf nineteenth-century Americans perceived between the family and the outside world was reflected in the characteristics they attributed to the inhabitants of these separate spheres. Men and women were no longer seen as partners making similar although unequal contributions to a common enterprise, as they had been in the preindustrial family, but as inhabitants of distinctly different and even conflicting worlds. Jeffrey concludes with a provocative suggestion: Although the literature of the nineteenth century encouraged individuals to think of their families as protected from outside intrusions, Jeffrey argues that this view obscured the ways in which society continued to penetrate the family. In fact, he suggests that the family may have become even more subject to outside influence and even less in control of its destiny than the family in previous eras.

In "Family Time and Industrial Time," Tamara K. Hareven explores the topic of the influence of external forces on family behavior in detail. In doing so, she extends our consideration of the American family into the early twentieth century and shifts the focus to the families of industrial workers. The conception of the family as a haven from the outside world may have borne a superficial resemblance to middle-class life. To the degree that women remained in the home and men were able to provide a sufficient and secure income, family and work may have appeared as distinct realms. However, as Hareven's article demonstrates, this conception of the family must have stood in stark contrast to the realities of the daily life of working-class Americans, many of whom were immigrants. For industrial workers at the turn of the century (as well as today), the effects of low wages, poor working conditions, and periodic unemployment on the family must have been all too clear.

To examine the relationship between work and the family among the working class, Hareven introduces the concepts of "family time" and "industrial time." Using evidence from employee records kept by the Amoskeag Corporation in Manchester, New Hampshire, as well as other records, Hareven is able to trace the relationship between the family and the organization of industrial employment. Hareven is careful to articulate the complex ways in which the lines of influence ran back and forth between the family and work.

Hareven raises two other issues relevant to our consideration of basic changes in the family accompanying industrialization and urbanization. First, Hareven's article demonstrates that industrialization affected working-class and middle-class women differently. Working-class women entered the paid labor force in large numbers, and the ideology of the separate spheres probably had little relevance for them. Second, Hareven's findings alert us to the importance of ethnicity in investigating the impact of industrialization on the family. In the peak migration years around the turn of the century, millions of immigrants arrived in the United States. For example, approximately seven and a half million Eastern and Central Europeans (one-third of whom were Jewish) and four million Italians immigrated to the United States between 1880 and 1914. Each of these groups may have adapted to the conditions of industrial life in somewhat different ways, based on their own cultural patterns. For example, in a study of working-class families in Buffalo, New York, around the turn of the century, Virginia Yans McLaughlin (1971) found important differences in the employment patterns of Italian and Polish women. Polish women were more likely to seek employment in factories or to work as domestics, while Italian women were more likely to take in boarders or to work seasonally in canneries. Many of America's "unmeltable ethnics" retain distinctive family patterns to the present day.

Although the wives and daughters of Amoskeag mill workers often joined men in the factory, less than 30 percent of single women and an even smaller minority of married women worked outside the home throughout the first half of the twentieth century in the United States. One can ask, as Hareven's article invites us to do, why working-class women behaved differently from so many of their contemporaries.

In the third article in this chapter, "Work, Leisure, and Family Roles," Joann Vanek raises an equally interesting but perhaps more perplexing question. Vanek examines the family roles of men and women in farm households between 1920 and 1950. She suggests that the contributions of these men and women to the family were symmetrical and concludes that they retained a division of labor like that in preindustrial economies. Vanek also describes the use of leisure time by farm men and women, emphasizing the ways these two activities were intertwined in farm households. Vanek concludes by suggesting that in addition to asking why the few women who entered the paid labor force in the first half of the twentieth century did so, we should also ask why so many women failed to join them. Vanek's question is exceedingly complex and is one to which we will return in Chapter 4.

In the final article, "Afro-American Adaptive Strategies," Earl Lewis examines the impact of urban migration on black Americans who left the rural South to seek opportunities in the industrial cities of the South and North in the first part of the twentieth century. Some sociologists (Frazier, 1939; Moynihan, 1965) have claimed that the black family, already disrupted by the experience of slavery, was further weakened by urban migration. Specifically, these sociologists argued that urban migration cut black Americans off from extended kin and the sources of support these kin provided. However, Lewis's research suggests that black urban migrants made extensive efforts to maintain contact with absent kin and that these contacts were among the strategies adopted by blacks to overcome the dislocations associated with migration. White Americans probably used similar adaptive strategies, belying the notion that urbanization cut individuals off from extended kin. Nevertheless, Lewis's research is important because it shows the continuing resilience of black families under the difficult conditions they have faced in this country, a resilience they continue to demonstrate today (Stack, 1974).

References

Adams, Bert. 1968. *Kinship in an Urban Setting*. Chicago: Markham.

Ankarloo, Brengt. 1979. "Agriculture and Women's Work: Directions of Change in the West, 1700–1900." *Journal of Family History* 4:111–120.

Basch, Norma. 1986. "The Emerging Legal History of Women in the United States: Property, Divorce, and the Constitution." *Signs* 12:97–117.

Berkner, Lutz. 1972. "The Stem Family and the Developmental Cycle of the Peasant Household: An Eighteenth-Century Austrian Example." *American Historical Review* 47:398–418.

———— .1975. "The Use and Misuse of Census Data for the Historical Analysis of Household Structure." *Journal of Interdisciplinary History* 4:721–738.

Demos, John. 1970. *A Little Commonwealth: Family Life in Plymouth Colony*. New York: Oxford University Press.

_____ . 1982. "Images of the American Family, Then and Now." In *Changing Images of the Family,* edited by Virginia Tufte and Barbara Myerhoff, 43–60. New Haven, Conn.: Yale University Press.

Ehrenreich, Barbara, and Deirdre English. 1978. *For Her Own Good.* Garden City, N.Y.: Doubleday, Anchor Press.

Frazier, E. Franklin. 1939. *The Negro Family in the United States.* Chicago: University of Chicago Press.

Goode, William. 1963. *World Revolution and Family Patterns.* New York: Free Press.

Greven, Phillip J., Jr. 1970. *Four. Generations: Population, Land, and the Family in Colonial Andover.* Ithaca, N.Y.: Cornell University Press.

Gutman, Herbert. 1976. *The Black Family in Slavery and Freedom, 1750–1925.* New York: Pantheon.

Hareven, Tamara K. 1976. "Modernization and Family History: Perspectives on Social Change." *Signs* 2: 190–206.

_____ .1982. "American Families in Transition: Historical Perspectives on Change." in *Normal Family Processes,* edited by Froma Walsh, 446–466. New York: The Guilford Press.

Lemon, James T. 1972. *The Best Poor Man's Country: A Geographical Study of Early Southeastern Pennsylvania.* Baltimore: Johns Hopkins University Press.

McLaughlin, Virginia Yans. 1971. "Patterns of Work and Family Organization: Buffalo's Italians." *Journal of Interdisciplinary History* 2:1–31.

Mintz, Steven, and Susan Kellog. 1988. *Domestic Revolutions: A Social History of American Family Life.* New York: Free Press.

Modell, John, and Tamara K. Hareven. 1973. "Urbanization and the Malleable Household: An Examination of Boarding and Lodging in American Families." *Journal of Marriage and the Family,* 35:467–479.

Morgan, Edmund. 1966. *The Puritan Family: Religion and Domestic Relations in Seventeenth-Century New England.* New York: Harper & Row.

Moynihan, Daniel Patrick. 1965. *The Negro Family: The Case for National Action.* Washington, D.C.: U.S. Department of Labor.

Ryan, Mary P. 1979. *Womanhood in America: From Colonial Times to the Present.* 2nd ed. New York: New Viewpoints.

Seward, Rudy Ray. 1978. *The American Family: A Demographic History.* Newbury Park, Calif.: Sage.

Stack, Carol B. 1974. *All Our Kin.* New York: Harper & Row.

Staples, Robert. 1988. "The Black American Family." In *Ethnic Families in America,* 3d ed., edited by Charles H. Mindel, Robert Habenstein, and Roosevelt Wright, Jr., 303–324. New York: Elsevier.

Young, Michael, and Peter Willmott. 1957. *Family and Kinship in East London.* Baltimore: Penguin.

The Family as Utopian Retreat from the City: The Nineteenth-Century Contribution

Kirk Jeffrey

Can society ever be constituted upon principles of universal Christian brotherhood? The believing Christian, the enlightened philosopher, answer—IT CAN. Will this organization commence with the entire race of man? with existing governments? or with small isolated communities? Doubtless, the principles of this new organization must be matured in the hearts and lives of individuals, before they can be embodied in any community, but when the new organization commences, it will doubtless be in small communities.[1]

The foundation of our free institutions is in our love, as a people, for our homes. The strength of our country is found, not in the declaration that all men are free and equal, but in the quiet influence of the fireside, the bonds which unite together the family circle. The corner-stone of our republic is the hearth-stone. . . . From the corroding cares of business, from the hard toil and frequent disappointments of the day, men retreat to the bosom of their families, and there, in the midst of that sweet society of wife and children and friends, receive a rich reward for this industry, and are reminded that their best interests are inseparable from public and social morality. . . . The feeling that here, in one little spot, his best enjoyments are concentrated. . . gives a wholesome tendency to [a man's] thoughts, and is like the healing oil poured upon the wounds and bruises of the spirit.[2]

During the years from about 1800 to 1870, and particularly after 1825, the values and expectations about family life which many Americans share today became implanted in middle-class American culture for the first time. These included beliefs about the nature and proper behavior of women and children, attitudes about sex which were widely accepted well into the twentieth century, and a general sense of sharp disjunction between the private world of the family and the larger society. This last assumption pervaded the writings of the popular moralists and advisers of that age—the physicians, phrenologists, clergymen, "scribbling women," and others who instructed middle-class Americans about their "duties and conduct in life." In the sermons and novels, the magazines and hortatory literature of the mid-nineteenth century, they asserted over and over that home was a distinct sphere, an enclave emphatically set apart from the

Reprinted from *Soundings: An Interdisciplinary Journal* Vol. 55, No. 1 (Spring 1972): 21–42. Used by permission of The Society for Values in Higher Education and *Soundings*.

activities and priorities of "the world," as they usually called the non-domestic part of their society. Associated with this idea was a second one which could be stated in a good many ways but which amounted to an affirmation that, ultimately, the individual found meaning and satisfaction in his life at home and nowhere else.

Our ancestors thus were encouraged to nurse extravagant hopes for the domestic realm. Whether they regarded home as an utter and permanent retreat from life in a shocking and incomprehensible social order, or as a nursery and school for preparing regenerate individuals who would go forth to remake American society, they agreed that domestic life ought to be perfect and could be made so. Through careful design of the home as a physical entity, and equally painstaking attention to the human relationship which would develop within it, the family could actually become a heaven on earth. Many of the significant features and patterns of middle-class family life in the nineteenth century, as well as significant points of strain, tension, and guilt, arose directly from these extravagant expectations.

A risky but potentially illuminating way of coming to terms with dominant American ideas about the family both in that day and in our own may be to analyze the middle-class family as a kind of utopian community, analogous in many respects to the more famous communities which some reformers attempted to plant and nurture during those same decades prior to the Civil War, when recognizably modern family patterns were developing in some parts of American society. Certainly three utopian themes—retreat, conscious design, and perfectionism—pervaded nineteenth-century writings about the family.[3]

What strikes one immediately, as one reads into the ephemeral popular literature of that era, is the intense seriousness with which middle-class writers discussed the home and the family. Often their words seem comical as they strain for the sonorous phrase, the classical allusion, which may succeed in capturing that intensity, that seriousness. "Home!—sweet word and musical!" wrote Mrs. Lydia Sigourney, a noted household poet, "key-tone of the heart, at whose melody, as by the harp of Orpheus, all the trees in its garden are moved, holy word! refuge from sadness and despair, best type of that eternal rest, for which we look, when the journey of life is ended!"[4] This gush was typical of many writers in a sentimental and declamatory age; beneath it, though, was a serious statement. Others could be equally effusive, equally serious: "Home! the very word calls up a thousand feelings of thrilling interest; what ear is there so dull as not to hear it with delight? what heart so cold as not to respond with pleasure to the welcome sound?"[5] Still another writer asked, "Is there any brain so dull into which [the word 'home'] does not flash with a gush of suggestive congruous fascinations?"[6]

In Mrs. Sigourney's statement the dominant theme is retreat. In this connection it is noteworthy that idealized homes of the nineteenth century were invariably described in the context of a generalized, usually sentimentalized rural setting, surrounded by gardens and orchards. An entirely typical description is the following, from Mrs. A. J. Graves's novel *Girlhood and Womanhood* (1844). Here one of the heroines gazes for the first time at the landscape around her family's new home:

A beautiful prospect stretched away before her. A fine range of green, softly swelling hills, bounded the horizon, behind which the sun was setting, in all the splendor of a richly tinted canopy of clouds. At their base, a lovely valley lay in shadow, through which a stream was gliding, fringed here and there with clumps of trees and shrubs, and upon its grassy banks, her father's herds were quietly grazing. A fine grove of old oaks rose beneath the window, whose trunks were lighted up with the red rays of the declining sun, and the green sward, from which they sprung, was beautifully varied by long lines of sunshine and lengthened shadows, as intervening trees or intermediate spaces admitted, or obscured the brilliant hues of sunset.[7]

The language of this description, clotted with "softly swelling hills," "grassy banks," and "green sward," suggests that such scenes—which can be found quite frequently in popular fiction and illustrations—were debased pastorals; middle-class Americans, that is, regarded the most important feature of the ideal home as its location in ordered natural surroundings. But so great was the gulf between aspiration and the social realities of the nineteenth century, and so unequipped were most writers for the task of discovering adequate ways of relating the two, that they fell back upon stale literary conventions.

The hortatory writings of the same period also betrayed the same assumptions. In their massive and famous compendium of domestic advice entitled *The American Woman's Home,* Catharine Beecher and her sister Harriet Beecher Stowe made the rural home their ideal model despite the fact that their audience was largely urban. Much of their instruction on matters domestic, the sisters explained, "is chiefly applicable to the wants and habits of those living either in the country or in such suburban vicinities as give space of ground for healthful outdoor occupation in family service. . . ." They offered advice on the cultivation of flowers, fruits, and vegetables, and the care of "horse, cow, and dairy." "Each and all of the family, some part of the day," they asserted, should "take exercise in the pure air, under the magnetic and healthful rays of the sun. Every head of a family should seek a soil and climate which will afford such opportunities. Railroads, enabling men toiling in cities to rear families in the country, are on this account a special blessing."[8]

This was in 1869. As the illustration of "The Christian Home" and phrases such as the one about "magnetic and healthful rays" suggest, the Beecher sisters too fell back upon a prettified image of country life which was probably far removed from the mundane realities confronting the average farm family. Home, they were suggesting, belonged neither in the city nor too far away from it on the American frontier. Like Mrs. Graves, they believed that it ought ideally to be found in an ordered but natural setting—that is, a timeless one.

The development of this middle-class cult of the rural home must be understood as a response to the historical experience which members of this group were undergoing during the middle decades of the nineteenth century. What is betrayed was an intense fear, a shock of non-recognition, with which such Americans greeted their society. As Marvin Meyers has remarked of them, they "were not inwardly prepared for the grinding uncertainties, the shocking changes, the complexity and indirection" of the economic and social order which was beginning to confront them by the 1830's and 1840's.[9] The trends toward rapid change, extreme diversity, and new psychic demands had developed most fully in the larger cities of the Republic by then, and we should recall that the forty years prior to 1860 witnessed a higher rate of urban growth in proportion to total population growth, for the Eastern part of the nation, than at any later time in the century. Hence it was appropriate that the city appear to popular moralists and their readers as a symbol of all that distressed them in society outside the home. The cities housed the slums and immigrants, the gambling-dens and saloons which the Protestant clergy so frequently attacked.

The shocking features of urban life were magnified for many middle-class Americans because they were themselves rural-bred migrants to the city. Their very notable propensity to idealize the villages and farms of their childhood years and to excoriate the cities of their adulthood ones is a good index to the "profound alteration in human experience" which they were undergoing.[10] The present discussion can do no more than offer a few examples from the considerable literature of wailing and gnashing of teeth about the city which was appearing as early as the 1830's. One typical volume by the Reverend John Todd, entitled *The Moral Influence, Dangers and Duties, Connected with Great Cities,* offered readers a comprehensive analysis of urban life. Most striking, according to Todd, was the set of purposes that men pursued in the city: "Wealth and Fashion are the deities which preside over the great city. . . . [There] you see the young, the ardent, the keen, and the gifted, rushing into these great marts of nations, to court the smiles of Mammon;—all hoping for his gifts." The frenzy and cultural diversity of the city thus alarmed him most. "On all sides. . . are the songs and the invitations of pleasure, the snares and the pitfalls covered with flowers. . . . To these very many yield. . . . All hope by-and-by to be able to retire on a competency. A few can do it; but what an amazing proportion fall in the race! and the tide rolls on, and they and their hopes are forgotten!"[11]

Here, then, was one central meaning of the city: the frantic and relentless pursuit of wealth, a quest at which few would succeed. It was *"the universal unconquerable desire for money,"* according to Todd, which both gave the city its *raison d'etre* and rendered it utterly iniquitous. The pursuit of riches was intrinsically evil; but it had some side consequences which further compounded the dangers of urban life, even for those few who might withstand its central mania for riches. Of particular importance among these was the transiency of human ties: "Your acquaintances come and go,—are here to-day, and off to-morrow, and you have hardly time, or opportunity, to form deep attachments. The unceasing hurry, and perpetual pressure for time, prevent our forming those deep attachments which we do in country life."[12]

Similar lessons were purveyed to Americans through the didactic fiction of the same era. In the Reverend Daniel Wise's *Young Man's Counsellor,* for instance, one finds the parable of Arthur—"Arthur in Babylon," as R. Richard Wohl calls it in his delightful evisceration of this cautionary tale. Arthur is a kind of failed Horatio Alger hero; everything he does turns out wrong. Aged nineteen, "educated, handsome, of fascinating manners, and manly spirit," Arthur arrives in "a certain city" determined to make his fortune. Here is the very archetype of the middle-class migrant. But the city, it transpires, contains perils that Arthur is wholly unprepared to withstand. The youth "unhappily fell into dissolute society, and began to run the giddy rounds of deep dissipation." Soon his money is gone and he must pay a bill. Arthur's next error brings down the catastrophe upon him: "he took the fatal step of selling an opera glass, which he had borrowed from a gay friend; and thus paid his bill." Next day Arthur learns to his dismay that friendship in the city it not to be counted upon; "his quondam friend had the heart of a Shylock, and hurried the astonished and mortified young man to the police."

At this point Arthur collapses; " 'Cut my throat! kill me! trample me to death!' " he howls to his astonished cell-mates. Delirious, he is pronounced by a physician to be "in imminent danger of dying." Bailed out by an anonymous philanthropist, Arthur collapses once again when told that his father has been summoned from the hinterland. " 'I can't see him! I can't—I can't!' " groans the piteous Arthur, and dies just as his "venerable father" enters the room.

Wohl's summary remarks are worth quoting in full:

> This brutal little yarn, so equally devoid of mercy and moderation, was printed as a true story; and was intended, and surely accepted by some, as an edifying and moral tale. Arthur's reckless hysteria, his pathological sense of guilt, his panic, and his egregious moral vanity, are blandly recounted by the author as something just and genteel. The story's excessive melodrama is in itself revealing. The fear and hatred of urban demoralization was so great that its condemnation was correspondingly enormous. The story serves well to polarize city and country, stigmatizing the one and, by implication, unreservedly approving the other. Arthur's downfall commences from the day he comes to the city; in the country he was happy, useful, and ornamental. The city is the villain and Arthur is its victim.[13]

Indictments of the city such as Todd's and Wise's were based on a common nineteenth-century psychological theory; "We all know," wrote Todd, "that familiarity with any thing has a wonderful effect upon our feelings, and that it is a principle in human nature, that what is in itself revolting, will, by familiarity, cease to disgust."[14] By implication, few if any city-dwellers could long hold out against the inevitable taint of experience; sophistication and virtue were incompatible. Indeed, such was precisely the lesson of "Arthur in Babylon."

Thus the necessary conclusion to such a despairing theory of the impact of urban experience was the recommendation that it be avoided entirely. And the only sure way to do so, naturally, was to remain in the country. But there was a second possibility—an outpost of the country, as it were, within city walls. This was, of course, the family; and for those who could not return to rural America, or who found the opportunities of city life too attractive to allow them to heed the warnings of the Todds and the Wises, the second-best choice was to establish a little sphere of peace and order to which they could retreat. Ideally the family ought to be rural; and a later generation, blessed with more efficient means of transportation, would discover that is was possible to commute to the city while still enjoying a home life far removed from its terrors, in houses surrounded by a few hundred square feet of well-trimmed grass. But more than a century ago the essential perception of the city had already been formulated, along with the response which has remained the most popular one for the American middle class; complete retreat.

> We go forth into the world, amidst the scenes of business and of pleasure; we mix with the gay and the thoughtless, we join the busy crowd, and the *heart* is sensible to a desolation of feeling: we behold every principle of justice and of honor, and even the dictates of common honesty disregarded, and the delicacy of our moral sense is wounded; we see the general good, sacrificed to the advancement of personal interest; and we turn from such scenes, with a painful sensation, almost believing that virtue has deserted the abodes of men; again, we look to the *sanctuary* of *home*; there sympathy, honor, virtue, are assembled; there the eye may kindle with intelligence, and receive an answering glance; there disinterested love, is ready to sacrifice every thing at the altar of affection.[15]

For the most part, as such statements indicate, popular writers tended to define the ideal home as an Edenic retreat, a rural haven utterly distinct from the terrors of urban life and the loneliness which could assail men there. As one clergyman put it, home was "a sweet bower of peace and joy in this desert world, where hope brightens, and love gathers its linked, confiding circle;—a blissful retreat for jaded and weary hearts when the busy world drives on its votaries in the train of Mammon and pampered self;—a safe and alluring shelter for *yourselves* amid the vicissitudes of life, becoming more and more the abode of peace and love as the world grows dark without."[16] This conception was nowhere more memorably stated than in Donald Grant Mitchell's bestseller of the 1850's, *Reveries of a Bachelor:*

> Sending your blood in passionate flow, is the ecstasy of the conviction that *there* at least you are beloved; that there you are understood; that there your errors will meet ever with gentlest forgiveness; that there your troubles will be smiled away; that there you may unburden your soul fearless of harsh, unsympathizing ears; and that there you may be entirely and joyfully—yourself.[17]

Retreat, companionship, possibly even the surcease from moral striving— these were the elements of Americans' notion of the Edenic home. Sometimes, to be sure, popular writers—often the very same ones—also asserted that home and the surrounding society were vitally connected: that the regenerate family would train up moral children and gradually reform adult males, so that ultimately, through thousands of such trickles of perfected individuals, a mighty tide of social reform would sweep aside all the evil features of nineteenth-century society. Through "family discipline and instruction," rather than any public institutions or agencies, Americans could achieve some deeply desired goals: "the preservation of manners, the maintenance of religion, and the perpetuity of national freedom."[18] But this second conception of the relationship between family and society, like the first, posited no extended day-to-day contact between the two "spheres." Middle-class Americans, that is, took care to define the social role of the family in such a way that it did not demand many significant forays from home out into the larger society, or even much detailed knowledge of it. Thus both definitions of the ideal home—as perfect retreat or as school for a moral citizenry—were premised upon the assumption that a serious and practically unbridgeable gulf existed between the two spheres, family and society.

In a more extended discussion of the nineteenth-century middle-class family it would be possible to consider the underlying structural changes which certainly stimulated the intense preoccupation with domesticity and the sense of a sharp disjunction. It was not merely the transformation of the outer society but rapid alterations in family patterns themselves which sensitized middle-class Americans to the problem of the family. Notable among these changes, but difficult as yet for the historian to examine with precision, were a disruption of the internal unity of the family due to the separation of the husband's work from the home in nineteenth-century cities, and the attenuation of informal ties to relatives and neighbors which had characterized rural and village life. The latter development was particularly significant, for without a rich web of kinship and friendship, urban middle-class family members were seriously hindered from meeting other city-dwellers on intimate terms, gaining detailed knowledge about the processes of urban life, or becoming more involved in these processes. In fact, one might hazard the guess that the isolation wrought by the withering of kin ties probably contributed as much as the chaos of the urban environment itself to the notable middle-class alienation from the city by mid-century.[19]

The middle-class sense of a gulf between family and society was by no means inevitable and natural, and it had not existed, as far as historians can tell, in colonial America. I have suggested that the growth of this perception can be understood as the *consequence* of social changes, some of them external to the family and others within the family and kinship system itself. Now I want to raise a different question: Did the nineteenth-century sense of a disjunction between the two realms in turn act as a *cause* of other changes in family and society, or at least reinforce changes already occurring?

Let us first consider the results for intimate family life of the cult of the idyllic home. It seems that life in the isolated, Edenic homes of the middle class, to the degree that the perfectionist definition of home was taken seriously, probably exacerbated the compulsive self-examination of many Protestant middle-class husbands and wives and enormously increased the burdens of anxiety and guilt which they bore. Here was an unexpected and particularly ironic result of the cult, for it encouraged is votaries to expect near-perfect repose and emotional fulfillment in the domestic sphere.

The precise nature of the difficulties differed for husbands and wives. For husbands, there arose what we may call the "commuting problem." If a virtuous sophistication in the city was truly impossible, as writers like Todd and Wise affirmed, how then could men dare to leave home at all to pursue careers in American society? Or if they did leave, even for a few hours a day, what would happen to their wives and families when they returned? This quandry, arising from the literal way in which middle-class Americans took their own definitions of the pure home and the depraved world, was at the center of many novels and stories of the period. In no case were popular authors able to fuse domestic and worldly experience into a coherent whole.

One typically spectacular expression of the problem appeared in a story entitled "The Prodigal's Return," by Timothy Shay Arthur.[20] Arthur, whose temperance novel *Ten Nights in a Bar-Room* rivalled even *Uncle Tom's Cabin* in sales, published over one hundred volumes of didactic fiction between 1840 and 1870. In "The Prodigal's Return" young William Enfield leaves home to go to college. His mother's anxious question as he sets out, " 'You won't forget your mother, William?' " sets the theme for the tale. At college William falls under the influence of evil companions, becomes a card-sharper and a prankster, and is finally expelled. He spends years as a professional gambler—the road from college high-jinks to adult depravity was apparently a broad and easy one—but finally experiences an instantaneous conversion in the form of a dream about home and mother. Resolving to put aside his evil ways, William returns to his childhood home and is forgiven by his parents. There he remains, presumably, forever after. This version of the prodigal son parable failed adequately to solve the dilemma of home's relation to the world. What would William Enfield *do* now that he had returned home? Could he be the kind of vigorous, ambitious, independent man that Americans admired, without venturing outside again? Equally important, was it really so easy to put aside everything he had learned and become since leaving home? And was it really true that all experience was worthy only of being forgotten?

A second and even more interesting pattern in popular fiction also tried to deal with the problem posed for men by the notion of two spheres. In this case we find that worldly men, instead of being saved by home and women, destroy the domestic enclave itself. Lydia Maria Child's story "Home and Politics" provides an example.[21] George Franklin and his wife are at first a happy, married couple preoccupied with their domestic life together. But "in an evil hour a disturbing influence crossed their threshold. It came in the form of political excitement; that pestilence which is forever racing through our land, seeking whom it may devour; destroying happy homes." George's increasing interest in caucuses and campaigns, growing largely out of desire for office and power, draws him away from home night after night. On election night, 1840, while he is gone, his child falls sick and dies. Then in 1844 he loses all his money by betting on Henry Clay; this time his wife goes mad. "When he visits her, she looks at him with strange eyes, and still clinging to the fond ideal of her life, she repeats mournfully, 'I *want* my home. Why don't George come and take me home?' "

Essentially Mrs. Child was wrestling with the same difficulty: experience in the world inevitably changes a person, but the cult of home demanded that one return absolutely intact. Implicit in both stories, and made fully explicit in the numerous volumes of advice to young men during the mid-nineteenth century, was the exhortation for American men to love domestic life and to model themselves after their wives. This suspicion of men and their worldly doings followed necessarily from the Victorian "cult of true womanhood," which placed middle-class women on pedestals and proclaimed that they were naturally more cultured, affectionate, and pious than their husbands.[22] Only by becoming women in significant respects could American men, it seemed, be considered fit for sustained presence in the home.

In concrete terms, this boiled down to a number of extreme demands which popular moralists quite literally expected men to meet. The first was that they stay home—indeed, this was their fundamental commandment to American men. *"Virtue, purity, spiritual excellence* are the great purpose of our being. And where can you acquire these qualities better than at home?"[23] Such writers regarded ambition for fame or fortune as a base impulse, the moral equivalent of uncontrollable lust for sex or gambling. One clergyman lamented, for example, that in many young men

> you may see in the very outset of life a passion for Gain towering above every thing else; so that ease, even the necessary rest of night, time, talents, and not seldom reputation itself, are sacrificed on the alter of Mammon. He, who feels this burning desire to get rich, cares usually but little for the pleasures of home. He is never, indeed, so uneasy as when seated by his own fireside; for he feels, while conversing with his kindred, that he is making no money. And as for fireside reading, there is to him no interest in that; "he reads no book but his ledger."[24]

Once at home, men must consult with their wives and defer to them. As purer beings, women were more trustworthy guides on matters of morals and often, too, with respect to more worldly decisions. "Nothing," wrote the health reformer William A. Alcott, "is better calculated to preserve a young man from the contaminations of low pleasure and pursuits, than frequent intercourse [of the Platonic variety, one judges] with the more refined and virtuous of the other sex."[25]

But how could women be safeguarded from the sexual lust of men? Might not husbands prove so coarse and passionate that the purity of their wives, and hence of the home itself, would be endangered? This was an issue of explicit discussion during the generation before 1860. Whether the passions of men resulted from their innately bestial natures or were vastly heightened by worldly experience, men were always perceived in middle-class writing about the home as extreme threats to the peace and unity of the family. The natural conclusion was that husbands must exercise a continual self-restraint in sexual matters, in order to enable wives to remain pure enough to save them through their mild influence. Clearly there was something circular about this line of thought, for if men successfully practiced sexual continence, was that not a good indication that they already had their base propensities well under control? Which was to come first, the influence of the pure wife or masculine self-restraint? Unaware of this problem with their regimen, domestic advisers went right ahead in affirming that "there is no lust in true marriage, and two rightly mated never run to excess in anything in any of the indulgencies [*sic*] of their natures."[26] In more explicit terms, physicians and others were not shy about spelling out precisely what this meant. Alcott, an extremely popular arbiter on matters of medicine and health, urged late marriage, told young married couples to live with their parents during the early months of marriage, and warned them to refrain from sexual relations during pregnancy and lactation. The rest of the time "one indulgence to each lunar month, is all that the best health of the parties can possible require."[27]

In the case of middle-class husbands, then, we might say that the demands upon them—that they stay home, practice a continual sexual continence, and model themselves upon their wives—were heavy and almost impossible to carry out to perfection. Yet popular moralists demanded perfection. Moreover, their advise disguised a significant contradiction, for the intimacy and affection which they promised American husbands and wives was probably difficult to achieve in the context of the rigid sexual formality and self-control which the same writers also urged.

For American wives the difficulties arising from the definition of home as a separate and perfect realm were, if anything, more poignant, for women had few alternatives to their domestic role. Curiously, though, the precise nature of these difficulties has been little noted and discussed by social historians.

While it is an overstatement to speak of the "oppression" or "subjection" of middle-class wives in the nineteenth century, there seems little doubt that they suffered a notable decline in autonomy and morale during the three-quarters of a century following the founding of the American republic. Essentially this decline occurred as an indirect result of underlying changes in family patterns, and particularly in expectations about family life, which we have been examining. Most women in this group failed to perceive the "correct" causes for the sense of desperation which many of them seem frequently to have felt. In particular, they failed to see the unfortunate side-effects of the "cult of true womanhood," which defined them as the pious, pure keepers of the hearthside and bearers of genteel culture.

Almost all middle-class American wives accepted these ideas quite seriously, as far as the historian can tell. They did not regard confinement to the home as an indication that they were oppressed. On the contrary, if home was more pure and joyful, as women were continually assured, then it was a definite privilege to be allowed to remain there, unsullied by the outside world. Over and over again, women writers commented on the exalted position of their sex and thanked men for treating them with the respect which was their due. Thus Mrs. Sarah J. Hale, editor of *Godey's Lady's Book* and probably the most influential spokeswoman for her millions of sisters in nineteenth-century America, dedicated her *Woman's Record* to American men, "who show, in their laws and customs, respecting women, ideas more just and feelings more noble than were ever evinced by men of any other nation."[28]

In the home middle-class wives had an arena in which they exercised much genuine responsibility and power. Their husbands were absent often; yet even when present, men were urged by popular moralists to model themselves after women and treat their wives with affection and deference. But is appears that the very set of ideas which endowed them with significant responsibility and power in the domestic sphere also weighted women with a heavy burden of anxiety and guilt. It was their duty to make home perfect, for only in a perfect home could husbands and children be redeemed and the outside society thereby reformed and saved. Or, to put it another way, only a perfect home could be a genuine alternative, a genuinely Edenic retreat from the horrors of the larger society.

Whether perfection was defined in terms of retreat and affection or training and order, it followed that every mundane household duty of women could be invested with the gravest implications. No matter how apparently routine and trivial, *every last chore* could be made to seem enormously significant. "Who knows but the Mexican war may be traced to an ill-cooked, ill-assorted, contradictory and irritating cabinet dinner?" asked "A Lady of New York" in *The American System of Cookery*.[29] This was an unusually bold claim, or at least an unusually specific one. But many others spoke in the same vein. "It is within your power," Daniel Wise told young American wives, "to create a domestic heaven in the lowliest cottage."[30] Catharine Beecher was especially prominent in the campaign to endow homemakers with a sense of the grave significance of their every action. Her advice books covered dozens of minute topics, abounded with technical illustrations, and always conveyed the message that if such seemingly unimportant matters were not attended to by American wives, the family and society would suffer grievously.

Ideas of this sort obviously led directly to a belief in the pressing need for conscious, sustained domestic training for women. Housekeeping, in fact, was a science "of broad extent, and minute detail. It cannot be grasped without due preparation, any more than a course of history could be achieved without laborious reading."[31] This notion could take ludicrous forms when combined with the ruthless perfectionism of popular moralists. "For my own part," wrote William A. Alcott in *Letters to a Sister; or Woman's Mission*, "I see not how a Christian woman of but common intelligence, should dare. . . to make a loaf of bread without a thorough knowledge of Chemistry."[32] In the same book he summarized the message to American wives: "There is not an act of your lives so small but you should labor with all your might, and resolve, and if necessary re-resolve concerning it."[33]

The task of perfecting the home through ceaseless work and attention to detail was ultimately an impossible one; indeed, the constant effort and bustle of trying to perfect it probably would have ensured that family life would never succeed in being perfectly restful and joyous. But American domestic advisers encouraged women to believe that perfection was really theirs to attain, and that if they failed at it the responsibility was their own and the consequences vast. Inevitably, in a culture which entertained perfectionist dreams and looked to the home for their attainment, women would bear much of the sense of failure and guilt when perfection failed of being achieved.

Perhaps, then, historians should seek indications that middle-class women felt a sense of futility and guilt arising from the inevitable gap between expectations and reality. Presumptive signs of such feelings abound, but as yet little systematic study of this problem has been done.[34] It appears, for one thing, that women devised a number of ways to "drop out" of the domestic role without explicitly rejecting it. One way, of course, was to develop a non-domestic avocation or career in which one continued to pay lip-service to domesticity without personally trying to live up to it. This path was the one taken by many "scribbling women," most of whom apparently felt somewhat uneasy about their effective rejection of domesticity in favor of a literary career, but few of whom were able to face the fact that they had indeed rejected it.[35] A second path was to develop interests in charity work, Sunday School societies, tract societies, sewing circles, or other similar activities which the historian William L. O'Neill has called "social feminism."[36] These pursuits, like journalism and literature, were premised upon two of the fundamental tenets of the "cult of true womanhood,": that women were too pure to associate safely with anybody except other women, and that nurture, religion, letters, and the like were peculiarly feminine activities. Still a third avenue was to become involved in movements for political reform, including feminism. Even this alternative to domesticity did not necessarily result in a rejection of prevailing expectations and ideals about women and the home, as O'Neill and others have shown.[37] Another path is less clearly understood from the distance of a century or more, but some women—how many is anybody's guess—dropped out, temporarily or permanently, through sickliness and the use of drugs. By developing vague physical or psychological maladies a women could reduce to more manageable proportions the expectations focused upon her in her roles as wife, mother, and housekeeper. By turning to patent medicines, many of which were laced with alcohol or narcotic drugs, she could find more immediate and temporary respite.[38]

Let us attempt to summarize the foregoing discussion, and in the process we can perhaps note some consequences for the society at large of the middle-class tendency to perceive a virtually unbridgeable gulf between the domestic and worldly realms.

It seems clear, first, that these nineteenth-century Americans entertained utopian aspirations about the family. At least, they told themselves that the domestic sphere could truly and literally become an isle of bliss in which their hopes for leisure, harmony, and joy could be fulfilled. Even when they affirmed that the family ought to concern itself with moral training of its members, they still emphasized that this would occur through gently, loving techniques. Thus the ends of family life were emphatically individualistic, libertarian, even anarchic. In the perfected American home that perennial American aspiration, individual freedom, could at last be attained—and without a corresponding increase in social disorder.

In practice, as we have seen, these aspirations were more difficult to realize, even in such a small theater as the family, than most Americans had anticipated. Indeed, it even appears that the aspirations were so high as to breed greater frustration with family life than they might otherwise have been forced to endure. Internally, the perfectionist expectations placed heavy burdens of guilt upon adults of both sexes.

In terms of the relationship between family and community, the middle-class yearning for a small corner of peace in the form of a happy family may actually have furthered the social trends which Americans deplored and which encouraged them to turn inward in the first place: the misgovernment of the city, the frantic race for status through conspicuous consumption, the degradation of politics in the Jacksonian era, and the rest. It is notable in this connection that nineteenth-century writings on the city and on other problems of American society usually betrayed a deep ignorance even as they lamented the national decline and called for reform and renewal. Popular writers and their audience strike one as unable to perceive their society in any complexity; they tended to view it, and particularly the city, in stereotyped images, as a hellish place dotted with brothels, saloons, gambling-dens, race-tracks, and Catholic churches. What brought about this ignorance? The retreat to domesticity was hastened by fear of the city, but also by structural changes such as the withering of ties to kin and neighbors. These probably resulted from the migration of many middle-class families from small towns to cities, and were further exacerbated by the high rates of geographical mobility which apparently prevailed in nineteenth-century cities.[39]

Whatever the cause of the fear of the city and the ignorance about its workings, the point is that middle-class Americans increasingly opted for retreat rather than for active engagement in the life of their society. They thereby ensured that the abuses they perceived would be perpetuated and that their reasons for despairing about their society would grow ever stronger.

The foregoing indictment also raises the question of the "privacy" of the family. Middle-class Americans valued privacy in the nineteenth century as never before. In a sense their isolated families enjoyed a significant amount of it. Certainly this was one of the things implied in the distinction they customarily drew between home and the world. But their privacy was far from complete, and in some ways it has declined further since that time. The family was being penetrated by society at large at the very moment that its members discerned a gulf between family and society. It was being penetrated, most significantly, by the popular novels, magazines, and advice-books of the day. Unthinking, traditional ways of proceeding—in sexual behavior, child nurture, task allocation—were being replaced by impersonal instruction provided by outsiders. Custom was being replaced by fashion.

Thus the vaunted privacy of the middle-class family, its emphatic otherness from the evil world beyond, did not run so deep as many believed. Uprooted, half-educated, self-scrutinizing, middle-class Americans turned eagerly to the new mechanisms which seemed ready to assume responsibility for telling them what to believe and how to behave. The "Jacksonian era," then, may have witnessed not a breakdown of institutions, as some historians contend, but rather the beginnings of a switch in the sources from which Americans would take their cues.[40]

And yet, if total privacy did not really exist, this was due to society's penetration of the family, not to any intense participation of family members in the life of the society. The emerging ideology of the happy family was an outgrowth of the pervasive American ideology called "privatism" by Sam B. Warner, Jr.:

Already [Warner writes] by the time of the Revolution privatism had become the American tradition. Its essence lay in its concentration upon the individual and the individual's search for wealth. Psychologically, privatism meant that the individual should seek happiness in personal independence and in the search for wealth; socially, privatism meant that the individual should see his first loyalty as his immediate family, and that a community should be a union of such money-making, accumulating families; politically, privatism meant that the community should keep the peace among individual money-makers, and, if possible, help to create an open and thriving setting where each citizen would have some substantial opportunity to prosper.[41]

One might conclude, then, that middle-class Americans in the mid-nineteenth-century city were able to isolate themselves with sufficient thoroughness to retreat from responsibility for dealing with urban governance and urban reform; but they were unable to isolate themselves to the degree needed for a genuinely different set of values, priorities, and configurations of personal interaction to take hold. Indeed, as one studies the supposedly Edenic family of the urban middle classes, one discovers that the very qualities by which Eden was defined—the possibility for isolation and individual fulfillment—and the implacable perfectionism with which such hopes were pursued, were quintessentially American. To these Americans of the nineteenth century there was no necessary conflict between the demands of domestic life and the desire for personal freedom. Huck Finn may have yearned to light out for the territory after exposure to domesticity as personified in Miss Watson. But to a great many less adventurous citizens, domesticity itself came to seem a pleasurable and emancipating escape-hatch from the cares and anxieties of life in nineteenth-century society. Or so they thought, at any rate. Huck encountered terrors and dangers in his travels to evade life in society. Perhaps it would have amused and heartened him to be told that his more conventional countrymen also came up against their own obstacles and disappointments in their search for a genuine alternative to urban life in the very midst of the city.

Notes

1. "Co-operative Associations," *Liberator*, X (December 25, 1840), p. 207; as quoted in Arthur E. Bestor, Jr., *Backwoods Utopias: The Sectarian and Owenite Phases of Communitarian Socialism in America: 1663–1829* (Philadelphia, 1950), p. 19.
2. William G. Eliot, Jr., *Lectures to Young Women* (Boston, 1880 [first published in 1853]), pp. 55–56.
3. The analysis which follows is based on my doctoral dissertation: *Family History: The Middle-Class American Family in the Urban Context, 1830–1870* (Department of History, Stanford University, 1972). For further discussion and many more examples the reader is invited to consult that work. I should add that the notion of the family as a utopian community occurred to me only as an afterthought and plays no part in the dissertation. The dissertation, however, contains discussions of several matters, such as kinship and conjugal role relationships, which I have largely omitted here.
4. Lydia H. Sigourney, *Whisper to a Bride* (Hartford, 1850), p. 25.
5. "Home," *Ladies' Magazine*, III (May, 1830), p. 217.
6. Timothy Shay Arthur, *Our Homes: Their Cares and Duties, Joys and Sorrows* (Philadelphia, 1856), p. 27.
7. Mrs. A. J. Graves, *Girlhood and Womanhood: or, Sketches of My Schoolmates* (Boston, 1844), pp. 179–80.

8. Catharine Beecher and Harriet Beecher Stowe, *The American Woman's Home: or Principles of Domestic Science* (New York, 1869), pp. 24–25.
9. Marvin Meyers, *The Jacksonian Persuasion: Politics and Belief* (New York, 1960), p. 11.
10. Michael B. Katz, *The Irony of Early School Reform: Educational Innovation in Mid-Nineteenth Century Massachusetts* (Cambridge, 1968), p. 5.
11. John Todd, *The Moral Influence, Dangers and Duties, Connected with Great Cities* (Northampton, Mass., 1841), pp. 18–20.
12. Ibid., p. 119.
13. Daniel Wise, *The Young Man's Counsellor; or, Sketches and Illustrations of the Duties and Dangers of Young Men,* 4th ed. (Boston, 1851), pp. 196–98; R. Richard Wohl, "The 'Country Boy' Myth and Its Place in American Urban Culture: The Nineteenth-Century Contribution," ed. Moses Rischin, *Perspectives in American History,* III (1969), p. 90.
14. Todd, p. 54.
15. "Home," *Ladies' Magazine,* p. 218.
16. William M. Thayer, *Pastor's Wedding Gift* (Boston, 1854), p. 36.
17. "Ik Marvel," pseud. [Donald Grant Mitchell], *Reveries of a Bachelor; or, A Book of the Heart* (New York, 1893 [first published in 1850]), p. 57.
18. Theodore Dwight, Jr., *The Father's Book; or Suggestions for the Government and Instruction of Young Children, on Principles Appropriate to a Christian Country,* 2nd ed. (Springfield, Mass., 1835), p. 23.
19. Kinship patterns in colonial America are discussed in John Demos, *A Little Commonwealth: Family Life in Plymouth Colony* (New York, 1970) and Philip J. Greven, Jr., *Four Generations: Population, Land, and Family in Colonial Andover, Massachusetts* (Ithaca, N.Y., 1970). For a modern sociological discussion of kinship which has implications for the nineteenth century, see Michael Young and Peter Willmott, *Family and Kinship in East London* (Baltimore, 1957).
20. Timothy Shay Arthur, "The Prodigal's Return," in idem, *Stories for Parents* (Philadelphia, 1854), pp. 92–111.
21. Lydia Maria Child, "Home and Politics," *Sartain's Union Magazine of Literature and Art,* III (August, 1848), pp. 43–48.
22. See Barbara Walter, "The Cult of True Womanhood: 1820–1860," *American Quarterly,* XVIII (Summer, 1966), pp. 151–74.
23. Artemus B. Muzzey, *The Young Man's Friend* (Boston, 1836), p. 103.
24. Ibid., p. 102.
25. William A. Alcott, *The Young Man's Guide* (Boston, 1833), p. 247.
26. Charles S. Woodruff, *Legalized Prostitution: or Marriage as It Is, and Marriage as It Should Be, Philosophically Considered* (Boston, 1862), p. 148.
27. Alcott, *The Physiology of Marriage* (Boston, 1855), passim.
28. Sarah J. Hale, *Woman's Record; or Sketches of All Distinguished Women, from "the Beginning" till A.D. 1850* (New York, 1853), p. 5.
29. Quoted in *Sartain's Union Magazine of Literature and Art,* I (December, 1847), p. 287.
30. Daniel Wise, *Bridal Greetings: A Marriage Gift* (New York, 1850), p. 84.
31. Lydia H. Sigourney, *Letters to My Pupils* (New York, 1851), p. 115.
32. William A. Alcott, *Letters to a Sister; or Woman's Mission* (Buffalo, 1850), p. 74.
33. Ibid., p. 32.
34. See, however, William R. Taylor and Christopher Lasch, "Two 'Kindred Spirits': Sorority and Family in New England, 1839–1846," *New England Quarterly,* XXXVI (March, 1963), pp. 23–41.
35. See Ann D. Wood, "The 'Scribbling Women' and Fanny Fern: Why Women Wrote," *American Quarterly,* XXIII (Spring, 1971), pp. 3–24. For an interesting older treatment see Gordon S. Haight, *Mrs. Sigourney: The Sweet Singer of Hartford* (New Haven, 1930).
36. William L. O'Neill, *Everyone Was Brave: The Rise and Fall of Feminism in America* (Chicago, 1969), Ch. iii. See also Keith Melder, "Ladies Bountiful: Organized Women's Benevolence in Early 19th-Century America," *New York History,* XLVIII (July, 1967), pp. 231–54.

37. O'Neill, *Everyone Was Brave;* Aileen S. Kraditor, *The Ideas of the Woman Suffrage Movement, 1890–1920* (New York, 1965), esp. Ch. iii.

38. I make this assertion without, as yet, having much evidence about drugs or their connection to the anxieties of women. Some nineteenth-century testimony is to be found in William. A. Alcott, *Forty Years in the Wilderness of Pills and Powders* (Boston, 1859); and Catharine Beecher, *Letters to the People on Health and Happiness* (New York, 1855).

39. The most important recent study of geographical mobility is Stephan Thernstrom and Peter R. Knights, "Men in Motion: Some Data and Speculations about Urban Population Mobility in Nineteenth-Century America," *Journal of Interdisciplinary History,* I (Autumn, 1970), pp. 7–35.

40. This idea was suggested by Professor Daniel H. Calhoun in an unpublished paper entitled "The Authoritarian Character of Jacksonian America," which was read in August, 1968, at the annual meeting of the Pacific Coast Branch of the American Historical Association.

41. Sam B. Warner, Jr., *The Private City: Philadelphia in Three Periods of Its Growth* (Philadelphia, 1968), pp. 3–4.

Family Time and Industrial Time: Family and Work in a Planned Corporation Town, 1900–1924

Tamara K. Hareven

The role of the family in the adaptation of workers to industrial life, a central concern for sociologists for some time, has only recently begun to interest historians. Neil Smelser has shown that during the early years of the industrial revolution in Britain, working families carried their own habits into the factory setting and often continued to function as units. William Goode went further to argue that the family was an independent agent in the process of industrialization.

This paper was subsequently developed into *Family Time and Industrial Time* (Cambridge University Press, 1982). The project was supported by Grant No. RO 8963–73–500 from the National Endowment for the Humanities, and by a research grant from the Merrimack Valley Textile Museum, with matching funds from Amoskeag Industries, the Cogswell Benevolent Trust, and the Norwin and Elizabeth Bean Foundation. The oral history interviews were supported by the New Hampshire Council for the Humanities and the United Textile Workers. I am indebted to Dr. Thomas Leavitt, Director of the Merrimack Valley Textile Museum, whose initial support helped launch this project. Research was carried out at the Manchester Historic Association and the Baker Library, Graduate School of Business Administration, Harvard University. I am indebted to Randolph Langenbach for his important discoveries in the history of the Amoskeag Corporation in his own study of the architectural and urban planning history of the Amoskeag Mills. Herbert Gutman, David Montgomery, Maris Vinovskis, John Modell, Howard Chudacoff, Daniel Walkowitz, and David Grimsted provided valuable criticisms.

Rather than being a passive recipient of social and economic change, the family acted as a catalyst in activating changes in the larger society.[1]

This revisionist sociological view of the role of the family in the process of industrialization has been reinforced by the work of some labor historians. Following the route of cultural anthropologists, they have demonstrated that workers, while adapting to the industrial system, also succeeded in modifying it in terms of their previous cultural traditions and work habits. The continuous influx of immigrants from the same or similar backgrounds tended to reinforce the impact of preindustrial immigrant traditions on the new system.[2]

Several recent historical studies have emphasized the active role of the family in the migration process and its function as a source of continuity and stability under the pressures of adjustment to new conditions. Some of these studies now argue that not only did the family not break down, it in fact retained active control over the careers of its members. As the transmitter of premigration culture, the family kept ethnic traditions alive, and its cultural heritage guided the family in its adaptation to new conditions.[3]

Such revisions of the stereotypes of family passivity and breakdown in the industrial process have engendered new extremes. The filiopietism which has been emerging over the past years tends to exaggerate the strength of the immigrant or working-class family and its autonomy as an institution. This neo-romantic interpretation of the role of the family could easily result in another stereotype, as removed from historical reality as earlier ones.

Now that the ghosts of social breakdown are being exorcised from historical scholarship, we must ask: to what degree, under varying circumstances, was the family in control of its own decisions, and to what degree was its behavior guided by external pressures and incentives? To answer these questions it is necessary to study more closely the family's role in the industrial environment, an approach which must be *contextual* as well as *dynamic*. Contrary to the prevalent approach which studies the family in isolation in the household, it is necessary to see the family as it actually existed in constant interaction with other social processes and institutions.[4]

For laborers such an approach links family organization and traditions to the experience of industrial work. It takes into account the interrelationships between the family and technological change, the work process, demands for work discipline, job mobility, ethnicity, and economic behavior, within the framework of industrial capitalism. Such a model by necessity views the "family" as a process which unfolds over its entire cycle rather than as a constant at one point in time. It takes into account the fact that family structures, functions, relationships, and needs differed at each stage of the family cycle and that these internal changes were related to larger societal processes.[5]

If the term "industrial time" designates the new time schedules and work discipline imposed by the industrial system, "family time" refers to the internal and external timing of family behavior at different stages of individual and family development, particularly to the timing of major demographic events. An understanding of how the two different times affected each other, the areas in which they conflicted or reinforced each other, provides a model for the study of the family's role in the larger society. While families responded to external pressures and adjusted their timing accordingly, they also often timed their own behavior in accordance with their internal "clock." It is the historian's task to determine to what degree, under what changing circumstances, the family's behavior was timed in response to external conditions, and to what degree it moved in accordance with the family's internal and traditional timepiece.[6]

This essay will explore the family's interaction with the industrial system on two levels: it will first examine the workers' adjustment to industrial life. Secondly, it will examine the internal timing of family behavior along the family cycle in response to the external pressures and demands of the world of work.

This exploration focuses on the experienced French-Canadian immigrant laborers of the Amoskeag Manufacturing Company in Manchester, New Hampshire, at the peak of the corporation's industrial development during the first two decades of the twentieth century. At the turn of the century Manchester had 70,000 inhabitants and was the seat of the world's largest textile mill—The Amoskeag Corporation—which employed an average of 14,000 workers each year in the period preceding World War I.[7]

Originally developed by the Amoskeag Corporation as a planned New England textile community, Manchester, unlike its sister communities of Lawrence and Lowell, continued to be dominated by the corporation that originally founded it in the 1830s.[8] Similar to the textile manufacturing towns on which it was patterned, the Amoskeag Corporation recruited its early labor force from rural New Englanders. From the 1850s on, immigrants from England, Scotland, and Ireland began to replace native American workers. In the 1870s, following the textile industry's discovery of the French Canadians as the most "industrious" and "docile" labor force, the corporation embarked on the systematic recruitment of laborers from Quebec. By 1900, French Canadians constituted about 40% of the labor force in the mill, and about one-half of the city's population. While their migration continued through the first two decades of the twentieth century, the corporation was also absorbing small numbers of Germans and Swedes, followed by increasing numbers of Polish and Greek immigrants in the second decade of the twentieth century.[9]

As a planned industrial town, Manchester did not experience the classic problems of social disorganization generally attributed to urban living. The carefully designed and maintained corporation space, encompassing the mill yard and housing for a large segment of the work force, enclosed the workers in a total environment. From the late nineteenth century on, Manchester developed cohesive ethnic neighborhoods which were organized along kinship and ethnic lines, and which surrounded the corporation housing, radiating east, south, and west of the mill yard.[10] The problems that Manchester's laborers were facing, therefore, did not derive from urban anomie, but rather from the pressures of industrial work and discipline. These conditions allow the historian to examine the role of the family in the process of industrialization without the interference of factors generally connected with the pressures of life in a large city.

The surviving historical record utilized for this study is unusually rich, allowing an exploration of conditions and developments from the perspectives of the workers as well as the corporation. The unique collection of cumulative, individual employee files which were recorded for the period 1910–1936, provides detailed data for the reconstruction of the workers' careers. Particularly important are the entries in each employee file listing the reasons for his or her leaving the job, as well as the reasons given by overseers for the dismissal of workers. The linkage of this data with marriage and insurance records, as well as with oral histories, permitted a reconstruction of the workers' life and work histories with a wealth of information unavailable in census records.[11]

Family Interaction with the Corporation

In their day-by-day relationships, the corporation and the family were two interacting institutions. Although the two were not equals, they were exercising checks and balances on each other. In a paternalistic system such as that of the Amoskeag Mills, the corporation not only perceived itself as a family, but also was aware of the family's powerful role in the workers' lives and consciously attempted to utilize that force as an instrument to control the workers. It therefore relied on the family to recruit the workers and to socialize them into industrial work.[12]

The Amoskeag Corporation and its immigrant workers demonstrated a remarkable fit in their respective ideologies of work and of social hierarchy and authority. Nineteenth-century paternalistic ideology, still alive in twentieth-century Manchester, viewed industrial management as a family affair. In the tradition of industrial paternalism the corporation perceived itself as a large family, and the workers within it as its children. "More than 15,000 persons work in these mills. . . . It is true that the large company to which they sell their labor treats them as its own children," read a typical corporation advertisement in French-Canadian newspapers. The corporation's own management and organization were structured along family and kinship lines. Even in the early part of the twentieth century, when workers were hired as individuals, the corporation continued to employ entire families where possible. Family hiring was more advantageous to the corporation since the effort invested in recruitment and transportation could be maximized through the number of textile workers provided by one family. This also held true for housing arrangements where the corporation preferred to utilize the space by placing families with several working members in the corporation tenements.[13]

In the beginning of the twentieth century, the corporation embarked on a series of new employee welfare programs. With the exception of the superannuation of a limited number of older workers, these programs were aimed primarily at the workers' families, rather than at individuals. They included a homeownership plan for workers who had stayed in the corporation's employ five years or longer, a playground and dental care program for children, and a visiting nurse and home instruction program for mothers. Management hoped to socialize the children through these programs, to Americanize the workers, and to develop a permanent, stable, and loyal industrial labor force.[14] The new welfare program introduced in 1910 was combined with an efficiency program which, under the influence of Taylorism, tried to centralize and rationalize hiring policies, and to increase the speed of production.[15]

Corporate paternalism struck a responsive chord in newly arrived immigrant workers. The work ethic and customs of a preindustrial culture were woven around the traditional view of the family as a work unit. The workers transferred this tradition into the industrial system and realigned their family work relationships in accordance with the needs and expectations of industrial work. This is not to argue that the tasks and division of labor which the French-Canadian farm family had traditionally carried out in rural Quebec were automatically transferred to the American industrial system. Child labor in the factory, the work of mothers outside the home, and the regimentation of life to an industrial schedule were all novel experiences.

The basic tradition of family work and of the economic role of each member, however, was carried over from the agricultural background. The important continuity was in the perception and experience of the family as a work unit, even when the locations of the job and the work process were different. Daughters and wives who had earlier contributed to the family's economic efforts on the farm transferred these work roles to industrial labor. Even though the tasks they were performing differed from those in their premigration setting, the basic traditional assumptions that guided family work roles were not disrupted.[16] The one area of conflict concerned the issue of women's work. The French-Canadian customs, reinforced by the Catholic Church, regarded women's work outside the home as a threat to the family. This did not stop two-thirds of all married French-Canadian women in the town from working in the factory. In their own minds, they reconciled the conflict by arguing that their work was temporary. Many, however, claimed such temporary conditions till the end of their lives. Married women continued to work over their entire careers with intermittent interruptions for childbirth.[17]

The relationship between the workers and the corporation was one of mutual interaction. The degree of their cooperation or withdrawal depended on a variety of factors for each: on the corporation's side, the relationship was governed by the availability of the labor force and by the fluctuation of the textile market. In periods of labor shortage prior to World War I, when the corporation had to compete with other industries over the labor supply in the city, it was forced to tolerate the autonomous behavior of the workers and their resistance to modernization. On the other hand, during it continuous decline in the post-World-War-I period, and until its shutdown in 1936, the corporation's gradual curtailment of its labor force allowed the workers less freedom to manipulate the system.[18]

The workers were by no means equals to the corporation in this balance of power, but they were able to exercise a certain degree of autonomy under limited conditions. The workers' response depended on the changing work conditions and demands of the corporation, and on individual and family considerations. The availability of alternative employment opportunities in the city, economic needs, traditional work habits, and family values all influenced their behavior. Demographic patterns had a crucial impact on the workers' careers, especially those of women. The degree of their dependence on industrial work or independence from it, especially mobility in and out of the mill, was determined by individual and family needs which changed over the stages of the family's development. Particularly significant in this scheme was the shifting margin of poverty and subsistence at different stages of the family cycle. Unmarried individuals in their late twenties had a different attitude toward work than fathers of families of five, for example, or widows in their fifties.[19]

This model suggests, therefore, that both the worker's family and the corporation were flexible institutions. Their relationships and patterns of interaction fluctuated and changed over time, in response to internal conditions as well as under the impact of larger historical processes. The family was most effective in making an impact on work patterns in two areas: (1) it facilitated the adjustment of its members by acting as a labor recruiter, a housing agent, and as a source of support in critical life situations, and (2) it exercised its own controls, even if limited ones, against the corporation by encouraging labor turnover, by influencing the job placement of its members, and by affecting job control in the daily routine of work.

The Role of Family and Kin in Industrial Adjustment

Acting as a conveyor belt, facilitating the workers' movements and cushioning the shock of adjustment, the family and the kin group served as the labor recruiters, the organizers of migration routes, and housing agents. Within the factory, the family group directed the work choices of its members, influenced their placement in different departments, and prepared them for industrial work. Kinship ties were especially instrumental in facilitating the workers' experimentation with alternative careers.[20]

French Canadians were streaming to Manchester in response to systematic recruitment propaganda issued out of Manchester through their own ethnic organizations and through communications from relatives. Their kin met them on arrival, placed them on their first job, and located them as temporary boarders until they found a corporation flat or rented an apartment in the growing French-Canadian section of the city's West Side.[21]

Chain migration through the kin group was not limited to Manchester. Kinship networks were pervasive throughout the entire industrial region in New England. The presence of clusters of kin in a variety of New England industrial towns offered laborers of the Amoskeag Mills the opportunity to migrate through a series of mill towns with the hope of improving their conditions. Their migration was not terminal. It followed a circuitous route through other textile mills in Maine, southern Massachusetts, and Rhode Island, where relatives were working.[22] Workers moved back and forth, from Manchester to Quebec and back to Manchester. Leaving the mills often for two or three summer months, they visited relatives in the Quebec countryside or took on temporary jobs, only to return again to the textile mills in Manchester.

Family ties thus formed a network of employment opportunities as well as temporary and permanent stations for migration. A reconstitution of the migration patterns on the basis of the employee records of the Amoskeag Company suggests that prior to 1922 about one-fourth of the employees studied immigrated to the other New England mill towns in search of better jobs. In most of these instances, the presence of relatives in other towns facilitated their temporary sojourns. Migration did not destroy the family and kin group. It transposed a formerly localized family pattern over an entire industrial region in New England.[23]

Flexibility in corporation employment policy, which emanated primarily from the need for cheap labor, enabled the family to exercise some controls over the recruitment and placement of its members. The continuous informality in corporation hiring policies, and especially the overseers' autonomy in their departments, facilitated personal connections between overseers and the workers' relatives. The character of a department was basically determined by its overseer, and a workroom frequently containing 100 or more workers was still identified by the overseer's name. Workers continued to obtain jobs directly from the overseer, even after the introduction of a formal employment office.[24] When there was a vacancy in a workroom, the overseers generally filled it by asking one of the workers to bring in someone he knew. Most workers ignored the employment office and turned directly to the overseers for jobs and the placement of relatives. Since the workers were continuously coming and going, this informal placement network was quite extensive.

The family group thus infiltrated the mill and made its direct impact on the composition of the workrooms. Kin and ethnic clusters developed in most departments. Members of one family often clustered in a variety of jobs working near each other in the same room, and childhood friends, cousins, and neighbors often worked side by side for years. About one-fourth of all French-Canadian workers studied in this group met their spouses in the mill and continued to work there after marriage.[25]

Such arrangements enabled the workers to exercise some controls over the work pace. Especially following World War I, as the corporation accelerated its pressures for speed-ups, workers assisted relatives and friends in meeting quotas, even if it meant a loss in pay on their own piece-rate work. The presence of relatives reinforced the workers' collective strength in resisting corporation pressure, especially when the demand for speed-up became overwhelming. The pervasiveness of family groups also enabled the workers to try out different jobs in various departments by passing for one of their relatives, to take turns going to work, and to substitute for each other by switching their employee passes, or by having several members utilize the same pass.

From the late 1920s on, the corporation was becoming nervous about the ethnic and kin alignment in the workrooms: "Refrain from requesting the employment of relatives of persons in charge of units in the same units," read the instruction of management to overseers. An inspector reporting his conversation with various overseers to the management concluded: "For instance, I did not believe it was really good for any unit of the mill to be wholly comprised of relatives and friends of the operatives also of the same race." In that particular workroom, 90% of the labor force was made up of the same ethnic group.[26]

The strength and resilience which workers derived from their families was reinforced by ethnic ties. Ethnicity provided the major organizational scheme for the workers' adjustment to the pressures of the factory work and life in the city. The ethnic group offered the commonality of a cultural heritage, language, residential cohesion, entertainment and rituals, religious ties, and mutual benefit associations. Most of the work and residential patterns were organized around the laborers' family and ethnic ties. Tight-knit clusters of ethnic residential areas appeared in Manchester from the 1880s on.[27] Ethnic enclaves developed in the corporation housing as well. Although corporation flats had to be secured through individual family applications, residents managed to cluster along ethnic lines in corporation housing in the same manner in which they succeeded in aligning themselves in the workroom. Officially, applications for residence in corporation housing had to be submitted long in advance, and workers had to wait their turn. In reality, friends and relatives notified prospective tenants of vacancies and managed to secure those flats ahead of their turn through the help of acquaintances in the office. Sons of former workers recall the invisible, but clearly reinforced, boundaries between ethnic youth gangs in the corporation tenements.[28]

Family Time: The Stages of the Family Cycle

Internal family considerations and demographic conditions, but primarily economic need, influenced the patterns of the workers' persistence and migration. In the pre-World-War-I period, families decided who of their members would go to work, what son or daughter should start first, at what point the wife should stop, when she should return to work, and who should explore alternative employment outside the mill.

This process of family decision-making emerges both in the analysis of the employment files, where workers frequently cited family reasons for leaving their jobs, as well as in the oral history interviews. Aside from involuntary reasons such as illness, accidents, retirement, and death, laborers left because: "husband did not want wife to work," "wife did not approve of husband's work in the night shift," "parents want son to go back to school," "girl takes care of young children at home." As long as the employment system was flexible, family members could decide whose labor was needed to maintain the family's income, who should work in the mill, who should stay home, and what department or workroom he or she should be sent to.[29]

What factors governed the family's decision on the timing of entrance into the labor force, taking on new family obligations, or migration into new areas? What were the internal and external factors which directed the family's interaction with the world of work?

The timing of behavior followed the family life cycle and was governed by the external pressures of the industrial system. The decision as to when people were leaving home, marrying, giving birth to their first child, spacing the births of their subsequent children, or sending their children to work or to school was timed by the internal clock of family traditions as well as by the external pressures of the factory system and by economic needs. Historians are only now beginning to unravel what specific processes were involved in this timing, and how they varied among different socioeconomic and cultural groups under different circumstances.[30]

For the French-Canadian immigrants, industrial work meant family employment. It is not surprising, therefore, that they were recognized as textile workers par excellence. French Canadians had the highest birth rate of all industrial workers in the United States. Their large numbers of children made them particularly suitable for family employment. In New England their average family size was 7.2, while the Irish, a group also well known for high fertility, had an average of 5 members per family. French Canadians also boasted the highest average number of family members working in the textile industry (3.9). Large family size, which had served well the work needs of farmers, continued to be an asset in industrial work in the late nineteenth century.

Changing conditions in the textile industry from the early part of the nineteenth century, however, dictated a modification of demographic behavior after the end of the nineteenth century.[31] The first major impact of the industrial system on demographic behavior was in the postponement of marriage, particularly for women. By the second decade of the twentieth century, women who had migrated to Manchester in their teens and second-generation immigrant women began to delay their marriage until their late twenties or early thirties. This was a direct response to the conditions of industrial work. Because much of the family's income depended on the work of more than one member, marriage did not offer an escape from work outside the home.[32]

Postponement of marriage was also dictated to women by their own parents. Since single women workers carried a significant share of the burden of their families' support from the moment they were able to work, parents counted on their daughters' wages as an essential addition to the family income. As unmarried daughters sixteen and older began to work full-time, their parents and younger siblings were gradually withdrawing from work. Several investigations of New England textile towns, including Manchester, which were carried out by the U.S. Bureau of Labor Statistics revealed that while sons committed only 83% of their income to their parents' budgets, daughters delivered 95% of their pay. Parents tried to influence daughters to delay their marriage in order to continue to rely on them as a source of income.[33]

Aside from economic need, women also worked because they enjoyed their occupations. Numerous testimonies in the oral history interviews provide this insight, which has escaped historians who rely on quantitative data only. "I loved my work," said one retired weaver (now ninety-four years old). Work in the mills provided an experience of partnership and sociability which was organized along sex lines, but which nevertheless carried a family ambiance into the workrooms. "We were all like a family," remarked another retired worker.[34]

For most young immigrant women workers, marriage did not provide an escape from industrial work; it actually added the new burden of housekeeping and childrearing to factory labor. Caught between the traditional definition of sex roles in their own culture and the economic needs of their family, women found themselves working in the mill as well as tending to their domestic tasks. Most female textile workers continued to work after marriage until giving birth, and returned to the mill as soon as they weaned their infants. They worked until the birth of their next child and then stopped temporarily, only to return again.[35] The woman's mother next door, or an aging aunt or other female relative provided day care. Where no relatives were available, women either left their children with a neighbor or deposited them each day at the orphanage, which, in addition to its regular inmates, by necessity took in children of working mothers.

About one-half of the married men working in the Amoskeag Mills also had their wives working with them, in order to supplement the family income. This experience was not unique to Manchester. It was characteristic of employment patterns in the textile and shoe industries in general, which in 1930, for example, had the highest ratio of females to males ten years and above reporting gainful employment.[36]

Once they had children, however, women's careers became more checkered and less stable. Married women with children made up the major proportion of the Amoskeag Mills' reserve labor force. While the group of regularly employed workers consisted of a higher percentage of young women under age thirty-five, the reserve labor force included a higher percentage of women between the ages of thirty-five and fifty-five. There was no comparable age discrepancy between males in the regular and the reserve force. Among workers older than fifty-five, there was no major difference in the percentage of men and women in the reserve labor force.[37]

The pattern of the work cycle of married women was thus articulated to the family cycle: during their childbearing and childrearing years, women did not work to their full capacity. Because of family reasons as well as corporation needs, they found themselves in the reserve labor force, rather than as regular workers. During the period of optimal family earnings, when their children were grown, but still living at home and working, the women worked only occasionally. The marriage or departure of the last child drove the mothers back to the mill. This explains why one finds a much higher proportion of married women aged fifty-five and up on the regular labor force, rather than on the reserve. The most intensive periods in the employment of married women came before age thirty-five and after age fifty-five. In the intervening periods, their intermittent work patterns depended on the availability of temporary jobs in the mill. Prior to 1922, there was almost always a job to be found in one department or another. After the strike in 1922, as a consequence of gradual and continuous curtailment, married women were most vulnerable to permanent job loss if they left work to raise children.

One of the important functions of delayed marriage, especially in the second generation of immigrants, was a curtailment in the number of children born. In some respects, this decline in fertility was a manifestation of a gradual secularization and relaxation of traditional norms. It also represented, however, changing conditions in the employment market. With the passing of the New

Hampshire Child Labor Law in 1905, the employment of children under sixteen became increasingly risky. In this case, the corporation decided to comply with the new law, since it had nothing to lose at a time when changes in production and experimentation with efficiency made the work of young children obsolete. The decline in the child labor market turned large numbers of children into economic burdens on the family. It was advantageous, therefore, to limit the number of children, especially since childbirth impaired the mother's effectiveness as a breadwinner; it imposed on her patterns of intermittent employment and therefore undermined her chances of occupational advancement.[38]

Even though they were not actually entering factory work before age sixteen, children were socialized to the work experience in the mill at an early age. Industrial labor became part of their lives even before they actually worked. The experience of their parents, and the proximity of their homes to the mills, prevented any real separation between the world of childhood and the world of work. Children carrying lunch pails to the mills at the noon hour were a familiar part of the Manchester scene, where school children earned their first money by bringing lunches from the boarding houses to the mills. Most youths attending high school worked regularly in the mills during the summer. The expectations that children would have to work as soon as the law permitted were strongly impressed on them from an early age by their parents. The family economy, as well as the family's work ethic, was built around the assumption that children would contribute to the family's economic effort from the earliest opportunity.

By the time they entered the mill, young people had become familiar with the entire work process. Parents and older brothers and sisters provided a variety of models of occupational behavior. Oral history interviews have revealed consistently that most young boys and girls commencing work in the mills learned initial tasks from relatives rather than from strangers. An informal family apprenticeship system was thus infused into the formal structure of the world's largest textile mill.

When they came to take their first job, the children were already familiar with the names of overseers and second hands, knew the gossip about various transactions in the workrooms, and were familiar with a number of shortcuts and tricks. They also knew from an early age that the Amoskeag Corporation was the single largest employer in the city and that they could not afford to be blackballed by the Amoskeag Company, because they would not be able to find work anywhere else in northern New England.

Work roles along sex lines were also inculcated at an early age. Girls knew that, until their marriage, their work would be regulated by parents and that most of their income would be ploughed back into the family's resources. They were also prepared for the fact that if the family could afford to send any of its children to school after age fourteen, the boys would go first. Within the limited occupational structure of the mill town, they were prepared for the fact that the highest rank of skill a woman could aspire to would be that of a weaver, while men could hope to become loom fixers, expert dye mixers, master mechanics, and eventually even overseer, the most coveted position.

This advance knowledge of the limits of opportunity cast the daughter into the role of back-up person for the son's career. It meant that her work would serve to facilitate her brother's occupational mobility. Girls were directed to the mill and were expected to work steadily, in order to plug the holes in the family's income, so that their brothers could afford the flexibility of experimentation in search of better occupations. As long as the daughter maintained a consistent income, the sons could afford the freedom to transfer from one department to another in the mill, or could take the risk of experimenting with outside jobs. It is not surprising, therefore, that unmarried women under thirty (who might generally be expected to have a higher turnover on the job) showed a higher persistence rate except for situations where they moved because they followed husbands or parents to another mill town or to another job.[39]

Commencement of work did not mean independence from parental and family controls. Young men and women working in the mill continued to live in their parents' or relatives' households until marriage. Those without parents boarded with relatives, usually with married brothers and sisters or with aunts and uncles under similar arrangements. They were paying, in effect, for their room and board and were using the remainder of their pay for supplies and personal savings. While in large commercial cities young men and women tended to leave their homes and to board with strangers, industrial workers in Manchester continued to live at home or with relatives until they married. They rarely boarded with strangers. Only those men and women in their twenties and thirties who had no relatives in the city turned to corporation or commercial boarding houses.[40]

Family regulation of the individual careers of its members significantly cut down initiative for migration and experimentation with other occupations. The employment of several members in the same enterprise made the entire family vulnerable to fluctuations of the labor market and the shifting of occupational opportunities. During periods of layoff and curtailment of production, an entire family group found itself without work. This particular vulnerability was dramatized during the strike of 1922, when whole families were unemployed and on the verge of starvation during the nine-month shutdown of the mills. The strike clearly revealed that workers who had spouses or other relatives employed in the shoe industry were more inclined to strike than those whose entire source of support depended on the textile industry. Disagreement over the strike tore families apart. Brothers and sisters stopped talking to each other after their initial disagreement over whether they should strike. The almost total dependency of entire families on the textile industry deprived them of the opportunity of assisting each other during that critical situation.[41]

Conclusion

Family or surrogate family organization thus provided the central organizing scheme in the workers' living and work experience. These arrangements had their own built-in flexibilities which were governed by the family's decisions, or by external pressures, as conditions might dictate. On what basis the family made its decisions and what considerations and motives were involved in the decision are questions still open for exploration.

Immigrant families in factory towns timed their behavior by the internal clocks which were wound by their traditional customs, as well as by the factory bells. Under what circumstances did they respond to their traditional rhythms of time, and under what circumstances did they conform to industrial time? This is one of the key issues of social, cultural, and economic history. The data in this study suggest that at certain stages of their cycle families were more independent than at other stages, and that the differences in their behavior at different points in time were governed by internal family conditions as well as by the pressures and requirements of the industrial system. While these tentative conclusions await careful testing and further detailed research, it is clear now that the family was a flexible institution, and that given the historical circumstances or the opportunity structure, it was a dependent agent at certain times and an independent agent at other times.

While sociologists have been arguing that the isolated nuclear family was the form most fit for the industrial environment, this study suggests that the most adaptable family type was the extended family. With elaborate kin networks in Manchester as well as in Quebec, and with extensions in several other industrial New England towns, such families were best able to offer their members flexibility in the immigration process and in adaptation to new industrial conditions. Their major strength was in their ability to manage their resources and to direct their members into the labor force in accordance with their own needs.[42]

Despite the sophisticated structures of industrial capitalism, families continued to function as production units, even though the workplace shifted from the home to the industrial plant. Within the limited flexibility of a corporation-controlled factory town, the family could continue to make its own labor force decisions and to maintain controls over the careers of its members, as long as the market was open. Migration to an urban setting and industrial work did not drastically challenge paternal authority and traditional sex roles.

The family's interaction with the system was based on cooperation and mutual exploitation of needs and opportunities. The family succumbed to the pressures of industrial work during periods of labor surplus, but maintained its own controls during periods of labor shortage. It offered its members important resources to fall back on during times of crisis or critical life situations. While it prepared its children for industrial work, it also cushioned them from the potential shock and disruptions which they encountered under new industrial conditions. In its effort to protect its members from such exposures, the family developed its own defense system and brought its cultural traditions to bear on its environment and the industrial system.

The immigrant laborers of Manchester, New Hampshire, offer the historian the rare opportunity to explore intensively a group of industrial villagers living in a twentieth-century city still dominated by nineteenth-century paternalism. Several unique facets of their experience might lead us to question the feasibility of generalizing to the experience of the family and industrial work: patterns of family employment were different in the textile industry, which is female-intensive, than in steel communities, where women's occupations were segregated from male occupations.[43] Secondly, the continuation of paternalism in a community this size is not typical of American industrial towns in general. Finally, the particular immigrant group studied here in detail—the French Canadians—had the flexibility of "commuting" to and from the homeland, which other immigrants did not enjoy.

Despite the unique conditions of Manchester, it is possible to generalize from its experience about most early twentieth-century textile communities in the northeastern United States. It is not surprising that the patterns found in Manchester have strong parallels in mid-nineteenth-century Lancashire, England, and in late-nineteenth-century Stockport, England, and Amiens, France—all of which were centers for the textile industry.[44] What is more surprising is that the kin and family patterns described in this study bear resemblance to patterns found in London's Bethnal Green and Boston's West End in the 1950s.[45]

This study does not provide a universal interpretation of the interaction of the family with the world of work. Instead, it invites historians to pursue these questions in a variety of communities under different historical conditions in order to derive deeper insights into the relationship between the family and the process of industrialization.

Notes

1. Neil Smelser, *Social Change and the Industrial Revolution* (Chicago, 1959); William Goode, *World Revolution and Family Patterns* (New York, 1963). See also Sidney Greenfield, "Industrialization and the Family in Sociological Theory," American Journal of Sociology, 67 (1961), 312–322.

2. For crucial revisions of traditional working-class historiography, see E. P. Thompson, *The Making of the English Working Class* (New York, 1963); Herbert Gutman, "Work, Culture and Society in Industrializing America, 1819–1918," American Historical Review, 78 (1973), 531–588; David Montgomery, "Immigrant Workers and Scientific Management, " in *Proceedings of the Conference on Immigrants in Industry. Eleutherian Mills, 1973.* On recent working-class historiography, see Paul Faler, "Working-Class Historiography," Radical America, 3 (1969), and Robert H. Zieger, "Workers and Scholars: Recent Trends in American Labor Historiography," Labor History, 13 (1972)

3. The most well-documented work in support of this thesis is Michael Anderson, *Family Structure in Nineteenth-Century Lancashire* (Cambridge, 1973). Specifically on American immigrant families, see Virginia Y. McLaughlin, "Patterns of Work and Family Organization: Buffalo's Italians," Journal of Interdisciplinary History, 2 (1970).

4. For the emphasis on family and household structure as the major unit of analysis, see Richard Sennett, *Families Against the City* (Cambridge, Mass., 1970). Sennett errs in defining "extended family" only within the household, thus ignoring the significant presence of kin outside the household.

5. See Tamara K. Hareven, "The Family as Process: The Historical Study of the Family Cycle," Journal of Social History, 7 (1974). For conceptualization and definition of the family cycle, see Paul C. Glick, "The Family Cycle," American Sociological Review, 12 (1947), 164–174; Reuben Hill, *Family Development in Three Generations* (Cambridge, Mass., 1970).

6. On the concept of "industrial time," see Pitirim A. Sorokin and Robert K. Merton, "Social Time: A Methodological and Functional Analysis," American Journal of Sociology, 42 (1937).

7. On the Amoskeag Mills, see Waldo Brown, *A History of the Amoskeag Company* (Manchester, N.H., 1915), a company history; Daniel Creamer and Charles W. Coulter, *Labor and the Shutdown of the Amoskeag Textile Mills,* Works Project Administration, National Research Project, Report No. L-5 (Philadelphia, 1939).

8. On classic planned New England textile towns, see Caroline F. Ware, *The Early New England Cotton Manufacture* (New York, 1942); John Armstrong, *Factory Under the Elms* (Cambridge, Mass., 1968); Vera Shlakman, *Economic History of a Factory Town; Chicopee, Massachusetts* (New York, 1935). On the significance of the architectural design of the Amoskeag Mills and the relationship between corporate paternalism and control of the city, see Randolph Langenbach, "An Epic in Urban Design," Harvard Bulletin (April 15, 1968), and "Architecture and Paternalism: A Study in Social Space," unpublished manuscript. For the corporation's Welfare Program, see Tamara K. Hareven, "Continuities and Discontinuities in Corporate Paternalism," unpublished manuscript.

9. In 1911, French Canadians constituted 37.6% of the labor force; native-born Americans (many of whom were of Irish and Scotch descent) constituted 18.6%; the Irish, 14.7%; the Poles, 10.8%; and the Greeks, 8%. By 1923, French Canadians constituted 46%. On the textile workers of Manchester in the context of other textile communities, see *Report on the Condition of Women and Child Wage-Earners in the United States,* vol. I, Cotton Textile Industry (Washington, D.C., 1910), Senate Doc. No. 65, 61st Congress, 2nd session. Manchester was one of the communities investigated in this report. See also Ralph Vicero, "The Immigration of French-Canadians to New England, 1840–1900." Ph.D. dissertation. University of Wisconsin, 1966.

10. A reconstruction and mapping of the neighborhoods from the Manchester City Census of 1881, from the Federal Manuscript Censuses of 1860 to 1880, and from the most recently opened census of 1900 is now in progress.

11. This project utilized the following data: a 5% random sample of the individual employee files kept by the corporation from 1912 to 1936. The sample consists of 2,000 individual files. Individual workers' careers were reconstructed from these files over each worker's entire work period. They were subsequently traced through city directories, and, wherever relevant and possible, workers' careers were reconstructed for the period prior and subsequent to their employment by the corporation, as well as during intermittent periods. The individual records were then linked with marriage records and were augmented by corporation records, newspapers, and a collection of oral history interviews of former employees. The records of French-Canadian workers were also linked with insurance records.

12. Recruitment before 1930 was carried out primarily through returning relatives to Quebec villages. From 1900 on, after the organization of the Association Canado-Americaine in Manchester, the corporation utilized the newspaper published by this organization for propaganda and recruitment of workers. The paper published major articles on the Amoskeag Mills, the copy for which was supplied by the Amoskeag Corporation. See *Le Canado-Americain* (1913–1915).

13. *Le Canado-Americain,* November 10, 1913. On corporation housing, see Langenbach, "Architecture and Paternalism: A Study in the Planning of Social Space."

14. The corporation published regular descriptions of the program in *The Amoskeag Bulletin,* 1–4 (1912–1918). The corporation's welfare and efficiency system is discussed in greater detail in Hareven, "Continuities and Discontinuities in Corporate Paternalism." On the strike, see *History of the Amoskeag Strike During the Year 1922* (Manchester, N.H., 1924).

15. On the French-Canadian background, see Phillippe Garigue, *La Vie Familiale des Canadiens Francais* (Montreal, 1967).

16. Compare with Semlser, *Social Change and the Industrial Revolution,* and Anderson, *Family Structure in Nineteenth-Century Lancashire.* See also Tilly, Louise A. and Joan W. Scott. 1978. *Women, Work, and the Family.* New York: Holt, Rinehart, and Winston.

17. This is based on oral history interviews as well as on an analysis of the women's employment patterns.

18. On the fluctuation of the textile market and its impact on the Amoskeag Company's hiring policies, see Creamer and Coulter, *Labor and the Shutdown*.

19. On the internal economic conditions of the family and their impact on labor market behavior, see U.S. Congress, *Report on the Condition of Women and Child Wage-Earners I;* John Modell, "Family, Economy and Insecurity," paper delivered at the annual meeting of the Organization of American Historians, April 1974, and "Economic Dimensions of Family History," The Family in Historical Perspective Newsletter, No. 6 (1974). Tamara Hareven and John Modell are embarking on a study of family budgets in the early part of the twentieth century. The margin of poverty has been defined by early social investigators of the urban poor. See B. Seebohm Rowntree, *Poverty: A Study of Town Life* (London, 1922), and Robert Hunter, *Poverty* (New York, 1904).

20. On the role of kinship in migration, see Charles Tilly and C. Harold Brown, "On Uprooting, Kinship, and the Auspices of Migration." Journal of International Comparative Sociology, 7 (1967). On French–Canadian kinship see Phillippe Garigue, "French Canadian Kinship and Urban Life," American Anthropologist, 58 (1956).

21. This is a recurring pattern described in the oral history interviews.

22. Labor turnover and patterns of migration are discussed in detail in Hareven, Tamara K. "Laborers of Manchester, New Hampshire: The Role of the Family and Ethincity in Adjustment To Industrial Life." *Labor History* 16:249–265. See also U.S. Congress, *Report on the Condition of Women and Child Wage-Earners I*. 127.

23. It is now possible for the first time to reconstruct such patterns of migration, because the employee records actually state where individuals went on leaving the corporation. See also U.S. Department of Labor, Women's Bureau, *Lost Time and Labor Turnover in Cotton Mills: A Study of Cause and Extent,* Publication No. 52 (Washington, D.C., 1926), Part I, 109–113.

24. The overseer was the man in charge of production, management, and discipline in an entire department, which consisted of several workrooms.

25. The trace of the original 2,000 employee files gathered for the study turned up an additional 500 of their relatives who were also working in the mill. This does not represent all the possible kin combinations. It contains only the immediate ones that could be traced through vital records. If one allowed for second cousins and a variety of relatives that are not mentioned in the interviews, the number of kin could be considerably higher.

26. Evidence for kin clustering in the workrooms is derived from the reconstruction of kin groups by place of work. See also "Memo to Mr. Hagan," October, 1934, Amoskeag Files, Baker Library, Harvard University.

27. Based on oral history interviews and on a preliminary survey of the residential clustering in the corporation's tenements and boarding houses by Tamara Hareven and Randolph Langenbach. For comparison, see two significant studies of the social space of the urban working class, Pierre Chombard de Lauwe, *La Vie Quotidienne des Familles Ouvrières* (Paris, 1956), and André Michel, "La Famille Urbaine et la parenté en France," in Rueben Hill and René Konig, *Families in East and West: Socialization Process and Kinship Ties* (Paris, 1970). On ethnicity and residential cohesion, see Herbert Gans, *The Urban Villagers* (New York, 1962). For a comparative experience in a textile community, see Donald B. Cole, *Immigrant City* (Cambridge, Mass., 1957).

28. Based on oral history interviews. See also Gerald D. Suttles, *The Social Order of the Slum: Ethnicity and Territory in the Inner City* (Chicago, 1968).

29. The reasons for leaving have been computed from the individual employee files.

30. Hareven, "The Family as Process," and Anderson, *Family Structure in Nineteenth-Century Lancashire*. For an analysis of women's family cycles, see Peter Uhlenberg, "A Study of Cohort Life Cycles: Cohorts of Native Born Massachusetts Women, 1830–1920," Population Studies, 23 (1968).

31. U.S. Congress, *Report on the Condition of Women and Child Wage-Earners I*.

32. U.S. Department of Labor, Women's Bureau, *The Share of Wage-Earning Women in Family Support,* Bulletin, No. 30 (Washington, D.C., 1923), 137–140.

33. Ibid.

34. Oral history interviews.

35. These patterns emerge from the reconstruction of the work careers of 1,000 women from the employee files, and from oral history interviews.

36. See *The Share of Wage-Earning Women*.

37. Creamer and Coulter, *Labor and the Shutdown*.

38. Wilson H. Grabill, Clyde V. Kiser, and Pascal W. Whelpton, *The Fertility of American Women* (New York, 1958), 404–406; J. Hill, "Fecundity of Immigrant Women," U.S. Congress, Immigration Commission, *Reports of First and Second Generations of Immigrants in the United States—Fecundity of Immigrant Women* (Washington, D.C., 1911), Senate Doc. No. 282. 61st Congress, 2nd session.

39. This is based on the reconstruction of the work histories and the computation of the number of times hired and dismissed for each worker. See also *Lost Time*, 29–32, 67–72, 84–87.

40. See John Modell and Tamara K. Hareven, "Urbanization and the Malleable Household: An Examination of Boarding and Lodging in American Families," Journal of Marriage and the Family, 35 (1973), 467–479.

41. Most of the interviewees still refer to the strike as the most traumatic experience of their lives. Some of them are still not on speaking terms with former friends and relatives.

42. See Talcott Parsons and R. F. Bales, *Family, Socialization and Interaction Process* (New York, 1955); Bernard Farber, *Guardians of Virtue* (New York, 1972); Sennett, *Families Against the City.*

43. For comparisons, see Susan Kleinberg, "Women's Work Patterns and the Occupational Structure of Cities, " paper presented at the Brockport Conference, October 1974, and Elizabeth Butler, *Women and the Trades* (Pittsburgh, 1907–1908).

44. Compare with Anderson, *Family Structure in Nineteenth-Century Lancashire,* and with Louise Tilly and Joan Scott, "Daughters, Wives, Mothers, Workers: Peasants and Working Class Women in the Transition to an Industrial Economy in France," paper presented at Second Berkshire Conference on the History of Women, October 1974, Cambridge, Mass. The study is based on data gathered and analyzed by Howard Chudacoff and Burt Litchfield.

45. See Michael Young and Peter Wilmott, *Family and Kinship in East London* (London, 1957, revised 1962), and Gans, *Urban Villagers*.

Work, Leisure, and Family Roles: Farm Households in the United States, 1920–1955

Joann Vanek

Over the past ten or fifteen years, studies of the history of the family have challenged popular and scholarly views about the impact of industrialization on social life. It had generally been assumed, as E. A. Wrigley points out, that "modernization and industrialization go hand in hand, the latter representing the upshot in the economy of the changes going forward in society more generally." But he continues, "The effects on the family produced by the early decades of the industrial revolution were confused, including some changes which by the canons of modernization would be regarded as regression" (1977:81). Particularly important is the perspective family historians provide on women's recent strides toward equality in the market and in the home. Rather than continuing to describe women's uninterrupted progress toward equality, historical studies reveal that women once had an important economic role and that with this came influence and power within the family.

For example, according to Louise Tilly and Joan Scott, the productive activity of married women takes on an "U-shaped pattern—from relatively high in the preindustrial household economy, to a lower level in industrial economies, to a higher level with the development of the modern tertiary sector" (1978:229). Tilly and Scott review data for eighteenth-century France and England which show that wives had an important role in the household economy and from this power within the family. In particular married women decided on the allocation of the family resources.

In the United States the household mode of production continued to be important well into the twentieth century; as recently as 1920, one-third of the nation's families still lived on the farm. On the farm, husbands and wives were partners not only in making a home but also in making a living. And as E. A. Ross, an early sociologist, points out, economic partnership affected the dynamics of family relationships:

The research reported in this article was supported by a grant from the Research Foundation of the City University of New York. The views expressed are the author's.

Reprinted from *Journal of Family History* Vol. 5, No. 4 (Winter 1980):422–431. Used with permission of JAI Press, Inc.

Nearly all that was eaten and worn in the family had been manufactured by the hands of its women folk. In those days nothing was heard as to "economic dependence" of the wife, or her being supported. My aunt, busy in and about the house was as strong a prop of the family's prosperity as my uncle afield with his team. Uncle knew it, and, what is more, she knew he knew it (1922:79).

During the 1940s and 1950s discussions of family change often ignored the economic partnership that was characteristic of marriage under the household mode of production. For example, in describing a trend toward equality in family relationships, Robert Blood and Donald Wolfe express the view that a husband's dominance was a basic and necessary characteristic of family life in preindustrial economies (1960:16–17). This once influential view ignores women's important role in the family economy and the power which accompanied it. Since wives produced the basic necessities for subsistence, their husbands were dependent on them, just as they were dependent on their husbands. And because farm wives also produced goods which were sold for cash, they had some control over a resource that was valuable in the world outside the home. The relationship of husbands and wives on the farm was not entirely equal, since according to custom and the law women were subordinate to men. But men's dominance was offset by the tangible value of women's contribution to the household economy.

Symmetry, defined by Michael Young and Peter Willmott as "opposite but similar" (1973:32), is as this paper will show an appropriate description of family roles on the farm. Paradoxically, it was chosen by Young and Willmott to describe the unique effect of modern life on family roles. Observing marked difference in modern society "in human rights, in the work opportunities and generally in the way of life of the two sexes," they felt that the term symmetry was more accurate than that of equality to capture the present relationship of husbands and wives (1973:31). Although data support this description of family relationships today, studies also show that a kind of symmetry had occurred earlier in the household mode of production of preindustrial economies and in an agrarian past.

This article will examine family roles in farm households in the United States during the period 1920 to 1955. The data for the study are daily activity schedules of farmers and farm wives. The accounts, known as time budgets, record the sequence and duration of activities engaged in by individuals over the 24-hour day. The allocation of time provides a good criterion for evaluating the economic contribution of couples on the farm since both spouses produced goods and neither (at least in the studies used here) worked for a salary or wage.

The earliest of the studies, the 1922–24 research of Ellis Kirkpatrick (1929), was part of an ambitious project. Although he had little in the way of technology to facilitate the collection and processing of data, his work covered 13 states and over 2,000 households. The aim of the project was to obtain information on the living standards of farm families comparable to the wealth of information collected by the Bureau of Labor Statistics and other agencies for urban families. In addition to data on the production and purchase of goods, Kirkpatrick collected information on the time spent in work and leisure in order to measure total household production and the quality of daily living.

J. O. Rankin's objectives in his 1924 research in Nebraska (1928) were similar. That both economists examined the schedules of wives as well as husbands to derive measures of family living standards in itself confirms the importance of women's economic role on the farm.

The third main source of data is the 1957 research of John Ross and Lloyd Bostian (1958). Although the focus of this study is communication patterns rather than living standards, it uses activity categories that are very close to those used in the other studies. In addition, these three studies are supplemented with time use research on the workday of farmers, on the workday of housewives, and on the leisure activities of farm families.

One may have reservations about drawing general inferences about farm families from so few widely scattered studies. With respect to socio-economic status, for example, the families are not representative of the farm population, for they mainly include owners rather than tenants or workers. Moreover, by the 1920s technology and the products of industry had already altered certain aspects of household production. Yet whether or not the data represent "typical" farm families, they do reflect certain characteristics of the household mode of production, i.e., the close integration of work and family life and a significant degree of self-sufficiency.

Several features of the findings also support the credibility of the data as measures of family behavior. First, the symmetry in family roles is shown consistently across the studies, and also across the status categories, owner and tenant, when the data were so reported.[1] Second, as one might expect, there are some differences between owners and tenants in types of leisure activities. Farm owners could afford to use their free time in more costly ways than tenants. Third, there were instances in which the data were remarkably sensitive to distinct characteristics of the population or households surveyed. For example, a South Carolina study showed comparatively greater participation in religious activities, as one would expect in an area where fundamentalist religions are strong. Again as expected, the time spent reading was lower in households with radio and lower still with television.

Daily Activities

Farm families worked a six-day week. Only Sunday, a day of relative leisure, was markedly different from the other days of the week. According to the three studies reported in Table 1, work dominated the daily routine and only a few hours remained for leisure. The job of operating a farm household—burdensome as it was—was shared equally by husbands and wives. Each devoted about 11 hours a day to work. The three studies, although quite diverse, are remarkably consistent as to the time spent in work, in leisure, and in personal care. Only the most recent study reports slightly less time in work, and this is probably because interviewing took place exclusively in the winter.

The workday for farmers includes field work, chores, going to the field, and attending to farm business. Studies other than those listed in Table 1 also report that the farmer's workday averaged about 11 hours.[2] This includes a number of 1936

Table 1   Daily Use of Time for Farmers and Farm Housewives,1922–1957[a]

Principal Investigator and Date of Data Collection	Work	Personal Care	Free Time	Total
Kirkpatrick, 1922–24 (2,179 Families)				
Housewives	11.4		2.7	
Farmers	11.3		2.6	
Rankin, 1924 (328 Families)				
Housewives	10.7	9.7	3.6	24.0
Farmers	11.1	9.5	3.6	24.0
Ross & Bostian, 1957 (488 Families)				
Housewives	10.4	10.8	2.8	24.0
Farmers	10.8	11.0	2.6	24.0

Numbers in parentheses indicate the number of families from which diaries were secured.

[a]Daily averages were based on weekdays and Saturdays.

Sources: Kirkpatrick, 1929; Rankin, 1928; Ross & Bostian, 1958.

studies which show little deviation from the 11-hour standard for farm operators and other full time helpers. Nor was there significant variation in the workday according to type of product, season or region (Hopkins, 1941). Only in southern cotton areas was the workweek shorter during the winter. Farmers in these areas seldom had cattle. But for farmers in others areas, livestock required additional work in winter and offset the time saved by having no field work. Nor does it appear that hours of work have declined for farmers since the 1930s, for a survey made by the Federal State Crop Reporting Service shows that in 1957 Wisconsin farm owners averaged a 10.7-hour workday (Ross and Bostian, 1958:28).

The estimates for the workday of housewives reported in Table 1 include both farm work and housework. These figures agree with a set of studies done by home economists which show that the standard workday for farm wives tended to be between 10 and 11 hours (cf. Vanek, 1974).

Division of Labor

Although the length of the workday was identical for husbands and wives on the farm, there was a sharp division of tasks. Housekeeping and family care were women's work. Farmers spent only about two hours a week in domestic tasks, and this was mainly in carrying wood and pumping water (Moore, 1930:242). Child care was rarely shared. Only one-fourth of the fathers with children under six years of age spent any time caring for children; the average amount of time was two and one-half hours a week (Moore, 1930:242).

Farm wives spent roughly 10 hours a week in tasks classified as farm work. This significant portion of their work time should not, however, be construed as "help" to their husbands, for women had distinct productive tasks on the farm. These included work in the garden and care of poultry. Washing the milking equipment was also a standard task. But not all of the cleaning chores on the farm were "women's work." Cleaning the barn and the chicken coop were typically men's chores. Milking was one of the few tasks that wives shared with their husbands. Helping with livestock and field work was done rarely and then usually by choice rather than on the orders of her husband. For example, women commented in one study that they did outside work "because they like to do it or because they preferred to do it rather than have a hired man to help and have to board and lodge him about the house" (Clark and Grey, 1930:26).

Not only did farm wives produce a great part of the family's subsistence goods, their earnings from extra household activities such as selling eggs or produce contributed substantially to the purchase of other supplies. For example, a 1915 study of farm homes in Michigan (Bailey and Snyder, 1921) shows that 80 percent of the living expenditures, as distinct from the expenses associated with producing the principal product on the farm, were met by cash earnings of farm wives.

Some wives kept the money they earned from the sale of goods for personal use rather than pooling it with the general farm earnings to meet family expenses. According to a 1919 Department of Agriculture study of 10,000 housewives, 22 percent of the women selling poultry kept their earnings, as did 16 percent of those selling eggs and 11 percent selling butter (Ward, 1920: 11). Farm wives also took a direct role in running the family business by keeping farm accounts (32 percent) and household accounts (30 percent) (Ward, 1920:10). Although a simple clerical activity, keeping the accounts is an integral part of running the household or family business. Frequently Rosalyn Carter comments that her widely acknowledged partnership with the President dates back to the days when she began to keep the accounts for the family peanut business. Since she knew more accurately than he what was happening in business, he needed to consult with her. Apparently this was the beginning of a pattern which has continued in what is sometimes known as the "Mom and Pop Presidency."

There is no evidence in these data that women worked under the economic leadership or domination of their husbands as Blood and Wolfe and others had suggested. Rather, these data suggest that a symmetrical pattern prevailed. Men and women had autonomous but interdependent spheres, each of which was essential to the family's survival. While under the canons of religion and the law a woman was subordinate to her husband, a man's superiority or dominance was tempered by the awareness that for much of his livelihood he depended on his wife.

The Texture of Farm Life

The symmetry in farm family roles extended beyond quantities of time and the interdependence of tasks to other aspects of the daily routine. The day began early for families on the farm, around five A.M. in the summer and about an hour later in winter. Before central heating, a farmer typically rose about 15 minutes earlier than his wife in winter to carry wood and start fires. Whether in the kitchen or in the barn, the work day began immediately and did not end until about 8:30 in the summer and 7:15 in the winter. Not long after, by 10 p.m. most nights of the week, families were in bed (cf. Rankin, 1928; Ross and Bostian, 1958). These simple features of the daily schedule point up the distinctive character of farm life. Since husbands and wives were part of the same productive enterprise, their day had a similar rhythm. It was shaped by the seasons, the weather, and the necessary daily tasks.

The seasonal cycle in women's work on the farm included gardening in the spring and summer, canning in summer and early fall, extra baking for the winter holidays, additional cleaning in the spring, and sewing and cheesemaking through the fall, winter, and spring (Wilson, 1929).

For farmers, seasons and weather conditions affected the daily scheduling of activities even more than for housewives. A 1915 Pennsylvania study showed that out of the total 78 or 79 weekdays in each yearly quarter, only 45 were suitable for field work in the spring quarter, 65 in the summer, and 52 in the fall (Hopkins, 1941:26). On the days when a farmer could not do field work, there were other things to do. In the winter, cattle and barn chores required more time. And certain chores were left for rainy days such as cleaning the barn and the chicken coop or repairing farm equipment.

Similarly women had long-range tasks they picked up when they could. One of my grandmother's was bleaching commercial bags which she later used to make family linens and underwear. The family purchased feed, flour, and sugar in 100-pound cotton bags which were covered at least on one side with an emblem. Since bleach was not available, the printed emblem could be removed only by a great deal of rubbing with strong bar soap. From time to time over a period of weeks my grandmother would turn to this project. Finally, after boiling, the result was a sturdy white cloth.

In writing about spare time activities such as my grandmother's bleaching, Sebastian de Grazia refers to pastimes—"some little thing to do when what you had to do didn't take as long as you thought" or "the long range things to do that could be picked up or dropped at will" (1962:189). De Grazia was interested in these activities because he believed they reveal one of the main changes in the nature of time that occurred with industrialization. Having pastimes suggests that one does not have unoccupied or free time, and that work and leisure are not separate spheres of life as they are for people who work outside the home. Moreover, because work extends throughout the day and occurred in the home, leisure and family life were integrated.

Rather than eating on the run with whomever happens to be home, mealtime for farm families was a kind of leisure activity. By the time breakfast was served, adults had already worked for a couple of hours and were ready to take time off. Each meal took about half an hour, and once a day the family remained at the table to visit for a least 20 or 30 minutes (Hill *et al.*, 1930:15). Only school-age children missed eating with the family and then only at the noon meal.

After eating at noon a farmer remained indoors, sometimes for as much as an hour, listening to the noon crop and livestock reports, reading and resting. In the winter months when there was a little less to do he often rested for a short time after breakfast. Of course, mealtime was not as relaxing for housewives as for their families. Rather than take time off right after meals, housewives relaxed in the afternoon for an hour or so before beginning supper. Supper was usually served between five and six P.M. before the evening barn chores began (cf. Ross and Bostian, 1958).

On the farm, Saturday was a routine workday although people took a little more time for resting during the day and went to bed later in the evening. Work was restricted on Sunday to "only" about three to six hours for farmers (Hopkins, 1941:26; Ross and Bostian, 1953:31). As a rule, housewives did not clean, wash, iron, sew, or garden on Sunday (Wasson, 1930:4). This reduced their working time to about five and one-half hours (Wilson, 1929:14; Ross and Bostian, 1958:31). However, housewives frequently spent more time in food preparation tasks on Sunday than on other days of the week when there was a greater likelihood of guests and meals were more elaborate.

The patterning of the daily routine on the farm did not have the character of fixed hours or a rigid scheduling of tasks. Even though work was never done, it could be interspersed with leisure and family activities. Unlike today, this was true for husbands and wives. Not only were their work experiences similar, leisure was as well. While the broad pattern of the daily routine suggests this is so, more detailed attention to leisure activities shows there are important similarities in what farmers and their wives did when not at work.

A popular view of leisure on the farm pictures the family gathered around the hearth in the evening popping corn and telling stories. There is some support for this nostalgic view of family life in that many leisure activities were shared. As mentioned earlier, one study showed that visiting after meals occurred daily in every home surveyed. In addition, two-thirds of the families listened to radio together daily, played games and musical instruments several times a week, told stories at least once a week, and either popped corn or made candy weekly (Hill *et al.*, 1930:15–16). In another study one-half of the families reported owning a musical instrument, usually either a piano or an organ, and the average time spent playing it was two or three hours a week. About one-third of these families had a phonograph and another two or three hours a week were spent listening to records (Frayser, 1930:58–60). Sundays were singled out as days for family leisure with church in the morning, a more elaborate meal at noon, and visiting neighbors in the afternoon (Anderson, 1953; Ross and Bostian, 1958; Wilson, 1929).

Of course, to a great degree "family togetherness" was based on necessity. The isolation, long hours of work, and limited resources of farm households meant that the opportunities for leisure were restricted; very little time could be spent off the farm. But husbands and wives also had independent activities, some occurring at home and others away. Even in these activities, which reflect individual preferences, there is evidence of symmetry. For example, two studies show that husbands and wives spent the same amount of time reading, the earlier study reporting about nine hours a week and the later study four and one half hours (Frayser, 1930:32–33; Ross and Bostian, 1958:14–15). The drop in hours between 1930 and 1958 may in itself be significant as a measure of the affect of modern consumption goods on the use of free time. Only 10 percent of the homes in the early study had radio. The figure, somewhat lower than the 20 percent average for all rural farm families in 1930, reflects the slower development of rural South Carolina (U.S. Census, 1930:10). By contrast, information collected around the same time in several studies reporting higher ownership of radios showed that wives spent only six and one-half hours reading (Wilson, 1929; Richardson, 1933). The more recent survey, occurring when many homes had television, showed even less time in reading for both husbands and wives (Ross and Bostian, 1958). The habit of reading, it would appear, was eroded by radio and then again by television.

Husbands and wives also did a variety of things off the farm. Women tended to spend more time visiting friends than their husbands (Frayser, 1930:66–67; Rankin, 1928; Ross and Bostian, 1958:19). But farmers made up for this with trips to market, which provided opportunities for visiting, as well as by hunting and fishing (Anderson, 1953:32; Frayser, 1930:64–65, 66–67; Rankin, 1928:8).

In the more formal leisure activities, wives attended church and Sunday school a little more frequently than farmers (Anderson, 1953; Rankin, 1928; Ross and Bostian, 1958:61–62). But a South Carolina study, reporting much more time in religious activities, found that husbands and wives spent the same amount of time attending church, Sunday school, and revival meetings (Frayser, 1930:41). This probably reflects the distinct character of Southern fundamentalist religion.

Housewives also attended school meetings more frequently than farmers (Anderson, 1953; Rankin, 1928). On the other hand, husbands spent more time attending farm association meetings than their wives (Anderson, 1953; Frayser, 1930:52). Altogether meetings excluding church took only a small amount of time for farm families. In a 1924 study, for the farmers and housewives attending any organizations (about 75 percent), the frequency of attendance was only about 15 times a year (Rankin, 1928:8). A more recent study reported that husbands and wives each averaged only an hour a week at meetings (Ross and Bostian, 1958:23).

In summary, there are important similarities in the leisure of husbands and wives on the farm. The nature of work is such that both are able to integrate leisure and family life with work. Consequently, a great deal of leisure is shared. Although husbands and wives also have separate activities these appear symmetrical, that is, each spends roughly the same amount of time in reading, in informal contact, in organizational participation as well as the same amount of time off the farm.

Conclusion

This study gives a somewhat biased view of farm life since it is based on quantities of time and not on data that report on qualitative aspects of life. A description drawn from data in which a long workday is the only evidence of the hardship and toil in the lives of these families is incomplete and tends to be unduly romantic. Moreover, the data do not provide a full picture of the relationship of husbands and wives. They reveal nothing of the psychological intimacy in marriage or of the internal conflicts that may arise from the pressures of working together and from spending so much time in proximity.

Despite these inherent weaknesses, time budget data provide a kind of objective evidence that is essential to an assessment of family roles. Since time budgets report activity by activity what a respondent does all day, they provide a more accurate view of the sharing of tasks in marriage than the method used in most studies, that is, asking who typically performs a sampling of tasks (cf. Blood and Wolfe, 1960; Young and Willmott, 1973). In fact, time budgets question a basic assumption made by those who argue that work is now divided equally in marriage, for in housework they show that little has changed (cf. Berheide, Berk, and Berk, 1976; Vanek, 1977).

The study of how people spend time can measure another dimension of equality, the intermingling of the social worlds of husbands and wives. Since on the farm activities of both spouses centered on the home, their daily routines were quite similar. There was symmetry in work time, in free time, and even in the time spent off the farm. There was an intermingling of the social spheres of husbands and wives on the farm that the growth of cities and industry to some degree reversed. Industrialization not only segregated the work activities of husbands and wives— which in a regime of 12-hour days, six-day weeks, was in itself considerable—but . . . also affected free time. It removed the opportunity for interweaving work and family activities throughout the day and provided new opportunities and reasons for segregated leisure for husbands but not for wives. For example, a turn of the century study of a mill community near Pittsburgh reports that after a grueling day of labor, alcohol and the companionship offered by the local saloon were preferred to drab, cramped homes, wives, and screaming children. As evidence, a mill community with a population of 25,000 was able to support over 55 saloons and other drinking places (Byington, 1974:112). Industrialization changed the nature of family interactions. For working-class families, and others as well, it effected a segregation not only in work but also in free time activities.

Against the perspective of this paper, the impact of industrial growth on the economic position of women in marriage is somewhat of a paradox. While it is true that the labor force participation of wives has increased rapidly over the past 35 years, there was a long time lag between the loss of women's gainful role in the home and a substantial change in their participation in the labor force. Was it simply that women were so difficult to pry away from their "natural" role in the home? Or did it take so long to transform the attitudes of employers about women's place? The dynamics of change are considerably more complicated than what these popular notions convey, and any consideration of them would, of course, extend beyond the bounds of this article. Rather, my point is that in terms of continuity with the past, it was reasonable to expect women to leave home as their husbands did to take jobs in the labor force.[3] What must be emphasized then is not only the forces that have led to the employment of wives, but also, as W. Elliot Brownlee argues, those that have held women in the home (1979). Both perspectives are necessary to understand the changes that modern economic developments have caused for the family, women's roles, and individual well-being.

Notes

1. William Sewell pointed to tenure status as the most common single-factor index of socio-economic status for farm families (1940:9).
2. Kirkpatrick reported that others had arrived at lower estimates of the farmer's workday, and explained that they had used a less precise method (1929:224). While Kirkpatrick asked

farmers to account for what they did all day, other researchers listed only the major tasks and asked farmers to report the corresponding time expenditures. By the latter method, some of the less important tasks were neglected.

3. Turn of the century writings of dispassioned observers as well as concerned reformers predicted that married women would soon be leaving home with their husbands to seek employment.

References

Anderson, W. A. 1953. Rural Social Participation and the Family Life Cycle. Part I, Formal Participation. Cornell Agricultural Experiment Station Memoir 314; Part II, Informal Participation, Memoir 318. Ithaca: Cornell University.

Bailey, Ilena, and Melissa F. Snyder. 1921. "A Survey of Farm Homes." The Journal of Home Economics 13:346–356.

Berheide, Catherine White, Sarah Fenstermaker Berk, and Richard Berk. 1976. "Household Work in the Suburbs." Pacific Sociological Review 19:491–518.

Blood, Robert, Jr., and Donald Wolfe. 1960. Husbands and Wives. New York: Free Press.

Brownlee, W. Elliot. 1979. "Household Values, Women's Work and Economic Growth." The Journal of Home Economics 18:123–127.

Byington, Margaret. 1974. Homestead: The Households of a Mill Town. Pittsburgh: University Center for International Studies.

Clark, M. Ruth, and Greta Gray. 1930. The Routine and Seasonal Work of Nebraska Farm Women. Nebraska Agricultural Experiment Station Bulletin 237. Lincoln: The University of Nebraska.

de Grazia, Sebastian. 1962. Of Time, Work and Leisure. Garden City, N.Y.: Anchor Books.

Frayser, Mary. 1930. The Use of Leisure in Selected Rural Areas of South Carolina. South Carolina Agricultural Experiment Station Bulletin 263. Clemson; Clemson College.

Hill, Randall, E. L. Morgan, Mabel Campell, and O. R. Johnson. 1930. Social, Economic and Homemaking Factors in Family Living. Agricultural Experiment Station Research Bulletin 148. Columbia: The University of Missouri.

Hopkins, John. 1941. Changing Technology and Employment in Agriculture. Works Projects Administration, National Research Project on Reemployment Opportunities and Recent Changes in Industrial Techniques. Report A, No. 15. Washington D.C.: U.S. Government Printing Office.

Kirkpatrick, Ellis. 1929. The Farmer's Standard of Living. New York: The Century Co.

Kneeland, Hildergarde. 1932. "Leisure of Home Makers: Studies for Light on the Standard of Living." U.S. Department of Agriculture, Yearbook of Agriculture. pp. 562–564. Washington, D.C.: U.S. Government Printing Office.

Moore, Ruth. 1930. "Farm Home Makers Get Little Aid in Housework from Others in Family." U.S. Department of Agriculture, Yearbook of Agriculture, pp. 241–243. Washington, D.C.: U.S. Government Printing Office.

Rankin, J. O. 1928. The Use of Time in Farm Homes. Nebraska Agricultural Experiment Station Bulletin 230. Lincoln: The University of Nebraska.

Richardson, Jessie. 1933. The Use of Time by Rural Homemakers in Montana. Montana Agricultural Experiment Station Bulletin 271. Bozeman: Montana State College.

Ross, Edward O. 1922. The Social Trend. New York: The Century Co.

Ross, John, and Lloyd Bostian. 1958. Time Use Patterns and Communications Activities of Wisconsin Farm Families in Wintertime. Department of Agricultural Journalism Bulletin 28. Madison: University of Wisconsin.

Sewell, William. 1940. The Construction and Standardization of a Scale for the Measurement of the Socio-Economic Status of Oklahoma Farm Families. Oklahoma Agricultural Experiment Station Technical Bulletin 9. Stillwater: Oklahoma Agricultural and Mechanical College.

Tilly, Louise, and Joan Scott. 1978. Women, Work, and Family. New York: Holt, Rinehart, and Winston.

U.S. Bureau of the Census. 1930. Population: Vol. VI, Families.

Vanek, Joann. 1974. "Time Spent in Housework." Scientific American 231:116–120.

———. 1977. "The New Family Equality: Myth or Reality?" Paper presented at annual meetings of the American Sociological Association, Chicago.

Ward, Florence. 1920. The Farm Woman's Problems. U.S. Department of Agriculture Circular 148. Washington, D.C.: U.S. Government Printing. Office.

Wasson, Grace. 1930. Use of Time by South Dakota Farm Homemakers. South Dakota Experiment Station Bulletin 247. Brookings: South Dakota State College of Agriculture and Mechanic Arts.

Wilson, Maud. 1929. Use of Time by Oregon Farm Homemakers. Oregon Agricultural Experiment Station Bulletin 256. Corvallis: Oregon State Agricultural College.

Wrigley, E. Anthony. 1977. "Reflections on the History of the Family." Daedalus 106:71–85.

Young, Michael, and Peter Willmott. 1973. The Symmetrical Family. New York: Pantheon.

Afro-American Adaptive Strategies: The Visiting Habits of Kith and Kin among Black Norfolkians during the First Great Migration

Earl Lewis

As a little girl growing up in Norfolk, Virginia, during the 1930s and 1940s, Virginia Carr often accompanied her parents on visits to what was commonly called the "country"—nearby Norfolk Country (Carr 1985). Her parents used such trips to narrow the social and physical distance between themselves and their family and friends. They began the practice in the late 1910s as individuals, and continued it in the 1920s and beyond, after marriage (James 1980, 1981). Mrs. Elizabeth Upshur also visited. For a month in the summer of 1916, Mrs. Upshur and daughter visited friends in Philadelphia. She later described her stay as a "delightful trip" (*Journal and Guide* 1916). As often as black Norfolkians left to visit, those who moved away returned. The death of Willie Lamb's mother hastened his return from New York City in March 1917 (*Journal and Guide* 1917).

The three stories are interesting, but given the historical context in which they occurred these anecdotal accounts assume a greater importance. Between 1900 and 1920 1.5 million Afro-Americans left the rural South for the cities and towns of the Northeast, Midwest, and South. This period, generally called the First Great Migration, witnessed the redistribution of one-sixth of the nation's total black population. The aforementioned accounts inform our knowledge of the efforts undertaken to circumvent the possible deleterious effect of such large out-migration on Afro-American institutions.

At first, few observers examined the impact of this relocation on the Afro-American family. Then in 1939 E. Franklin Frazier argued that first slavery and then migration had undermined the stability of the dyadic structure of the black family. He viewed as absolute the power of the slave master to sexually exploit black women and wantonly separate black families. He also believed that disunion was further increased by migration to the city. According to Frazier, such movement, particularly during the period 1900–1920, induced blacks to severe their ties with kin and kith (family and friends) who remained behind (Frazier [1939] 1973, pp. 17–69, 209–255).

The author would like to thank Jon Gjerde, William Banks, and Jayne London for their helpful comments and suggestions, and the University of Minnesota Computer Center for a grant that made the analysis of these data possible.
Reprinted from *Journal of Family History* Vol. 12, No. 4 (Winter 1987):407–420. Used with permission of JAI Press, Inc.

Frazier simply expounded upon an argument advanced by many urban sociologists, most notably his former teachers at the University of Chicago. They viewed that movement to the city as an alienating process which led to social disorganization (Sennett 1969). By linking these prominent beliefs with his thesis that slavery disrupted black family organization, Frazier was able to explain what he found in contemporary Chicago and other centers of large black in-migration before World War Two.

Frazier's thesis went unchallenged until 1965, when the U.S. Department of Labor published Daniel Patrick Moynihan's study of the crisis in the black family (Moynihan 1965). With greater emphasis than Frazier, Moynihan attributed the structure of the contemporary black family to the legacy of slavery. Unlike Frazier, however, Moynihan used the word *pathology* when describing that structure. As a result of Moynihan's emphasis, scholars debated the extent of slavery as the root of the alleged dysfunctional black family. Intensive research revealed that if the two-parent household was the norm, then upon exiting slavery the black family was meeting the norm. Historians who joined the debate argued that when there were deviations from this pattern, it was because of a complex of factors that had little to do with an intrinsic predisposition to shun lasting familial bonds (Rainwater and Yancey 1967; Pleck 1972; Furstenberg, Hershberg, and Modell 1975).

As slavery became the centerpiece of the debate, most scholars ignored Frazier's second premise: the role of migration to the city in causing family disorganization. Herbert Gutman (1976), the one notable exception, found that neither slavery nor migration has a substantive impact on the structure of the Afro-American household. Working with state-level census data and the U.S. manuscript censuses, Gutman discovered that between 68 and 90% of all Afro-Americans lived in two-headed households through the 1920s (Gutman 1976, pp. xviii, 443–475, 511).

While Gutman's findings constituted a major contribution, he dealt only with part of the migration component of Frazier's thesis. Whereas the cross-sectional analysis of the household portrayed the structure of the Afro-American family, he noted that it failed to capture the workings of kin networks (Gutman 1976, p. 433). While migration did not cause disunion, it did produce periods of isolation. Thus, what is lacking is some discussion of the strategies adopted by blacks to counter the potential for dislocation caused by residential separation.

This neglect is not due to a lack of data. Historians of the urban Afro-American experience have long known of a source that could shed some light on the tactics employed by the migrants. Writing in *Harlem: The Making of a Negro Ghetto* in 1968, Gilbert Osofsky observed:

> It was common practice for migrants who lived within a day's journey of their former homes, to shuttle back and forth for regular visits. If European immigrants found the Atlantic no great barrier to such journeys, . . . the Negro migrant was even less restricted by distance and cost. Practically every issue of the *New York Age* carried some report of such movement   [*Osofsky 1968, p. 30*].

Neither Osofsky nor others who studied black urbanites submitted the accounts found in such black journals as the *Age,* Chicago *Defender,* or Norfolk *Journal and Guide* to a systematic examination (Spear, 1967; Kusmer 1976; Trotter 1985). Yet from this type of detailed microlevel information, it is possible to take a new look at the Afro-American family.

Blacks, like other migrant groups, utilized what I call *adaptive strategies,* cultural adjustments to changes in their social world stemming from migration. Much of the current literature on migration's impact on family bonds focuses on white ethnic immigrants. Scholars of the immigrant experience have described the relationship between migration and the desire to re-create elements of their cultural past (Gjerde 1985; Hareven 1982; Bell 1979; Vecoli 1964). In their discussions two patterns are apparent: (1) migrants who came to the United States with the intent of returning home; and (2) those who came to stay. The returnees sought to remain true to their cultural values of land ownership and economic independence by emigrating, obtaining the material wealth abroad and returning home (Bodnar, Simon, and Weber 1982; Bell 1979). But those who did not intend to return also hoped to remain true to their cultural past even if by different means. Cognizant of their inability to re-create sacred elements of their cultural heritage at home because of declining opportunity, this group struggled to re-create as much of that world as was possible (Gjerde 1985; Hareven 1982; Vecoli 1964). In each case, the European migrants devised a strategem for adapting to perceived changes in their environment.

Similar impulses motivated Afro-Americans as well. Opportunities to acquire land, wealth, and respect appeared unlikely in many parts of the rural South; as a result, many blacks were induced to migrate. But unlike those Europeans who returned home, most blacks who left the South between 1900 and 1920 intended to migrate permanently. Unlike the nonreturnees, however, Afro-Americans did go back for social visits and emergency-induced trips (see Grossman 1982; Borchert 1980; Gottlieb 1977). Black Americans, in many ways, behaved unlike either European group. For them the social visit afforded an opportunity to maintain key relationships, mend strained family ties, and rekindle old friendships without relinquishing the dream of better opportunities. As the migration intensified, visiting developed as a way of bridging the spatial distance. As such, of course, it became a strategy for adapting to changes in conditions.

Within this context we are drawn again to the stories mentioned at the outset. This article suggests that Afro-Americans used such visits as a means of bridging the separation caused by migration. The essay will also outline the role women and men played in maintaining interpersonal ties with family and friends. And, it will discuss the complexity of the visiting social travel fields, which had a direct bearing on how visits helped maintain kin and friendship links.

As a means of revealing extra-local kinship ties, I have sampled travel behavior illustrated in every fourth issue (a total of 37 issues) of the Norfolk (VA) *Journal and Guide* for the years September 1916–September 1917, 1921, and 1925. The *Journal and Guide* was the South's best edited black weekly for much of this century (Suggs 1976, 1983, p. 397–407). It was published in a city strategically located in the east-coast transportation complex, one which functioned as the embarkation point for many who later migrated to the North. For our purposes, the paper featured a section chronicling travel behavior. Each weekly issue highlighted those going out of town as well as those receiving out-of-town guests.

This study is periodized according to the availability of data, and changes in the character of the data. I sought to select a time frame that paralleled the peak of the Great Migration and a period that encompassed the less intense post-migration years, when strategies might have become institutionalized. But, because issues of the *Guide* for the period October 1917 to December 1920, excluding a few extant copies, were lost to fire, I decided to examine visitation patterns at evenly spaced intervals between 1917 and 1925. This accounts for the years selected. Furthermore, after 1925, and paralleling the greater social stratification of the black community, one's appearance in the travel column became linked to one's status in the community. As a result, by 1925 the newspaper covered the travel habits of the middle class more than their proportion in the population would warrant, a bias that had not been true before.[1]

A typical citation in the newspaper listed the name of a person coming into or leaving Norfolk or some adjacent area, the person he or she visited, the length of the trip, the size of the party traveling, and the type of traveling group. The following is a fairly representative example of how the information appeared:

> Mrs. W. H. Miller of Ave. B was the guest of her parents, Mr. and Mrs. Robert Harris of Smithfield, VA last week. . . .

From this illustration we can infer several things about visiting, familial contact, and Afro–American culture. We know Mrs. W. H. Miller of Ave. B resided in Norfolk. We also know she probably was married. In addition, the description is phrased to indicate that Mrs. Miller visited her parents in Smithfield. From the example it is hard to say with absolute certainty how long she stayed in Smithfield, but it seems reasonable to surmise more than one day but less than a week (2–6 days), simply because the *Guide* generally reported if it was a day trip or a week trip. Further, it is clear Mrs. Miller traveled alone, and that she was a daughter returning to her family of origin, albeit for a short time. Finally, the weekly appearance of such citations suggests that black Norfolkians, and their relatives and friends elsewhere, derived some pleasure from knowing that others knew of their efforts to sustain and renew important relationships.

This study used 840 such citations.[2] In this sample population, females out–numbered males two to one.[3] Further, approximately as many of the travelers were coming into the Norfolk area as were leaving (48.8% versus 51.2%).

The weakness of this approach is its reliance on self-reported data. Only those individuals able and inclined to report their visiting were included. Yet a sample of the occupational makeup of those reported in the *Guide* through 1921 revealed that they mirrored the community's class composition, which was, at this time, overwhelmingly working class.[4] In all probability the newspaper columns underenumerated the activities of the very poor. Whereas in other communities the black elite may have escaped enumeration as well, such was not the case in Norfolk. Norfolk's leading black citizens were educators, fraternal leaders, and small business people (Lewis 1984, chapter 4). Because their welfare so closely paralleled that of the larger community, they made no attempts to disassociate themselves from the community. Indeed, the travel of individuals in this group appeared in the newspaper repeatedly. Hence only one tail of the distribution—the very poor—is likely omitted. But even the very poor, over the course of several years, may have traveled; the only difference between them and the community's other residents would have been the frequency of such trips, and possibly a trip's duration.

Not only did females outnumber males, but individuals traveled more often than groups. Nearly 62% of all social migrants traveled alone. When persons traveled in a group, 75.7% of them did so with just one other person. Almost one-third (30.4%) of these dyadic groups consisted of a parent and child, while another 21.1% consisted of a husband and a wife. Not surprisingly, the nuclear family—mother, father, and children—were considerably underrepresented (4.8%).

In 815 of the 840 cases a description is provided of the purpose of the trip. Just over three-fourths (or 77.4%) of travelers described their visit as social, suggesting thereby the nurture of kith and kin bonds. Bereaved travelers like Mrs. William Marsh, who journeyed to attend the funeral of her stepmother, accounted for another 6.5% (*Journal and Guide* April 1921). The remaining proportion traveled to a convention, for business reasons, for unspecified personal reasons, to be at the bed of a sick relative or friend, or to move to another locale (see Table 1).

The percentages in Table 1 also indicate that four out of every five travelers engaged in behavior designed to facilitate the maintenance of direct affective bonds. Unfortunately, none of the black travelers left diaries and letters, and, therefore, unlike in studies of the migrant-kinship ties of rural whites, it is difficult to establish attitudes (Pederson 1984). Psychologists, however, have found that the patterning of behavior is often suggestive of the underlying attitude (Fishbein and Ajzen 1974; Oskamp 1977, pp. 165–245). In addition, James Grossman's research on black migration to Chicago and Peter Gottlieb's study of migration to Pittsburgh underscore how visiting, along with letter writing, functioned as a means of bridging

Table 1   Reason for Trip

Reason	Number	Percentage
Visit (i.e., holiday, vacation, and so forth)	631	77.4
Death	53	6.5
Convention	38	4.7
Business	34	4.2
Other	33	4.1
Illness	19	2.3
Move	6	.7
Revival (church)	1	.1
Total	815	100.0

the distance caused by relocation, allowing it to be called an adaptive strategy (Grossman 1982, pp. 57–61; Gottlieb 1977, pp. 105, 109). Given the volume of visiting, we can safely suggest blacks attached an importance to maintaining contact with kin and kith when separated geographically.

Because visiting constituted an adaptation to spatial separation one would also expect that travelers would decide that some relationships were more important to maintain than others. Of the 600 cases where the data are complete, 42.5% indicated that the person visited was a member of the family of procreation or the family of orientation, hereafter called a *first-order relative*. In contrast, only 16.1% of the individuals visited second–order kin, such as grandparents and grandchildren, uncles, aunts, cousins or in–laws. Of the second–order kin, 56% had lateral links to the travelers—e.g., aunts, uncles, and nephews. The remaining 44% had lineal ties to those visiting. Even fewer people visited persons of unspecified relation to the travelers. The remaining 30.5% traveled to see friends. Bruce (1970) has suggested that for white males in the contemporary city visiting among first–order kin is not a high priority and that is correlates negatively with occupational mobility. Although we have no data on occupational mobility, the behavior illustrated by the sample suggests that blacks believed contact with immediate family members important. The contact became less frequent only after the blood ties became more distant (see Table 2).

Further, we find a strong association between gender and the nature of the trip taken (see Table 3). Ostensibly, as part of the adaptation to out-migration, rules developed that prescribed the gender of the primary visitor. Both men and women, we discover, tended to travel if a relative or friend was seriously ill or had died. So too did they travel in equal proportions when the trip was to attend a convention. But as the evidence indicates, women were more often social visitors than men, and as such the primary "kinkeepers,"[5] thus duplicating patterns found among other groups (Adams 1968; Young and Willmott 1957; Hareven 1982, pp. 105–106).

When we examine the travel dyad composed of the husband and wife, we see that males comprised the primary visitor in 87.1% of the cases. (A primary visitor was the person inferred from the description as determining the person or persons visited.) Moreover, in the small number of cases where both parents and children traveled together, men figured as the primary visitors in 81.2% of the

Table 2   Categories of Persons Visited by Migrants

Category	Number	Percentage
First–order kin[a]	265	42.5
Second–order kin[b]	100	16.1
Unspecified relations	68	10.9
Kith	190	30.5
Total	623	100.0

Notes: [a]First–order kin consists of members of either the family of origin, such as parents, siblings; or the family of procreation.
[b]Second–order kin comprise aunts, uncles, nephews, nieces, in–laws, step-relations, and grandparents.

Table 3   The Association between Gender of Primary Visitor and the Type of Trip

	Male		Female		Total	
Type of Trip	*Number*	*Percentage*	*Number*	*Percentage*	*Number*	*Percentage*
Social visit	193	71.1	437	81.2	630	78.1
Death	17	6.3	36	6.7	53	6.6
Illness	6	2.2	13	2.4	19	2.4
Business	24	8.9	10	1.9	34	4.2
Convention	13	4.8	25	4.6	38	4.7
Other	16	5.9	17	3.2	33	4.1

Note: Chi-square = 26.78588 with 5 *df*, significance = .0001.

cases. Consequently, when the group consisted of one parent and child(ren), fathers were the primary visitors in only 13% of the cases.

This pattern suggests several possible explanations. In part, the conditions under which men traveled with their families may have been related to the larger issue of intrafamilial gender politics. Restrained by work or constitution, men may have decided to travel only when they could decide who would be visited. It is also possible that because fewer men than women traveled under any condition, both husbands and wives may have decided that it was important that the male have an opportunity to visit his kith or kin whenever he could. Conceivably the pattern highlights the little-addressed patriarchal and patrilineal structure of the black family in which wives were viewed as part of the male line, but husbands did not belong to the female line. Of course there is another possibility: in certain instances the travel of men may have resulted from prodding by their spouses, who said "It is time you visit your. . . ." But because of the nature of the reporting, the male, rather than the female who inspired the trip, was noted as the primary visitor. In such instances, the female was actually the real functional kinkeeper because she provided the impetus for the trip. More likely, however, the pattern noted above is not the result of any one of these factors but the aggregation of many factors. As such, the woman's role as kinkeeper is highlighted by the fact that she visited in all situations—alone, with children, and as a member of the conjugal and nuclear family.

An association also existed between gender and the length of stay. When men traveled, they limited the length of their stay, unless the move required them to be away for more than six months. Typically a trip with the male as the primary traveler lasted somewhere between one day and two to five days. For the 174 cases where the data are complete, 110, or 63.2%, of the men stayed away for less than a week. Whereas many women also took short trips (less than a week), they were more inclined, and, we must assume, able, to stay longer. In turn the greater availability for travel no doubt enhanced their role as contact persons between kin and kith who lived elsewhere. The difference in the length of this visit as determined by gender bears a strong statistical association (*df* 6, significance = .0009).

The length of one's stay was also affected by the point of departure. Due to a strong correlation between place of origin and distance (Although not neces-

Table 4 Interpersonal Relation and Length of Stay (in Percent)

Length of Stay	First-Order Kin N = 115 (36.7)*	Second-Order Kin N = 48 (15.3)*	Friends N N = 150 (47.9)*
1 day	25.4	13.4	61.2
2–6 days	37.4	13.9	48.7
1 week	42.9	14.3	42.9
2–3 weeks	38.6	19.3	42.1
1 month	36.4	27.3	36.4
2–5 months	57.1	14.3	28.6

Note: *Proportion of total observations.

sarily ease of transit) persons from North Carolina and Virginia (excluding Norfolk and vicinity) made short trips lasting no more than a week. On the other hand, very few persons coming from the North stayed just one day. While the modal length of their visit was a few days, more than one-quarter of all visitors stayed between a week and three weeks. One can speculate that the cost of travel did not make it economical for Northerners to come South for short visits, as implied by Osofsky (1968, p. 30). A family of four traveling by ship from Norfolk to New York, for example, could anticipate spending $25. For a male oyster-shucker or fertilizer worker, such a trip amounted to the pay from the previous week's work (Henri 1976; Virginia Report 1920).

In addition, the length of stay was related to the blood ties between migrant and host. Travelers reserved much of their one-day trips for friends and not family. This supports the findings of Schwarzweller, who studied the migration habits of Appalachian whites. He found that longer trips, implying vacations, were reserved for family and not friends (Schwarzweller, Brown, and Mangalam 1971, p. 133). Thus if visiting was an adaptation to dislocation caused by out-migration, then it is not surprising that immediate family members were honored with the longest stays (Table 4). . . .

Conclusion

Blacks who left and came to Norfolk between 1916 and 1925 resembled the many who fled rural America in the early twentieth century. Just as for whites in rural Wisconsin during this period, the maintenance of primary relationships remained important to Afro-Americans (Pederson 1984). As with any cultural expression, the act of visiting took on its own characteristics. Among the Afro-Americans in our study, women visited more than men. Individuals also visited more than families. When families visited, women functioned as the primary kinkeepers unless they were visiting the first-order kin of their husbands.

These travel habits suggest the evolution of a complex interactional mechanism in an era before the telephone, which helped blacks overcome geographic separation. That there are similar accounts to be found in newspapers for the entire country would indicate that instead of being overawed by change, Afro-Americans adjusted and restructured their lives to meet their primary needs. Although additional research is needed, the data presented here indicate that visiting arrested the breakdown of primary relationships between black migrants and those who remained behind, and therefore constituted an important adaptive strategy of the black family (Feagin 1968, 1970; Stack 1974; Bethel 1981; Bodnar et al. 1982).

Notes

1. The composition of Norfolk's black community changed appreciably after World War One through the growth of an active middle class (see Lewis 1984, chapters 3 and 4). Black communities nationwide experienced similar social stratification after the war. See, for example, Kusmer (1976, chapter 11).
2. Some wonder if 840 citations represents a small or large sample of such visits. Given that possible visits (N) equal some factorial of all black Norfolkians plus their family members and friends elsewhere, we must conclude that the sample is small. If the question, however, is whether 840 represents a sizable number of available citations, the answer is positive. The 840 citations represent roughly one-fourth of all citations for the three years selected.
3. The sex of the primary visitor was determined by asking whose family member or friend(s) was being visited.
4. Again, see Lewis (1984, chapters 3 and 4).
5. *Kinkeepers* is a neologism used to convey the importance of the social function.

References

Adams, Bert M. 1968. *Kinship in an Urban Setting*. Chicago: Markham Publishing Company.

Bell, Rudolph M. 1979. *Fate and Honor, Family and Village*. Chicago: University of Chicago Press.

Bethel, Elizabeth Rauh. 1981. *Promiseland: A Century of Life in a Negro Community*. Philadelphia, PA: Temple University Press.

Bodnar, John, Roger Simon, and Michael P. Weber. 1982. *Lives of Their Own*, Urbana: University of Illinois Press.

Borchert, James. 1980. *Alley Life in Washington: Family, Community, Religion, and Folklife in the City, 1850–1978*. Urbana: University of Illinois Press.

Bruce, J. M. 1970. "Intragenerational Occupational Mobility and Visiting with Kin and Friend." *Social Forces* 49:117–127.

Carr, Virginia. 1985. Conversation, June 7.

Feagin, Joe R. 1968. "The Kinship Ties of Negro Urbanites." *Social Science Quarterly* 69:660–665.

————. 1970. "A Note on the Friendship Ties of Negro Urbanites." *Social Forces* 49:303–308.

Fishbein, Martin, and Icek Ajzen. 1974. "Attitudes Toward Objects as Predictors of Single and Multiple Behavior Criteria." *Psychological Review* 81:59–74.

Frazier, E. Franklin. [1939] 1973. *The Negro Family in the United States*. Chicago: University of Chicago Press.

Furstenburg, Frank F., Jr., Theodore Hershberg, and John Modell. 1975. "The Origins of the Female-Headed Black Family: The Impact of the Urban Experience." *Journal of Interdisciplinary History* 6:211–233.

Gjerde, Jon. 1985. *From Peasants to Farmers: The Migration from Balestrand, Norway, to the Upper Middle West*. New York: Cambridge University Press.

Gottlieb, Peter. 1977. "Making Their Own Way: Southern Blacks' Migration to Pittsburgh, 1916–30." Ph.D. dissertation, University of Pittsburgh.

Grossman, James R. 1982. "A Dream Deferred: Black Migration to Chicago, 1916–1921." Ph.D. dissertation, University of California, Berkeley.

Gutman, Herbert, 1976. *The Black Family in Slavery and Freedom, 1750–1925*. New York: Pantheon Books.

Hareven, Tamara K. 1982. *Family Time and Industrial Time*. Cambridge: Cambridge University Press.

Henri, Florette. 1976. *Black Migration: Movement North, 1900–1920*. Garden City, NY: Anchor Books.

James, Susan. 1980. Untaped conversations.

––––––. 1981. Interview, January 2.

Journal and Guide [Norfolk, Virginia] 1916. September 30.

––––––. 1917. March 3.

––––––. 1921. April 23, September 17.

Kusmer, Kenneth L. 1976. *A Ghetto Takes Shape: Black Cleveland, 1870–1930*. Urbana: University of Illinois Press.

Lewis, Earl. 1984. "At Work and at Home: Blacks in Norfolk, Virginia. 1910–1945." Ph.D. dissertation, University of Minnesota.

MacDonald, John S., and Leatrice D. MacDonald, 1964. "Chain Migration, Ethnic Neighborhood Formation and Social Networks." *Milbank Memorial Fund* 42:82.

Moynihan, Daniel Patrick. 1965. *The Negro Family: The Case for National Action*. Washington, DC:U.S. Department of Labor.

Oskamp, Stuart. 1977. *Attitudes and Behavior*. Englewood Cliffs, NJ: Prentice-Hall.

Osofsky, Gilbert. 1968. *Harlem: The Making of a Negro Ghetto*. New York: Harper & Row.

Pederson, Jane Marie. 1984. "The Country Visitor: Patterns of Hospitality in Rural Wisconsin, 1880–1925." *Agricultural History* 58:347–364.

Pleck, Elizabeth. 1972. "The Two-Parent Household: Black Family Structure in Late Nineteenth Century Boston." *Journal of Social History* 6:3–31.

Rainwater, Lee, and William Yancy. 1967. *The Moynihan Report and Politics of Controversy*. Cambridge: MIT Press.

Schwarzweller, Harry K., James S. Brown and J. J. Mangalam. 1971. *Mountain Families in Transition*. University Park, PA: Pennsylvania State University Press.

Sennet, Richard, 1969. *Classic Essays on the Culture of Cities*. Englewood Cliffs, NJ; Prentice-Hall.

Spear, Allan H. 1967. *Black Chicago: The Making of a Negro Ghetto, 1890–1920*. Chicago: University of Chicago Press.

Stack, Carol B. 1974. *All Our Kin*. New York: Harper & Row.

Stutz, Frederick P. 1973. "Distance and Network Effects on Urban Social Travel Fields." *Economic Geographer,* 49:135.

Suggs, Henry Lewis. 1976. "P. B. Young and the Norfolk Journal and Guide. 1910–1954." Ph.D. dissertation, University of Virginia.

_____ . 1983. *The Black Press in the South, 1865–1979*. Westport, CT: Greenwood Press.

Trotter, Joe William, Jr. 1985. *Black Milwaukee: The Making of an Industrial Proletariat, 1915–1945*. Urbana: University of Illinois Press.

U.S. Census. 1920. *[Fourteeneth] United States Census,* Vol. 2: *Population.* Washington, DC: U.S. Government Printing Office.

Vecoli, Rudolph J. 1964. "Contadini in Chicago; A Critique of the Uprooted." *Journal of American History* 51:404–417.

Virginia Report. 1920. *Virginia Annual Reports of the Offices, Boards and Institutions of the Commonwealth of Virginia.* Report of the Labor Commission.

Young, Michael, and Peter Willmott. 1957. *Family and Kinship in East London.* Baltimore: Penguin.

3

Dating and Mate Choice

> I had made some courtship during this time to Miss Read. I had a great
> respect and affection for her, and had some reasons to believe she had the
> same for me; but as I was about to take a long voyage and we were both
> very young, only a little above eighteen, it was thought most prudent by
> her mother to prevent our going too far at present, as a marriage, if it was
> to take place, would be more convenient after my return, when I should
> be as I hoped set up in my business.   [*Benjamin Franklin,* Autobiography]

In Chapter 2, we viewed the American family in broad sociohistorical perspective. In this and subsequent chapters, we turn our attention to specific features of
the American family. An appropriate beginning is a consideration of the
relationships between young women and men who are unmarried. For most
young people these relationships eventually end with the selection of a marriage
partner. However, some young people in every era have remained unmarried,
either by choice or because of factors beyond their control. Therefore, although
this chapter focuses on the paths that lead most young people to marriage, it is
important to recognize that these paths sometimes lead others to different
destinations.

Societies exhibit great variation in the frequency, duration, and degree of
intimacy of relationships between young people and in the amount of freedom
given in the selection of marriage partners. At one extreme, relationships between
young men and women who are unmarried are virtually nonexistent, and
marriage partners are selected by parents or other adult kinfolk. In these kin- or
parent-run courtship systems, prospective mates may actually see each other for
the first time on the day of their marriage ceremony. At the other extreme are
societies in which young people are allowed great latitude in their relationships

with members of the opposite sex, sometimes having intimate emotional and sexual relationships outside of marriage. In these participant-run systems, young people have the right to choose their own marriage partners. Actually, few societies fall at the extreme ends of this continuum because even in a participant-run system parents find ways to influence their children and even in a parent-run system participants find ways to have their wishes taken into account.

Relationships between young people in the United States and other industrialized countries most closely approximate participant-run courtship systems. In this introduction, we consider the historical antecedents of these relationships and some important findings of sociologists about the process and the outcomes of mate choice.

Courtship in Early America

In colonial America and in the years immediately following the Revolution, parents exercised substantial control over their children's activities and choices of marriage partners. Although it would be inaccurate to characterize courtship practices prior to the nineteenth century as parent-run, the term *parent-directed* is appropriate. As we have seen, the preindustrial family was a unit of production, and marriage was primarily an economic partnership. Consequently, the selection of a marriage partner was a matter of great significance, and parents were prepared and sometimes had the legal right to assure that their children made timely decisions and wise choices. As the opening quotation from Benjamin Franklin's autobiography illustrates, the wishes of parents were not discounted by those contemplating marriage.

Young men and women in this period were unable to marry without the wherewithal to establish their own households. For this they were often dependent on the man's father, although the woman's parents would also make some contribution to the new couple's means of support. Usually a man could marry only when his father was willing to divide his property and do without his son's labor (Rothman, 1984:27). Although fathers were obligated to provide a "portion" to their sons, the age at which they did so was apparently discretionary. If a father was unwilling to divide his property, a young man was left in the unenviable position of waiting until his father died before he could marry.

Daniel Scott Smith's (1973) study of average ages at marriage in colonial New England provides evidence that the inheritance of land and other property did influence the behavior of young men. Smith found that men whose fathers died over the age of sixty-five had higher mean ages of marriage than did those whose fathers died before the age of sixty-five. He concluded that fathers often delayed their sons' marriages by retaining control of their property to an advanced age. As a consequence of this dependence of young men on their fathers for means of support, most men married in their middle to late twenties. Their brides were typically a few years younger.

Although parents had less to say about whom their children married than about when they married, they did guide their children to an appropriate partner and had the authority to prevent marriages of which they disapproved. Edmund Morgan's (1966) description of courtship patterns in Puritan New England illustrates the mechanisms parents used to direct their children to the choice of a suitable spouse. According to Morgan, the choice of an individual to court or, for a woman, an appropriate suitor to accept was left to young people. However, numerous restrictions applied. First, the prospective partners needed to be of the same social status, of "equal birth" in the language of the time. Second, to assure that children exercised good judgment, the laws of New England required young men wishing to begin courtship to obtain "liberty and allowance" from women's parents. Third, after young men and women decided they were suitably matched, they had to obtain consent from their parents, and a contract for marriage had to be negotiated by the parents. In these contracts, parents spelled out the contributions each would make to the future partners. The bride's parents were expected to give approximately half the amount contributed by the parents of the groom.

In Puritan beliefs about marriage, reason was the appropriate basis for choosing a marriage partner. A marriage partner needed to be an individual with whom one could spend the rest of one's life in a close cooperative endeavor, and Puritans believed that decisions about compatibility were best made with the mind instead of the heart. Individuals would eventually develop love for their mates after they married, but love was not a firm basis for the choice of a partner. Therefore, according to Puritan ideals, young men and women should not marry individuals they loved but should marry those they judged they could learn to love in the process of working together. In Morgan's (1966:53) words, a man "allowed reason to choose the object of his love and then commanded his affections to act accordingly." While women did not take the initiative in courtship, they were also expected to select a compatible individual from among their suitors. Puritans recognized that decisions about whom one could love were best made by young people themselves, and parents were warned not to force matches. For Puritans, the choice of a marriage partner was both far too important to be left to the participants alone and too personal a matter to be decided solely by others.

In the 1800s, relationships between young men and women gradually began to change, paving the way for patterns that would develop in the twentieth century. Lying behind these changes in courtship patterns were alterations in the position of young people in the family. Joseph Kett (1977) suggests that in the early decades of the nineteenth century boys and girls continued to experience a prolonged period of "semidependence" between childhood and adulthood. Both boys and girls began to assume adult work roles early, and their responsibilities grew as they became older. Young people often went to work in the households of others. However, their early departures from home were not permanent, and periods of living and working away from home alternated with periods of living at home. In the early decades of the nineteenth century, most young people remained dependent on their parents for the means to make the transition to adulthood, just as they had in colonial America.

As the nineteenth century progressed, a subtle but extremely important alteration in the period of semidependence occurred. The change was most pronounced in urban areas, but rural youth also felt its impact. Industrialization decreased the chances that young people would work for their parents and increased the likelihood that they would work in a factory, shop, or commerical establishment. Eventually, this shift in the locus of employment and the potential for independence it held allowed young people to leave home, marry, and establish their own households at younger ages than at any previous time in American history.

However, these changes in the transition to adulthood did not occur abruptly. In industrial cities, young people went to work and often left home in their teens, but they did not marry or set up households until their mid- to late twenties, postponing these events just as their predecessors had done in the previous century. However, the delays in marriage and household headship were not the result of dependence on parents to provide the necessary means of support. Instead marriage and household headship depended on the success of young people in securing and advancing in employment. Young people were, in short, dependent on their own abilities to take advantage of the opportunities provided by an occupational world that their parents did not control. Michael Katz (1975) captures the subtle nature of this shift in the transition to adulthood among nineteenth-century urban youth by substituting the term *semiautonomy* for Kett's *semidependence*.

It it important to distinguish between the experiences of men and women and between those of young people in different social classes in nineteenth-century cities. In rural areas, prior to the expansion of market-oriented farming, the labor of both women and men in home production was essential. In industrializing cities, the sphere of women's activities in the household was restricted without a corresponding increase in opportunities outside the household. As a result, young men were likely to enter the labor force as soon as they finished their schooling. Young women, however, were likely to spend a period before marriage living with their parents when they neither went to school nor were employed. The divergence in the experiences of men and women was more marked for middle-class than working-class youth because working-class women often worked in factories or as domestic servants in the homes of the upper-middle class. It also is likely that middle-class men remained more dependent on their parents than their working-class counterparts because they went to school longer and had the possibility of inheriting a family-owned business.

It is often thought that the transition to adulthood takes place later today than it did in the past. A study by John Modell, Frank Furstenberg, and Theodore Hershberg (1976) demonstrates both why this perception exists and why it is not completely accurate. Using census data from Philadelphia in 1880 and a sample of the U.S. population in 1970, the authors compared the timing of five transitions on the pathway to adulthood: departure from school, employment, residence away from home, household headship, and marriage. Only two of these transitions, departure from school and entry into the labor force, occurred later in the life course in 1970 that in 1880. In fact, entry into the adult world of employment occurs later in the twentieth century primarily because of the delay in the departure from school. However, after completing school and obtaining a job, young people tend to move away from home, establish households, and marry earlier than their nineteenth-century predecessors. Therefore, the transition to adulthood begins later for contemporary youth, but independence comes earlier.

The subtle shift from semidependence to semiautonomy in the nineteenth century gave young people additional control over when they married. The potential for independence also increased both young people's freedom in the choice of marriage partners and their latitude in relationships with each other because parental approval had lost much of its significance. It is difficult to document when these changes occurred. Ellen Rothman's (1984) study of middle-class courtship, *Hands and Hearts*, demonstrates that young people had considerable, and growing, freedom in their relationships with one another throughout the nineteenth century. According to Rothman (p. 35), "young men and women born in the years following Independence enjoyed a high level of self-determination. This meant not only that they were free to choose their own mates but that they socialized with little supervision." Much of the interaction of young people occurred in the homes of their parents, but men and women also met at churches, dances, picnics, and simply while traveling about. In this connection, Rothman (p. 23) notes the distinction made between courting and courtship. In the nineteenth century, *courting* referred generally to informal socializing between unmarried men and women, while *courtship* referred specifically to the interaction of couples who had declared, or were soon expected to declare, their intent to marry. While pairing was allowed in courting, most of this socializing took place in groups.

The emphasis on freedom of action and choice in courtship is consistent with the changing place of the family in the community. As middle-class Americans began to view the family as a private retreat, the emotional relationship between husband and wife began to occupy a place of special significance. The perceived isolation of the family from the rational and impersonal world of the factory and business establishment was reflected in the increasing emphasis on love as a prerequisite for marriage rather than as an emotion that was best left to develop after marriage. According to Rothman (p. 35), when a man proposed marriage in the nineteenth century, "love was his most important qualification. When a woman responded, love was her first consideration." In contrast to the practice in colonial New England, matches needed to be something more than suitable, and love needed to be something more than a potential. In the diaries and letters of nineteenth-century Americans, Rothman found numerous examples of the intense self-examination young men and women conducted in their search for a partner they loved.

By the beginning of the twentieth century, American courtship patterns had assumed many of the basic characteristics they retain to the present day. Young people were able to interact with others in relative freedom and could marry when they had the economic resources to do so. Although young men may have occasionally asked parents for their daughters' hands in marriage, these requests had probably become little more than anxiety-producing rituals. Exceptions to the freedom of mate choice continued to exist among some groups, particularly the very wealthy. However, a participant-run courtship system had become the rule.

Theories of Mate Selection and Homogamy

When sociologists turned their attention to mate selection, this participant-run system had been in place for several decades. Two initial concerns of sociologists were how individuals chose marriage partners and what social patterns of mate choice resulted from a system in which young people were theoretically free to marry any individual they wished. Investigation of the first topic resulted in the development of theories of mate selection, and research on the second topic led to the documentation of patterns of homogamy.

Robert Winch (1958) proposed an early and influential theory of mate selection. According to Winch, a principle of complementary needs governs mate choice so that individuals choose marriage partners whose personalities are the opposites of their own. For example, a dominant man will seek a passive woman, and a nurturing woman will seek a succorant man. In this way, the personality needs of each individual are gratified, forming the basis of a lasting relationship. Although this sociological version of the folk wisdom that "opposites attract" has intuitive appeal, research has failed to provide much evidence that supports it (Murstein, 1980:781).

Other theories of mate selection have emphasized the importance of factors such as value similarity, the relative quality of the contributions each partner can make, and role compatibility. Although these theories have received some empirical support, it is now clear that no single-factor theory will explain mate choices. Instead, sociologists have proposed that various factors act in sequence or conjunction in decisions to marry. For example, Bernard Murstein (1976) has proposed a multistage stimulus–value–role theory of mate selection in which individuals (1) are initially attracted to one another by factors such as similar interests, attractive physical appearance, or valued personality traits, (2) develop a deeper attraction to one another because of perceived value similarity, and (3) discover that they enjoy participating in various activities together.

While Murstein and other proponents of sequential models can demonstrate that many couples pass through stages of deepening compatibility, even these multifactor theories have difficulty capturing the extreme complexity of mate choice. For example, many couples successfully traverse the stages proposed by a model but fail to marry because of external factors such as financial insecurity, lack of support from others, and career aspirations. More critical for the validity of these theories are cases in which individuals who have not gone through the stages marry. Finally, to deepen the complexity even more, some factors may have relatively more importance for some individuals than others, and some factors may vary in importance over time. Several decades of research have thus demonstrated that mate selection is a complex and, to a certain extent, unpredictable process. Some would argue that this is as it should be.

Despite the difficulty that theories of mate selection have in predicting who will marry whom, individuals do tend to choose marriage partners from among those in the same broad social categories as themselves. Sociologists refer to this pattern of like-marrying-like as *homogamy*. Among the most important social characteristics influencing mate choices are ethnicity, education, social class, race, intelligence, and age (Murstein, 1980:777). For example, studies show rates of racial homogamy of between 95 and 99 percent and rates of religious (interfaith) homogamy between 80 and 90 percent. Rates of social class and ethnic homogamy depend on how classes and ethnic groups are divided. Bruce Eckland (1968), for example, reports rates of 80 percent for class homogamy when the division is between the middle class and the working class, and rates of 50 percent when more divisions are used. Similarly, rates of ethnic homogamy depend on the specific groups considered. For example, research in the 1960s demonstrated that Puerto Ricans, Italians, the Polish, and the Irish had a greater tendency to marry within their own groups than others did (Bogue, 1969).

Patterns of homogamy are related to opportunities for interaction. It is obvious that people in a participant-run system are unlikely to marry individuals they have never met, and studies have demonstrated that people are likely to marry individuals who live near them (Burr, 1973). For example, racial segregation in the United States makes it likely that blacks will meet and interact with other blacks. Similarly, because many individuals meet their future mates in their late teens and early twenties, high rates of social-class homogamy are supported by the differential rates of college attendance among middle- and working-class youth. High rates of homogamy are also supported by differences in values between groups. Even if young people of different classes do meet, they may not evaluate each other highly as prospective mates because they do not share the same interests or have the same goals. Finally, even in a participant-run courtship system, parents have some control over whom their children meet.

Opportunities for interaction, value similarity, and parental influence thus all play a significant part in maintaining patterns of homogamy. However, it is likely that many people simply do not define members of other groups as potential marriage partners. Research demonstrating the negative societal reaction to interracial couples provides one reason why this may be the case (Gallup, 1978). Although rates of homogamy for all the social characteristics we have discussed have been declining since the 1970s (Murstein, 1980:777), each of these characteristics remains a powerful factor in mate selection.

Readings

The articles in this chapter examine several additional features of premarital relationships in the United States. In "Was Waller Ever Right? The Rating and Dating Complex Reconsidered," Michael Gordon considers the history of dating. He does so in a reassessment of the well-known work of Willard Waller (1937) on dating among college students in the 1930s. According to Waller, dating was a form of status seeking in which one collected dates with high-status individuals just as one might collect valuable objects. He maintained that relationships between individuals who dated were superficial, exhibiting little in the way of commitment or emotional involvement.

Gordon defines dating as any form of socializing between young people who are not yet ready to marry. This use of the term leads him to conclude that dating existed in the nineteenth century. Most historians and sociologists use the term in a more restrictive way, referring to the paired and sometimes exclusive relationships between young men and women that appeared in the twentieth century. In contrast to the home-based socializing of men and women in the nineteenth century, dates, in this view, are prearranged meetings between couples that take place away from home. John Modell (1983:93) suggests that the emergence of dating represented a further step in the development of participant-controlled courtship. Although disagreement exists on this point, parents probably did lose control as socializing between young people moved away from the home and particularly as the automobile gave young people additional freedom of movement. The expansion of high school and college education, which increased the importance of peer groups, also eroded the influence of parents.

Gordon describes the changes that took place in relationships between young men and women in the first part of the twentieth century and explores the causes of these changes. He goes on to argue that "rating and dating" has disappeared and has been replaced by more humanistic relationships. Finally, Gordon suggests that dating has given way to group-based activities, perhaps signaling the development of a new stage in the courtship process.

In the second article in this chapter, "Sex Differences in Bases of Power in Dating Relationships," Susan Sprecher examines the experiences of men and women in dating. Modell (1983:92) suggests that "asymmetries of gender roles were the armature around which the dating system evolved." In other words, the rules of participation were different for young men and women, and the two groups had different expectations of what they would receive from dating. Men initiated dates, although they certainly had to build up the courage to make their first request. Women had to wait to be "asked out," although they certainly developed ways to encourage or discourage invitations. Men also paid the expenses on dates and often took responsibility for planning the couple's activities. Most important, perhaps, a double standard of sexual behavior governed dating. Young men sought and expected sexual intimacy on a date, and it was young women's responsibility to keep things from "going too far." The emergence of the dating system may actually have done much to soften the double standard of sexual conduct, as the Kinsey studies (Kinsey, Pomeroy, and Martin, 1953) of changes in the sexual behavior of women born in the early part of the century suggest. Nevertheless, young women were more likely than their partners to emphasize the nonsexual aspects of dating such as companionship and emotional commitment.

An important topic of investigation is the impact of the women's movement on the asymmetric gender roles traditionally associated with the dating system. Several studies shed light on this issue. For example, Leslie Ann Peplau, Zick Rubin, and Charles Hill (1977) examined sexual intimacy among dating couples in a group of college students. They found that the sexual experiences of the men and women studied were quite similar, confirming the results of other studies that have shown that men and women are becoming similar in their sexual behavior. However, beneath this emerging symmetry in sexual experience, important differences concerning the meaning of sexual activity remain. The authors found that "traditional" role playing, in which men attempted to initiate sexual intimacy while women attempted to postpone or limit it, was very common. Among the couples studied, men emphasized the importance of sex, either as an aspect or a goal of their relationships, more often than did women. In addition, although many men and women agreed that sexual intimacy was an acceptable part of a loving relationship, women were more likely to think that emotional intimacy should precede sexual activity. In another study, Korman (1983) found that date initiation and expense sharing were more common among feminist than nonfeminist women. Although certainly not surprising, this finding reveals another crack in the asymmetric armature of the dating system.

Sprecher's study focuses on power and decision making among dating couples. She points out that power among married couples has been extensively studied by sociologists but that power among dating couples has not been studied directly. (In the next chapter we will consider the results of studies of marital power.) Sprecher's conceptualization of the sources of power reveals the ways that both men and women gain power in dating relationships, and her findings contribute to our understanding of the continuing asymmetries of gender roles in dating.

In the final article in this chapter, "Institutionalization of Premarital Cohabitation," Patricia Gwartney-Gibbs examines the emergence of a new stage in the mate-selection process. Statistics on the number of couples sharing a household without marrying are not available prior to 1970. However, the data show that since 1970 a substantial increase in cohabiting couples has occurred. The U.S. Census Bureau estimates that the number of unmarried couples living together more than doubled between 1970 and 1980, rising to 1,346,000. The increase was greatest among individuals under twenty-five, whose rate of cohabitation rose more than eightfold (Cherlin, 1981:12–13). A large proportion of the total rise was among college students. Studies show that about one-quarter of all college students in the 1970s were cohabiting or had cohabited at a previous time (Macklin, 1978:2). However, cohabitation is not only a practice of the well-educated. Cherlin (p. 13) suggests that cohabitation has also increased among another group of young adults—less educated individuals who are more likely to have been previously married. Therefore, he suggests that cohabitation is emerging as a common living arrangement for two groups occupying very different positions in the class structure.

Although this increase in the number of cohabiting couples is easily documented, the meaning of this trend is not yet clear. The increase could mean that men and women are abandoning traditional marriage or that cohabitation is emerging as a new stage in the courtship process between dating and marriage. It is also possible that cohabitation is a substitute for marriage among some groups and the precursor to marriage among others. Also unclear is the degree to which cohabitation has contributed to the rising age at marriage since 1970 and how cohabiting couples differ from noncohabiting couples.

Gwartney-Gibbs attempts to answer some of these questions. To do so she uses information from applications for marriage licenses in Lane County, Oregon, in 1970 and 1980. With this information she is able to estimate the percentage of couples who cohabited prior to marriage, investigate the characteristics of individuals who cohabited prior to marriage and those who did not, and examine the characteristics cohabiting couples have in common. In addition, she is able to assess the changes that occurred in patterns of cohabitation over the ten-year period. Gwartney-Gibbs concludes her analysis of premarital cohabitation with the suggestion that a "new normative pattern in courtship and marriage rituals may be emerging."

References

Bogue, Donald. 1969. *Principles of Demography*. New York: Wiley.

Burr, Wesley R. 1973. *Theory Construction in the Sociology of the Family*. New York: Wiley.

Cherlin, Andrew J. 1981. *Marriage, Divorce, Remarriage*. Cambridge: Harvard University Press.

Eckland, Bruce K. 1968. "Theories of Mate Selection." *Eugenics Quarterly* 15:17–23.

Gallup, George. 1978. "A Question of Race. Report No. 160." The Gallup Opinion Index. Princeton, N.J.: American Institute of Public Opinion.

Katz, Michael. 1975. *The People of Hamilton, Canada West*. Cambridge: Harvard University Press.

Kett, Joseph T. 1977. *Rites of Passage: Adolescence in America 1790 to the Present*. New York: Basic Books.

Kinsey, Alfred C., Wardell B. Pomeroy, and Clyde E. Martin. 1953. *Sexual Behavior in the Human Female*. Philadelphia: Saunders.

Korman, Sheila. 1983. "Non-Traditional Dating Behavior: Date Initiation and Date Expense Sharing Among Feminists and Non-Feminists." *Family Relations* 32:575–581.

Macklin, Eleanor D. 1978. "Nonmarital Heterosexual Cohabitation: A Review of Recent Literature." *Marriage and Family Review* 1:1–12.

Modell, John. 1983. "Dating Becomes the Way of American Youth." In *Essays on Family and Historical Change*, Edited by Leslie Page Moch and Gary D. Stark, 91–126. College Station, Tex.: Texas A&M University Press.

Modell, John, Frank F. Furstenberg, Jr., and Theodore Hershberg. 1976. "Social Change and Transitions to Adulthood in Historical Perspective." *Journal of Family History* 1:7–32.

Morgan, Edmund. 1966. *The Puritan Family: Religion and Domestic Life in Seventeenth-Century New England*. New York: Harper & Row.

Murstein, Bernard I. 1976. *Who Will Marry Whom? Theories and Research in Marital Choice*. New York: Springer.

_____. 1980. "Mate Selection in the 1970s." *Journal of Marriage and the Family* 42:777–92.

Peplau, Leslie Ann, Zick Rubin, and Charles T. Hill. 1977. "Sexual Intimacy in Dating Relationships." *Journal of Social Issues* 33:86–109.

Rothman, Ellen K. 1984. *Hands and Hearts: A History of Courtship in America*. New York: Basic Books.

Smith, Daniel Scott. 1973. "Parental Power and Marriage Patterns: An Analysis of Historical Trends in Hingam, Massachusetts." *Journal of Marriage and the Family* 35:419–28.

Waller, Willard. 1937. "The Rating and Dating Complex." *American Sociological Review* 2:727–34.

Winch, Robert. 1958. *Mate Selection*. New York: Harper & Row.

Was Waller Ever Right? The Rating and Dating Complex Reconsidered

Michael Gordon

Every now and then an article is published which sets the tone of subsequent research in an area for some time to come. Willard Waller's (1937) "The Rating and Dating Complex" is unquestionably such an article. It has provided three generations of family sociologists with a benchmark against which change in courtship customs can be compared. Yet, oddly enough, in view of its influence, few researchers have questioned the historical accuracy of the picture presented by Waller.[1] In what follows, I shall argue that Waller described patterns at "X College" (Pennsylvania State) which were already on the decline in the 1930s and which, perhaps, were never representative of the nation's young people, on or off campus.

To reread Waller's paper today is to be struck both by its sketchiness and the number of provisos it contains. It begins with the following statement (Waller, 1937:727): "*In the present paper we propose to discuss the customs of courtship which prevail among college students.*" Therefore, it is not surprising that many, if not all, of Waller's readers accepted it as a widely applicable image of campus dating. However, upon reading further one can see that Waller was basing this image on a campus that may have been rather special and on a methodology that was less

I would like to thank Jerold Heiss for his comments on an earlier draft of this article. This research was partially supported by the National Endowment for the Humanities.

From Michael Gordon, *Journal of Marriage and the Family*, Vol. 43, No.1, (February 1981): 67–76.

than clearcut. Moreover, he recognized at the time of writing that dating patterns varied from campus to campus (Waller, 1937:732).

What did Waller mean by the "Rating and Dating Complex"? Its key elements were supposedly *thrill seeking and exploitiveness,* and from a structural perspective, plurality (*i.e.,* one dated several [people] rather than one person). The ascent of thrill seeking as an element in heterosexual relationships was seen by Waller as part and parcel of the decline of the "formal modes of courtship" (with their associated "moral structure") which had traditionally moved people step-by-step towards the altar. Waller (1937:728) defined a thrill as "a physiological stimulation and release of tension."

> Whether we approve or not, courtship practices today allow for a great deal of pure thrill-seeking. Dancing, petting, necking, the automobile, the amusement park, and a whole range of institutions and practices permit or facilitate thrill-seeking behavior.

Thus, courtship, at least in its early stages, had become an amusement and a release of organic tensions instead of a serious business of mate selection.

According to Waller (1937:728), the relationship between thrill seeking and exploitiveness arose because of the persistence of certain understandings regarding [the] courtship process.

> According to the old morality a kiss means something, a declaration of love means something, a number of Sunday evening dates in succession means something, and these meanings are enforced by customary law, while under the new morality such things may mean nothing at all—that is, they may imply no commitment of the total personality whatsoever.

Thus, false commitment and involvement were offered in exchange for thrills. Women, Waller felt, exploited as "gold diggers," men exploited in searching for sexual liberties which would not be otherwise offered.

This thrill seeking and exploitiveness took place within a dating system that was oriented, toward prestige seeking (*i.e.,* rating). Men and women were rated according to their desirability on a variety of criteria. For a man to be highly rated required that he (Waller, 1937:730):

> belong to one of the better fraternities, be prominent in activities, have a copious supply of spending money, be well-dressed, "smooth" in manners and appearance, have a "good line," dance well, and have access to an automobile.

The factors which resulted in a woman receiving a high rating were not all that different: "good clothes, a smooth line, ability to dance well, and popularity as a date" (Waller, 1937:730). The last criterion, popularity, was obtained by creating the impression of being sought after and not frequently seen with the same person, while being seen often in the right places with a diversity of high-ranking people. Hence, the system was based upon plural, rather than exclusive dating.

Relations between men and women on campus were described by Waller in terms such as "antagonistic" and "wary." This was not surprising, given the

emphasis on rating, thrill seeking, and exploitiveness. Therefore, it is understandable that he saw this system as not being oriented toward actual mate choice,
although he did feel that every now and then, in spite of all the forces militating
against it, mate choice resulted from it. In general, however, the move to more
serious (*i.e.*, mate-choice oriented) dating would require a shift in values.

In commenting that "the rating and dating complex varies enormously
from one school to another" and that "in other schools, where the sex ratio is
about equal, and particularly in the smaller institutions, going steady is probably
a great deal more common than on the campus described," Waller (1937:732)
certainly covered himself. Still, it seems that no one who read the article
remembered these provisos, and it could be argued, as I have already done, that
they were legitimately ignored, since Waller presented his material as though it
characterized American college students as a whole.[2]

In order to adequately convey reservations about Waller's work, it is
necessary to do more than just consider the literature of the 1930s. Nevertheless,
it is the place to begin looking, since the literature of this period offered a
somewhat different picture of courtship at that time. Writing in the same year as
Waller, Newcomb (1937:662) maintained that the Depression had wrought
considerable change in the courtship behavior of America's undergraduates.

> The major effects of these changes may be listed as follows: (1) less
> compulsive and more spontaneous demonstration of affection between
> boys and girls, (2) less soul struggle on the part of the socially timid, who
> are freer than before to do as they please, (3) more widespread acceptance,
> particularly by females, of the 'naturalness' of sex intimacies with or
> without coitus; (4) less extreme "petting" on first or early acquaintance,
> and (5) more "steady dating" with fewer inhibitions as to sex intimacy
> following long acquaintances. The apparent change in the last decade is
> great: "sex is no longer news" to American youth. The change is most
> conspicuous, perhaps, in the degree to which and the manner in which it
> is talked about.

It would seem rather difficult to reconcile this picture with the one offered
by Waller. One, however, is immediately tempted to say that *if* Newcomb's
observations were based largely upon Bennington, where he taught from 1934 to
1941, they can hardly be seen as reflective of the patterns being followed by Joe
and Jane College on the campuses of America, most of which resembled Penn
State much more than they did this avant-garde woman's college. Yet, Newcomb
was not alone in his sense that things were changing. Similar views were offered
by no less conservative an organ of America's economic establishment than
Fortune magazine.

In June of 1936, *Fortune* looked at campus life as it existed in the Ivy League.
The Seven Sisters, The Big Ten, and a handful of other schools (*e.g.*, Stanford).
It offered the assessment that the "flaming youth" of the 1920s (with Jazz Age
tastes for fast cars, bootleg liquor, and loose morality) was giving way to a more
sedate sort of undergraduate, who, while hardly averse to the pleasures of drink
and sex, nonetheless pursued them, if not less avidly, at least more sedately and

on a campus that was now more supportive of serious academic matters than it had been a decade earlier. While courtship patterns were not specifically discussed, *Fortune* offered profiles of typical days in the lives of students at various campuses. From these, one gets a picture which seems to better fit the image offered by Newcomb than it does the one offered by Waller.

Given the reports of Newcomb, the editors of *Fortune,* and some other sources as well (*e.g.,* Cole, 1957), it would be easy to simply dismiss Waller as a poor observer who was not able to separate the most conspicuous patterns from the most common ones or as a sociologist so wedded to his interpretation of behavior which he had previously observed that he failed to perceive how it was changing. Probably neither of these interpretations [is] correct. Instead, it may be that the picture Waller presented of Pennsylvania State rating and dating was a fairly accurate one for a segment of that school's undergraduates at that time. Nevertheless, it is probable that a cooling of the intensity of the rating and dating game was already evident if one were to look for it.[3] Moreover, it is also probable that a system of heterosexual socializing, based more upon going steady than on competitive-pluralistic dating, was already coexisting with rating and dating throughout the nation, and even at Pennsylvania State. To support these assertions, a brief picture of the direction courtship patterns have taken during the last century and a half will be presented.

With courtship, as with many other phenomena, the more we learn about it in the past the more continuity we see with the present. What supposedly makes 20th century courtship customs unique is the degree to which parental involvement in mate choice has declined to what is at best a very weak "veto power" and, more importantly, the extent to which much of what is seen as courtship is actually not oriented toward mate selection, but is instead largely recreational.[4] As a result of the work of social historians in recent years, it has become clear that nearly complete parental control over the choice of mate was never the dominant pattern in the United States (Demos, 1970). Even in early-Modern England, this pattern was primarily restricted to the nobility and squirarchy (Stone, 1977). Regarding the separation of heterosexual socializing from actual mate choice (*i.e.,* the appearance of dating) there is some evidence to suggest that patterns *resembling,* though not identical to, dating had already begun to appear before the 20th century.

The research of several historians suggests that, as early as the beginning of the 19th century, young people in parts of the country as remote from each other as Maine and North Carolina were engaging in dances, sleigh rides, and parties with members of the opposite sex well before they were marriageable age (Kett, 1977; Fritsch, 1970). Joseph Kett (1977:42) has noted:

> If "dating" is defined as social meetings between young people of opposite sex who have no intention to marry, then it is a more accurate term than "courtship" to describe social engagements in the early 19th century. The presence of so many unescorted young people at social gatherings probably reduced pressures to establish formal courtship but at the same time distinguished such meetings from our own style of dating,

which places a premium on physical intimacy in public and exclusive pairing.

John Fritsch (1970:207–208) has argued that not only did young men and women who were *not* courting have the opportunity to interact socially with each other, but that there also existed considerable opportunity for them to be alone together. The importance of the work of Kett, Fritsch, and others is that it seems to make evident the fact that "dating" is not an invention of this century. Nevertheless, we must not assume that there was a perfect structural correspondence between dating as it existed in the 19th century and as it has existed in the 20th century.

If the notion is accepted that young people who were not ready to marry did "date" in the 19th century, then the problem becomes one of establishing what changes, if any, took place in the form of this activity during the 20th century. Relatively little of a scholarly nature has been written on early 20th century American courtship patterns (*e.g.,* McGovern, 1968). Therefore, it is necessary to resort to fiction as an alternative source of data, albeit one that must be used with great care, the assumption here being that the routine presentation of certain patterns is indicative of their acceptance, if not their general presence, in the society. To be sure, one cannot build too large an edifice on such a foundation, but fiction can provide some general outlines of behavior patterns. It is important to attempt to establish two things from these fictional sources. One, is there evidence of exclusive relationships which are not oriented toward marriage ("going steady") and, two, what evidence, if any, is there for the existence of a "rating and dating" complex prior to the 1920s?

Willa Cather's *My Antonia,* (1954, first published in 1918) represents a rather interesting description of socializing patterns of high school youth in a small Nebraska town at the end of the 1880s. In the story, a "dancing pavilion" is built at the edge of town and becomes the focal point of the townspeople's activities (Cather, 1954:196).

> At least there was something to do in the long empty summer evenings, when the married people sat like images on their front porches, and the boys and girls tramped and tramped the broad sidewalks—northward to the edge of the open prairie, south of the depot, and back again to the post office, the ice cream parlor, the butcher shop. Now there was a place where the girls could wear their new dresses.

There is considerable continuity between this picture of the early 20th century and the one of the early 19th century presented by Kett (1977), especially in regard to the socializing of young people. In each of these periods, socializing in rural communities was to some extent both communal in nature and under the direct scrutiny of adult members of the community.

In the 20th century novel, different patterns begin to emerge. One example of changing patterns is presented in Kilbourne's (1919) *Betty Bell,* which describes the romantic life of a 16-year-old high school girl in a small midwestern city in the early 1900s. This book discusses a number of interesting and important points relevant to courtship. For example, the telephone is used by a young man to ask Betty to a high school dance. Later in the novel she is asked by her "beau" to go to "the Orpheum Tuesday night" and to stop at the ice cream parlor for some refreshment afterwards. For a while she seems to be "going steady" with this boy, although it is not referred to as such. However, later on in the book she does go out with other young men. Perhaps the single most important factor contained in the book is what might be described as an incipient rating-dating complex. Not only do her discussions with her friends smack strongly of this, but when she is asked by a member of the football team if he may walk her home from school, she hopes that they will be observed by her friends. Also notable is a section toward the end of the novel when Betty seriously considered becoming engaged to an older man (Kilbourne, 1919:244):

> It was the first time in Betty's life that she had thought seriously of being engaged. High school "affairs" did not look toward matrimony as a climax; being a belle with ever-changing "crushes" or the "girl" of a certain boy—when Central [high school] dreamed of romance it was in such symbols.

This excerpt is important for several reasons. First, it indicates that, during the World War I period, there existed a dating system for middle-class young people which was pretty much independent of courtship. (It is not without significance that the man Betty considered becoming engaged to was older.) Second, it may *suggest* that "going steady" and "rating and dating" coexisted or, more likely, were part and parcel of the same system. However, going steady did not seem to have the exclusive quality (*i.e.,* seeing only one person at a time) that it would later acquire.

In the 1920s, several novels appear which describe high school courtship practices. While these descriptions reveal a continuity with the past, they also contain notable departures. For example, Louise Dutton's (1923) *Going Together* describes a situation which is rather traditional. The novel (which appears to be set in the early 1920s, although it could be earlier) deals with the social life of the heroine, Sally Belle, from age 12 through 16. At one point she speaks of what "going together" means (Dutton, 1923:20–21):

> There was a thing you called going together. That was what Sally Belle wanted. You went with a boy. He was your fellow then, and you were his girl. When you were old enough you got engaged and married. Engaged girls marked towels and napkins and had to be kissed. They never had any fun. Being engaged was stupid, but going together was beautiful. You had fun then; all the fun there was. You were not an odd girl. You were not left out. You could go to straw rides and barge rides, where there had to be even numbers. You could belong to a crowd. You had somebody to walk home with you, pay for your ticket at shows, send you valentines, candy at Christmas. You were—well—going together.

This is a very rich passage. It indicates, on the one hand, that there is a relationship between "going together" and mate choice and to this extent it is reminiscent of much older patterns. On the other hand, the heroine is involved in a going-together relationship when she is 12 and her downgrading of the engaged state indicates the value young people placed on such relationships, independent of their relationship to mate choice. The types of activities and obligations she sees as befitting a pair of people involved in such a going-together relationship are also interesting. Apart from those activities mentioned above, the novel also describes teenagers going on horse and buggy rides, picnics at the local lake, and other similar and equally tame activities. What is important about this novel (and it should be pointed out that it appears to be written for young people and has a rather didactic tone) is that it portrays a teenage culture, which, while very much oriented toward cross-sex socializing, nevertheless contains little that can be related to Waller's rating and dating game. This is not true of other novels published at the same time.

Waller's rating and dating complex, as well as various other more general aspects of "roaring twenties" culture, are depicted in numerous novels set in urban high schools during the 1920s. Robert S. Carr's [*The*] *Rampant Age* (1928) and Harold Brecht's *Downfall* (1929) are two good examples. Carr's novel is especially noteworthy because it compares the situation in two midwestern high schools. When the novel opens, the 16-year-old protagonist, Paul, is living with his family in a small city. He is actively involved in the school's social life and even has a girl friend (Carr, 1928:22):

> Mary Bartham was a plump, rosy-cheeked brunette, Paul's 'girl' inasmuch as he had escorted her (on foot) to the annual Halloween Party at the high school, where he sat an uneasy six inches away from her and juggled pumpkin pie and cider in nervous agony and had a swell time.

He moves on to the family car, the automobile being presented as an important part of high school socializing: "Stepping out in the Ford to the Junior party . . . hot rocks!" (Carr, 1928:62). Dating requires a phone call to the girl early in the week, patterns of double dating are also described, and the ice cream parlor looms large in the high school social scene. Paul is presented as being overwhelmed when a girl throws herself at him in a necking session and the author describes him as being relieved that it does not result in his loss of innocence. Yet, it is clear that Carr is preparing us for what is to come when Paul's family moves to a large city.

The situation encountered in East High School is rather more sophisticated than what Paul had previously known. The standard by which students judge each other is a "collegiate" one and there are even high school fraternities. Dance halls are part of the scene and the young "sheiks" see them as good hunting grounds for young women who may be free with their sexual favors. What is perhaps most notable is the extent to which the reigning standards are hostile to academic matters, something which commentators on college culture of the 1920s also have noted (Fass, 1977). At one point in the book, Paul reflects (Carr, 1928:183):

> He realized that no Collegiate Sheik dare be a star student in anything. A boy may be the pride of the school and president of the Senior Class, but

never really a Collegiate Sheik at the same time. If he shows any indication of scholarship his more lurid social habits begin to wane till, although he may be a popular youth, he has lost the sterling quality called Being Collegiate.

Along with elements of the rating and dating complex, Carr's (1928) novel also depicts a going steady complex. Going steady, however, is not as apparent in Brecht's (1929) novel. In this novel, high school students are credited with a much more complete emulation of collegiate culture. In addition to the depiction of fraternities as central to high school life, and the use of the term "petting" to describe certain sexual behaviors, the novel also presents an elaborate rating and dating complex.

The novels discussed above indicate the importance of "collegiate" styles and values in determining the social life of high school youth. Since it is probable that campuses were in the vanguard on these patterns, it might be useful to consider if there were any changes in the structure and character of campus life during the 1920s that could have contributed to the growing intensity of undergraduate social life and to the genesis of rating and dating. Paula Fass's (1977) recent study, *The Damned and the Beautiful,* is very relevant in this regard. Prior to the 1920s, she claims campus social life was largely dominated by the importance of class (freshman, sophomore, etc.); however, in the 1920s, this gave way to fraternity and sorority domination. Greek letter societies had been growing in numbers since the beginning of the century, but the 1920s witnessed an explosion in their membership (Fass, 1977:143):

> In 1912 there were 1560 national fraternity and sorority chapters. The surging increase in enrollments during the twenties caused the number of chapters to more than double to 3900 in 1930.

When the classes ran campus social life, a basically equalitarian ethic was at work, since classes, by their very nature, are nonexclusive. Classes, however, were replaced by organizations which prided themselves on their selectivity and elitism. Nevertheless, if Fass's (1977:153) interpretation is accepted, the selection criteria employed by the Greeks "usually had more to do with superficial attractiveness and personality than rigid socioeconomic class." This is not to say that the latter was irrelevant (Fass, 1977:153);

> The criteria of acceptability for most fraternities were attributes of manner, dress and style. These were certainly related to family background, economic position, and prep-school training, but they could also be cultivated.

This emphasis on style, personality, and looks obviously articulates well with the ethic of rating and dating as described by Waller. Not only did fraternities and sororities set the standards for social acceptability, they also created much of the campus social life. For example, "The University of Wisconsin was reported to have hosted 30 college dances and 80 fraternity and sorority dances each month in 1925" (Fass, 1977:199).

Through their control of campus social life, the fraternities and sororities were able to establish certain standards which were highly supportive of rating and dating. While Fass has argued that the standards used to select members were based more on style than economics, it cannot be denied that such organizations existed in a prestige hierarchy on American campuses, a hierarchy whose shape was well-known and generally agreed upon in each campus setting. If, in fact, Fass is correct in her claim that the differences in family background between members of these organizations were not that great, then it can be assumed that the maintenance of individual positions in the hierarchy required continuous reaffirmation. Rating and dating evolved, in part, as a device to support such status claims.[5]

If this link between the Greek letter societies and the rating and dating complex is correct, it may partially explain why rating and dating and less exploitive and pluralistic dating appear to have existed simultaneously. It may be that rating and dating only became significant on those campuses where fraternities and sororities were an important force in social life. Moreover, even on those campuses, non–Greeks were involved in socializing patterns that could not be characterized as rating and dating. Thus, it is likely that a majority of America's young people in or out of college were never involved in rating or dating to a significant degree, but that as part of the general national romance with things collegiate during the 1920s this pattern received more attention than its actual pervasiveness deserved. Nevertheless, rating and dating was a pattern that did rise to prominence in the 1920s and which continued to influence courtship patterns for 30 or 40 years. There are several factors which led to the eventual decline of this form of dating.

The coming of the Depression altered the character of undergraduate culture. To begin with, it had a negative effect on student enrollment. Willey (1937:234) notes that prior to 1930, college enrollments only dipped once (in 1918, presumably a result of students serving in the armed forces during World War I); however, between 1932 and 1934 they declined again. This decline was seen as being clearly related to the economic problems created by the Depression (Willey, 1937:234). Shrinking undergraduate enrollments took their toll on the Greek letter societies:

> Despite the fact that what then was regarded as a normal world was shattered by World War I, probably never to be restored, the college fraternity was little changed by the event. The depression which followed in 1929 was, however, a different story. The financial situation, for instance, became so serious that college enrollments suffered, and the majority who did attend college felt they could not afford to belong to a fraternity. Some chapter houses were closed because of resulting financial difficulties. Chapters were necessarily withdrawn in a number of cases. Membership in all slumped. Expansion on the part of many fraternities and sororities came to a standstill, for in the great majority of cases, locals, some of them long standing, ceased to exist (Lasher, 1957:31).

Given a situation such as this, it would seem evident that it would have become increasingly difficult for the fraternities and sororities to maintain the dominant role they had previously played on certain campuses, and in fact this appears to have been the case. Then, just when colleges were beginning to recover from the worst effects of the Depression, World War II came along and curtailed male enrollment. This created a crisis for many undergraduate institutions. Those institutions that depended heavily upon student fees for funding or that were unable to become involved in military education programs were especially hard hit. Some fraternities responded to the situation by closing their houses for the duration of the war and those that remained open had to cope with serious enrollment and financial problems. All of this had an effect on campus social life. For example, the following report concerning Cornell appeared in *Fortune* as early as 1942 (Editors of *Fortune,* 1942:136):

> Outward changes in college life have been few. On the lovely hill above Cayuga's waters in Ithaca, New York, automobiles no longer crowd the curbs in front of Willard Straight Hall and the fraternity and sorority houses. House parties too are out for the duration—including the traditional festivities of Junior Week and Spring Day. Classes may be cut for illness only. Every man must turn up for three hours of physical training per week, one hour of it over the difficult new commando course. Football crowds have slumped badly.

The Depression had brought a certain seriousness to American undergraduate life, though it hardly robbed it of its lighter moments. However, Pearl Harbor furthered this trend and gave relationships a weightier character, as young men reconciled themselves to the possibility of not returning from overseas or returning disabled. This would hardly seem to have been an atmosphere in which the frivolous rating and dating game would have continued to flourish.

The specific ways in which changes brought by the Depression influenced campus social life have been to some extent indicated by the previous discussion of Newcomb's (1937) article and the *Fortune* magazine study published in 1936. A more focused look at the degree to which rating and dating dominated the campus scene in the 1920s and then subsequently declined is offered by Charles Cole, who was president of Amherst College from 1946 to 1960. An undergraduate himself in the 1920s, he notes (Cole, 1957:20):

> It was an autumn Saturday in 1935 when I was eight years out of college that I first realized I belonged to an older generation. But I did not understand that I was witnessing the first stages of a revolution which has dramatically altered the folkways of American youth and created a new and strange chasm between my generation and the next.

He goes on to describe a fraternity dance that he and his wife were chaperoning and which they both found perplexing because of the diminutive stag line and the fact that one of his students danced with the same girl for the whole evening. His concern for the young man reached such a level, he tells us, that he finally asked one of the young man's fraternity brothers to cut in and save him, only to be told (Cole, 1957:29):

> "Oh no! That's Fred's girl." It was another five years (1940) before "going steady" was fully established as the standard and persuasive pattern for the social life of the young.

He follows this with as elaborate a description of the going-steady complex as can be found in the literature, even speculating on the norms that dictate how many prior dates define a couple as having such a relationship (Cole, 1957:30).

There is one final and, in view of earlier comments in this paper, interesting note in Cole's article. He maintains that going steady represents a return to patterns of an earlier era (Cole, 1957:32–33):

> The oddest thing about the revolution in the social life of the last twenty years is that it constitutes the triumph of rural nineteenth-century America mores in the urban and suburban society of the mid-twentieth century. Anybody over seventy who was brought up in a country village or town finds the social customs of young people today strangely familiar. In the 1880s or 1890s it was normal to have boys and girls pair off in a more or less stable fashion, and such pairings often ended eventually in marriage. The very phrase "going steady" has the ring of rural America under President Cleveland.

This statement would seem to support the view that rating and dating represented a brief, albeit important, episode in American courtship whose persistence was exaggerated by the too-ready acceptance of Waller's 1937 paper. However, what Cole witnessed was not a revolution. Rather the "pairing off" he saw as a return to older rural values never disappeared, it just became less conspicuous during the heyday of rating and dating, and *very much* less linked to marriage.

What has been seen in the 50 years between 1930 and 1980 is the virtual disappearance of the rating and dating complex as a significant aspect of adolescent socializing. This is not to say that on both high school and college campuses there are no prestige dimensions to cross-sex socializing, but rather that the elaborate system of pluralistic dating that Waller described (oriented it would seem almost solely to the gleaning of prestige) has given way to a system that is both less pluralistic and more humanistic.[6] Writing more than 20 years ago, David Riesman (1959:213) observed:

> There can be no doubt that what many young men and women today are looking for in each other is not the rating-dating game of twenty years ago. To be sure there are still fraternities and sororities on the campus and still an interest in good looks, popularity, good grooming and smoothness. But all this is more subdued and the relationships increasingly sought for are more searching, more profound, more sincere.

This trend has continued. Now, even noncompetitive, pluralistic dating is giving way to more group-based activity. Young men and women are socializing together in groups as the path that ultimately leads to exclusive, though not necessarily mate choice-oriented, relationships.[7]

Notes

1. Most family sociologists are familiar with the literature published since the 1940s which questions whether the values that informed the rating and dating scheme continued to be

relevant on American campuses. (*e.g.,* Blood, 1955). For the most part, in the later studies the values students reported finding desirable in a date were not those that Waller saw being at the heart of the rating and dating complex. Even at Waller's own campus, Pennsylvania State, in the 1950s (Smith, 1952) rating factors loomed nowhere near as large as personality factors (e.g., sense of humor, being considerate). While authors of these studies have viewed these results as evidence of changes in campus values, they generally have not questioned the accuracy of Waller's depiction of the values prevalent in the 1930s. It is this paper's contention that, had similar studies been carried out in the 1920s, findings corresponding more closely to Waller's thesis would have been discovered on those campuses whose social life was dominated by fraternities and sororities and perhaps only among members of these organizations. However, by the late 1930s, when Waller (1937) published his paper, even among this group, these would not have been the dominant dating criteria.

2. Additional problems are created by the ambiguity concerning the period to which his article refers. Blood (1955) has remarked: "The heart of Waller's article consists of a description of the 'rating complex' at Penn State College. . . . According to Howard Becker [comments at an NCFR Research Section in 1953] the observations by Waller were made during academic year 1929–1930, when the 'Roaring Twenties' had not yet succumbed to the Depression" (1955:42). While this sounds plausible, it is factually incorrect. Waller did not begin teaching at Pennsylvania State until the fall of 1931 (Goode *et al.,* 1970:38–42). Moreover, Waller himself, writing again in 1938 about the rating and dating complex, makes it clear that the period he is talking about is the current one and that his own research on dating was done in the 1930s (Waller, 1983:230–235).

3. It could be argued that Pennsylvania State was a rather special institution in several respects. First, it was relatively isolated, creating a situation in which social life, by necessity, became focused on the campus. Second, competitive dating may have been fostered by an unusually high sex ratio of 6 males to every one female (Waller, 1937:729); at Cornell, for example, the ratio was 3 to 1 and at Michigan it was 2 to 1 (Edwards *et al.,* 1928: Appendix). Third, its student body was probably drawn from the lower reaches of the middle class to a greater degree than was true for many other state universities where there were no older private institutions to draw off the elite of the state. Consequently, status striving may have played an unusually important role in campus social life (Waller, 1937:729). Taken together, these three factors alone may have accounted for the persistence and salience of rating and dating at Pennsylvania State during the 1930s, although the role of fraternities and sororities also should be considered.

4. This distinction between courtship behavior (*i.e.,* behavior oriented toward the selection of a mate) and dating (recreational cross-sex socializing) is a very important one and one which is relevant to an understanding of the rating and dating complex since Waller contended that the complex was not courtship behavior. In certain respects it could be argued that, while most dating is largely unrelated to choosing a mate, rating and dating represents a variant whose structure is the most antithetical to it. In other words, one could see how a "going steady" relationship, given its premises, might eventuate in engagement. However, both the pluralism and competiveness of rating and dating militates against its becoming a courtship device.

5. Waller suggests that this was the case at Pennsylvania State (1937:729).

6. While fraternities and sororities are still part of college life and may even be experiencing a renaissance on some campuses, their members do not seem to be involved in rating and dating (Krain *et al.,* 1977). At the same time the values of these organizations do continue to perpetuate prestige homogamy and ultimately, presumably, endogamy of similarly ranked fraternity and sorority members (see Krain *et al.,* 1977).

7. It would appear that what determines the likelihood of an exclusive relationship leading to engagement probably has more to do with age and general feasibility of marriage than anything else. Nevertheless, what is notable is that young people today enter these relationships well before marriage is a likely outcome.

References

Blood, R. 1955. "A retest of Waller's rating complex," Marriage and Family Living 17 (February):41–47.

Brecht, H. 1929. Downfall. New York: Harper and Row, Publishers.

Carr, R. S. 1928. The Rampant Age. Garden City, New York: Doubleday and Company.

Cather, W. 1954. My Antonia. Boston: Houghton Mifflin Company. (Originally published, 1918.)

Cole, C. W. 1957. "American youth goes monogamous." Harper's Magazine 214 (March):29–32.

Demos, J. 1970. A Little Commonwealth: Family Life in Plymouth Colony. New York: Oxford University Press.

Dutton, L. 1923. Going Together. Indianapolis, Indiana: Bobbs-Merrill Company.

Editors of Fortune. 1936. "Youth in college." Fortune 13 (June):99–102, 155–162.

———. 1942. "Education for war." Fortune 26 (December):133–141, 175–181.

Edwards, R. H., J. M. Hartman, and G. M. Fisher. 1928. Undergraduates: A Study of Morale in Twenty-Three American Colleges and Universities. Garden City, New York: Doubleday and Company.

Fass, P. S. 1977. The Damned and the Beautiful. New York: Oxford University Press.

Fritsch, J. R. 1970. "Youth culture in America, 1790–1865." Unpublished doctoral dissertation. University of Wisconsin.

Goode, W. J., F. F. Furstenberg, and L. R. Mitchell (Eds.). 1970. Willard Waller on the Family, Education and War. Chicago: University of Chicago Press.

Kett, J. F. 1977. Rites of Passage: Adolescence in America 1790 to the Present. New York: Basic Books.

Kilbourne, F. 1919. Betty Bell, New York: Harper and Brothers, Publishers.

Krain, M., D. Cannon, and J. Bagford. 1977. "Rating-dating or simple prestige homogamy? Data on dating in the Greek system on a midwestern campus." Journal of Marriage and the Family 39 (November):663–676.

Lasher, G. S.. 1957. "1937–1957: Fraternity developments." Pp. 31–38 in G. S. Lasher (Ed.), Baird's Manual of American College Fraternities. Menasha, Wisconsin: George Banta.

McGovern, J. R.. 1968. "The American woman's pre-World War I freedom in manners and morals." Journal of American History 55 (September):315–333.

Newcomb, T. 1937. "Recent changes in attitude toward sex and marriage." American Sociological Review 2 (October):659–667.

Riesman, D. 1959. "Permissiveness and sex roles." Journal of Marriage and the Family 21 (August):211–217.

Smith, W. M. 1952. "Rating and dating: A restudy." Marriage and Family Living 14 (November):312–316.

Stone, L. 1977. The Family, Sex and Marriage in England 1500–1800. New York: Harper and Row, Publishers.

Waller, W. 1937. "The rating and dating complex." American Sociological Review 2 (October):727–734.

_____. 1938. The Family. New York: Cordon Company.

Willey, M. M. 1937. Depression: Recovery and Higher Education. New York: McGraw-Hill.

Sex Differences in Bases of Power in Dating Relationships

Susan Sprecher

While a great deal of research has explored power in intimate relations, almost all of the research has been of marital or family power. Virtually unexplored is the operation of power in dating relationships. However, because dating is a critical stage from which later marriages and families are formed, a theoretical understanding of power in intimate relationships must incorporate power as it is manifested in the dating stage of a relationship. The purpose in the present study is to examine bases of power for dating relationships, and to see how these differ for men and women.

As pointed out in a recent review of family power (McDonald, 1980), power is *both* a behavioral and a peceptual phenomenon. The importance of perceptions of power in a social relationship cannot be overestimated. Viewing the balance of power in the relationship from the perspective of the participants suggests that there may really be two power relations in a heterosexual dyad—a "hers" and a "his." Bernard (1972), for example, has suggested that wives and husbands objectively and subjectively experience two different marriages—e.g., that no such entity as a "real" marriage common to both spouses exists. This distinction between each partner's perception of the relationship would apply to all relationships, including dating relationships.

Because each partner experiences a slightly different relationship, there will not always be agreement between the man and woman on how power is distributed in the relationship. Although "real" power may be thought of as a property of the relationship (McDonald, 1980), the process through which power arises depends on individual definitions of the power relation. As several theorists have argued, it is the individual's perception of the power distribution that

I would like to give a special thanks to Elizabeth Thomson for her assistance throughout the writing of this manuscript. Gratitude also goes to Elaine Hatfield and John DeLamater for their advice at earlier stages of the research.

From Susan Sprecher, *Sex Roles* Vol. 12 (Fall 1985):449–462. Reprinted by permission of Plenum Publishing Corporation and the author.

Rothschild, 1970). Reflecting this importance of power as a perc~~~ enon, the focus in this study will be on power *as perceived* by each phenom- dating relationship.

Several theorists have argued that the dyadic property of power one partner's dependence on the other (Blau, 1964; Emerson, 1962; T~~ Kelley, 1959). Dependence can arise from exchange both within the dy~ within the larger network in which the dyad is located. As defined by Cook Emerson (1978), dependence is a joint function of the relative value of resources provided by each partner and the availability of similar resources outside the relationship. The more powerful (less dependent) person is one for whom (a) the value of resources potentially provided to her/his partner is greater than the value of resources potentially obtained from her/his partner, and/or (b) there are alternative exchange relations through which she/he may obtain at least the same value of resources the partner has to offer.

Studies of marital power have dealt with both parts of this dependence function. Several studies report that the greater the socioeconomic resources of one partner relative to the other, the more powerful is that partner (for a review, see McDonald, 1980). The effects on power of alternative exchange relations has usually been assessed by examining the relationship between an individual's control of socioeconomic resources and her/his power (Blood & Wolfe, 1960; Michel, 1967). It is assumed that the greater absolute resources controlled by an individual, the more likely she/he can find alternative relationships that would be as rewarding or more so than the present relationship.

There are several limitations of previous research on power. The first major limitation of studies examining bases of power is that a relatively narrow range of resources has been used. In studies examining the relationship between resources and power, resources have primarily been operationalized in terms of socioeconomic indicators. Safilios-Rothschild (1970, 1976) has suggested that the focus on socioeconomic resources represents a male bias in research on power. Stereotypically feminine resources such as love have not been included in these studies, despite their importance in intimate relationships. Safilios-Rothschild identifies five such categories of feminine resources that are exchanged in intimate heterosexual relationships: affection, expression, companionship, sex, and services. In studies of power it is important to examine this wider range of resources.

A second major limitation of past research is that resources *controlled* in an intimate relationship (for example, the level of education or income of each partner) have been examined rather than resources actually *contributed* to the relationship. However, it is less clear whether contributions of resources, and especially of particular types of resources, will be positively related to having power in the relationship. In fact, a social psychological theory of bargaining (Michener & Suchner, 1972) states that power involves the capacity to influence the behavior of the other in order to acquire needed and desirable resources: "Social power involves both the *capacity to influence* the behavior of the other, which enables a person to obtain valued outcomes, and the *capacity to resist* the influence of the other, which permits him to deny others the outcomes they want from him" (p. 239). According to this theory, then, contributions of resources should be negatively related to power.

d limitation of past research is that no studies have directly assessed
lity of attractive alternatives to the present relationship. Having access
the ble alternative relationships entails both being desirable (e.g., having
to e resources to potentially offer someone) *and* having alternative others in
va vironment.
th As pointed out in the introduction, most of the research on power in
mate relationships concerns marital power. Few studies have examined
xchange and power in dating relationships. In one early classic study ("The
Rating and Dating Complex"), Waller (1937) illustrated that the courtship process
could be best described as bargaining behavior. He found that young men and
women try to advance themselves by dating the most desirable partner. Desirable
personal resources controlled by unmarried women included such things as
sorority membership, physical attractiveness, and being a good dancer. Personal
resources found desirable in men included possession of a car, money for social
activities, and fraternity membership. Waller found that if relationships of
unequal status occur, the partner with higher status (more desirable resources)
may "exploit" the other. In general terms, exploitation may be thought of as the
exercise of power. He also found that the person who is least involved in the
relationship can usually exercise more power. Waller (1937) wrote, "That person
is most able to dictate the condition of the association whose interest in the
continuation of the affair is least."

In a more recent study of dating couples, perceived power was directly
assessed and related to other aspects of the relationship. Based upon an interview
study of 231 dating couples, Peplau (1978) found that the partner who was least
involved in the dating relationship tended to be more powerful. Peplau also found
that a very important factor related to the balance of power in the dating
relationship was the educational and career goals of women. The higher the
educational goals of a woman, the more powerful she was perceived to be. In this
study, bases of power in dating relationships are further explored.

What about gender differences in power? In general, it has been reported that
husbands are more powerful than wives (Bernard, 1972; Blood & Wolfe, 1960;
Gillespie, 1971). This sex difference in power has also been reported for dating couples (Peplau, 1978). Resource and social exchange theorists have tended to view
the gender power differential (male having more power than the female) as the "natural" and equitable result of the differential resources possessed by men and women
and/or the differential alternative exchange relations available to men and women.
As indicated above, most of the empirical research on marital power has used socioeconomic indicators to represent personal resources. Since men are more likely
to be employed and generally have greater earnings than women, their greater
power has been attributed to the operation of an equitable exchange process.

Although women have fewer opportunities than men to acquire income and
status in the existing gender-stratification system, there are other ways in which
women may acquire power. Evidence suggests that women who do not have
access to socioeconomic resources may gain power by controlling love and sex in
the relationship. As long as her partner is very much in love with her, the woman
may gain power by controlling the reciprocation of the partner's love. In a
cross-cultural study, Safilios-Rothschild (1976) found that women who thought

their husbands were the partner more in love perceived that they themselves had power to make important decisions more often than those women who perceived themselves to be the partner more in love. While this general trend was also found for men, the difference was not significant. In addition, it has also been found that women who have little direct access to money and prestige may use sex as a resource to gain power in the relationship (Safilios-Rothschild, 1976, 1977). It is possible, then, that socioeconomic resources may be an important basis of power for males, while controlling the reciprocation of love may be an important basis of power for females. Such sex differences will be explored in this study.

♂ have socioecon. resources
♀ have love + sex

Method

Sample

Fifty dating couples participated in an interview study on relationships. Volunteers were sought from a sorority and fraternity at the University of Wisconsin. It was required that their partner, who also was often a Greek member, participate in the study. Because the respondents were volunteers, they may not be representative of all young dating couples (see Hill, Rubin, Peplau, & Willard, 1979, for a discussion of how volunteer couples differ from other couples). The analyses reported here, therefore, must be considered somewhat exploratory, providing preliminary evidence upon which future studies of more representative samples may be based.

The majority of the respondents were undergraduate students ranging in age from 18 to 22. In general, the couples had been going together for at least six months and were dating exclusively at the time of the study. None of the couples were cohabiting.

Procedure

The questionnaire was self-administered, and was completed by each individual separately from her/his partner. All respondents were guaranteed that the information would be kept strictly confidential. The questionnaire, which took approximately 45 to 60 minutes to complete, examined several aspects of the relationship.

Measures

Power   Responses to three items were summed to form an index of perceived power in the relationship. The three items were:

1. In your relationship, who has the most power? Responses ranged on a seven-point scale from "My partner has much more power than I do" to "I have much more power than my partner."
2. In your relationship, who do you think has more of a say about what the two of you do together? Responses ranged on a five-point

scale from "My partner has much more of a say" to "I have much
more of a say."

3. In your relationship, who makes the most sacrifices? Responses ranged
on a five-point scale from "I make many more sacrifices than my
partner does" to "My partner makes many more sacrifices than I do."

Responses to the three items were scaled such that the higher the number,
the greater the perceived power. Alpha coefficients of scale reliability for males
and females were .58 and .68, respectively, which were considered satisfactory for
a scale of three items.

Contribution of Resources   To measure resources contributed in the relationship,
respondents were given a list of eight resources and asked to describe their own
contributions to the relationship and their partner's contributions. The list of resources was a modified version of those identified by Safilios-Rothschild (1976)
as being resources potentially exchanged in the intimate relationship. They include:
(1) socioeconomic, (2) affective, (3) expressive, (4) physical appearance, (5) intellectual, (6) companionship, (7) sex, and (8) service resources. The response scale
provided to describe the contributions ranged from $(+4)$ = extremely positive to
(-4) = extremely negative. Using the evaluative descriptors allows the respondents to answer with respect to both the amount they contribute and how they
value the contributions. See the Appendix for more detail on these measures.

Relative Involvement   Because of the importance of the exchange of love in the
relationship, a more specific question was asked about who loved more in the
relationship. Responses ranged on a seven-point scale from "Partner loves much
more" to "I love much more."

Access to Alternatives   Access to alternatives was measured directly by asking the
respondents how easy or difficult it would be to find a new dating partner—given
what they had to offer and how many "eligibles" were available:

1. If you found yourself unattached again, for whatever reason, and
wanted to find a new partner, how easy/difficult would that be
given the number of "eligibles" you are aware of?
2. How easy/difficult would it be to find a new partner, given what
you feel you have to offer?

Responses ranged from (1) = very difficult to (4) = very easy. Responses
to the two items were summed to form the index of "access to alternatives."

Results

Who Is More Powerful—Men or Women?

In spite of the fact that today most men and women subscribe to an egalitarian
philosophy, the evidence reviewed suggests that males perceive themselves as

Table 1   Bases of Power and Perceived Power
in the Relationship[a]

| | Perceived power | |
Basis	*Males*	*Females*
Absolute contributions	.27[b]	−.21
Relative contributions	−.18	−.49[c]
Access to alternatives	.23[b]	−.15
Relative involvement	−.04	−.45[d]

[a]Pearson correlation coefficients represent these relationships.
[b]$p < .05$.   [c]$p < .01$.   [d]$< .001$.

having more power than do females. However, a gender difference was not found in this sample of dating couples. There was *no* significant difference between men and women daters in how powerful they perceived themselves to be in the relationship. The overall power index score for males was 10.84 ($SD = 2.24$); for females it was 10.76 ($SD = 2.36$). The scores were slightly in the direction of perceiving oneself as being powerful in the relationship.

Bases of Power

1. *Relative Contributions of Resources* Based upon resource theory it was expected that the more resources an individual contributed to the relationship relative to what her/his partner contributed, the more power the individual would perceive her/himself as having. Relative contributions were calculated by subtracting perception of partner's contributions from own contributions. The more positive (or less negative) this difference, the more powerful the individual was expected to perceive her/himself to be.

As indicated in Table 1, there was *no* positive correlation between relative contributions and perceived power for either males or females. In fact, there was a significant *negative* correlation between contributions of resources and perceived power for females. The more females perceived themselves as contributing relative to their partner, the *less* powerful they felt.

We also explored the association between relative contributions of *specific* types of resources and power perceptions. The results of these analyses are displayed in Table 2.

For males, only contributions of affective resources seemed to be significantly correlated with feeling powerful—and it was a negative correlation. The more affective resources males perceived they contributed relative to their partner, the less powerful they perceived themselves to be. For females, there were four significant negative correlations between relative contributions of specific resources and perceiving the self as powerful: affection, expressiveness, physical attractiveness, and services. Another way of phrasing this is that the less females contributed of these resources, the more powerful they perceived themselves to be. Thus, resource theory was not supported either overall, or for any specific resource, for either males or females.

Table 2   Absolute and Relative Contributions of Specific
Resources and Perceived Power in the Relationship[a]

Resource	Absolute contributions		Relative contributions	
	Males	*Females*	*Males*	*Females*
Socioeconomic	.11	.01	−19	−.02
Affective	.24[b]	−.17	−.24[b]	−.41[c]
Expressive	.10	−.09	−.16	−.27[b]
Physical appearance	.29[b]	−.23[b]	.04	−.24[b]
Intelligence	.28[b]	−.05	.16	−.08
Companionship	.24[b]	.03	−.12	.00
Sex	.37[c]	−.16	−.14	−.20
Services	.04	.25[b]	−.18	−.49[c]

[a]Pearson correlation coefficients represent these relationships.
[b]$p < .05$.   [c]$p < .001$.

In general, the more affective resources (i.e., love, affection) that males or females contributed *relative* to what their partners contributed, the less powerful they perceived themselves to be. This tendency, as we had expected, was stronger for females than for males. This relationship was also found when we examined the item asking *who loves more in the relationship*. The more women perceived they loved relative to their partner, the less power they perceived themselves as having ($r = -.45; p < .001$). For males, on the other hand, there was no significant correlation between relative involvement and perceived power (see Table 1).

2. *Absolute Contributions of Resources and Access to Alternatives* Based upon social exchange theory, it was expected that the greater the absolute contributions to the relationship, the more powerful the individual would perceive her/himself to be. This was based on the assumption that the more the individual has to contribute to the relationship, the more she/he is probably also desirable to available alternative dates.

For absolute contributions, the correlation with power was found to be positive and significant for males ($r = .27; p < .05$). For females on the other hand, the correlation was negative (but not significant). (See Table 1.) In general, then, the more males perceived they contributed to the relationship, the more power they perceived they had. Conversely, the more females contributed, the less power they perceived they had.

It was also explored more specifically how absolute contributions of particular types of resources were associated with being powerful. The results from these analyses are displayed in Table 2. For males, the greater absolute contributions of five categories of resources were positively correlated with power: affection, physical attractiveness, intelligence, companionship, and sex. For females, on the other hand, there were *no* categories of resources for which absolute contributions were positively associated with feeling powerful. Instead, there were two types of resources that were negatively correlated with having power: physical attractiveness and services. It is interesting to note that the relation between absolute contributions of physical attractiveness and being powerful was the opposite for males and females—significantly positive for males and significantly negative for females.

By examining absolute contributions of resources it was assumed that the more resources an individual has to contribute, the more potential others she/he would be able to attract—and this potential serves as a basis of power. In addition, "access to alternatives" was directly assessed by summing the items asking how easy it would be to find a new partner given: (1) the number of "eligibles" available, and (2) what the individual has to offer. As indicated in Table 1, the relationship was significantly positive for males ($r = .23$; $p < .05$). The easier it was perceived to develop alternative relationships, the more power the male perceived he had. However, the correlation was negative (but not significant) for females. Having access to alternatives did not seem to affect the perceived power of females.

Summary and Discussion

No evidence was found that contributing more resources than one's partner was positively related to feeling powerful in the relationship. In fact, there seemed to be a general tendency for both men and women to perceive themselves as having less power the greater their relative contributions. Surprisingly, this was true even for socioeconomic resources, the type of resource examined in past studies.

This negative relationship between contributing more resources than one's dating partner and feeling powerful in the relationship suggests the importance of distinguishing between resources *contributed* and resources *controlled*. In general, past studies testing resource theory have used resources that were controlled by the individual (i.e., an income, an education). In such studies, resource theory was supported. In this study, however, resources contributed were measured, and no support was found for resource theory. The relationship between resources and power may depend, then, on whether resources controlled or resources contributed are examined. As suggested by the bargaining theory by Michener and Suchner (1972), being powerful may involve convincing the partner to contribute desirable resources, but being able to resist contributing in return the desirable resources one controls.

While no support was found for resource theory, it was found that the higher the absolute level of resources men perceived themselves as contributing to the relationship, the more powerful they perceived themselves to be. Presumably, this power is based on their ability to use resources to attract alternative dating partners who can provide desirable rewards. For females, the relationship between absolute contributions of resources and perceived power was actually negative, but not significant. In addition, the easier men thought it would be to find a new dating partner, the greater their perceived power. The relationship was negative (nonsignificant) for females. These combined results suggest that males and females differ in the degree to which factors outside the relationship are a basis of power within the relationship. Males may be more likely than females to derive power within the relationship from their standing in a wider social network. Males have the upper hand in the initiation of dating relationships—and thus are in a better position to use the ability to attract alternative dating partners as a basis of bargaining power in the relationship. If females are dissatisfied with their present relationship they often have to passively wait for someone to show an interest in them; dissatisfied men, on the other hand, can more actively seek alternative others.

Absolute and relative contributions of specific types of resources seemed to be related differently for males and females to perceived power. In general, there was a tendency for stereotypically female characteristics (i.e., physical attractiveness, sexual favors, personal services) to be negatively correlated with perceived power for women, perhaps because those women who contribute high levels of such resources have developed less assertive (powerful) feelings about themselves. These resources, however, tended to be positively correlated with perceived power for men.

Physical appearance was, for example, a type of resource for which there was a gender difference in how contributions were associated with perceived power. The higher the level of physical appearance the men perceived they contributed to the relationship (e.g., the more physically attractive they perceived themselves to be), the more likely they were to feel powerful. This is what can be expected considering that physical attractiveness is a characteristic of the self that often determines one's market-value in attracting alternative dating partners (Walster, Aronson, Abrahams, & Rottman, 1966). However, the more women perceived they contributed in physical appearance, the *less* powerful they perceived themselves as being. There was also a negative correlation for women between relative contributions of physical attractiveness and being powerful. Perhaps physically attractive and physically unattractive women are treated in different ways that lead unattractive women to be more assertive than attractive women. In a recent study of undergraduate men and women (Reis, Wheeler, Spiegel, Kernis, Nezlek, & Perri, 1982), it was found that although attractive men scored higher than unattractive men on a scale to measure assertiveness, unattractive women scored higher than attractive women.

Males and females also differed in how sexual and affective contributions were related to power. In general, the higher the absolute level of contributions of sex, the more powerful males perceived themselves to be. This relationship, however, was negative (but nonsignificant) for females. That the ability to perform sexually may be more of a basis of power for males than for females is consistent with sexual stereotypes. Similarly, the more affection men contributed, the more power they perceived they had. For women, on the other hand, the more absolute contributions of affection, the less power they perceived themselves as having.

For both males and females, the more affective resources contributed *relative* to the partner, the *less* power they perceived themselves as having. This finding is consistent with the principle of least interest (Waller, 1937) and recent empirical research (Safilios-Rothschild, 1976; Peplau, 1978). This relationship was stronger for females than for males, as we had predicted. For women, it was found that the less they loved relative to the partner, the more power they perceived themselves as having. For males, this relationship was not significant. Thus, it appears that for women an important basis of power appears to be the control of the reciprocation of love in the relationship.

Women probably have traditionally had to become skilled at controlling their emotions in their heterosexual relationships in order to acquire any bargaining power. Indeed, evidence has been found that men are more romantic than women. For example, men are more likely than women to endorse such beliefs as "To be truly in love is to be in love forever" and "A person should marry whomever he loves regardless of social position," and to have other similar romantic attitudes (Dion & Dion, 1973, 1979; Hobart, 1958; Knox & Sporakowski, 1968). It has also been found that men are the first to fall in love (Coombs & Kendell, 1966; Kanin, Davidson, & Scheck, 1970) and the last to fall out of love (Rubin, Peplau, & Hill, 1981). Thus the evidence suggests that men may value and need the love from women more than women value and need the love from men. Often unable to have access to other desirable resources (money, status), women have had to use the control of love as a means to gain some power in the relationship.

While love may be treated as a "resource" that is contributed to the relationship, there is an alternative way of understanding love as it relates to the exchange of resources in the relationship. Love *may* act as a barometer to indicate how much the individual needs the partner. In general, dependence is often equated with romantic love (Reik, 1944); furthermore, dependency often arises because the other person is providing the desirable resources one needs. Those who perceive themselves as loving more in the relationship may feel less powerful in the relationship because of their greater need for the other. A woman's sense of power in the relationship may be especially dependent on how much she feels she needs (or loves) the partner.

In general, then, it appears that the bases of power may differ for males and females. Females seem more likely to gain power if they control the reciprocation of their partner's love. For males, on the other hand, the ability to attract alternative other dating partners seems to be an important basis of power. In addition, while past research and cultural stereotypes would suggest that males are more powerful than females, we did not find a significant difference between males and females in perceived power.

The results for this study suggest that further research should examine more clearly how contributions versus control of resources may be related to power. In addition, these findings demonstrate the importance of expanding the range of resources considered to include both stereotypically "male" and "female" resources as potential bases for power in intimate relationships.

References

Bernard, J. *The future of marriage*. New York: Bantam, 1972.

Blau, P. M. *Exchange and power in social life*. New York: Wiley, 1964.

Blood, R. O., & Wolfe, D. M. *Husbands and wives.* New York: Free Press, 1960.

Cook, K. S., & Emerson, R. M. Power, equity, commitment in exchange networks. *American Sociological Review,* 1978, *43,* 721–739.

Coombs, R. H., & Kendell, W. F. Sex differences in dating aspirations and satisfaction with computer-selected partners. *Journal of Marriage and the Family,* 1966, *28,* 62–66.

Dion, K. L., & Dion, K. K. Correlates of romantic love. *Journal of Consulting and Clinical Psychology,* 1973, *41,* 51–56.

_____. Correlates and behavioral correlates of romantic love. In M. Cook & G. Wilson (Eds.), *Love and attraction.* London: Pergamon, 1979.

Emerson, R. Power-dependence relations. *American Sociological Review,* 1962, *27,* 31–41.

Gillespie, D. L. Who has the power? The marital struggle. *Journal of Marriage and the Family,* 1971, *33,* 445–458.

Hill, C. T., Rubin, Z., Peplau, L. A., & Willard, S. G. The volunteer couple: Sex roles, couple commitment, and participation in research on male-female relationships. *Social Psychology Quarterly,* 1979, *42,* 415–420.

Hobart, C. W. The incidence of romanticism during courtship. *Social Forces,* 1958, *36,* 362–367.

Kanin, E. J., Davidson, D. K. P., & Scheck, S. R. A research note on male-female differentials in the experiences of heterosexual love. *The Journal of Sex Research,* 1970, *6,* 64–72.

Knox, D. H., & Saporakowski, M. J. Attitudes of college students toward love. *Journal of Marriage and the Family,* 1968, *30,* 638–643.

McDonald, G. W. Family power: Reflection and direction. *Pacific Sociological Review,* 1977, *20,* 607–621.

_____. Family power: The assessment of a decade of theory and research, 1970–1979, *Journal of Marriage and the Family,* 1980, *42,* 841–854.

Michel, A. Comparative data concerning the interaction in French and American families. *Journal of Marriage and the Family,* 1967, *29,* 337–344.

Michener, H. A., & Suchner, R. Tactical use of social power. In J. Tedeschi (Ed.), *The social influence processes* (pp. 239–270). Chicago: Aldine, 1972.

Peplau, L. A. Power in dating relationships. In J. Freeman (Ed.), *Women: A feminist perspective* (2nd ed.) (pp. 106–121). Palo Alto: Mayfield, 1978.

Reik, T. *A psychologist looks at love.* New York: Farrar and Rinehart, 1944.

Ries, H. T., Wheeler, L., Spiegel, N., Kernis, M. H., Nezlek, J., & Perri, M. Physical attractiveness in social interaction: II. Why does appearance affect social experience? *Journal of Personality and Social Psychology,* 1982, *43,* 979–996.

Rubin, Z., Peplau, L. A., & Hill, C. T. Loving and leaving: Sex differences in romantic attachments. *Sex Roles,* 1981, *7,* 821–835.

Safilios-Rothschild, C. The study of family power structure: A review 1960–1969. *Journal of Marriage and the Family,* 1970, *32,* 539–552.

_____. *Love, sex, and sex roles.* Englewood Cliffs, N.J.: Prentice-Hall, 1977.

_____. A Macro- and Micro-Examination of Family Power: An Exchange Model. *Journal of Marriage and the Family* 1976, 38:355–362.

Thibaut, J., & Kelley, H. H. *The social psychology of groups.* New York: Wiley, 1959.

Waller, W. The rating and dating complex. *American Sociological Review,* 1937, *2,* 727–734.

Walster, E., Aronson, V., Abrahams, D., & Rottman, L. The importance of physical attractiveness in dating behavior. *Journal of Personality and Social Psychology,* 1966, *4,* 508–516.

Appendix

To measure contributions of resources, each respondent was asked to indicate how much of each of the following resources he/she contributed and how much his/her partner contributed. Each description of the resource was followed by a response scale. The response scale for self and partner is also reproduced below.

Socioeconomic Contributions (money, social mobility, prestige)

Affective Contributions (affection, love, feeling needed—needing the other)

Expressive Contributions (understanding, concern, emotional support, special attention, appreciation, respect)

Physical Appearance Contributions (physical attractiveness, concern for health)

Intellectual Contributions (education, knowledge, information, commonsense)

Companionship Contributions (social, leisure, communication)

Sexual Contributions (the physical relationship)

Service Contributions (housekeeping, child care, personal services)

+4. My contributions are extremely positive.
+3. My contributions are very positive.
+2. My contributions are moderately positive.
+1. My contributions are slightly positive.
−1. My contributions are slightly negative.
−2. My contributions are moderately negative.
−3. My contributions are very negative.
−4. My contributions are extremely negative.

+4. My partner's contributions are extremely positive.
+3. My partner's contributions are very positive.
+2. My partner's contributions are moderately positive.
+1. My partner's contributions are slightly positive.
−1. My partner's contributions are slightly negative.
−2. My partner's contributions are moderately negative.
−3. My partner's contributions are very negative.
−4. My partner's contributions are extremely negative.

The Institutionalization of Premarital Cohabitation: Estimates from Marriage License Applications, 1970 and 1980

Patricia A. Gwartney-Gibbs

The number of unmarried heterosexual couples living together in the United States is estimated to have increased three- to fourfold since 1970 (Glick, 1984; Glick and Norton, 1979; Spanier, 1982, 1983; Sweet, 1979; U.S. Bureau of the Census, 1983a). This nonmarital heterosexual cohabitation comprises two subcategories that suggest different social implications and consequences. The first category includes unmarried cohabiting couples who, regardless of their original intentions, eventually separate. The second category includes cohabiting couples who eventually marry. Prior research has not systematically distinguished between these two groups in examining the determinants and consequences of cohabitation, although unmarried heterosexual cohabitation in general has received generous attention (for reviews, see Macklin, 1978, 1983). The research reported here partially addresses this deficiency by focusing on the second category, premarital cohabitation.

The proportion of married couples who have lived together prior to marriage is of interest to family sociologists and demographers alike. Several family sociologists have suggested that cohabitation is becoming institutionalized as part of the American mate-selection process (e.g., Henze and Hudson, 1974; Macklin, 1978; Reiss, 1980; Risman, Hill, Rubin, and Peplau, 1981). From this perspective, living together is an additional step that intervenes in the movement of couples' relationships from dating to marriage. Rapid increases in the number of couples who cohabit prior to marriage may signal fundamental shifts in values, attitudes, and behavior regarding courtship and marriage rituals in recent decades. For demographers, to the extent that cohabitants delay marriage, increasing rates of premarital cohabitation may be related to secular increases in the average age at first marriage (Cole, 1977; Spanier, 1983). This, in turn, may be related to increasing fertility control and changing roles of women. Still, not much is known about the extent to which premarital cohabitation occurs in the United States among couples who eventually marry.

An earlier version of this article was presented at the annual meeting of the Population Association of America, Boston, 1985. The research was supported in part by a grant from the Center for the Study of Women in Society, University of Oregon. Comments from Jean Stockard, Walt Martin, Miriam Johnson, Kingsley Davis, Patricia Roos, and two anonymous referees, and the research assistance of Jill L. Solberg, Susann Bartley, and Vicki Van Nortwick are gratefully acknowledged.

What little is known about premarital cohabitation is often limited by nongeneralizable samples and inadequate data (cf. Newcomb, 1979). Risman et al. (1981) followed a sample of 231 "going together" college students, of whom 40 were cohabiting, for two years and found no differences in marriage or breakup rates between cohabiting and noncohabiting couples. In an eight–month follow–up study of 23 dating couples and 15 living–together couples, Lyness (1978) found that the former were more likely to marry than the latter. Clayton and Voss's (1977) retrospective sample survey of 2,510 young men found that 12% of those currently married had cohabited for six months or more at least once, and that 35% of those married two or more times had cohabited at least once, but accurate data on the extent to which cohabitation preceded marriage was not available. Other studies have asked retrospective questions of college students about their cohabitation experiences (e.g., Henze and Hudson, 1974; Macklin, 1972; Peterman, Ridley, and Anderson, 1974), or have compared married couples who did and did not cohabit premaritally, to assess the quality or success of their subsequent marriages (e.g., Hanna and Knaub, 1981; Jacques and Chason, 1979; Newcomb and Bentler, 1980; Rank, 1981). While several of these studies suggest that cohabitation serves as a "trial marriage," particularly for couples in which one or both partners have been previously married, none . . . can fully address the question of the prevalence of premarital cohabitation. Prospective data on the marriage expectations of cohabiting college students have been reported in several studies, and most indicate that large proportions hope or plan to marry someone (not necessarily their current partner) someday (e.g., Arafat and Yorburg, 1973; Bower and Christopherson, 1977; Danziger, 1978; Lyness, Lipetz, and Davis, 1972; Peterman et al., 1974; Risman et al., 1981). But again, without linking marriage expectations to specific marital events, the extent to which students' cohabitation preceded marriage is unknown.

In order to answer questions about the extent to which cohabitation leads to marriage, many cohabitation researchers have called for the gathering of longitudinal data. Although such an undertaking for large, representative samples would be costly in time and money, such data are necessary to address the question of how many cohabitants eventually marry. A corollary question, however, has not been asked. That is, *to what extent have married couples cohabited prior to their marriages?* The difference in the phrasing of the two questions is subtle but important, since it involves changing the unit of analysis from cohabiting couples to married couples. Such a shift still allows the testing of valuable research questions, and data to answer this corollary question are readily available, although infrequently used, in the United States (see, however, Carmichael, 1984, on New Zealand).

Marriage registration data can be examined to estimate the proportion of married couples who have cohabited before marriage. In most states, couples who wish to marry must fill out marriage license applications at their local county seat. These applications are open for public examination and contain, among other items, the applicants' addresses. Brides and grooms who supply the same home addresses may be assumed to be cohabiting prior to marriage. Questions about the validity of this assumption are addressed below.

In the case study of a county reported here, data from marriage license applications in 1970 and 1980 are used to address four research questions. First, to what extent did married couples cohabit with one another prior to their marriages, and how has this changed over time? Prior research provides us with no firm hypotheses on prevalence rates, but if increases in premarital cohabitation parallel national estimates of increases in nonmarital heterosexual cohabitation in general, we can expect growth of 300% to 400% in the decade.

Second, what are the characteristics of premaritally cohabiting brides and grooms, and how has this changed over time? Answers to these questions not only provide descriptive baseline information; they can also be used to test the hypotheses derived from previous research. On the basis of Spanier's (1983) findings for the nation, premarital cohabitation is expected to be more prevalent among young persons, and growth in premarital cohabitation is expected to be concentrated mainly among those who are young and/or previously divorced. Previously divorced applicants for marriage licenses are expected to show higher rates of premarital cohabitation than never-married persons, since "trial marriages" may be a strategy for avoiding future divorces. If these data parallel national data, nonwhites can be expected to cohabit at higher rates than whites, but the gap should be diminishing, and there should be a convergence in the occupational and employment characteristics of premarital cohabitants and noncohabitants as cohabitation spreads in the population.

Third, how are the joint characteristics of couples who live together prior to marriage different from those who do not, and how did this change between 1970 and 1980? Again from Spanier's (1983) findings, we can expect that cohabiting couples are more likely than noncohabiting couples to have brides older than grooms, are equally likely to be interracial, and are more likely to have employed brides supporting unemployed grooms. The joint characteristics of couples can also be used to explore the relative extent to which cohabiting and noncohabiting couples are demographically homogamous, that is, the degree to which partners are similar in age, race, previous marital status, and employment status. Previous research consistently indicates that heterogamous marriages are less successful and less stable than homogamous marriages (Bumpass and Sweet, 1972; Dean and Gurak, 1978; Udry, 1974). To the extent that heterogamous couples attempt to avoid these negative outcomes by trial marriages, we can expect greater demographic heterogeneity among premaritally cohabiting couples than among noncohabiting couples. Moreover, if premarital cohabitation is becoming institutionalized as part of the American mate-selection process, we can expect less heterogamy among cohabiting couples in 1980 than in 1970, as premarital cohabitation becomes more pervasive over the decade.

Fourth, is there any evidence that couples who live together delay marriage longer than couples who do not? Several researchers have found evidence indicating that cohabitants delay, or plan to delay, marriage longer than persons who do not cohabit (Clayton and Voss, 1977; Bower and Christopherson, 1977; Danziger, 1978). The degree to which premarital cohabitants delay marriage may be explored by comparing the average age at marriage for cohabitants and noncohabitants. If the average age at marriage of premarital cohabitants is greater than that of noncohabitants, and if we consider this difference to reflect a greater tendency among cohabitants to delay marriage (rather than a predisposition to delay marriage, independent of cohabitation), then we can conclude that premarital cohabitants postpone marriage longer than those who do not cohabit prior to marriage. Among those who have been divorced or widowed, the average age at remarriage is greater than that of persons at first marriage; therefore previous marital status must be controlled.

Methods

Data

All persons wishing to marry in Oregon must fill out a marriage license application at their local county seat. Lane County, Oregon, was chosen for this exploratory case study purely for convenience. Lane County comprises 4,620 square miles, with one major urban center, the Eugene-Springfield MSA, and four additional cities of 2,500 or more persons. The population was approximately 215,000 in 1970 and 275,000 in 1980, of which 27% is rural. Forestry and wood products are the principal industries of the county. Compared to the nation, Lane County has no characteristics that would suggest that cohabitation would be substantially higher, although the western states in general seem to have higher rates of cohabitation (Clayton and Voss, 1977).In 1980, 23.3% of the Lane County population were single, 60.1% married, and 16.6% widowed, divorced, or separated, compared to 26.3%, 57.4% and 16.3%, respectively, in the nation (Population Reference Bureau, 1981). And the sex ratio for persons aged 15 to 64 was .99 compared to .96 in the nation (calculated from the U.S. Bureau of the Census, 1983b, 1983c). The presence of a large state university in Lane County may help make premarital cohabitation more socially acceptable, but, as this study shows, students neither comprised a large proportion of marrying cohabitants nor were more likely to cohabit premaritally than nonstudents.

In Lane County, 1,714 marriage license applications were completed in 1970 and 2,582 in 1980. Couples who filled out applications but did not subsequently marry are excluded from these populations. All applications were coded with both brides' and grooms' ages (ranging from 15 to 88); race/ethnicity (white, black, Asian, other); previous marital status (never married, divorced/annulled, widowed); and occupation (detailed 1970 Census occupation codes, with additional codes for students, homemaker, unemployed, and retired). Couples were coded as cohabiting if they supplied identical home addresses on their marriage license application.

Vital reports hold promise for the study of the relationship between cohabitation and marriage because they come as close as possible to a complete count of the number of marital events that take place in a given year in a given locale. The disadvantage of marriage registration data, at least in Oregon, is that it exists only on paper or microfiche and must be hand-coded for analysis. This problem will probably preclude the widespread use of marriage license applications as a source of information on premarital cohabitation.

Because marriage license applications are official documents, the information reported is likely to be more accurate than that obtained by surveys. Despite the official importance of these applications, however, some marriage license applicants may report the address of their future home for convenience, which would lead to overestimates of premarital cohabitation. On the other hand, some couples may wish to conceal the fact that they are cohabiting by supplying different addresses. The extent and net effect of these countervailing possibilities cannot be disentangled when nonreactive data are used. In addition, cultural norms about the acceptability of premarital cohabitation seemingly relaxed in the decade between 1970 and 1980, which would result in less underreporting in the latter year. Thus, the increase in premarital cohabitation reported below may reflect both absolute increases in the number of premarital cohabitants as well as increases due to less underreporting. The present data provide no basis for evaluating these two influences.

Analysis

For an examination of trends and differentials in premarital cohabitation in Lane County, the major dependent variable is the percentage of brides and grooms who were cohabiting prior to marriage. To test hypotheses about the extent to which premarital cohabitants postpone marriage, the average age at marriage is used as the dependent variable. As is appropriate for an exploratory case study such as this, simple descriptive statistics (i.e., percentages, means, *t* tests of differences in means, and confidence invervals) are used to examine the results.

Findings

Trends and Differentials in Premarital Cohabitation

Changes in the extent to which marrying couples cohabited premaritally, the first research question, are evident in the population numbers in Table 1. In 1970, 13.2% of all marriage license applicants in Lane County gave identical home addresses and thus are assumed to have been cohabiting prior to marriage. In 1980 the percentage cohabiting increased to 52.7%. This fourfold increase parallels national esimates of the increase in cohabitation between 1970 and 1980 based on Current Population Survey (CPS) data (Glick, 1984; Glick and Spanier, 1980; Spanier, 1982, 1983; U.S. Bureau of the Census, 1983a; Sweet, 1979).

The second research question, regarding the characteristics of premaritally cohabiting brides and grooms and how these have changed over time, is addressed in Tables 1 and 2. In 1970 the majority of marriage license applicants who cohabited were less than 25 years old (71.2% of cohabiting brides and 57.1% of cohabiting grooms were less than 25). By 1980 the age distribution of premarital cohabitants had spread considerably into the next-older age group, with 48.9% and 32.4% of cohabiting brides and grooms, respectively, who were less than 25 years old, and 39.8% and 49.8%, respectively, aged 25 to 34. The proportion of each age group cohabiting increased by roughly 200% to 400%

Table 1 Percentage Frequency Distributions of Premarital Cohabitants and Noncohabitants, Brides and Grooms, for Age Group, Previous Marital Status, Race/Ethnicity, and Occupation/Employment, 1970 and 1980

| | 1970 | | | | 1980 | | | |
| | Cohabitants (N = 226) | | Noncohabitants (N = 1,488) | | Cohabitants (N = 1,361) | | Noncohabitants (N = 1,221) | |
Characteristic	Brides	Grooms	Brides	Grooms	Brides	Grooms	Brides	Grooms
Age group								
<25	71.2	57.1	79.8	67.2	48.9	32.4	61.5	49.1
25–34	15.5	27.0	11.6	20.3	39.8	49.8	24.0	31.0
35–44	8.0	7.5	3.4	6.0	7.5	11.2	6.3	9.7
45–64	4.9	7.5	3.5	4.3	3.3	5.9	5.7	6.8
65+	.4	.9	1.7	2.2	.4	.7	2.5	3.5
	100.0	100.0	100.0	100.0	99.9	100.0	100.0	100.1
Previous marital status								
Never married	65.5	66.8	78.1	77.4	59.2	59.6	71.8	67.8
Ever married	34.5	33.2	21.9	22.6	40.8	40.3	28.2	32.2
	100.0	100.0	100.0	100.0	100.0	99.9	100.0	100.0
Race/ethnicity								
Whites	97.3	95.6	98.9	98.3	97.4	96.2	97.9	97.5
Blacks	.9	1.3	.2	.8	.3	1.2	.7	.7
Asians	1.3	1.3	.6	.8	1.6	.7	.6	.8
Others	.4	1.8	.3	.1	.7	1.8	.9	1.1
	99.9	100.0	100.0	100.0	100.0	99.9	100.1	100.1
Occupation/employment								
White collar	22.1	16.9	29.9	19.4	43.2	35.4	47.0	35.9
Blue collar, farm	3.5	44.0	2.3	51.2	6.5	46.0	5.9	45.3
Service	11.1	2.7	12.6	3.1	11.8	6.0	13.1	5.4
Student	18.1	26.7	26.1	22.1	9.1	7.1	10.6	7.5
Homemaker	7.5	0	2.5	0	9.8	0	4.1	0
Unemployed, retired	37.6	9.8	26.7	4.2	19.6	5.5	19.3	5.8
	99.9	100.1	100.1	100.0	100.0	100.0	100.0	99.9

Table 2 Percentage of Group Cohabiting at Date of Marriage License Application, and Percentage Increases for Brides and Grooms, 1970 and 1980

| Characteristic | Percentage Cohabiting | | | | Percentage Increase 1970 to 1980 | |
| | 1970 (N = 1,714) | | 1980 (N = 2,582) | | | |
	Brides	Grooms	Brides	Grooms	Brides	Grooms
Age group						
<25	11.9	11.4	47.0	42.4	395	372
25–34	16.9	16.8	64.9	64.2	384	382
35–44	26.1	16.0	57.0	56.3	218	352
45–64	17.5	21.0	39.5	49.1	226	234
65+	3.8	5.7	16.2	18.9	426	332
Previous marital status						
Never married	11.3	11.6	47.9	49.5	424	427
Ever married	19.4	18.2	61.7	58.3	318	320
Race/ethnicity						
White	13.0	12.9	52.6	52.4	405	406
Nonwhite	26.1	27.8	57.3	62.7	220	226
Occupation/employment						
White collar	10.1	11.7	50.6	52.3	501	447
Blue collar, farm	19.5	11.5	55.6	53.1	285	462
Service	11.7	11.5	50.0	55.4	427	482
Student	9.6	15.4	49.0	51.3	510	333
Homemaker	31.5	—	72.7	—	231	—
Unemployed, retired	17.6	26.2	53.0	50.7	301	194

during the decade (the last two columns of Table 2). By 1980 those most likely to cohabit were brides and grooms aged 25 to 34, at 64.9% and 64.2%, respectively.

In 1970 only about 11% of the marriage license applicants who had never been married before were cohabiting (Table 2), compared to 19.4% of brides at 18.2% of grooms who had previously been divorced or widowed. In 1980, nearly half of the never-married persons were cohabiting at the date of their marriage license application, while 60% of those previously married were. In both years, never-married persons accounted for the majority of premarital cohabitants, about 66% in 1970 and 59% in 1980 (Table 1).

When age and previous marital status are simultaneously controlled (Table 3), the proportion of each group cohabiting in 1970 is widely spread with little pattern. Previously divorced applicants for marriage licenses had a somewhat greater tendency to cohabit than never-married applicants (among those previously divorced, 14.3% to 25.5% of four age groups cohabited, while among never-married persons, 10.0% to 22.2% of three age groups cohabited). A distinctly small tendency to cohabit prior to remarriage in 1970 is evident among all widowed men and among widowed women aged 65 or more (7.1% or less). By 1980, large proportions of all age and previous-marital-status groups cohabited prior to marriage, except again for older widows. Among never-married persons, those aged 25 to 34 were most likely to cohabit, with about 60% of brides and grooms doing so, compared to just over 40% of brides and grooms less than 25 years old. Among those previously divorced, fully 71.1% of women less than 25 years old and about 68% of men and women aged 25 to 34 cohabited prior to remarriage. For all persons remarrying, including those previously widowed, age seems to be an important factor in the likelihood of cohabitation; with one exception, the proportion of each group cohabiting declines successively with age. The percentage increases over the decade were high for all age and marital-status groups, ranging from 154% to 535%, and, contrary to expectations, the greatest increases were not particularly concentrated among the young or previously divorced.

In 1970 twice as many nonwhites as whites cohabited prior to marriage, about 26% and 13%, respectively (Table 2). But by 1980 this gap was reduced to just 4.7% for brides (57.3% for nonwhites and 52.6% for whites) and 10.3% for grooms (62.7% and 52.4% for nonwhites and whites, respectively). Nonwhites, however, comprised less than 5% of the pool of marriage license applicants in both years.

With regard to employment in 1970, a larger proportion of cohabitants than noncohabitants were unemployed or out of the labor force (i.e., students, homemakers, or retired persons), which suggests that some couples cohabited for economic advantages. Specifically, 63.2% and 36.5% of cohabiting brides and grooms, respectively, compared to 55.3% and 26.3% of noncohabiting brides and grooms, were unemployed or out of the labor force (Table 1). But by 1980 this difference evaporated, with 38.5% and 12.6% of cohabiting brides and grooms, and 34.0% and 13.3% of noncohabiting brides and grooms, respectively, unemployed or out of the labor force. The pervasiveness of premarital cohabitation is especially clear when one examines occupation/employment

Table 3 Percentage Cohabiting at Date of Marriage License Application by Previous Marital Status and Age, and Percentage Increases for Brides and Grooms, 1970 and 1980

Characteristic	1970		1980		Percentage Increase 1970 to 1980	
	Brides	Grooms	Brides	Grooms	Brides	Grooms
Never married	(N = 1,309)	(N = 1,303)	(N = 1,683)	(N = 1,639)		
<25	11.0	11.0	44.5	41.5	405	377
25–34	15.0	14.8	59.5	61.7	397	417
35 +	22.2	10.0	48.1	53.5	217	535
Divorced	(N = 337)	(N = 346)	(N = 803)	(N = 861)		
<25	22.1	20.4	71.1	56.9	322	279
25–34	17.9	20.0	69.4	67.8	388	339
35–44	24.1	19.5	58.6	55.9	243	287
45 +	14.3	25.5	41.3	53.6	289	210
Widowed	(N = 66)	(N = 65)	(N = 94)	(N = 78)		
<45	23.5	0.0	56.5	44.4	240	444
45–64	22.2	7.1	34.1	29.6	154	417
65 +	4.5	4.0	11.1	14.3	247	358

groups in Table 2. In 1980, 49% or more of the brides and grooms in every occupation/employment category were cohabiting at the date of their marriage license applications. Those least likely to cohabit in both years were female students, of whom 9.6% in 1970 and 49.0% in 1980 reported identical home addresses as their partners (but there may be underreporting here if students used parents' home addresses). Those most likely to cohabit in both years were female homemakers, at 31.5% in 1970 and 72.7% in 1980.

The picture that emerges from these findings shows that premarital cohabitation in Lane County increased between 1970 and 1980 at high rates for virtually every demographic subgroup that can be identified by using marriage license application data. This finding is dissimilar to results from CPS data for the nation. Spanier (1983) found increases in cohabitation to be concentrated among young and previously divorced persons. In addition, Glick and Spanier (1980) and Spanier (1983) reported roughly equal proportions of never-married and previously married cohabitants, whereas in Lane County never-married persons comprised about 66% of all premarital cohabitants in 1970 and about 59% in 1980. Whether these differences are due to something unique about Lane County or to differences in data sources, or to some combination of the two, remains to be studied. The fact that premarital cohabitation increased at roughly the same rate as national estimates of cohabitation provides suggestive evidence of the reliability of cohabitation data based upon vital reports.

Joint Characteristics of Cohabiting and Noncohabiting Couples

The third research question concerns an examination of the joint characteristics of premarital cohabitants and noncohabitants, and this is addressed in Table 4. Here we switch the unit of analysis from individual brides and grooms to couples. This approach provides a basis for testing whether those living together were less homogamous than those who did not live together, and whether heterogamy among cohabitants decreasd over the decade.

In both 1970 and 1980 cohabiting brides and grooms were about 10% less likely to be of similar ages than noncohabiting brides and grooms. In 1970, 59.7% of cohabiting partners were within three years of age of each other, compared to 68.8% of noncohabiting partners; and in 1980, 53.6% of cohabitants and 63.2% of noncohabitants were of similar ages. Among those couples in which the bride was four or more years older than the groom, there was a distinctly greater tendency to cohabit. In 1970, 29.0% of the couples with older brides cohabited, compared to 11.7% of the couples close in age, and in 1980 the parallel figures were 69.9% and 48.6%.

Cohabiting partners were about 10% less likely than noncohabiting partners to have the same previous marital status in both 1970 and 1980. In the earlier year, 77.5% of cohabiting partners had the same previous marital status (i.e., both partners were never married before or both had previously married), compared to 86.4% of noncohabitants. In 1980, 72.2% of cohabitants and 81.8% of noncohabitants had the same previous marital status. Comparisons across the decade indicate that 5% fewer cohabitants and noncohabitants had the same previous marital status in 1980 than in 1970.

Table 4 Characteristics of Brides and Grooms—Age Differentials, Previous Marital Status, Race/Ethnicity, and Employment Status: Percentage Frequency Distribution and Percentage of Group Cohabiting Prior to Marriage, 1970 and 1980

	1970			1980		
	% Frequency Distribution		% of Group Cohabiting	% Frequency Distribution		% of Group Cohabiting
Joint Characteristics	Cohabitants (N = 226)	Noncohabitants (N = 1,488)		Cohabitants (N = 1,361)	Noncohabitants (N = 1,221)	
Age differential						
Brides ≥ 4 years older	8.8	3.3	29.0	8.5	4.1	69.9
Ages within 3 years +/−	59.7	68.8	11.7	53.6	63.2	48.6
Groom 4–10 years older	25.7	23.5	14.3	28.7	26.2	55.0
Groom ≥ 11 years older	5.8	4.5	16.3	9.1	6.5	42.3
	100.0	100.1		99.9	100.0	
Previous marital status						
Both never married	54.9	71.0	10.5	45.6	60.8	45.6
Both previously married	22.6	15.4	18.2	26.6	21.0	41.4
Bride previously married, groom never married	11.9	6.5	22.0	14.1	7.1	69.0
Groom previously married, bride never married	10.6	7.1	18.5	13.7	11.1	59.1
	100.0	100.0		100.0	100.0	
Race/ethnicity						
Both white	94.7	97.7	12.9	94.3	96.1	52.3
Both nonwhite	1.8	.6	30.8	.8	.7	63.2
Mixed	3.5	1.7	24.2	4.9	3.2	52.6
	100.0	100.0		100.0	100.0	
Employment status						
Both employed	26.1	34.9	10.2	55.7	60.2	50.7
Groom employed, bride not	37.6	38.8	9.1	31.8	26.5	57.2
Bride employed, groom not	10.6	9.9	14.0	5.9	5.8	53.0
Both notworking	25.7	16.4	19.2	6.7	7.5	49.7
	100.0	100.0		100.1	100.0	

[a]Not working includes those unemployed and those out of the labor force.

Moreover, approximately 15% more cohabiting than noncohabiting couples in both years included one or more partner who had been previously married. In 1970, 45.1% of cohabiting couples, compared to 29.0% of noncohabiting couples, had one or more never-married partner; in 1980 the corresponding proportions were 54.4% and 39.2%. In 1970 these couples were twice as likely to cohabit as those who entered their first marriages (roughly 20% compared to 10.5%). By 1980 the pattern was more mixed, as the proportion of never-married couples that cohabited (45.6%) actually surpassed the proportion of couples who were both previously married that cohabited (41.4%). In both years, the couples most likely to live together before marriage were those in which the bride had been married before and the groom had not, with 22.0% of such couples cohabiting in 1970 and 69.0% in 1980.

Racially homogamous couples comprised a slightly smaller percentage of cohabitants than noncohabitants in both years. In 1970, 96.5% of cohabiting partners were the same race (i.e., both white or both nonwhite), compared to 98.3% of couples who did not live together, while for 1980 the parallel figures are 95.1% and 96.8%. Increases over the decade in mixed-race couples were about 1.5% for both cohabitants and noncohabitants. Although couples with one or more nonwhite partner were two times more likely to cohabit than white couples in 1970, by 1980 the magnitude of these differences mostly disappeared, when 63.2% of nonwhite couples lived together before marriage and nearly equal proportions of white and mixed-race couples cohabited (about 52%).

The information on employment status in 1970 provides evidence of the extent to which premarital cohabitation may have been used by couples in order to save money by pooling resources. Fully 25.7% of all of the cohabiting partners in that year were both not working, compared to 16.4% of noncohabiting couples. Indeed, unemployed couples were the most likely to cohabit in that year, with 19.2% doing so, compared to 9.1% of then-traditional couples in which grooms worked and brides did not. Although economic conditions in Lane County were much worse in 1980, only 6.7% of cohabitants and 7.5% of noncohabitants were both not working in that year. Unemployed couples in 1980 were the least likely to cohabit of the four joint-employment-status groups, at 49.7%. This change does not necessarily mean that economic movitations to cohabit were less important in 1980 than in 1970, but rather that premarital cohabitation spread across the other joint-employment statuses of couples. In 1980 over half of couples in which one or both partners were employed lived together before marriage. In neither year were cohabiting brides in Lane County substantially more likely than noncohabiting brides to be supporting nonworking partners. In 1970, 10.6% and 9.9% of cohabiting and noncohabiting brides, respectively, worked and had partners who did not, and in 1980 the parallel figures were 5.9% and 5.8%.

The joint characteristics of couples indicate that premarital cohabitants in Lane County in 1970 and 1980 were somewhat less homogamous than noncohabiting couples in age, previous marital status, and race characteristics, but not in employment. Since heterogamous marriages have been found to be less successful than homogamous ones, these findings suggest that premarital cohabitation may serve as a means of reducing the risk of unsuccessful marriages among unlike partners. Contrary to predictions, heterogamy did not decrease over the decade for cohabiting couples as cohabitation spread in the population. Rather, cohabiting and noncohabiting couples both became slightly more heterogamous in age, race, and previous marital status. The findings for the joint characteristics of cohabiting and noncohabiting couples generally parallel Spanier's (1983) findings for the nation, with the exception of cohabiting females supporting their partners.

Marriage Postponement among Premarital Cohabitants

Table 5 presents data to test the hypothesis that the average age at marriage for cohabitants is greater than for noncohabitants, by previous marital status. In 1970 none of the age differences between cohabiting and noncohabiting brides and grooms were found to be significant (using a two-tailed *t* test of differences in means). However, among those who had never married previously, the cohabiting brides' average age at marriage was 20.5 years compared to 20.0 years for non-cohabiting brides, and the cohabiting grooms' average age at marriage was 22.6 years compared to 22.2 years for noncohabiting grooms. These differences of approximately one-half year are in the predicted direction. By 1980 never-married cohabitant brides averaged 22.8 years of age ($\pm.32$ years with 95% confidence) compared to 21.7 ($\pm.29$) years for noncohabitant brides. Never-married cohabitant grooms averaged 25.0 ($\pm.31$) years of age, compared to 23.6 ($\pm.37$) for noncohabitant grooms. These differences, 1.1 years between cohabitant and non-cohabitant brides and 1.4 years between cohabitant and noncohabitant grooms, are statistically significant, and using the 95% confidence intervals, the age ranges do not overlap. Assuming that this age difference reflects a greater tendency among cohabitants to delay first marriages, rather than a predisposition to do so, we can conclude, as predicted, that premarital cohabitants delay marriage just over one year longer than those who do not cohabit prior to marriage.

Table 5 also reflects the general secular trend between 1970 and 1980 to delay first marriages. The average age at first marriage was several years later in 1980 then in 1970 for both cohabitant and noncohabitant brides and grooms. It is important to note, however, that cohabitant brides' and grooms' average ages at first marriage were 2.3 and 2.4 years later, respectively, in 1980 than in 1970, compared to just 1.7 and 1.4 years for noncohabitant brides and grooms. These differences, combined with the results in the paragraph above, suggest that premarital cohabitation may be a contributing factor to the general secular trend in delaying first marriages.

Unlike first-marrying persons, cohabitants in 1980 who had been divorced or widowed were significantly younger than previously married noncohabitants, contrary to expectations. Among those who were previously divorced, cohabitant brides averaged 30.7 ($\pm.67$) years old when remarrying, compared to 34.3 (±1.28) years for noncohabitant brides. And remarrying cohabitant grooms averaged 34.6 ($\pm.77$) years compared to 36.7 (±1.15) years for noncohabitant grooms. For those previously widowed, cohabiting and noncohabiting brides

Table 5 Average Age at Marriage for Cohabitants and Noncohabitants by Previous Marital Status, for Brides and Grooms, 1970 and 1980 (Standard Deviations in Parentheses)

Previous Marital Status	Cohabitants		Noncohabitants		t Test of Mean Difference	
	Brides	Grooms	Brides	Grooms	Brides	Grooms
1970						
Never married	20.5	22.6	20.0	22.2	1.60	1.09
	(3.5)	(5.4)	(3.5)	(4.5)		
Divorced	30.1	35.0	31.2	34.1	−.86	.60
	(9.0)	(10.8)	(10.2)	(11.0)		
Widowed	47.1	58.3	55.4	57.1	−1.69	.16
	(14.7)	(13.1)	(15.7)	(15.1)		
1980						
Never married	22.8	25.0	21.7	23.6	5.10***	5.86***
	(4.6)	(4.5)	(4.4)	(5.5)		
Divorced ·	30.7	34.6	34.3	36.7	−4.88***	−2.94**
	(7.8)	(9.0)	(10.9)	(10.7)		
Widowed	46.4	56.6	58.0	65.3	−3.89***	−2.31*
	(13.9)	(14.6)	(12.8)	(11.7)		

*$p < .05$.   **$p < .01$.   ***$p < .001$.

were 46.4 (± 4.91) and 58.0 (± 3.17) years of age, and grooms were 56.6 (± 6.77) and 65.3 (± 2.97) years of age, respectively. This pattern suggests either that previously married cohabitants do not delay remarriage or that those who cohabit are simply younger than those who do not. As noted above in Table 3, the latter appears to be the case; the proportion of each age group of those previously divorced or widowed who cohabited prior to remarriage declines successively with age in 1980, with one exception.

Thus, the data for 1980 appear to support the hypothesis that never-married cohabitants postponed marriage by a little more than a year. It should be noted, however, that cohabitation per se is not necessarily a causal factor; those who cohabit may be predisposed to delaying first marriages, independent of cohabitation. Among never-married persons in 1970 the age differentials were in the predicted direction, but insignificant. Among those remarrying in 1980, cohabitants were significantly younger than noncohabitants, probably because living together is socially more acceptable among younger persons.

Summary and Conclusions

Marriage registration data from 1970 [and] 1980 in Lane County, Oregon, were used in this research to examine four questions regarding premarital cohabitation. First, we examined the prevalence of premarital cohabitation. Of all couples who filled out marriage license applications, 13% in 1970 and 53% in 1980 reported identical home addresses and thus are assumed to have been cohabiting before marriage. This fourfold increase is similar to increases in all types of cohabitation reported for the nation.

The second research question concerned the characteristics of premaritally cohabiting brides and grooms, and how they changed in the decade. Unlike findings on nonmarital cohabitation in the nation, the growth in premarital cohabitation in Lane County was widely spread across demographic subgroups; it was not particularly concentrated among young persons or those previously divorced, although previously divorced persons did cohabit before marriage at higher rates than never-married persons. The findings of this study also indicate that the racial gap in premarital cohabitation has diminished in Lane County, as in the nation, and the occupational and employment characteristics of cohabitants and noncohabitants have converged as cohabitation has spread in the population.

For the third research question, the joint characteristics of premaritally cohabiting couples were compared to those of noncohabiting couples, and changes over time were examined. As others have found among nonmarital cohabitants in the nation, brides are more likely to be older than grooms among premaritally cohabiting couples than among noncohabitants. But premaritally cohabiting brides in Lane County were not more likely than noncohabitants to be supporting nonworking grooms. We predicted that, to the extent that heterogamous couples attempt to avoid unsuccessful and unstable marriages, cohabiting couples would be more heterogamous demographically than noncohabiting couples. This prediction was supported. Partners living together before marriage were less homogamous in age, previous marital status, and race than those who did not cohabit. This in turn suggests that premarital cohabitation may serve as a "trial marriage" and a means of enhancing the success of marriage among partners with dissimilar characteristics. Contrary to expectations, however, demographic heterogamy among premarital cohabitants did not decrease in the decade as cohabitation became more pervasive. Rather, both cohabitants and noncohabitants became slightly more heterogamous.

The fourth research question addressed whether premaritally cohabiting couples postponed marriage longer than noncohabiting couples. This case study provides the first empirical evidence to suggest that this is true. With average age at marriage used as a criterion, the hypothesis that cohabitants delay first marriage longer than noncohabitants was only partially supported in the 1970 data, but in 1980 the average age at first marriage was 1.1 and 1.4 years later for premaritally cohabiting brides and grooms, respectively, compared to noncohabitants. Although the possibility that cohabitants are predisposed to delay marriage cannot be ruled out, these results tentatively suggest that increasing rates of cohabitation may be associated with the general secular trend of increasing age at first marriage. Whether formerly married premarital cohabitants delay marriage, however, is uncertain. Among those who were previously divorced or widowed in 1980, the average age at remarriage was significantly lower for cohabitants than for noncohabitants, but this difference seems to be due to the fact that young, never-married persons are much more likely to cohabit than older ones.

Findings from Spanier's 1983 study of nonmarital cohabitation in the United States have provided a framework for several of the research questions addressed in this study. While many of the results presented here parallel Spanier's, some do not. Most notably, Spanier found the greatest increases in cohabitation among young persons and those who were previously divorced, while in this study large increases in premarital cohabitation were found for all age and previous–marital–status subgroups. The differences between the two studies most likely stem from the fact that this study has examined premarital cohabitation from marriage registration data, whereas Spanier's study examined all forms of cohabitation from CPS data. Premarital cohabitants, a subset of all cohabitants, are likely to have different social and demographic characteristics compared with cohabitants who do not marry. Young cohabitants, in particular, may not yet have reached a life cycle stage in which social pressure or economic or reproductive motivations are sufficient to result in a decision to marry. Differences between the two studies may also be due to something unique about Lane County, although I have argued above that Lane County has no glaring characteristics that would suggest that cohabitation there should be higher than in the nation as a whole. Finally, some differences may be due to the fact that in the present study we measured cohabitation directly, by examining addresses of marriage registrants. The CPS has no specific question that directly measures cohabitation; individuals counted as cohabitants may, in fact, be platonic roommates.

This case study highlights marriage registration data as a potentially rich source for the study of premarital cohabitation. Although the many similarities in findings from cohabitation data for the nation and from marriage registration data for Lane County provide suggestive evidence of the reliability of the latter, additional research needs to be done in a variety of locales to explain variations in levels and correlates of premarital cohabitation. Marriage registration data cannot, however, address an important alternative question: To what extent is cohabitation *not* premarital? A new approach could be to triangulate upon nonmarital and premarital cohabitation by comparing census estimates of cohabitation to estimates based on marriage license applications in particular locales.

The extensiveness of premarital cohabitation in Lane County suggests that social norms regarding the acceptability of sexual relations prior to marriage have relaxed substantially. This, in turn, may be associated with increased availability of effective means of birth control and fundamental changes in attitudes toward the roles of women. When over half of a marrying population cohabits premaritally, as was the case in Lane County in 1980, it signals that a new normative pattern in courtship and marriage rituals may be emerging. Premarital cohabitation may indeed become institutionalized as a new step between dating and marriage for many couples.

References

Arafat, Ibithaj, and Betty Yorburg. 1973. "On living together without marriage." Journal of Sex Research 9:97–106.

Bower, Donald W., and Victor A. Christopherson. 1977. "University student cohabitation: A regional comparison of selected attitudes and behaviors." Journal of Marriage and the Family 39:447–452.

Bumpass, Larry, and James A. Sweet. 1972. "Differentials in marital instability, 1970." American Sociological Review 37:754–766.

Carmichael, Gordon A. 1984. "Living together in New Zealand: Data on coresidence at marriage and on de facto unions." New Zealand Population Review 10 (October):41–53.

Clayton, Richard R., and Harwin L. Voss. 1977. "Shacking up: Cohabitation in the 1970s." Journal of Marriage and the Family 39:273–283.

Cole, Charles Lee. 1977. "Cohabitation in social context." Pp. 61–79 in Roger W. Libby and Robert N. Whitehurst (eds.), Marriage and Alternatives: Exploring Intimate Relationships. Glenview, IL: Scott, Foresman.

Danziger, Carl. 1978. Unmarried Heterosexual Cohabitation. San Francisco: R and E Research Associates.

Dean, Gillian, and Douglas T. Gurak. 1978. "Marital homogamy the second time around." Journal of Marriage and the Family 43:559–570.

Glick, Paul C. 1984. "American household structure in transition." Family Planning Perspectives 16:205–211.

Glick, Paul C., and Arthur J. Norton. 1979. "Marrying, divorcing, and living together in the U.S. today." Population Bulletin 32 (February):1–40.

Glick, Paul C., and Graham B. Spanier. 1980. "Married and unmarried cohabitation in the United States." Journal of Marriage and the Family 42:19–30.

Hanna, Sharon L., and Patricia Kaine Knaub. 1981. "Cohabitation before remarriage: Its relationship to family strengths." Alternative Lifestyles 4:507–522.

Henze, Laura F., and John W. Hudson. 1974. "Personal and family characteristics of cohabiting and noncohabiting college students." Journal of Marriage and the Family 36:722–727.

Jacques, Jeffrey M., and Karen J. Chason. 1979. "Cohabitation: Its impact on marital success." Family Coordinator 28:35–39.

Lyness, Judith F. 1978. "Happily ever after? Following-up living-together couples." Alternative Lifestyles 1:55–70.

Lyness, Judith F., Milton E. Lipetz, and Keith E. Davis, 1972. "Living together: An alternative to marriage." Journal of Marriage and the Family 34:305–311.

Macklin, Eleanor D. 1972. "Heterosexual cohabitation among unmarried college students." Family Coordinator 21:463–472.

_____. 1978. "Nonmarital heterosexual cohabitation: A review of recent literature." Marriage and Family Review 1:1–12.

_____. 1983. "Nonmarital heterosexual cohabitation: An overview." Pp. 49–74 in Eleanor D. Macklin and Roger H. Rubin (eds.), Contemporary Families and Alternative Lifestyles: Handbook on Research and Theory. Beverly Hills, CA: Sage Publications.

Newcomb, Michael D., and Peter M. Bentler. 1980. "Cohabitation before marriage: A comparison of married couples who did and did not cohabit." Alternative Lifestyles 3:65–85.

Newcomb, Paul R. 1979. "Cohabitation in America: An assessment of consequences." Journal of Marriage and the Family 41:597–605.

Peterman, Dan J., Carl A. Ridley, and Scott M. Anderson. 1974. "A comparison of cohabiting and noncohabiting college students." Journal of Marriage and the Family 36:344–354.

Population Reference Bureau, Demographic Information Services Center. 1981. Population Profile of Oregon. Washington, DC: PRB.

Rank, Mark R. 1981. "The transition to marriage: A comparison of cohabiting and dating relationships ending in marriage or divorce." Alternative Lifestyles 4:487–506.

Reiss, Ira L. 1980. Family Systems in America (3rd ed.). New York: Holt, Rinehart and Winston.

Risman, Barbara J., Charles T. Hill, Zick Rubin, and Letitia Anne Peplau. 1981. "Living together in college: Implications for courtship." Journal of Marriage and the Family 43:77–83.

Spanier, Graham B. 1982. "Living together in the eighties." American Demographics 4 (November):17–19, 42.

_____. 1983. "Married and unmarried cohabitation in the United States, 1980." Journal of Marriage and the Family 45:277–288.

Sweet, James A. 1979. "Estimates of levels, trends, and characteristics of the 'living together' population from the Current Population Survey." Working Paper 79–49, Center for Demography and Ecology, University of Wisconsin-Madison.

Udry, J. Richard. 1974. The Social Context of Marriage (2nd ed.). Philadelphia: J. B. Lippincott.

U.S. Bureau of the Census. 1983a. Households, Families, Marital Status, and Living Arrangements: March 1983 (advance report). Current Population Reports, Series P-20, No. 382. Washington, DC: Government Printing Office.

_____. 1983b. U.S. Census of the Population, 1980. Characteristics of the Population: General Social and Economic Characteristics, U.S. Summary, PC80-1-C1. Washington, DC: Government Printing Office.

_____. 1983c. U.S. Census of the Population, 1980. Characteristics of the Population: General Social and Economic Characteristics. Oregon, PC80-1-C39. Washington, DC: Government Printing Office.

4

Love, Marriage, and Intimate Relationships

Do you love me? I'm your wife. *But do you love me?* Do I love him? For twenty-five years I've lived with him, fought with him, starved with him. Twenty-five years my bed was his: If that's not love what is? *Then you love me?* I suppose I do. *And I suppose I love you too.*   [*Tevye and Golde in* Fiddler on the Roof]

Family sociologists have focused much of their attention on the study of husband/wife relationships. In fact, historian Christopher Lasch (1978:39) claims that the sociology of the family, for many years, was little more than the sociology of marriage. This imbalance has been at least partially corrected since the 1960s. However, the interaction of husbands and wives continues to be the subject of extensive research, and its study covers a vast array of topics. In recent years, attention has expanded to include the study of less traditional relationships, such as those between cohabiting heterosexual couples and gay and lesbian couples. In this chapter we consider some findings of the rich tradition of sociological research on marriage and other intimate relationships.

It is important to begin our consideration, however, with a brief examination of some statistics on the timing and prevalence of marriage in the United States. Contrary to popular belief, teenage brides and grooms were a rarity in the American past. As we have already discovered, men and women in colonial America usually married in their mid- and late twenties, waiting until they were economically independent and able to set up their own households. This pattern continued in the nineteenth century. In 1890, American men married at an average age of twenty-six and women at an age of twenty-two, average ages only slightly lower than those in colonial New England over two hundred years earlier. Not only did young men and women delay marriage in previous centuries, but a greater percentage of the population never married at all. As a result, "maiden aunts" and "bachelor uncles" were a more common part of American families than they are today.

In the twentieth century, the average age at marriage declined, reaching a low of twenty-two for men and twenty for women in the 1950s. As the average age at marriage declined, so too did the proportion never marrying. Only 5 percent of women born between 1930 and 1934 had not married by age fifty. Seventy-five percent of all women born between 1940 and 1944 had married by age twenty-three, and 95 percent of this birth cohort will almost certainly have married by age fifty.

Since the 1960s the average age at marriage has inched upward. In 1970, men married at an average age of 22.5 and women at 20.6. In 1983 the average age at marriage for men was 24.4 and for women, 22.5. A larger proportion of men and women are also remaining unmarried in their mid- and late twenties than was the case in the recent past. In 1985, 26 percent of women and 38 percent of men between the ages of twenty-five and twenty-nine had never married. It is not yet clear whether increasing numbers of young men and women born in the 1960s are simply delaying marriage or are forgoing marriage altogether. However, it is unlikely that in the near future the proportion never marrying will rise much above the 10 percent level recorded at the turn of the century. Therefore, despite current trends, Americans continue to marry earlier and a greater percentage eventually marry than in previous centuries.

From Institution to Companionship

In a 1945 textbook, Ernest Burgess and his colleague Harvey Locke suggested that the family was in the process of evolving from an institutional to a companionate form. According to Burgess and Locke, this evolution was dramatically altering the relationships between family members and, consequently, changing the basis of family solidarity. As they stated in a later edition of their textbook, the institutional family was held together by "traditional rules and regulations, specified rights and duties, and other social pressures impinging on family members" (Burgess, Locke, and Thomas, 1971:8). The rights and duties of family members centered around the family's economic function: Each individual had a prescribed role and made tangible contributions to the family. Burgess and Locke did not claim that affection and rapport were absent in the institutional family, but they did suggest that the emotional quality of marriage was subordinate to familistic objectives. Like Tevye and Golde in *Fiddler on the Roof,* husbands and wives in the past may not have given their love for one another much thought. And while Tevye and Golde did conclude that they indeed loved one another, the continuation of their marriage did not depend on a positive response from Golde to Tevye's persistent questioning. It depended instead on the degree to which each had fulfilled their traditional rights and obligations to one another.

In the emerging companionate family, Burgess and Locke (1945:28) argued, interpersonal bonds of affection were released from subordination to familistic objectives and, along with congeniality and common interest, became the primary basis of family unity. Burgess and Locke also believed that the transition from institution to companionship meant the demise of the hierarchical and patriarchal family and the emergence of the democratic family. They argued that industrialization and urbanization undermined the basis of patriarchal authority because men no longer owned and controlled productive property. As a result, the companionate family was "based on equality of husbands and wives, with consensus in decision making and increasing participation of children as they grew older" (p. 28).

Burgess and Locke wrote at a time of great concern about the future of the family. Divorce rates had been rising for several decades, birth rates had been declining, and many Americans were concerned about the apparent decline of parental authority. Burgess and Locke's ideas provided a basis of optimism about the family's future. Although the family would eventually become an affectional group united by interpersonal relationships, the process of adaptation to new social conditions would take time. As Burgess stated, "much of what is termed the instability of the family arises from the shift to a democratic companionship family from the old rural family of this country and the transplanted old-world family forms of immigrant groups" (1957:484). For Burgess and Locke a new, stronger, and more personally satisfying family life, a "unity of interacting personalities" as they called it, was evolving.

From the perspective of the 1980s, the prediction of the emergence of a strengthened family reconstituted around the emotional bonds between family members does not appear to have been fulfilled. However, Burgess and Locke's belief that expectations of marriage were developing that contrasted sharply with those of previous eras has been amply demonstrated by historical research. Analyses of popular literature, correspondence between husbands and wives, and divorce records from the late nineteenth and early twentieth centuries show an emerging emphasis on the qualitative aspects of marriage and the increasing importance individuals placed on companionship in marriage (Degler, 1980; Griswold, 1982; May, 1980). Changing expectations were reflected in legal changes as well. Divorce laws gradually became more liberal in the decades following the Civil War, making it less difficult for couples to divorce if the quality of their interpersonal relationship was unsatisfying. The Married Women's Property Acts, passed in all states in the mid-nineteenth century, gave married women increased control over their property and earnings and reflected a move, however small, toward the legal equality of husbands and wives.

Burgess and Locke's characterization of the family as a unity of interacting personalities began a long tradition of research on husband/wife relationships. Sociologists of the family initially focused their attention on the definition, measurement, and prediction of "marital adjustment" (Lasch, 1978:42). If the companionate marriage depended on the quality of the interpersonal relationships between husbands and wives, then the characteristics of "successful" marriages and the correlates of marital success needed to be identified. Burgess, Locke, and Mary Thomas (1963:294) defined the adjusted and "successful" marriage in the following way:

A well-adjusted marriage may be defined as a union in which the husband and wife are in agreement on the chief issues of marriage, such as the handling of finances and dealing with in-laws; in which they have come to an adjustment on interests, objectives, and values; in which they are in harmony on demonstrations of affection and sharing confidences; and in which they have few or no complaints about their marriage.

Locke (1951:48–52) developed an early and widely used measure of marital adjustment. The scale asked individuals to rate their overall marital happiness, their satisfaction with their marital partner, and the extent to which they agreed with their spouses about specific issues and activities related to their marriage. The scale also asked individuals to report the extent to which they confided in their mates and the extent to which they shared outside activities and interests with one another. The greater the happiness, togetherness, agreement, and communication an individual reported, the higher his or her marital-adjustment score and the more successful the marriage was judged to be.

Sociologists using the Locke scale of marital adjustment, or similar measures, sought to discover the demographic, personality, or social factors associated with high marital-adjustment scores (Spanier and Lewis, 1980). By identifying these factors, researchers believed that they could establish the bases for successful marriages and perhaps even hasten the evolution of marriage to the companionate form. They found that individuals from untroubled backgrounds who marry individuals like themselves tend to score higher on marital-adjustment scales than do those with troubled backgrounds who marry individuals unlike themselves. In addition, longer engagements, older ages at marriage, and higher levels of education are associated with higher adjustment scores. Unfortunately, these results are not particularly astounding, nor are these factors very strongly associated with marital adjustment.

Although attempts to locate variables predictive of marital adjustment have not been very successful, studies have consistently shown that marital adjustment is related to length of marriage. In general, couples start out with high scores only to become less adjusted in the middle years of marriage. Various explanations have been offered for this seemingly inevitable decline in marital adjustment over time. Pineo (1961), for example, hypothesized that individuals become "disenchanted" with one another over time, not because they idealized their partners prior to marriage but because inevitable personal changes and alterations in external circumstances make it likely that the initial "good fit" between partners will worsen over time. Others, who take into account that marital adjustment tends to rise again in the later years of marriage, suggest that the growing responsibilities in the middle years of marriage (child care, housework, financial obligations) decrease companionship and increase the opportunities for disagreement. This interpretation is supported by the rather dramatic drop in marital adjustment that occurs with the birth of the first child. Deutscher (1967) explains the increase in marital happiness in the later years of marriage as the result of the freedom experienced by couples who have fewer responsibilities than in the middle years and time for one another again.

Clearly, many factors are required to explain the tendency for marital adjustment to decline after the initial years of marriage only to rebound in couples' later years together. However, the decline in marital adjustment in the middle years of marriage presents an additional problem. If marital adjustment declines over time and if marital adjustment is equated with marital success, then one is faced with the uncomfortable implication that enduring marriages in which partners are adequately fulfilling their responsibilities are not successful. As a result, many have called into question the concept of marital adjustment itself, arguing that it presents an unrealistic and value-laden picture of successful marriages. Marital-adjustment scales judge marriage against a standard of total companionship and openness, absence of conflict, and consistent and complete expressions of marital happiness and satisfaction with one's partner. As Arlene Skolnick (1987:282) suggests, the concept of marital adjustment is based on a utopian model of marriage that few couples can expect to approximate. In addition, the concept classifies marriages in which husbands and wives do not share interests or engage in outside activities together as unadjusted even if the partners are quite satisfied with their marriages.

One result of the criticism of the concept of marital adjustment was the realization that there may indeed be many types of "successful" marriages, and thus several researchers have attempted to develop typologies of enduring marriages. For example, John Cuber and Peggy Harroff (1965) described five types of marriages based on interviews with over 200 men and women who had been married at least ten years and who had never considered divorce. In "conflict-habituated" marriages, tension and conflict are the dominant and cohesive forces. "Devitalized" marriages initially approximate the marital-adjustment model, but the partners soon find less satisfaction in their activities with one another and go their separate ways. Although nostalgia and disappointment are sometimes expressed by individuals in devitalized marriages, many simply feel they have made a realistic adjustment to married life. In "passive-congenial" relationships, individuals start their marriages with low expectations of sharing and companionship; each partner wishes to pursue his or her own interests and goals. The marriage is simply a matter of convenience and is felt by the partners to be necessary for comfortable living. The "vital" and "total" relationships are similar to the adjustment model, total marriages being more multifaceted and having more numerous "points of vital meshing" than vital marriages. Cuber and Harroff were careful to point out that the five types do not represent degrees but kinds of marital happiness and adjustment. In this way, they attempted to avoid the value judgments that plagued previous conceptions of marital adjustment. They judged enduring marriages that partners considered to be satisfactory as successful regardless of the characteristics of the relationships.

Other sociologists have been less willing to abandon the concept of marital adjustment as a fixed standard against which marriages can be judged. However, the concept of marital quality has been substituted for marital adjustment, and the more value-laden aspects of marital-adjustment scales have been discarded. For instance, Spanier (1976:127–28) defines marital quality as "a process, the outcome of which is determined by the degree of (1) troublesome marital differences; (2) interspousal tension and anxiety; (3) marital satisfaction; (4) dyadic cohesion; and (5) consensus on matters of importance to marital functioning." Thus, the emphasis on total companionship and harmony has been replaced by an emphasis on aspects of marriage that reflect the ability to function as a couple without debilitating differences or unhappiness. In short, Spanier has attempted to develop a realistic measure of marital quality. Like previous researchers, Spanier and his colleagues have attempted to discover factors associated with marital quality, and they have developed a sophisticated multidimensional predictive model for it.

It is likely that sociologists of the family will continue to investigate marital quality. As Spanier and Lewis (1980:825) pointed out, marital quality may be the most frequently studied topic in the field. The concept is also unlikely to remain a static one as relationships between men and women continue to change.

Marital Power and Decision Making

Another subject of research growing out of Burgess and Locke's ideas about the companionate family is the relative power of husbands and wives and resulting patterns of decision making in marriage. Power is the ability to influence the behavior of others. Authority is legitimate power—that is, power supported by beliefs about who should rightfully hold it. In the family, power and authority are reflected in the ability to make decisions that affect other family members. As we have seen, Burgess believed that the companionate family was egalitarian, industrialization having removed the basis of patriarchal authority from the family. Indeed, the Locke marital-adjustment measure gives a higher score to marriages in which partners report shared decision making.

Robert Blood and Donald Wolfe (1960) made one of the first and most influential attempts to systematically study marital decision making. Their method of studying decision making and the conclusions they drew from their research generated much controversy and substantial theoretical and empirical work on family power. Like Burgess, Blood and Wolfe believed that the material basis of male power in the family was disappearing. Although they thought vestiges of patriarchal authority may have survived in various corners of American society (for example, in rural areas and among older couples), they believed the emerging and dominant pattern to be egalitarian decision making.

Blood and Wolfe developed a method of study that served as a model for much subsequent research. Recognizing that an assessment of the relative power of husbands and wives could not include all decisions ever made in a marriage, they selected eight decisions that were relatively important and that were faced by nearly all couples at one time or another. The eight decisions were:

1. What job the husband should take.
2. What car to get.
3. Whether to buy life insurance.

4. Where to go on vacation.
5. What house or apartment to take.
6. Whether a wife should go to work or quit work.
7. What doctor to have when someone is sick.
8. How much money the family can afford to spend per week on food.

Blood and Wolfe interviewed 738 wives from metropolitan Detroit and 178 wives from the surrounding rural area. They asked the wives to report who usually made the final decisions in each of the eight decision areas: "husband always," "husband more than wife," "husband and wife exactly the same," "wife more than husband," or "wife always." On the basis of the wives' responses, Blood and Wolfe divided the marriages into four types. In husband-dominated marriages, the majority of the eight decisions were made by husbands, and in wife-dominated marriages the reverse was true. In shared-authority marriages, husbands and wives made decisions together, and in divided-authority marriages husbands made decisions in some areas and their wives, in others. They classified 25 percent of the marriages as husband dominated and 3 percent as wife dominated. Thirty-one percent of the marriages exhibited a shared-authority pattern, and 41 percent a divided-authority pattern. Contrary to their expectations, they found that husband-dominated marriages were not concentrated in particular subgroups. Because almost three-quarters of the wives in their sample reported making decisions together or dividing power somewhat equally with their husbands, Blood and Wolfe concluded that American marriages had become primarily egalitarian and that the patriarchal family was dead.

To explain their findings, Blood and Wolfe suggested that the relative power of husbands and wives was based on the personal resources that were brought to marriages. They defined a resource as anything an individual could make available that would satisfy the needs of his or her partner—for example, money and interpersonal competence. They suggested that "insofar as partners can contribute to each other's satisfaction in life, they will build up a mutual respect that expresses itself naturally in mutual consultation" (p. 12). However, as partners contribute more than their share, they acquire the basis for having more than a fifty-fifty say in decisions. Blood and Wolfe maintained that because of changes in the family, the power to make decisions was now a matter of personal resources and husbands and wives were on an equal footing in bringing these resources to marriage. Just as Burgess believed that the family had become a unity of interacting personalities, Blood and Wolfe claimed that the balance of power in marriage had become an interpersonal affair. Summing up their resource theory of marital power, they stated:

> Under former historical circumstances, the husband's economic and social role automatically gave him pre-eminence. Under modern conditions, the roles of men and women have changed so much that husbands and wives are potential equals—with the balance of power tipped sometimes one way and sometimes another. It is no longer possible to assume that just because a man is a man, he is the boss. Once upon a time

the function of culture was to rationalize the predominance of the male sex. Today the function of culture is to develop a philosophy of equal rights under which, as the saying goes, "May the best man win!"—and the best man is sometimes a woman [pp. 29–30].

Blood and Wolfe's study has been criticized on both methodological and theoretical grounds. Constantina Safilios-Rothschild (1969) suggested that although Blood and Wolfe gave equal weight to the eight decisions in assessing marital power, these decisions are actually of varying importance and are made with varying frequency. For example, decisions about what house or apartment to take have a greater impact than decisions about where to go on vacation, and decisions about food expenditures are made more frequently than decisions about what doctor to visit. In addition, Safilios-Rothschild (1970:542) took Blood and Wolfe to task for relying only on the responses of wives. Subsequent studies have shown that wives tend to attribute more power to themselves than do their husbands and that husbands perceive their marriages as more egalitarian than do their wives. Finally, Safilios-Rothschild (1976:359) stressed the importance of the distinction between "orchestration" power and "implementation" power. Partners with orchestration power are able to delegate less important and time-consuming decisions to their spouses, who then implement this higher-level decision. This behind-the-scenes process is ignored by Blood and Wolfe's method of studying marital power.

At the theoretical level, Dair Gillespie (1971) maintained that Blood and Wolfe's personal-resource theory of marital power is inaccurate and is not even supported by their own data. She pointed out that when the eight decisions are examined individually, the findings show that husbands made the most important of the eight decisions and dominated in more decision-making areas. Husbands were more likely to prevail than wives in decisions about the husband's job, what car to buy, whether to buy life insurance, and where to go on vacation. Wives were more likely to prevail in decisions about their own employment and about food expenditures. The other decisions were likely to be shared equally.

To explain why the balance of power tips more often in favor of husbands, Gillespie offered an alternative approach to marital power. According to Gillespie, Blood and Wolfe erred in assuming that the basis of male power in the family eroded as industrialization shifted production out of the home and in concluding that the distribution of power in marriages was now simply an interpersonal affair. Instead, she maintained, structural factors continue to operate to make it likely that husbands have more power than their wives. To support her contention, Gillespie again drew on Blood and Wolfe's results: They found that the higher a husband's occupational prestige, the greater his income, and the higher his social status (based on education, income, occupation, and ethnic background), the greater was his power.

For Gillespie, these findings suggested that the tendency of men to predominate in marriage was based on their connection with and success in the economic-opportunity structure. Although lower-status husbands had less power than their higher-status counterparts, both derived their power from resources obtained in the occupational world. When wives did work outside the home, which was much less common at that time than it is today, Blood and Wolfe found that the relative power of husbands declined. Because men are more likely to be in the paid labor force than their wives and to have higher-status occupations than those women who do enter the labor force, Gillespie concluded that the distribution of resources was not random but was structurally predetermined in favor of men. Although Gillespie discussed other structural sources of male power (for example, socialization and the laws governing marriage), she concluded that the distribution of power in marriage would be unequal until women gained equal access to the economic-opportunity structure.

Safilios-Rothschild (1976) also contributed to the critique of resource theory and attempted to resolve some of its theoretical problems in her own research on marital power. She maintained that resource theory does not take into account the "costs" involved in receiving resources or in the withdrawal of resources. The cost of a resource is determined by the degree to which an individual has direct access to the resource or can receive it from another source. For example, if a husband contributes the financial resources to the family and his wife cannot make the same amount herself or find another husband who will provide the same income, the husband will be able to exercise greater power because the cost to the wife of the withdrawal of his income would be very high. Safilios-Rothschild also faulted Blood and Wolfe's version of resource theory for its failure to take into account resources such as love, sex, and physical attractiveness. For example, a wife with no economic resources may be so attractive that her husband could not find an equally beautiful woman willing to marry him. This woman may be able to compensate for the structural basis of inequality described by Gillespie. As Safilios-Rothschild (p. 356) noted:

> Because of the existing sex stratification system and the unequal status of men and women in practically all societies, unequal exchange models have been the rule in marital exchanges. Sex or services have been exchanged for money or status; love and/or sex have been exchanged for services; love has been exchanged for power and money; and status for other resources.

In her study in Athens, Greece, Safilios-Rothschild interviewed both husbands and wives about decisions of varying frequency and importance. Her data showed that husbands in general had more power to make important and infrequent decisions (orchestration power). However, when wives worked outside the home, their power increased. To investigate the relative "cost" to each spouse of the contribution and withdrawal of resources and to explore the importance of nonsocioeconomic resources, Safilios-Rothschild also classified couples according to which spouse was more in love with the other. She found that in cases where women perceived their husbands to be "more in love," women were more likely to claim the power to make important and infrequent decisions than when they were "more in love" than their husbands. Therefore, in the context of pervasive and structurally supported husband dominance in marriages, women are able to exchange love for power, particularly when they love their husbands less than their husbands love them. Like Gillespie, Safilios-

Rothschild concluded that only when women gain direct access to socioeconomic resources on a par with men will power in marriages be more equally distributed than it is at present. At that time, marital power may become the interpersonal affair that Blood and Wolfe claimed it to be in 1960.

Readings

The selections that follow are important contributions to the study of the quality of relationships between couples. Although the focus of the selections is primarily on marriage, the findings presented have implications for less traditional relationships as well. The first selection, "Marriage," is taken from the landmark work of Robert and Helen Lynd, *Middletown: A Study in Contemporary American Culture*. First published in 1929, *Middletown* looks at the "interwoven trends that are the life of a small American city" (p. 3). In the 1920s, Middletown (actually Muncie, Indiana) was a city of approximately 30,000 with a varied industrial base and a fairly rapid rate of growth. The Lynds thought Muncie had many features common to a wide group of communities and was therefore a good laboratory in which to observe the dynamics of American culture. In Muncie, the Lynds investigated attitudes and behavior in six main areas: work, family, education, religion, leisure, and community activities. The result is a rich description of life in a single American community in the first part of the twentieth century.

The Lynds were contemporaries of Ernest Burgess and Harvey Locke, and their work contains many similar ideas. Like Burgess and Locke, the Lynds believed that expectations of marriage were changing, with an increased emphasis being placed on the qualitative aspects of the relationship. Like Burgess and Locke, the Lynds believed that the process of change from the institutional family to the companionate family was a difficult one. They also thought that the rising rate of divorce in the 1920s was in part the result of changing expectations of marriage, and they too were hopeful that couples would make increasingly successful adjustments to marriage as these expectations became widely shared.

On the basis of the Lynds' discussion of companionship between husbands and wives in Middletown, it is not difficult to understand why sociologists who shared Burgess's view of adjusted marriages were concerned about the state of marriage. These couples would have scored low on Locke's marital-adjustment measure, and the Lynds' research probably did much to stimulate interest in the study of marital quality. Today, their findings also provide a good source of comparison for studies of contemporary marriage.

The Lynds also discovered important differences between marriages in the business and working classes in Middletown, and they were the forerunners in a long tradition of research on class differences in husband/wife relationships. Lillian Rubin's *Worlds of Pain,* the source of the second selection in this chapter, is a more recent and an important contribution to this tradition. Rubin interviewed fifty working–class husbands and wives about their upbringings, their courtships and marriages, their leisure activities, and their attitudes toward work. As a basis of comparison, Rubin also interviewed twenty-five middle-class couples.

The working-class couples Rubin interviewed had married relatively young, women at an average age of eighteen and men at twenty. Likewise, they began their families early. In fact, many of the women were pregnant when they married. For most of the couples, the early years were difficult, and the reality of marriage stood in sharp contrast to their expectations. Particularly difficult were the financial problems created by low-paying and unstable employment. In this selection, "Marriage: The Dream and the Reality," Rubin follows the couples into the middle years of marriage, and she identifies several distinctive features of working-class marriages and their material bases. For example, she explores why working-class women have different expectations of marriage than middle-class women do and why working-class husbands are willing to turn over the handling of family finances to their wives.

Rubin's work helps explain an interesting puzzle evident in studies of marital power. As we have seen, studies show that working-class husbands have less power than their middle-class counterparts. Gillespie and Saffilios-Rothschild attribute this difference to the greater economic resources controlled by middle-class husbands. However, working-class husbands tend to be less egalitarian and more overtly authoritarian in their views of marriage than middle-class husbands. Rubin's study helps explain this apparent paradox.

Both the Lynds and Rubin discovered differences in the expectations of men and women for the behavior of their partners. For example, the Lynds found that some wives expected greater sharing in the handling of family finances than their husbands granted and some hoped for a greater "community of interest" with their husbands. Rubin found disagreements between husbands and wives about the division of labor in the household and also indications that some wives were discontent with the emotional aspects of their marriages. Many other studies amply confirm that discrepancies in the expectations of husbands and wives are persistent features of contemporary marriages (Blumstein and Schwartz, 1983; Rubin, 1983). As Jesse Bernard (1972) concluded, every marriage actually contains two marriages, his and hers.

The third selection, "The Feminization of Love" by Francesca Cancian, examines one source of the discrepancies in the expectations of husbands and wives. Cancian suggests that men and women have different styles of love and therefore have different perceptions of how their partners should express love. She believes that these differences arise out of the division of gender roles in our society, and she suggests that many problems are caused by these differences in love styles. This thought-provoking essay also has important implications for studies of marital quality because it suggests that men and women may have different perceptions of the components of a successful marriage.

In the next selection, "Role Making among Married Mexican American Women: Issues of Class and Ethnicity," Norma Williams examines changing marital roles among the second largest ethnic minority in the United States. Black Americans are the largest ethnic minority, numbering over twenty-eight million in 1985. However, in the same year, nearly seventeen million people of Hispanic descent resided in this country (U.S. Bureau of the Census, 1986). Although the Hispanic population shares a common language, it includes groups that trace their origins to Puerto Rico, Cuba, Mexico, and other Latin American countries. These groups have different cultural traditions and occupy different positions in American society. Mexican Americans are the largest of these Hispanic groups. In 1985, the U.S. Bureau of the Census placed the number of people of Mexican descent at slightly over ten million, almost certainly an underestimate because of the number of illegal immigrants from Mexico in the United States.

Much writing on marriage among Mexican Americans has emphasized the passivity of women and the dominance of men. However, as Williams points out, this characterization is in need of modification. It is true that Mexican American women have traditionally drawn their social and personal identities from their roles as wives and mothers and that male dominance is an important feature of traditional Mexican American culture. Nevertheless, in the sphere of home and family women often exercise considerable autonomy (Becerra, 1988). Therefore, the subordination of Mexican American women has involved their relegation to family roles rather than their powerlessness within the family. Williams examines the ways in which Mexican American women are attempting to remake their marital roles to allow the development of identities apart from the family. She discovers that important class differences exist in this role-making process and that Mexican American women encounter special problems in their role-making efforts because of their ethnicity.

In "The Balance of Power in Lesbian Relationships," Mayta Caldwell and Letitia Peplau turn attention to the dynamics of relationships between same-sex couples. Statistics do not exist on the number of gay and lesbian couples who live together in ongoing relationships. However, over one-third of American households include unrelated adults, and some proportion of these households consist of homosexual couples. Other homosexuals maintain long-lasting relationships without living together. These same-sex couples provide "naturally occurring experiments" that allow investigation of relationships in which gender differences are absent (Blumstein and Schwartz, 1983:14). Lesbian couples are particularly interesting because some have argued that relationships between women are more likely to be egalitarian than are relationships between males and females or between two males. According to this line of reasoning, women in intimate relationships with other women are sensitive to issues of dominance and are likely to have rejected traditional sex roles.

Caldwell and Peplau seek to discover the extent of power differences among lesbian couples and investigate the factors associated with equality and inequality in these relationships. Briefly, they discover that many of the same factors that influence the balance of power in heterosexual relationships operate in lesbian relationships. However, women in lesbian relationships are likely to value egalitarian relationships and to express dissatisfaction with imbalances of power.

In the final selection, "The Decision to Leave an Abusive Relationship: Economic Dependence and Psychological Commitment," Michael Strube and Linda Barbour address the tragic problem of wife abuse. Although evidence now shows that wife battering has a long history, it was not considered a serious social problem until the late 1960s (Glenn, 1987:363). Since that time, efforts have been made to protect women from physical violence through the establishment of shelters for battered women and changes in the law and police practice. However, few would argue that these efforts have been adequate to meet the needs of women who are victims of marital violence.

Sociological research on wife battering began in earnest in the 1970s, and it demonstrated both the prevalence of violence in the contemporary family and the widespread approval of the use of physical force against women by their husbands (e.g., Gelles, 1972, and Straus, 1978). In past times, men had the legal right to chastise their wives for "misbehavior," although various limits were placed on the exercise of violence. For example, eighteenth-century common law held that a man could beat his wife as long as he used a stick no bigger than his thumb. A state court in North Carolina upheld that law as recently as 1867 (Straus and Gelles, 1986:466). Apparently, current cultural attitudes continue to legitimate the control of women through violence.

Strube and Barbour examine the situation of women who are victims of domestic violence, specifically the conditions that prevent women from escaping relationships that hold the potential for serious injury. As these authors state, many battered women continue to live with their abusive husbands. Early research on this topic often blamed the battered women for failing to leave their husbands, locating the problem in some personal failing of the abused women. However, Strube and Barbour examine the structural and cultural factors that hold women in destructive relationships. Instead of "blaming the victim," Strube and Barbour locate the problem in the gender inequalities that perpetuate the dependency of women on men.

References

Becerra, Rosina M. 1988. "The Mexican American family." In *Ethnic Families in America,* 3d ed., edited by Charles H. Mindell, Robert W. Habenstein, and Rossevelt Wright, Jr., 141–59. New York: Elsevier.

Bernard, Jesse. 1972. *The Future of Marriage.* New York: Bantam.

Blood, Robert O., Jr., and Donald M. Wolfe. 1960. *Husbands and Wives: The Dynamics of Married Living.* New York: Free Press.

Blumstein, Phillip, and Pepper Schwartz. 1983. *American Couples.* New York: Morrow.

Burgess, Ernest W. 1957. "The Family in a Changing Society." In *Cities and Society,* edited by Paul K. Kett and Albert J. Reiss, Jr., 481–89. New York: Free Press.

Burgess, Ernest W., and Harvey J. Locke. 1945. *The Family: From Institution to Companionship.* New York: American Book.

Burgess, Ernest W., Harvey J. Locke, and Mary Margaret Thomas. 1963. *The Family: From Institution to Companionship.* 3d ed. New York: American Book.

———. 1971. *The Family: From Institution to Companionship.* 4th ed. New York: Van Nostrand Reinhold.

Cuber, John F., and Peggy B. Harroff. 1965. *Sex and the Significant Americans.* Baltimore: Penguin.

Degler, Carl N. 1980. *At Odds: Women and the Family in America from the Revolution to the Present.* New York: Oxford University Press.

Deutscher, Irwin. 1967. "The Quality of Postparental Life." In *Middle Age and Aging,* edited by B. L. Neugarten, 263–68. Chicago: University of Chicago Press.

Gelles, Richard J. 1972. *The Violent Home: A Study of Physical Aggression between Husbands and Wives.* Newbury Park, Calif.: Sage.

Gillespie, Dair. 1971. "Who Has the Power? The Marital Struggle." *Journal of Marriage and the Family* 33:445–58.

Glenn, Evelyn Nakano. 1987. "Gender and the Family." In *Analyzing Gender: A Handbook of Social Science Research,* edited by Beth B. Hess and Myra Marx Ferree, 348–80. Newbury Park, Calif.: Sage.

Griswold, Robert L. 1982. *Family and Divorce in California, 1850–1890: Victorian Illusions and Everyday Realities.* Albany: State University of New York Press.

Lasch, Christopher. 1978. *Haven in a Heartless World: The Family Besieged.* New York: Basic Books.

Locke, Harvey J. 1951. *Predicting Adjustment in Marriage: A Comparison of Divorced and Happily Married Groups.* New York: Holt, Rinehart & Winston.

May, Elaine Tyler. 1980. *Great Expectations: Marriage and Divorce in Post-Victorian America.* Chicago: University of Chicago Press.

Pineo, Peter C. 1961. "Disenchantment in the Later Years." *Marriage and Family Living* 4:825–39.

Rubin, Lillian. 1983. *Intimate Strangers: Men and Women Together.* New York: Harper & Row.

Safilios-Rothschild, Constantina. 1969. "Family Sociology or Wive's Family Sociology? A Cross-Cultural Examination of Decision Making." *Journal of Marriage and the Family* 31:290–301.

———. 1970. "The Study of Family Power: A Review 1960–1969." *Journal of Marriage and the Family* 32:539–52.

———. 1976. "A Macro- and Micro-Examination of Family Power: An Exchange Model." *Journal of Marriage and the Family* 38:355–62.

Skolnick, Arlene. 1987. *The Intimate Environment: Exploring Marriage and the Family.* 4th ed. Boston: Little, Brown.

Spanier, Graham B. 1976. "Toward Clarification and Investigation of Marital Adjustment." *International Journal of the Sociology of the Family* 6:121–46.

Spanier, Graham B., and Robert A. Lewis. 1980. "Marital Quality: A Review of the Seventies." *Journal of Marriage and the Family* 42:825–39.

Straus, Murray A. 1978. "Wife-Beating: How Common and Why?" *Victimology* 2:443–58.

Straus, Murray A., and Richard J. Gelles. 1986. "Societal Change and Change in Family Violence from 1975 to 1985 as Revealed by Two National Surveys. *Journal of Marriage and the Family* 48:465–479.

U.S. Bureau of the Census. 1986. *Statistical Abstract of the United States: 1987.* 107th ed. Washington, D.C.: U.S. Government Printing Office.

Marriage

Robert S. Lynd and Helen M. Lynd

In each of Middletown's homes lives a family, consisting usually of father, mother, and their unmarried children, with occasionally some other dependents. These family groups are becoming smaller. According to the Federal Census, which defines a family as one person living alone or any number of persons, whether related or not, who live together in one household, Middletown families shrank from an average of 4.6 persons in 1890 to 4.2 in 1900, to 3.9 in 1910, and 3.8 in 1920. Both the decrease in the number of children and the decline in the custom of having other dependents in the home are factors in this change.[1] The 40 business class families interviewed by the staff in 1924 averaged 4.7 persons and the 124 working class families 5.4, but only those families were interviewed which had one or more children of school age.

Within the walls of each house this small family group carries on the activities concerned with sex, child-rearing, food, clothing, sleep, and to some extent play and religion. These activities center about the institution of marriage.

The country over, a smaller percentage of the population is unmarried today than a generation ago, and while earlier figures by which the trend within Middletown can be observed are not available, in 1920 the city had a smaller proportion of both males and females single than had either state or nation [Table 1]. While only 22.8 percent of the population of the urban United States aged fifteen to twenty-four in 1920 were married, 31.4 percent of this group in Middletown were married. It would appear that more people are marrying young in Middletown today.[2] Explanation of this apparent drift toward more and earlier marriages may lie in part in such changes, noted elsewhere, as the cessation of apprenticeship, which gives a boy of eighteen a man's wages at a machine, the increased opportunities for wives to supplement the family income by working, the relatively greater ease and respectability of dissolving a marriage today, the diffusion of knowledge of means of contraception, and the growing tendency to engage in leisure-time pursuits by couples rather than in crowds, the unattached man or woman being more "out of it" in the highly organized paired social life of today than a generation ago when informal "dropping in" was the rule.

Marriage consists in a brief ceremonial exchange of verbal pledges by a man and woman before a duly sanctioned representative of the group. This ceremony, very largely religious in the nineties, is becoming increasingly secularized. In 1890, 85 percent of the local marriages were performed by a religious represen-

Table 1

	Percentage single males constitute of all males aged 15 and over		Percentage single females constitute of all females aged 15 and over	
	1890	1920	1890	1920
United States, all classes	41.7	35.1	31.8	27.3
United States, urban	Not available	35.5	Not available	29.0
State, all classes	38.9	30.9	29.6	23.9
State, urban	Not available	31.1	Not available	24.5
Middletown	Not available	28.5	Not available	20.8

tative and 13 percent by a secular agent, while in 1923 those performed by the religious leaders had fallen to 63 percent, and the secular group had risen to 34 percent of the total.[3] A prominent local minister accounted for the prevalence of divorces in Middletown in 1924 by the fact that "there are too many marriages in secular offices away from the sanctity of the churches." The marriage ceremony relaxes the prohibition upon the mutual approaches of the two persons to each other's persons and as regards the sexual approach makes "the wrongest thing in the world the rightest thing in the world."[4] The pair usually leave the homes of their parents at once and begin to make a home of their own; the woman drops the name of her father for the name of her husband.[5]

A heavy taboo, supported by law and by both religious and popular sanctions, rests upon sexual relationships between persons who are not married. There appears to be some tentative relaxing of this taboo among the younger generation, but in general it is as strong today as in the county-seat of forty years ago. There is some evidence that in the smaller community of the eighties, in which everybody knew everybody else, the group prohibition was outwardly more scrupulously observed than today. A man who was a young buck about town in the eighties says, "The fellows nowadays don't seem to mind being seen on the street with a fast woman, but you bet we did then!" That all was not serene underneath, particularly after the influx of population accompanying the gas boom, appears from various items in the local press in 1890: "In looking over the Board of Health statistics . . . I noticed in the birth records . . . that some of our prominent citizens are given the credit of being the father of offspring of which women of very loose character are the mothers." An editor "hopes that something can be done about the large number of 'street walkers' which are to be seen every evening." "This morning an officer requested the *Times* to state that he had of late seen a number of married men in company with disreputable characters and that after this date every one so detected will be arrested and exposed." By 1900 the rough-and-tumble industrial influx is reflected in the press in such headlines as "The Bowery Outdone in [Middletown]": "A traveling man who has visited both the universally notorious Bowery in New York City and the locally notorious High Street theater asserts that for downright lewdness and immorality the former is outdone by the latter." Editorials posed the question, "What does [Middletown] need?" and answered: "Mayors and police officers who will guard boys and girls from dens of evil like High Street theater." The city, according to a local historian, bore an "ill repute during its early career as a manufacturing city."

A former proprietor of one of the largest saloons in the city estimates the number of houses of prostitution about 1890 as twenty-five, and an old iron puddler estimates twenty, both agreeing on four to eight girls per house. In 1915 a state act was passed providing for injunction and abatement of houses of prostitution, thereby driving the institution underground.[6] Today conditions fluctuate in Middletown. Within ten years a group of public officials is reported to have conducted Middletown as a "wide-open town" in which city officials, later sent to the Federal penitentiary, were alleged to have a financial interest in "the red-light district." At the present time there are reported to be only two or three fly-by-night, furtively conducted houses of prostitution, catering exclusively to the working class, but a comparison with 1890 on this point is fruitless, because, as the judge of the juvenile court points out, "the automobile has become a house of prostitution on wheels."

The choice of a mate in marriage is nominally hedged about by certain restrictions—legal, religious, and customary. Legal stipulations, substantially the same as a generation ago, prohibit marriage between a white and a negro, by an insane person, an imbecile or epileptic, by a person having a transmissible disease, or, within certain limits, by a male who has within five years been a public charge, by a person whose former marriage has not been dissolved, by a person under the influence of liquor or narcotics, and by a man under eighteen and a woman under sixteen years. Other requirements implicitly recognized by law appear from the allowable grounds for dissolution of a marriage: sexual exclusiveness, living together in the same home, financial support of the wife by the husband, sufficient mutual consideration to exclude "cruel" treatment, sufficient "sobriety" and "morality" to avoid charges of "habitual drunkenness" and "criminal conviction." Religious requirements, today as in the nineties, vary somewhat from one religious group to another, but concern two main points: the nominal prohibition by Catholics of marriage "outside the Church" and a corresponding though weaker sentiment among Protestants against marriage to a Catholic; and, second, a varying but somewhat lessening emphasis upon the permanence of marriage whereby a few religious leaders refuse to remarry a divorced person. Some ministers would refuse to marry persons living in "open [sexual] sin," though the marriage ceremony is commonly regarded as the accepted means of regularizing such individuals.

Further informal demands, made by the fluid sentiments of the group, have apparently altered little since the nineties, although they have been given somewhat greater legal recognition.[7] Foremost among these is the demand for romantic love as the only valid basis for marriage. Theoretically, it is the mysterious attraction of two young people for each other and that alone that brings about a marriage, and actually most of Middletown stumbles upon its partners in marriage guided chiefly by "romance."[8] Middletown adults appear to regard romance in marriage as something which, like their religion, must be believed in to hold society together. Children are assured by their elders that "love" is an unanalyzable mystery that "just happens"— "You'll know when the right one comes along," they are told with a knowing smile. And so young Middletown grows up singing and hearing its fathers sing lustily in their civic clubs such songs as "It had to be you, It had to be you. . . . *For nobody else gave me a thrill. With all your faults I love you still.* It had to be you."

And yet, although theoretically this "thrill" is all-sufficient to insure permanent happiness, actually talks with mothers revealed constantly that, particularly among the business group, they were concerned with certain other factors; the exclusive emphasis upon romantic love makes way as adolescence recedes for a pragmatic calculus. Mothers of the business group give much consideration to encouraging in their children friendships with the "right" people of the other sex, membership in the "right" clubs, deftly warding off the attentions of boys whom they regard it as undesirable for their daughters to "see too much of," and in other ways interfering with and directing the course of true love.

Among the chief qualifications sought by these mothers, beyond the mutual attraction of the two young people for each other, are, in a potential husband, the ability to provide a good living, and, in a wife of the business class, the ability, not only to "make a home" for her husband and children, but to set them in a secure social position. In a world dominated by credit this social function of the wife becomes, among the business group, more subtle and important; the emphasis upon it shades down as we descend in the social scale until among the rank and file of the working class the traditional ability to be a good cook and housekeeper ranks first.

"Woman," as Dorothy Dix[9] says, "makes the family's social status. . . . The old idea used to be that the way for a woman to help her husband was by being thrifty and industrious, by . . . peeling the potatoes a little thinner, and . . . making over her old hats and frocks. . . . But the woman who makes of herself nothing but a domestic drudge . . . is not a help to her husband. She is a hindrance . . . and . . . a man's wife is the show window where he exhibits the measure of his achievement. . . . The biggest deals are put across over luncheon tables; . . . we meet at dinner the people who can push our fortunes. . . . The woman who cultivates a circle of worth-while people, who belongs to clubs, who makes herself interesting and agreeable . . . is a help to her husband. . . ."

Not unrelated to this social skill desired in a wife is the importance of good looks and dress for a woman. In one of Marion Harland's *Talks,* so popular in Middletown in the nineties, one reads, "Who would banish from our midst the matronly figures so suggestive of home, comfort, and motherly love?" Today one cannot pick up a magazine in Middletown without seeing in advertisements of everything from gluten bread to reducing tablets instructions for banishing the matronly figure and restoring "youthful beauty." "Beauty parlors" were unknown in the county-seat of the nineties; there are seven in Middletown today.

"Good looks are a girl's trump card," says Dorothy Dix, though she is quick to add that much can be done without natural beauty if you "dress well and thereby appear 50 percent better-looking than you are, . . . make yourself charming," and "cultivate bridge and dancing, the ability to play jazz and a few outdoor sports."

Emphasis upon the function of the man in marriage as "a good provider" and of the woman as home-maker, child-rearer, and, among the bulk of the business group, social pace-setter, is far-reaching as affecting the attitude of the sexes toward each other. In general, "brains" tend to be regarded as of small importance in a wife; as one of the city's most "two-fisted" young business men announced to the high school seniors at a Rotary high school "chapel:" "The thing girls get from high school is the ability to know how to choose a 'real one' from a 'near one.' When a girl gets around eighteen or so I begin to expect her to get married."

Middletown husbands, when talking frankly among themselves, are likely to speak of women as creatures purer and morally better than men but as relatively impractical, emotional, unstable, given to prejudice, easily hurt, and largely incapable of facing facts or doing hard thinking. "You simply cannot criticize or talk in general terms to a woman," emphatically agreed a group of the city's most thoughtful men. "There's something about the female mind that always short-circuits a general statement into a personal criticism." A school official, approached regarding the possibility of getting a woman on the school board, replied that "with only three people on the board there isn't much place for a woman." In a group of prominent Middletown men a suggested new form of social grouping came up in conversation and was promptly downed because "the women couldn't abide by it. Woman is the most unselfish creature on earth within her family, but with outsiders she is quick to imagine snubs to her family, bristle up, and become unsocial."

Middletown wives appear in part to accept the impression of them that many of their husbands have. "Men are God's trees; women are his flowers," and "True womanliness is the greatest charm of woman," the recent mottoes of two of the local federated women's clubs, suggest little change from the prevailing attitude reflected in a commencement essay in 1891, "Woman Is Most Perfect When Most Womanly."[10] At a local political dinner the talk about one of the tables turned to women's smoking and a woman politician said with an air of finality: "Women have to be morally better than men. It is they who pull men up or cause their downfall." Women, on the other hand, are frequently heard to express the opinion, accompanied by a knowing smile, that "Men are nothing but big little boys who have never grown up and must be treated as such."

In general, a high degree of companionship is not regarded as essential for marriage.[11] There appears to be between Middletown husbands and wives of all classes when gathered together in informal leisure-time groups relatively little spontaneous community of interest. The men and women frequently either gravitate apart into separate groups to talk men's talk and women's talk, or the men do most of the talking and the women largely listen. Even since women have been allowed to vote with men some tendency persists for women of all classes to depend in such practical matters upon the opinions of their husbands "coming in from the outside," as Dorothy Dix puts it, "with the breath of the fighting world about them."

Companionship between husband and wife in sheer play varies greatly in different families; among the business group who belong to the country club, e.g., husbands frequently play eighteen holes of "real golf" with a male "foursome" Sunday morning and possibly a concessionary "one round with the wife in the afternoon just to make her feel good." One wife who makes "a definite effort to do things" with her husband says that she has achieved this at the cost of cutting herself off from much of the routine social life of the community: "My husband, my children, and what community work I have time for after them are my job. I have gradually withdrawn from the social activities of the wives of my husband's business associates because most of these women seem absorbed in activities that do not include their husbands. That is just the sort of thing that leads to the break-up of families and I don't see why I and my family should be exempt from the things that befall other people."

One of the commonest joint pursuits of husbands and wives is playing cards with friends. A few read aloud together, but this is relatively rare, as literature and art have tended to disappear today as male interests. More usual is the situation described by one prominent woman: "My husband never reads anything but newspapers or the *American Magazine*. He is very busy all day and when he gets home at night he just settles down with the paper and his cigar and the radio and just rests." The automobile appears to be an important agency in bringing husbands and wives together in their leisure, counteracting in part the centrifugal tendency in the family observable in certain other aspects of Middletown's life.

Among the working class, leisure activities and other relations between married couples seem to swing about a somewhat shorter tether than do those of business folk. Not infrequently husband and wife meet each other at the end of a day's work too tired or inert to play or go anywhere together; many of them have few if any close friends. In families where there is some financial leeway there are plans for an addition to the house or perhaps the possibility of normal school for the children, which are spontaneous centers of interest and conversation between husband and wife; in the 60 out of 122 families reporting who had automobiles, these and the trips they make possible form a chief center of interest; in some cases there is talk of lodge affairs or the movies. But if, as in many families, the necessities of shelter and food overshadow other plans, such conversation as there is may be of a bickering sort, or may lapse into apathetic silence. In a number of cases, after the interviewer had succeeded in breaking through an apparently impenetrable wall of reserve or of embarrassed fear, the housewife would say at the close of the talk, "I wish you could come often. I never have any one to talk to," or "My husband never goes any place and never does anything but work. You can talk to him, but he never says anything. In the evenings he comes home and sits down and says nothing. I like to talk and be sociable, but I can hardly ever get anything out of him."[12]

This frequent lack of community of interests, together with the ideas each sex entertains regarding the other, appears in many families in a lack of frankness between husband and wife, far-reaching in its emotional outcome. "One thing I always tell my young men when they marry," said the only one of the six leading ministers who gives any instruction to people he marries, "is that they must get over any habit of thinking that they must be frank and tell everything they know to their wives." Dorothy Dix urges: " 'Let well enough alone' is a fine matrimonial slogan and as long as husband and wife are good actors it is the part of wisdom for their mates not to pry too deeply into the motives that inspire their conduct. . . . What we don't know doesn't hurt us in domestic life, and the wise do not try to find out too much." And again, "Nothing does more to preserve the illusions that a man and woman have about each other than the things they don't know."

Notes

1. Fewer "old-maid" sisters live with married relatives now when women commonly work outside the home for pay, move about town freely at night unescorted, and live in small flats of their own. Smaller houses without "spare" rooms are diminishing the custom, according to the head of the Social Service Bureau, of having elderly parents live in the homes of married children. This modern tendency towards the non-support of parents was openly recognized in 1920, when, among the recommendations made by the State Board of Charities and Correction to the Legislature, was one stating that "we believe that there should be legislation to prevent the abandonment of parents by children who are able to support them."

   The presence of outsiders as boarders at the family table is somewhat less sanctioned today, though roomers are still not uncommon; business class families who take in roomers are likely to do so to help pay children's expenses in college, and this explanation lessens any social stigma that may attach to this procedure.

2. While the single males in the United States declined between 1890 and 1920 from 41.7 to 35.1 percent of all males fifteen and over, and the percentage of single males aged thirty-five to forty-four showed an actual slight increase from 15.3 to 16.1, the single males aged fifteen to nineteen dropped from 99.5 to 97.7 of all males of this age and the twenty to twenty-four group from 80.7 to 70.7. In other words, the increase in marriage is occurring in the younger age groups. Likewise, throughout the state in which Middletown is situated the percentage of single men in the group aged thirty-five to forty-four increased from 11.5 percent to 13.6 between 1890 and 1920, while those aged fifteen to nineteen fell from 99.6 to 97.3 percent and those aged twenty to twenty-four from 80.6 to 66.5 percent. It is noteworthy that Middletown had, in 1920, 64.9 percent of its population fifteen years old and over married, while in all cities in the United States of 2,500 and over there were but 58.3 percent of this age group married. Neither race nor age or sex distribution of the population accounts for the difference between the age of marriage in Middletown and in the urban United States. Probably various cultural factors are responsible.

3. Two percent of the 1890 officiating persons and 3 percent of the 1923 group could not be identified. Figures here are for the entire county.

4. Advances prior to marriage are traditionally made entirely by the man, but, . . . , there is an increasing aggressiveness on the part of the girls in the activity preliminary to mating.

5. There is occasional talk in the community of a woman's "keeping her own name," but no woman in Middletown follows this practice, and it is sharply frowned upon by the group.

6. The description in the *Cleveland Hospital and Health Survey* of this new type of prostitution to some extent among girls nominally employed at other occupations probably applies in

a general way to Middletown; it concludes, "How far the activities of such amateur prostitutes make up for the reduction in the activities of the professionals no one knows. The doctors testify, however, that a large number of their men patients claim to have been infected by such amateurs." Part V, *Venereal Disease* (Cleveland: Cleveland Hospital Council, 1920), pp. 420–21.

7. Loss of affection after marriage was not legally recognized as sufficient reason for dissolving a marriage until recent years, but in 1924 divorces were granted to couples who came into court frankly saying, "We have no affection for each other and do not want to live together," and, "She says she does not love me and does not want to live with me."

8. [By an] equally casual method . . . Middletown youths stumble upon the kind of work by which they forever after earn their living. The casualness of procedure in both these cases is probably traceable in part to the same inherited conceptions regarding the individual's "freedom" and "rationality."

   The close identification of love with the religious life of the group has tended to import into courtship some of the same inscrutability that envelops the religious life of Middletown. By the same token the religious taboo upon "carnal love" has carried over into the situation so that, although sexual exclusiveness in marriage is demanded by both law and custom, virtually no direct consideration is given prior to marriage to the physical and sexual compatibility of the two contracting parties. . . .

9. References will be made to Dorothy Dix from time to time in the following discussion of what the group demands of marriage. Day after day two columns of syndicated advice to "Desolate," "A Much-disturbed Husband," "Young Wife," etc., appear in the leading Middletown paper from this elderly lady. This is perhaps the most potent single agency of diffusion from without shaping the habits of thought of Middletown in regard to marriage and possibly represents Middletown's views on marriage more completely than any other one available source. Of the 109 wives of working men interviewed giving information on this point, 51 said that they read Dorothy Dix regularly and 17 occasionally, while of 29 wives of the business class answering on this point 16 read this column regularly and 10 occasionally. Her advice is discussed by mothers and daughters as they sew together at Ladies' Aid meetings and many of them say that her column is the first and sometimes the only thing which they read every day in the paper. Her remarks were quoted with approval in a Sunday morning sermon by the man commonly regarded as the "most intellectual" minister in town.

10. The following is part of a tribute to woman read with general approval at the close of a meeting of another of the local women's federated clubs in 1924: "There is a being, the image and reflection of whom is ever present in the mirror of my soul. Her words are like enchanted echoes in a beautiful dell and her laughter like the sweetness of the bursting magnolia and her beauty like the smiling violet and the laughing morning glory. The sound of her footstep is like that of a messenger bearing gifts from a queen, and her touch like the gentle zephyrs fanning the tired brow of a weary traveler, and her presence like an altar of holiness and benediction. That spirit has taught me to revere heaven's divinest gift to the world—womanhood."

11. It may not be wholly fantastic to surmise that there may be some significance for the understanding of the basis of local marital association in the hierarchy of terms by which local women speak of their husbands. There is a definite ascent of man in his conjugal relations as one goes up in the social scale, from "my old man" through "the man," "he" (most frequent), "the mister," "John," "My husband," to "Mr. Jones." The first four are the common terms among the working class families and the last two among business class families.

12. This is the kind of maladjustment which may later figure in the divorce courts as "cold, grouchy, never says anything" or may lead to more violent reactions which figure as "cruel treatment."

Marriage: The Dream and the Reality—The Middle Years

Lillian Breslow Rubin

> I guess I can't complain. He's a steady worker; he doesn't drink; he doesn't hit me. That's a lot more than my mother had, and she didn't sit around complaining and feeling sorry for herself, so I sure haven't got the right.   [*Thirty-three-year-old housewife, mother of three, married thirteen years.*]

"He's a steady worker; he doesn't drink; he doesn't hit me"—these are the three attributes working-class women tick off most readily when asked what they value most in their husbands. Not a surprising response when one recalls their familiarity with unemployment, alcoholism, and violence, whether in their own families or in those around them.[1] That this response is class-related is evident from the fact that not one woman in the professional middle-class families mentioned any of these qualities when answering the same question. Although there was no response that was consistently heard from the middle-class wives, they tended to focus on such issues as intimacy, sharing, and communication and, while expressed in subtle ways, on the comforts, status, and prestige that their husbands' occupation affords. Janet Harris, writing about middle-class women at forty, also comments that she never heard a women list her husband's ability to provide or the fact that he is "good to the children" as valued primary traits. "The security and financial support that a husband provides are taken for granted," she argues; "it is the emotional sustainment which is the barometer of a marriage."[2]

Does this mean, then, that working-class women are unconcerned about the emotional side of the marriage relationship? Emphatically, it does not. It says first that when the material aspects of life are problematic, they become dominant as issues requiring solutions; and second that even when men are earning a reasonably good living, it is *never* "taken for granted" when financial insecurity and marginality are woven into the fabric of life. These crucial differences in the definition of a good life, a good husband, a good marriage—and the reasons for them—often are obscured in studies of marriage and the family because students of the subject rarely even mention class, let alone analyze class differences.[3]

Still, it is a mixed message that these working-class women send; for while many remind themselves regularly that they have no right to complain, their feelings of discontent with the emotional aspects of the marriage are not so easily denied. Indeed, once the immediate problems and preoccupations of the early

From Lillian Breslow Rubin, *Worlds of Pain: Life in the Working Class Family*, 93–113. Copyright© 1976 by Lillian B. Rubin. Reprinted by permission of Basic Books, Inc., Publishers.

years subside, once the young husband is "housebroken," an interesting switch occurs. Before the marriage and in the first years, it is the wife who seems more eager to be married; the husband, more reluctant. Marriage brings her more immediate gains since being unmarried is a highly stigmatized status for a woman, especially in the working-class world. Both husband and wife subscribe to the "I chased-her-until-she-caught-me" myth about courtship in America; both believe that somehow, using some mysterious feminine wiles, she contrived to ensnare him. It is no surprise, then, that it is he who has more trouble in settling down at the beginning—feeling hemmed in, oppressed by the contours and confines of marriage, by its responsibilities.

With time, he begins to work more steadily, to earn more money. The responsibilities seem to weigh a little lighter. With time, he finds ways to live with some constraints, to circumvent others. For him, marriage becomes a comfortable haven—a place of retreat from the pressures and annoyances of the day, a place where his needs and comforts are attended to by his wife, the only place perhaps where he can exercise his authority. He begins to feel he's made a good bargain. It's true, it costs plenty. He has to commit to a lifetime of hard work—sometimes at a job he hates, sometimes not. But the benefits are high too; and there's no other way he can get them:

> I like being married now. I don't even feel tied down anymore. I'm out all day and, if I want to have a drink with the boys after work, I just call her up and tell her I'll be home later. When I get home, there's a meal—she's a real good cook—and I can just relax and take it easy. The kids—they're the apples of my eyes—they're taken care of; she brings them up right, keeps them clean, teaches them respect. I can't ask for any more. It's a good life.   [*Thirty-eight-year-old plumber, father of three, married seventeen years*]

For his wife, time works the other way. She finds herself facing increasing constraints or, at least, experiencing them as more oppressive.[4] For her, there are few ways to circumvent them—no regular work hours:

> When I was a kid and used to wish I was a boy, I never knew why I thought that. Now I know. It's because a man can go to work for eight hours and come home, and a woman's work is just never done. And it doesn't make any difference if she works or not.

. . . no stopping off for a relaxing moment after work:

> He gets to stop off and have a drink when he feels like it. But me, I have to rush home from work and get things going in the house.

. . . no regular time off in which to develop her own interests and activities:

> I know I shouldn't complain. Bringing home a check and food for the family and keeping a roof over our heads is a lot of responsibility. But it's his *only* responsibility. I work too, and I still have to worry about everything else while he comes home and just relaxes. He has time to do other things he wants to do after work, like getting out there and fooling

around fixing his truck, or other projects he likes to do. Me, I don't have time for anything.

. . . no night out she can count on:

> He gets out once a week, at least. I don't always know what he does. He goes to a ball game or something like that; or he just goes out with some of the guys. Me, if I'm ever dumb enough to take a night off to do something, I pay for it when I come home. He can't—or maybe he won't—control the kids, so the house looks like a cyclone, and he's so mad at the kids and me, you can't live with him for days.

. . . and perhaps more important, no way, short of years of nagging or divorce, to defy her husband's authority and dicta about what she may or may not do with her life:

> I begin to worry what's going to happen to me after the kids are grown up. I don't want to be like my mother, just sort of hanging around being a professional mother and grandmother. So I thought I could go to school—you know, take a few courses or something, maybe even be a teacher eventually. But he says I can't and no matter how much I beg, he won't let me.

"He won't let me"—a phrase heard often among working-class women. "He won't let me"—a phrase spoken unselfconsciously, with a sense of resignation, as if that's the way of the world. Indeed, that is the way for most of these women.

It is not only in the working class that this is true, however. Rather, it is only there that a *language* exists which speaks of husbands "permitting" wives. Not once did a professional middle-class man speak about refusing his wife persmission to do something—whether to go to work, to school, or to have an abortion. Not once was a wife in a professional family heard to say, "He won't let me." Such talk would conflict with the philosophy of egalitarianism in the family that finds its fullest articulation among men and women of this class. But the tension between ideology and reality is high and, as William Goode writes in *World Revolution and Family Patterns,* ". . . the more educated men are more likely to concede more rights ideologically than they in fact grant." The mere fact that the discussion takes place around what men will "grant" is itself a telling statement. For in relations between equals, one need not grant rights to another; they are assumed as a matter of course.

To understand the reality of middle-class life around this issue, the shell of language with which the more highly educated protect themselves must be pierced. When it is, the behavior with which men effectively deny women permission stands revealed. Thus, referring to an unplanned pregnancy and his wife's wish for an abortion, one professional man said:

> It's her choice; she has to raise the kids. I told her I'll go along with whatever she decides. [*After a moment's hesitation.*] But, you know, if she goes through with it, I'll never agree to have another child. If we destroy this one, we don't deserve to have another.

Have you told her that?

[*Defensively.*] Of course! She has to know how I feel.

How did she respond?

She cried and got angry. She said I wasn't giving her much of a choice. But it seems to me she ought to know what the consequences of her actions will be when she makes the decision, and those are the consequences. Anyhow, it's all over now; she's decided to have the baby.

Such are the "choices" that confronted this woman as she struggled to make the decision.

The difference, then, is not that middle-class marriages actually are so much more egalitarian, but that the *ideology* of equality is more strongly *asserted* there. This fact alone is, of course, not without consequences, paradoxical though they may be. On the one hand, it undoubtedly is a central reason why middle-class women are in the vanguard of the struggle for change in the family structure. On the other hand, an ideology so strongly asserted tends to obscure the reality, leaving middle-class women even more mystified than their working-class sisters about how power is distributed in their marriages. Thus, the middle-class wife who wants an abortion but decides against it because of her husband's threats, doesn't say, "He won't let me." Instead, she rationalizes:

It was a hard choice, but it was mine. Paul would have accepted anything I decided, but it just didn't seem right or fair for me to make that kind of decision alone when it affects both of us.

For the working-class woman, the power and authority of her husband are more openly acknowledged—at least around issues such as these. She knows when he won't let her; it's direct and explicit—too much so for her to rationalize it away.

Such differences in ideology are themselves a concomitant of class and the existential realities which people confront in their daily lives. First, there are important differences in what is expected of wives—in how they relate to their husbands' work, for example—and important consequences that flow from those expectations. Wives in professional middle-class families actually are expected to participate in their husbands' professional lives by cultivating an appropriate social circle, by being entertaining and charming hostesses and companions.[5] Most large corporations, after all, do not hire a middle or top executive without meeting and evaluating the candidate's wife. By definition, the tasks of such a wife are broader than those of the working-class wife. The wife of the executive or professional man must be active in the community, alert to world events, prepared to "shine"—only not *too* brightly—at a moment's notice. Husbands who require wives to perform such services must allow them to move more freely outside the home if they are to carry out their tasks properly.

The working-class man has no need of a wife with such accomplishments since his work life is almost wholly segregated from his family life. His wife has no positive, active role in helping him to get or keep a job, let alone in his advancement. No one outside the family cares how she keeps the house, raises the children, what books she reads, what opinions she holds on the state of the nation, the world, or the neighborhood. Her husband, therefore, is under no pressure to encourage either her freedom of movement or her self-development; and she has no external supports to legitimate whatever longings she may feel. Among the wives of the professional middle class, those longings and the activities they generate are supported by the requirements of the role. A charming hostess must at least be conversant with the world of ideas; an interesting companion must know something about the latest books. But for the working-class woman to develop such interests would require a rare order of giftedness, a willingness to risk separation from the world of family and intimates, and a tenacity of purpose and clarity of direction that few of us can claim.

In other ways, too, the realities of class make themselves felt both inside and outside the home. The professional man almost invariably is more highly educated than his wife—a fact that gives him an edge of superiority in their relationship; not so with his working-class counterpart. The professional man has the prospect of a secure and orderly work life—his feet on a prestigious and high-salaried career ladder; not so with his working-class counterpart. The professional man is a respected member of the community outside his home—his advice sought, his words valued; not so with his working-class counterpart.

Thus, the professional middle-class man is more secure, has more status and prestige than the working-class man—factors which enable him to assume a less *overtly* authoritarian role within the family. There are, after all, other places, other situations where his authority and power are tested and accorded legitimacy. At the same time, the demands of his work role for a satellite wife require that he risk the consequences of the more egalitarian family ideology. In contrast, for the working-class man, there are few such rewards in the world outside the home; the family usually is the only place where he can exercise power, demand obedience to his authority. Since his work role makes no demands for wifely participation, he is under fewer and less immediate external pressures to accept the egalitarian ideology.

Yet, despite the fact that, under these conditions, egalitarianism in the family—whether ideal or real—offers little benefit to working-class men, these men are not wholly without some understanding of the difficulties of their wives' position in the family. Listen to this twenty-eight-year-old assistant pressman, father of two, married ten years:

Whose life would you say is easier—a man's or a woman's?

Actually, I would say the man's life is easier because even though I do go to work every day and it's hard, when the day's over, that's it for me. But for her, when the kids are sick, she has to take care of them. And after supper, she's still doing things around the house.

I kind of rely on her for a lot of stuff, too. You know, like, "Where's my socks?" and all that sort of stuff. I only have one thing to think about. She has all these things. I mean, I have worries too, about how much money I'm going to make, and how we're going to do this thing or that, but that's not every day. She's got to worry every day about whether she's got enough money for groceries and for the kids' shoes and all the stuff she takes care of. And on top of that, she's got to worry about if I'm going to come home in a bad mood.

Indeed, there are more than twice as many husbands and wives who think that a man's life is simpler than a woman's than those who think the converse. And the answers—whether from women or men—are remarkably similar in content, although very different in tone.

The men tend to express these thoughts with a cool calmness—mildly regretful that life is so for their wives but with the assumption that it is ordained:

That's just the way life is. It's her job to keep the house and children and my job to earn the money. My wife couldn't do my job, and I couldn't be as good a cook and housekeeper as she is. So we just ought to do what we do best.

The women more often express themselves with heated frustration—angry that life is thus and wondering how they can change it:

It seems like I do everything. It's just taken for granted that I'm supposed to get it all done—as if it were natural.

I like sports, too. I wonder what would happen if I sat down in front of the TV and watched all the time like he does.

Especially when they also work outside the home, the women feel keenly the weight of all the burdens. For regardless of class, there is plenty of evidence that the amount of time husbands spend in family roles is unrelated to whether their wives work or not.[6] The major difference among the people I met is that the employed wives of professional middle-class men are more likely to hire someone to help with at least the heavy household chores. Not so among working-class women, for whom household help is almost nonexistent.

Whose life would you say is easier—a man's or a woman's?

A thirty-year-old beautician, mother of two, married twelve years says:

Definitely, I'd say the man's life is simpler. He goes to work at a certain time, he comes home at a certain time, and it's over. We get up and it's there, and we go to bed and it's there. It's always there.

Another working mother of three, married seven years, replies:

The man's life is a lot easier; there's no doubt about it. He gets up in the morning; he gets dressed; he goes to work; he comes home in the evening; and he does whatever he wants after that.

As for me, I get up in the morning; I get dressed; I fix everybody's breakfast; I clean up the kitchen; I get the children ready for school and the baby ready to go to his baby-sitter; I take him to the baby-sitter. Then I first go to work. I work all day; I pick up the baby; I come home. The two older kids come home from my neighbor who takes care of them after school. Everybody wants me for something but I can't pay them any mind because I first have to fix dinner. Then I do the dishes; I clean up; I get the kids ready for bed. After the kids are finally asleep, I get to worry about the money because I pay all the bills and keep the checking account.

Doesn't your husband do anything at all?

Sometimes he helps get the kids to bed, but he won't touch a dish—not even to help clear the table. Mostly he's doing some project he likes or he's watching TV.

Her husband says:

It's not as bad as she says. I do a lot more around here than she gives me credit for. I won't do the dishes; that's her job, not mine. I didn't get married so I could do the dishes. But I help her out with some other things if she asks.

"If she asks"—that's precisely the issue in contest so much of the time, the issue about which women so often cry out:

Why do I have to ask? It's his house, too. They're his kids, too. Don't you think most women would like to have a husband help out once in a while without having to ask? It makes me feel like I'm begging him to do me a favor or else that I'm nagging him to death since he'll *never* do anything without my asking.

Interestingly, however, almost no one argues about the language of "him helping her." All agree that it's *her* job; the only difference between a couple is whether he *ought* to help her with it.[7]

Such are the contours of modern marriage. With all the talk about the changing structure of family roles, a close look reveals that when it comes to the division of labor in the family, it's still quite traditional. Over and over, that's the story: He does man's work; she does woman's work:

I make the money for her to bake the bread. Only women today don't bake bread anymore.

He "helps her out" when he feels like it:

If he wants to do something, then he does it. Yesterday, he helped clean up the yard, but that's because he wanted to do it. If he doesn't feel like it, he won't do anything, no matter what I say.

Household chores, when shared at all, are divided as they have been historically: he does the outside work; she does the inside. That means: he cleans the garage twice a year; she cleans the house every day. The one inside task he does most consistently is to take out the garbage but that, too, often doesn't get done without a struggle:[8]

I'll leave it in front of the door so he has to trip over it to get out. Even then, he'll walk around it sometimes, and I have to ask him to do it.

More often than not, work in the yard is shared, with the wife doing the lion's share. But even where the sharing is real, it is usually she who must take the responsibility for organizing and planning, she who reminds him of what needs to be done and when.

The big change, then, may lie in the fact that more women than ever before are now in the labor force, giving them the doubtful privilege of doing two days work in one—one on the job and the other after they get home at night. This is true not just in working-class families but in the professional middle class as well. Again, the ideology and rhetoric are different, but the reality is much the same. Thus, in the vast majority of those homes as well, there is more talk than action when it comes to the allocation and distribution of household and childrearing tasks.[9] With only a few exceptions, when a man does anything around the house that falls within the domain traditionally defined as the woman's, it is spoken of also as "helping her" and is almost always at the wife's instigation. The difference is in the women's attitudes toward the situation. For whether they work outside the home or not, more middle-class wives are angry about the burdens they carry in the family and more are able to express that anger with less fear and ambivalence than their working-class counterparts.

Among the working-class women, those who do not have outside jobs are least likely to complain about the division of labor in the family:

I think a woman should do all the housework. If I was working at a job, then I would expect him to do more.

That reasonable expectation, however, is quickly tempered with:

I wouldn't ever ask him to do something unless he wanted to do it, though.

Even those who spend many hours each week on jobs outside the home often try to assuage their anger with injunctions to themselves not to complain, and with reminders about how lucky they are compared to others. Indeed, hardly are the words out of their mouths than they try to modify or take back their complaints. Typical are these comments of a twenty-nine-year-old woman who, remembering her alcoholic father and mindful of her sister's violence-prone husband, says:

Help around the house? Walter? I'm satisfied if he doesn't throw his clothes around when he comes home or, when he changes, if he puts his old clothes in the hamper instead of just dropping them.

But I really haven't got a right to gripe. I don't have a lot of problems that a lot of women I know do. I feel very lucky. My husband doesn't drink; he never does anything mean to me; he's nice to anyone that comes over; he doesn't gamble. So I really can't complain too much.

Another, aged thirty-two, qualfies her remarks:

I don't want you to think I'm complaining now. He's a good man, a lot better than most. Any woman who's got a man who hardly ever gets violent and who doesn't drink much hasn't got a lot to complain about.

But when I'm working, I sure wish I could have more help. With five kids and all, it's hard to work and do everything yourself. The kids help, but there's a lot they can't do.

When I'm not working, I think it's perfectly natural and right that I should do everything. Even now, I still feel it's my job; but it would be nice if he could help a little when I'm gone at work so much.

If they're not qualifying their complaints, they're denying them, and suffering all the anguish, pain, and depression that come when conflicts are repressed:

I don't know what's the matter with me. For the last few years it feels like there's two "me"s in there [*pointing to her head*]. One pulls me one way and the other pulls me the other way. It's like they're trying to pull me apart, and I keep trying and trying not to let it happen. I get so tired.

And I feel so quilty because I know I ought to be happy, and I can't figure out why I'm not. I have nothing to complain about, yet there's that "me" in there that keeps pulling at me and making me miserable and depressed all the time. [*Twenty-four-year-old clerk, mother of two, married seven years*]

It is not just the household chores that so many women find so burdensome, however. Rather it is the very shape and structure of their lives, the sense that in every way they bear the responsibility for the family—its present and future:

Whose life would you say is easier—a man's or a woman's?

The question opens the floodgates of pain and frustration, especially for the women:

He just goes to work and brings some money home, but I have all the responsibilities. I tell him what the bills are. I know when there's not enough money to pay them all. I know when something's wrong in the family. I know when his brother and sister-in-law are splitting up. I know when his mother's unhappy. I know when there's a problem with the kids. Why, I'm even the one who knows when there's a problem in our marriage. I have to tell him about all those things and most of the time he just listens to a few words and tunes it out. I'm the one who knows about it; and I'm the one who gets stuck worrying what to do about it. [*Twenty-nine-year-old sandwich maker, mother of three, married ten years*]

It is true that some men think their lives are harder than women's, and some women agree with them. Always, the reason is the same: she doesn't have to go to work every day. Yet, even those men who assert that view most adamantly, recoil with distaste when asked if they could conceive of changing places with their wives:

I couldn't stand being home every day, taking care of the house, or sick kids, or stuff like that. But that's because I'm a man. Men aren't supposed to do things like that, but it's what women are supposed to be doing. It's natural for them, so they don't mind it.

Few women would agree that they "don't mind it." They may believe it's their job, that it's what they *ought* to want to do. They may be frightened at the thought of having to support a family; they may even prefer the tasks of housewifery to a job once held that was dull and constricting. But no woman reacts with repugnance to the idea of changing places with her husband. Indeed, even those who say they would like it least refer only to his role as breadwinner, finding other aspects of their husbands' lives appealing:

I guess I wouldn't like to change places with him because I couldn't support the family like he does. Anyhow, it's not much fun knowing you have all the responsibility on your head. On the other hand, that's all men have to do. I don't mean it's easy, but it's *all* they do. We—women I mean—have a lot more to do and to worry about all the time. I guess what it boils down to is that the man does the harder physical work, but the woman does the harder emotional work. I mean, he has to get up every morning and go to work; I don't. It's true, I work three days a week; but it's different. The family doesn't depend on my working; it does on his. But when it comes down to the emotional work in the family, that's mine, all mine. In the long run, I guess that's harder because it never ends; the worries are always there—whether it's about the kids, or our families, or how we're getting along, even about money. He makes most of it, but it's never enough. And I have to worry how to pay the bills.

I get mad sometimes and wish I could change places with him. It would be such a relief to worry only about one thing. It feels like I drag around such a heavy load.

In well over three-quarters of the families, that "heavy load" includes the responsibility for paying the bills in a household where often there's either not enough income to match outgo or . . . they're just balanced. The median income in these families is $12,300—a figure that sounds high until one looks at the Bureau of Labor Statistics figures which estimate that, in late 1974, a typical urban family of four in the San Francisco Bay Area needed $9,973 just to get by and $15,127 to maintain a moderate standard of living. Over 70 percent of these working-class families fall well below the amount designated for a moderate living standard. Of the remaining 30 percent, most barely reach that level, and all except two require two incomes and lots of overtime to get there. For most, then, there is little discretion in how earnings are allocated and spent:

Who manages the money in the family?

There's nothing to manage; it's all very predetermined. He puts his pay check in the bank, and I figure out what bills *have* to be paid this week, and write the checks.

So then, you decide how the money will be spent?

There's nothing to decide. I told you! It's already decided before we get the pay check. I have a budget, and there's nothing extra. If we ever *have* to buy something extra, we put it on Bank Americard, and then it's just another bill.

Decisions, then, are limited to which bills to pay now, which can be deferred—in effect, to assessing the best strategy for juggling the creditors:

I pay all the bills and manage the money—if you can call it managing. All it means is that I get stuck with all the scut work. When there's a problem with dun notices, or what have you, I'm the one who faces it. If there's anything that has to be explained or worked around so that things like the electric don't get turned off, I'm the one who gets stuck with it. Like, just the other day, P. G. & E. was going to shut off the electric, and I was the one who had to face them and figure out a way so they wouldn't do it. [*Thirty-four-year-old sales clerk, mother of three, married fourteen years*]

Observers of American family life often point to the fact that so many women handle the family finances as evidence that they wield a great deal of power and influence in the family. A look *behind* that bare fact, however, suggests some other conclusions.[10] Among the professional middle-class families, for example, where median income is $22,000—a level that allows for substantial discretionary spending—the figures flip over almost perfectly; the *men* manage the money in three-quarters of the families. Moreover, among those working-class families where some discretion in spending exists, almost always the husband handles the money, or the wife pays the bills while he makes the decisions. A thirty-three-year-old housewife, mother of three, married fifteen years, says:

I handle the money, but he makes the decisions. Like, he decided about whether we were going to buy this house or not, or whether we should buy a car, and how much we should spend for it. Some things I decide, like when the kids need shoes. But he watches out for what we're spending money on, and I pretty well know what it's okay for me to do and what's not okay.

Her husband, a thirty-six-year-old plumbing foreman, agrees:

Yeah, I make the major decisions as far as financial things, as far as any important things are concerned, I guess. I don't think she minds, though. She agrees with me that I'm used to making decisions and she's not, and that I know more about making decisions and have more experience in that type of thing.

Conversely, in the few professional families where the women manage the money, almost invariably they are families just beginning the climb upward—incomes are still quite low, and the choices around spending are very limited. It seems reasonable to conclude, then, that men manage the money when there is enough of it so that the task involves some real decision-making. Only then is the job worth their while. A thirty-five-year-old automobile bodyman says:

She used to handle the money. It was a pretty cut-and-dried affair then, and I didn't need to spend my time on it. But now there's more of it, and there are decisions that have to made about what we need to buy and when we should buy it. So I do it now.

His wife comments acidly:

Now that we're better off, he takes care of the money. When there wasn't enough, he was glad for me to do it because then he didn't have to worry about what bills to pay. As soon as we got a little more money, he started to butt in all the time. So it was okay with me when he decided to take it over. When I was doing it, I was just handling the chores. I didn't have any control over the money or the decisions about how it was spent. So what was I giving up?

While it's true that no one likes to do the difficult or tedious tasks of life, and that men have the option of turning some, such as these, over to their wives, this is not the *only* reason why they do so. At least as compelling, perhaps, is the fact that it permits them to avoid confronting the painful reality that they are not bringing home enough money to buy all the necessities they need and the comforts they would like. If he hands over his pay check and it doesn't stretch quite far enough, he can behave as if the problem lies not with his inadequate income but with her shortcomings as a manager. Listen to this couple, parents of three children, married eight years. The wife:

It takes quite a bit of managing to run the house with so little money, and with taxes and prices going up all the time, and his wages not going up. Every time we fix up the house a little bit, they call it an improvement and increase the property tax. But it's really just that we're trying to keep the place together so it shouldn't fall down on our heads.
   It's really a problem because I never know how much the new taxes are going to be. I save a little every week to put away for taxes and then all of a sudden the new tax bill comes and it's higher than I expected. So we have to go into debt to pay the taxes again. And he gets mad because he says if I managed better, it wouldn't happen.

The husband:

She spends too much. I don't know why she can't manage better. We always seem to be behind; she just can't save anything. As soon as she's got a couple of bucks in her hands, she finds something to spend it on. It makes me mad as hell sometimes when I work so hard and there's not enough money for me to spend on something I want.
   You know, I'm dying to get away on vacation, to see some of the country. But there's never any money. Can you believe it, I've been to Vietnam but I've never seen the Grand Canyon. Hell, I've never even been to Lake Tahoe.

One husband, at least momentarily aware of the bind he puts his wife in, comments:

I know it's not fair to her sometimes. I let her take care of the money, and then she has to listen to me asking her why we don't have enough, as if it's her fault.

Under such circumstances, managing the money in the family becomes yet another onerous chore to which the woman must attend. Adding to her burdens is the wife's knowledge that this is a difficult issue for her husband, and that almost anything she says on the subject is likely to turn out badly:

It's hard to talk about it because if I complain about money or that things are hard, he thinks it's a reflection on him. So I really try not to do that.

There couldn't be a harder-working person, so it's not his fault. It's just the way it is, and I try not to make him feel bad because there's not enough money sometimes. But even if I don't talk about it, he knows it. And sometimes he just needs to blame me even though we both know it's not my fault any more than it's his fault.

It is not only around decisions that involve spending money that men remain dominant, but in almost every other sphere of domestic life as well. Indeed, the studies of family power which tote up the number of decisions each spouse makes without reference to their relative importance, then conclude that wives and husbands are equally powerful, are absurd.[11] But the myth of egalitarianism runs so deep that even the marriage partners can be deluded by it:

How are the decisions made in the family?

Most people say "fifty-fifty." Yet, when one pushes the question a little further the illusion is quickly dispelled.

Who has veto power over a decision?

Almost all agree: the husband. One man's comments are typical:

It's kind of a joint effort up to a point. We'll talk it over and, if we agree, we do it. But if I say a flat "Forget it," that's it.

What happens if she says no to something you want?

Then she has to convince me. But she very seldom says no if I want it. Maybe that's because she knows she'd have a hard time convincing me.

In general, "fifty-fifty" turns out to mean that when both agree, they act. If he wants something she doesn't want, he can usually get it. If it's the other way around, she has to convince him or find ways to "get around him." When they decide together, he makes policy, she executes it:

How are decisions made in the family?

They're mutual, you know, fifty-fifty. She asks me whether we can buy some furniture, let's say. If I say okay, she goes out and looks around. When she picks out something she likes, she asks me to go look at it. If I approve of it, she buys it. If not, she looks some more.

. . . On the surface, working-class women generally seem to accept and grant legitimacy to their husbands' authority, largely because they understand his need for it. If not at home, where is a man who works on an assembly line, in a warehouse, or a refinery to experience himself as a person whose words have weight, who is "worth" listening to? But just below the surface, there lies a well of ambivalence; for the cost of her compliance is high. In muting her own needs to be responsive to his, she is left dissatisfied—a dissatisfaction that makes her so uncomfortable she often has difficulty articulating it even to herself. What right have I to complain? she is likely to ask herself. After all, I'm so much better off than my mother, she keeps reminding herself. But ask her what her dreams are for her children, and the dissatisfaction comes tumbling out:

What would you like for your children when they grow up?

Almost every woman in the study was unequivocal in her hope that her daughter would not marry so young:

I'd like her to be independent and not to have to rush into marriage.

I'd like my girls to think about getting a job and getting out and seeing a little of the world after high school before they settle down to family life.

I sure hope she doesn't get married until she's at least twenty-two or -three.

I don't want the girls to have the regrets I've had, so I hope they take their time and do whatever they want to do before they get married and can't do anything more. Don't misunderstand! I'm glad I'm married, and I want them to be married; only not so young.

Could anything more clearly reveal the feelings these women have about their own lives?

Notes

1. Lopata (1971:123) also notes that "white working class women . . . consider themselves lucky if their husbands are 'good to them,' do not use physical violence, and bring home a paycheck."
2. *The Prime of Ms. America* (New York: Putnam's, 1975):127.
3. See, for example, Blood and Wolfe (1960), a much-cited study that has achieved the status of a classic in the field, in which the word "class" does not appear in the text.
4. Cf., Bernard (1973) who presents a review and re-analysis of the literature and data on marriage and concludes that, on the whole, marriage is less satisfying and contains within it more "structured strain" for women than for men.
5. Papanek (1973).
6. See Walker (1969, 1970) whose time-budget data show that, in the aggregate, husbands contribute the same amount of time to the family—about 1.6 hours a day—whether their wives work or not. Furthermore, husbands' family time remains independent of wives' employment when age, class, and number of children are controlled for. See also Pleck (1975) for a fine analysis of the sex-patterned relationship between work and family roles; and Cook (1975) for a cross-national analysis of the problems of working mothers.

7. Cf., Lopata (1971:113–122) who telegraphs her findings by the subheading of this section of her book, "The Division of Labor and Husband's *Help* in the Home." [*emphasis mine*] On the issue of childcare as well, Lopata comments: "the fact that so many respondents feel that their husbands 'help with the children' is significant, even when stated as a form of praise. It suggests that *childcare is not part of the role of father and is done as a favor to the wife. . ."* [*emphasis mine*]

8. Cf., Holmstrom (1972:68) who studied two-career professional families and found that "the tasks most likely to be done by the husband were emptying the garbage and trash, repair work, and heavy yard work."

9. Although there may be some changes from the findings of earlier eras (see, for example, Blood and Wolfe, 1960; Komarovsky, 1962), my data for both working-class and professional middle-class families strongly support his contention. Cf., also Lopata (1971) and Epstein (1971), whose findings also support those reported here. In fact, in her study of husband-and-wife law partnerships, Epstein (1971) found that, even among those where the language of equality is most frequently heard, the wife has the major responsibility for house and children. Even more striking, the division of labor in the law practice generally broke down along traditional female-male lines.

   After a careful and perceptive examination of the literature, Bernard (1973:140–175), too, argues that there is no research proof that egalitarianism has been increasing between husbands and wives. "Talking a good egalitarian game," she comments acidly, "does not . . . prove that we are playing it." Cf., Nye (1974) who, in a study of 210 couples, reports that while there are some changes taking place in the functions of the family, the traditional role divisions (where wives are expected to assume responsibility for socialization and childcare and husbands for providing for the family) still are adhered to strongly. For an insightful exposition of the struggle between husbands and wives on this issue, see Mainardi (1970).

10. For a recent critical review of the family-power literature and the resource theory of family power which has dominated the field since its formulation by Blood and Wolfe (1960), see Safilios-Rothschild (1970). For critical comments on her review, see Bahr (1972) and Safilios-Rothschild (1972) for her rejoinder.

11. See for example, Bahr (1974); Blood and Hamblin (1958); Blood and Wolfe (1960); Heer (1958, 1962); Hoffman (1960); Olson and Rabunsky (1972); Sprey (1972); Turk and Bell (1972). Larson (1974) also argues that a major methodological weakness in family studies is the reliance on the response of one family member—usually the wife—from which inferences about family power and decision-making are made. His recent study shows that perceptions of family power vary systematically by both sex and age—that fathers, mothers, sons, and daughters tend to perceive "family reality" differently. Cf., Safilios-Rothschild (1969) who aptly describes family research as "wives' family sociology."

References

Bahr, Stephen J. "Comment on 'The Study of Family Power Structure: A Review 1960–1969.' " *Journal of Marriage and the Family* 34 (1972):239–243.

———. "Effects on Family Power and Division of Labor in the Family." In *Working Mothers*, edited by Lois W. Hoffman and F. Ivan Nye. San Francisco: Jossey Bass, 1974.

Bernard, Jessie. *The Future of Marriage*. New York: Bantam Books, 1973.

Blood, Robert O., Jr., and Robert M. Hamblin. "The Effects of Wife's Employment on the Family Power Structure." *Social Forces* 36 (1958):347–352.

Blood, Robert O., Jr., and Donald M. Wolfe. *Husbands and Wives: The Dynamics of Married Living*. New York: Free Press, 1960.

Cook, Alice H. *The Working Mother.* Ithaca: New York State School of Industrial and Labor Relations, Cornell University, 1975.

Epstein, Cynthia Fuchs. "Law Partners and Marital Partners." *Human Relations* 24 (1971):549–564.

Heer, David M. "Dominance and the Working Wife." *Social Forces* 36 (1958) 341–347.

_____ . "Husband and Wife Perceptions of Family Power Structure." *Marriage and Family Living* 24 (1962):65–77.

Hoffman, Lois Wladis. "Effects of the Employment of Mothers on Parental Power Relations and the Division of Household Tasks." *Marriage and Family Living* 22 (1960):27–35.

Holmstrom, Lynda L. *The Two-Career Family.* Cambridge, Mass.: Schenkman Publishing, 1972.

Komarovsky, Mirra. *Blue-Collar Marriage.* New York: Vintage Books, 1962.

Larson, Lyle E. "System and Subsystem Perception of Family Roles." *Journal of Marriage and the Family* 36 (1974):123–138.

Lopata, Helena Znaniecki. *Occupation Housewife.* New York: Oxford University Press, 1971.

Mainardi, Pat. "The Politics of Housework." In *Sisterhood Is Powerful*, edited by Robin Morgan. New York: Vintage Books, 1970.

Nye, F. Ivan. "Emerging and Declining Family Roles." *Journal of Marriage and the Family* 36 (1974):238–245.

Olson, David H., and Carolyn Rabunsky. "Validity of Four Measures of Family Power." *Journal of Marriage and the Family* 34 (1972):224–234.

Papanek, Hana. "Men, Women, and Work: Reflections on the Two-Person Career." *American Journal of Sociology* 78 (1973):852–872.

Pleck, Joseph H. "Work and Family Roles: From Sex-Patterned Segregation to Integration." Delivered at the Seventieth Annual Meeting of the American Sociological Association, San Francisco, California, August 25–29, 1975.

Safilios-Rothschild, Constantina. "Family Sociology or Wives' Family Sociology? A Cross-Cultural Examination of Decision Making." *Journal of Marriage and the Family* 31 (1969):290–301.

_____ . "The Study of Family Power Structure: A Review 1960–1969." *Journal of Marriage and the Family* 32 (1970):539–552.

_____ . "Answer to Stephen J. Bahr's 'Comment on the Study of Family Power Structure: A Review 1960–1969.' " *Journal of Marriage and the Family* 34 (1972):245–246.

Sprey, Jetse, "Family Power Structure: A Critical Comment." *Journal of Marriage and the Family* 34 (1972):235–238.

Turk, James L., and Norman W. Bell. "Measuring Power in Families." *Journal of Marriage and the Family* 34 (1972):215–223.

Walker, Kathryn E. "Time Spent in Household Work by Homemakers." *Family Economic Review* (1969):5–6.

_____ . "Time Spent by Husbands in Household Work." *Family Economic Review* (1970):8–11.

The Feminization of Love

Francesca M. Cancian

A feminized and incomplete perspective on love predominates in the United States. We identify love with emotional expression and talking about feelings, aspects of love that women prefer and in which women tend to be more skilled than men. At the same time we often ignore the instrumental and physical aspects of love that men prefer, such as providing help, sharing activities, and sex. This feminized perspective leads us to believe that women are much more capable of love than men and that the way to make relationships more loving is for men to become more like women.[1] This paper proposes an alternative, androgynous perspective on love, one based on the premise that love is both instrumental and expressive.[2] From this perspective, the way to make relationships more loving is for women and men to reject polarized gender roles and integrate "masculine" and "feminine" styles of love.

The Two Perspectives

"Love is active, doing something for your good even if it bothers me," says a fundamentalist Christian. "Love is sharing, the real sharing of feelings" says a divorced secretary who is in love again. In ancient Greece, the ideal love was the adoration of a man for a beautiful young boy who was his lover. In the thirteenth century, the exemplar of love was the chaste devotion of a knight [to] another man's wife. In Puritan New England, love between husband and wife was the ideal, and, in Victorian times, the asexual devotion of a mother [to] her child seemed the essence of love.[3] My purpose is to focus on one kind of love: long-term heterosexual love in the contemporary United States.

What is a useful definition of enduring love between a woman and a man? One guideline for a definition comes from the prototypes of enduring love—the relations between committed lovers, husband and wife, parent and child. These relationships combine care and assistance with physical and emotional closeness. Studies of attachment between infants and their mothers emphasize the importance of being protected and fed as well as touched and held. In marriage, according to most family sociologists, both practical help and affection are part of enduring love, or "the affection we feel for those with whom our lives are deeply intertwined."[4] Our own informal observations often point in the same direction:

I am indebted to Frank Cancian, Steven Gordon, Lillian Rubin, and Scott Swain for helpful comments and discussions.

From Francesca M. Cancian, *Signs,* Vol. 11, No. 4 (Autumn 1986):692–709. Copyright © 1986 by The University of Chicago. All rights reserved. Reprinted by permission of The University of Chicago Press and the author.

if we consider the relationships that are the prototypes of enduring love, it seems that what we really mean by love is some combination of instrumental and expressive qualities.

Historical studies provide a second guideline for defining enduring love, specifically between a woman and a man.[5] In precapitalist America, such love was a complex whole that included work and feelings. Then it was split into feminine and masculine fragments by the separation of home and workplace. This historical analysis implies that affection, material help, and routine cooperation all are parts of enduring love.

Consistent with these guidelines, my working definition of enduring love between adults is a relationship wherein a small number of people are affectionate and emotionally committed to each other, define their collective well-being as a major goal, and feel obliged to provide care and practical assistance for each other. People who love each other also usually share physical contact: they communicate with each other frequently and cooperate in some routine tasks of daily life. My discussion is of enduring heterosexual love only; I will for the sake of simplicity refer to it as "love."

In contrast to this broad definition of love, the narrower, feminized definition dominates both contemporary scholarship and public opinion. Most scholars who study love, intimacy, or close friendship focus on qualities that are stereotypically feminine, such as talking about feelings.[6] For example, Abraham Maslow defines love as "a feeling of tenderness and affection with great enjoyment, happiness, satisfaction, elation and even ecstasy." Among healthy individuals, he says, "there is a growing intimacy and honesty and self-expression."[7] Zick Rubin's "Love Scale," designed to measure the degree of passionate love as opposed to liking, includes questions about confiding in each other, longing to be together, and sexual attraction as well as caring for each other. Studies of friendship usually distinguish close friends from acquaintances on the basis of how much personal information is disclosed, and many recent studies of married couples and lovers emphasize communication and self-disclosure. A recent book on marital love by Lillian Rubin focuses on intimacy, which she defines as "reciprocal expression of feeling and thought, not out of fear or dependent need, but out of a wish to know another's inner life and to be able to share one's own."[8] She argues that intimacy is distinct from nurturance or caretaking and that men are usually unable to be intimate.

Among the general public, love is also defined primarily as expressing feelings and verbal disclosure, not as instrumental help. This is especially true among the more affluent; poorer people are more likely than they to see practical help and financial assistance as a sign of love.[9] In a study conducted in 1980, 130 adults from a wide range of social classes and ethnic backgrounds were interviewed about the qualities that make a good love relationship. The most frequent response referred to honest and open communication. Being caring and supportive and being tolerant and understanding were the other qualities most often mentioned.[10] Similar results were reported from Ann Swidler's study of an affluent suburb: the dominant conception of love stressed communicating feelings, working on the relationship, and self-development.[11] Finally, a contemporary dictionary defines love as "strong affection for another arising out of kinship or personal ties" and as attraction based on sexual desire, affection, and tenderness.[12]

These contemporary definitions of love clearly focus on qualities that are seen as feminine in our culture. A study of gender roles in 1968 found that warmth, expressiveness, and talkativeness were seen as appropriate for women and not for men. In 1978 the core features of gender stereotypes were unchanged although fewer qualities were seen as appropriate for only one sex. Expressing tender feelings, being gentle, and being aware of the feelings of others were still ideal qualities for women and not for men. The desirable qualities for men and not for women included being independent, unemotional, and interested in sex.[13] The only component perceived as masculine in popular definitions of love is interest in sex.

The two approaches to defining love—one broad, encompassing instrumental and affective qualities, one narrow, including only the affective qualities—inform the two different perspectives on love. According to the androgynous perspective, both gender roles contain elements of love. The feminine role does not include all of the major ways of loving; some aspects of love come from the masculine role, such as sex, and providing material help, and some, such as cooperating in daily tasks, are associated with neither gender role. In contrast, the feminized perspective on love implies that all of the elements of love are included in the feminine role. The capacity to love is divided by gender. Women can love and men cannot.

Some Feminist Interpretations

Feminist scholars are divided on the question of love and gender. Supporters of the feminized perspective seem most influential at present. Nancy Chodorow's psychoanalytic theory has been especially influential in promoting a feminized perspective on love among social scientists studying close relationships. Chodorow's argument—in greatly simplied form—is that, as infants, both boys and girls have strong identification and intimate attachments with their mothers. Since boys grow up to be men, they must repress this early identification, and in the process they repress their capacity for intimacy. Girls retain their early identification since they will grow up to be women, and throughout their lives females see themselves as connected to others. As a result of this process, Chodorow argues, "girls come to define and experience themselves as continuous with others; . . . boys come to define themselves as more separate and distinct."[14] This theory implies that love is feminine—women are more open to love than men—and that this gender difference will remain as long as women are the primary caretakers of infants.

Scholars have used Chodorow's theory to develop the idea that love and attachment are fundamental parts of women's personalities but not of men's. Carol Gilligan's influential book on female personality development asserts that women define their identity "by a standard of responsibility and care." The predominant female image is "a network of connection, a web of relationships that is sustained by a process of communication." In contrast, males favor a "hierarchical ordering, with its imagery of winning and losing and the potential for violence which it contains." "Although the world of the self that men describe at times includes 'people' and 'deep attachments,' no particular person or relationship is mentioned. . . . Thus the male 'I' is defined in separation.[15]

A feminized conception of love can be supported by other theories as well. In past decades, for example, such a conception developed from Talcot Parsons's theory of the benefits to the nuclear family of women's specializing in expressive action and men's specializing in instrumental action. Among contemporary social scientists, the strongest support for the feminized perspective comes from such psychological theories as Chodorow's.[16]

On the other hand, feminist historians have developed an incisive critique of the feminized perspective on love. Mary Ryan and other social historians have analyzed how the separation of home and workplace in the nineteenth century polarized gender roles and feminized love.[17] Their argument, in simplified form, begins with the observation that in the colonial era the family household was the arena for economic production, affection, and social welfare. The integration of activities in the family produced a certain integration of expressive and instrumental traits in the personalities of men and women. Both women and men were expected to be hard working, modest, and loving toward their spouses and children, and the concept of love included instrumental cooperation as well as expression of feelings. In Ryan's words, "When early Americans spoke of love they were not withdrawing into a female byway of human experience. Domestic affection, like sex and economics, was not segregated into male and female spheres." There was a "reciprocal ideal of conjugal love" that "grew out of the day-to-day cooperation, sharing, and closeness of the diversified home economy."[18]

Economic production gradually moved out of the home and became separated from personal relationships as capitalism expanded. Husbands increasingly worked for wages in factories and shops while wives stayed at home to care for the family. This division of labor gave women more experience with close relationships and intensified women's economic dependence on men. As the daily activities of men and women grew further apart, a new worldview emerged that exaggerated the differences between the personal, loving, feminine sphere of the home and the impersonal, powerful, masculine sphere of the workplace. Work became identified with what men do for money while love became identified with women's activities at home. As a result, the conception of love shifted toward emphasizing tenderness, powerlessness, and the expression of emotion.[19]

This partial and feminized conception of love persisted into the twentieth century as the division of labor remained stable: the workplace remained impersonal and separated from the home, and married women continued to be excluded from paid employment. According to this historical explanation, one might expect a change in the conception of love since the 1940s, as growing numbers of wives took jobs. However, women's persistent responsibility for child care and housework, and their lower wages, might explain a continued feminized conception of love.[20]

Like the historical critiques, some psychological studies of gender also imply that our current conception of love is distorted and needs to be integrated with qualities associated with the masculine role. For example, Jean Baker Miller argues that women's ways of loving—their need to be attached to a man and to serve others—result from women's powerlessness, and that a better way of loving would integrate power with women's style of love.[21] The importance of combining activities and personality traits that have been split apart by gender is also a frequent theme in the human potential movement.[22] These historical and psychological works emphasize the flexibility of gender roles and the inadequacy of a concept of love that includes only the feminine half of human qualities. In contrast, theories like Chodorow's emphasize the rigidity of gender differences after childhood and define love in terms of feminine qualities. The two theoretical approaches are not as inconsistent as my simplified sketches may suggest, and many scholars combine them;[23] however, the two approaches have different implications for empirical research.

Evidence on Women's "Superiority" in Love

A large number of studies show that women are more interested and more skilled in love than men. However, most of these studies use biased measures based on feminine styles of loving, such as verbal self-disclosure, emotional expression, and willingness to report that one has close relationships. When less biased measures are used, the differences between women and men are often small.

Women have a greater number of close relationships than men. At all stages of the life cycle, women see their relatives more often. Men and women report closer relations with their mothers than with their fathers and are generally closer to female kin. Thus an average Yale man in the 1970s talked about himself more with his mother than with his father and was more satisfied with his relationship with his mother. His most frequent grievance against his father was that his father gave too little of himself and was cold and uninvolved; his grievance against his mother was that she gave too much of herself and was alternately overprotective and punitive.[24]

Throughout their lives, women are more likely to have a confidant—a person to whom one discloses personal experiences and feelings. Girls prefer to be with one friend or a small group, while boys usually play competitive games in large groups. Men usually get together with friends to play sports or do some other activity, while women get together explicitly to talk and to be together.[25]

Men seem isolated given their weak ties with their families and friends. Among blue-collar couples interviewed in 1950, 64 percent of the husbands had no confidants other than their spouses, compared to 24 percent of the wives.[26] The predominantly upper-middle-class men interviewed by Daniel Levinson in the 1970s were no less isolated. Levinson concludes that "close friendship with a man or a woman is rarely experienced by American men."[27] Apparently, most men have no loving relationships besides those with wife or lover; and given the estrangement that often occurs in marriages, many men may have no loving relationship at all.

Several psychologists have suggested that there is a natural reversal of these roles in middle age, as men become more concerned with relationships and women turn toward independence and achievement; but there seems to be no evidence showing that men's relationships become more numerous or more intimate after middle age, and some evidence to the contrary.[28]

Women are also more skilled than men in talking about relationships. Whether working class or middle class, women value talking about feelings and relationships and disclose more than men about personal experiences. Men who deviate and talk a lot about their personal experiences are commonly defined as feminine and maladjusted.[29] Working-class wives prefer to talk about themselves, their close relationships with family and friends, and their homes, while their husbands prefer to talk about cars, sports, work, and politics. The same gender-specific preferences are expressed by college students.[30]

Men do talk more about one area of personal experience: their victories and achievements; but talking about success is associated with power, not intimacy. Women say more about their fears and disappointments, and it is disclosure of such weaknesses that usually is interpreted as a sign of intimacy.[31] Women are also more accepting of the expression of intense feelings, including love, sadness, and fear, and they are more skilled in interpreting other people's emotions.[32]

Finally, in their leisure time women are drawn to topics of love and human entanglements while men are drawn to competition among men. Women's preferences in television viewing run to daytime soap operas or, if they are more educated, the high-brow soap operas on educational channels, while most men like to watch competitive and often aggressive sports. Reading tastes show the same pattern. Women read novels and magazine articles about love, while men's magazines feature stories about men's adventures and encounters with death.[33]

However, this evidence on women's greater involvement and skill in love is not as strong as it appears. Part of the reason that men seem so much less loving than women is that their behavior is measured with a feminine ruler. Much of this research considers only the kinds of loving behavior that are associated with the feminine role and rarely compares women and men in terms of qualities associated with the masculine role. When less biased measures are used, the behavior of men and women is often quite similar. For example, in a careful study of kinship relations among young adults in a southern city, Bert Adams found that women were much more likely than men to say that their parents and relatives were very important to their lives (58 percent of women and 37 percent of men). In measures of actual contact with relatives, though, there were much smaller differences: 88 percent of women and 81 percent of men whose parents lived in the same city saw their parents weekly. Adams concluded that "differences between males and females in relations with parents are discernible primarily in the subjective sphere; contact frequencies are quite similar."[34]

The differences between the sexes can be small even when biased measures are used. For example, Marjorie Lowenthal and Clayton Haven reported the finding, later widely quoted, that elderly women were more likely than elderly men to have a friend with whom they could talk about their personal troubles— clearly a measure of a traditionally feminine behavior. The figures revealed that 81 percent of the married women and 74 percent of the married men had confidants—not a sizable difference.[35] On the other hand, whatever the measure, virtually all such studies find that women are more involved in close relationships than men, even if the difference is small. In sum, women are only moderately superior to men in love; they have more close relationships and care more about them, and they seem to be more skilled at love, especially those aspects of love that involve expressing feelings and being vulnerable. This does not mean that men are separate and unconcerned with close relationships, however. When national surveys ask people what is most important in their lives, women tend to put family bonds first while men put family bonds first or second, along with work.[36] For both sexes, love is clearly very important.

Evidence on the Masculine Style of Love

Men tend to have a distinctive style of love that focuses on practical help, shared physical activities, spending time together, and sex.[37] The major elements of the masculine style of love emerged in Margaret Reedy's study of 102 married couples in the late 1970s. She showed individuals statements describing aspects of love and asked them to rate how well the statements described their marriages. On the whole, husband and wife had similar views of their marriage, but several sex differences emerged. Practical help and spending time together were more important to men. The men were more likely to give high ratings to such statements as: "When she needs help I help her," and "She would rather spend her time with me than with anyone else." Men also described themselves more often as sexually attracted and endorsed such statements as: "I get physically excited and aroused just thinking about her." In addition, emotional security was less important to men than to women, and men were less likely to describe the relationship as secure, safe, and comforting.[38] Another study in the late 1970s showed a similar pattern among young, highly educated couples. The husbands gave greater emphasis to feeling responsible for the partner's well-being and putting the spouse's needs first, as well as to spending time together. The wives gave greater importance to emotional involvement and verbal self-disclosure but also were more concerned than the men about maintaining their separate activities and their independence.[39]

The difference between men and women in their views of the significance of practical help was demonstrated in a study in which seven couples recorded their interactions for several days. They noted how pleasant their relations were and counted how often the spouse did a helpful chore, such as cooking a good meal or repairing a faucet, and how often the spouse expressed acceptance or affection. The social scientists doing the study used a feminized definition of love. They labeled practical help as "instrumental behavior" and expressions of acceptance or affection as "affectionate behavior," thereby denying the affection- ate aspect of practical help. The wives seemed to be using the same scheme; they thought their marital relations were pleasant that day if their husbands had directed a lot of affectionate behavior to them, regardless of their husbands' positive instrumental behavior. The husbands' enjoyment of their marital relations, on the other hand, depended on their wives' instrumental actions, not on their expressions of affection. The men actually saw instrumental actions as affection.[40] One husband who was told by the researchers to increase his affectionate behavior toward his wife decided to wash her car and was surprised when neither his wife nor the researchers accepted that as an "affectionate" act.

The masculine view of instrumental help as loving behavior is clearly expressed by a husband discussing his wife's complaints about his lack of communication: "What does she want? Proof? She's got it, hasn't she? Would I be knocking myself out to get things for her—like to keep up this house—if I didn't love her? Why does a man do things like that if not because he loves his wife and kids? I swear, I can't figure what she wants." His wife, who has a feminine orientation to love, says something very different: "It is not enough that he supports us and takes care of us. I appreciate that, but I want him to share things with me. I need for him to tell me his feelings."[41] Many working-class women agree with men that a man's job is something he does out of love for his family,[42] but middle-class women and social scientists rarely recognize men's practical help as a form of love. (Indeed, among upper-middle-class men whose jobs offer a great deal of intrinsic gratification, their belief that they are "doing it for the family" may seem somewhat self-serving.)

Other differences between men's and women's styles of love involve sex. Men seem to separate sex and love while women connect them,[43] but, paradoxically, sexual intercourse seems to be the most meaningful way of giving and receiving love for many men. A twenty-nine-year-old carpenter who had been married for three years said that, after sex, "I feel so close to her and the kids. We feel like a real family then. I don't talk to her very often, I guess, but somehow I feel we have really communicated after we have made love."[44]

Because sexual intimacy is the only recognized "masculine" way of expressing love, the recent trend toward viewing sex as a way for men and women to express mutual intimacy is an important challenge to the feminization of love. However, the connection between sexuality and love is undermined both by the "sexual revolution" definition of sex as a form of casual recreation and by the view of male sexuality as a weapon—as in rape—with which men dominate and punish women.[45]

Another paradoxical feature of men's style of love is that men have a more romantic attitude toward their partners than do women. In Reedy's study, men were more likely to select statements like "we are perfect for each other."[46] In a survey of college students, 65 percent of the men but only 24 percent of the women said that, even if a relationship had all of the other qualities they desired, they would not marry unless they were in love.[47] The common view of this phenomenon focuses on women. The view is that women marry for money and status and so see marriage as instrumentally, rather than emotionally, desirable. This of course is at odds with women's greater concern with self-disclosure and emotional intimacy and lesser concern with instrumental help. A better way to explain men's greater romanticism might be to focus on men. One such possible explanation is that men do not feel responsible for "working on" the emotional aspects of a relationship, and therefore see love as magically and perfectly present or absent. This is consistent with men's relative lack of concern with affective interaction and greater concern with instrumental help.

In sum, there is a masculine style of love. Except for romanticism, men's style fits the popularly conceived masculine role of being the powerful provider.[48] From the androgynous perspective, the practical help and physical activities included in this role are as much a part of love as the expression of feelings. The feminized perspective cannot account for this masculine style of love; nor can it explain why women and men are so close in the degrees to which they are loving.

Negative Consequences of the Feminization of Love

The division of gender roles in our society that contributes to the two separate styles of love is reinforced by the feminized perspective and leads to political and moral problems that would be mitigated with a more androgynous approach to love. The feminized perspective works against some of the key values and goals of feminists and humanists by contributing to the devaluation and exploitation of women.

It is especially striking how the differences between men's and women's styles of love reinforce men's power over women. Men's style involves giving women important resources, such as money and protection, that men control and women believe they need, and ignoring the resources that women control and men need. Thus men's dependency on women remains covert and repressed, while women's dependency on men is overt and exaggerated; and it is overt dependency that creates power, according to social exchange theory.[49] The feminized perspective on love reinforces this power differential by leading to the belief that women need love more than do men, which is implied in the association of love with the feminine role. The effect of this belief is to intensify the asymmetrical dependency of women on men.[50] In fact, however, evidence on the high death rates of unmarried men suggests that men need love at least as much as do women.[51]

Sexual relations also can reinforce male dominance insofar as the man takes the initiative and intercourse is defined either as his "taking" pleasure or as his being skilled at "giving" pleasure, either way giving him control. The man's power advantage is further strengthened if the couple assumes that the man's sexual needs can be filled by any attractive women while the woman's sexual needs can be filled only by the man she loves.[52]

On the other hand, women's preferred ways of loving seem incompatible with control. They involve admitting dependency and sharing or losing control, and being emotionally intense. Further, the intimate talk about personal troubles that appeals to women requires of a couple a mutual vulnerability, a willingness to see oneself as weak and in need of support. It is true that a woman, like a man, can gain some power by providing her partner with services, such as understanding, sex, or cooking; but this power is largely unrecognized because the man's dependency on such services is not overt. The couple may even see these services as her duty or as her response to his requests (or demands).

The identification of love with expressing feelings also contributes to the lack of recognition of women's power by obscuring the instrumental, active component of women's love just as it obscures the loving aspect of men's work. In a culture that glorifies instrumental achievement, this identification devalues both women and love.[53] In reality, a major way by which women are loving is in the clearly instrumental activities associated with caring for others, such as preparing meals, washing clothes, and providing care during illness; but because of our focus on the expressive side of love, this caring work of women is either ignored or redefined as expressing feelings. Thus, from the feminized perspective on love, child care is a subtle communication of attitudes, not work. A wife washing her husband's shirt is seen as expressing love, even though a husband washing his wife's car is seen as doing a job.

Gilligan, in her critique of theories of human development, shows the way in which devaluing love is linked to devaluing women. Basic to most psychological theories of development is the idea that a healthy person develops from a dependent child to an autonomous, independent adult. As Gilligan comments, "Development itself comes to be identified with separation, and attachments appear to be developmental impediments."[54] Thus women, who emphasize attachment, are judged to be developmentally retarded or insufficiently individuated.

The pervasiveness of this image was documented in a well-known study of mental health professionals who were asked to describe mental health, femininity, and masculinity. They associated both mental health and masculinity with independence, rationality, and dominance. Qualities concerning attachment, such as being tactful, gentle, or aware of the feelings of others, they associated with femininity but not with mental health.[55]

Another negative consequence of a feminized perspective on love is that it legitimates impersonal, exploitive relations in the workplace and the community. The ideology of separate spheres that developed in the nineteenth century contrasted the harsh, immoral marketplace with the warm and loving home and implied that this contrast is acceptable.[56] Defining love as expressive, feminine, and divorced from productive activity maintains this ideology. If personal relationships and love are reserved for women and the home, then it is acceptable for a manager to underpay workers or for a community to ignore a needy family. Such behavior is not unloving; it is businesslike or shows a respect for privacy. The ideology of separate spheres also implies that men are properly judged by their instrumental and economic achievements and that poor or unsuccessful men are failures who may deserve a hard life. Levinson presents a conception of masculine development itself as centering on achieving an occupational dream.[57]

Finally, the feminization of love intensifies the conflicts over intimacy between women and men in close relationships. One of the most common conflicts is that the woman wants more closeness and verbal contact while the man withdraws and wants less pressure.[58] Her need for more closeness is partly the result of the feminization of love, which encourages her to be more emotionally dependent on him. Because love is feminine, he in turn may feel controlled during intimate contact. Intimacy is her "turf," an area where she sets the rules and expectations. Talking about the relationship, as she wants, may well feel to him like taking a test that she made up and that he will fail. He is likely to react by withdrawing, causing her to intensify her efforts to get closer. The feminization of love thus can lead to a vicious cycle of conflict where neither partner feels in control or gets what she or he wants.

Conclusion

The values of improving the status of women and humanizing the public sphere are shared by many of the scholars who support a feminized conception of love; and they too, explain the conflicts in close relationships in terms of polarized gender roles. Nancy Chodorow, Lillian Rubin, and Carol Gilligan have addressed these issues in detail and with great insight. However, by arguing that women's identity is based on attachment while men's identity is based on separation, they reinforce the distinction between feminine expressiveness and masculine instrumentality, revive the ideology of separate spheres, and legitimate the popular idea that only women know the right way to love. They also suggest that there is no way to overcome the rigidity of gender roles other than by pursuing the goal of men and women becoming equally involved in infant care. In contrast, an androgynous perspective on love challenges the identification of women and love with being expressive, powerless, and nonproductive and the identification of men with being instrumental, powerful, and productive. It rejects the ideology of separate spheres and validates masculine as well as feminine styles of love. This viewpoint suggests that progress could be made by means of a variety of social changes, including men doing child care, relations at work becoming more personal and nurturant, and cultural conceptions of love and gender becoming more androgynous. Changes that equalize power within close relationships by equalizing the economic and emotional dependency between men and women may be especially important in moving toward androgynous love.

The validity of an androgynous definition of love cannot be "proven"; the view that informs the androgynous perspective is that both the feminine style of love (characterized by emotional closeness and verbal self-disclosure) and the masculine style of love (characterized by instrumental help and sex) represent necessary parts of a good love relationship. Who is more loving: a couple who confide most of their experiences to each other but rarely cooperate or give each other practical help, or a couple who help each other through many crises and cooperate in running a household but rarely discuss their personal experiences? Both relationships are limited. Most people would probably choose a combination: a relationship that integrates feminine and masculine styles of loving, an androgynous love.

Notes

1. The term "feminization" of love is derived from Ann Douglas, *The Feminization of Culture* (New York: Alfred A. Knopf, 1977).

2. The term "androgyny" is problematic. It assumes rather than questions sex-role stereo-types (aggression is masculine, e.g.); it can lead to a utopian view that underestimates the social causes of sexism; and it suggests the complete absence of differences between men and women, which is biologically impossible. Nonetheless, I use the term because it best conveys my meaning: a combination of masculine and feminine styles of love. The negative and positive aspects of the concept "androgyny" are analyzed in a special issue of *Women's Studies* (vol. 2, no. 2[1974]), edited by Cynthia Secor. Also see Sandra Bem, "Gender Schema Theory and Its Implications for Child Development: Raising Gender-Aschematic Children in a Gender-Schematic Society," *Signs: Journal of Women in Culture and Society* 8, no. 4 (1983):598–616.

3. The quotations are from a study by Ann Swidler, "Ideologies of Love in Middle Class America" (paper presented at the annual meeting of the Pacific Sociological Association, San Diego, 1982). For useful reviews of the history of love, see Morton Hunt, *The Natural History of Love* (New York: Alfred A. Knopf, 1959); and Bernard Murstein, *Love, Sex and Marriage through the Ages* (New York: Springer, 1974).

4. See John Bowlby, *Attachment and Loss* (New York: Basic Books, 1969), on mother-infant attachment. The quotation is from Elaine Walster and G. William Walster, *A New Look at Love* (Reading, Mass.: Addison-Wesley Publishing Co., 1978), 9. Conceptions of love and adjustment used by family sociologists are reviewed in Robert Lewis and Graham Spanier, "Theorizing about the Quality and Stability of Marriage," in *Contemporary Theories about the Family,* ed. W. Burr, R. Hill, F. Nye, and I. Reiss (New York: Free Press, 1979), 268–94.

5. Mary Ryan, *Womanhood in America,* 2d ed. (New York: New Viewpoints, 1979), and *The Cradle of the Middle Class: The Family in Oneida County, N.Y., 1790–1865* (New York: Cambridge University Press, 1981); Barbara Ehrenreich and Deirdre English, *For Her Own Good: 150 Years of Experts' Advice to Women* (New York: Anchor Books, 1978); Barbara Welter, "The Cult of True Womanhood: 1820–1860," *American Quarterly* 18, no. 2 (1966):151–74; Carl N. Degler, *At Odds: Women and the Family in America from the Revolution to the Present* (New York: Oxford University Press, 1980).

6. Alternative definitions of love are reviewed in Walster and Walster; Clyde Hendrick and Susan Hendrick, *Liking, Loving and Relating* (Belmont, Calif.: Wadsworth Publishing Co., 1983); Ira Reiss, *Family Systems in America,* 3d ed. (New York: Holt, Rinehart & Winston, 1980), 113–41; Margaret Reedy, "Age and Sex Di   nces in Personal Needs and the Nature of Love" (Ph.D. diss., University of Southern California, 1977).

7. Abraham Maslow, *Motivation and Personality,* 2d ed. (New York: Harper & Row, 1970), 182–83.

8. Zick Rubin's scale is described in his article "Measurement of Romantic Love," *Journal of Personality and Social Psychology* 16, no. 2 (1970):265–73. Lillian Rubin's book on marriage is *Intimate Strangers: Men and Women Together* (New York: Harper & Row, 1983), quote on 90.

9. The emphasis on mutual aid and instrumental love among poor people is described in Lillian Rubin, *Worlds of Pain* (New York: Basic Books, 1976); Rayna Rapp, "Family and Class in Contemporary America," in *Rethinking the Family,* ed. Barrie Thorne (New York: Longman, Inc., 1982), 168–87; S. M. Miller and F. Riessman, "The Working-Class Subculture," in *Blue-Collar World,* ed. A. Shostak and W. Greenberg (Englewood Cliffs, N.J.: Prentice-Hall, Inc., 1964), 24–36.

10. Francesca Cancian, Clynta Jackson, and Ann Wysocki, "A Survey of Close Relationships" (University of California, Irvine, School of Social Sciences, 1982, typescript).

11. Swidler. (n. 3 above)

12. *Webster's New Collegiate Dictionary* (Springfield, Mass.: G. C. Merriam Co., 1977).

13. Paul Rosencrantz, Helen Bee, Susan Vogel, Inge Broverman, and Donald Broverman, "Sex Role Stereotypes and Self-Concepts in College Students," *Journal of Consulting and Clinical Psychology* 32, no. 3 (1968):287–95; Paul Rosencrantz, "Rosencrantz Discusses Changes in Stereotypes about Men and Women," *Second Century Radcliffe News* (Cambridge, Mass., June 1982), 5–6.

14. Nancy Chodorow, *The Reproduction of Mothering* (Berkeley: University of California Press, 1978), 169. Dorothy Dinnerstein presents a similar theory in *The Mermaid and the Minotaur: Sexual Arrangements and Human Malaise* (New York: Harper & Row, 1976). Freudian and

biological dispositional theories about women's nurturance are surveyed in Jean Stockard and Miriam Johnson, *Sex Roles* (Englewood Cliffs, N.J.: Prentice-Hall, Inc., 1980).

15. Carol Gilligan, *In a Different Voice* (Cambridge, Mass.: Harvard University Press, 1982), 32, 159–61; see also L. Rubin, *Intimate Strangers*.

16. Talcott Parsons and Robert F. Bales, *Family, Socialization and Interaction* (Glencoe, Ill.: Free Press, 1955). For a critical review of family sociology from a feminist perspective, see Arlene Skolnick, *The Intimate Environment: Exploring Marriage and the Family* (Boston: Little, Brown & Co., 1978). Radical feminist theories also support the feminized conception of love, but they have been less influential in social science; see, e.g., Mary Daly, *Gyn/Ecology: The Metaethics of Radical Feminism* (Boston: Beacon Press, 1979).

17. I have drawn most heavily on Ryan, *Womanhood* (n. 5 above); Ryan, *Cradle* (n. 5 above); Ehrenreich and English (n. 5 above); Welter (n. 5 above).

18. Ryan, *Womanhood,* 24–25.

19. Similar changes occurred when culture and religion were feminized, according to Douglas (n. 1 above). Conceptions of God's love shifted toward an image of a sweet and tender parent, a "submissive, meek and forgiving" Christ (149).

20. On the persistence of women's wage inequality and responsibility for housework, see Stockard and Johnson (n. 14 above).

21. Jean Baker Miller, *Toward a New Psychology of Women* (Boston: Beacon Press, 1976). There are, of course, many exceptions to Miller's generalization, e.g., women who need to be independent or who need an attachment with a woman.

22. In psychology, the work of Carl Jung, David Bakan, and Bem are especially relevant. See Carl Jung, "Anima and Animus," in *Two Essays on Analytical Psychology: Collected Works of C. G. Jung* (New York: Bollinger Foundation, 1953), 7:186–209; David Bakan, *The Duality of Human Existence* (Chicago: Rand McNally & Co., 1966). They are discussed in Bem's paper, "Beyond Androgyny," in *Family in Transition,* 2d ed., ed. A. Skolnick and J. Skolnick (Boston: Little, Brown & Co., 1977), 204–21. Carl Rogers exemplifies the human potential theme of self-development through the search for wholeness. See Carl Rogers, *On Becoming a Person* (Boston: Houghton Mifflin Co., 1961).

23. Chodorow (n. 14 above) refers to the effects of the division of labor and to power differences between men and women, and the special effects of women's being the primary parents are widely acknowledged among historians.

24. The data on Yale men are from Mirra Komarovsky, *Dilemma of Masculinity* (New York: W. W. Norton & Co., 1976). Angus Campbell reports that children are closer to their mothers than to their fathers, and daughters feel closer to their parents than do sons, on the basis of large national surveys, in *The Sense of Well-Being in America* (New York: McGraw-Hill Book Co., 1981), 96. However, the tendency of people to criticize their mothers more than their fathers seems to contradict these findings; e.g., Donald Payne and Paul Mussen, "Parent-Child Relations and Father Identification among Adolescent Boys," *Journal of Abnormal and Social Psychology* 52 (1956):358–62. Being "closer" to one's mother may refer mostly to spending more time together and knowing more about each other rather than to feeling more comfortable together.

25. Studies of differences in friendship by gender are reviewed in Wenda Dickens and Daniel Perlman, "Friendship over the Life Cycle," in *Personal Relationships,* vol. 2, ed. Steve Duck and Robin Gilmour (London: Academic Press, 1981), 91–122; and Beth Hess, "Friendship and Gender Roles over the Life Course," in *Single Life,* ed. Peter Stein (New York: St. Martin's Press, 1981), 104–15. While almost all studies show that women have more close friends, Lionel Tiger argues that there is a unique bond between male friends in *Men in Groups* (London: Thomas Nelson, 1969).

26. Komarovsky, *Blue-Collar Marriage* (New York: Random House, 1962), 13.

27. Daniel Levinson, *The Seasons of a Man's Life* (New York: Alfred A. Knopf, 1978), 335.

28. The argument about the middle-age switch was presented in the popular book *Passages,* by Gail Sheehy (New York: E. P. Dutton, 1976), and in more scholarly works, such as Levinson's. These studies are reviewed in Alice Rossi, "Life-Span Theories and Women's Lives," *Signs* 6, no. 1 (1980):4–32. However, a survey by Claude Fischer and S. Oliker reports an increasing tendency for women to have more close friends than men beginning

in middle age, in "Friendship, Gender and the Life Cycle," Working Paper no. 318 (Berkeley: University of California, Berkeley, Institute of Urban and Regional Development, 1980).

29. Studies on gender differences in self-disclosure are reviewed in Letitia Peplau and Steven Gordon, "Women and Men in Love: Sex Differences in Close Relationships," in *Women, Gender and Social Psychology,* ed. V. O'Leary, R. Unger, and B. Wallston (Hillsdale, N.J.: Lawrence Erlbaum Associates, 1985), 257–91. Also see Zick Rubin, Charles Hill, Letitia Peplau, and Christine Dunkel-Schetter, "Self-Disclosure in Dating Couples," *Journal of Marriage and the Family* 42, no. 2 (1980):305–18.

30. Working-class patterns are described in Komarovsky, *Blue-Collar Marriage.* Middle-class patterns are reported by Lynne Davidson and Lucille Duberman, "Friendship: Communication and Interactional Patterns in Same-Sex Dyads," *Sex Roles* 8, no. 8 (1982):809–22. Similar findings are reported in Robert Lewis, "Emotional Intimacy among Men," *Journal of Social Issues* 34, no. 1 (1978):108–21.

31. Rubin et al., "Self-Disclosure."

32. These studies, cited below, are based on the self-reports of men and women college students and may reflect norms more than behavior. The findings are that women feel and express affective and bodily emotional reactions more often than do men, except for hostile feelings. See also Jon Allen and Dorothy Haccoun, "Sex Differences in Emotionality," *Human Relations* 29, no. 8 (1976): 711–22; and Jack Balswick and Christine Avertt, "Gender, Interpersonal Orientation and Perceived Parental Expressiveness," *Journal of Marriage and the Family* 39, no. 1 (1977):121–28. Gender differences in interaction styles are analyzed in Nancy Henley, *Body Politics: Power, Sex and Non-Verbal Communication* (Englewood Cliffs, N.J.: Prentice-Hall, Inc., 1977). Also see Paula Fishman, "Interaction: The Work Women Do," *Social Problems* 25, no. 4 (1978):397–406.

33. Gender differences in leisure are described in L. Rubin, *Worlds of Pain* (n. 9 above), 10. Also see Margaret Davis, "Sex Role Ideology as Portrayed in Men's and Women's Magazines" (Stanford University, typescript).

34. Bert Adams, *Kinship in an Urban Setting* (Chicago: Markham Publishing Co., 1968), 169.

35. Marjorie Lowenthal and Clayton Haven, "Interaction and Adaptation: Intimacy as a Critical Variable," *American Sociological Review* 33, no. 4 (1968):20–30.

36. Joseph Pleck argues that family ties are the primary concern for many men, in *The Myth of Masculinity* (Cambridge, Mass.: MIT Press, 1981).

37. Gender-specific characteristics also are seen in same-sex relationships. See M. Caldwell and Letitia Peplau, "Sex Differences in Same Sex Friendship," *Sex Roles* 8, no. 7 (1982):721–32; see also Davidson and Duberman (n. 30 above), 809–22. Part of the reason for the differences in friendship may be men's fear of homosexuality and of losing status with other men. An exploratory study found that men were most likely to express feelings of closeness if they were engaged in some activity such as sports that validated their masculinity (Scott Swain, "Male Intimacy in Same-Sex Friendships: The Impact of Gender-Validating Activities" [paper presented at the annual meeting of the American Sociological Association, August 1984]). For discussions of men's homophobia and fear of losing power, see Robert Brannon, "The Male Sex Role," in *The Forty-Nine Percent Majority,* ed. Deborah David and Robert Brannon (Reading, Mass.: Addison-Wesley Publishing Co., 1976), 1–48. I am focusing on heterosexual relations, but similar gender-specific differences may characterize homosexual relations. Some studies find that, compared with homosexual men, lesbians place a higher value on tenderness and verbal self-disclosure and engage in sex less frequently. See, e.g., Alan Bell and Martin Weinberg, *Homosexualities* (New York: Simon & Schuster, 1978).

38. Unlike most [researchers], Reedy (n. 6 above) did not find that women emphasized communication more than men. Her subjects were upper-middle-class couples who seemed to be very much in love.

39. Sara Allison Parelman, "Dimensions of Emotional Intimacy in Marriage" (Ph.D. diss., University of California, Los Angeles, 1980).

40. Both spouses thought their interaction was unpleasant if the other engaged in negative or displeasurable instrumental or affectional actions. Thomas Wills, Robert Weiss, and Gerald

Patterson, "A Behavioral Analysis of the Determinants of Marital Satisfaction," *Journal of Consulting and Clinical Psychology* 42, no. 6 (1974):802–11.

41. L. Rubin, *Worlds of Pain* (n. 9 above), 147.

42. See L. Rubin, *Worlds of Pain;* also see Richard Sennett and Jonathan Cobb, *Hidden Injuries of Class* (New York: Vintage, 1973).

43. For evidence on this point, see Morton Hunt, *Sexual Behavior in the 1970s* (Chicago: Playboy Press, 1974), 231; and Alexander Clark and Paul Wallin, "Women's Sexual Responsiveness and the Duration and Quality of Their Marriage," *American Journal of Sociology* 21, no. 2 (1965):187–96.

44. Interview by Cynthia Garlich, "Interviews of Married Couples" (University of California, Irvine, School of Social Sciences, 1982).

45. For example, see Catharine MacKinnon, "Feminism, Marxism, Method, and the State: An Agenda for Theory," *Signs* 7, no. 3 (1982):515–44. For a thoughtful discussion of this issue from a historical perspective, see Linda Gordon and Ellen Dubois, "Seeking Ecstasy on the Battlefield: Danger and Pleasure in Nineteenth Century Feminist Thought," *Feminist Review* 13, no. 1 (1983):42–54.

46. Reedy (n. 6 above).

47. William Kephart, "Some Correlates of Romantic Love," *Journal of Marriage and the Family* 29, no. 3 (1967):470–74. See Peplau and Gordon (n. 29 above) for an analysis of research on gender and romanticism.

48. Daniel Yankelovich, *The New Morality* (New York: McGraw-Hill Book Co., 1974), 98.

49. The link between love and power is explored in Francesca Cancian, "Gender Politics: Love and Power in the Private and Public Spheres," in *Gender and the Life Course,* ed. Alice S. Rossi (New York: Aldine Publishing Co., 1984), 253–64.

50. See Jane Flax, "The Family in Contemporary Feminist Thought," in *The Family in Political Thought,* ed. Jean B. Elshtain (Princeton, N.J.: Princeton University Press, 1981), 223–53.

51. Walter Gove, "Sex, Marital Status and Mortality," *American Journal of Sociology* 79, no. 1 (1973):45–67.

52. This follows from the social exchange theory of power, which argues that person A will have a power advantage over B if A has more alternative sources for the gratifications she or he gets from B than B has for those from A. See Peter Blau, *Exchange and Power in Social Life* (New York: John Wiley & Sons, 1964), 117–18.

53. For a discussion of the devaluation of women's activities, see Michelle Rosaldo, "Woman, Culture and Society: A Theoretical Overview," in *Woman, Culture and Society,* ed. Michelle Rosaldo and Louise Lamphere (Stanford, Calif.: Stanford University Press, 1973), 17–42.

54. Gilligan (n. 15 above), 12–13.

55. Inge Broverman, Frank Clarkson, Paul Rosenkrantz, and Susan Vogel, "Sex-Role Stereotypes and Clinical Judgments of Mental Health," *Journal of Consulting Psychology* 34, no. 1 (1970):1–7.

56. Welter (n. 5 above).

57. Levinson (n. 27 above).

58. L. Rubin, *Intimate Strangers* (n. 8 above); Harold Rausch, William Barry, Richard Hertel, and Mary Ann Swain, *Communication, Conflict and Marriage* (San Francisco: Jossey-Bass, Inc., 1974). This conflict is analyzed in Francesca Cancian, "Marital Conflict over Intimacy," in *The Psychosocial Interior of the Family,* 3d ed., ed. Gerald Handel (New York: Aldine Publishing Co., 1985), 277–92

Role Making among Married Mexican American Women: Issues of Class and Ethnicity

Norma Williams

Introduction

Some have argued that the family system in the United States has changed more during the last 30 years than in the previous 250 (cf. Blumstein & Schwartz, 1983). Although one may not completely agree with this, the family has undergone dramatic changes, and we have witnessed a growing diversity of family forms in the United States.

Unfortunately, most of the research on changing family forms has emphasized those belonging to the majority group of this society. Some research has addressed black families (e.g., Stack, 1974; Willie, 1983), but few empirical studies have been made of family patterns of the second-largest minority group in the United States: Mexican Americans.

This article seeks to contribute to our understanding of the Mexican American family in several ways. First, it attempts to document how married Mexican American women—and men—are redefining traditional role expectations and basic conjugal relationships. Second, it highlights important differences between working-class Mexican Americans and those in the business/professional class. Third, it analyzes how women in minority groups, by being "twice a minority," face special obstacles.

The resulting data have significant implications for social policy. We must recognize that most major social policies in both the private and the public spheres are related, either directly or indirectly, to family life. We thus cannot understand family life without relating it to organizational structures implementing these policies. More specifically, organizational structures—both business and governmental, with the latter category including schools—must consider changing family arrangements among Mexican Americans, and, as suggested below, must assume new shapes if necessary to enhance the quality of life of this minority group.

Financial assistance for field work on the Mexican American family in Corpus Christi, Texas, during the summer of 1985 was provided by the Liberal Arts College of Texas A&M University. The author also gratefully acknowledges the National Science Foundation—through the Minority Research Initiation Program (Document No. RII-8509893)—for supporting research in Corpus Christi for two months during the academic years 1985–1986 and 1986–1987 and full-time field work during the summer of 1986. The author also thanks the anonymous *JABS* reviewers for their helpful comments on this article.

From *The Journal of Applied Behavioral Science* Vol. 24, No. 2 (1988):203–17. Reprinted by permission of JAI Press Inc. and the author.

Current State of Knowledge

When generalizing about Mexican American gender roles and family life, social scientists have drawn upon the older ethnographic work of Madsen (1964), Rubel (1966), and Clark (1959). Madsen and Rubel have emphasized machismo and the passivity of women (cf. Horowitz, 1983). Although their work remains uncritically accepted (e.g., Queen, Habenstein, & Quadagno, 1985), it is flawed (Paredes, 1977). Yet some of their data can be useful if interpreted in light of recent theoretical advances regarding gender roles (cf. Rosaldo, 1974).

A second body of literature addresses decision-making patterns of married couples. Some researchers (Cromwell & Cromwell, 1978; Hawkes & Taylor, 1975; Ybarra, 1977, 1982), building upon the work of Blood and Wolfe (1960), have concluded that the Mexican American family is essentially egalitarian. The results of the study reported herein question these findings.

A third body of literature (Baca Zinn, 1984) focuses on Mexican American women and includes three edited publications—Mora and Del Castillo (1980), Melville (1980), and *Chicana Voices* (Editorial Committee, 1986)—and a monograph by Mirandé and Enriquez (1979). Except for research by sociologists such as Baca Zinn (1980) and Romero (1986), most of these writings are theoretical critiques of the stereotypical depictions of gender roles—including the image of married women as passive—and indicate the need for research on the nature of interactions between wives and husbands, and how these may be shaped by the broader community and organizational structures.

We thus have only limited data on contemporary Mexican American family life, and the policy implications of changing family patterns have not been explored.

Theoretical Background

In this study, I adopted a modified version of symbolic interactionism for analyzing the qualitative data collected. In particular, I built upon the work of Turner (1962, 1985), who reshaped the orientation of Mead (1934) and Blumer (1969). Turner emphasized that actors not only take the roles of others—thereby sustaining some conformity to others' expectations—but . . . also actively reshape and remake roles for themselves. Thus, human agents engage in "role making" as well as "role taking."

Turner has found that roles have varying degrees of concreteness and consistency, and that when actors attempt to make aspects of roles explicit they often modify or create new ones for themselves. The role-making framework is a useful corrective to the work of Linton (1936), Parsons (1951), and Goode (1973), who typically view persons as passive rather than active agents. Although Turner's framework is not typically cited by behavioral scientists writing about the remaking of women's roles (e.g., Gerson, 1985), research in this area indirectly supports the usefulness of the role-making framework.

Turner's framework must be modified in several ways.[1] One must distinguish between two types of role making. Turner emphasizes role making in situations with vague, ill-defined expectations and a limited time frame. He has not analyzed role making in situations that are rather fixed and have a historical context.

This article considers both types of role making, but pays special attention to that occurring in situations with well-defined patterns. In these situations, two subtypes arise. One relates to the traditional cultural expectations existing for men's and women's role within the Mexican American community, which require us to consider how the actor's memory of expectations shapes that person's current actions. The second relates to the resistance of the broader community's organizational structure (cf. McCall & Simmons, 1982) to role making by members of an ethnic minority. Women face especially significant constraints, which seem to vary somewhat according to social class. The implications of these issues for social policy are, as I shall demonstrate, rather far reaching.

Research Design

My research was first conducted in Austin, Texas. It was then replicated in Corpus Christi, Texas, so as to verify and elaborate upon my original findings. In 1980, about 17% of Austin's population of 345,109 could be identified as "Mexican, Mexican American, Chicano" (U.S. Bureau of the Census, 1983a), and about 44% of Corpus Christi's population of 231,999 belonged to this ethnic group (U.S. Bureau of the Census, 1983b).[2]

I selected Austin as a research site for theoretical and practical reasons. Its recent rapid changes made it a useful setting for studying the family in transition. I chose Corpus Christi because of its less rapid growth, large Mexican American population, and classification as part of the Mexican American region of South Texas. Because these two cities exhibit rather similar patterns, the data obtained for both are combined in this article.

The research in Austin took place over two years, during 1981–1983 (excluding summers). The data from Corpus Christi were collected during the summers of 1985 and 1986 and on several field trips during academic years 1985–1986 and 1986–1987. All the data are qualitative in nature, and were collected through in-depth interviews and participant observation (cf. Lofland & Lofland, 1984). I focused upon the working class and business/professional class, for change within the family seems to be greater in these social and economic sectors than among the poor.

In-Depth Interviews

I conducted in-depth interviews with 75 married couples. Of the Austin couples, 21 belonged to the business/professional class and 22 to the working class; of the Corpus Christi couples, 16 belonged to each class.[3]

I used occupation and education level to delineate social status. Of each couple assigned to the business/professional class, one of the spouses had a college degree and the other at least two years of college education; in the cases of 29 of these 37 couples, both spouses had at least one degree each. Of each working-class couple, both spouses had completed at least five years of elementary school, and neither had any college education. Of these 38 couples, in 27 cases both spouses had high school diplomas. The spouses making up one working-class couple had only an eighth grade education, but in all the others at least one spouse had some high school education.

The sample was limited to persons 25–50 years of age, which ensured some diversity yet kept the research manageable.

Among the business/professional couples, only one woman had never worked. Seven were temporarily unemployed at the time of the research, but all of them were involved in community activities. Of the working-class women, only two had never worked, and ten were temporarily unemployed.

I selected couples from both cities by using snowball sampling procedures (Bailey, 1987, p. 95). I became involved with each group through different social contacts; many of the couples from each group did not know one another. Typically, I interviewed husbands and wives separately. A common criticism of qualitative research is that it is not conducted systematically. To partially overcome this objection, I employed an interview guide and asked all the respondents certain questions. I did, however, emphasize collecting qualitative data, probing to obtain information on specific problem areas through follow-up questions and comments for about three or four hours per respondent. The interviews were conducted in either English or Spanish, with the latter used more frequently with working-class respondents.

Participant Observation

I conducted extensive participant observation in Austin and, within a more restricted time frame, in Corpus Christi. In Austin I observed one-third of the working-class couples and two-thirds of the business/professional couples in various social settings. In Corpus Christi I engaged in participant observation with more than two-thirds of the respondents in each class.[4]

The data from my participant observation serve several significant functions.[5] First, they are important for checking the validity of the interview data (Kirk & Miller, 1986, pp. 29–32); they enabled me to determine whether what respondents said corresponded to what they actually did (Deutscher, 1973). Second, the participant observation provided a broader social context for the role patterns discussed in the interviews. Third, they also permitted me to collect data concerning many married women (and often their husbands, too) whom I did not formally interview.

Findings

Traditional Mexican American Women

As indicated above, earlier research on the traditional role of Mexican American women has provided the base line for interpreting role making among married Mexican American women in some contemporary urban settings. The most important of these earlier works are ethnographic accounts published several decades ago (e.g., Madsen, 1964; Rubel, 1966). I supplemented these, however, by asking respondents about the role patterns of their mothers and fathers and how these differed from or resembled those of the respondents. The comments of those respondents more than 40 years old proved especially useful.[6]

The above-mentioned early ethnographic accounts defined the traditional role of women with respect to their passivity versus the "machismo" of their husbands. Madsen and Rubel have greatly distorted certain role patterns of Mexican American women, and some of their data must be recast in terms of more recent cross-cultural research. In many traditional societies, women have had considerable influence in the private sphere, although not the public one (Rosaldo, 1974). For example, when writing about Korean women, Kendall spoke of their lives as reflecting "public powerlessness and private strength" (1985, p. 164). The same can be said of traditional Mexican American women.

The distinction between the private and the public helps one understand the image of the "good/bad" woman of Mexican American cultural tradition (cf. Moore, 1976). The image of the good woman is upheld through the private sphere, especially in motherhood. In the public sphere, the bad woman's image has sexual overtones and is exemplified by prostitutes.

Traditionally although women had considerable influence in the private sphere, their personal and social identities came from their husbands, who were considered the dominant figures of the family and community. This pattern was dramatically symbolized in funeral ceremonies, especially the mourning patterns of widows (Williams, 1987). Typically, a Mexican American widow was supposed to wear black for the remainder of her life to symbolize respect for her deceased husband, and secluded herself from all but family and religious activities. Although some role making took place in the traditional setting, conforming to well-defined role expectations was emphasized.

Role Making by Working-Class Women

All of the working-class women studied are in the process of reshaping their roles (cf. Zavella, 1987). They are striving to attain new personal—and social—identities for themselves. Although the two often merge, one's personal identity is quite private, and one's social identity public (cf. Weigert, 1983). What seems striking, however, is that these women are not seeking "equality" with their husbands, but instead a "separate identity."

These women's new personal and social identities set them apart from traditional Mexican American women. None of the working-class women expected to adhere to the traditional mourning patterns, nor did their husbands expect them to. A somewhat separate identity is essential if a widow is to pursue various activities in the public sphere, as today she cannot rely upon her relatives to conduct everyday activities in the community on her behalf. Moreover, the demands of the work place do not allow women to engage in extended mourning rituals. These women thus must reshape traditional role expectations in response to structural changes in modern urban communities.

To remake their roles, women need social support. When provided from relatives or friends and acquaintances—especially at work—working-class married women can generally attain a degree of identity, or autonomy, apart from that of their husbands. For example, one woman whose friends from work regularly attended Friday evening "happy hours" told her husband she wanted to join them. This created tension between them, for traditional expectations define women who go to bars as "loose." She persisted, however, and managed to persuade her husband to revise his expectations and allow her to attend happy hours without him. The woman had thus taken the role of her fellow workers, but was only able to act upon it after getting her husband to change his expectations.

Kinship relationships also support many of the women as they develop a new sense of identity vis-à-vis their husbands. In one case a woman encouraged her daughter-in-law not to be passive. Her remarks prove quite revealing: "Your father-in-law was the kind that you have to wait on. Don't get my son used to that. Make him help you" (translated from Spanish). This woman reacted negatively to her own passivity—and lack of social identity—with respect to her husband, who had left her. She did not want her daughter-in-law to suffer a similar fate.

In several cases, women attending a university in another community encouraged their mothers to visit them there. In one case, a husband only reluctantly permitted his wife to travel without him. She made the following comments: "I used to drive all that way to see my daughter. My husband could not go, so I drove it. I was not familiar with the road, but I did it." Through concrete actions, she took a significant step in creating her own sense of identity and autonomy.

Often, the women—especially educated ones—socialize their mothers to create new identities for themselves, and occasionally they persuade their fathers to hold less rigid expectations of their mothers' role.

Developing a personal and social identity, however, depends not only upon a support system, but also upon attaining new social skills and knowledge that college-educated women often take for granted. Thus, many working-class women are learning the importance of impression management (Goffman, 1959) as they move from one situation to the next. They realize the need to act differently at home than at work so as to handle the tensions resulting from the different expectations of their husbands and persons at work. Because of this, some women conceal information about their jobs from their husbands. One respondent had baked a cake to take to a party at work, only to have her husband eat some of it. She had not told him why she had baked it because she believed he would have disapproved of her "partying" at work, and feared he would have insisted she quit her job. The husband did not know that through role making his wife had created a somewhat new social identity for herself in the public sphere.

The new identities of these working-class women receive credibility because of the organizational skills they have acquired through their jobs. By guiding some of her fellow workers in acquiring their high school GEDs, one woman proved to herself that she could act independently of her husband.

Moreover, many women feel proud of having learned to budget effectively and shop for bargains, thus providing their children with opportunities they might otherwise have lacked. This new knowledge makes many respondents aware of their having created identities greatly different from those of their mothers and grandmothers.

In general, the role-making process of working-class women does not result from a fixed formula. Constraints and opportunities vary considerably among the respondents (cf. Gerson, 1985). These women reshape their roles by using opportune situations as they arise.

Role Making by Business/Professional Women

In comparing role making by working-class and business/professional women, a major difference emerges. All the business/professional women—even the most traditional ones—have already achieved a personal and social identity, both in the private and the public spheres, that the working-class women were still in the process of constructing at the time of this study. The business/professional women had attended college, where success required a certain social identity apart from that of their fathers and husbands. Moreover, success at work or in other public activities reinforced their sense of identity, which they recognized as greatly different from the traditional role expected of Mexican American women.

Five of the business/professional couples I interviewed in depth were striving to attain equality in decision making. Although these couples—some were in their 20s, some in their 40s—had not achieved the egalitarian ideal, they had departed from traditional expectations in this area. That only five couples attempted this causes me to question earlier research findings that equality in decision making exists among Mexican American couples (Cromwell & Cromwell, 1978; Ybarra, 1977, 1982).

The role-making patterns of the women (and their husbands) in the business/professional class also differ markedly from those of the working class. Moreover, I found considerable diversity in role making among the business/professional women, which does not exist among those in the working class.

Four types of patterns stood out, and these rested primarily on two interrelated criteria: the patterns of authority between husbands and wives, and the emphasis women gave to their obligations at home versus those of the public sphere, particularly their jobs.[7] The following is a brief discussion of each of these four types.

Type I: Reluctant dependent   Of those formally interviewed, four women—perhaps five—fell into this category. Several of the wives I talked with while conducting participant observation also fit this description. All of these women worked outside the home.

These women, [like] all those in the business/professional class, had achieved an identity the working-class women were seeking to attain. This self-recognition of autonomy was captured by one woman's stating, "If we ever divorce, I know I can support myself and my children." I never heard a working-class women speak in this vein.

Still, women in this category accept their husbands' position as the authority figure in the home who delegates tasks to his wife. Their husbands expect them to be at home with their children in the evening, and control the family's choice of friends. Because of their new personal and social identity, however, these women express reservations about their own actions. One woman, a former administrator in a government agency, complained privately about her husband's control:

> I felt like I was forced to quit my counseling job. I didn't like the idea of opening a clothing store. We don't need the money, but he [her husband] went ahead with his ideas and opened it up.

Although she was unhappy with her husband's constraints on her, she did not complain to him, wishing to avoid overt conflict.

These women may have accepted their husbands' authority because each of them had experienced severe trauma during childhood and youth, which led to personal insecurity reflected in their early life experiences. Moreover, because their husbands tightly control their circle of friends, these women have had few opportunities to develop the support they could have used to reshape their marital relationships.

In summary, the reluctant-dependent woman's husband wants his wife to work and earn money, but also expects her to maintain a rather traditional role as homemaker and mother. The wife accepts this definition of herself, but only reluctantly.

Type II: Semi-independent, family-oriented   The majority of the business/professional women fell into this category, including those articulating the egalitarian ideal discussed above.

For these women, the family takes precedence over public activities, including their careers. They do, however, have a more well-defined sense of their own personal worth than the reluctant-dependent women, and are less dependent on their husbands. They often emphasize their independence by contrasting their lives with those of their mothers. One woman observed:

> She [her mother] relied a lot on my father. She didn't start making decisions until he died. It was a different time. The men worked and made all the decisions. She told me I'm a professional, [and said,] "Stand on your own and defend yourself."

The strain their role causes these women, most of whom worked outside the home, reflects their struggle to maintain their identities as career women along with their identities as wives and mothers. One woman's comments underscored this pattern.

> My children are more important to me than my career. He [my husband] says that I am old fashioned because I prefer to stay at home with my children. I admire my mother, who stayed at home. I work because I have to. I work very hard with the schoolchildren during the year. I put all my

efforts into teaching. But I feel very guilty when I leave the children at the
sitter's home.

This woman readily acknowledged the contradictions between the roles she
sought to maintain.

Their careers give these women considerable personal and social satisfaction, enhance their feelings of self-worth, and provide income, giving their
families a sounder economic base. But they also seek to be supportive wives and
caring mothers. One way to try and reduce the resulting "role strain" is to
"compartmentalize" their lives and give motherhood priority over their careers.

The women fulfill their commitment to motherhood in various ways, including intervening with teachers on behalf of their children. The respondents
expressed guilt about the lack of time they spent with their children. As one
woman noted, "It is difficult with my work schedule to spend time with the kids.
I don't have enough time. I get home late and I read them a story or they read me
a story."

These women create new roles for themselves in managing their time so
that they can perform domestic and child care duties while also participating in
work-related activities. To accommodate the resulting role strain, they not only
compartmentalize certain activities, but also employ "symbolic gestures." One
woman said, "I will make time to bake for them [her children]. My husband tells
me not to do it, but I feel I have to." Baking a cake indicates her commitment to
being a good mother.

Many women in this category distinguished between their roles as wife and
mother. Unlike the reluctant-dependent women, they tried hard to maintain communication with their husbands. The following statement is typical of this type.

As a wife . . . communication is very important. We [her husband and
she] enjoy talking to each other, and we know exactly what we are
thinking. Our lives have changed because we both have heavy loads at our
job[s] and we have to help each other.

Tensions arise, however, because spouses lack the time and financial resources to
be alone together, even during vacations.

The men's expectations for their wives' roles correspond to those of the
women. Men expect their wives to care for the house and children, assuming this
arrangement to be proper. The women complain about this, however.

It's unfair. Women have to do things that they are expected to do, hold on
to housekeeping responsibilities. We are supermoms. I teach, and as a
mother I work all night.

Such women engage in role making to cope with "supermom" expectations,
something their mothers and grandmothers never had to face.

Type III Semi-independent, career-oriented   These women constituted the second-
largest group, and are far more committed to their careers than the Type II
women. Many intend to continue their education so as to achieve occupational or

career goals. They are somewhat less committed to being homemakers and mothers than the Type II women, and far less so than the Type I women. They take child care seriously, however, and experience strain between being a mother and being a career woman. Several respondents cried when they spoke of how the demands of their careers conflicted with those of motherhood.

Typically, the husband of a Type III woman does not want to surrender control of the family's resources. Nevertheless, these men profess to support their wives' careers. Their ambivalance is reflected in one man's comment: "I was shocked when she said that she was more qualified than I was for that job." Another said, "She has done some things that I never thought she would finish."

Although these women gain a strong sense of personal and social identity from their work, they nevertheless consider their husbands' careers more significant than their own, at least economically. One respondent asked for a job transfer so that a position could become available for her husband. Moreover, several of the men married to Type III women hastened to tell me they made more money than their wives. The women's careers create strain, as they are perceived as undermining their husbands' authority.

Type IV: Independent with constraints   This kind of role-making pattern is uncommon. Only two of the women I interviewed fit this type, although I met several others while conducting participant observation.

The Type IV woman considers her career to be more important than her husband's. She has not, however, achieved equality in the conjugal relationship. Husbands of these women typically are disadvantaged—in education or some other respect—compared to their wives; one was a "househusband." The role strain the Type IV woman faces differs greatly from that of women in the other categories. Such women engage in a role-making pattern whereby they minimize their own importance within the conjugal relationship. One woman carefully avoided emphasizing her own career or monetary success because this made her husband feel threatened; he conceded that he had difficulty accepting his wife's role in having a successful career and being chief wage earner of the family.

"Twice a Minority"

Thus far I have focused primarily on internal relationships within the family. To understand role making by Mexican American women more fully, they and their husbands must be examined in a broader community and organizational context (McCall & Simmons, 1982). Moreover, we should recognize that although most behavioral scientists focus on the shared experiences of all women, some—including Dill (1987)—question this orientation. One must consider class and ethnicity in any study of the conjugal relations of Mexican American women. Only by understanding the community's social resistance to role making by persons of a particular gender and ethnic group can we grasp the problems married Mexican American women confront in role making. Too often, those who study the family fail to examine such interactions and the complex relationship between the family and the broader social order.

As twice a minority, married Mexican American women encounter resistance to role making within organizational structures, sometimes because of their gender, sometimes because of their ethnicity. These patterns emerged through my participant observation and in-depth interviews. Yet significant differences exist between the constraints encountered by working-class women and business/professional women.

The husbands of the working-class women—because of their commitment to and memory of a cultural tradition that calls for women to defer to men's authority—exert greater control over their wives than those married to business/professional women. In addition to being limited by their social and educational resources when remaking their roles, the working-class women also seem to encounter greater restraints in the public sphere because of their ethnicity than do the business/professional women. In their public roles, the working-class women have more contact with majority-group members whose actions are overtly discriminatory. As one woman said, "They [Anglo Americans] do not care for Mexican Americans. They call you anything." This undermines the women's self-esteem and their search for an identity separate from their husbands, and prevents them from fully using their abilities in the work place. Of even greater significance, discrimination limits their initiative in intervening on behalf of their children in such community spheres as the school system. I repeatedly encountered working-class women who wanted me to tell them how they might assist their children with school.[8] Lacking sufficient knowledge of how the schools operate and a well-defined personal and social identity, and recognizing that the society excludes members of their ethnic group, they have difficulty acting for their children's sake.

The business/professional women faced more subtle discrimination, but are more conscious of it than the working-class women. For example, they are sensitive about negative stereotypes of Mexican Americans as incompetent and uninterested in education. These stereotypes are carried into organizational settings, often indirectly.

In examining role making by the business/professional women, I found that their husbands typically feel less constrained by cultural traditions than those of the working class. Still, a subgroup of educated men justified their dominance over their wives by referring to their heritage, telling their wives "Don't forget your culture" or "Put your culture first" as they sought to depart from traditional expectations.

The professional women often observed, however, that they were more frequently demeaned for their gender than for their ethnicity, something not mentioned by the working-class women. Apparently, those with whom the professional women interacted considered remarks against Mexican Americans less socially acceptable than remarks against women, and Mexican American men in general seemed to accept discrimination based on gender more readily than that based on ethnicity.

Still, the business/professional women recognize that their ethnicity prevents them from achieving certain goals at work. Their sensitivity to discrimination has been reinforced by their children's exclusion from various social groups in their communities. Several of the women told me their children were prevented from participating in various social activities at school.

Thus, a duality appears to exist with respect to the exclusion of women from participation in the organizational structure of the community. Sometimes discrimination is based on gender, sometimes it is based on ethnicity, and often it is based on both to varying degrees that are difficult to determine.

The married Mexican American women of both classes also feel constrained by the lack of successful women from their culture who could serve as role models (cf. Fischer, 1986). Although women in the majority society also encounter serious difficulties in achieving equality with men at home and at work, they can emulate some role models from their culture. For example, those in the feminist movement have highlighted notable women from the past, and the communications media pay attention to women who are successful in the public sphere. Although those in intellectual circles know of a few accomplished Mexican American women (cf. Ruiz, 1985, 1987), they are not generally known to most in this culture.

Under these circumstances, one may ask whether Mexican Americans are emulating role models from the majority sector of society. This suggests an adherence to an assimilationist model (Gordon, 1964). Except for one couple, those I interviewed and encountered during participant observation did not view themselves as assimilated.[9] Acculturation has occurred, but not assimilation; Mexican American women are still excluded from key segments of the community structure. Although this may have led them to rely on their husbands more than they might have otherwise, these women nonetheless were striving to reshape their roles, despite social resistance.

We must seek to understand role making by minority-group women in terms other than those of the assimilationist model. Industrialization, urbanization, and bureaucracy—along with changing cultural values—have led these women to remake their roles. We should also recognize that although women in the majority sector may have more role models to emulate, they too are having to invent new roles for themselves that have no historical equivalents. Thus, women in both the majority and minority groups of this nation are responding to similar social forces, although their responses differ greatly, as the Mexican American women belong to an ethnic group excluded from various sectors of society.

Summary and Discussion

This article reports a study of how married Mexican American women in the working class and business/professional class are creating new roles for themselves and reshaping their conjugal relationships. I used a modified symbolic interaction framework to interpret the data obtained through in-depth interviews and participant observation.

Despite the limitations of the sample, I have drawn several tentative conclusions from this research.

1. *Mexican American women are doing more than taking the roles of others and responding to existing expectations* These women are reacting to changing circumstances and contradictory expectations by creating new roles for themselves. Contrary to common stereotypes, these women—in both the working class and the business/professional class—are not passive. They are actively remaking their roles in the community and especially in their marriages. Both the men and women explicitly described the differences between their own roles and those of their parents and grandparents.

2. *The women, rather than their husbands, have taken the lead in the role-making process* (cf. Araji, 1977; Lein, 1984) The husbands' expectations for their wives' roles are also changing, albeit more slowly (cf. Goode, 1986), resulting in important shifts in the marital relationship. My findings, however, do not support the conclusions of Cromwell and Cromwell (1978) and Ybarra (1977, 1982) that an egalitarian pattern exists among Mexican American couples.

3. *The role-making patterns of the working-class and business/professional women differ significantly* This has not been documented in the literature. Moreover, women in both groups are doing more than engaging in role-making in ambiguous situations: They are reshaping the traditional role expectations for Mexican American wives. Their husbands are adapting to this new definition of the situation.

The working-class women are creating new personal and social identities for themselves apart from their husbands. The business/professional women have already developed, and taken for granted, such identities. The differences in role making between the two groups seem to result from the greater resources and opportunities available to business/professional women (cf. Coser, 1975). Consequently, role-making patterns of the former are more diverse than those of the latter.

4. *When roles are remade during periods of rapid change, contradictions and strain become more apparent* The working-class women must address strains associated with their new identities primarily by maintaining some ambiguity in their relationships with their husbands, and thus avoiding direct confrontations with them. Often they act first and then inform their husbands indirectly about what they are doing. The business/professional women seek to reduce tension, to varying degrees, through compartmentalization of their public and domestic roles. These women also make accommodations to the demands of family life through symbolic gestures emphasizing their commitment to their families.

In general, Mexican American women cope with role contradictions and the resulting strain by feeling personally and socially satisfied with what Stryker and Stathan (1985) term ''role diversity'' (cf. Zurcher, 1977). These women address the strain associated with their new roles by defining them in positive terms, and viewing themselves as having far more satisfying lives than those of their mothers and grandmothers, who adhered more closely to traditional roles.

5. *Role making by Mexican American women is restricted by discrimination based on gender and ethnicity in community and societal organizations* Although discrimination based on ethnicity is not as severe as it was several decades ago (Montejano, 1987), it, along with discrimination based on gender, continues to exist. This

limits Mexican American women's ability to remake their roles within their families and to improve the quality of life they and their families can experience within the community.

Implications for Theory and Policy

The findings of this research must also be examined in a broader social context (cf. Marcus & Fischer, 1986, chap. 4). The intersection of family and organizational structures within the community and the broader society has been neglected in the literature. True, attention has been paid to welfare policies and their impact on the family (cf. Stack, 1974), and some research has examined dual-career couples and organizational structures. Nevertheless, behavioral scientists have typically ignored the complex interrelationship between family policy and organizational policy, particularly with respect to minority-group families.

One implication of the findings of this research is that those who formulate organizational policies, in both the public and private spheres, should recognize that significant diversity often exists among minority-group families. I have uncovered some important differences between working-class Mexican Americans and those in the business/professional class, and some meaningful variations among those in the latter group. The family patterns of these two groups also differ from those of the poor with whom I have interacted. Corporations and government agencies—including school systems—generally tend to label minority-group families as being of one type and to view minority-group women as facing similar problems. Bureaucratic organizations emphasize standardization, which leads to policies that do injustice to the varying patterns among Mexican Americans.

The interrelationships among family patterns and formal organizations can have even greater implications for policy. Many scholars and policy makers (e.g., Moynihan, 1986) have called for the strengthening of family bonds among those in minority groups, especially blacks. Most of these analysts, however, have not considered that strengthening the family will also require major revisions in the organizational structure of the community and broader society. I have observed that Mexican American women encounter constraints imposed by a cultural tradition giving men greater authority in the public—although not necessarily the private—sphere. As women seek to better the quality of life for themselves and their children in the public sphere, they encounter resistance from their husbands. This is particularly true for minority-group women, who face the additional problem of remaking their roles within the family and community while faced with discrimination based not only on gender but also on ethnicity. Policies formulated without regard for community and societal resistance to change cannot address the basic problems faced by those in minority-group families, especially women.

Behavioral scientists writing about organizational theory are now beginning to incorporate the issue of gender into their analyses (Morgan, 1986). These theorists, however, have yet to address effectively the problems associated with ethnicity. Specifically, those writing about organization development conceptualize the basic theoretical and practical problems in rather narrow terms, typically speaking of advancing the goals of the organization. If members of minority-group families, especially women, are to receive more equal treatment, social scientists addressing organization development must view issues not just in narrow organizational terms, but also with respect to the broader community and society. Those who do not will be unable to address the basic concerns of minority groups in American society. Most of the Mexican American women I studied wished to do more for their families—especially their children—but were hindered in various organizational settings by discrimination based on both gender and ethnicity.

One of the themes I have advanced is that to understand organizational issues, one must examine them not only from the perspective of the managers of organizations, but also from the perspective of various social groups who interact with these organizations, some of whom are excluded from full participation in the organizational structures. This article examines only those in the more privileged social and economic sectors of the Mexican American community. If we examined the situation of the poor, the problems of exclusion would appear greatly compounded.

Unless the leaders of organizations in the public and private sectors begin viewing the problems of minority groups such as Mexican Americans more comprehensively, the quality of life of those in minority-group families—especially women and children—cannot be improved.

Notes

1. For a critical theoretical analysis of the theory of role making, see Williams (in press).
2. One faces several problems when trying to identify Mexican Americans through the 1980 U.S. Census. The census presented a main category of persons of Spanish/Hispanic origin or descent, which was subdivided into various groups with which respondents were asked to identify themselves. One such subgroup was "Mexican, Mexican American, Chicano" (cf. Tienda & Ortiz, 1986, p. 5). This included "undocumented persons" from Mexico along with Mexican Americans born in the U.S. who do not identify themselves with Mexico.

   Many social scientists confuse Mexican Americans with undocumented persons from Mexico and with residents of Mexico. True, waves of immigration from Mexico have resulted in generational differences among Mexican Americans. We should recognize, however, that many Mexican Americans are descended from persons living in the Southwest when that area was incorporated into the U.S. under the Treaty of Guadalupe Hidalgo in 1848.

   The Mexican Americans I interviewed and observed viewed themselves as sharing a culture that is neither Anglo American nor Mexican national in character. They typically had no ties with relatives in Mexico, and if they visited that country they traveled as tourists. Mexican Americans identify with the U.S. and have been socialized in school systems substantially different from those of Mexico.
3. All the persons interviewed had professional training, and a few owned small businesses or were independent consultants. Thus, the terms "business/professional" and "professional" are used synonymously to identify this group of respondents.
4. Colvard (1967) has discussed the ethical problems of sociologists' collecting data by playing the role of a friend rather than that of a researcher. Because I conducted participant observation while in the role of a friend rather than researcher, I have used this information only as background data for formulating my generalizations.
5. Zurcher (1983, pp. 229–261) justified the use of participant observation for studying roles in natural settings.

7. The few women unemployed at the time of this research were all active in community (i.e., public) activities.
8. Because the respondents provided me with much significant information about themselves, I felt morally obligated to assist them whenever possible (for an analysis of reciprocity in field work, see Wax, 1952).
9. The sample for this study did not include persons married to members of the majority group (Murguia, 1982). My own field observations indicate, however, that intermarriage is not equivalent to assimilation. This area needs careful study.

References

Araji, S. (1977). Husbands' and wives' attitude-behavior convergence on family roles. *Journal of Marriage and Family Living, 39,* 309–321.

Baca Zinn, M. (1980). Employment and education of Mexican-American women: The interplay of modernity and ethnicity in eight families. *Harvard Educational Review, 50,* 47–62.

_____. (1984). Mexican heritage women: A bibliographic essay. *Sage Race Relations Abstracts, 9,* 1–12.

Bailey, K. D. (1987). *Methods of social research* (3rd ed.). New York: Free Press.

Blood, R., Jr., & Wolfe, D. M. (1960). *Husbands and wives: The Dynamics of Married Living.* Glencoe, IL: Free Press.

Blumer, H. (1969). *Symbolic interactionism.* Englewood Cliffs, NJ: Prentice-Hall.

Blumstein, P., & Schwartz, P. (1983). *American couples.* New York: William Morrow.

Clark, M. (1959). *Health in the Mexican-American culture.* Berkeley: University of California Press.

Colvard, R. (1967). Interaction and identification in reporting field research: A critical reconsideration of protective procedures. In G. Sjoberg (Ed.), *Ethics, politics, and social research* (pp. 319–358). Cambridge, MA: Schenkman.

Coser, R. L. (1975). The complexity of roles as a seedbed of individual autonomy. In L. H. Coser (Ed.), *The idea of social structure: Papers in honor of Robert K. Merton* (pp. 237–264). New York: Harcourt Brace Jovanovich.

Cromwell, V. L., & Cromwell, R. E. (1978). Perceived dominance in decision-making and conflict resolution among Anglos, Black and Chicano couples. *Journal of Marriage and the Family, 40,* 749–759.

Deutscher, I. (1973). *What we say/what we do.* Glenview, IL: Scott, Foresman.

Dill, B. T. (1987). Race, class and gender: Prospects for an all-inclusive sisterhood. In M. J. Deegan & M. Hill (Eds.), *Women and symbolic interaction* (pp. 159–175). Boston: Allen & Unwin.

Editorial Committee, Center for American Studies. (1986). *Chicana voices: Intersections of class, race, and gender.* Austin: University of Texas at Austin.

Fischer, M. M. J. (1986). Ethnicity and the postmodern arts of memory. In J. Clifford & G. E. Marcus (Eds.), *Writing culture* (pp. 194–233). Berkeley: University of California Press.

Gerson, K. (1985). *Hard choices: How women decide about work and motherhood.* Berkeley: University of California Press.

Goffman, E. (1959). *The presentation of self in everyday life.* Garden City, NY: Doubleday/Anchor.

Goode, W. J. (1973). *Explorations in social theory*. New York: Oxford University Press.

———. (1986). Why men resist. In A. S. Skolnick & J. H. Skolnick (Eds.), *Family in transition* (pp. 145–161). Boston: Little, Brown.

Gordon, M. M. (1964). *Assimilation in American life*. New York: Oxford University Press.

Hawkes, G. R., & Taylor, G. (1975). Power structure in Mexican and Mexican-American farm labor families. *Journal of Marriage and the Family, 37,* 807–811.

Horowitz, R. (1983). *Honor and the American dream*. New Brunswick, NJ: Rutgers University Press.

Kendall, L. (1985). *Shamans, housewives, and other restless spirits: Women in Korean ritual life*. Honolulu: University of Hawaii Press.

Kirk, J., & Miller, M. L. (1986). *Reliability and validity in qualitative research*. Beverly Hills: Sage.

Lein, L. (1984). *Families without villains*. Lexington, MA: D. C. Heath.

Linton, R. (1936). *The study of man*. New York: Appleton-Century.

Lofland, J., & Lofland, L. H. (1984). *Analyzing social settings: A guide to qualitative observation and analysis*. Belmont, CA: Wadsworth.

Madsen, W. (1964). *The Mexican-Americans of South Texas*. New York: Holt, Rinehart and Winston.

Marcus, G. E., & Fischer, M. M. J. (1986). *Anthropology as cultural critique*. Chicago: University of Chicago Press.

McCall, G., & Simmons, J. L. (1982). *Social psychology: A sociological approach*. New York: Free Press.

Mead, G. H. (1934). *Mind, self and society*. Chicago: University of Chicago Press.

Melville, M. B. (Ed.). (1980). *Twice a minority: Mexican American women*. St. Louis: C. V. Mosby.

Mirandé, A., & Enriquez, E. (1979). *La Chicana*. Chicago: University of Chicago Press.

Montejano, D. (1987). *Anglos and Mexicans: In the making of Texas, 1836–1986*. Austin: University of Texas Press.

Moore, J. (1976). *Mexican Americans*. Englewood Cliffs, NJ: Prentice-Hall.

Mora, M., & Del Castillo, A. R. (Eds.). (1980). *Mexican women in the United States: Struggles past and present*. Los Angeles: Chicano Studies Research Center Publications.

Morgan, G. (1986). *Images of organization*. Beverly Hills: Sage.

Moynihan, D. P. (1986). *Family and nation*. San Diego: Harcourt Brace Jovanovich.

Murguia, E. (1982). *Chicano intermarriage*. San Antonio, TX: Trinity University Press.

Paredes, A. (1977). On ethnographic work among minority groups. *New Scholar, 4,* 1–32.

Parsons, T. (1951). *The social system*. Glencoe, IL: Free Press.

Queen, S. A., Habenstein, R. W., & Quadagno, J. D. (1985). *The family in various cultures*. New York: Harper and Row.

Romero, M. (1986). Twice protected? Assessing the impact of affirmative action on Mexican-American women. In W. A. Van Horne (Ed.), *Ethnicity and women* (pp. 135–156). Milwaukee: University of Wisconsin System American Ethnic Studies Coordinating Committee/Urban Corrido Consortium.

Rosaldo, M. Z. (1974). Women, culture, and society: A theoretical overview. In M. Z. Rosaldo & L. Lamphere (Eds.), *Woman, culture and society* (pp. 17–42). Stanford, CA: Stanford University Press.

Rubel, A. (1966). *Across the tracks: Mexican-Americans in a Texas city.* Austin: University of Texas Press.

Ruiz, V. L. (1985). Obreras y madres: Labor activism among Mexican American women and its impact on the family. In I. Garcia & R. R. Goldsmith (Eds.), *La Mexicana/Chicana* (The Renato Rosaldo Lecture Series Monograph Vol. I) (pp. 19–32). Tucson: University of Arizona Mexican American Studies Research Center.

———. (1987). *Cannery women/cannery lives.* Albuquerque: University of New Mexico Press.

Stack, C. (1974). *All our kin.* New York: Harper and Row.

Stryker, S., & Statham, A. (1985). Symbolic interaction and role theory. In G. Lindsey & E. Aronson (Eds.), *The handbook of social psychology* (Vol. I), (pp. 311–378). New York: Random House.

Tienda, M., & Ortiz, V. (1986). Hispanicity and the 1980 Census. *Social Science Quarterly, 67,* 3–20.

Turner, R. (1962). Role taking: Process versus conformity. In A. Rose (Ed.), *Human behavior and social processes* (pp. 20–39). London: Routledge and Kegan Paul.

———. (1985). Unanswered questions in the convergence between structuralist and interactionist role theories. In H. J. Helle & S. N. Eisenstadt (Eds.), *Microsociological theory perspectives on sociological theory* (Vol. 2), (pp. 22–36). Beverly Hills: Sage.

U.S. Bureau of the Census. (1983a). Census tracts, Austin, Texas, SMSA, PHC80-2-80. In *Census of Population and Housing, 1980.* Washington, DC: U.S. Government Printing Office.

———. (1983b). Census tracts, Corpus Christi, Texas, SMSA, PHC80-2-129. In *Census of Population and Housing, 1980.* Washington, DC: U.S. Government Printing Office.

Wax, R. (1952). Field methods and techniques: Reciprocity as a field technique. *Human Organization, 11,* 34–37.

Weigert, A. J. (1983). Identity: Its emergence within sociological psychology. *Symbolic Interaction, 6,* 183–206.

Williams, N. (1987). Changes in funeral patterns and gender roles among Mexican Americans. In V. L. Ruiz & S. Tiano (Eds.), *Women on the U.S.-Mexico border: Responses to change* (pp. 197–217). Boston: Allen & Unwin.

———. (in press). Theoretical and methodological issues in the study of role making. In N. Denzin (Ed.), *Studies in symbolic interaction* (Vol. 10). Greenwich, CT: JAI Press.

Willie, C. V. (1983). *Race, ethnicity, and socioeconomic status.* Bayside, NY: General Hall.

Ybarra, L. (1977). *Conjugal role relationships in the Chicano family.* Unpublished doctoral dissertation, University of California, Berkeley.

_____. (1982). When wives work: The impact on the Chicano family. *Journal of Marriage and the Family, 44,* 169–178.

Zavella, P. (1987). *Women's work and Chicano families.* Ithaca, NY: Cornell University Press.

Zurcher, L. A., Jr. (1977). *The mutable self: A self-concept for social change.* Beverly Hills: Sage.

_____. (1983). *Social roles: Conformity, conflict and creativity.* Beverly Hills: Sage.

The Balance of Power in Lesbian Relationships

Mayta A. Caldwell and Letitia Anne Peplau

Despite the American ideal of equality, women in heterosexual relationships often have less power than their boyfriend or husband. In a study of college dating couples (Peplau, 1979), less than half the students reported that both dating partners shared equally in power, and 40% said that the boyfriend had greater power than the girlfriend. Research on married couples also indicates that male-dominant relationships are common (Bernard, 1972; Centers, Raven, & Rodrigues, 1971; Gillespie, 1971; Poloma & Garland, 1971). Explanations for the male power advantage have emphasized the impact of traditional sex-role ideology, which legitimates male superiority (Bernard, 1972; Millet, 1970), and the importance of men's greater personal resources (Gillespie, 1971; Safilios-Rothschild, 1976).

The present study extends research on interpersonal power to lesbian romantic/sexual relationships. Although social scientists have speculated about power in lesbian couples, empirical evidence on it is lacking. Chafetz (1974) suggested that lesbians reject traditional sex roles and that "real equality between partners is easier between two females than between a male and a female or two males" (p. 189). Similarly, Kelly (1972) argued that love relationships between women are more likely to be free of factors that cause inequality. Others (Barnhart, 1975; Peplau, Cochran, Rook, & Padesky, 1978) have emphasized that lesbians strongly value equality in personal relationships. The present study investigated empirically the nature of power in lesbian relationships.

The authors wish to thank Susan D. Cochran, Naomi McCormick, Karen S. Rook, and Richard R. Lau for their helpful comments on an earlier version of this article, and Christine Padesky for her assistance in data analysis.

From Mayta A. Caldwell and Letitia Ann Peplau, *Sex Roles* Vol. 10 (1984):587–99. Reprinted by permission of Plenum Publishing Corporation and the authors.

The first goal of the study was to assess both the balance of power that lesbians want and the balance of power they perceive in their current romantic/sexual relationship. Power is defined as the ability of one partner to influence the other partners' behavior (e.g., Blood & Wolfe, 1960). A relative imbalance of power is manifest when one partner has greater say about the relationship or about specific decisions made by the couple. An egalitarian balance of power is reflected in both partners' having equal say in the relationship. We predicted that lesbians would strongly support an egalitarian ideal, but we expected that a number of women would not achieve power equality in their relationship. Research suggests that endorsement of an egalitarian ideal does not ensure an egalitarian relationship. For example, Peplau (1979) found that nearly all the heterosexual dating couples in her college sample supported an egalitarian ideal for power, but less than half believed that both partners actually shared equally in power.

The second goal of our study was to investigate factors that tip the balance of power away from equality. By selecting variables derived from social exchange theory, the applicability of an exchange perspective to the unstudied population of lesbian women was tested. Social exchange theory (e.g., Blau, 1964; Rollins & Bahr, 1976; Thibaut & Kelley, 1959) proposes that the balance of power in dyadic relationships is affected by the relative dependence of the two partners on the relationship and by their relative resources. Waller (1938) described the impact of dependence as the "principle of least interest." In this view, the partner who is less interested or less involved in a relationship has greater influence. Research with heterosexual dating couples indicates that imbalances of involvement are often accompanied by imbalances of power (Peplau, 1979). It was predicted that a similar pattern would be found for lesbian relationships.

The impact of relative resources has been emphasized by Blood and Wolfe (1960): "Power accrues spontaneously to the partner who has the greater resources at his [sic] disposal" (p. 13). Resources have often been assessed by measures of level of education, income or social class, but are defined more broadly as "anything that one partner may make available to the other, helping the latter satisfy his [sic] needs or attain his goals" (Blood & Wolfe, 1960, p. 12). Relative resources do appear to be a determinant of power in heterosexual married couples (e.g., Blood & Wolfe, 1960; Rollins & Bahr, 1976; Safilios-Rothschild, 1976). We predicted that in lesbian relationships, a partner with greater educational attainment and income would have greater power.

Two factors not related to social exchange theory—sex-role attitudes and butch-femme role playing—were also investigated for their impact on the balance of power. Among heterosexual dating couples, a significant association has been found between sex-role attitudes and the balance of power (Peplau, 1979). Men and women with pro-feminist attitudes were more likely to report that their dating relationship was egalitarian than were students with traditional sex-role attitudes. Among lesbians, a concern with equality in relationships has been linked to more general feminist beliefs (Barnhart, 1975; Peplau et al., 1978). Thus, lesbians who are active feminists may be more sensitive to power issues and perhaps also more likely to achieve equality in their personal relationships.

A common stereotype is that lesbians engage in butch-femme role playing that mimics heterosexual roles. Thus, one partner might adopt a more "masculine" and dominant role, while the other partner might play the more "feminine" and submissive role. The present study assessed the extent of role-playing patterns in the division of household activities and examined possible links between such role playing and power. Since recent evidence (reviewed in Peplau & Gordon, 1982) indicates that role-playing behavior is uncommon among contemporary lesbians, we anticipated that it would not be a significant determinant of power.

The final goal of our study was to examine links between the balance of power and satisfaction in lesbian relationships. Since lesbians lack a cultural ideology that legitimates power imbalances, they may be unhappy with non-egalitarian relationships. Thus, we predicted that lesbians would report greater satisfaction and would anticipate fewer problems if their relationship was equal, rather than unequal, in power.

The present study investigated the balance of power and factors that affect it in lesbian relationships. We should, however, note that we have borrowed heavily from research on heterosexual relationships in making predictions about the impact of relative involvement, resources, and sex-role attitudes on power. This approach sets up implicit comparisons between lesbian and heterosexual relationships. Such research may help us identify aspects of interpersonal power that operate in all close relationships and aspects that are specific to particular types of relationships.

Method

Recruitment

Women were recruited from the Los Angeles area for a study of "lesbian relationships" by advertisements placed in a university newspaper, a feminist student publication, and a gay community newsletter. Leaflets were distributed at a women's center and university campus. Contacts were also made with a community feminist center, gay community services center, and a church-related lesbian rap group.

Participants spent approximately one hour filling out a detailed questionnaire. Most women completed the questionnaire in a group setting, either at the University of California, Los Angeles, or at one of five meetings scheduled at community locations in the Los Angeles area. Other participants were scheduled individually. Responses were completely anonymous. All data were collected in 1976.

The Sample

A total of 127 women participated in the study. We report data for only the 77 women who indicated that they were currently in a "romantic/sexual relationship" with a woman at the time of our testing. Of these 77 women, 44 were currently living with their romantic/sexual partner. All women were white. Ages ranged from 19 to 59, with a median age of 27. About 55% of the women worked full-time for pay, and 40% were students in college or graduate school. The majority (87%) either held a B.A. or were currently college students; the remaining 13% held a high school diploma or less.

The religious backgrounds of participants were diverse—40% were raised as Protestants, 35% as Catholics, and 13% as Jews. Participants indicated that they were not currently very religious (mean of 3.8 on nine-point scale of religiousness). Only 19% said they attended religious services weekly, and 59% went to services less than once a year.

In general, women in the sample were fairly experienced in lesbian relationships. The women had had an average of four lesbian relationships. The length of the women's longest lesbian relationship ranged from two months to 25 years, with a median of just under 3 years. The women's age when their first lesbian relationship began ranged from 13 to 47, with a median of 20.

Many of the women in the sample had previously had romantic/sexual relationships with men. Over 95% reported having dated or gone out with a man; 84% said they had been in a romantic/sexual relationship with a man. The median number of heterosexual relationships was 3.6. Almost 80% of the women had had sexual intercourse with a man; among these women, the median number of heterosexual partners was 4.8.

Although the women in our sample were fairly diverse in religion, education, and occupation, they clearly do not include a full spectrum of lesbians (see Morin, 1977). Women in this sample were relatively young, middle-class whites. The experiences of working-class and minority lesbians were not represented in our volunteer sample. Furthermore, our recruitment was probably most likely to come to the attention of women involved in lesbian or feminist groups; hence, the sample may overrepresent such women. The women who volunteered for this study may well have been more interested in psychological research and more trusting of psychologists than other lesbians. Caution is obviously warranted in making generalizations from this limited sample to other segments of the lesbian population.

The Questionnaire

Participants completed a 23-page questionnaire. Development of the questionnaire was based on extensive two-hour interviews with 12 lesbians about their relationships and on group discussions held with lesbian students. The questionnaire benefited from previous research with heterosexual dating couples (Hill, Rubin, & Peplau, 1976; Peplau, 1979; Peplau, Rubin, & Hill, 1976), and a number of questions were adapted for the present questionnaire. The first part of the questionnaire concerned the participant's background, attitudes and characteristics. The second part of the questionnaire focused on a specific "romantic/sexual relationship," and included questions about power, love and commitment, sexual behavior, satisfaction, problems in the relationship, and characteristics of the partner.

The assessment of power in close relationships is a complex matter (see discussions by Cromwell & Olson, 1975; Olson & Rabunsky, 1972; Safilios-Rothschild, 1970). The present study followed Blood and Wolfe (1960) and Rollins and Bahr (1976), who have focused on individuals' perceptions of power in their relationships. The specific power questions used in the present study had proved to be reliable and useful measures in an earlier study of power in heterosexual dating couples (Peplau, 1979; Peplau et al., 1976). Beliefs about the ideal balance of power were measured by the question "Who do you think should have more say in your relationship—your partner or you?" Perceptions of the overall balance of power in the relationship were assessed by "Who do you think has more of a say about what you and your partner do together—your partner or you?" Other questions concerned perceptions of power in deciding how much time the partners spent with each other and how much time the couple spent with other people. Responses to all power questions were made on five-point scales. For example, in responding to the question of who actually has more say, participants checked one of five responses: "My partner has much more say," "My partner has somewhat more say," "We both have exactly the same amount of say," "I have somewhat more say," "I have much more say."

Relative dependence on the relationship was assessed by two items: "Who do you think is more involved in your relationship—your partner or you?" and "Who do you think is more committed to the relationship—your partner or you?" As for the power questions, five-point response scales were provided for each question. To examine the effects of relative resources, questions were included about two personal resources—level of education and monthly income. Participants indicated their own and their partner's level of education. Education was considered equal when both partners had attained the same level of schooling (e.g., both had master's degrees, or both had finished junior college). One partner was considered to have greater relative education if she had more schooling than the other (e.g., one had a master's degree and the other had a bachelor's degree). Relative income was determined by the differences between a participant's report of her own monthly income and of her partner's monthly income.

Sex-role attitudes were measured by a ten-item Sex-Role Traditionalism scale (Peplau, 1973) assessing general attitudes about proper roles for men and women. Also included was an eight-item index of involvement in feminist activities (see detailed description in Peplau et al., 1978), which inquired about participation in feminist groups, attendance at feminist social and political events, and self-ratings of involvement in feminist activities.

For the 44 women in the sample who were currently living with their partner, additional questions explored possible butch-femme role playing in the division of household tasks. Questions asked which partner more often performed each of five traditionally "feminine" tasks (i.e., cooking, decorating, cleaning, laundry, and food shopping) and three traditionally "masculine" tasks (i.e., household repairs, household accounting, and driving). Scores for the five feminine tasks and for the three masculine tasks were totaled separately.

Other closed-ended questions asked about closeness and satisfaction in the relationship. Also included were Rubin's (1973) nine-item "Love Scale" and

"Liking Scale." The Love Scale assesses feelings of attachment, intimacy, and caring for the partner; the Liking Scale measures attitudes of respect and affection toward the partner. Finally, participants were presented with a list of 17 "factors that may cause difficulties in close relationships" (adapted from Hill et al., 1976). These included such possible problems as jealousy, differences in attitudes and background, and the desire for greater independence. Respondents indicated on a three-point scale how likely it was that each factor might create problems in their own relationship during the coming year.

Results

Balance of Power

The lesbians in this sample were virtually unanimous in their support for the ideal of equal power. Ninety-seven percent thought that both partners should have "exactly equal" say in their relationship. Not all women believed that their current relationship achieved this ideal, however. Although a majority of women (61%) indicated that both partners had "exactly equal" say in their relationship, a sizable minority (39%) said that one partner had greater influence than the other.

When women were asked more specific questions about power in particular areas, a comparable pattern was found. About two-thirds of women (66% in both cases) reported that they and their partners contributed equally to "deciding how much time the two of you spend together" and "deciding how much time you two will spend with other people." As expected, reports of the overall balance of power were significantly correlated with reports of who decided about time together, $r(73) = .22$, $p < .05$, and who decided about time with others, $r(74) = .33$, $p < .05$. These correlations are modest but reasonable, given the complex relationship between decisions in any particular area and the overall balance of power in a relationship (see Safilios-Rothschild, 1970). In later sections, results are presented based on the more general measure of overall balance of power.

Factors Influencing the Balance of Power

Relative dependence   As predicted, imbalances in relative involvement were linked to imbalances in power. The partner who was relatively less involved in the relationship was perceived as having greater power in the relationship, $r(74) = -.36$, $p < .001$. Most women (62%) reported that they and their partner were equally involved in their relationship. Among those equally involved women, 72% also reported equal power. In contrast, among the 38% of women who reported unequal involvement, 82% perceived the less involved partner as having relatively greater power.

A similar pattern of findings emerged from analyses of commitment. As might be expected, women's reports of relative involvement and relative commitment were significantly correlated, $r(75) = .48$, $p < .01$. As with relative involvement, a majority (61%) of women described both partners as equally committed to the current relationship. When unequal commitment occurred, the partner who was less committed tended to have greater power in the relationship, $r(74) = -.30$, $p < .01$. Thus results provide clear support for the effect of the "principle of least interest" on power in lesbian relationships.

Relative resources   Inequality in personal resources was also related to power in lesbian relationships. As predicted, women with relatively less education than their partner had less power, $r(71) = .37$, $p < .001$. Similarly, women with a lower monthly income also tended to have less power in the relationship, $r(44) = .28$, $p < .05$.

Sex-role attitudes and butch-femme role playing   It was predicted that adherence to traditional sex-role patterns would affect the balance of power in lesbian relationships. It should be noted at the outset that women in this sample held fairly nontraditional views about sex roles. Most women scored in a feminist direction on the ten-item Sex-Role Traditionalism scale, and over half of the women belonged to a feminist group or organization. Contrary to popular stereotypes, no evidence was found that women in the sample engaged in butch-femme role playing. If role playing occurs, there should be a negative correlation between the performance of traditionally masculine and feminine tasks. Results, however, showed no significant relationship between performing male and female activities, $r(42) = .14$, $p = .18$.

Analyses examining the links between sex roles and the perceived balance of power yielded mixed results. Women in equal power relationships were more feminist in their responses to the Sex-Role Traditionalism scale than women in unequal power relationships, $t(75) = 1.05$, $p < .05$, a one-tailed test. But no association was found between the balance of power and women's recent participation in feminist groups or activities. Nor, as might be suggested by sex-typed role playing, was there any relationship between how often a partner performed traditionally masculine tasks or traditionally feminine tasks and how much power she had, $r(42) = -.06$, *ns,* and $r(42) = -.13$, *ns,* respectively. It appears that the absence of butch-femme role playing and the general feminist orientation of the majority of women in this sample limited the impact of sex-role attitudes on the balance of power.

Predicting power   Previous bivariate analyses examined how various individual factors affected the balance of power. Statistically significant associations were found between relative power and the following variables: relative involvement, relative commitment, relative education, relative income, and sex-role attitudes. A multiple regression analysis with pairwise deletion showed that these five variables accounted for 31% of the variance, $R = .55$, $F(5, 38) = 3.35$. Part correlations indicated that relative education, $r = .25$, made the largest contribution to predicting power after the four other variables were taken into account. The contributions of relative involvement, $r = .21$, and relative income, $r = .20$, were somewhat less. Relative commitment, $r = .10$, contributed least,

Table 1   Mean Scores for Lesbians in Equal Power
and Unequal Power Relationships[a]

	Equal Power	Unequal Power	t	df
Satisfaction measures				
Overall satisfaction in relationship (Maximum score = 9)	7.85	6.00	4.14[e]	75
Sexual satisfaction with partner (maximum = 9)	6.29	5.27	3.16[d]	73
Closeness to partner (maximum = 9)	8.17	6.97	3.03[d]	74
Love Scale (maximum = 9)	7.00	6.91	.26	74
Liking Scale (maximum = 9)	7.30	6.52	2.54[c]	74
Likelihood relationship will exist in one year (maximum = 7)	5.75	4.92	1.88[b]	68
Anticipated problems (scale of 0 to 2)				
My desire to be independent	.54	1.00	2.69[d]	73
Partner's desire to be independent	.43	.93	2.93[d]	73
My dependence on partner	.36	.62	1.96[b]	72
Partner's dependence on me	.41	.66	1.50[f]	73
Conflicts about exclusivity	.38	.72	2.24[c]	74
Differences in background	.21	.45	1.97[b]	74
Differences in intelligence	.15	.31	1.38[f]	74
Differences in interests	.49	.76	1.61[f]	74
Total of 17 problems (maximum = 34)	6.44	9.21	2.31[c]	71

[a]Degrees of freedom *(df)* vary slightly due to missing data. Significance tests are one-tailed.
[b]$p < .05$.   [c]$p < .025$.   [d]$p < .01$.   [e]$p < .001$.   [f]$p < .10$.

probably because of its substantial correlation with relative involvement. Sex-role attitudes, $r = .12$, added little and accounted for only 1.5% of the variance in power.

Satisfaction and Anticipated Problems

A final set of analyses examined links between the perceived balance of power and measures of satisfaction and problems in the relationship.

Satisfaction   Since most women endorsed an ideal of equal power for their relationship, it was predicted that women in unequal relationships would be less satisfied than women in equal relationships. Comparisons of equal power and unequal power relationships provided clear support for this prediction. As shown in Table 1, women in equal power relationships reported greater satisfaction with the overall relationship and with the sexual aspect of their relationship. They also rated their relationships as significantly closer. These differences occurred even though women in the sample generally felt quite satisfied and close to their partner. The mean level of overall satisfaction with the relationship fell midway between "moderately satisfied" and "extremely satisfied" (mean of 7.14 on a nine-point scale). Similar results were obtained for satisfaction with sex (mean of 5.88 on a seven-point scale) and for closeness (mean of 7.68 on a nine-point scale).

Additional analyses examined the association of perceived power and scores on Rubin's (1973) Love and Liking Scales. Consistent with the findings for satisfaction, women in equal power relationships reported greater liking for their partners than did women in unequal power relationships (see Table 1). Strong feelings of respect and affection were concomitants of power equality among the lesbians in this sample. In contrast, no association was found between power and scores on Rubin's Love Scale, a measure of feelings of attachment, caring, and intimacy.

No differences were found in the duration of equal and unequal power relationships. Women in equal power relationships were, however, more likely to predict that their relationship would continue for the next year. This may reflect the greater satisfaction of women in egalitarian relationships and their anticipation of fewer problems in their relationship.

Anticipated problems   It was expected that women in equal power relationships would anticipate fewer problems in their relationship. Women indicated how likely each of 17 factors was to lead to difficulties in their relationship in the next year. Included were such potential problems as desire to be independent, differences in interests, pressure from parents, and jealousy. In general, lesbians anticipated few problems in their relationships. Most women reported that the potential problems listed were unlikely to lead to difficulties or would be only minor problems. Nonetheless, as shown in Table 1, women in unequal power relationships anticipated a greater number of problems than women in egalitarian relationships.

An examination of specific problems that were of greater concern to women in unequal power versus equal power relationships highlighted the importance of issues of dependence and independence. Women in unequal power relationships were significantly more worried about possible problems caused by "my partner's desire to be independent," "my desire to be independent," "my dependence on my partner," and "conflicting attitudes about exclusivity in our relationship." Only one related item, "my partner's dependence on me," fell short of statistical significance. These results, as a whole, are consistent with earlier data directly linking imbalances of involvement with imbalances of power.

There was also a tendency for women in unequal power relationships to anticipate greater problems due to differences in background, intelligence, and interests. But only differences in background reached statistical significance. Other problems not linked to power were differences in political views, pressure from parents, feelings about being a lesbian, societal attitudes toward lesbian relationships, conflicting attitudes about sex, jealousy and living too far apart.

To reiterate, women in egalitarian and unequal power relationships did not differ in their love for their partner or in the duration of their current relationship. An imbalance of power in lesbian relationships was not the result of lack of love for the partner, nor a "phase" in relationship development. Results clearly indicated that women in unequal power relationships were less satisfied with the relationship, felt less closeness, scored lower on a measure of liking for their partner, anticipated more problems in the relationship, and were less confident that the relationship would continue. These findings seem to suggest that for lesbians, egalitarian relationships may function better than unequal power relationships. Imbalances in dependency and resources may produce strains in relationships, leading to lower satisfaction and greater problems.

Discussion

Although the lesbian women in our sample were strong supporters of the egalitarian ideal of shared power in love relationships, nearly 40% of the women perceived the balance of power in their current relationship as unequal. Social exchange theory proved a useful framework for understanding power imbalances in lesbian relationships. Women were likely to be at a power disadvantage if they were more involved in the relationship than their partner and if they had relatively less education or less income than their partner. Four variables measuring relative dependence and resources (i.e., involvement, commitment, education, and income) accounted for over a quarter of the variance in power.

This study examined a rather limited set of personal resources. Safilios-Rothschild (1976) has suggested that other important resources in interpersonal relationships may include prestige, affection, understanding, intellectual companionship, and housekeeping services. Future research might profitably examine a wider range of resources. It may be that women in lesbian and heterosexual relationships differ in the availability and the importance of particular resources. For example, in contemporary society, men have greater access to socioeconomic resources than do women; thus, women are likely to enter heterosexual relationships with a power disadvantage (Bernard, 1972) that is not present in lesbian relationships. Lesbians and heterosexuals may also differ in the value or importance they place on particular resources. One stereotype suggests that a woman's physical beauty is a greater asset in a heterosexual relationship than in a lesbian relationship. A detailed account of the personal resources that are central in lesbian relationships is currently lacking.

Links between feminism and power in lesbian relationships were ambiguous, perhaps because a majority of the women in our sample had pro-feminist beliefs. The balance of power was significantly related to a measure of sex-role attitudes, but was not related to personal involvement in feminist activities. The impact of feminist beliefs on power may be complex. For example, while feminism may increase a woman's desire for an egalitarian relationship, it may also provide her with more exacting standards of what constitutes equality. It appears that egalitarian attitudes alone can not always compensate for major imbalances in dependency or resources. Contrary to cultural myth, no evidence was found that lesbians engaged in a sex-typed division of household activities. Butch-femme role playing did not occur and was not a determinant of the balance of power in the relationships we studied.

Among the lesbians in this study, there was a clear association between power equality and satisfaction with a relationship. Women in equal power relationships reported greater personal satisfaction and closeness, and anticipated fewer problems in their relationships than did women in unequal power relationships. This contrasts with findings using similar power measures in a sample of heterosexual dating couples (Peplau, 1979). Among that college sample, men and women were equally satisfied in egalitarian and male-dominant relationships, but were dissatisfied in female-dominant relationships. Lacking a cultural ideology that endorses the superiority of one partner as boss and decision maker, lesbians may be less comfortable than heterosexuals with unequal power relationships.

Our study provides a first attempt to describe and analyze the balance of power in lesbian relationships. Research on this topic with women from other segments of the lesbian population (e.g., women who are older or from working-class backgrounds) would be valuable. Nonetheless, the present study does suggest that being in a lesbian relationship is no sure guarantee of avoiding power imbalances. Even among lesbian feminists who have been sensitized to power issues in personal relationships, the balance of power can be tipped away from equality if the two partners are not equally involved and do not possess equal resources. The determinants of the balance of power go beyond attitudes and reflect processes of social exchange that can occur regardless of ideology or affectional preference.

References

Barnhart, E. Friends and lovers in a lesbian counterculture community. In N. N. Glazer-Malbin (Ed.), *Old family, new family.* New York: Van Nostrand, 1975.

Bernard, J. *The future of marriage.* New York: Bantam Books, 1972.

Blau, P. M. *Exchange and power in social life.* New York: Wiley, 1964.

Blood, R. O., Jr., & Wolfe, D. M. *Husbands and wives: The dynamics of married living.* Glencoe, Ill.: Free Press, 1960.

Centers, R., Raven, B. H., & Rodrigues, A. Conjugal power structure: A reexamination. *American Sociological Review,* 1971, *36,* 264–277.

Chafetz, J. S. *Masculine/feminine or human: An overview of the sociology of sex roles.* Itasca, Ill.: Peacock, 1974.

Cromwell, R. E., & Olson, D. H. (Eds.). *Power in families.* New York: Wiley, 1975.

Gillespie, D. Who has the power? The marital struggle. *Journal of Marriage and the Family,* 1971, *33*(3), 445–458.

Hill, C. T., Rubin, Z., & Peplau, L. A. Breakups before marriage: The end of 103 affairs. *Journal of Social Issues,* 1976, *32*(1), 147–168.

Kelly, J. Sister love: An exploration of the need for homosexual experience. *Family Coordinator,* 1972, *21*(4), 473–475.

Millett, K. *Sexual politics.* Garden City, N.Y.: Doubleday, 1970.

Morin, S. F. Heterosexual bias in psychological research on lesbianism and male homosexuality. *American Psychologist,* 1977, *32,* 329–337.

Olson, D. H., & Rabunsky, C. Validity of four measures of family power. *Journal of Marriage and the Family*, 1972, *34*, 224–234.

Peplau, L. A. *The impact of fear of success, sex-role attitudes and opposite-sex relationships on women's intellectual performance*. Unpublished doctoral dissertation, Harvard University, 1973.

_____. Power in dating relationships. In J. Freeman (Ed.), *Women: A feminist perspective* (2nd ed.). Palo Alto: Mayfield, 1979.

Peplau, L. A., Cochran, S., Rook, K., & Padesky, C. Loving women: Attachment and autonomy in lesbian relationships. *Journal of Social Issues*, 1978, *34*(3), 7–28.

Peplau, L. A., & Gordon, S. L. The intimate relationships of lesbians and gay men. In E. R. Allgeier & N. B. McCormick (Eds.), *Changing boundaries: Gender roles and sexual behavior*. Palo Alto: Mayfield, 1982.

Peplau, L. A., Rubin, Z., & Hill, C. T. The sexual balance of power. *Psychology Today*, November 1976, 142–151.

Poloma, M. A., & Garland, T. N. The married professional woman: A study in the tolerance of domestication. *Journal of Marriage and the Family*, 1971, *33*, 531–540.

Rollins, B. C., & Bahr, S. J. A theory of power relationships in marriage. *Journal of Marriage and the Family*, 1976, *38*, 619–629.

Rubin, Z. *Liking and loving: An invitation to social psychology*. New York: Holt, 1973.

Safilios-Rothschild, C. The study of family power structure: A review, 1960–1969. *Journal of Marriage and the Family*, 1970, *32*, 539–552.

_____. A macro- and micro-examination of family power and love: An exchange model. *Journal of Marriage and the Family*, 1976, *38*, 355–362.

Thibaut, J. W., & Kelley, H. H. *The social psychology of groups*. New York: Wiley, 1959.

Waller, W. *The family: A dynamic interpretation*. New York: Gordon, 1938.

The Decision to Leave an Abusive Relationship: Economic Dependence and Psychological Commitment

Michael J. Strube and Linda S. Barbour

Introduction

Recently, social scientists have begun to examine the problem of wife abuse in depth, and a small but growing literature has begun to accumulate (for several useful treatments of the topic, see Gelles, 1979; Hilberman, 1980; Martin, 1977; Roy, 1977; Straus, Gelles and Steinmetz, 1978; Straus and Hotaling, 1980). Estimates of prevalance suggest that as many as 1.8 million women are beaten by their husbands each year (Straus, 1978), a figure that is almost certainly an underestimate given the likely occurrence of massive underreporting (see Straus, Gelles and Steinmetz, 1978). For many women the problem is not simply one of being shoved once or twice. Rather, the abuse is a severe, chronic problem. For example, in the national survey conducted by Straus and his colleagues (Straus, Gelles and Steinmetz, 1978), two thirds of the women who reported a beating (which *did not* include pushing or slapping) also indicated that such abuse occurred two or more times during the interview year. Indeed, nearly half of those women had experienced five or more attacks (see also Fojtik, 1978). For nearly 1700 women each year, the violence ends in death (Steinmetz, 1978; see also Fields, 1978; Ohrenstein, 1977).

One somewhat puzzling aspect of wife abuse is the fact that many women choose to remain in the abusive relationship. For example, Snyder and Fruchtman (1981) interviewed 119 battered women admitted to a shelter in Detroit. At intake, only 13% of the women intended to return to their assailants. However, at discharge 34% indicated such an intention, and at follow-up six-to-ten weeks later fully 60% of those contacted had returned. Gelles (1974) likewise found a majority of battered women still living with their abusive partners (78%), as did Pfouts (1978—57%), Labell (1979—64%), Fojtik (1978—59%) and Hilberman and Munson (1978—53%). Obviously, substantial pressures must be operating to keep a woman in a relationship where she risks severe injury or death. The

Portions of this paper were previously presented at the annual meeting of the American Psychological Association, Washington, DC, August 1982. We would like to thank Jetse Sprey and two anonymous reviewers for their helpful comments.

From Michael J. Strube and Linda S. Barbour, *Journal of Marriage and the Family* Vol. 45, No. 4 (November 1983):785–793. Copyright © 1983 by the National Council on Family Relations. Reprinted by permission.

present study examined the role of economic dependence and psychological commitment as two such factors in the decision to leave or remain in an abusive relationship.

Economic Dependence

Lack of economic resources has long been suspected of playing a major role in a battered woman's tolerance of abuse (e.g., Fields, 1978; Gelles, 1974, 1976; Hilberman, 1980; Roy, 1977; Truninger, 1971). Many battered women lack the education, skills, or motivation to obtain employment. Responsibility for child care likewise can preclude the acquisition of work outside the home. Not surprisingly, unemployment among battered women is high (57.4% in Fojtik, 1978; 56% in Gelles, 1974; 65% in Hilberman and Munson, 1978; 72% in Snyder and Fruchtman, 1981). In short, economic dependence appears to be a major factor that prevents termination of an abusive relationship.

While commentaries concerning the importance of economic dependence in maintaining abusive relationships are abundant, clear empirical verification is surprisingly sparse. For example, Gelles (1976) examined the factors that lead to seeking various forms of intervention in an abusive relationship. Women who were divorced or separated from their assailants were more likely to be employed than were married women who sought no mode of intervention (44% vs. 25%). However, divorced or separated women were *not* more likely to be employed than women who were still married but had sought help from police or agencies (52%). In fact, when the divorced or separated women are compared with all those still married, the employment rates are the same (i.e., 44%). In addition, it is not possible to determine whether the divorced or separated women obtained their employment before or after the end of the relationship (a point that Gelles also makes). As a result, firm conclusions concerning the role of economic dependence in divorce or separation decisions in this study are not possible.

More convincing evidence comes from a recent study by Kalmuss and Straus (1982). These investigators used national survey data to examine the relationship of dependence to the incidence of minor and severe violence in intact couples. The results quite clearly demonstrated that higher rates of severe marital violence (actions carrying a high risk of serious injury) were associated with higher economic dependence. Women with fewer economic resources were more likely to tolerate severe abuse: they had no alternatives (however, see also Hornung, McCullough and Sugimoto, 1981). While this study indicates that economic dependence moderates tolerance of severe abuse, it also must be recognized that only intact couples were surveyed. Although termination of an abusive relationship is logically related to tolerance of abuse, it remains an empirical question whether economically dependent women are less likely to *leave* their abusive partners.

In summary, the available evidence is suggestive, but not conclusive, concerning the relationship of economic dependence and the decision to leave an abusive relationship. It appears that women who are more economically dependent on their partners may be more tolerant of abuse and, thus, less likely to leave. This study was aimed at providing more direct evidence bearing on this question.

Psychological Commitment

A second factor in the decision to terminate an abusive relationship—psychological commitment—was also examined in this study. Traditionally, society has been biased in the emphasis placed on the husband/wife roles. As Straus (1980) points out, traditional values suggest that being a wife and mother are the most important roles for a woman (though this value system is shifting) and that one cannot be a full woman unless one is married (see also Marsden, 1978). Not surprisingly, society places the burden of family harmony on the woman, with the implication that a failed marriage is her fault. This suggests that commitment to the relationship may be a salient factor in the decision to tolerate abuse. Although no direct evidence for the role of commitment in relationship decisions exists in the literature, discussions of related topics suggest that it may be an important factor.

A number of researchers (e.g., Hilberman, 1980; Hilberman and Munson, 1978; Prescott and Letko, 1977; Walker, 1978, 1979) have noted the parallels between the shame, guilt, depression, and low self-esteem exhibited by many battered women, and the phenomenon of learned helplessness (Seligman, 1975). Furthermore, recent developments within the learned-helplessness paradigm indicate that the cognitive, motivational, and affective deficits are most pronounced in individuals who blame themselves for their inability to control their outcomes (e.g., Abramson, Garber and Seligman, 1980). In other words, only those women who feel it is their responsibility to make the relationship work (i.e., high commitment) should exhibit the self-blame characteristic of learned helplessness. Self-blame should lead to greater tolerance of abuse and a lower likelihood of leaving the relationship, since the woman will be more likely to feel that the abuse is justified.

Greater commitment also may contribute to a common and recurrent pattern evidenced in many abusive relationships: separation followed by reconciliation (e.g., Hilberman, 1980; Hilberman and Munson, 1978; Labell, 1979; Walker, 1979). Women committed to "saving" the relationship (Pfouts, 1978) appear more willing to cling to the belief that their partners will change (Truninger, 1971). The end result is that the woman, in order to fulfill her role as a good wife and mother, agrees to "try to make it work one more time." However, a woman committed to making the relationship work may be condemning herself to a life of repeated abuse.

The above comments suggest that the more committed a woman is to her relationship, the more tolerant she will be of abuse, and the more reluctant she will be to leave her partner. The present study was designed to provide direct empirical evidence addressing this issue.

Objective vs. Subjective Assessment

This study had one additional purpose: to assess the relative utility of objective and subjective measures of the conceptual variables (i.e., economic dependence and psychological commitment). Kalmuss and Straus (1982) examined this issue in their recent investigation of marital dependence and marital violence. Not only were different results obtained for the objective and subjective measures of dependence, but a very low correlation between the measures was found ($r = .147$). This suggests that women who were economically dependent on their husbands were not necessarily aware of that dependence.[1] The present study also included objective and subjective measures in order to assess their relative merits.

In summary, this study was designed to examine the role of economic dependence and psychological commitment in the decision to leave an abusive relationship. It was expected that women who were more economically dependent on their partners would be less likely to leave the abusive relationship. Likewise, women more committed to making the relationship work were expected to be less likely to leave. Given no evidence to the contrary, these factors were expected to operate independently. Finally, these relationships were expected to hold for both objective and subjective measures, with variation in the strength of relationships anticipated as a possibility.

Method

Sample

The sample consisted of 98 women (84 Caucasian) who had contacted a counseling unit associated with the county attorney's office in a medium-sized western city. Their ages ranged from 17 to 62 ($M = 31$), with socioeconomic status in the low- to high-middle-income range. The abuse had occurred more than once and usually was a chronic problem. The violence included moderate to life-threatening physical abuse encompassing punching, kicking, biting, being thrown down or against objects, being knifed, or being shot with a gun. Injuries ranged from bruising to broken bones and scarring. All women were in, or had been in, an intimate, sexual, live-in relationship with their husbands or lovers.

Procedure

All women in the sample had contacted the counseling unit voluntarily or at the request of law enforcement officials, attorneys, relatives, or friends. Upon initial intake, a counselor collected demographic and abuse background information from which data for the present study were obtained. A follow-up contact made when a case was closed (from 1 to 18 months following intake) indicted whether a woman had remained in the relationship or had left with no intention of returning. This measure constituted the dependent variable.

Two types of data, objective and subjective, were obtained from the intake form. Objective measures were taken from the demographic section of the form, while subjective measures were abstracted from the women's responses to the counselor's open-ended request for the reasons they had remained with their partners thus far. It is important to note that at intake, when this information was obtained, all women were living with their partners. As a result, this study has the advantage of being prospective in nature, with responses at intake uncontaminated by decisions to leave or remain in the relationship.

Objective economic dependence   The objective measure of economic dependence was the presence/absence of employment outside the home. Other factors may contribute to economic dependence, such as the presence of young children in the home (Gelles, 1976; Truninger, 1971) or the inability to find a job that allows complete self-sufficiency (Kalmuss and Straus, 1982) or maintenance of current standard of living (Kinsley, 1977). While these factors are certainly important, the most basic component of economic independence is the acquisition of employment, regardless of its stature. Any job, even one that does not permit complete self-sufficiency, allows the woman an economic base with which to begin a new life and social contacts that can provide much needed support. Thus, it was expected that women employed outside the home would be more likely than unemployed women to end an abusive relationship.

Objective commitment   Length of relationship was chosen as the objective measure of commitment for several reasons. First, the more committed a woman is, the more attempts she should make to "save" the relationship. These repeated attempts should result in a longer relationship than one in which the woman is less committed and, thus, less tolerant of abuse. Furthermore, the longer a woman remains in an abusive relationship, the more effort she exerts to make the relationship function, and the more likely she will feel compelled to "justify" her past efforts with continued efforts to make the relationship work. This process of effort justification is a rather widespread phenomenon based on the psychological state of cognitive dissonance (Festinger, 1957; Wicklund and Brehm, 1976). This theory proposes that individuals attempt to avoid the uncomfortable state of having inconsistent cognitions. For example, the cognition, "I've worked very hard to make this relationship work" is inconsistent with the cognition "This relationship, for which I'm responsible, is not working." Such inconsistency is resolved by altering the most easily modified cognition. In the case of an abusive relationship in which commitment is high, the woman cannot change the fact that she has exerted much effort, so she attempts to alter the "failure of the relationship" cognition by continuing her efforts to make the relationship work. To do otherwise would be to admit that a lot of time and effort have been wasted. Moreover, the more time and effort invested, the harder it becomes to give up without success, and the less likely that the battered woman will "call it quits."

In one sense this is a somewhat paradoxical prediction. The longer the woman stays in the relationship, the more abuse (in an absolute sense) she will suffer. However, considerable psychological evidence suggests that in many "investment" situations, people will "entrap" themselves (Rubin and Brockner, 1975) in the pattern of continued investment (time, effort, money, etc.) which is undertaken to justify past investment, even to the point where total costs far exceed the value of the original goal (see Brockner, Rubin and Lang, 1981;

Brockner, Shaw and Rubin, 1979; Teger, 1980). In such situations, the individual has "too much invested to quit" (Teger, 1980) and continues to invest even though goal attainment may be low.

As a result it was expected that the more committed a battered woman is to making her relationship work, the more tolerant of abuse she will be. Furthermore, this tolerance should lead to longer relationships and continuously escalating effort justification. The end result is that the longer a woman remains in the abusive relationship, the less likely that she will leave (cf. Pfouts, 1978).

Subjective economic dependence   The reasons given by women for initially remaining in their relationships at the time of intake were classified into seven different categories (interrater agreement 91%), one of which was "economic hardship." The presence/absence of this reason was used as the subjective measure of economic dependence. It should be noted that the answers women gave were in response to the general question, "Why are you staying with him?"—not to specific questions like, "How economically dependent on your partner are you?" As such, the answers represent the most salient, self-generated reasons for the women, uncontaminated by the content of the counselor's question.

Subjective commitment   Another major category of reasons for staying with the partner—love—seemed to map adequately onto the concept of commitment. Presumably, women committed to making their relationships work would be more likely to say they remain because they still love their partners.

Additional subjective categories   The remaining reasons women gave for initially staying with their abusive partners fell into the following categories: (a) nowhere else to go, (b) staying for the sake of the children, (c) partner promised he would change, (d) fear, (e) dependence other than economic. An additional, miscellaneous category was used for idosyncratic, less frequently given reasons. These categories were included in the analysis for exploratory purposes.

Results

Overall, 61 of the 98 women decided to separate from or divorce their assailants. This percentage (62.2%) is somewhat higher than that reported in recent studies (e.g., 40% in Snyder and Fruchtman, 1981), perhaps due in part to the overall higher rate of employment in the present sample (57.1% vs. 28% in Snyder and Fruchtman's study).

Objective Measures

As expected, employment was significantly related to relationship decisions. Of the 56 women employed at intake, 41 (73.2%) had left the abusive relationship at follow-up, while only 20 (47.6%) of the 42 unemployed women chose to do so ($\chi^2(1) = 6.69$, $p < .01$). Also consistent with hypotheses, length of relationship was found to be significantly related to relationship decisions (point-biserial

Table 1 Relationship Decisions as a Function of Employment and Length of Relationship

Variables	Percentage of Women Who Had Left Relationship at Follow-up	n
Length of relationship less than four years		
Employed	75.0%	24
Unemployed	62.5%	24
Length of relationship four years or more		
Employed	71.9%	32
Unemployed	27.8%	18
Total	62.2%	98

r (96) = .21, $p < .05$). Women who had left their partners at follow-up had been in their relationships a shorter period of time ($M = 5.15$ years) than women who chose to remain with their assailants ($M = 8.27$ years). Furthermore, these two factors—employment and length of relationship—were found to be independent of each other (point-biserial r (96) = −.031).

Although no hypotheses were advanced, the combined effect of dependence and commitment was examined. To carry out this analysis, the length-of-relationship variable was dichotomized and cross-tabulated with the employment variable (see Table 1). Examination of the percentages reveals an interesting pattern. A majority of women left the relationship when they had been with their partners for less than four years *or* were employed (or both). But, when a woman was both unemployed *and* a member of a long-term relationship, it was particularly unlikely that she would leave. These results must be interpreted with caution, however, since this latter cell differs only marginally from expectation ($\chi^2(1) = 3.43$, $p < .10$) and since the overall pattern is not significant ($p > .10$).

Subjective Measures

Subjective data were available for only 79 of the 98 women. However, the missing data were equally distributed among women who eventually left the relationship (18.0%) and those who remained (21.6%).

Analyses of the subjective measures also provided support for the hypotheses. Of the 11 women who cited economic hardship as a reason for initially remaining with their partners, only 2 (18.2%) subsequently left the relationship (see Table 2). By contrast, 48 (70.6%) of the 68 women not citing economic hardship as a reason for initially remaining had left the relationship at follow-up. The difference in these percentages is significant (Yates corrected $\chi^2(1) = 9.05$, $p < .01$). In addition, of the 17 women who said they initially remained because of love, only 6 (35.3%) had left at follow-up, while 44 (71.0%) of the 62 women not citing love as a reason for remaining chose to leave their abusers (Yates corrected

Table 2 Percentages of Self-Reported Reasons for
Initially Remaining in an Abusive Relationship

| | Final Outcome | | | |
| | Remained (n = 29) | | Left (n = 50) | |
Initial Reason for Remaining	f	%	f	%
1. Promised he would change	10	34.5	30	60.0
2. Dependence other than economic	7	24.1	11	22.0
3. Love	11	37.9	6	12.0
4. For the sake of the children	7	24.1	8	16.0
5. Economic hardship	9	31.0	2	4.0
6. Fear	0	0.0	4	8.0
7. Nowhere else to go	2	6.9	0	0.0
8. Miscellaneous	4	13.8	10	20.0

Note: Percentages are summed to greater than 100% because more than one reason could be given.

$(\chi^2(1) = 5.85, p < .025)$. These two reasons were found to be relatively independent of each aother $(\chi^2(1) = 1.17)$. In correlational terms, women who used "economic hardship" as a reason for initially remaining were slightly less likely (though not significantly so) to also cite "love" as a reason (phi coefficient $r(77) = -.12$).

An analysis of relationship decisions as a joint function of love and economic hardship also was carried out to examine their combined effect (see Table 3). Women who listed either love *or* economic hardship (or both) as reasons for initially staying were unlikely to have left at follow-up. Thus, whereas it took both unem-

Table 3 Relationship Decisions as a Function
of Self-Rated Love and Economic Hardship

Variables	Percentage of Women Who Had Left Relationship at Follow-up	n
Love not given as a reason for initially remaining		
Economic hardship not given as a reason for initially remaining	80.8%	52
Economic hardship given as a reason for initially remaining	20.0%	10
Love given as a reason for initially remaining		
Economic hardship not given as a reason for initially remaining	37.5%	16
Economic hardship given as a reason for initially remaining	0.0%	1
Total	63.3%	79

ployment *and* a long-term relationship to keep a woman in an abusive situation (see Table 1), it took only love *or* economic hardship to do so. Once again, however, the results must be interpreted with caution. Only one woman listed both reasons, precluding a reliable statistical analysis of combined effects.

The percentages of women endorsing the remaining subjective categories for initially remaining in abusive relationships are given in Table 2. One additional finding emerges: 30 (75.0%) of the 40 women who initially remained because their partners promised they would change subsequently left the relationships, while 20 (51.3%) of the 39 women not citing this reason chose to leave ($\chi^2(1) = 4.78$, $p < .05$). The baseline data suggest that this is a commonly given reason for remaining with an abusive partner (50.1% of all women). However, the differential percentages for those leaving and those remaining in the relationship indicate that it is not a very convincing or salient reason.

Relationship Between Objective and Subjective Measures

As pointed out earlier, an important consideration is the relationship between objective and subjective measures of the same conceptual variable. Consider first the economic-dependence measures. Overall, a small but significant relationship between the objective and subjective measures was found. Eight (22.8%) of the 35 unemployed women cited economic reasons for remaining with their partners, while only three (6.8%) of the 44 employed women did so (phi coefficient $r(77) = .23$, $p < .05$). At first glance this may appear to be a rather low correlation, and the percentages are certainly small in magnitude. However, it must be recognized that correlations computed from dichotomous data are limited in the maximum value they can achieve as the marginal proportions deviate from a .50/.50 split. Using a formula for estimating this upper boundary (Guilford and Fruchter, 1973), it can be shown that the maximum correlation obtainable in this instance is .36. When the obtained correlation is considered as a proportion of this maximum possible value (i.e., 64), it becomes clear that a substantial positive relationship between objective and subjective economic dependence may exist. By contrast, virtually no relationship was found between length of relationship and endorsement of love as a reason for remaining (point-biserial $r(77) = .01$).

Two additional results, pertaining to potential competing explanations for the length-of-relationship effect, require mention. First, it's possible that marital status could underlie the length-of-relationship variable. To the extent that a marital contract promotes commitment and longer relationships, marital status would qualify as a more basic cause of the length-of-relationship effect. This proved not to be the case in the present sample. Nearly equal percentages of women who remained in (89.2%) or who left (86.9%) abusive relationships were married at intake. A second potential mediating variable is onset of abuse. While women who chose to remain with their abusers had been in their relationships longer than women who decided to leave, it's possible that the abuse began later and, thus, was less chronic in the former case. Such an explanation would be simpler than the somewhat paradoxical commitment explanation. It was found, however, that length of relationship and time of abuse onset (length of abuse) were very highly correlated (r (75) = .93, p < .001) indicating their virtual psychometric equivalence. Furthermore, the abuse began at about the same time for women who eventually left (M = 60.8 weeks after the beginning of the relationship) and those who remained (M = 43.5 weeks after beginning of relationship), t (75) = .48. If anything, the abuse began slightly sooner for women who remained with their abusers. The means suggest that abuse began nearly a year after the initiation of the relationship. This is somewhat of a distortion due to a high degree of skew in the data. In 60% of the cases, the onset of abuse was simultaneous with the beginning of the relationship

Discussion

The results of the present investigation provided support for the major hypotheses and also suggested several patterns of data worthy of future study. As expected, economic dependence was found to be a significant factor in the decisions by battered women to leave or remain in their abusive relationships. Furthermore, this proved to be the case for both the objective and subjective measures. Indeed, a moderate relationship between the measures suggests that economic dependence is a particularly salient factor to women in their decisions.

By contrast, the two measures of commitment were found to be unassociated with each other, though both were associated to relationship decisions. There are several possible reasons for this finding. It may be that both measures tap different aspects of the conceptual domain of commitment (i.e., it is multidimensional, cf. Kalmuss and Straus, 1982); or the lack of association may indicate an absence of subjective awareness by women of their objective commitment (cf. Nisbett and Wilson, 1977). Finally, it's possible that both measures are tapping completely different conceptual domains. This latter explanation seems unlikely given the face validity of love as a measure of commitment and the substantial research base suggesting length of relationship as a valid operationalization. Obviously, it will take further study to untangle the problem. Nonetheless, the present results indicate that commitment is an important factor in the decision to terminate an abusive relationship— independent of economic considerations.

An important practical issue is the degree to which objective and subjective measures differ in their predictive utility. As noted above, both sets of measures and each of their components were significantly associated with relationship decisions. However, it is also useful to determine if one type of measure is better than the other. When multiple regression techniques are applied to the two sets of results, it is found that the objective measures account for 11.6% of the variance in relationship decisions but that the subjective measures account for 26.6% of the variance. This over twofold increase indicates that the greater effort typically required to obtain self-report data may be justified when investigating relationship decisions.

Two intriguing patterns of data were uncovered when the joint effects of economic dependence and commitment were examined. With the objective measures it was found that if a woman was both unemployed *and* a member of a long-term relationship it was unlikely that she would leave her partner; neither factor alone resulted in a large percentage of women remaining with their abusers. On the other hand, with the subjective measures it was found that if economic hardship *or* love was cited as a reason for initially remaining in the relationship it was likely that the woman would still be in that relationship at follow-up. The questionable statistical reliability of these data dictate that one proceed with caution in interpretation. These patterns do suggest, however, that the objective and subjective measures might be tapping different processes (in which case it becomes important to use both measures). While future research is necessary, these data underscore the importance of considering both objective and subjective variables (Kalmuss and Straus, 1982).

One more set of results deserves mention. In addition to economic dependence and love, women gave several other reasons for initially remaining in abusive relationships. Of these, only the promise by the partner that he would change was related to subsequent relationship decisions. This suggests that, while a variety of factors may be involved in initial tolerance of abuse (e.g., fear, nowhere to go, presence of children), not all are salient or important factors when a decision to leave the relationship is made. Of particular note is the fact that 18 women cited noneconomic dependence as a reason for initially staying with their partners. That this factor was not related to subsequent decisions indicates that discriminating among types of dependence is important in the present context.

Although this study indicates that economic dependence and commitment are two important factors in the decision to terminate an abusive relationship, several limitations must be recognized. First, the causal role of these factors is not entirely discernable. As many researchers have noted, the dynamics of marital violence are exceedingly complex (see, e.g., Gelles, 1974; Straus, Gelles and Steinmetz, 1978; Straus and Hotaling, 1980). It seems unlikely that economic dependence and commitment are direct causes of violence. Rather, as Kalmuss and Straus (1982) suggest with their data on dependence, the present factors most likely mediate the woman's tolerance for abuse. The prospective nature of our study does lead us to suspect, however, that economic dependence and commitment are directly linked to decisions regarding relationship maintenance. Second, while the two factors investigated in this study account for a substantial proportion of the variance in relationship decisions, other factors require examination. For example, it seems likely that the woman's prior exposure to violence in her family of origin (e.g., Gelles, 1976), the extensiveness of her social-support system, and her emotional and physical well-being all contribute to her tolerance of abuse and ultimately to the decision to leave. In addition, the role of guilt about one's participation in an abusive relationship may play an important role in the woman's decision to "give the relationship another chance." This seems particularly likely given the reciprocal nature of abusive relationships (e.g., Straus, Gelles and Steinmetz, 1978). Third, the complex nature of this decision process requires that future research examine the interactive effects of decision components. This study could only partly address the issue of interaction among decision factors, but it suggested that this may be a particularly fruitful line of investigation. Finally, certain sample limitations must be noted. All of the women in this study sought help voluntarily and, thus, are not a random sample. In particular, the sample is biased toward the lower and middle socioeconomic classes and is predominantly white. As a result generalizations must be made with care.

The continued study of decisions by battered women to leave their abusive partners will provide information of both practical and theoretical importance. This decision process lies at the heart of the woman's perception of her violent relationship. By further application of current sociological and psychological theory, a better understanding of abusive relationships will be gained. For example, this study suggests that the principles of entrapment (e.g., Rubin nd Brockner, 1975) found in many decision-making contexts also may exist in relationship decisions. Further examination of this possibility is warranted. In addition, the identification of factors that are important in the decisions of women who leave their relationships can pinpoint those factors that may be modified for women who cannot leave. By changing the battered woman's beliefs concerning her role in the relationship, both her tendency toward self-blame and the likelihood of escalating entrapment may be reduced.

In summary, this study has provided direct empirical evidence for the role of economic dependence and psychological commitment in decisions to leave an abusive relationship. The multiple measures of each variable and the prospective nature of the data collection indicate that these relationships are both robust and not a function of retrospective biases. Future research will be necessary, however, in order to clarify possible interactions among these factors. Furthermore, the theoretical and practical importance of understanding the dynamics of marital violence mandates that other decision-relevant factors be investigated.

Note

1. While the tendency for people to be inaccurate in reporting on the reasons for their behavior has been well established (e.g., Nisbett and Wilson, 1977), one must be aware of other possibilities. Specifically, both the objective and subjective measures must be equally valid indices of the underlying conceptual variable; otherwise the lack of correlation between the two may be due to the fact that they are tapping the same conceptual variable with differential success, or that they are tapping different conceptual variables. In practice, these possibilities can be difficult to discriminate.

References

Abramson, L. Y., Garber, J., and Seligman, M. E. P. 1980. "Learned helplessness in humans: an attributional analysis." In J. Garber and M. E. P. Seligman (Eds.), Human Helplessness: Theory and Applications. New York: Academic Press.

Brockner, J., Rubin, J. E., and Lang, B. 1981. "Face-saving and entrapment." Journal of Experimental Social Psychology 17:68–79.

Brockner, J., Shaw, M. C., and Rubin, J. Z. 1979. "Factors affecting withdrawal from an escalating conflict: quitting before it's too late." Journal of Experimental Social Psychology 15:492–503.

Festinger, L. 1957. A Theory of Cognitive Dissonance. Stanford, CA: Stanford University Press.

Fields, M. D. 1978. "Wife beating: facts and figures." Victimology: An International Journal 2:643–647.

Fojtik, K. M. 1978. "The NOW domestic violence project." Victimology: An International Journal 2:653–657.

Foss, J. E. 1980. "The paradoxical nature of family relationships and family conflict." In M. A. Straus and G. T. Hotaling (Eds.), The Social Causes of Husband-Wife Violence. Minneapolis, MN: University of Minnesota Press.

Gelles, R. J. 1974. The Violent Home: A Study of Physical Aggression between Husbands and Wives. Beverly Hills, CA: Sage.

_____. 1976. "Abused wives: why do they stay?" Journal of Marriage and the Family 38 (November):659–668.

_____. 1979. Family Violence. Beverly Hills, CA: Sage.

Guilford, J. P., and Fruchter, B. 1973. Fundamental Statistics in Psychology and Education (5th ed.). New York: McGraw-Hill.

Hilberman, E. 1980. "Overview: the 'wife-beater's wife' reconsidered." American Journal of Psychiatry 137:1336–1347.

Hilberman, E., and Munson, K. 1978. "Sixty battered women." Victimology: An International Journal 2:460–470.

Hornung, C. A., McCullough, B. C., and Sugimoto, T. 1981. "Status relationships in marriage: risk factors in spouse abuse." Journal of Marriage and the Family 43 (August):675–692.

Kalmuss, D. S., and Straus, M. A. 1982. "Wife's marital dependency and wife abuse." Journal of Marriage and the Family 44 (May):277–286.

Kinsley, S. 1977. "Women's dependency and federal programs." In J. R. Chapman and M. Gates (Eds.), Women into Wives: The Legal and Economic Impact of Marriage. Beverly Hills, CA: Sage.

Labell, L. S. 1979. "Wife abuse: a sociological study of battered women and their mates." Victimology: An International Journal 4:258–267.

Marsden, D. 1978. "Sociological perspectives on family violence." In J. P. Martin (Ed.), Violence and the Family. New York: Wiley.

Martin, D. 1977. Battered Wives. New York: Pocket Books.

Nisbett, R. E., and Wilson, T. D. 1977. "Telling more than we can know: verbal reports on mental processes." Psychological Review 84:231–259.

Ohrenstein, M. 1977. Battered Women: Statewide Task Force Study on Battered Women. New York Senate Publication (available from the Office of New York State Senate Minority Leader, 270 Broadway, New York, NY 10007).

Pfouts, J. S. 1978. "Violent families: coping responses of abused wives." Child Welfare 57:101–111.

Prescott, S., and Letko, C. 1977. "Battered women: a social psychological perspective." In M. Roy (Ed.), Battered Women: A Psychosociological Study of Domestic Violence. New York: Van Nostrand Reinhold.

Roy, M. (Ed.). 1977. Battered Women: A Psychosociological Study of Domestic Violence. New York: Van Nostrand Reinhold.

Rubin, J. Z., and Brockner, J. 1975. "Factors affecting entrapment in waiting situations: the Rosencrantz and Guildenstern effect." Journal of Personality and Social Psychology 31:1054–1063.

Seligman, M. E. P. 1975. Helplessness: On Depression, Development, and Death. San Francisco, CA: Freeman.

Snyder, D. K., and Fruchtman, L. A. 1981. "Differential patterns of wife abuse: a data-based typology." Journal of Consulting and Clinical Psychology 49:878–885.

Steinmetz, S. K. 1978. "Violence between family members." Marriage and Family Review 1:1–16.

Straus, M. A. 1978. "Wife beating: how common and why?" Victimology: An International Journal 2:443–458.

_____. 1980. "Sexual inequality and wife beating." In M. A. Straus and G. T. Hotaling (Eds.), The Social Causes of Husband-Wife Violence. Minneapolis, MN: University of Minnesota Press.

Straus, M. A., Gelles, R. J., and Steinmetz, S. K. 1978. Behind Closed Doors: Violence in the American Family. Garden City, NY: Anchor Books.

Straus, M. A., and Hotaling, G. T. (Eds.). 1980. The Social Causes of Husband-Wife Violence. Minneapolis, MN: University of Minnesota Press.

Teger, A. I. 1980. Too Much Invested to Quit. New York: Pergamon.

Truninger, E. 1971. "Marital violence: the legal solutions." Hastings Law Review 13:159–176.

Walker, L. E. 1978. "Battered women and learned helplessness." Victimology: An International Journal 2:525–534.

_____. 1979. The Battered Woman. New York: Harper & Row.

Wicklund, R. A., and Brehm, J. W. 1976. Perspectives on Cognitive Dissonance. Hillsdale, NJ: Erlbaum.

5

Paid Work and Family Work

The housewife is held to her work by duty and by love; also by necessity. She cannot "better herself" by leaving; and indeed without grave loss and pain, she cannot leave at all. So the wife struggles on, too busy to complain; and accomplishes, under this threefold bond of duty, love, and necessity far more than can be expected of a comparatively free agent [*Charlotte Perkins Gillman, 1903*].

As we have seen, the growth of industry in the nineteenth century disrupted the intergration of production and family life. By the mid-nineteenth century a conception of a radical disjunction between the home and the workplace had taken hold and, because of increasingly efficient communication networks, had spread to virtually every corner of the United States. Men and women viewed the home sentimentally, as a place to escape the harsh realities of "the world" and a place where the human solidarity absent in the world of work could be nurtured (Ehrenreich and English, 1980:221).

Although the doctrine of separate spheres was apparently widely shared, its acceptance camouflaged important variations in gender roles by class and the ways in which women escaped the confines of the home (Ryan, 1979:79). For many working-class women, particularly immigrant and black women, the doctrine may have served only as a reminder of a less difficult and seemingly unobtainable way of life. For many middle-class women, the doctrine obscured the many ways in which their activities extended beyond the boundaries of the family. For example, nineteenth-century women played crucial roles in reform movements, from abolition to temperance, and organized and operated charitable activities. Although both charity and reform were aimed at human betterment and were considered consistent with women's sphere, these activities led the way out of the home and laid the foundation for direct challenges to restrictions on women's roles by nineteenth-century feminists.

The tenuous cultural hegemony of the doctrine of separate spheres also camouflaged the relationship between work done inside and outside the home. Although some nineteenth-century thinkers such as Karl Marx and Charlotte Perkins Gilman examined these connections, students of the family have drawn on the work of these scholars only recently. Louise Lamphere (1986), for example, uses the ideas of Karl Marx to show that paid work and family work are simply two sides of the same coin. Marx suggested that human beings use their labor power to create material goods to satisfy their needs. As they do so, their labor power must be replenished through physical and psychological care and by the upbringing and education of new laborers. Production, therefore, is sustained only by the reproduction of labor power.

As production moved out of the home in the nineteenth century, much reproductive labor remained behind as the unpaid work of women in the family. Because the work of housewives was private and uncompensated, it was not considered work. Nevertheless, the work of paid laborers is made possible only by those working in the home and receiving payment indirectly through wage earners. In fact, as Gilman observed at the turn of the century, housewives may accomplish much more under the bonds of duty, love, and economic dependence on wage earners than if they were working for wages alone.

Lamphere (p. 119) maintains that it is important not the think of production and reproduction simply as "glosses for the terms 'work place' and 'family' but to think of them as analytical concepts which point to important relationships and changes in either place." For example, productive work moved out of the home only gradually, and the two spheres remain partially integrated even today for owners of small businesses, farmers, and migrant workers. Equally important, but less easily recognized, reproductive work also takes place outside the home. Workers and managers must be taught their jobs and to accept the division of labor and the unequal distribution of resources as legitimate. In this sense, reproduction takes place in schools, factories, and through the media.

In this chapter we examine the changing relationships of productive and reproductive work to the family. Our focus is on the participation of women in the paid labor force and its impact on the organization of labor in the home.

Women in the Labor Force

In the years prior to the Civil War, most white women worked on family-owned farms, and most black women labored in servitude as field hands and domestic workers. However, some women did engage in occupations that took them away from farms and domestic labor. Women were silversmiths, barbers, and wood-workers, and owned taverns, inns, and shops of various kinds. However, these craftswomen and "she merchants" were usually widows who had taken over their husbands' businesses. That they did so attests to their familiarity with the family enterprise and to the belief that women were capable of taking the place of their husbands if necessity required (Degler, 1980:365). Women were most likely to take over family businesses when shop and home were closely connected. As production and the family began to separate physically and the percentage of independent entrepreneurs declined in the nineteenth century, so too did the percentage of female proprietors. According to Gerda Lerner (1979:22), there were fewer female storekeepers and businesswomen in the 1830s than in colonial days.

Lerner (pp. 18–21) also suggests that opportunities for women declined in many professions in the nineteenth century. Prior to the Revolution, for example, there were no medical schools and few laws regulated medical practice. One became a doctor by serving an apprenticeship with an established practitioner. Although the number of female physicians in the years before 1800 is unknown, Lerner suggests that the "occasional 'doctress' was fully accepted and frequently well rewarded." The establishment of medical schools and medical licensing standards in the nineteenth century effectively barred women from the practice of medicine. In 1850, admission to nearly all of the forty-two medical schools in the United States was closed to women. The picture improved toward the end of the century, but as late as 1920 one-third of all medical schools did not admit women. The practice of law was similarly closed to women throughout the century. Arabella Mansfield of Iowa became the first women attorney in 1869, but by 1891 only 200 women were practicing law in the United States (Degler, 1980:382).

In some occupations, however, the number of female workers increased rapidly throughout the nineteenth century. A severe labor shortage marked the first decades of industrialization in the United States. Men were engaged primarily in agriculture, where the slow pace of mechanization kept labor requirements high. As a result, factory owners depended on the labor of women and children. For most of the nineteenth century, women outnumbered men in the textile industry and accounted for a substantial proportion of laborers in other industries as well. In 1850, 25 percent of all workers employed in manufacture were female. The proportion had declined to 20 percent by 1860 as immigration increased the supply of cheap male labor. Nevertheless, the number of women working in factories continued to climb, increasing by 500 percent between 1850 and 1900 (Degler, pp. 368–72).

Although manufacturing was an important source of female employment in the nineteenth century, the greatest number of women were employed in domestic service. The growth of cities and of the urban middle class increased the demand for servants, and 45 percent of all employed women worked as domestic servants by 1880 (Degler, p. 377). The wages for domestic service were lower than for factory work, and women considered the work less desirable. However, the number of women seeking factory work was greater than the number of jobs available, and many women had few options other than entering domestic service. As the century progressed, some women found employment in retail sales and clerical work. These jobs were more desirable than either factory work or domestic service and were taken primarily by better-educated and native-born women (Kessler-Harris, 1982:135).

One profession in which the number of women increased substantially in the nineteenth century was teaching. Lerner (1979:23) suggests that women were available to fill the demand created by the expansion of public schooling just as they had filled a labor shortage in the factory. In 1860, 78 percent of all teachers and approximately 90 percent of all teachers in cities were women. Although only a small percentage of women were schoolteachers at any one time, teaching was a part of the lives of many women in the nineteenth century. A study in Massachusetts found that 20 percent of all women had worked as teachers at one point in their lives (Degler, 1980:381). Women educators worked cheaply, receiving 30 to 50 percent less than male teachers.

Employment in factories, domestic service, and teaching contributed to the increasing percentage of women in the labor force during the nineteenth century. Fifteen percent of all women sixteen years of age and older were employed in 1860, 18 percent in 1880, and 20 percent in 1900. However, these figures mask important differences in the prevalence of wage-earning women in different groups. First, married women were much less likely to work outside the home than single women. In 1990, approximately 5 percent of married women were employed, accounting for less than 15 percent of all employed women. Second, immigrant women, both single and married, were more likely to be employed than native-born women. In 1900, 15 percent of white women with native-born parents, 25 percent of native-born women with foreign-born parents, and 19 percent of foreign-born women worked outside the home. Third, married and single black women were much more likely to be in the paid labor force than white women. Forty-three percent of black women were employed in 1900 (Degler, p. 384). Therefore, the female labor force was composed primarily of single women and those women who faced economic hardship. Most women withdrew from the labor force when they married to concentrate their energies on the tasks necessary to maintain a household. These patterns remained substantially unchanged for the first half of the twentieth century.

An important factor in institutionalizing women's secondary position in the labor force at the turn of the century was legislation regulating women's participation in the workplace (Kessler-Harris, 1982:181). This protective legislation limited the number of hours women could work, restricted the conditions under which they could labor, and prohibited them from working in certain occupations. Support for protective legislation came from diverse sources including labor unions, women's groups, and reform organizations, and its ultimate effect was to contribute to women's unequal participation in the labor force. Proponents of this legislation argued that women, like children, were a special group requiring the protection of the state. Women, they maintained, were weaker than men and could not work under the same conditions. In addition, the health of women needed to be protected since they would give birth to and raise the next generation of workers. Some went so far as to suggest that women were not only constitutionally but morally different and needed to be restricted from occupations and conditions that threatened their innocence.

Although male-dominated labor unions publicly supported protectionist legislation for these reasons, they had other motives as well. If the hours per day that women worked were limited or the conditions under which they could work were restricted in other ways, the competition of women with men for jobs would be reduced. Thus, for example, when New York City passed a law in 1919 prohibiting women from working on streetcars during rush periods (because it was supposedly too stressful), 800 women lost their jobs (Kessler-Harris, p. 194). The relegation of women to a secondary position in the labor force served another goal of organized labor—the "family wage," which would be paid to each male worker and which would be enough to support a wife and children (Sidel, 1986:52). Although the family wage was never a reality for many workers, unions were in a better position to demand higher wages and could make a better case for receiving them if women were not competing with men for jobs.

States began to pass protective legislation in the 1870s, and state courts upheld the constitutionality of the laws on the grounds of the inherent physical weaknesses of women. In 1908, the Supreme Court gave its seal of approval to protective legislation in *Muller* v. *Oregon*. In that case, an Oregon law establishing a ten-hour work day for women was upheld on the grounds that it was necessary to protect women's health. A brief submitted to the Court by Louis Brandeis and his sister-in-law, Josephine Goldmark, claimed that "women are fundamentally weaker than men in all that makes for endurance: muscular strength, nervous energy, in powers of persistent persuasion and application" (Kessler-Harris, 1982:187). The Court was persuaded, and its decision opened the way for the passage of numerous protectionist laws. By 1917, thirty-nine states had laws limiting the workday for women. As late as 1969, twenty-six states had laws barring women from some jobs (Degler, 1980:404).

Although support for protectionists legislation was widespread, it was not without its opponents. Some in the women's movement opposed laws restricting women's participation in the labor force because they conflicted with the struggle for equal rights for women. If protection and restrictions were extended to women in occupations, the way was open for special treatment and discrimination in other areas. This branch of the women's movement eventually urged the passage of an equal rights amendment eliminating all discrimination against women, fully recognizing that its passage would strike down all protectionist legislation. The amendment was introduced in Congress in 1923. It remains unratified, testifying to the persistence of the beliefs that inspired protectionist legislation at the turn of the century.

Because of beliefs about the proper roles of women, protectionist legislation, and other barriers, the percentage of women in the labor force rose slowly in the first four decades of this century, from 20 percent in 1900 to 27 percent in 1940. A significant change did take place in the kinds of work women did during this period, however. In 1900 nearly 1.5 million women were manual workers, and about 1.5 million were in private domestic service. Approximately 1 million women worked in clerical, sales, and other white-collar jobs. However, by 1940 the number of women engaged in white-collar occupations had increased to over 5.6 million. The numbers of women in manual work and private domestic work had barely doubled, to approximately 2.7 million and 2.3 million, respectively.

Beginning with World War II, the employment situation for women changed dramatically. During the war women entered the work force in large numbers to replace men and to fill the demand for labor in the war industries, such as metals, chemicals, and rubber (Sidel, 1986:56). Between 1940 and 1944, the percentage of women in the labor force increased more than it had in the previous four decades (from 27 to 35 percent), and the number of women workers rose by more than five million. By the end of the war, union restrictions against female membership had ended, and women had moved into many occupations that had previously been closed to them. In addition, many women were able to leave low-paying jobs because the demand for their labor was high. For example, Degler (1980:42) reports that 600 laundries closed in 1942 because their female workers obtained more lucrative employment and no replacements could be found.

Many expected these trends in female employment to reverse when the war ended and men returned to the labor force, and indeed the percentage of women in the labor force declined between 1944 and 1947. However, the percentage then began to rise again and has continued to increase ever since. By 1965 the percentage of employed women had surpassed its World War II high, and 55 percent of all women sixteen years of age and over were employed in 1986. More dramatic than the overall rise in female employment is the increase in the employment of married women. Between 1948 and 1986 the percentage of married women in the labor force rose from 22 to 55 percent, while the percentage of single women rose only from 51 to 65 percent. Married women composed 59 percent of the total female labor force in 1985.

A number of factors operated to draw married women into the paid labor force in the postwar years. First, the demand for white-collar workers continued its prewar climb. For example, between 1960 and 1982, the number of women in clerical jobs increased from 6.6 to 14.9 million. During the same period, the number of women in all types of blue-collar work rose from 3.6 to just 5.5 million. Second, declines in fertility meant that women spent less time caring for children. From 1960 to 1980 the birthrate (per 1,000 women 15–44 years of age) fell from 118 to 66. On average, women born in the 1960s will have one or two children, while their mothers had three or four. Third, the family wage, a goal of organized labor since the turn of the century, has become less of a reality than it ever was. Most families can now earn a family wage only when husbands, wives, and sometimes children work (Ehrenreich, 1983:173). Fourth, the women's movement has increased the desire of many women to work outside the home and has campaigned to end job and wage discrimination against women.

Although women's participation in the labor force has increased dramatically, women are concentrated in certain occupational categories. The majority of women are employed in 20 of the 420 occupations listed by the Bureau of Labor Statistics (Sidel, 1986:61). For example, 98 percent of all secretaries, 98 percent of all receptionists, 95 percent of all registered nurses, 92 percent of all bookkeeping clerks, and 96 percent of all private domestic workers were women in 1985. Women have entered the professions, skilled trades, and other prestigious occupations in increasing numbers but remain substantially underrepresented in most. Partly as a result of job segregation in lower-status jobs, women's wages remain lower than men's. Women in full-time work earn about 70 percent of what men working full time earn. However, even when women work in the same general occupational fields as men, they earn significantly less. For example, women in sales jobs make only 40 percent of the average salaries of salesmen, and women in the professions earn only 64 percent of the salaries of male professionals (Degler, 1980:425).

Increases in women's employment, however, have still not eliminated differences in the patterns of labor-force participation of men and women. Despite the gains women have made, men still participate in the labor force at substantially higher rates than do women. In 1985, 78 percent of all men and 55 percent of all women sixteen and over were employed. In addition, 27 percent of employed women worked part time and only 10 percent of men did so. Women are also more likely to move in and out of the labor force than men. Finally, an inverse correlation continues to exist between married women's employment and their husbands' incomes. (The higher a husband's income, the less likely is his wife to work outside the home.)

Therefore, although women now integrate paid work and family work to a much greater extent than in the past, their involvement in the labor force remains secondary to men's in several ways. In this respect, the increase in women's employment appears less revolutionary than evolutionary. To understand why this is the case, we must turn our attention to the distribution of labor in the household.

Family Work

As industrialization gradually organized the production of material goods as paid work in shops and factories and reproductive labor as unpaid work in the family, the conditions and principles of each type of work diverged as well. Paid work is hierarchical and routinized, while family work is unsupervised and is more likely to be organized according to the preferences of individual workers. Paid work is competitive and rewards individuals differentially, while family work is cooperative and is based on service to others (Brown, 1982:153). Finally, paid work encompasses a huge variety of activities and takes place in a variety of settings. Family work may vary with income, standards, and tastes, but it usually occurs in individual households and encompasses the same basic activities—child rearing, cooking, cleaning, and the related activities necessary to accomplish these tasks.

The division of productive and reproductive work into paid work and family work had a profound impact on men and women and their lives together, and it is worthwhile to consider briefly how this change took place. A rough gender-based division of labor existed in preindustrial families, with women responsible for cleaning, cooking, and child care and men responsible for fieldwork. However, both men and women produced material goods for sale and barter, and both men and women processed goods for home consumption. This intertwining of reproduction and production unraveled as material goods began to be produced outside the home. Cloth, leather goods, candles, furniture, foodstuffs, and numerous other essential items could then be purchased instead of manufactured at home. At the same time, technological developments reduced the time necessary to accomplish various household tasks. For example, the wood stove drastically cut the amount of fuel necessary to heat homes and cook meals and, consequently, reduced the amount of time required to provide wood for family use. The coal stove eliminated this task altogether. Indoor plumbing eliminated the task of carrying water from wells, and the meat-packing industry reduced the time spent butchering and processing meat.

Ruth Schwartz Cowan (1983:64) suggests that the availability of manufactured goods and labor-saving technological developments had the greatest impact on men's work. In fact, Cowan maintains that "virtually all the stereotypical male household occupations were eliminated by technology in the nineteenth century." However, women's work in the home changed relatively little and may even have increased during this period. Many nineteenth-century families possessed a greater variety of material goods, lived in more spacious houses, and had a more varied diet than their preindustrial predecessors. However, larger homes needed to be kept clean, manufactured goods required maintenance, and more elaborate meals required preparation. These tasks traditionally belonged to women. As a result, Cowan (p. 67) argues, "the material conditions of domestic life during the first phases of industrialization required women to stay at home so as to protect (and even enhance) the standard of living of their families." Therefore, women continued to labor in the household while men were freed to enter the paid labor force.

Some men and women challenged this gender-based division of labor, arguing that women too should be freed from the burdens of housework. For example, Gilman claimed that the home was backward because cooking, cleaning, and other household tasks had not been taken over by industry as had other kinds of work. In *The Home,* first published in 1903, she wrote: "Back of history, at the bottom of civilization, untouched by thousands of whirling centuries, the primitive woman, in the primitive home, still toils at her primitive tasks" (Gilman, 1972:83). The remedy was organizing the few "crude industries" remaining in the home as businesses. Restaurants, laundries, and house-cleaning services could take over these tasks just as the factory had taken over household manufacture. Women would then be able to pursue occupations, free of the primitive conditions that had tied them to the home. To those who feared that family life would suffer if women left the home each day, Gilman (p. 102) responded: "The house will not be 'neglected' by her doing so; but is even now most shamefully neglected by her antique methods of labor. The family will not be less loved because it has a skilled worker to love it. Love has to pass the muster of results, as well as intentions."

Others hoped that household tasks could be organized cooperatively. In 1869 Melusina Fay Pierce founded the Cooperative Housekeeping Society in Cambridge, Massachusetts. This group operated a cooperative laundry, grocery store, and bakery, and planned to open a cooperative kitchen. The experiment lasted only two years but was followed by many others. For example, in 1915 Alice Constance Austin devised an ambitious plan for a community of kitchenless houses connected to centralized kitchen and laundries by underground tunnels. Railway cars would bring cooked food and laundry to the basements of the houses. All gas, water, and electric lines would be in these same underground tunnels producing an aesthetically pleasing and restful city. Although the planned community, Llana del Rio in California, encountered financial difficulties and was not developed, Austin's plan still provides an imaginative alternative to the organization of domestic work in private households (Hayden, 1978:283).

However, advocates of alternative approaches to housework remained a minority, and most women continued to labor full time in the home for most of this century. (The number of employed married women outnumbered full-time housewives for the first time in 1980.) Labor-saving devices such as washing machines, electric and gas ranges, and refrigerators, as well as the availability of processed goods, have reduced the time required for some household tasks. However, many modern "conveniences" added other tasks to housewives' duties. For example, processed goods have to be purchased, which often requires travel, and indoor plumbing means that some housewives have several bathrooms to clean (Cowan, 1983).

Standards of housekeeping have also changed. As early as 1869, Catharine Beecher and Harriet Beecher Stowe, in *The American Woman's Home,* urged women to make "the art of housekeeping" a scientific study. The Beechers claimed that housewives needed to be versed in chemistry, economics, horticulture, hygiene, and other sciences to care adequately for their families (Strasser, 1982:188). In 1899 the first meeting of the Lake Placid Conference on Home Economics took place, formally beginning the domestic science movement, and the American Home Economics Association was formed in 1908. Home economists maintained that housework required technical training and an understanding of the principles of health, sanitation, and nutrition (Laslett, 1973:109). In addition, home economists advocated that housework be organized according to principles of efficiency to increase productivity. In short, housewives were urged to make their work a profession and organize their homes as businesses.

As a result of the creation of new household tasks and increasing standards of housekeeping, the time full-time housewives spend on domestic chores has remained relatively constant. Joan Vanek (1984) found that full-time housewives spent slightly over fifty hours a week on housework in the 1920s and the 1960s. (The distribution of labor had shifted, however. Housewives spent less time in food preparation and more time in house care, shopping and management tasks, and care for family members in the 1960s than they did in the 1920s.) Although the time housewives spend in housework has declined slightly since the 1960s (Robinson, 1977), one may still ask how married women who worked close to fifty house per week in the household were able to enter the labor force in large numbers. The answer appears to be that they reduced the number of hours devoted to housework by lowering their standards of housekeeping and finding alternative ways of accomplishing essential tasks. Employed wives spend about half as much time on housework as full-time housewives. They simply cook and clean less and rely more heavily on labor-saving devices, convenience foods, and sometimes hired help. Although research is scarce, women may be relying more on the help of older children (Zelizer, 1985:225).

What employed wives have not done is rely extensively on their husbands for help with housework. Studies show that men, as a group, do little household labor when their wives enter the labor force. For example, Shelley Coverman and Joseph Sheley (1986) found that in 1975 men with wives employed twenty or more hours per week spent an average of eleven minutes more per day on housework than men with nonemployed wives (ninety-three and eighty-two minutes respectively). Men with employed wives spent the same amount of time on child care (twenty-four minutes per day) as did men whose wives were full-time housewives. A study (Barnett and Baruch, 1987) based on more recent data does show small but statistically significant differences in the time spent on housework and child care between men with employed and nonemployed wives. However, the convergence of men's and women's labor in the household is still far from a reality. As a result, when married women enter the labor force, their overall work loads increase significantly while their husbands' do not. Vanek (1983) reports that in the 1960s employed married men worked 62.5 hours per week in family and paid work combined, while employed married women worked 71 hours per week. Employed wives with young children worked 80 hours per week, while husbands with young children worked 65 hours a week. According to Vanek, the picture had not changed in the 1970s.

Therefore, despite the impressive gains women have made in the labor force, the household remains primarily their responsibility. Their continuing obligations to the family help explain their concentration in part-time and lower-status jobs. For example, part-time work allows women to contribute to their families' incomes while fulfilling their responsibilities for household chores and child care. Similarly, lower-status jobs often require one to put in fewer hours than more prestigious occupations. Perhaps most important, women are less able than men to pursue careers because they leave and reenter the labor force as their family responsibilities expand and contract. Women's need to organize their participation in the labor force around their responsibilities to their families is only a partial explanation for women's secondary involvement in paid work. Nevertheless, it is unlikely that men and women will be equal participants in such work until they share family work equally.

Readings

More adults engage in housework full time than in any other occupation, and virtually all adults participate in it to some extent (Brown, 1982:151). However, sociologists have only recently examined the significance of housework in the economy. One way to assess its importance is to estimate its monetary value based on its replacement cost. For example, one can calculate how much it would cost to pay for all the house cleaning, food preparation, child care, transportation, and other services that homemakers provide for their families. Such estimates yield total figures for all housework from one-sixth to one-quarter of the gross national product (Vanek, 1984:99). However, this method underestimates the value of housework for several reasons. First, families need too few hours per day of many services to purchase them conveniently. Few people are available to be hired for an hour or two each day. Therefore, more than the needed service would have to be purchased in order to receive it. Second, a housewife must be available twenty-four hours a day because the need for many of her services is unpredictable. The cost of providing this flexibility would also be far more than an hourly wage figure. Finally, the cost of some services housewives provide (for example, personalized attention to the sick, listening to individual problems and resolving arguments) cannot be estimated or could be provided only at great expense. Therefore, the housewife provides services that are essential for the economy and worth far more than the wages for the total hours she devotes to her tasks.

The first selection here, a chapter from Susan Strasser's book, *Never Done: A History of American Housework,* illustrates another way to assess the significance of housework in the economy. In "Selling Mrs. Consumer," Strasser examines the historical development of one aspect of the contemporary housewife role and explains its importance for the development of an industrial economy. Industrialization did far more than simply offer goods for purchase that were formerly produced by the home economy. It also provided goods never produced in the home and therefore required the creation of a new role for housewives. As you read the article recall Kirk Jeffrey's claim (in Chapter 2) that the ideology of separate spheres obscured the ways in which outside forces impinge on the family. Strasser's discussion of housewives as consumers, standing "at the intersection of the previously separate spheres," is one illustration of this influence.

In "The Division of Labor in Contemporary Marriage: Expectations, Perceptions, and Performance," Dana Hiller and William Philliber help explain why household tasks continue to be divided by gender. Hiller and Philliber interviewed husbands and wives about their role expectations, their perceptions of their spouses' role expectations, their attachment to their roles, and their perceptions of the division of labor in their households. By comparing expectations, perceptions of expectations, attachment, and perceived divisions of labor, the authors attempt to identify how contemporary couples think household labor should be divided and what factors influence its division. It is important to keep these four factors in mind when reading the article because each plays a part in the conclusions the authors reach.

One aspect of Hiller and Philliber's methodology requires explanation. In one section, they employ a statistical technique called *multiple regression analysis* to discover which of several variables are most important in explaining the division of labor in households. Multiple regression analysis assigns numbers to each variable Hiller and Philliber think may predict the division of labor. The numbers indicate the relative contributions of each variable to variations in the division of labor in marriages. The higher the number (either positive or negative), the greater the contribution of that variable to the division of labor. The results of this analysis appear in their Table 6. In this case, negative numbers indicate that wives take less responsibility for a particular task the higher the value of the predictive variable and more responsibility the lower the predictor's value. For example, the analysis showed that if a wife is employed (a high value on wife's employment), she has less responsibility for child care than if she were not employed (a low value on wife's employment). Consequently, a relatively high negative number ($-.25$) appears in the table. A positive number in Table 6 indicates that the values of the predictors and wives' participation in a particular task area rise and fall together. For example, the analysis showed that if a husband expects his wife to manage money (a high value on husband's role expectations about money management), his wife is more likely to participate in money management than if he does not think she should be involved (a low value on husband's role expectations about money management). Consequently, a relatively high positive value (.31) appears in the table. As you read the section explaining Table 6, simply identify the predictors which have the most influence (the highest values) on the division of labor and try to understand the meaning of positive or negative signs.

Hiller and Philliber conclude that the division of labor in the household is "still heavily colored by traditional expectations." However, they found that some areas are more influenced by these expectations than others. The authors also discovered differences between expectations for role behavior on the one hand and the reported division of labor on the other. These discrepancies were greater in some areas than others.

Two-thirds of the couples Hiller and Philliber interviewed were dual-earner couples. The authors were interested in these couples because the way in which they divide tasks provides clues about the directions of change in the household division of labor. Many sociologists, including Hiller and Philliber, think that a "new definition of an equitable marital role bargain is emerging which suggests men should take a more active role in housekeeping and child care." Although an equal division of labor is not yet a behavioral reality, recent books such as *Becoming a Two-Job Family* (Hood, 1983) and *Role Sharing Marriage* (Smith and Reid, 1986) indicate that many sociologists also believe that sharing household tasks is a likely if not inevitable direction of change. Ultimately, this change holds the potential for men and women to compete equally in "the public worlds of work and politics" and for gender inequality to disappear.

To a certain extent, Janet and Larry Hunt, authors of "The Dualities of Careers and Families: New Integrations or New Polarizations?", share this assessment of the evolution of the household division of labor. However, they are concerned about the broader implications of this change. The Hunts agree that the participation of women in the labor force will eventually lead to a more equitable division of labor in households and that the United States is "evolving toward a social order which is less overtly sexist." These changes will mean that, within couples, household labor and participation in the labor force will be divided more fairly than they now are. However, the Hunts suggest that these trends will also lead to a less equitable division of resources between couples. As they see it, the outcome will be a polarization between couples who pursue careers and those who "choose" to have families. The Hunts have identified troublesome features of the organization of work and family life, and some recent research on the attempts of men and women to combine careers and child rearing provide empirical support for their arguments (Gerson, 1985; Hertz, 1986).

The final article in this chapter demonstrates still another way in which participation in the paid labor force influences the organization of family life. In this case, however, the focus is on the consequences of men's experiences. In "Changes in Black Family Structure: The Conflict Between Ideology and Structural Conditions," Robert Staples examines the sources of the high incidence of female-headed households among black Americans, a topic that has occupied the attention of sociologists for several decades.

Among the first seeking to explain the prevalence of female-headed households among blacks was Daniel Patrick Moynihan. Writing in 1965, Moynihan asserted that the weakened condition in which the black family emerged from slavery was one factor contributing to the relatively high incidence of female-headed households among contemporary blacks. However, subsequent research failed to support this claim. Throughout the rural South, in the immediate Civil War period, over 80 percent of black households contained both husband and wife, scarcely convincing evidence of a weakened black family (Gutman, 1976).

It appears, instead, that the prevalence of female-headed families occurred as a result of the economic conditions blacks encountered subsequent to slavery. In a study of household composition in Philadelphia in 1880, Furstenberg, Hershberg, and Modell (1975) found that blacks were much more likely than whites to live in female-headed households. Approximately 25 percent of black households with children were female-headed, compared with about 12 percent of white households. However, these differences in the composition of black and white households essentially disappeared when the economic status and the high mortality rates of black males were taken into account. Furstenberg and his coauthors concluded that the high incidence of female-headed households among blacks was a result of the inability of black males to support families and of the early deaths of black husbands and fathers. The large-scale black migrations to the urban North dramatically increased the number of blacks subject to these conditions. Therefore, what Moynihan observed in the 1960s was the impact of the "destructive conditions of the northern urban life" on the families of black rural migrants to the city rather than the legacy of slavery.

Staples demonstrates that the characteristics of the black family that concerned Moynihan have become even more prevalent today. He attributes the increase of female-headed households to the deteriorating position of black males in the labor market in the 1970s and 1980s. In short, he argues that black women face a severe shortage of men "qualified" to be marriage partners. In interpreting Staple's argument, it is important not to conclude that the increase in female-headed households is exclusively a black phenomenon. In fact, the percentage of all households that are female-headed has increased. Neither should one conclude that female-headed households are necessarily dysfunctional. The fact that black women and their dependent children are likely to be poor does not tell us that the lack of attachment to men is the cause of their poverty. Instead, it suggests that black women occupy a disadvantaged position in the labor force, along with black men. From Staple's perspective, the important point is that black men and women who wish to establish families together are often unable to do so because of the problems faced by black men.

References

Barnett, Rosalind C., and Grace K. Baruch. 1987. "Determinants of Fathers' Participation in Family Work." *Journal of Marriage and the Family* 49:29–40.

Brown, Clair (Vickery). 1982. "Home Production for Use in a Market Economy." In *Rethinking the Family: Some Feminist Questions,* edited by Barrie Thorn and Marilyn Yalom, 151–61. New York: Longman.

Coverman, Shelley, and Joseph F. Sheley. 1986. "Changes in Men's Housework and Child-Care Time, 1965–1975." *Journal of Marriage and the Family* 48:413–22.

Cowan, Ruth Schwartz. 1983. *More Work for Mother: The Ironies of Household Technology from the Open Hearth to the Microwave.* New York: Basic Books.

Degler, Carl N. 1980. *At Odds: Women and the Family in America from the Revolution to the Present.* New York: Oxford University Press.

Ehrenreich, Barbara. 1983. *The Hearts of Men: American Dreams and the Flight from Commitment.* Garden City, N.Y.: Doubleday/Anchor.

Ehrenreich, Barbara, and Deirdre English. 1980. "Reflections on the 'Woman Question.'" In *Family in Transition,* 3d ed., edited by Arlene Skolnick and Jerome Skolnick, 217–31. Boston: Little, Brown.

Furstenberg, Frank F., Jr., Theodore Hershberg, and John Modell. 1975. "The Origins of the Female-Headed Black Family: The Impact of the Urban Experience." *Journal of Interdisciplinary History* 6:211–33.

Gerson, Kathleen. 1985. *Hard Choices: How Women Decide about Work, Career, and Motherhood.* Berkeley: University of California Press.

Gilman, Charlotte Perkins. 1972. *The Home: Its Work and Influence.* Reprint of the 1903 edition. Urbana: University of Illinois Press.

Gutman, Herbert. 1976. *The Black Family in Slavery and Freedom, 1750–1925.* New York: Pantheon.

Hayden, Delores. 1978. "Two Utopian Feminists and Their Campaigns for Kitchenless Households." *Signs* 4:274–90.

Hertz, Rosanna. 1986. *More Equal Than Others.* Berkeley: University of California Press.

Hood, Jane. 1983. *Becoming a Two-Job Family.* New York: Praeger.

Kessler-Harris, Alice. 1982. *Out to Work: A History of Wage Earning Women in the United States.* New York: Oxford University Press.

Lamphere, Louise. 1986. "From Working Daughters to Working Mothers: Production and Reproduction in an Industrial Community." *American Ethnologist* 13:118–30.

Laslett, Barbara. 1973. "The Family as a Public and Private Institution: A Historical Perspective." In *Intimacy, Family, and Society,* edited by Arlene Skolnick and Jerome Skolnick, 94–114. Boston: Little, Brown.

Lerner, Gerda. 1979. "The Lady and the Mill Girl: Changes in the Status of Women in the Age of Jackson." Chap. 3 in *The Majority Finds Its Past,* New York: Oxford University Press.

Moynihan, Daniel Patrick. 1965. *The Negro Family: The Case for National Action.* Washington, D.C.: U.S. Government Printing Office.

Robinson, J. 1977. *Changes in Americans' Use of Time: 1965–1975.* Cleveland: Communications Center of Cleveland State University.

Ryan, Mary P. 1979. *Womanhood in America: From Colonial Times to the Present.* 2d ed. New York: New Viewpoints.

Sidel, Ruth. 1986. *Women and Children Last: The Plight of Poor Women in Affluent America.* Baltimore: Penguin.

Smith, Audrey D., and William J. Reid. 1986. *Role Sharing Marriage*. New York: Columbia University Press.

Strasser, Susan. 1982. *Never Done: A History of American Housework*. New York: Pantheon.

Vanek, Joann. 1983. "Household Work, Wage Work, and Sexual Inequality." In *Family in Transition,* 4th ed., edited by Arlene Skolnick and Jerome Skolnick, 176–89. Boston: Little, Brown.

_____. 1984. "Housewives as Workers." In *Work and the Family: Changing Roles of Men and Women,* edited by Patricia Voyanhoff, 89–103. Palo Alto, Calif.: Mayfield.

Zelizer, Viviana A. 1985. *Pricing the Priceless Child: The Changing Social Value of Children*. New York, Basic Books.

Selling Mrs. Consumer

Susan Strasser

As mass production removed productive work from the private sphere, mass marketing and mass distribution introduced a new task and a new pastime: buying things. A new kind of consumer, courted by new kinds of advertising, purchased new kinds of goods at new kinds of stores. American consumerism is a historical phenomenon: at one time nonexistent, it became pervasive; the wholesale transformation of most Americans' daily life from near-subsistence farming to mass participation in the money economy both as workers and as consumers, like any other long historical process, proceeded piecemeal. Many seemingly unconnected events, each in itself of minor historical importance, combined over two centuries to produce a changed world; although this complexity defies precise dating, an enormous transformation occurred during the few decades on either side of the turn of the twentieth century. Advertisers came to see women as their audience; home economists taught women how to shop and how to plan for shopping; new, interrelated products like washing machines and soap powders appeared on the market, each encouraging the use of another; mail-order houses, department stores, supermarkets, and chain stores, emphasizing impersonal relationships between buyer and seller and dominated by large corporations, replaced small shops, country stores, and public markets. By the time of the Great Depression, which delayed the full expression of the new trends, consumption was established as the new task of the private sphere, now completely dominated by the public.

As long as households produced most of the goods they used, consumption in the modern sense of the word meant little. Until the middle of the nineteenth century, farmers bought things, but not much and not often; a trip to town or to the country store at the crossroads was an occasion. City people produced as much as possible. Often men did the shopping; handling money clearly belonged within their sphere, the world outside the home. "The smartest men" in Cincinnati, wrote Frances Trollope in the 1820s, "and those of the 'highest standing' do not scruple to leave their beds with the sun, six days in the week, and, prepared with a mightly basket, to sally forth in search of meat, butter, eggs, and vegetables," returning home for breakfast, which their wives prepared in their absence. Few cookbooks or manuals of household advice before the last decades of the century offered any instruction whatever in buying things—no charts distinguishing chuck from rump, no directives on bulging fish eyes and fresh-looking gills, little guidance on quality in food or fabrics or household equipment. As Catharine Beecher revised her successive comprehensive house-keeping manuals, she added increasing amounts of consumer advice, finally writing a chapter entitled "Marketing and the Care of Meats" for her 1873 *Housekeeper and Healthkeeper.* "Every young woman, at some period of her life, may need the instructions of this chapter," it began, indicating that women with trustworthy servants sent them to market, although even they "should have the knowledge which will enable them to direct their servants what and how to buy." Beecher admitted that thousands of her readers were "obliged to go to market," but evidently those who could avoid such indelicate activity in the world outside the home would do so.

With trustworthy servants in short supply by the end of the century, with husbands working long hours in factories, and with households increasingly dependent on manufactured products, women of all classes began to assume the function of buying household goods. In 1891, readers of *Printer's Ink,* a new weekly journal for the advertising industry later to become *Advertising Age,* encountered a series of arguments among advertisers on the issue of women consumers. Nathaniel C. Fowler, Jr., a newspaper publisher soon to found the Fowler School of Advertising, began the controversy by asserting that women made the purchasing decisions and that advertisers ought therefore to direct their campaigns at them. Even goods used exclusively by men, he said, sold better when advertised in women's magazines; he had experimented with this concept many times, "until I believe I have a right to claim that the experiment has passed into fact." Nonsense, responded William H. Maher, citing his advertisements for scissors and cutlery in the *Ladies Home Journal,* which cost more than they paid in sales receipts, and in the *Farm Journal,* which, "with rates about the same, pays me well and has always paid well." Women, more timid than men about ordering anything but seeds by mail, rarely even wrote business letters; men, in any case, controlled the purse strings. "In selling cutlery," Maher wrote, "where one woman orders a knife for a man one thousand men will order knives for women, and ten thousand men buy for themselves where one woman orders for herself." Fowler defended himself three weeks later, claiming that he had been "overwhelmed with opinions unconditionally substantiating the ground which I attempted to assume." Maher, "one of the shrewdest advertisers in the country," had based his singular reply on the fact that men's names appeared on the cutlery firm's orders: "He seems to be of the opinion that because men order these things the advertisement is read by the men, not the women." Fowler felt this illustrated a limited understanding of marriage: "Is Mr. Maher a married man? Has he brothers [who are] married? One would almost suppose he knew nothing of the links of the chain of matrimony, that he never had experienced that delightful thrill which comes to every married man when his wife, kissing him on the doorstep, says, 'My dear, be sure and order so-and-so for me from Mr. Somebody.'" Within a few decades, nobody would debate who decided what scissors to buy, although advertisers would carry on identical arguments with regard to major purchases such as houses, automobiles, and large appliances.

The advertisers attempted to attract whoever did the deciding. Although their ultimate decision to advertise most products to the woman consumer undoubtedly bolstered the development of the consumer role, creating that role and establishing a new function for the household in the world of mass production and mass distribution was, for them, a means to their clients' financial ends. The home economists, on the other hand, consciously created and defined a place in the new economic order for the private home and for the married women who stayed in it. From the start, they taught educated consumption. When Juliet Corson took classes from her New York Cooking School to the Fulton Market, she paraded them around the stalls to point out high-quality poultry ("the best is plump, fat, and nearly white"), fish ("Lobsters and crabs must be bright in color and lively in movement, like these"), meat ("Good mutton is bright red"), and vegetables ("Roots and tubers must be plump"). For those who consulted cookbooks instead of taking classes, writers introduced instructions in written form, emphasizing food values in the new scientific terms: calories, vitamins, and protein. Issues of quality intersected with issues of cost. "Economizing on food," wrote Florence Nesbitt in a manual on low-cost cooking, "is a most dangerous thing to try unless the housekeeper has an understanding of food values. She must know what foods are necessary for the health of her family and in what food materials she gets the most for her money, to be able to decide where it is wise and safe to cut and where unsafe." Social workers who translated scientific principles of housekeeping to poor women while they oversaw their spending of relief money often required them to keep written budget accounts, providing "uncolored facts as to how the money has gone and what has been secured for it"—and an examination procedure to test their progress. Although they held no such financial power over their students, home economics teachers in public schools and colleges likewise linked quality with price and encouraged careful shopping and conscious budgeting.

Household engineer Christine Frederick took careful shopping and conscious budgeting to their extremes, as she had done with efficient use of time; again, her ideas are important because more moderate home economists adopted her general principles and taught them to millions of women, and her statements of those principles provide their most straightforward exposition. Every large business, Frederick pointed out, employed "persons called 'purchasing agents,' who are trained, informed on market conditions, and able to buy to the best advantage for their particular firms," thereby saving thousands of dollars. Housewives, who spent family funds, must similarly learn about market conditions (when to buy and what to pay) and make their decisions according to their particular needs, family incomes, and express goals. "In other words, every woman running the business of homemaking must *train herself* to become an efficient 'purchasing agent' for her particular firm or family, by study, watchfulness, and practice." This new role offered housewives a truly managerial position in the modern household that stood at the intersection of the previously separate spheres; even those who failed to plan their dishwashing must plan their purchases or else fail at the "entirely new responsibilities" that replaced the work of the old-fashioned household where women made soap and candles, wove and sewed, and produced food for daily and future use.

The modern household purchasing agent, like her factory counterpart, oversaw an extensive record-keeping system; budget records, of course, predominated. Frederick, writing the textbook version of her ideas in 1920, carefully distinguished between "household accounts," recording expenditures after the fact, and her "budget system," based on annual planning in advance. Husband and wife must sit down together to assess their financial situation and determine the family goals; "otherwise it would be just as if a ship were to start on a voyage without a port toward which to sail. The budget is to the family what a charted course is to the navigator with a settled harbor in view and definite sailing directions to guide." The family could then apportion expenses among shelter, food, clothing, operating expenses, savings, personal luxuries, and "advancement" (education, music, books, church, charity, and vacations—luxuries that benefited the entire family): "typical divisions for all incomes." Instead of spending their money "just as each need seems to arise—$30 for food one month, $20 the next, 'squeezing' down the food some other month because the entire family needs winter clothing," they could account for all needs throughout the year. The object of such annual planning, Frederick maintained, "is not so much *skimping, economy* or *saving,* as it is *proportionate, balanced spending.*" Although Frederick offered possible apportionments for six income levels, ranging from $600 to $2,400 a year, she emphasized that budgets must be designed by and for individual families, based on their temperaments, social and professional standing, locale (climate and proximity to markets), and size, as well as on income.

Once made, the budget was to be followed; household accounts provided a record of success or failure. Frederick outlined two account plans, one to be kept in a notebook, the other in a card file, both based on simplified versions of double-entry bookkeeping, to be totaled daily and balanced weekly or monthly. Monthly checks against the annual budget helped to avert financial disaster by discouraging long-term extravagance in every category, while the budget records for any given year furnished information for even better planning for the following year. . . .

Frederick thus placed consumption in the category of a household task, specifying its performance more carefully than the home economists who preceded her, and anticipating the popularizers who communicated the idea through the women's magazines during the 1920s. An article on shopping for linens in the *Ladies' Home Journal* in 1928 stated the historical case that Melusina Fay Pierce had made clear in 1869: "A woman's virtue and excellence as a housewife do not in these days depend upon her skill in spinning and weaving." But whereas Pierce, and later Charlotte Perkins Gilman, fretted about women's consequent status as parasites, the *Journal* crowed about the new world of consumption, where "an entirely different task presents itself, more difficult and more complex, requiring an infinitely wider range of ability, and for these very reasons more interesting and inspiring."

The *Journal's* pep talk on inspirational consumption flew in the face of truth: women bought machine-made products because they made life easier, not more complex, interesting, or inspiring. A character in *Bread Givers,* a Yiddish novel of the period, described her Old World dowry: pillows full of down plucked by hand, embroidered sheets and towels, curtains that took her a whole year to knit, and a hand-crocheted tablecloth in all the colors of the rainbow. "It was like dancing sunshine lighting up the room when it was spread on the table. . . . There ain't in America such beautiful things like we had home." "Nonsense, Mamma!" her daughter replied. "If you only had the money to go on Fifth Avenue you'd see the grand things you could buy." "Yes, buy!" repeated the mother. "In America, rich people can only buy, and buy things made by machines. Even Rockefeller's daughter got only store-bought ready-made things for her dowry. There was a feeling in my tablecloth—" That feeling, the feeling of craft satisfaction, disappeared with all the new products, and the supposed interest and inspiration of consumption never replaced it.

Time spent on consumption tasks did replace time spent on other household tasks. Probably few women elevated consumption to the level Frederick recommended; few established the elaborate files and records and devoted hours solely to planning. Sociologists' studies from the 1920s onward, however, indicate that women continued to spend about as many hours doing their housework as they had done before, substituting extra hours spent with children and in shopping and managerial work for the arduous labor of the old-fashioned laundry and kitchen. Indeed, unlike the old-style work, consumption was an expandable task: nobody would eat without a fire in the fireplace or stove, and the laundry had required a certain amount of water hauling, but consumption, the new women's work, never ended at all. The thrifty housewife could always go to yet another store for yet another sale, clip yet another coupon from yet another magazine, read yet another article about yet another kind of appliance. It was the perfect task to occupy the full-time housewife while increasing numbers of married women went off to work outside the home. The time studies suggest that employed women devoted considerably less time to housework than full-time housewives; they probably more often called on other family members to help, and substituted industrial products and services for their own labor, but they also had less time for consumption. People still had to eat and the laundry still got dirty, but the employed woman would more likely ignore the fact that peaches cost four cents less per pound at the store down the block.

By far the most potent and pervasive force fostering the new consumer role, advertising shaped the concepts in the interest of business. As large firms combined the methods of mass production and mass distribution to create and control a national market, they linked the activities of the consumer housewife to their own through advertising. The small merchants and tradespeople of the old economic order had advertised in newspapers since colonial times; the advertising industry itself began to develop in the 1850s, with advertising agencies that promoted products on local levels. After the 1880s, national agencies worked with the sales departments of the developing national manufacturers; then as now, the manufacturers hired the ad agencies and ultimately controlled the content, location, and volume of their advertising.

The manufacturers' new products required advertising to create demand: consumers did not know they wanted or "needed" products they had never seen. Furthermore, many of the early manufactured consumer goods—packaged cereals, cigarettes, canned foods, and the like—had low unit costs; because manufacturers could not increase demand by lowering the already low price of a package of oatmeal or a can of soup, they had to concentrate on ways of selling more of them to increase their profits. Advertising therefore developed in tandem with mass production: both the ads and the products appeared before the turn of the century and developed consistently, but without infiltrating most people's daily lives until after World War I. Along with the new products, the advertising industry boomed during the 1920s: magazine advertising revenues more than tripled between 1918 and 1929, to become a $200 million business on the eve of the Depression, while commercial radio, inaugurated by KDKA in Pittsburgh in 1920, offered an entirely new and increasingly popular medium for promoting the new products and for connecting the private household with the outside world.

As the industry developed, its techniques changed; the relatively straightforward advertising of the turn of the century gave way during the 1920s to ads that established corporate products as solutions for fearful individuals in a hostile world. Woodbury Soap equipped women with beautiful skin to meet people "proudly—confidently—without fear"; a baby-food ad suggested the infant death rate ("If we only had the nerve to put a hearse in the ad, you couldn't keep the women away from the food," the ad agency head told the copywriter); and numerous ads promoted terror of the new corporate diseases—' "sneaker smell,' 'paralyzed pores,' 'vacation knees,' . . . 'underarm offense,' and 'ashtray breath.' " . . .

All the new manufactured goods appeared on the shelves of new kinds of stores. Mass retailing began with the urban department stores that appeared almost simultaneously in many cities during the 1870s, but even the largest of these remained primarily local, except for those like Marshall Field's of Chicago, which did much of its business wholesaling to country storekeepers. At the end of the century, those country stores felt the competition of the first national retailers, the mail-order houses. Montgomery Ward, founded in 1872 and supported by the largest national farmers' association, the Grange, marketed a wide range of goods by mail from its inception. Its first serious competition came in the 1890s, when Sears, Roebuck & Company, originally a watch and jewelry concern, began to expand, surpassing Ward's sales around 1900 by taking on nearly every product line that existed—a move so successful that the firm nearly went under from too many orders. It was saved by drastic reorganization of the order-filling process. "The new system," writes historian Alfred Chandler, "permitted the filling of over 100,000 orders a day. That involved as many transactions as most traditional merchants in pre-railroad days handled in a lifetime."

During the years before the Depression, Sears and Wards, suffering from the decline of the rural market, established retail outlets; in doing so, they essentially imitated their newest and greatest competitors, the chain stores. The variety chains, beginning with Woolworth's in the 1880s, followed the lead of the grocery chains. By 1865, when the Great Atlantic and Pacific Tea Company added a grocery line to its business, it operated 26 stores; over the next fifteen years it expanded to 100 stores all over the Northeast and as far west as Saint Paul, Minnesota. Other chains followed before the end of the century: Grand Union in the 1870s, Kroger in the 1880s, and Jewel Tea in the 1890s. The most rapid growth for grocery and variety chains came during the first decades of the twentieth century. By the end of 1913, A&P had 585 stores; it opened 1,600 more in 1914–1915, another 2,600 before the end of 1919, and 11,500 during the twenties. The number of food chains doubled during that time, and the number of stores they operated multiplied nearly eightfold. Because the chains had trade margins (overhead and net profit) lower than the independent grocers, they charged lower markups; people from lower-income groups patronized them, while their wealthier neighbors continued to use the credit and the personal service the independents offered their trusted customers.

The original chain stores bore little resemblance to the modern supermarket; clerks served customers in stores that specialized in groceries, handling no fresh meat or produce. In 1912, John A. Hartford of the A&P introduced cash-and-carry "economy stores," small operations with low overhead, run by one clerk, offering no delivery service and carrying no credit accounts. Four years later, a Memphis entrepreneur named Clarence Saunders opened his first Piggly-Wiggly store, introducing the turnstile and the idea of self-service with great fanfare; Piggly-Wiggly operated 2,660 stores at its peak. Self-service spread during the 1920s, along with the combination store, which handled fresh meats and produce as well as groceries. In 1930, Michael Cullen opened his first King Kullen store in Jamaica, Long Island, and with it the era of the modern supermarket; Cullen, who called himself "the world's greatest price wrecker," emphasized high-volume selling with low markups, running splashy ads in local newspapers. "Cheapy" supermarkets, located in empty factory and warehouse buildings and featuring drugs, auto accessories, clothing, hardware, soda fountains, and other variety store goods along with food, spread throughout the East during the Depression. These huge new stores and their low prices quickly ate into the business of the chains, which began to close their small stores and open their own supermarkets during the middle thirties.

Each one of the supermarket's innovations destroyed the personal relationships that had prevailed at the independent grocery, the country store, and even the stall at the larger public market. Customers and storekeepers stopped bargaining about prices and making credit deals; delivery men stopped coming around the neighborhood; one-stop shopping and self-service cut the number and altered the quality of the interactions the housewife had with the people she bought from. No longer dependent on daily shopping thanks to home refrigeration, women now went to stores with narrow check-out aisles and no room to stand and chat with the clerks. At first the combination store retained the custom-service butcher and the produce man, but eventually they too fell prey to prepackaging and to the cheaper, more detailed division of labor that has characterized work in the twentieth century. The supermarket fit the new task of consumption as the home economists defined it. The trained consumer studied and planned at home for the goods she would need and went to the store ready to buy; armed with the advice of experts, she needed no guidance from the butcher or the grocer.

In fact, she received her guidance not from experts on the products but from experts on selling, advertisers not merely in league with the manufacturers but dependent on them for their livelihood. Under that guidance, the new task of the private sphere became a pastime of a sphere private only in rhetoric. The corporations dominated consumption—apparently the exercise of free, private, individual choice—with the products they offered and the methods they used to sell them.

Industrialization replaced the arduous productive work of the nineteenth-century household with products that raised the standard of living and made life easier for many people by the 1930s; the large, centralized concerns that manufactured those products invaded daily life with their advertising, creating new needs to establish economic demand. The very activity of buying came to represent happiness, and perhaps indeed to produce it, if only temporarily. The new consumerism declared that things that cost money had more value than those that did not; it even revised the seasons, as January white sales and end-of-summer clearances defined the time of year as tasks like spring housecleaning and laying in the wood for winter once did. The expandable task of consumption, like the other new task of motherhood, capable of taking up whatever time the new products released, became ever more necessary as families adapted their daily lives to manufactured existence.

The Division of Labor in Contemporary Marriage: Expectations, Perceptions, and Performance

Dana V. Hiller and William W. Philliber

Married women have moved into the labor market at a dramatic pace during the second half of the twentieth century. In 1950, 12 percent of wives with pre-schoolers were employed, while, in 1980, 50 percent of this group were employed (Bianchi and Spain, 1983). However, the institutions of North American society are still geared to meet the needs of two-parent families with only one employed partner.

Partners in a two-job marriage may be overloaded with demands on their time and energy, and that pressure in turn may generate rigid role performances as well as emotional exhaustion. Such conditions create an environment ripe for marital dissent. Two outside jobs demand that couples take time to negotiate a household division of labor that once was a given, while at the same time employment absorbs more time and requires greater efficiency in the performance of household tasks.

The underlying issue for individual spouses is equity and fairness in the distribution of costs and rewards within the relationship. With a majority of wives employed in the United States, a new definition of an equitable marital role bargain is emerging which suggests men should take a more active role in housekeeping and childcare. Yet, sharing the responsibilities for housework, parenting, and nurturing others is difficult when tradition has delegated those tasks solely to women. Not surprisingly, Huber and Spitze (1983) have found that "thought of divorce" is strongly related to division of labor in the family. We believe that the extent to which the role expectations of a husband and wife differ will be critical to their ability to negotiate a mutually acceptable role bargain and, ultimately, to their marital stability.

We interviewed 489 midwestern married couples (two-thirds of them were dual-earner couples) to discern what each partner's expectations were and how they actually behaved, and to determine what factors were likely to influence those expectations and behaviors. Assuming that a couple's situational definitions

We are indebted to the National Science Foundation for the grant (SES-8121064) that supported the collection of data reported in this study.

From Dana V. Hiller and William W. Philliber, *Social Problems* Vol. 33, No. 3 (February 1986): 191–201. Copyright © 1986 by the Society for the Study of Social Problems Inc. Reprinted by permission of The University of California Press and Dana Yannoy.

are also important, we studied the perceptions spouses have of their partners' expectations. The specific purpose of this study was to answer the following questions: (1) Do husbands and wives hold different role expectations?; (2) How accurately does each partner perceive the other's expectations?; (3) How do expectations and behavior differ?; and (4) How is the division of labor between a couple affected by the expectations of husbands or wives? In general, we find that tradition endures even in modern, dual-earner families, and that the husband's view of marital roles strongly influences actual behavior.

Previous Research

The literature on gender role attitudes and marital role expectations suggests more attention should be paid to the perceptions partners have of their spouses' attitudes. Research indicates that men and women hold differing marital role expectations, with men tending to have somewhat more traditional expectations (Komarovsky, 1973; Mason and Bumpass, 1975; Osmond and Martin, 1975). Both men and women—but especially women—have come to prefer less rigid gender roles in the labor market and in family relationships (Mason et al., 1976; Parelius, 1975a).

It is unclear whether men really lag behind women in their preference for more egalitarian roles or whether women simply perceive that they do. Very early, McKee and Sheriffs (1959) found that women perceive men as wanting them to show more feminine qualities than men actually do. Parelius (1975b) concluded that women's expectations for themselves have changed, but that women perceive the expectations of men to have changed little. Osmond and Martin (1975) found more men saying their own self-esteem would not be hurt if their wives earned more money, while most women thought that their husband's self-esteem would be hurt.

Others have found that expectations and perceptions of expectations influence married women's decisions to work. Scanzoni (1979) found that a wife's attitude toward her gender role affects the probability that she will participate in the labor force. Spitze and Waite (1981) demonstrated that whether the wife perceived her husband's attitude to be positive or negative was important for her employment.

Husbands and wives also have different perceptions about behavior. Condran and Bode (1982) point out what they call the Rashomon effect—a significant disjuncture between wives' and husbands' perceptions about how much the husbands participate in household duties. Husbands see themselves as participating more than wives believe they do. Regardless of the perceptions, actual behavior with respect to housework and childcare has been slow to change (Meissner et al., 1975; Vanek, 1974). Typically only one partner is interviewed in these studies. Thus, there has been no way to determine whether partners actually differ in their expectations, or whether they just believe that they have different expectations than their partners. By using couples in our sample, we hope to clarify this issue.

Sample

In 1983, personal interviews were conducted with a stratified sample of 489 married couples in Hamilton County (Cincinnati), Ohio. Participants were selected by randomly dialing households in the target area and securing appointments for interviews to be conducted separately but simultaneously with husbands and wives in their home. Men interviewed husbands, and women interviewed wives. The overall acceptance rate was 47 percent.[1] Because we were particularly interested in professional and managerial women, the sample was stratified to over-sample dual-earner couples, and especially dual-earner couples in which wives held professional and managerial positions. This stratified sample was drawn as callers dialed random numbers and screened subjects. In the final sample, husbands only were employed in 153 couples, wives only were employed in 39 couples, both spouses were employed with the wife in a non-professional or non-managerial occupation in 240 couples, and both spouses were employed and the wife held a professional or managerial position in 57 couples.

Comparing this sample with the 1980 census and with a sample of the non-respondents suggests that the socio-economic status of these subjects is somewhat higher than in the general population and among those who refused to participate. The average family income for the comparable population in Hamilton County is $28,711; in the sample it is $38,260. The census indicates this population to be 12.5 percent black; the sample is 7 percent black. Equal percentages in the census data and the sample were in their first marriages. Demographic variables appear sensitive to response rates, but we believe marital variables to be less so (see Hiller and Philliber, 1985). In all analyses the sample has been weighted to match the actual proportions of Hamilton County households which are dual-earner households, husband-only-earner households, and wife-only-earner households.

Measures

Role Expectations

The four family roles for which expectations were analyzed were childcare, housework, money management, and income earning. The first two are traditionally considered to be in the wife's domain, and the second two in the husband's. Participants were asked to indicate on a five-point scale whether they thought each of these four family roles should be carried out entirely or mostly by themselves, by both partners equally, or mostly or entirely by their spouses.

Perceptions of Spouse's Role Expectations

Using the same five-point scale, we asked participants who they thought their spouses thought should take responsibility for these family roles. In addition, husbands were asked how they felt about their wives being employed, and wives were asked how they thought their husbands felt about their being employed.

Accuracy of Perception

We computed a three-fold difference score for the relationship between an individual's expectation and his or her spouse's perception of that expectation. Individuals were classified either as having a *more traditional* expectation than perceived by their partners, having an expectation *congruent* with their partner's perception, or having a *less traditional* expectation than perceived by their partners.

Attachment to Roles

Marriage partners were asked how important it was to them to be better than their spouses at each of the four family roles: raising children; keeping house; managing finances; and earning income. Responses were scored on a four-point scale from very important to not important at all.

Perception of Division of Household Labor

Both husbands and wives were presented with a list of 20 household and childcare tasks, and were asked whether these tasks were done mostly by themselves, mostly by their spouses, equally by both, mostly by children, or mostly by someone hired. In these analyses, the children and hired help responses are eliminated.

Findings

Differences in Expectations

Within each couple, we compared the spouses' views of who should do what.[2] Table 1 indicates that, irrespective of the family role in question, over two-thirds of the couples had similar expectations. However, for roles traditionally thought to be the wife's, 84 percent agree that childcare should be shared, but only 38 percent agree housework should be. Almost as many couples, 30 percent, agree that housework should be the wife's responsibility. For the roles traditionally assigned to husbands, 69 percent agree that the management of money should be shared, but only 24 percent agree that earning it should be. Almost twice as many—43 percent—agree that earning money is the husband's responsibility.

When couples disagree, the spouses who traditionally perform a given role believe they should continue to do so, while their partners believe those tasks should be shared. A greater number of husbands wish to maintain traditional roles in money matters, and more women than men thought they, the women, should be responsible for domestic matters. This suggests that few husbands or wives want to give up the prerogatives belonging to their traditional marital roles, yet some are interested in expanding their activities into non-traditional roles.

Differences Between Expectations and Partner's Perceptions

Table 2 compares one partner's expectations about the division of family roles with his or her spouse's perceptions of those expectations. First, spouses

Table 1 Comparison of Spouses' Expectations about
Who Should Perform Marital Roles

Expectations for Wife's Traditional Roles:	*Childcare*	*Housework*
Agree job should be shared	84%	38%
Agree it is wife's job	2	30
Husband: wife's job/Wife: should share	7	13
Husband: should share/Wife: wife's job	8	20
Total	101%	101%
(N)	(483)	(488)

Expectations for Husband's Traditional Roles:	*Money Management*	*Income Earning*
Agree job should be shared	69%	24%
Agree it is husband's job	9	43
Wife: husband's job/Husband: should share	5	9
Wife: should share/Husband: husband's job	17	25
Total	100%	101%
(N)	(487)	(484)

misperceive their partner's expectations fairly often. In five of the nine compar-isons, over 40 percent inaccurately perceive their partners' expectations. In two of those comparisons—wife's perceptions of husband's attitude about her working and about who should manage money—their majority were incorrect. Second, husbands perceive their spouses' expectations more accurately than their wives perceive theirs. On each of the four items which were available for both husbands and wives, husbands were accurate more often than wives.

Third, inaccurate perceptions about housekeeping and childcare roles occur most often because husbands are less traditional and wives more traditional than their partners expect. On the one hand, sizeable percentages of wives believe their husbands expect them to do housework and childcare when, in fact, their husbands believe these should be shared roles. On the other hand, husbands are especially likely to believe their wives expect them to share housework when, in fact, wives do not expect this.

Finally, inaccuracies in perceptions of expectations for roles traditionally assigned to men occur most often because husbands are more traditional and wives less traditional than their partners expect. Wives tend to perceive husbands' expectations about managing money to be less traditional than they actually are. Husbands more often perceive wives' expectations about both managing and earning money to be more traditional then they actually are.

Differences Between Expectations and Behavior

How do the expectations spouses have of themselves and each other match the actual behavior in their marriages? The discrepancies between expectations and

Table 2 Accuracy of Spouse's Perception of Partner's Expectations for Marital Roles

	Accuracy of Wife's Perception				Accuracy of Husband's Perception			
	Husband More Traditional	*Perception Accurate*	*Husband Less Traditional*	*Total (N)*	*Wife More Traditional*	*Perception Accurate*	*Wife Less Traditional*	*Total (N)*
Having a working wife	26%	38	36	100% (482)	a	a	a	a
Doing childcare	6%	73	21	100% (483)	11%	82	7	100% (485)
Doing housework	9%	55	36	100% (487)	27%	65	8	100% (487)
Managing money	37%	44	19	100% (488)	18%	51	31	100% (485)
Earning income	22%	55	23	100% (484)	13%	61	26	100% (484)

Note: a. Variable not measured.

actual behavior become apparent when Table 1 is compared to data on task performance in Table 3. Fifty-eight percent of husbands say housework should be shared; yet, except for two tasks listed in Table 3, not more than a third of the husbands either share or do regular household tasks, even by their own estimate. Thirty-three percent of the husbands report they shop for food, and 43 percent wash dishes. Note that the percentage of wives who see their husbands doing or sharing these tasks is lower than the percentages of husbands who see themselves doing them (although the percentages tend to vary in the same direction across all tasks). Both husbands and wives report that money management is the only regular household task either done or shared by a majority of husbands.

Although wives perform the more regular household tasks, a number of husbands do household tasks which are less regular or are needed on an occasional basis. Almost all husbands take primary responsibility for household repairs and yard work, and most share in making major purchases, planning recreation, and planning vacations. Many also share in the supervision of help and in preparations for entertainment.

Analyses of perceptions of childcare task performance were limited to those couples who still have children at home (which accounts for the reduced sample size for these items in Table 3). While 84 percent of all these couples agree that childcare should be shared, a majority of fathers say they participate equally or more in only three of the six childcare tasks—staying with ill children, getting children ready for bed, and helping kids with homework. Moreover, according to wives' reports, only about a third of their husbands participate equally or more in any childcare tasks, except for helping with homework.

As shown in the far right-hand column of Table 3, couples generally agree about who does what around the house. With the exception of money management, at least three-quarters agree about whether regular household tasks are done primarily by the wife, the husband, or are shared. There is somewhat lower agreement about who does non-regular household tasks and even less about who does childcare; but for every task the majority of couples agree. Across the board, both husbands and wives see themselves participating more than their spouses see them participating. Husbands are especially more likely to see tasks as shared, while wives see themselves with major responsibility.

Personal Attachment to Roles

Table 4 shows that 58 percent of husbands consider it important to be better than their wives at earning income—suggesting that the men are still very attached to their traditional breadwinning role. Neither husbands nor wives are overwhelmingly attached to the role of managing finances. However, 43 percent of wives still consider it important to be better than their husbands at childcare, and 38 percent feel that way about housekeeping. The majority of wives do not consider it important to exceed their husbands in performance of the traditional female roles.

Table 5 indicates husbands' feelings about their wives' employment. While the majority of men in this sample consider it important to earn more income

Table 3 Husband's and Wife's Perceptions of Division of Labor

	Wife's Perception				Husband's Perception				Percent Agreement Between Spouses
	Wife Does %	Both Do %	Husband Does %	(N)	Wife Does %	Both Do %	Husband Does %	(N)	
Regular Household Tasks									
Food shopping	70	20	10	(489)	67	23	10	(489)	86
Meal preparation	85	10	5	(481)	82	13	5	(487)	81
House cleaning	80	17	3	(453)	73	23	4	(456)	78
Washing dishes	66	29	5	(451)	57	36	7	(453)	87
Washing clothes	84	10	6	(475)	81	14	5	(473)	76
Ironing	90	7	3	(489)	90	7	3	(450)	90
Managing money	42	31	27	(489)	30	38	32	(488)	65
Less Regular Household Tasks									
Household repairs	7	13	80	(440)	2	7	91	(458)	82
Yard work	11	29	60	(382)	6	24	70	(405)	71
Supervision of help	72	24	4	(174)	51	34	15	(226)	56
Entertaining preparation	52	46	2	(487)	44	53	3	(489)	61
Major purchases	14	82	4	(489)	9	85	6	(488)	79
Planning Recreation	16	80	4	(476)	11	83	7	(476)	72
Planning vacations	8	85	7	(472)	8	82	10	(482)	79
Childcare Tasks									
Arranging activities	61	36	3	(280)	58	40	2	(325)	63
Take kids to doctor	74	23	3	(309)	62	34	4	(333)	73
Stays home when kids are sick	62	36	2	(332)	48	48	4	(340)	52
Gets kids ready for bed	60	34	6	(253)	48	47	5	(300)	71
Get kids ready for school	82	11	7	(218)	80	16	4	(267)	81
Help kids with homework	45	41	14	(235)	35	54	11	(266)	65

Table 4 Importance of Superior Role Performance for Husband and Wife

Importance of Role	Childcare		Housework		Money Management		Income Earning	
	Husband	*Wife*	*Husband*	*Wife*	*Husband*	*Wife*	*Husband*	*Wife*
Very important	4%	15%	2%	14%	9%	7%	26%	2%
Somewhat important	22	28	7	26	30	25	32	10
Not very important	43	30	43	33	36	41	24	44
Not at all important	31	27	48	27	25	27	18	44
Total	100%	100%	100%	100%	100%	100%	100%	100%
(N)	(481)	(481)	(488)	(486)	(487)	(486)	(488)	(485)

Table 5 Husbands' Attitude Toward Wife's Employment

	Husbands with Employed Wife	*Husbands with Non-Employed Wife*	*All Husbands*
Likes wife working	74%	37%	63%
Does not care	11	26	15
Dislikes wife working	15	37	22
Total	100%	100%	100%
(N)	(341)	(141)	(482)

than their wives, three-fourths of those with employed wives like the fact that their spouses are working, and over a third with unemployed wives would like their wives to be working. Less than a fourth of the total sample of husbands prefer that their wife be unemployed.

Effects of Expectations and Perceptions on Performance

To discern how expectations and perceptions of expectations affect performance, measures of the division of labor in four major areas were subjected to multiple regression analysis. We constructed a summary measure of who does childcare by adding responses to the six childcare items. Similarly, we obtained a measure of who does housework by adding the six regular household tasks, excluding money management. Money management was kept as a separate item. We calculated income earning as the percent of family income earned by the wife. On all four measures, a high score indicates the wife takes greater responsibility for the role.[3]

The four regression equations included as predictors each spouses's expectations for the specific marital role, perceptions of partner's expectations, and husband's and wife's attachments to the role.[4] In addition, we included family income, wife's employment, presence of children in the home, and length of marriage to examine and control their possible effects on performance of each role.

Table 6   Standardized Effects of Independent Variables on Household Division of Labor as Reported by Husband

	Marital Role			
Predictor	Childcare (N = 209)	Housework (N = 336)	Money Management (N = 395)	Income Earning (N = 185)
Family income	−.01	−.13**	.01	−.19**
Wife's employment	−.25***	−.14**	.09**	b
Children in the home	a	.06	−.05	−.11
Length of marriage	−.10	.07	−.05	−.13
Husband's role expectations	.12	.17**	.31***	.02
Wife's role expectations	.01	−.09	−.08	−.04
Husband's perception of wife's expectation	−.05	−.23***	−.22***	.21*
Wife's perception of husband's expectation	.11	.27***	.28***	−.18*
Importance of role to husband	.09	−.11*	−.09**	−.01
Importance of role to wife	.08	.07	.08*	.01
R^2 =	.16	.42	.56	.15

Notes:
  a. Analysis limited to couples with children in the home.
  b. Analysis limited to couples with an employed wife.
    *$p < .05$ **$p < .01$ ***$p < .001$.

Table 6 indicates that the only variable with a significant effect on childcare is the wife's employment. Specifically, the husband is more likely to share in childcare if the wife is employed than if the wife stays at home.

Several variables significantly affect performance of housework. The wife does more of the housework if she is not employed, has a husband who believes she should do the housework, perceives that to be his expectation, and has a husband who perceives it to be her expectation. She does less housework if her husband feels it is important for him to be able to do it well, or if the family has a relatively high income. The strongest effect is that of wife's perception of husband's expectation. In general, the husband's attitudes about housework appear to be more important than the wife's.

Money management is affected by expectations, perceptions, and role attachment in much the same way as housework, except that the wife's attitudes are somewhat more important. The wife is more likely to manage the money if she is employed, if both she and her husband feel she should do it and perceive the other to feel that way, and if performance of that role is important to her and unimportant to him. Again, the most influential variables are husband's expectation and wife's perception of that expectation.

Three predictors are significantly related to income earning. First, the lower the total income of a family, the higher the percentage earned by the wife. Also, the percentage of income earned by the wife is greater if (a) the husband perceives that his wife expects to earn money, and (b) the wife perceives that her husband expects her to share in income earning.

Discussion and Conclusions

What do partners in contemporary marriages expect of one another? How do they see their spouses' expectations? And how do these definitions of the marital relationship relate to the traditional division of labor in the household? We have attempted to move beyond previous efforts to answer these questions by basing our inquiry on the perspectives of both husbands and wives. The picture of their marriages portrayed in our results is complex, but it is still heavily colored by traditional expectations about spouses' respective role responsibilities.

We did find widespread agreement among couples that childcare and money management should be shared responsibilities. Most couples expected to share childrearing equally, and two-thirds expected to take equal responsibility for managing money. However, differences between and within couples were more apparent for two other areas of responsibility—housework and income earning. Although many spouses agreed that these tasks should be shared equally, nearly a third of the couples agreed that housework is the wife's job, and 43 percent agreed that income earning is the husband's job. In another third of these couples, partners held different expectations about housework and income earning. In these cases, the wife tended to be more traditional with respect to responsibility for housework, and the husband was more likely to hold traditional expectations toward income earning. These results suggest that many spouses were willing to share in the traditional roles of the opposite sex but did not expect to relinquish primary responsibility for their own traditional roles in marriage.

Focusing specifically on the key issue of income earning in these households, we found that nearly two-thirds of the husbands liked (or would have liked) their wives being employed. Yet, a majority of the men in our sample (58 percent) felt that it is important to earn more than their wives earn, and nearly three-fourths of them held to the traditional view that income earning is the husband's job. Apparently, most husbands were comfortable with having their wives work—as long as the man is still the main breadwinner. While over half of the wives similarly expected the husband to be the primary earner of household income, our results seemingly contradict Osmond and Martin's (1975) finding that women were more likely than men to believe that a husband would be hurt if his wife earned more money.

Turning to the question of how partners perceive their spouses' expectations about household responsibilities, we found that husbands' perceptions were consistently more accurate than were wives' perceptions. Perhaps wives are more likely to express their feelings about who should perform household tasks, giving their husbands a better reading of these expectations. When partners misperceived their spouses' expectations, this often occurred because the spouse actually expected to take more responsibility for the traditional roles of the opposite sex than the partner perceived. For instance, many wives underestimated their husbands' willingness to share childcare and housework. Likewise, substantial proportions of the husbands seemed unaware that their wives expected to share in managing and earning household income. On the other hand, spouses tended to be more traditional about their own sex-specific responsibilities—i.e., husbands expecting to manage the money and wives expecting to do the housework—than their partners thought they would be.

Spouses' respective perceptions of the actual division of labor in their household were generally consistent with one another. In those instances where spouses disagreed about who performed a given task, both husbands and wives tended to see themselves as doing more than their spouses said they did. These discrepancies reflect the Rashomon effect noted previously by Condran and Bode (1982). However, the dominant pattern in spouses' ratings of task performance, especially for routine tasks, was one of agreement. Consequently, we focused on husbands' reports in our subsequent analyses of the household division of labor.

Even when measured by husbands' reports of behavior, the performance of key household tasks departed markedly from spouses' expectations about shared responsibilities. For instance, over four-fifths of these couples expected to share childcare, but less than half actually did so. Over half of these spouses expected to share housekeeping chores, but only a third of the husbands reported sharing even two tasks equally (dishwashing and shopping). For most couples, then, these activities continued to follow traditional patterns in spite of spouses' expectations for greater equality in their relationship.

This brings us to our final question: What factors do affect the household division of labor? Perhaps the most important and far-reaching finding of our multivariate analysis is that perceptions of partners' expectations strongly influence spouses' behavior. Spouses' views of what their partners expected significantly affected performance of housework, money management, and income earning. Clearly, these definitions of the marital situation have real consequences for the behavior of married men and women, even when they define their partners' expectations incorrectly. This important link between perceptions and behavior in the marital relationship deserves attention in future research.

Our analysis also indicated that the husband's prerogatives continue to have a more pronounced impact on marital role bargains than do the wife's employment or other family characteristics. We found that money management was more strongly affected by the husband's expectations—and by the wife's perception of those expectations—than by whether the wife worked. Similarly the husband's expectations and wife's perceptions of his preferences were the most important factors in the allocation of housework. The only area where the wife's employment had a leading influence was in childcare.

Therefore, despite the fact that 69 percent of the wives in our sample were working outside the home, the traditional division of labor and dominant role of the male "head-of-household" were still very much in evidence in these marriages. Although some signs of change were apparent in spouses' expectations about sharing certain household tasks, we did not find indications of dramatic change in the husband's position as the "primary" wage earner or in the wife's day-to-day responsibilities for housework and childcare. As Pleck (1977) has argued, the traditional priorities of work and marital roles reflected in our results form an interdependent system that will be difficult to alter. Until women's earnings are more comparable to men's, it seems unlikely that role bargaining in the intimate marital relationship will change drastically. Conversely, the ability of women to compete equally with men in the public worlds of work and politics will suffer until they are equally free of—or equally burdened by—the constraints of housework and childcare.

Notes

1. Callers contacted 1,037 households in which a married couple lived and at least one spouse was employed. Of these, 489 couples agreed to be interviewed, producing an acceptance rate of 47 percent. Both men and women callers screened households between 6 and 9 P.M. weeknights and on Saturdays, and interviews were scheduled at the convenience of the subjects. Addresses were sought from eligible couples who hesitated to make interview appointments, and information about the study was mailed. This letter was followed by a call back, and, if necessary, a second letter and call back. Those who refused to give addresses or who initially refused to answer the screening question were also called a second time. Subjects were not paid but gave their time voluntarily. More details about the sampling and data collection processes for this study appear in Hiller and Philliber (1985).
2. For roles traditionally fulfilled by wives, responses were dichotomized by grouping perceptions that the role should be carried out entirely or mostly by wife as "wife's job," while perceptions that the role should be shared or done entirely or mostly by husband were classified as "shared job." The same procedure was followed for roles traditionally carried out by husbands with the categories reversed accordingly.
3. Because of the reasonably high agreement between husbands and wives, only husbands' perceptions of who does childcare, housework, and money management were analyzed.
4. Zero-order, correlations, means, and standard deviations for the variables in the four regression equations are available from the first author [University of Cincinnati]. As might be expected, several of the independent variables in these analyses are significantly correlated, but none so highly that multicollinearity would be of great concern. The total N varies across the four analyses because of different levels of missing data (deleted listwise) and sub-sample selection on the dependent variable (i.e., analysis only of couples with children or a working wife).

References

Bianchi, Susanne M., and Daphne Spain. 1983. American Women: Three Decades of Change (DCS-80-8). Washington, DC: U.S. Bureau of the Census.

Condran, John G., and Jerry G. Bode. 1982. "Rashomon, working wives, and family division of labor: Middletown, 1980." Journal of Marriage and the Family 44:421–26.

Hiller, Dana V., and William W. Philliber. 1985. "Maximizing confidence in married couple sample." Journal of Marriage and the Family 47:729–32.

Huber, Joan, and Glenna Spitze. 1983. Sex Stratification: Children, Housework, and Jobs. New York: Academic Press.

Komarovsky, Mirra. 1973. "Cultural contradictions and sex roles: the masculine case." American Journal of Sociology 78:873–84.

Mason, Karen Oppenheimer, and Larry L. Bumpass. 1975. "U.S. women's sex-role ideology, 1970." American Journal of Sociology 80:1212–19.

Mason, Karen Oppenheimer, John L. Czajka, and Sara Arber. 1976. "Changes in U.S. women's sex-role attitudes, 1964–1974." American Sociological Review 41:573–96.

McKee, John P., and Alex C. Sheriffs. 1959. "Men's and women's beliefs, ideals, and self-concepts." American Journal of Sociology 64:356–63.

Meissner, Martin, Elizabeth Humphreys, Scott Meis, and William Scheu. 1975. "No exit for wives: sexual division of labor and the cumulation of household demands." Canadian Review of Sociology and Anthropology 12:424–39.

Osmond, Marie Withers, and Patricia Yancey Martin. 1975. "Sex and sexism: a comparison of male and female sex-role attitudes." Journal of Marriage and the Family 37:744–53.

Parelius, Ann P. 1975a. "Change and stability in college women's orientations toward education, family, and work." Social Problems 22:420–32.

———— .1975b. "Emerging sex-role attitudes, expectations, and strains among college women." Journal of Marriage and the Family 37:146–53.

Pleck, Joseph H. 1977. "The work-family role system." Social Problems 24:417–27.

Scanzoni, John. 1979. "Sex-role influences on married women's status attainments." Journal of Marriage and the Family 41:793–800.

Spitze, Glenna D., and Linda J. Waite. 1981. "Wife's employment: the role of husband's perceived attitudes." Journal of Marriage and the Family 42:117–24.

Vanek, Joann. 1974. "Time spent in housework." Scientific American 231:116–20.

The Dualities of Careers and Families: New Integrations or New Polarizations?

Janet G. Hunt and Larry L. Hunt

That dual-career families, while statistically few, hold important keys to broader social change is generally assumed to be self-evident by both the popular and research literature (Bird, 1979; Epstein, 1971; Pepitone-Rockwell, 1980; Rapoport and Rapoport, 1969, 1971, 1976, 1980). The work involvement of dual-career wives, the literature suggests, signals a more radical break with the conventional pattern of subordination of women's personal development to the demands of families and husbands' careers than do more typical job roles for women.

An earlier version of this paper was presented at the 76th annual meeting of the American Sociological Association, August 1981, Toronto.

In dual-career families, both husband and wife have continuous and self-fulfilling extra-domestic work roles as well as meaningful and involving family roles. As "lifestyle pioneers" (Bird, 1979; Rapoport and Rapoport, 1976), they are the vanguard of "new integrations of work and family" (Rapoport and Rapoport, 1976) that will characterize the more equitable role sharing of men and women in the future.

In this paper, we challenge the prevailing view. Dual-career families have not represented a radical departure from conventional sex roles, we argue. As careers become more legitimate for women, careers and families will become increasingly polarized rather than more effectively integrated. The new forms of role sharing that will evolve as women become more active in the labor force will involve men's withdrawal from—more than women's entry into—work roles that can be called "careers."[1]

Dual Careers and the Two-Person Career

Social analysts have highlighted the distinctive features of dual-career families by contrasting dual careers and "two-person careers" (Bird, 1979; Hunt and Hunt, 1977; Pepitone-Rockwell, 1980). The two-person career is a uniquely North American phenomenon in which highly educated women have channeled their talents and energies into an auxiliary role relative to their husbands' careers, rather than pursuing their own mobility (Papanek, 1973). This concept of the "companionate" or "egalitarian" marriage emphasizes the wife's emotional support rather than her physical labor in the household and does not question the breadwinner/homemaker distinction. In the dual-career family, the wife invests in her own career development, moving toward a principle of equity based on role "symmetry" between spouses (Young and Willmott, 1973). This principle assumes that as women pursue their own careers, men engage in more domestic work, resulting in a more balanced sharing of breadwinning and homemaking responsibilities in families.

This emphasis on the differences between dual careers and two-person careers ignores some important contextual and structural similarities between the two. The same circumstances that facilitated the growth of the two-person careers made dual careers a viable lifestyle option. In the 1980s, the historical moment for both of these family types may be passing.

The dual-career families described in the research literature were products of a time that predates the supportive cultural atmosphere that stimulated their study. Most of the data were collected in the 1960s and early 1970s from couples who grew up and embarked on their lifestyle after the Second World War. This was a period when feminist voices were unusually quiet. Return to family values was the dominant cultural ethos, embodied in what has been referred to as "the togetherness doctrine" (Skolnick, 1978), "the feminine mystique," (Friedan, 1963), and "the cult of domesticity" (Filene, 1974). It was a time when women's place in the home was idealized, and employed women, especially employed mothers, were portrayed unsympathetically. The myth of expanding affluence prevailed, minimizing perceptions of social inequality and many women's need for paid jobs (Skolnick, 1978).

In this context, high-income families exploited the captive labor of women denied sufficient alternative employment opportunities as cheap domestic help. This facilitated the emergence of the "idle wife," whose relative freedom from domestic chores permitted an active public life of social and volunteer activities. The idleness of these wives, however, was more apparent than real. Their activity was a form of "status production work" for their families (Papanek, 1979). They displayed their husbands' success, managed the couple's strategic social connections, and ran the household, despite their exemption from much of the physical labor. In short, they performed the auxiliary role in the most successful of two-person careers.

Domestic help, often live-in, was also considered essential for dual-career couples of the past (Holmstrom, 1972; Rapoport and Rapoport, 1971, 1976). It allowed highly educated women to substitute at least a "career of limited ambition" (White, 1979) for the non-paid public role of the idle wife. In both cases, one class of women escaped some of the constraints of sex stratification by using the labor of the class of women most severely limited by this stratification. Moreover, both the idle wife and the dual-career wife extricated themselves without challenging the male role. There has been little departure from the conventional domestic division of labor among dual-career couples (Garland, 1972; Holmstrom, 1972; Paloma, 1972; Rapoport and Rapoport, 1971, 1976). The career wife instead has managed to perform "two roles" (Myrdal and Klein, 1956) through skillful allocation of her own time and energies and effective use of the labor of other women.

The survival strategies of career women have benefited also from the particularistic treatment of career women in the past. Restricted employment and professional opportunities for women were legitimated by saying that women did not need or want jobs because of their primary identification with the family. But the other side of the coin was that the token women who were sponsored into professional and business roles were expected to pursue career paths that differed from men's—career paths that were slowly paced, often interrupted, and "neither upward-moving nor 'success-oriented' but [which recognized] their commitment to family responsibilities" (White, 1979:365). It was not a universalistic world of sex-blind policies; it was a world that largely excluded women but had special rules for those allowed to enter. This permitted the lives of dual-career men to be similar to those of other career men, while the lives of dual-career women were carefully balanced to provide a measure of career involvement as long as the family was not inconvenienced.

By today's standards, the lack of equity and role symmetry in the marriages of early dual-career couples seems odd. But compared to women around them, dual-career women were privileged. At the same time, their husbands could compare themselves to other men and feel they were doing their full share by "letting" their wives pursue careers and making the smallest of concessions to the arrangement (Miller, 1972). Domestic tensions were probably further reduced by the need of dual-career couples to maintain a low profile and project normalcy in order to minimize "environmental sanctions" (Rapoport and Rapoport, 1971, 1976). That is, while sex-role asymmetries may have generated some internal strain, they contributed to the management of tension with the social environment. Moreover, for dual-career couples to have scrutinized themselves too closely and questioned seriously the imbalances in their relationship would have been to risk alienating their most important source of support—each other (Johnson and Johnson, 1980).

Dual-career couples, then, could survive most comfortably in the 1950s and 1960s by retaining a high degree of structural similarity to other high-status families. This included having children. The presence of children made it possible to construe male success-striving as "breadwinning" and to justify women's non-involvement in their own careers in the name of "homemaking"—a prerequisite role division for two-person careers. Children were also essential for the legitimation of dual careers. More than anything else, children established normalcy and minimized the salience and visibility of the wife's career. Further, the pressure to conform and the couple's own probable inability to clearly articulate an alternative to parenting undoubtedly reduced conflict over the decision to parent and the competing demands of career and motherhood.

In sum, as long as the dual-career family was a deviant form, it was necessary for dual-career couples to conform in most areas of their lives to conventional sex roles. This ensured asymmetries in these marriages but minimized the resulting marital tensions. It also encouraged dual-career couples to have children but reduced the conflicts of employed mothers. With the growing cultural emphasis on sex equality in the 1970s and 1980s, the viability of the old dual-career pattern has begun to break down. Women who used to be available for domestic help are looking increasingly to other forms of employment. The old particularistic treatment of career women has given way to greater universalism—and the expectation that women's career development and involvement more closely approximate men's. In addition, the environmental pressures on dual-career couples are shifting. While Rapoport and Rapoport (1976) emphasized the reduction in strains that has resulted from growing social acceptance of dual careers, this new, more positive social atmosphere has placed new burdens on these couples. They are no longer expected to maximize their conventionality but to live up to the ideal of symmetry. Finally, women especially may now find more support for role change outside the marriage—from women's support groups, for example—than from their husbands. All of this means that the potential for marital tension over perceived inequities has increased considerably in recent years, and there is less tolerance for the compromises of the past. This raises the question: will these changes generate more, and more equitable, dual-career families, or is the dual-career family a transitional phenomenon relative to the lifestyles of the future?

The Polarization of Careers and Families

A sex-role ideology that allocates primary breadwinning responsibility to men and primary homemaking responsibility to women has reduced the family demands placed on husbands, contained the career aspirations of wives, and produced the phenomenon of the two-person career. It has also conditioned heavily the shape and meaning of dual careers. The developments of recent years are eroding both of these patterns, and with them the prospects for combining careers and families in the same households.

The decline of the two-person career is quite evident. New attitudes are stimulating women's labor force behavior, and [are] reshaping their increased labor-force activity attitudes; the once-modal single-breadwinner family has diminished, and so has both the availability of and the justification for wives as the second persons in men's careers (Bird, 1979; Pepitone-Rockwell, 1980). Most U.S. women in married households are now in the labor force (U.S. Department of Labor, 1980). Moreover, highly educated women—the source of two-person careers in the past—are the most likely to be employed, to want to be employed, and to desire changes in the sex-role division of labor in the family (Bird, 1979).

Less obvious, perhaps, is the way recent changes weaken the dual-career family. The literature on dual careers generally assumes that the increasing participation of women in the labor force, combined with rising standards of sex equity, imply inevitable movement toward more symmetrical families, especially among the highly educated. Fewer two-person careers and more dual-career families are predicted (Bird, 1979; Pepitone-Rockwell, 1980).

Lorber (1980) argues the more radical view that changes in sex roles undercut the very basis of the family. The principle of sex equality calls into question more than the division of labor and rewards between the sexes. It challenges the structural mechanisms that have maintained the institution of the family. Heterosexual union and procreation were ensured in the past by the functional interdependence of men and women. Women depended on men economically; women, in return, performed essential services for men and reared their children. While the sentiment of love may have embellished this functional interdependence and has provided a strong incentive to marry in modern times, love—particularly romantic love—is not by itself conducive to stable and permanent coupling. Thus, Lorber concludes, as women gain independence from marriage through employment, and men derive fewer automatic and/or indispensable services from their wives, heterosexual unions will become less permanent, sexuality will be less linked with procreation, and women will become less available to rear children. Equality between the sexes, in other words, implies more than modification of family roles. It means a diminishing place for the family in society.

While the literature on dual careers takes the incentives to form families too much for granted, Lorber's more radical analysis dismisses these incentives too easily, we believe. For some men and women, especially among the highly educated, the likelihood of family formation is declining. In a social climate that endorses sex equality, independence in women is seen increasingly as a positive attribute, and "childless" has become "child-free." Marriage and motherhood are not only less essential for women with careers than in the past, they are also more problematic. The dual-career family means the addition of a high-demanding work role to the couple's commitments and creates the problem of career coordination between spouses. No matter how housekeeping and childcare are apportioned, the dual-career family is over-extended and faces great logistic difficulties. The strain is probably greater today than it was in the past, as career women are forced to pace themselves with men, household help is less available, and the ability to choose or reject parenthood heightens ambivalence over competing role demands. Without positing a total lack of interest by women in families, we anticipate that, with the old stigmas removed, more career women will—either eagerly or reluctantly—avoid stress and risk to their careers by bypassing marriage and especially motherhood. Men, too, probably feel less need to justify their careers by having families, and the prospect of having to assume a greater share of domestic responsibilities and give their wives' careers more equal billing may diminish the attractiveness and feasibility of dual-career families from their standpoint as well. Thus, for the success-oriented of either sex, families will become less necessary, less helpful, and more of a liability than in the past. Some analysts try to minimize the significance of this trend by claiming that declining birthrates are due primarily to smaller families rather than childlessness (Bane, 1976). Others, however, stress real growth in the proportion of young adults who expect to have no children (Glick, 1975; Westoff, 1978). Moreover, two recent, detailed studies of childlessness establish clear links between avoiding parenting and the desire to achieve personal, adult-centered goals—especially careers (Burgwyn, 1981; Veevers, 1980).

Meanwhile, many people in the United States continue to marry and have children, and the family is probably "here to stay" (Bane, 1976). Commitment to family values still runs deep, despite a growing tolerance and even idealization of the alternatives. The great upsurge of pro-family rhetorics in the United States in the early 1980s reflects not only a residual traditionalism but certain realities of modern life. For most people, neither paid work nor any other links to the public world are sufficient to provide a sense of efficacy, purpose, accomplishment, and security. For many, including a large portion of the highly educated, there is nothing compelling enough to draw them away from family life. This is not to say that these people lack need or interest in employment and even a measure of self-fulfillment through their paid work roles. Rather, for these people, all-consuming careers are either unavailable or undesirable, and family remains the primary source of satisfaction in life (Skolnick, 1978). Where this is the case, women undoubtedly will continue to compromise their careers as they have in the past, and men will be forced increasingly to do so as well. Men have been slow to assume more domestic responsibilities (Bird, 1979; Hofferth and Moore, 1979; Vanek, 1980). But women appear to be in the labor force to stay, and it is probably inevitable that men's roles will eventually adjust to this reality. Men, we predict, will be less free in the future to pursue careers without sacrifices, if they also wish to have families.

We are arguing, then, that what is becoming incompatible with family life is not women's participation in the labor force, or the principle of sex equality, but *careers*. Careers and families could be integrated in the past because of the sex-role division of labor between spouses, but *career and family involvement have never been* *combined easily in the same person*. As Hochschild (1976;256) observed, "the career system is shaped for and by the man with a family who is family-free." As more women have careers, and fathers are held more responsible for the care of their children, the pursuit of careers will foster more extreme forms of individualism. We foresee, as a consequence, a growing polarization of career-centered and family-centered lifestyles. Those who give priority to their careers will more often in the future be child-free. Many probably will continue to marry— producing dual-career couples—while others will prefer to avoid formal and/or long-term commitments entirely. Those who emphasize family life will gravitate toward greater role symmetry, which will preclude availability for the most competitive, demanding, and often rewarding careers. For highly educated men and women who are technically qualified to enter the career market, having families will mean scaling down aspirations and often settling for jobs instead of careers.

This polarization of careers and families that we anticipate contrasts with the new forms of career and family integration envisioned in the literature on dual careers. This literature assumes that, in response to men's and women's fuller participation in each other's worlds, U.S. society will evolve toward what Rossi (1969) has termed the "hybrid model of sex equality." According to this model, on both a personal and institutional level, the patterns of the future will synthesize aspects of men's and women's roles, values and perspectives. Work and political institutions will reflect values other than rationality and efficiency—values that are socially responsible, flexible, and responsive to family obligations and circumstances. Families will no longer "greedily" (Coser, 1974) consume the services of wives to promote the success and fulfillment of husbands and children.

This literature fails to acknowledge the self-defeating adjustments that would be required of those institutions most committed to "masculine" values in order for the hybrid model to be realized. Institutions whose primary goals are power and profit have a vested interest in rewarding most highly those whose personal orientations give priority to political and corporate success over family well-being. It is only in such institutions that the concept of "career" makes sense.

> "Career" is in itself a masculine concept (i.e., designed for males in our society). When we say "career" it connotes a demanding, rigorous, preordained life pattern, to whose goals everything else is ruthlessly subordinated—everythng pleasurable, human, emotional, bodily, frivolous. It is a stern Calvinistic word. When a man asks a woman if she wants a career, it is intimidating. He is saying, are you willing to suppress half of your being as I am, neglect your family as I do, exploit personal relationships as I do, renounce all personal spontaneity as I do? Naturally she shudders a bit and shuffles back to the broom closet   [*Slater, 1970:72*].

The very idea that women as well as men could embrace careers and, at the same time, become more humane and responsive to families is a contradiction. Employers may make concessions to the fact that more workers have parental responsibilities by providing childcare during working hours, permitting flexible schedules, and granting workers leave to care for infants and sick children. But as long as there is another tier of workers who do not value these benefits, who will apply themselves instead to occupational and professional advancement, the "gains" made by parents will only serve to differentiate their work orientations from those of serious careerists. As more of the latter are women, what used to be a tracking system that separated elite men from the rest of the work force will become one that assigns different institutional destinies to careerists and parents.

We are suggesting, then, that U.S. society is evolving toward a social order which is less overtly sexist yet which extends the legacy of patriarchy. What has been polarized by sex roles will remain polarized: public power versus family involvement. In the past this meant that men were assigned work roles that resulted in truncated family lives, while women were assigned family roles that often precluded satisfying work lives. Now women can become "sociological men"—persons who emphasize their public work lives and enjoy the resulting power and independence—and men can become "sociological women"—persons who invest themselves primarily in their families and forfeit power and control of their personal destinies. But U.S. society does not appear to be developing roles and institutions which transcend these two types.

> Today, the cast of characters is changing. It isn't only men in high-powered work lives and women at home. But the choices have remained the same. There seems to be an inherent contradiction between the commitment to become No. 1, the best, the first, and the commitment to a rich family life. A contradiction between family-first people and work-first people [*Goodman, 1979:158*].

Finally, as the axis of career/family polarization shifts from gender to parental status, and the differentiation becomes less ascribed and more achieved, the consequences for families may in some respects be even more damaging than in the past. While the old polarization combined careers and families in the same households, the new polarization implies more complete institutional separation. While the old polarization provided a structural basis for families—albeit not symmetrical or often equitable—the new polarization is more clearly anti-family in its implications. In the dual-*earning* but not dual-*career* families of the future, symmetry will be more a matter of shared limitations than expanded opportunities. The true pace-setters are those who forego families; those with families will increasingly suffer psychic and economic costs.

A Gap in Standard, as Well as Style, of Living

U.S. society has been slow to recognize what Europe has observed for decades: as the child-free option becomes more available and acceptable, a "class" distinction between parents and non-parents arises.

In a society where there is a normative obligation to have children, and not having children is treated as undesirable or deviant, the costs of children are shared extensively. Most people have children of their own to provide for, and the legitimacy of using collective resources, such as public space and tax revenues, is usually well-established. The use of collective resources is seen as an investment in society's future. Moreover, most are conscious of benefitting personally, whether or not they have children. The use of taxes to provide public education, for example, produces schools that enhance property values for non-parents as well as parents.

This all changes, however, in a society that makes parenting truly voluntary, and the costs of children become increasingly concentrated. Those without children not only escape the direct costs but begin to question the appropriateness of being asked to support "other people's children" through taxes and other collective resources. Instead, they argue that those who derive the rewards of having children should pay and care for them, and that non-parents should be free to establish and invest in their own adult worlds—separate housing developments, restaurants, theaters, and the like.

The result is not only a sense of exclusion on the part of those with families, but a widening gap in the standard of living between parents and non-parents. Those without children can monopolize the highest-paying jobs and combine their resources (through marriage and other alliances) to drive up the price of everything from housing to health care to transportation. Those with children will tend to have lower incomes, in addition to absorbing the expenses of children, and will fall further and further behind their child-free counterparts. This trend, already observed in Europe since the 1930s (Myrdal, 1968), has been obscured in the United States by the recent growth of labor-force participation by wives and mothers. By deploying the earning power of wives, U.S. families have sustained an illusion of "getting ahead," or at least "staying even," in the recession of the 1970s (Bird, 1979). But as we approach the full utilization of wives' earning power, it will become apparent that families cannot compete effectively in a market stimulated by the spending and investing power of child-free adults.

In countries where a larger proportion of the female population has been in the labor force since the Second World War and/or voluntary parenthood has already become fully sanctioned, the disadvantaged economic position of families is already recognized (Kamerman and Kahn, 1978). Liljeström refers to the plight of families in Sweden as a "new kind of poverty."

> The researchers spoke of a relative poverty, which seems to be bound up with the usages of resources by different groups. . . . The new poverty was to be found in families that did *not* suffer from unemployment or from alcoholism or other aberrations. Nor were they immigrants; these were families with full-time employed breadwinners who could not make both ends meet   [*1978:28*].

One consequence of this trend in Sweden and much of Europe has been declining birthrates (Kamerman and Kahn, 1978).

> The Population Commission saw as the most important cause of the declining birthrate the lower living standard of families with children *relative* to that of the childless at corresponding income levels   [*Liljeström, 1978:26*].

This cycle, if unchecked, produces more child-free couples and accentuates the divergence in living standards.

Seen in this light, the liberal emphasis in the United States on voluntary parenthood, increasingly evident in the literature on dual-career families, seems naive (Bird, 1979; Rapoport and Rapoport, 1976; Safilios-Rothschild, 1976). According to this view, when people are truly free to choose whether or not to have children, families will be healthier and children will receive better care. In the words of Bird (1979:xiv), "the most probable future of family life is fewer and better marriages, fewer and more cherished children. . . ." Choice alone, however, does not guarantee well-being. As adults acquire freedom to choose whether or not to parent, families will experience greater difficulties in attaining the middle-class standard of living flaunted by the media. Failure to "make it" will detract from the quality of life for families, and the belief that one's financial circumstance was chosen, not inevitable, will accentuate the sense of cost or opportunities forfeited.

The phenomenon of single parenting illustrates the hollowness of the United States' celebration of choice. At a time when even two-income families are at a disadvantage, single parenting (in spite of some women's higher earnings) is perhaps less economically feasible than ever before.[2] Yet not only is single parenting becoming more common (Glick, 1979), it is becoming, for some, a lifestyle of choice. Just as some people are limiting their commitments by seeking marriage without children, others are limiting their family involvement by raising children without marriage. As career-centered and family-centered lifestyles become more polarized, single parenting seems to offer a logical compromise: a way of participating in family life while maximizing adult autonomy. The film *Paternity*, made in the United States in 1981, suggests that men as well as women are considering this alternative. The cultural discovery of the single-parent life-style, however, ignores its economic implications. Most single parents experience financial difficulties (Bane, 1976; Glick, 1979), and most, as a result, find it necessary to share households with others (Glick, 1979). While this may be quite workable, it suggests that the consequences of choice may alter substantially the meaning of the choice. Single parenting for many may actually restrict, rather than enhance, life-style flexibility and control of personal destiny.

A Social Policy to Reduce Polarization

We have argued that the movement of women into careers and of men into family involvement will break down the integration of these spheres and promote the evolution of more distinct lifestyles organized around either careers *or* families. Families, in the process, will become more symmetrical but also more financially strained. Without more tangible social support, the choice of parenthood will become too costly to remain an attractive option. This has the potential to become a serious social problem. The birth of fewer children and/or their failure to develop into healthy and productive adults would be economically depressing and would increase the ratio of non-employed to the population of employed adults. This ratio, in turn, determines the viability of benefit systems such as social security (Kamerman and Kahn, 1978).

It is largely in response to these concerns that most of the developed countries of the world have formulated family policies designed to promote the well-being of families and stimulate birthrates. While the justifications for these policies and the goals toward which they are aimed vary from country to country, the policies have in common the subsidy of family incomes to reduce the disparity in living standards between families and non-families. These policies provide for greater sharing of the costs of children through tax-financed services and income transfers. Specifically, they include such things as publicly funded childcare and health care, family allowances (payments per child), housing allowances, and paid maternal (or paternal) leave to care for infants and sick children.[3]

The United States has been slow to consider any kind of explicit family policy, much less seriously entertain such direct and extensive subsidies to families as are provided throughout much of Europe. Former U.S. president Jimmy Carter promised to develop a family policy in his presidential campaign of 1976 (Kamerman and Kahn, 1978), but President Ronald Reagan has retreated even from that unrealized pledge. The absence of a family policy in this country, we believe, is due in part to the slower rate of development of such trends as the movement of women into the labor force and declining birthrates and a generally higher standard of living that has delayed awareness of the relative hardship experienced by families. It is, therefore, curious that Bird (1979:240) seems to take for granted in her discussion of the "most probable future" that resources will be more fairly distributed and children will have their health and educational needs provided for as a birthright through public funds. We predict that European-style family policies will eventually be adopted in the United States, but not before the problems of families become far more acute and visible.

Implementation of policies now common in Europe would, we believe, reduce the disparity in living standards between families and non-families in the United States, and increase the flow of resources to children. But these measures alone can alleviate only the external symptoms of the polarization problem. The kind of family policy we have described is, on closer inspection, not a family policy at all; it is an individual policy. As it has been developed in the countries of northern Europe, this policy directs benefits not so much to families as to individuals within families, and minimizes, if not eliminates, the economic dependence of family members on the family *per se*. Such a policy does not directly promote families, but protects freedom of choice. It is not aimed at the rights of families but of individuals, some of whom choose to have families. Although an admitted goal of the policy in most countries has been to stimulate birthrates or stem their decline—the latter, at best, representing the actual trends (Adams and Winston, 1980; Questiaux and Fournier, 1978; Westoff, 1978)—it is presented as a means of removing the obstacles to having families rather than explicitly favoring families. Freedom of choice for the individual is overtly emphasized as the primary basis for family policy in Sweden (Liljeström, 1978; Myrdal, 1968). Similarly, Bird (1979) stresses that it is individuals and not families that should be directly promoted in the United States. There will be fewer but better families in the future, Bird claims, because families will no longer be promoted or needed, but will be formed voluntarily and for non-economic reasons.

We disagree. Family well-being, we believe, requires a genuine family policy aimed at supporting an institution, and not simply individuals who may participate in it. This presumes that the family is more than a personal lifestyle option: it is the institution that best serves certain essential social functions. This idea, in itself, is not highly controversial. While there are differing views on the economic functions of the family in industrialized societies, there is considerable agreement that the family as a unit for the procreation and nurturing of children remains vital. All societies have a stake in children and the quality of their care and socialization. Though the family is not the only possible institutional arrangement for raising children, it is probably best suited to the bonds essential for the child's emotional security and initial formation of the self-concept (Bane, 1976; Kamerman and Kahn, 1978; Leik and Hill, 1979).

Despite relatively high consensus on the value of the family, a coherent and directly supportive family policy has yet to emerge in the United States. Clearly, government involvement in families is perceived as a threat to the most cherished of American values: individualism (Dumon and Aldous, 1979; Schorr, 1979). This concern is shared, in different forms, by both conservatives and liberals. For conservatives, most of whom consider themselves "pro-family," individualism means family autonomy, privacy, and freedom from government intervention or regulation. The family idealized in conservative rhetoric is conventional and patriarchal (the old polarization). It must be preserved in the face of developments that would alter or broaden the concept of family, reduce its power, redistribute its intergenerationally transmitted wealth, and legitimate alternative, non-family lifestyles. From a conservative point of view, the best family policy is no policy at all.

Liberals have a conception of individualism that stresses personal freedom and equality of opportunity. They want to avoid policies that promote conventional lifestyles over more egalitarian or more individualized ones (Feldman, 1979; Leik and Hill, 1979), and they want to diminish the family's function as a status-transfer institution (Bane, 1976). Liberals prefer policies which emphasize androgynous socialization, to free future generations from gender-stereotyped adults roles and lifestyles, and individual benefits that reduce stress for families and equalize life chances for children.

We submit that promoting families represses personal choice and conflicts with equality goals only in societies unwilling to dismantle the real structures of domination that lie outside the family. It is not families but mass institutions such as the news and entertainment media that generate uniformity of personhood and lifestyle. Families, moreover, do not generate socio-economic inequality; they simply mediate the intergenerational transfer of inequities produced by political and economic institutions. Individualism is an ideology that legitimates and strengthens those profit- and control-oriented institutions that most threaten the quality of personal life and the economic well-being of average citizens. Individualism fosters concern with private lifestyle rather than structural change. It focuses attention on equality of opportunity rather than equality of outcomes. It diffuses rather than integrates, and it undermines the capacity for collective action and genuine pluralism. A humane and egalitarian society should have nothing to fear from strong families. But a society which is fundamentally hierarchial must become increasingly wary of a family system not grounded in or central to the maintenance of dominance structures.

The polarization of careers and families is an inevitable consequence of the need to preserve the structures, if not the gender composition, of dominance institutions by promoting individuals. Careerists serve those structures and give individualism a glamorous face for the consumption of mass culture. Families absorb the frustrations of alienated individuals and divert attention from status injuries by offering an alternative reward system. A policy of individual benefits will preserve these family functions. With some form of income maintenance and health insurance for all persons—including children—the economic gap between families and non-families will be reduced, but it will never close. Families will survive, but not thrive. They will be idealized like motherhood and ignored like mothers. They will be forced to trade efficacy for security. Under these conditions, people will be free to choose families, but those who do so will continue to suffer the age-old effects of being women in a man's world.

Notes

1. The term "career" is used in this paper to designate a form of work involvement that is continuous and developmental, demands a high level of commitment, and is intrinsically rewarding (Rapoport and Rapoport, 1976:9). While careers are usually associated with business management and the professions, the concept does not coincide precisely with specific occupational titles or fields. A conscientious clerical worker may treat her work as a career, while a burned-out executive may give a perfunctory role performance. The job-versus-career distinction is partly subjective and represents a continuum rather than discrete categories of work involvement. Our arguments with respect to careers apply to work roles that require more than a nine-to-five (or conventional full-time) investment of self for success or satisfaction. By careers we mean work roles that, for reasons other than economic necessity, consume more time than, and take priority over, other roles and commitments.
2. The association between single parenthood and financial distress is long-standing and well-documented. In absolute terms, the likelihood of U.S. children in single-parent households experiencing poverty has declined since 1960, due to increased public assistance. But relative to children in general, the disadvantage of these children has increased. Further, apart from public assistance, the capacity of a single parent, especially if female, to provide for children is probably declining. For a discussion of these trends, see Bane (1976).
3. See Kamerman and Kahn (1978) for a review of these policies in 14 countries.

References

Adams, Carolyn Teich, and Kathryn Teich Winston. 1980. Mothers at Work: Public Policies in the United States, Sweden, and China. New York: Longman.

Bane, Mary Jo. 1976. Here to Stay: American Families in the Twentieth Century. New York: Basic Books.

Bird, Caroline. 1979. The Two-Paycheck Marriage. New York: Rawson, Wade.

Burgwyn, Diana. 1981. Marriage without Children. New York: Harper and Row.

Coser, Lewis A. 1974. Greedy Institutions. New York: Free Press.

Dumon, Wilfried, and Joan Aldous. 1979. "European and United States political contexts for family policy research." Journal of Marriage and the Family 41:497–505.

Epstein, Cynthia F. 1971. "Law partners and marital partners: Strains and solutions in the dual career family enterprise." Human Relations 24:549–563.

Feldman, Harold. 1979. "Why we need a family policy." Journal of Marriage and the Family 41:453–455.

Filene, Peter Gabriel. 1974. Him/Her/Self: Sex Roles in Modern America. New York: New American Library.

Friedan, Betty. 1963. The Feminine Mystique. New York: Dell Publishing Company.

Garland, T. Neal. 1972. "The better half: The male in the dual profession family." Pp. 199–215 in Constantina Safilios-Rothschild (ed.), Toward a Sociology of Women. Lexington, Mass: Xerox College Publishing.

Glick, Paul C. 1975. "A demographer looks at American families." Journal of Marriage and the Family 37:15–27.

———. 1979. The Future of the American Family. Current Population Reports Special Studies Series P-23, No. 78. Washington, D.C.: U.S. Department of Commerce.

Goodman, Ellen. 1979. Close to Home. New York: Fawcett Crest.

Hochschild, Arlie R. 1976. "Inside the clockwork of male careers." Pp. 251–266 in Jerome H. Skolnick and Elliott Currie (eds.), Crisis in American Institutions. Boston: Little, Brown.

Hofferth, Sandra L., and Kristin A. Moore. 1979. "Women's employment and marriage." Pp. 99–125 in Ralph E. Smith (ed.), The Subtle Revolution. Washington, D.C.: The Urban Institute.

Holmstrom, Lynda L. 1972. The Two-Career Family. Cambridge, Mass.: Schenkman.

Hunt, Janet G., and Larry L. Hunt. 1977. "Dilemmas and contradictions of status: The case of the dual-career family." Social Problems 24:407–416.

Johnson, Coleen L., and Frank A. Johnson. 1980. "Parenthood, marriage, and careers: Situational constraints and role strain." Pp. 143–161 in Fran Pepitone-Rockwell (ed.), Dual-Career Couples. Beverly Hills: Sage.

Kamerman, Sheila B., and Alfred J. Kahn (eds). 1978. Family Policy: Government and Families in Fourteen Countries. New York: Columbia University Press.

Leik, Robert K. and Rueben Hill. 1979. "What price national policy for families?" Journal of Marriage and the Family 41:457–459.

Liljeström, Rita. 1978. "Sweden." Pp. 19–48 in Sheila B. Kamerman and Alfred J. Kahn (eds.), Family Policy: Government and Families in Fourteen Countries. New York: Columbia University Press.

Lorber, Judith. 1980. "Beyond equality of the sexes: The question of children." Pp. 522–533 in James M. Henslin (ed.), Marriage and Family in a Changing Society. New York: Free Press.

Miller, S. M. 1972. "The making of a confused, middle-aged husband." Pp. 245–253 in Constantina Safilios-Rothschild (ed.), Toward A Sociology of Women. Lexington, Mass: Xerox College Publishing.

Myrdal, Alva. 1968. Nation and Family. Cambridge: Massachusetts Institute of Technology Press.

Myrdal, Alva, and Viola Klein. 1956. Women's Two Roles. London: Routledge and Kegan Paul.

Paloma, Margaret M. 1972. "Role conflict and the married professional woman." Pp. 187–198 in Constantina Safilios-Rothschild (ed.), Toward a Sociology of Women. Lexington, Mass: Xerox College Publishing.

Papanek, Hanna. 1973. "Men, women, and work: Reflections on the two-person career." Pp. 90–110 in Joan Huber (ed.), Changing Women in a Changing Society, Chicago: University of Chicago Press.

_____ . 1979. "Family status production: The 'work' and 'non-work' of women." Signs 4:775–781.

Pepitone-Rockwell, Fran (ed.). 1980. Dual-Career Couples. Beverly Hills: Sage.

Questiaux, Nicole, and Jacques Fournier. 1978. "France." Pp. 117–182 in Sheila B. Kamerman and Alfred J. Kahn (eds.), Family Policy: Government and Families in Fourteen Countries. New York: Columbia University Press.

Rapoport, Rhona, and Robert Rapoport. 1969. "The dual-career family: A variant pattern and social change." Human Relations 22:2–30.

_____ . 1971. Dual-Career Families. London: Penguin.

_____ . 1976. Dual-Career Families Re-examined: New Integrations of Work and Family. London: Martin Robertson.

_____ . 1980. "Three generations of dual-career family research." Pp. 23–48 in Fran Pepitone-Rockwell (ed.), Dual-Career Couples. Beverly Hills: Sage.

Rossi, Alice. 1969. "Sex equality: The beginnings of ideology." The Humanist 29:3–6, 16.

Safilios-Rothschild, Constantina. 1976. "Dual linkages between the occupational and family systems: A macrosociological analysis." Signs 1:51–60.

Schorr, Alvin L. 1979. "Views of family policy." Journal of Marriage and the Family 41:465–467.

Skolnick, Arlene. 1978. The Intimate Environment. Boston: Little, Brown.

Slater, Philip. 1970. The Pursuit of Loneliness. Boston: Beacon Press.

U.S. Department of Labor. 1980. U.S. Department of Labor News, December 9. Washington, D.C.: Bureau of Labor Statistics.

Vanek, Joann J. 1980. "Household work, wage work, and sexual equality." Pp. 275–291 in Sarah F. Berk (ed.,), Women and Household Labor. Beverly Hills: Sage.

Veevers, Jean E. 1980. Childless by Choice. Toronto: Butterworths.

Westoff, Charles F. 1978. "Marriage and fertility in the developed countries." Scientific American 139:51–57.

White, Martha S. 1979. "Women in the professions: Psychological and social barriers to women in science." Pp. 359–370 in Jo Freeman (ed.), Women: A Feminist Perspective. Palo Alto, Calif.: Mayfield.

Young, Michael, and Peter Willmott. 1973. The Symmetrical Family. New York: Penguin.

Changes in Black Family Structure: The Conflict between Family Ideology and Structural Conditions

Robert Staples

Historically, family theorists have argued that family structure and acheivement interact with one another (Goode, 1963; Parsons and Bales, 1955). While that may have some validity for certain ethnic groups in America, none of those groups share the history and current social conditions of the black population in the United States. The peculiar history of black Americans, combined with structural conditions inimical to family formation and maintenance, have precipitated a crisis in the black family.

The basic theoretical perspective that informs the present analysis of black family life is that of exchange theory. This theory focuses on the reinforcement patterns, the history of rewards and costs, that lead people to do what they do. Essentially it argues that people will continue to do what they have found rewarding in the past. The basic premise here is that certain kinds of family structures exist when there is an exchange of rewards; on the other hand, family arrangements that are costly to one or both parties are much less likely to continue (Blau, 1964; Homans, 1961).

We assume, first, that being married is important to the majority of blacks, especially women. The fact that a near majority of black Americans are not married and living in traditional nuclear family units is not a result of any devaluation of marriage qua institution but rather a function of limited [chances] to find individuals in a restricted and small pool of potential partners who can successfully fulfill the normatively prescribed familial roles. While many blacks fail to marry, the history of black marriages shows only a minority surviving a lifetime with the same people. Exchange theory suggests that a person will not remain in a relationship where the services provided seem relatively meager compared with what the person knows about other relationships. It appears, then, that blacks do not marry because the perceived outcome, derived from knowledge of past rewards and costs, is one where alternative sources of goal mediation are preferred risks (Thibaut and Kelley, 1959). This cost-benefit analysis is mediated by structural conditions among the black male population

The author is grateful to Paul Rosenblatt for his comments on an earlier draft of this paper.

From Robert Staples, *Journal of Marriage and the Family* Vol. 47, No. 4, (November 1985):1005–1013.

that give rise to dissonance between black family ideology and actual family arrangements.

Black Family Ideology

The popular image of blacks as a group pressing for change in the area of race relations and economic opportunities often is translated into the image of a radical group in the forefront of social change. Other than being opposed to unfair discrimination against any group and favoring liberal social and economic policies, blacks often hold very traditional even conservative, attitudes on other social issues—attitudes that place them in the mainstream of American mores and folkways. Some years ago Robert Hill (1972) noted that blacks have a strong work, achievement, and religious orientation. In particular, they believe strongly in the institution of the family. Gary and his associates (1983) found that the greatest source of life satisfaction among their black subjects was family life.

Their unconventional family arrangements and lifestyles easily can mislead outsiders to assume that blacks are strongly in accord with newly emerging alternative family lifestyles. While they are tolerant of people—especially blacks—who live in other than nuclear families, the family ideology of most blacks is in the direction of traditional family forms. Several studies, for instance, show that black women wish to marry and maintain traditional roles in the conjugal relationship (Broderick, 1965; Kulesky and Obordo, 1972). One indication of the black value of marriage is the fact that in the past more black women entered into a marital union than their white counterparts. In 1973, among black women 65 years and over, only 3.5% had never married, compared with 6.9% of white women (U.S. Bureau of the Census, 1978).

Among the most traditional of values is that of motherhood and childrearing. Except for college-educated black women, almost all black women bear children unless infertile. The role of mother is regarded as more important than any other role, including that of wife (Bell, 1971). While respectful of a woman's right to control her body, blacks tend to have a more negative attitude towards abortion. The Zelnik and Kantner (1974) study revealed that 35% of white teenagers terminated their first pregnancy by abortion compared with only 4% of black teenagers. However, some of this racial variation may reflect differential access to abortion rather than differential inclination. The black mother's childrearing techniques are also more traditional. She is more likely than the white mother to use physical, rather than verbal, punishment to enforce child discipline. Threatening the child with withdrawal of the mother's love, used by some white mothers, is uncommon among black women, which is one reason that the black mother-child bond remains strong throughout adult life (Nolle, 1972; Scanzoni, 1971).

Although there has been a noticeable increase in feminist ideology among women in the last 20 years, black women are greatly underrepresented in the women's liberation movement. Many black women continue to perceive racism—not sexism—as the biggest obstacle to their career and family goals. They are relatively uninvolved in such prominent feminist issues as pornography, sexual harassment, abortion, comparable pay, rape, etc. Moreover, they are more traditional in their definition of the roles that men and women should play in society and the family (Hershey, 1978). While their attitudes remain very traditional, the family lifestyles and arrangements of blacks are definitely unconventional. After examining the contemporary forms of black families, I explain it as a conflict between family ideology and structural conditions.

Changes in Black Family Structure

Probably the most significant change in the black family during the last 30 years has been the proliferative growth of female-headed households. When the Moynihan Report (1965) was first issued in 1965, more than three-fourths of all black families with children were headed by a husband and wife. In 1982 barely one-half of all such families included parents of both sexes. Those households headed by black women had a median income of $7,458 in comparison with the median income of $20,586 for black married couples and $26,443 for white married couples (U.S. Bureau of the Census, 1983).

One of the most visible reasons for the dramatic increase in households headed by women has been a corresponding increase in out-of-wedlock births as a proportion of all births to black women. Approximately 52% of all children born to black women in 1982 were conceived out-of-wedlock. This high percentage of out-of-wedlock births is attributed largely to teenage pregnancies. Among women who turned 20 during the second half of the 1970s, 41% of blacks but only 19% of whites had already given birth. Within that same group of young black women, about 75% of all births were out-of-wedlock, compared with only 25% of births to young white women (U.S. Bureau of the Census, 1984). Although black women were twice as likely to have had nonmarital sexual intercourse as whites by the age of 19, their rate of sexual activity was remaining constant, while such activity was rapidly increasing among white teenagers (Zelnik and Kantner, 1977).

Not only has the number and proportion of black female-headed households grown rapidly, but the majority of adult black women are not married and living with spouses. In 1982 approximately 56% of all black women over the age of 14 were separated, divorced, widowed, or never married. Under the age of 30, the majority of them fall into the never-married category; past age 30 most of them are listed as divorced or separated, with a small percentage counted among the widowed. The high divorce rate creates a number of female-headed households among black women over age 30. While one out of two white marriages will end in divorce, two out of three black marriages will eventually dissolve; moreover, black women who divorce are less likely than their white counterparts to remarry. Currently, one in four adult black women is divorced (U.S. Bureau of the Census, 1983).

Some 20 years since the publication of the Moynihan Report (1965), the figures he cited as evidence that the black family was deteriorating have doubled, almost tripled in some areas. How is it that a group that regards family life as its most important source of satisfaction finds a majority of its women unmarried?

Why does a group with more traditional sexual values than its white peers have a majority of its children born out-of-wedlock? Finally, we must ask how a group that places such importance on the traditional nuclear family finds a near majority of its members living in single-parent households. While a number of reasons have been cited by theorists, I suggests that the dominant force can be found in structural conditions of the black population.

Family Ideology vs. Structural Conditions

The basis of a stable family rests on the willingness, and ability, of men and women to marry, bear and rear children, and fulfill socially prescribed familial roles. In the case of women, those roles have been defined traditionally as the carrying out of domestic functions such as cooking and cleaning; giving birth to children and socializing them; providing sexual gratification, companionship, and emotional support to their husbands. There is abundant evidence that black women are willing and able to fulfill those roles (Staples, 1973). Conversely, the roles of men in the family are more narrowly confined to economic provider and family leader, but there are indications that a majority of black American males cannot implement those roles. When it comes to a choice between remaining single or getting married, individuals often do a cost-benefit analysis. Marriage is frequently a quid pro quo arrangement. The desire to enter and maintain a conjugal relationship is contingent on their perception of the benefits that can be acquired and, conversely, of the anticipated costs (Blau, 1964).

When selecting a mate, black women must consider the nature of the pool from which they will draw. In 98% of marriages with a black female bride, the groom will be a black male. Hence, her pool consists of unmarried black males with a variety of attributes. The most distinguishing characteristics of that pool is the shortage of men relative to the number of women during the marriageable years. According to the U.S. Bureau of the Census (1983), there are almost 1.5 million more black women than men over the age of 14. By the Census Bureau's own account, the undercount of black males means that about 925,000 black males exist that were not added to the black population total. It should be noted that the uncounted black male is likely to be transient and unemployed (Joe and Yu, 1984). Since there is an excess number of black males at birth, the subsequent shortage of black males over the age of 14 must be attributed to their higher infant mortality rate and the considerably greater mortality rate of young black males through such causes as homicide, accidents, suicide, drug overdose, and war casualty (Staples, 1982; Stewart and Scott, 1978).

The major problem for black women, however, is not the quantity in the available supply of potential mates, but the quality. Whereas black women may select a mate on the basis of a number of attributes, a minimum prerequisite is that he be gainfully and regularly employed. According to a study by Joe and Yu (1984), almost a majority of working-age black males fail to meet those minimum prerequisites. After an analysis of the economic and census data, they concluded that 46% of the 8.8 million black men of working age were not in the labor force. Based on 1982 statistics, they found that 1.2 million black men were unemployed,

1.8 million had dropped out of the labor force, 186,000 were in prison, and 925,000 were classified as "missing" because the Census Bureau said it could not locate them.

Furthermore, their study overstates the number of "desirable" and available black males in the marriage pool. Even with the census undercount, there are still a half million more black women over the age of 14 than black men. Also, we must subtract from the marriage pool black men with certain characteristics by which they substantially outnumber black women. Among those characteristics would be blacks serving in the Armed Forces. Approximatley 90% of them will be male. The U.S. Bureau of the Census (1983) reports that there were 415,000 blacks under arms in 1982, representing 20% of all United States military personnel. It can be stated reliably that a large number of those black males had poor prospects for employment in the civilian labor force (Steward and Scott, 1978). While the salaries and other benefits of military personnel have improved in recent years and a number of black soldiers are currently married, the military does take out of circulation a number of marriage-age black males by stationing them in foreign posts and isolated military stations. Furthermore, once their period of enlistment ends, black veterans experience a higher rate of unemployment, even in relation to black civilian males with no military service (Stewart and Scott, 1978). Hence, military service only postpones the entry of black males into the ranks of the unemployed, one reason black males have a higher rate of re-enlistment than their white counterparts.

Included in the factors that reduce the number of desirable black males in the marriage pool is the high rate of underemployed black males. The U.S. Civil Rights Commission (1982) reported that black men are overeducated for their jobs and have greater difficulty translating education into suitable occupations. Even college-educated black males have an unemployment rate four times greater than their white peers. Among black males employed in the labor force, one out of three will suffer from unemployment in a given year (Staples, 1982). However, these facts serve to explain why black marriages dissolve, not why they never take place. In Hampton's (1980) study, the respondents who reported the highest number of employment problems had a marital disruption rate three times higher than the overall rate for the sample.

Another group of black males regarded as undesirable or unavailable are those confined to mental institutions or who are otherwise mentally unstable. While their exact number is unknown, black males are more likely to be committed to mental institutions than are black women, and the strictures of racism are such that blacks are more likely to suffer from mental distress. In 1970, 240 nonwhites per 100,000 population were confined to mental institutions compared with 162 whites per 100,000 population. Blacks also used community mental health centers at a rate almost twice their proportion in the general population. The rate of drug and alcohol abuse is much greater among the black population—especially males—based on their overrepresentation among patients receiving treatment services (U.S. Dept. of Health, Education and Welfare, 1979:163–183). It is estimated that as many as one-third of the young black males in the inner city have serious drug problems (Staples, 1982). Many of the mentally unstable, drug and alcohol abusers will have been included in the figures on black males who have dropped out of the labor force or are incarcerated in prison. The magnitude of the problem simply reinforces the fact that black women are seriously disadvantaged in choosing from the eligible and desirable males in the marriage pool.

A large category of black males who fit into the desirable group must also be considered not available. By all reliable estimates, the black male homosexual population is considerably larger than the black female homosexual population (Bell and Weinberg, 1978). Based on the often-quoted Kinsey estimate (Kinsey et al., 1948) that 10% of the adult male population is homosexual, that would mean about 800,000 black men are not available to heterosexual black women. Of course, many of these gay males do marry, for a variety of reasons, and serve well in the roles of husband and father; but, due to the increasing public tolerance of overt male homosexuality, it is reasonable to expect that fewer gay males will choose to enter into heterosexual marriages in the future. Finally, it should be noted that black men marry outside their race at a rate twice as great as that of black women (Heer, 1974; Staples, 1982).

Although the shortage and desirability of black males in the marriage pool largely affects the non-college-educated black woman's marriage chances, the college-educated black female is not spared the problem if she desires to marry within her race and socioeconomic level. In 1980 there were 133,000 more black women enrolled in college than black men—about 57% of all black college students. Moreover, black male students have a much higher attrition rate than their female peers. In the University of California system, for instance, only 12 of every 100 black male students graduate within four years. Thus, in 1981, 36,200 of 60,700 bachelor's degrees awarded to blacks went to women (60%); and between the years 1976 and 1981, black women receiving bachelor's degrees increased by 9%, and comparable black males declined by 9%. These same trends existed for graduate degrees during the years 1976–1981: black women declined by 12% and black men by 21% in the receipt of the master's degree; in the receipt of the first professional degree, black women increased by 71% while black men declined by 21%; and at the doctoral level, black men declined by 10%, while black women increased at a rate of 29% (National Center for Education Statistics, 1983).

College-educated black women do have the option of marrying men with less education and making a viable choice. In the past as many as 50% of college-educated black women married men of a lower socioeconomic level (Noble, 1956), but increasingly there is resistance among these women to marrying down. Almost one-third of college-educated black women remain unmarried past the age of 30 (Bayer, 1972; Staples, 1981). Of course, they face a similar shortage in the marriage pool of male high school graduates and must compete with lesser educated black women for these same men. Also, such middle-level men tend to marry early and have the most stable marriages in the black community (Glick and Mills, 1974). The marriage patterns of college-educated black males tend to put college-educated black women at a disadvantage. Many of these men marry women of a lower educational level, and the interracial marriage rate is highest in this group of black men (Heer, 1974; Staples, 1981).

Structural Conditions and the Changing Black Family

There is no great mystery as to what has happened to the black family in the last 20 years; it is an acceleration of trends set in motion during the 1960s. A highly sexualized culture—via media, clothing and example—has conveyed to American youth the notion that nonmarital sexual relations are not only acceptable but required for individual fulfillment. Women are reaching puberty earlier and emotional maturity later. Furthermore, the consequences of teenage sexual behavior are counteracted somewhat by easier access to effective contraceptives and abortion; and the number of pregnant teenagers has not really increased— only the proportion of births to that group of women as a result of the rapid decline in births to older married women.

While the nonmarital sexually activity rate of black and white teenage women is converging, the black female is more likely to be engaged in unprotected intercourse and less likely to marry or have an abortion if she becomes pregnant. According to Zelnik and Kantner (1974) only 8.5% of their black sample (15–19 years) entered into marriage as an outcome of premarital pregnancy, compared with 50.8% of comparable white women. In addition, 35.5% of white women had their premarital pregnancies terminated by abortion, in contrast to 4.9% of similar black women.

While it is reasonable to question the wisdom of young black women attaining motherhood at such an early age, their decision to bear the children and raise them alone reflects their traditional values and limited options in life. Among black males their age, the official unemployment rate is 52%, and as many as 75% of young black men remain outside the work force (Malabre, 1980). While employment may be easier for black women to obtain, it often will be in dead-end jobs that pay only half the wages earned by white males. Rather than remain childless and husbandless, these women choose to have the children and raise them alone. A good explanation of these life choices is given by Hortense Canady, President of Delta Sigma Theta Sorority (1984:40): "Having a child is probably the best thing that's ever going to happen to them in their whole lifetime and the only thing they can contribute—this is not true in most other countries in the world. But if you belong to a class or a group of people who have no educational opportunities stretching out before them, no other goals, that's probably the single, best thing that's ever going to happen to you in your life."

Having limited educational and career options to set against bearing a child is not the only reason for the increase in female-headed households. A welfare system that often requires men to be absent from the home is part of the problem; and black women realize that the meager welfare payments are more reliable than a class of men who may never know gainful employment in their entire lives. In general, unemployed men do not make good husbands and fathers. Since employment and income are the measure of a man's masculinity in this society, men who have neither do not tend to feel good about themselves or act very positively toward their wives and children. In the Hampton (1980) study, for example, husbands who were not satisfied with themselves had a fairly high level of marital disruption.

However, the major reason for the increase in black female-headed households is the lack of "desirable" men with whom to form monogamous marriages. According to Joe and Yu (1984), between 1976 and 1983 the number of black families headed by women rose by 700,000, and the ranks of black men out of the labor force or unemployed increased by the same number. The same trend has existed for the last 25 years; almost 75% of black men were working in 1960, and black families headed by women accounted for 21% of all black families in the same year; but by 1982 only 54% of all black men were in the labor force, and 42% of all black families were headed by women (Joe and Yu, 1984).

Having a child out-of-wedlock and failing to marry accounts for 41% of all black households headed by women. Another 51% are divorced or separated from their spouses (U.S. Bureau of Census, 1983). These marriage disruptions are generally susceptible to the same structural conditions that plague never-married black women. Unemployment and underemployment, the public assistance complex, the educational system, and the health care system all produce economic and psychological alienation in the black male. As Hampton (1980) found, the pressures that push many black males out of other social institutions within society also work to push them out of marital relationships. For every 1,000 black married persons with spouses present, the number of divorces increased from 92 in 1971 to 233 in 1981; the comparable increase for whites was from 48 to 100. Black separations increased from 172 to 225 per 1,000 married persons in the same period; white separations rose from 21 to 29 (U.S. Bureau of the Census, 1983).

A number of social characteristics place blacks at risk for divorce. They have a higher rate of urbanization, greater independence of women, earlier age at marriage, earlier fertility, a higher education and income levels for the wife and lower income status for the husband (Cherlin, 1981). Most black marriages involve a wife who is more highly educated than her husband (Spanier and Glick, 1980). In one out of five black marriages, the wife earns a higher income than her husband (U.S. Bureau of Census, 1983). This incongurity between the socially assigned roles of the male as the primary provider and the wife as a subordinate member of the marital dyad may undermine the husband's self-esteem, frustrate the wife, and create marital dissatisfaction for both partners. In Hampton's (1980) study, the highest percentage of disrupted marriages (27.4%) was observed among wives with incomes accounting for 40% or more of the family's income. His explanation is that, when women have other means of support in the form of welfare or their own earnings, they may be less constrained to remain in a personally unsatisfying relationship. Alternatively, the wife may be satisfied with the husband's role; but her high income may threaten the husband's authority and status, undermining his self-concept so that *he* becomes unhappy.

These problems of the black family are only variations of the general problems of American families. The direction of change in the family structure is basically the same for all racial groups in the United States and for the same reasons. Guttentag and Secord (1983) demonstrated that unbalanced sex ratios have certain predictable consequences for relationships between men and women. They give rise to higher rates of singlehood, divorce, out-of-wedlock births, and female-headed households in different historical epochs and across different societies. According to Ehrenreich (1983) the breakdown of the family began in the 1950s, when men began a flight from commitment to the husband and father role. In the case of the black family, it stems from the institutional decimation of black males.

Discussion

The basic thesis here is that the dissonance between black family ideology and actual family arrangements is caused by the intervention of structural conditions that impede the actualization of black aspirations for a traditional family life and roles. The central factor in this situation is the inability of black males to meet the normative responsibilities of husband and father. Questions may be raised as to how the problem has reached its present magnitude and why it is so pronounced among the black population. The answer appears to involve a combination of cultural and economic forces which have been ascendant in the last 20 years.

A basic cause of black male unemployment has been the change in the economy and composition of the work force: automation and foreign competition have eliminated large numbers of jobs in manufacturing industries in the United States over the last couple of decades. Because black males were disproportionately concentrated in these industries, black males with years of seniority were displaced, and there were no high-paying unionized occupations for younger and newer workers to enter. Even low-paying menial jobs were automated or taken over by new immigrants, both legal and illegal. The expansion of the economy was in the private sector's high technology and service industries, which brought black males into competition (or noncompetition) with the bourgeoning numbers of white women entering and re-entering the labor force.

Women, both black and white, were better prepared to deal with the educational qualifications of an economy based on high technology and service industries. They required basic reading and writing skills precisely at the time when the public school system began to decline in its ability to produce students with those attributes. During this period black and Hispanic males had the highest rate of functional illiteracy among the 23 million Americans so classified; estimates are that as many as 40% of the black male population is not able to read and write well enough to function in a technological society (Staples, 1982). Moreover, the black male's functional illiteracy can be traced to problems in

America's urban school system. One explanation is that when a black male perceives the opportunity structure as not allowing for his upward mobility through education, he is more likely to divert his energy into sports, music, or hustling. On the other hand, black females—with fewer opportunities—continue to progress in the same educational system, possibly because, as Hale (1983) has noted, traditional classrooms are generally oriented toward feminine values; teachers are disproportionately female, and the behaviors tolerated and most encouraged are those that are more natural for girls.

The same general trends also occur to varying degrees among whites, but they affect their family structure differently. White male teenagers have an unemployment rate half that of the officially recorded rate for similar black males. Moreover, the white male teenager ultimately uses his kinship and friend-of-the-family networks more effectively to secure employment, while many black male teenagers who lack such networks drop out or never join the work force. The poor employment prospects for young black males are illustrated by the fact that some employers refused to hire them for jobs that were totally subsidized by federal funds (Malabre, 1980). Lack of steady employment largely accounts for the black male's high enlistment in the military, drug and alcohol abuse, and participation in criminal activities, ultimately leaving less than half the black male population as rational husband and father candidates (Glasgow, 1979).

One other distinguishing characteristic of the black population is the early age at which black women give birth to their first children. More than 40% of black women have given birth at least once by the time they reach 20 years of age. Estimates are that only one-sixth of the black males in that age range have jobs (Cummings, 1983). Should they marry before age 20, more than 7 out of 10 such marriages fail (Cherlin, 1981). Exacerbating this situation is the fact that even gainfully employed black men earn significantly less than white men. In 1982 the median income of black men was $10,510, compared with $15,964 for white men (U.S. Bureau of the Census, 1983).

Under positive conditions there are good indications that the black family is strong. College-educated black women, for example, have their children later and in smaller numbers than any other socioeconomic or racial group in the United States. While probably as sexually active as lower income black women, they are more effective in the use of birth control and more likely to resort to abortion if pregnancy occurs (Gebhard et al, 1958). Although college-educated black males earn less income than white male high school dropouts, approximately 90% of them are married and living with their spouses (U.S. Bureau of the Census, 1978). Where negative social conditions are absent, family ideology prevails.

A central question that remains is why black family ideology has not changed or adjusted to changing conditions. One answer is that it *has* changed among one stratum of the black population: the middle class. Within that segment of the black community, mainstream values—even changing ones—are stronger because they have a higher level of acculturation into those norms due to their greater participation in the majority group's institutions (Staple, 1981). Even among this group, however, traditional values are still strong and exert an influence on [this group's] ideological posture toward the family. In part, that is a function of their recent entry into the middle class and the retention of values from their class of origin. Another factor, however, is that their participatation in mainstream institutions and embrace of normative ideologies are still marginal, keeping traditional values attractive to many. Gary and his associates (1983) found that their middle-class black subjects cited their family life as the source of most satisfaction, while the source of least satisfaction was their jobs. Hence, traditional family life remains the one viable option for black American of all socioeconomic strata because it is less subject to the vagaries of race than any other institution in American life.

Similarly, lower income blacks sustain traditional beliefs about marriage and the family because the many traumas experienced by this group have cultivated a stronger belief in the value of the family as resource for their survival in a society not always hospitable to their aspirations. Other than the church, the family has been the only institution to serve as a vehicle for resisting oppression and facilitating their movement toward social and economic equality. Another factor may be the continued physical and social isolation of blacks—especially lower income blacks—from members of the majority group who are in the forefront of social and cultural change. In any context of social change, there is a gap between the ideal statements of a culture and the reality in which people live out their lives—a time lag between the emergence of new cultural forms and their internalization by the individuals who must act upon them. Thus, it would appear that black family ideologies will change only as their social and economic isolation diminishes.

In many ways this situation is nothing new for the black population. Social scientists continue to view the deterioration of the family as the problem when, in reality, the raison d'être of black family structure is the structural conditions that prevent the fulfillment of black family ideology. Given the present political and economic trends, there is little reason to expect an abatement of these trends in the black family. In fact, female-headed families are projected to be 59% of all black families with children by the year 1990 (Joe and Yu, 1984). Almost 75% of black children will live in such families, and 70% of blacks with incomes below the poverty level will belong to these families. The problem of the black family cannot be solved without resolving the economic predicament of black men. They are one and the same.

References

Bayer, A. 1972. "College impact on marriage." Journal of Marriage and the Family 34 (November):600–610.

Bell, A., and Weinberg, M. 1978. Homosexualities. New York: Simon and Schuster.

Bell, R. 1971. "The related importance of mother and wife roles among black lower class women." Pp. 248–255 in R. Staples (Ed.), The Black Family: Essays and Studies (2nd ed.). Belmont, CA: Wadsworth.

Blau, P. 1964. Exchange and Power in Social Life. New York: John Wiley.

Broderick, C. 1965. "Social heterosexual development among urban Negroes and whites." Journal of Marriage and the Family 27 (May):200–203.

Canady, H. 1984. Quoted in "Words of the week." Jet Magazine (March 19):40.

Cherlin, A. 1981. Marriage, Divorce, Remarriage. Cambridge, MA: Harvard University Press.

Cummings, J. 1983. "Breakup of the black family imperils gains of decades." The New York Times (November 20):1, 36.

Ehrenreich, B. 1983. The Hearts of Men: American Dreams and the Flight from Commitment. Garden City, NY: Doubleday.

Gary, L., Beatty, L., Berry, G., and Price, M. 1983. Stable Black Families: Final Report. Washington, DC: Institute for Urban Affairs and Research, Howard University.

Gebhard, P., Pomeroy, W., Martin, C., and Christenson, C. 1958. Pregnancy, Birth and Abortion. New York: Harper and Brothers.

Glasgow, D. 1979. The Black Underclass. San Francisco: Jossey-Bass.

Glick, P., and Mills, K. 1974. Black Families: Marriage Patterns and Living Arrangements. Atlanta: Atlanta University.

Goode, W. 1963. World Revolution and Changing Family Patterns. Glencoe, IL: The Free Press.

Guttentag, M., and Secord, P. 1983. Too Many Women: The Sex Ratio Question. Beverly Hills, CA: Sage.

Hale, J. 1983. Black Children. Provo, UT: Brigham Young University Press.

Hampton, R. 1980. "Institutional decimation, marital exchange and disruption in black families," Western Journal of Black Studies 4 (Summer): 132–139.

Heer, D. 1974. "The prevalence of black-white marriages in the United States 1960 and 1970." Journal of Marriage and the Family 35 (February):246–258.

Hershey, M. 1978. "Racial differences in sex role identities and sex stereotyping: evidence against a common assumption." Social Science Quarterly 58 (March):583–596.

Hill, R. 1972. The Strengths of Black Families. New York: Emerson Hall.

Homans, G. 1961. Social Behavior: Its Elementary Forms. New York: Harcourt, Brace and World.

Joe, T., and Yu, P. 1984. The "Flip-Side" of Black Families Headed by Women: The Economic Status of Black Men. Washington, DC: The Center for the Study of Social Policy.

Kinsey, A., Pomeroy, W., and Martin, C. 1948. Sexual Behavior in the Human Male. Philadelphia: W. B. Saunders.

Kulesky, W., and Obordo, A. 1972. "A racial comparison of teenage girls' projections for marriage and procreation." Journal of Marriage and the Family 34 (February): 75–84.

Malabre, A., Jr. 1980. "Recession hits blacks harder than whites." The Wall Street Journal (August 21):1.

Moynihan, D. P. 1965. The Negro Family: The Case for National Action. Washington, DC: U.S. Government Printing Office.

National Center for Education Statistics. 1983. Participation of Black Students in Higher Education: A Statistical Profile from 1970–71 to 1980–81. Washington, DC: U.S. Department of Education.

Noble, J. 1956. The Negro Woman College Graduate. New York: Columbia University Press.

Nolle, D. 1972. "Changes in black sons and daughters: a panel analysis of black adolescents' orientation toward their parents." Journal of Marriage and the Family 34 (August):443–447.

Parsons, R., and Bales, R. 1955. Family, Socialization and Interaction Process. Glencoe, IL: The Free Press.

Scanzoni, J. 1971. The Black Family in Modern Society. Boston: Allyn and Bacon.

Spanier, G., and Glick, P. 1980. "Mate selection differentials between blacks and whites in the United States." Social Forces 58 (March):707–725.

Staples, R. 1973. The Black Woman in America: Sex, Marriage and the Family. Chicago: Nelson-Hall.

_____ . 1981. The World of Black Singles: Changing Patterns of Male-Female Relations. Westport, CT: Greenwood Press.

_____ . 1982. Black Masculinity: The Black Male's Role in American Society. San Francisco: The Black Scholar Press.

Stewart, J., and Scott, J. 1978. "The institutional decimation of black males." Western Journal of Black Studies 2 (Summer):82–92.

Thibaut, J. W., and Kelley, H. W. 1959. The Social Psychology of Groups. New York: John Wiley.

U.S. Bureau of the Census. 1974. Marital Status and Living Arrangements: March 1973, Series P-20, Washington, DC: Government Printing Office.

_____ . 1978. Current Population Reports: March 1977, Series P-20, No. 314. Washington, DC: Government Printing Office.

_____ . 1983. America's Black Population, 1970 to 1982: A Statistical View, July 1983, Series P10/POP83. Washington, DC: Government Printing Office.

_____ . 1984. Fertility of American Women: June 1983, Series P-20, No. 386. Washington, DC: Government Printing Office.

U.S. Civil Rights Commission. 1982. Unemployment and Underemployment among Blacks, Hispanics and Women (November). Washington, DC: Government Printing Office.

U.S. Dept. of Health, Education and Welfare. 1979. Health Status of Minorities and Low-Income Groups. Washington, DC: Government Printing Office.

Zelnik, M., and Kantner, J. F. 1974. "The resolution of teenage first pregnancies." Family Planning Perspectives (Spring):74–80.

_____ . 1977. "Sexual and contraceptive experience of young unmarried women in the United States, 1976 and 1971." Family Planning Perspectives 9 (May/June):55–59.

6

Fertility and Childbirth

Patriarchy has told the woman in labor that her suffering was purposive—was the purpose of her existence; that the new life she was bringing forth (especially if male) was of value and that her own value depended on bringing it forth. As the means of reproduction, without which cities and colonies could not expand, without which the family would die out and its property pass into the hands of strangers, she has found herself at the center of purposes not hers, which she has often incorporated and made her own   [*Adrienne Rich, 1976.*]

Fertility and childbirth are biological processes, shaped by the unique characteristics of human organisms. (Fertility refers to the production of live births in a population. Childbirth refers to the act of bringing forth a child.) However, they are also social processes, organized and given meaning by the values, beliefs, and social relations of specific societies (Folbre, 1984:261). It is perhaps more difficult to appreciate the social influences governing reproduction than it is to understand the social origins of other human activities. However, the diversity in fertility patterns and childbirth practices discovered by cross-cultural and historical studies amply demonstrates the malleability of the human reproductive process. In some societies, most women give birth to their first child as teenagers. In others, childbearing is delayed for most women until they are in their twenties. In some societies almost all women have children, while in others many do not. Childbirth exhibits a similar diversity. In some societies women continue to work until they give birth and return to work relatively quickly afterward. In others women remain in seclusion both before and after giving birth. Historically, childbirth was a woman-centered event in Europe and the United States, while more recently women in childbirth have been attended primarily by male physicians.

The impressive variation in human reproductive processes requires that we examine fertility and childbirth in social context. We begin with a brief examination of fertility trends in the United States and some alternative explanations that demographers have proposed for these trends.

The Demographic Transition

In the nineteenth century, fertility began to fall dramatically in the United States. (Fertility is measured in many ways. The rates reported here are "total fertility rates." The total fertility rate for a given year is an estimate of the average number of children that women of childbearing age in that year will have in their lifetimes. Unless otherwise noted, the fertility statistics cited are from the U.S. Bureau of the Census (1986b).) In 1800 the fertility rate among white Americans was 7 children per woman. By 1850 the rate had dropped to 5.4, and by 1900 it had reached 3.6 (Wells, 1985:29). The decline in fertility was widespread, occurring among rural as well as urban women and among native-born as well as immigrant women. Although statistics for black women are not available for the first part of the century, the decline in the fertility of blacks paralleled that of whites in the last half of the nineteenth century. This century-long decline in fertility was so great that demographers sometimes refer to it as the "demographic transition" (Degler, 1980:178).

Although social historians do not agree completely about the causes of this precipitous decline in the fertility of American women, three explanations have received considerable attention. The first focuses on the declining economic value of children and rests on the assumption that couples make childbearing decisions based on calculations of the contributions that children can make to their economic well-being. If the value of these contributions outweighs the costs of raising children, couples will not attempt to limit their fertility. However, as the relative costs of raising children increase, couples will pursue various methods of controlling their fertility.

Advocates of this explanation suggest that industrialization played a crucial role in the nineteenth-century decline in fertility rates (Folbre, 1984:266). Industrialization eliminated much of the productive work that children could perform and required a skilled and educated work force. As a result, the economic contributions of children declined and the costs of preparing them for adult occupational roles increased. Industrialization did not reduce the demand for children's labor immediately, and many children continued to contribute to family incomes by working in factories in the nineteenth and early twentieth centuries. In fact, industrialization may have temporarily increased the value of children among the working class. Nevertheless, children were gradually excluded from industrial work as the demand for a skilled and educated labor force grew.

Industrialization reduced the economic value of children in another way. In preindustrial societies men owned and controlled the land, and children had no independent access to sources of income. As young people approached adulthood, it was difficult for them to marry and establish their own households unless their fathers provided them with the resources to do so. Therefore, fathers were able to prolong the dependence of their grown children and exploit their labor by withholding these resources (Folbre, 1984:269–70). The work of Daniel Scott Smith (1973), mentioned in Chapter 3, provides some evidence that fathers did exercise control over the labor of their sons in this way in preindustrial communities. In his study of Hingham, Massachusetts, Smith found that men whose fathers died before the age of sixty married earlier than men whose fathers lived longer. He concluded that the longer-lived fathers had retained control of the property that would provide their sons with sources of livelihood. Industrialization eventually undermined this mechanism of patriarchal control by providing young people with an independent source of income in the form of wage labor. As a result, children could leave home earlier than before, and parents could no longer rely on their economic contributions.

Although industrialized societies generally do have lower fertility rates than agricultural societies, fertility began to fall in the United States long before the period of significant industrialization (Degler, 1980:181). In 1850 the United States was just beginning to industrialize, yet the fertility rate fell as much between 1800 and 1850 as it did between 1850 and 1900. However, changes in the balance between the economic costs and contributions of children may also have played a role in the preindustrial decline in fertility. In 1800 the fertility rate in the United States was much higher than it was in most European countries, as it had been throughout the colonial period. One reason for this unusually high fertility rate was the abundance of cheap land, which allowed early American settlers to establish large farms. Because the labor requirements of families with many acres to cultivate were high, the potential economic contributions of children increased. The availability of land also reduced the cost of raising children because it lowered the cost of establishing children on their own land when they reached adulthood.

Many studies have shown that the fertility rates in rural areas in the United States declined as the land became increasingly densely populated in the nineteenth century (Wells, 1985:41). For example, fertility rates declined earlier in the East than they did in the West, where the land was more sparsely populated. Therefore, the decline in the economic value of children and the associated decline in fertility rates appear to have taken place in two stages in the nineteenth century. First, as agricultural land became increasingly scarce, the unusually high American fertility rates began to fall. By the mid-nineteenth century, fertility rates in the United States had fallen to approximately the same level as European rates. Second, as industrialization accelerated in the last half of the nineteenth century, fertility rates continued the decline that had commenced earlier in the century.

A second explanation for the decline in fertility in the nineteenth century stresses the importance of changes in individuals' motivations for controlling the number of children they had. For example, Robert Wells (1978) argues that fertility rates began to fall in Europe and the United States because of the emergence of "modern values." According to Wells, those with "traditional values" believe that they are powerless to control their own fates and must accept the world as they have found it. In contrast, Wells (p. 521) states, "persons with modern values believe not only that the world is knowable and controllable but that it is also to the individual's advantage to plan his or her life and attend to the future." From this perspective, couples begin to control their fertility only when they have adopted a set of future-oriented values and conclude that family limitation may well materially improve their lives. According to Wells, these values became prevalent in the United States during the eighteenth century and explain why the drop in fertility began before the Industrial Revolution. In fact, Wells suggests that both the Industrial Revolution and the demographic transition were the result of the development of values that led people to attempt to control their environments. Wells (1985:45) also thinks that the absence of modern values keeps fertility rates high and retards economic development in many Third World countries today.

In a third explanation, Carl Degler (1980:188–90) emphasizes the role of women in the decline in fertility in the nineteenth century. According to Degler, an emerging consciousness of themselves as individuals led American women to attempt to limit the number of children they had. He argues that women have always had reasons to limit their fertility that men have not shared—having and raising children, particularly large numbers of them, is physically strenuous, emotionally stressful, and all consuming. From this perspective, when women and men calculate the relative costs and benefits of having children, they do not use the same set of variables. However, women have usually been unable to act on the basis of their self-interest because of their subordination to men. As Adrienne Rich observes, in patriarchal societies women's reproduction is exploited for purposes that are not necessarily their own. These societies are "coercively pronatal," controlling women's reproductive behavior in various ways (in Folbre, 1984:270–71). For example, women have been denied access to abortion and birth control, and husbands have had the right to intercourse with their wives even when their wives did not consent. Women in patriarchal societies also have few opportunities to pursue activities outside of those associated with family roles and few options other than marriage and childbearing.

Women's struggle to gain equal individual rights with men was only beginning in the nineteenth century, but Degler suggests that women's attempt to control their fertility was an important and early part of this struggle. American women who bore an average of seven children at the beginning of the nineteenth century were pregnant or responsible for children for almost all of their adult lives. By attempting to free themselves from constant childbearing, women sought the opportunities that men already possessed for the expression of goals and interests apart from their role in the family. In other words, Degler thinks that in the nineteenth century women began to seek the power to control their own lives instead of passively accepting their position in the family. As evidence, he cites nineteenth-century writings that stressed the positive consequences of fertility limitation for women and the statements of women in diaries and letters.

Most likely a decline in fertility of the magnitude experienced in the nineteenth century is the result of many factors and each of the preceding explanations has some validity. Whatever the explanation, couples began to limit the number of children they had. Because no major advances in birth-control techniques took place in the nineteenth century, family limitation was accomplished primarily through the increasingly widespread practice of methods that were already known, such as *coitus interruptus* and avoidance of intercourse during what were thought to be "unsafe times" in women's menstrual cycles (Degler, 1980:221). Birth control did encounter significant opposition in the nineteenth century, an indication that its practice was becoming widespread. This opposition led to the passage of the Comstock Act in 1873, which made it a crime to send information about birth control through the mail. Despite opposition however, couples continued to practice birth control as the nineteenth century progressed. Although the motives of men and women were complex and may often have been different, the result was a decline in fertility that dramatically reduced the size of the typical American family.

From the Baby Boom to the Birth Dearth

The fertility rate continued its downward plunge in the first several decades of the twentieth century, dropping from 3.6 to 2.5 between 1900 and 1930. It continued to fall during the early years of the Depression but rebounded slightly to stand at 2.2 in 1940. As most demographers expected, the numbers of births increased after World War II as those who had delayed having children because of the Depression and the war made up for lost time. In May 1946, nine months after the war ended, 233,452 babies were born in the United States. In October over 300,000 babies were born. By the year's end, American women had given birth to 3.4 million babies, the highest number ever recorded. The record was topped the next year with 3.8 million births (Jones, 1980:10). However, demographers predicted that after a brief period of reproductive catch-up fertility would continue its inexorable decline.

This prediction was wrong. The number of births continued to rise in the postwar years, reaching four million for the first time in 1954. The fertility rate reflected these increases. In 1950 the rate had risen to 3.0, and it peaked at 3.7 in 1957, somewhat greater than the rate in 1900. After 1957 the number of births declined annually and in 1965 finally dropped below the four million mark again. However, seventy-four million babies were born in the United States between 1946 and 1965, a group now familiarly known as the "baby boomers."

Numerous explanations have been proposed for the baby boom. In one of the best known and most controversial, Richard Easterlin (1987) suggests that the fertility rate increased among those coming of age in the postwar years for two reasons. First, these individuals were members of the very small birth cohorts of the late 1920s and early 1930s. When they began to enter the labor force in the 1940s and 1950s, the scarcity of young adults created a high demand for new workers. As a result wages increased and young people were able to move more quickly up career ladders than they had previously. Therefore, couples in the 1950s could afford to have more children than their parents. Second, Easterlin argues that individuals who grew up in the Depression years were satisfied with relatively modest improvements in their standard of living. He believes that "the material expectations of young adults are largely the unconscious product of the environment in which they grew up" (p. 40). For those who had experienced the deprivations of the Depression, the 1950s were a period of comparative luxury. Therefore, Easterlin concludes that young couples chose to spend their money on children rather than other things because their material aspirations were low.

Most demographers agree that fluctuations in cohort size have an impact on fertility rates, particularly as they affect wages. However, some believe that the baby boom can be adequately explained by the economic conditions of the 1950s without reference to values rooted in childhood experiences. For example, Norman Ryder (1979) argues that the economic growth of the postwar period favored increases in fertility rates simply by making it possible for more people to conform to widely shared ideals of family size. Americans experienced an unprecedented wave of economic prosperity in the 1950s. The gross national product mushroomed, personal incomes grew, and consumer spending skyrocketed, all leading economist John Kenneth Galbraith to label the United States the "affluent society." Furthermore, many government policies contributed to the economic well-being of young families—for example, income tax deductions for each child and for interest paid on home mortgages, federal housing loans, and a highway program that made the suburbs more accessible than they had been. Together, these developments allowed more people to marry and have children.

Ryder points out that there was no real increase in the desired family size in the 1950s. Instead, the relative prosperity of the period allowed more couples than in less affluent times to have at least two children. In Ryder's (1979:361) words, "postwar conditions permitted almost universal adherence to the norm [of two children]: both economic improvement and parenthood were possible." He concludes that much of the increase in the fertility rate in the 1950s was due to a rise in the percentage (from 55 to 82) of women having at least two children rather than to substantial increases in the number of women having three or more children. Ryder also argues that many of the births to women with at least two children in the 1950s were unintended. He thinks that couples were being less careful in their practice of birth control because the consequences of having more than the desired number of children were not as dire as they were in less prosperous times. In addition, people were marrying earlier in the 1950s than in previous generations and, as a result, were exposed to the risk of unintended pregnancies for a longer time.

The approaches of Easterlin and Ryder are not necessarily mutually exclusive, and it would be difficult to rule out one in favor of the other. It is probably the case, as Andrew Cherlin (1981:43) concludes, that the early experiences of those who grew up in the Depression and the economic prosperity of the 1950s reinforced one another to produce a temporary upswing in fertility. And, in retrospect, it does appear that the baby boom was a single yet massive deviation from the long-term decline in fertility rates that began 150 years earlier. The baby boomers, the first of whom reached childbearing age in the mid-1960s, have rejected the procreative behavior of their parents *en masse*. From its 1950s high of 3.7, the fertility rate plummeted in the 1960s and 1970s. By 1965 the rate had declined to 2.9. It was 2.5 in 1970 and 1.7 in 1975. From 1976 to 1985, the fertility rate remained a constant 1.8.

Demographers generally agree on the importance of two factors in explaining the return to lower fertility. First, the postwar economic expansion slowed, and both inflation and slow wage growth eroded the gains in income made by American workers in the 1950s and 1960s. By the 1970s, young people began to face the prospect of having relatively lower incomes than their parents for the first time since the Depression (The Urban Institute, 1984:12). At the same time, the costs of raising children remained high and may even have increased. Housing costs have risen at a faster rate than inflation, putting the American dream of home ownership out of reach for many people. Adjusting for inflation, the average cost of a single-family home rose from slightly over $60,000 in 1960 to just over $80,000 in 1985 (U.S. Bureau of the Census, 1986a:13). The demand for skilled workers has also continued to increase so that the price of a college education must be added to the cost of raising a child for many parents.

The second powerful force that operated to lower fertility was the increasing proportion of women in the paid labor force. As we saw in Chapter 5, the percentage of women working outside the home increased only slightly in the 1950s, from 31.4 percent in 1950 to 34.8 percent in 1960. However, in the 1960s the trend accelerated. By 1970, the proportion of women in the labor force had reached 42.6 percent. The percentage has continued to rise, reaching 55.4 in 1987. In addition, the characteristics of women in the labor force began to change. In 1950, 31.6 percent of female workers were single, 16.3 percent were widowed or divorced, and 52.1 percent were married. These percentages had changed only slightly by 1960. However, in 1970 only 22.3 percent of the female labor force were single and 14.3 percent were widowed or divorced, while 63.4 percent were married. Furthermore, there have been large increases in the percentage of married women of childbearing age in the labor force since the 1950s. In 1960, 30.0 percent of women between the ages of twenty and twenty-four and 27.7 percent of women between twenty-five and thirty-four were in the labor force. By 1970 the percentages had risen to 47.4 and 39.3, respectively, and had reached 67.4 and 67.5 by 1987 (U.S. Bureau of the Census, 1986:373).

Participation in the paid labor force does not preclude having children. However, women who work outside the home do have lower fertility rates than those who do not (Wilkie, 1981:584). In addition, women with college and postgraduate educations, many of whom have high commitments to the occupational world, have lower fertility rates than women of all other educational levels (Sweet and Rindfuss, 1984:135).

As Cherlin (1981:33) points out, changes in family life often take scholars by surprise. Nevertheless, a return to the high fertility levels of the 1950s appears unlikely in the immediate future. Women's participation in the paid labor force is indicative of their increasing commitment to goals and purposes apart from those associated with their family roles of wife and mother. Furthermore, the decline in the economic prospects of young workers and the high costs of raising children today have once again shifted the balance of economic costs and benefits in a direction unfavorable to children. As Ryder (1979:365) comments, it is no surprise that fertility has fallen; a more intriguing question may be what keeps it from declining even further. We consider some answers to this question in Chapter 7. However, in the articles in this chapter, we turn our attention to the subjects of childbirth and voluntary childlessness.

Readings

The first article in this chapter, "Confidence in Survival," is from the book *Inventing Motherhood* by British author Ann Dally. In her book Dally traces the changing ideas in Britain and the United States about the attachment of mothers to their children and the role of mothers in children's care and development. Specifically, she examines the emergence and widespread acceptance in the twentieth century of the idea that children require the full-time care of their mothers. "Confidence in Survival" is the first chapter in her book, and it describes the improved chances of survival of both infants and women in childbirth. The statistics Dally cites are primarily from Britain and do not correspond exactly with those from similar periods in the United States. For example, infant and maternal mortality were lower in colonial America than they were in Britain. However, the United States had the highest rates of infant and maternal mortality in the Western world at the beginning of the twentieth century (Dye, 1980:101; Dye, 1986:36). Nevertheless, the general downward trend that she describes in mortality statistics occurred in both countries.

Prior to the nineteenth century, childbirth was almost exclusively a female event in which the woman giving birth was attended by a midwife and female friends and kin (Dye, 1980:99). This circle of females provided not only assistance with the birth but emotional support as well, and childbirth was one of the many rituals of the female world that created lasting bonds between women (Smith-Rosenberg, 1975). However, childbirth was also a time of pain and fear, and probably for this reason many women turned eagerly to the physicians who began to take an interest in childbirth in the late eighteenth century (Dye, 1986:28).

The control of childbirth by physicians did not immediately lead to safer deliveries because many physicians were poorly trained and many early surgical procedures may actually have caused more deaths than they prevented. It was not until the 1930s that increased supervision of practitioners by the medical profession brought a reduction in maternal deaths. However, as Dally observes, improvements in the safety of childbirth have been gained at very high emotional costs, and the development of obstetrics began a conflict that continues to this day over the management of childbirth.

Physicians redefined childbirth from a "natural" process to one that must be monitored and controlled. Accompanying this redefinition was the development of a model of the "ideal" or "normal" birth and the medical interventions necessary at various stages in the process (Eakins, 1986:7–8). The medicalization of childbirth transferred power from women to the professionals who possessed scientific knowledge about pregnancy and birth and the technical skills to intervene at the "appropriate" times. At the same time, childbirth moved to hospitals, where it could be more conveniently managed by physicians than at home. Although most women gave birth at home throughout the nineteenth century, virtually all births now take place in clinical settings that are organized primarily for the delivery of medical services. These developments have drastically altered the experience of childbirth for women. Instead of being central and active figures, women now have a more passive role. Instead of taking place among friends, relations, and the familiar sights and sounds of home, birth now takes place in unfamiliar and isolated settings.

Dissatisfaction with these new practices developed relatively quickly following the consolidation of the medical control of childbirth. The natural-childbirth movement, which originated in the 1950s, advocated a more active role for women and less medical intervention, although it did not reject professional oversight (Rothman, 1986). More recently, women have criticized the role of physicians in the control of childbirth, arguing that many decisions are made on the basis of what is most efficient and convenient from the medical standpoint rather than what is best for mothers and their babies. From this perspective, women need to regain control of childbirth, while retaining the improvements made in safety. In Pamela Eakins' (1986:14) words, a new vision is required that "combines excellent outcomes with a truly woman-centered experience." The development of this new vision requires that women's views of childbirth be understood.

In "Working-Class Women, Middle-Class Women, and Models of Childbirth," Margaret Nelson examines women's expectations of childbirth and their evaluations of their hospital experiences. As the title of the article suggests, Nelson discovered that women do not all have the same views of childbirth and that the differences between women tend to follow class lines. Her findings have important implications for those who wish to restructure childbirth because any changes must be broad enough to encompass these diverse views. Also important is Nelson's finding that women with different desires for their babies' birth were equally unlikely to have their wishes met in the hospital. In other words, the physicians' wishes often predominated.

Attempts to restructure childbirth are complicated not only by the diversity of views among women and the resistance of physicians but by the recent and rapid developments in reproductive technologies. Michelle Stanworth (1988:11–12) divides these technologies into four groups: those aimed at fertility control, those that deal with the management of childbirth, those that allow monitoring and intervention in the prenatal period, and those developed primarily as remedies for infertility. Developments in each of these areas have raised a host of controversial issues. Perhaps the most obvious example is contraception. The pill and the IUD have made it possible to effectively—although not necessarily safely for women—separate sexual relations from conception. However, those who believe that sex should be confined to monogamous marriage and those who wish to liberate sexual expression from the confines of marriage have different opinions about who should have access to contraceptive technologies. Even more controversial are those technologies that allow conception without sex and make it possible for children to be conceived and raised outside of heterosexual relation-ships (Stanworth, p 26). These technologies also create ambiguities about genetic parenthood and about who has social and legal claims to children (p. 21).

In the third article in this chapter, "Technology and Motherhood: Repro-ductive Choice Reconsidered," Robyn Rowland considers the impact of these technologies on control of the reproductive process. She focuses attention primarily on the new methods that allow infertile women to conceive children. These methods have the potential for increasing the reproductive choices of women who may otherwise be unable to bear children, although access to them is currently limited primarily to the affluent. However, Rowland argues that the development of these sophisticated technologies has an impact on all women, and she considers several ways in which they may decrease the control that women have over reproduction.

In the final article, "Gender-Role Orientations in Older Child-Free and Expectant Couples," Kristine Baber and Albert Dreyer consider voluntary childlessness, a phenomenon facilitated by the advances in reproductive technol-ogies. During the baby-boom years, the percentage of ever-married women who did not have children was so low that some demographers concluded that voluntary childlessness was virtually nonexistent among married couples (Pol, 1984:319). For example, only 6.6 percent of ever-married women who were twenty to twenty-four in 1960 were childless at the ages of forty to forty-four in 1980, when most had completed their childbearing careers. However, the sharp decline in fertility rates that began in the mid-1960s was accompanied by an increase in the percentage of couples remaining childless. Nearly 10 percent of ever-married women who were twenty to twenty-four in 1966, at the end of the baby boom, were childless by the time they reached the ages of forty to forty-four in 1986 (U.S. Bureau of the Census, 1987b:66).

Several indicators suggest that the percentage of childless couples will continue to increase in the years to come. First, more married women now in their twenties and thirties are childless than were their counterparts in previous years. Currently, approximately 40 percent of ever-married women between the ages of twenty-five and thirty-four do not have children, compared to about 25 percent in 1970 (U.S. Bureau of Census, 1987b:66). Although many of these women will eventually have children, it is unlikely that they will do so in large enough numbers to prevent the percentage of couples who never have children from increasing. Second, as we learned in Chapter 4, an increasing number of women are delaying marriage until their late twenties and early thirties. If and when these women do marry, they may choose to continue a child-free lifestyle. Third, childlessness is most common among women who have professional or managerial jobs (U.S. Bureau of the Census, 1987a:15). As the percentage of women in these occupations increases, so too may the number of couples without children. Fourth, it is likely that negative stereotypes of the voluntarily childless have become less prevalent in recent years, thereby reducing the social pressures to have children.

Baber and Dreyer explore the factors that distinguish couples who choose to remain child-free from those who have simply delayed having children. As they point out, the two types of couples are similar on many social demographic variables. However, they discovered that the postponers and the voluntarily childless differ on several "psychosocial factors" that may be related to the fertility decisions of the two groups. Baber and Dreyer's research illustrates how complex fertility decisions have become, particularly for women, as couples begin to develop egalitarian relationships and equal career commitments. The differences between those who are child-free and those who are not are often subtle. However, the consequences of the choices that couples make are not, as we shall see in the next chapter.

References

Cherlin, Andrew J. 1981. *Marriage, Divorce, Remarriage*. Cambridge: Harvard University Press.

Degler, Carl N. 1980. *At Odds: Women and the Family in America from the Revolution to the Present*. New York: Oxford University Press.

Dye, Nancy Schrom. 1980. "History of Childbirth in America." *Signs* 6:97–108.

———. 1986. "The Medicalization of Childbirth." In *The American Way of Birth*, edited by Pamela S. Eakins, 21–46. Philadelphia: Temple University Press.

Eakins, Pamela S. 1986. "The American Way of Birth." In *The American Way of Birth*, edited by Pamela S. Eakins, 3–15. Philadelphia: Temple University Press.

Easterlin, Richard A. 1987. *Birth and Fortune: The Impact of Numbers on Personal Welfare*. 2d ed. Chicago: University of Chicago Press.

Folbre, Nancy. 1984. "Of Patriarchy Born: The Political Economy of Fertility Decisions." *Feminist Studies* 9:261–84.

Jones, Landon Y. 1980. *Great Expectations: America and the Baby Boom Generation*. New York: Ballantine.

Packard, Vance. 1983. *Our Endangered Children: Growing Up in a Changing World*. Boston: Little, Brown.

Pol, Louis. 1983. "Childlessness: A Panel Study of Expressed Intentions and Reported Fertility." *Social Biology* 30:318–27.

Rich, Adrienne. 1976. Of Woman Born: Motherhood as Experience and Institution. New York: Bantam Books, Inc.

Rothman, Barbara Katz. 1986. "The Social Construction of Birth." In *The American Way of Birth*, edited by Pamela S. Eakins, 104–15. Philadelphia: Temple University Press.

Ryder, Norman. 1979. "The Future of American Fertility." *Social Problems* 26:359–70.

Smith, Daniel Scott. 1973. "Parental Power and Marriage Patterns: An Analysis of Historical Trends in Hingham, Massachusetts." *Journal of Marriage and the Family* 35:419–28.

Smith-Rosenberg, Carol. 1975. "The Female World of Love and Ritual: Relations between Women in Nineteenth-Century America." *Signs* 1:1–29.

Stanworth, Michelle. 1988. "Reproductive Technologies and the Deconstruction of Motherhood." In *Reproductive Technologies: Gender, Motherhood and Medicine*, edited by Michelle Stanworth, 10–35. Minneapolis: University of Minnesota Press.

Sweet, James A., and Ronald P. Rindfuss. 1984. "Those Ubiquitous Fertility Trends: United States, 1945–1979." *Social Biology* 30:127–39.

The Urban Institute. 1984. "Are Baby-Boomers Selfish?" *The Urban Institute Policy and Research Report* 14(3):12–14.

U.S. Bureau of the Census. 1986a. *How We Live: Then and Now.* Washington, D.C.: U.S. Government Printing Office.

———. 1986b. *Statistical Abstract of the United States: 1987.* 107th ed. Washington, D.C.: U.S. Government Printing Office.

———. 1987a. "Fertility of American Women: June 1986." *Current Population Reports*, Series P-20, No. 421. Washington, D.C.: U.S. Government Printing Office.

———. 1987b. *Statistical Abstract of the United States: 1988.* 108th ed. Washington, D.C.: U.S. Government Printing Office.

Wells, Robert. 1978. "Family History and Demographic Transition." In *The American Family in Social-Historical Perspective,* 2d ed., edited by Michael Gordon, 516–32. New York: St. Martin's Press.

———. 1985. *Uncle Sam's Family: Issues in and Perspectives on American Demographic History.* Albany: State University of New York Press.

Wilkie, Jane Riblett. 1981. "The Trend Toward Delayed Parenthood." *Journal of Marriage and the Family* 43:583–91.

Confidence in Survival

Ann Dally

Most of us assume that our children will survive. So confident are we about this that few of us even question it. Yet we can have little understanding of families and child-rearing today unless we realize how new this assumption is, and understand something of the extent to which our ideas and our practice are now based on it.

The development of confidence in the survival of children has been a basic change not only for parents but for society as a whole all over the western world. This confidence has come rapidly, extensively and recently. Nearly everything that is said, written or thought about children now takes it for granted that children will survive. Confidence in the survival of ourselves and our children is the basis of modern parenthood and is essential to virtually all our ideas about it.

Whatever else we may think, hope and fear, we expect to have children if and when we want them and we expect those children to be born healthy and to grow up and, like ourselves, to lead a long life. If our lives do not conform to this pattern we are likely to feel that there is something wrong with us or that life has cheated us. If we cannot have children or if they are damaged or unhealthy or die or lose their parents or do not "develop their potential," these matters are to us problems or tragedies.

Yet only in recent years has such confidence been possible. Our ancestors, even our near ancestors in the last century, were accustomed to losing a high proportion of their children, sometimes most of them. Exact figures are impossible to find,[1] but even the official figures show that in England and Wales in 1885–74 [sic], out of every hundred infants registered alive, some fourteen to sixteen died in their first year of life. In some areas and in some groups the death rate was much higher. In a typical enquiry in 1872, it was found that sixty-two mothers who went out to work had borne 185 children, of whom 127 (68.6%) had died under the age of five years. One hundred ten mothers who did not go out to work had borne 544 children, of whom 248 (45.5%) had died before they were five years old.[2]

The development of confidence in our children's healthy survival is now so much the foundation on which the ideas and customs of the western world are built that we tend to take it for granted. This lack of awareness has important implications for the modern tendency to idealize motherhood and also for our understanding of it. For if we are to reach some understanding of ourselves, our families and the various aspects of modern motherhood it is essential to look at this new confidence carefully, examine its origins, nature and significance. and have some idea of how different it is from former times and other societies in which it did not and does not prevail.

Throughout history until recent times motherhood was always close to death. A high proportion of babies always died, and in certain times and places *most* babies died. If they did survive infancy they were likely to die as children, adolescents or young adults. At any time one might lose the new baby, or an epidemic might carry off two or three of one's older children within a few days or weeks. Improved nutrition and social conditions together with increasing knowledge of and control over health, disease and death has been one of the most spectacular aspects of post-industrial technical advance and social change.

Never before in history have people been so healthy or lived for so long. In these days of healthy security it is difficult to imagine the time when one in three adults died of infection, many thousands died of starvation or malnutrition and only a minority of babies born lived to adult life. But anyone who thinks seriously about these things is bound to be impressed by the profound change that this trend from disease to health, from death to life, has brought to the mothering of young children. The situation was even worse for mothers and children than for the rest of the population because the incidence of sickness and death among them was even higher. Two centuries ago, of every four babies born alive, only one was likely to be alive on its first birthday, as gravestones in any eighteenth century churchyard remind us. Moreover, these figures exclude stillbirths, which were almost never recorded, and also exclude many infants who lived for a few days or more, for it was often more convenient and cheaper to take a small corpse to the undertaker and say that it had died at birth. Ecclesiastical lawyers and theologians took the view that "a child before he is baptized is not a child of God but a child of the Devil."[3] Charles Dickens once asked the Rector of a parish in a large English town: "What do they do with the infants of the mothers who work in the mill?" "Oh," replied the cleric, "they bring them to me and I take care of them in the churchyard!"[4]

Because exact figures are impossible to obtain, small studies are particularly valuable. A doctor's records in one probably fairly typical time and place showed that no less than one third of all infants died within fourteen days of birth and many more, unspecified, during the first year. The death rate between the ages of one and five was a further 18%,[5] and the death rate throughout the rest of youth was also very high. Thus large numbers of those who survived the hazardous first months of life died in childhood. This was just as true in royal and aristocratic families as among peasants. To mention just a few, Queen Anne of England had fifteen pregnancies: all except one of her children were born dead or died during infancy. The survivor, William, Duke of Gloucester, died at the age of eleven. Because of all these deaths there was no direct heir to the throne and the succession passed to George, elector of Hanover. Another royal, the Duc d'Orléans ("Monsieur"), brother of Louis XIV and ancestor of every Roman Catholic royal family, had eleven legitimate children of whom seven died in infancy or were born dead. These were not exceptional cases. Although mortality in infants and young children seems to have been somewhat lower in colonial America than in Europe, the situation was basically the same. Examples can be seen everywhere, such as in the early colonial families of Sewall and Mather. Samuel Sewall and Cotton Mather each had fourteen children. One of Sewall's was stillborn, several died as infants and several more as young adults. Seven Mather babies died soon after birth, one died at two years and of the six who survived to adult life, five died in their twenties. Of these twenty-eight children, only three outlived their fathers.[6].

Although infant mortality has fallen fairly steadily for the past two hundred years it was still high during the early part of the present century. Only since World War I and still more since World War II have parents been able to have reasonable confidence that all their children would survive. Stillbirths and neonatal deaths, of course, occur, but in industrialized countries in only about eight to twenty per thousand births. Children die, notably from accidents, cancer and inherited disease, but these deaths are even rarer. After the first month of life death has become extremely rare.

What was it like to be a mother with the possibility that at least half one's children would fail to survive birth or infancy or would die during childhood? What was it like to be a mother whose apparently healthy child suddenly sickens and dies? We cannot be sure, even though both these situations occasionally occur today. Today children occasionally die, and there still are a few individual mothers, such as those whose children suffer from inherited diseases, who have to face the problem. For these mothers it is a personal tragedy, but it is different from what it would have been in former times because it is rare and unexpected. The very fact that such mothers are few means that, although many of their feelings may be the same, their situation is different from that in the past, when it was the likely lot of every mother. In the past, mothers who lost children were unlikely to feel isolated in the way they do today. It happened around them all the time and to nearly everyone they knew. When things, however sad or tragic, are the same for everyone, they are different for all. Society supported bereaved families in what was likely to be regarded more as a sad little happening than as a deep family tragedy. They would have been less likely to blame themselves, as they might today, and they were less likely to feel that they had failed. Moreover, other people would not condemn them, as they might today, believing it to be irresponsible to bring sickly children into the world. Losing one's children by death was regarded as a normal hazard of life and hence it was important to have many children so that at least some might survive. This led to a resigned, even a detached attitude to the deaths of children epitomized by Montaigne: "I have lost two or three children at nurse, not without regret but without grief."

In the 1770s, Mrs. Thrale, devoted mother of many children, was extremely upset when one of her older children died but showed no grief over the deaths of infants. She took an instant dislike to one baby since "she is so very poor a creature I can scarce bear to look on her." Later, when another newborn baby died, she commented, "One cannot grieve after her much, and I have just now other things to think of."[7] It is difficult to imagine a modern mother saying such a thing. Philippe Ariès, who has made an extensive study of iconography in his search for evidence, points out that there were no portraits of individual children during the Middle Ages, and no children's tombs until the sixteenth century. Even then children appeared not on their own but on their parents' tombs. No one thought of keeping a picture of a dead child. The general feeling was, and for a long time remained, writes Ariès, "that one had several children in order to keep just a few." In the Basque country it was long the custom to bury children who died without baptism in the house, on the threshold or in the garden.[8] And sometimes the deaths of children were positively encouraged or hoped for. Ariès quotes the seventeenth century *Le Caquet de l'accouchée;* in which a neighbour, standing at the bedside of a woman who has just given birth, the mother of five "little brats," calmed her fears with these words: "Before they are old enough to bother you, you will have lost half of them or perhaps all of them." In Bavaria "people are generally pleased with the quick death of children and say 'they're well provided for.' "[9] Lebrun writes of eighteenth century Angevin peasants, "The death of a small child, provided it had been baptized, is considered in the religious plane as a deliverance, for the infant has had the grace of acceding directly to paradise without knowing the bitterness of this life. . . . On the human plane infant death is almost a banal accident, which a subsequent birth will recuperate."[10]

Thus one big difference between today and the past is in the nature of realistic and unrealistic expectations. In the past mothers hoped that their children would survive but it was unrealistic to expect them to do so. A young woman embarking on motherhood knew that she was likely to lose several children, especially babies. Nowadays for most women it is realistic to expect that every child will survive and grow up. Many women today have fears that they will lose their children or hidden suspicions that they are incapable of producing normal, healthy children, but these, though understandable, are usually neurotic projections of personal anxieties, or manifestations of the problems of personal identity that are so characteristic of our time.

Another result that one would expect if every mother was in danger of losing her children and knew no other state of affairs is that she would not and could not have the strong individual feelings about each child that are customary today, when each child is regarded as unique from the moment it is born or even before. Only with the new confidence is it possible to regard each new life as unique, valuable, personal and permanent for the rest of one's life. In the past a woman who became pregnant was extremely unlikely to feel this way. People are likely to invest less time and love on something or somebody whose existence is likely to be transitory and there is a good deal of evidence to show that this was so, quite apart from the evidence of the easy acceptance of death. It was, for instance, long the custom to give the same name to several children in the hope that at least one John or William or Richard would live to carry on the family name. In the medieval period the same name was often given to two living children. Later, from the sixteenth to the eighteenth centuries, it was more the practice to give a newborn child the name of one who had recently died. This practice was brought [from] England [to] colonial New England. When John Wesley was born in 1703 both his names, John Benjamin, were those of elder brothers who had died three and four years before.[11] But the older practice lingered on, as Edward Gibbon tells us. After his birth in 1737 "so feeble was my constitution, so precarious my life, that in the baptism of my brothers, my father's prudence successively repeated my Christian name of Edward, that, in the case of the departure of the eldest son, this patronymic appelation might still be perpetuated in the family."[12] One wonders what effect this custom had on family relationships. Such practices would be inconceivable today and would be regarded as both an insult to the memory of the dead child and a monstrous imposition on the living, a threat to its unique existence and personality.

Another way in which our ancestors indicated that their attitude to the individuality of children was different from ours was their frequent failure to record their births. Parish Registers of Birth were introduced in England in 1538 but long after that the records were inexact.[13] It was not possible to ascertain a person's age precisely until after the Registration of Births Act of 1836, and even after that in by no means every case. Judges decided people's ages, simply by looking at them or by consulting relatives. When, in 1620, E. Chamberlayne first published *Reflections on the Present State of England* he wrote so that "the whole state of England might be seen at once." Out of its 516 pages he devotes less than four to a section "Concerning Children in England" and then deals exclusively with the legal rights of children in the holding and disposing of property.

Lack of confidence in survival applied not only to children but also to their mothers; and to a lesser extent, their fathers. Health and death in young mothers have also changed profoundly. Stone[14] cites evidence that throughout the Early

Modern period nearly one in ten of all children under three and one in five of all children living at home had lost at least one parent. Until recent times death was frequent at all ages and killing diseases such as tuberculosis, diphtheria and typhoid were rampant. Epidemics of cholera were frequent in the nineteenth century. The last big outbreak, in 1887, is said to have killed 250,000 people in Europe and 50,000 in America,[15] and in 1892 a million people are said to have died from the disease in Russia.[16] Yet amidst all this, one of the greatest hazards that women had to face was childbirth. At times and in certain places it killed as many as fifteen or even twenty mothers out of every hundred and was particularly likely to occur in maternity hospitals expressly designed for their protection. In the seventeenth century John Donne referred to the womb as the "house of death."

"Death in childbirth" as a fact and a concept was once widespread everywhere, but few people now come into contact with it in the western world. Few have much idea of what it entails and most doctors never encounter it. Yet until the 1930s every woman embarking on pregnancy knew that her life was in danger. Death in childbirth was so common that it shaped royal dynasties and influenced the course of history. For instance, it killed three Tudor queens, Elizabeth of York, wife of Henry VII and mother of Henry VIII; Jane Seymour, third wife of Henry VIII, following the birth of the future Edward VI; and Catherine Parr, his sixth wife, who died in childbirth after Henry's death, when she was married to Thomas Seymour.

"Death in childbirth" covers a number of different conditions. The best known is probably puerperal or "childbed" fever. This is an infection, most commonly associated with the organism *haemolytic streptococcus,* but sometimes with other organisms such as those which cause gas gangrene in war wounds. The infection usually occurs during delivery but only manifests itself some days later, leading to septicaemia with fever and a high mortality rate. Death usually occurred eight to twelve days after the baby was born. The disease was known to the ancients, including Hippocrates, but became particularly common after the development of dirty, crowded towns, especially where charitable organizations established hospitals where the poor might give birth! Between the years 1652 and 1862 there were two hundred so-called epidemics of the disease. In 1660 it killed two thirds of the women confined in the Hôtel Dieu in Paris. In 1773 it killed more than a tenth of the population of lying-in hospitals in Europe. It was reported that in Lombardy for more than a year no woman survived childbirth.[17] Though commonest in hospitals it was also found elsewhere, for example in America, where there were few hospitals. Jane Seymour caught it in Greenwich Palace. Mary Wollstonecraft, one of the first pioneers of English feminism, caught it and died of it after a home confinement. The description of her suffering is typical of what women went through.

Puerperal fever is much commoner after deliveries that have been compli-cated and in which there has been some operative interference. So it was with Mary Wollstonecraft. She was full of good spirits when she went into labour with the future Mary Shelley, wife of the poet and author of *Frankenstein*. Her experience during her previous confinement had been so good that she planned to present the new baby to her husband herself as soon as it was born and to get up for dinner next day.[18] This was to give a pioneering example to other women, whose custom was to stay in their rooms for a whole month after delivery. She hired Mrs. Blenkinsop, the chief midwife from the Westminster Lying-In Hospital. The labour was slower and more painful than is usual with a second child, but after eighteen hours the baby was born. Now came the first serious difficulty. The placenta, which is usually born a few minutes after the baby, did not arrive. Moreover, it had separated partially which meant that the womb could not expel it. The partial separation caused bleeding and, because the retained placenta kept the womb distended, the bleeding was likely to continue danger-ously until the placenta was removed. Nowadays a retained placenta is usually removed in sterile conditions under anaesthetic and lost blood is replaced by transfusion. In 1797, without anaesthetics or blood transfusion, and without knowledge of the source or nature of infection, a retained placenta was extremely dangerous. Mrs. Blenkinsop sent for Dr. Poignard, the chief obstetrician at the Westminster Lying-In. Mary was already half-conscious from loss of blood and could easily have died from this alone. When Dr. Poignard arrived he did the only thing which could save her life, though it could also easily kill her. He put his hand [and] arm right up into the womb and extracted the placenta in pieces with his fingers, working through the night till dawn. Without an anaesthetic, Mary could easily have died from shock but in fact she survived this second danger to her life and later slept. When she woke she was much better and for two days everything seemed to be fine. Then she began to feel ill and had an attack of shivering so bad that the bed shook. This was a typical "rigor," a common start of puerperal fever. Late that evening she had another rigor in the presence of her husband who described it: "every muscle of her body trembled, the teeth chattered, and the bed shook under her. This continued probably for five minutes. She told me, after it was over, that it had been a struggle between life and death, and that she had been more than once, in the course of it, at the point of expiring." Mary tried to fight back but she was exsanguinated from the bleeding and exhausted. There was no treatment for the infection. The disease developed relentlessly during the next few days until she was clearly dying. She lingered on for yet a few more days.

Ironically, Mary Wollstonecraft died of puerperal fever at a time when the incidence seems to have been remarkably low. No national figures exist before the Act of 1836, but at the City of London Lying-In Hospital in the year 1797 only one mother died in 402 deliveries, an incidence of 2.4 per thousand deliveries. Over the next eighty years the figure fluctuated from two to as many as fourteen deaths per thousand births. Although the cause of puerperal fever was discovered in the nineteenth century and ways of preventing it were known, it continued to be common far into the twentieth century and killed many healthy women until the 1930s.

Eclampsia was another common killer. This is a disease which only occurs in pregnancy, usually develops slowly and, if not detected and prevented, proceeds to severe fits and often rapid and dramatic death. It is fairly common (perhaps three to four per thousand births) where pregnancy is left to nature but almost wholly preventable with good antenatal care. Its marked decline with medical effort was shown dramatically in Sydney, Australia. At the Women's Hospital, Crown Street, between 1936 and 1948 the incidence among booked cases was one in 400. In 1948 it was decided to attack this high incidence by the simple measures of meticulous observation of blood pressure and control of weight gain. After this was organized there was only one case of eclampsia in approximately 15,000 booked cases. Nowadays eclampsia still occurs in the western world, but it is almost always in women whose antenatal care has been poor or non-existent.

Obstructed labour was another common cause of death and old textbooks of obstetrics are full of heroic measures to deal with a situation that had gone too far to save the life of the child and often, especially in the days before anaesthetics, of the mother. Every obstetrician carried destructive instruments designed to kill and crush or decapitate the foetus in the hope of saving the mother's life. The operation or craniotomy is much older than the procedures which eventually replaced it, forceps and Caesarian section. Decapitation seems barbarous to us and to modern obstetricians. It is virtually never performed today in the western world but it is perhaps salutary to note that as late as the present century a new device was invented for performing it—the Blond-Heidler thimble, which, placed on the thumb, carries a fine wire-saw round the neck of the child.

Another constant hazard in childbirth is, and remains, haemorrhage, particularly post-partum haemorrhage, usually from a retained placenta. Even in a "normal" birth, it can strike suddenly and dangerously despite every precaution and the most skilled care during pregnancy and labour. It is one of the main reasons why many obstetricians say that no delivery is "normal" until it is finished and believe that all births should take place in hospital.

One serious condition attacks women early in pregnancy. This is *hyperemesis gravidarum* which is an exaggeration of the common "morning sickness." The expectant mother, usually of a nervous disposition, vomits so much that if she is treated inadequately or not at all she may lose her life. This seems to be what happened to Charlotte Brontë. Although her death during pregnancy is often attributed to tuberculosis, in fact Mrs. Gaskell's description of her last illness supplemented by Charlotte's own letters is a classical description of *hyperemesis gravidarum*.[19] In November 1854, just over three months after her return from a honeymoon in Ireland, Charlotte developed a cold, which lingered but does not seem to have been serious. In the new year (1855) "she was attacked by new sensations of perpetual nausea, and ever-recurring faintness."[20] Charlotte wrote in January 19th to her friend Ellen Nussey. "My health has been really very good since my return from Ireland till about ten days ago, when the stomach seemed quite suddenly to lose its tone—indigestion and continual faint sickness have been my portion ever since." She seems to associate this with her pregnancy for she continues, "Don't conjecture—dear Nell—for it is too soon yet though I certainly never before felt as I have done lately." Her husband called in Dr. MacTurk from Bradford, who "assigned a natural cause for her miserable indisposition."[21] Martha the maid "tenderly waited on her mistress, and from time to time tried to cheer her with the thought of the baby that was coming. "I dare say I shall be glad sometime," she would say: "but I am so ill—so weary—." Then she took to her bed, too weak to sit up. Some time in February she wrote to Amelia Taylor: "Let me speak the plain truth—my sufferings are very great—my nights indescribable—sickness with scarce a reprieve—I strain until what I vomit is mixed with blood." Mrs. Gaskell tells us: "About the third week in March there was a change; a low wandering delirium came on: and in it she begged constantly for food and even for stimulants. She swallowed eagerly now; but it was too late." On March 31st she died.

Hyperemesis gravidarum still occurs. But no one would leave a sufferer to vomit her life away in her own home. A few days in hospital with suitable diet, drugs, fluid replacement and perhaps some psychotherapy are usually all that is required. Probably never again will it be possible to follow so closely the natural, untreated course of the illness.[22]

Death in childbirth was often precipitated or hastened by ignorance, impotence, neglect, interference or a mixture of these according to the knowledge and custom of the time. Throughout the history of obstetrics there has been conflict between those who believe in leaving everything to Nature and those who believe in interfering whenever any delay or abnormality became apparent. Today this conflict is as strong as ever, though the criteria have changed. A period in which leaving matters to Nature was very much in vogue was the early nineteenth century. This idea and also the belief in "meddlesome midwifery" can both be studied in the story of the labour of Princess Charlotte in November 1817. The hour-to-hour notes of Sir Richard Croft, Bart., Accoucheur-in-Chief have enabled us to follow the progress of labour in some detail. Thirty-eight years before Charlotte Brontë's death [the person after whom she was named], the Princess Charlotte, daughter of the Prince Regent, died in childbirth. Her death and the circumstances that surrounded it are of interest for several reasons. First, it created a crisis in the succession to the throne of England; second, it was a turning point in the history of midwifery; third, it can be seen as part of a conflict that continues in the present time and is of particular interest to feminists: the conflict in the management of childbirth between control and interference by a male obstetrician and leaving it to Nature.

Princess Charlotte was the only child of her estranged parents, the Prince Regent, later George IV, and Queen Caroline. King George III had had fifteen children. He was now seventy-nine years old, sick, and likely to die soon. His heir was already fifty-five years old and estranged from his wife. Charlotte was the king's only legitimate grandchild. If no new heirs were born the crown would pass to the Duke of Brunswick, aged thirteen, and mentally weak. Charlotte's death meant that the dissolute pleasure-loving princes were urged to attend to the important matters of royal marriage and producing an heir. The Duke of Cambridge won the race with a son. But two months later the Duchess of Kent, wife of his older brother, gave birth to a daughter. The child, in the aftermath of her cousin's tragic death, was destined to become Queen Victoria.

The story of the Princess Charlotte's labour has been ably told by Sir Eardley Holland, and named "a triple obstetric tragedy" because not only did the mother and child both die as a result of it but also the obstetrician.[23] Sir Richard

Croft, the obstetrician who conducted the labour, became severely depressed amid all the criticism and shot himself three months later. Only during the reign of George III had midwifery become respectable, and as it became respectable it also became ultra-conservative. Smellie, a brilliant man-midwife and careful operator who invented a number of techniques that are still used today, had retired in 1760. There followed a period in which forceps were used so freely that William Hunter, who became England's most prominent man-midwife, is said to have told his class that it was "a thousand pities that it was ever invented." When Hunter died the next leading society obstetrician was Thomas Denman, an exponent of the non-intervention school. Denman trained Richard Croft according to the principles he had laid down in his *Introduction to the Practice of Midwifery*, first published in 1788, which went into many editions. In his conduct of Princess Charlotte's labour Croft followed Denman's precepts, which meant that, despite the length of the labour and the complications that arose, he did nothing and left it all to Nature.

Charlotte's labour started with the breaking of the waters at 7 P.M. on Monday, 3 November, 1817. Her contractions were irregular and the first stage of labour lasted for twenty-six hours. There is nothing unusual in this, but Croft bled her and refused to allow her food or drink. The second stage of labour began. This is the stage during which the child is actually born. In modern practice it is allowed to last no longer than an hour and often less because of the risks to child and mother. Charlotte's second stage lasted for twenty-four hours, including five to six hours when the head was actually pressing on the perineum and any but the most ultra-conservative practitioner would have lifted the baby out with forceps. At 9 P.M. on November 5, Charlotte, exhausted after this immense labour, gave birth to a 9 lb. stillborn boy. We can find the reason for this long delay in Denman's book. He tells us the "cessation of pains, which is the consequence of long continued fruitless action, and of great debility is to be considered the only justification for the use of the forceps." He also formulated what came to be known as "Denman's Law," "that the head of the child shall have rested for six hours as low as the perineum before the forceps are applied, though the pains should have ceased during that time." Even by the most conservative obstetrician today, this would be regarded as malpractice.

This delay was disastrous for Charlotte. Her baby was dead and she was exhausted. Twenty minutes later, as is liable to happen after a long hard labour, she had a post-partum haemorrhage. Croft removed the placenta manually as Poignard had done twenty years before on Mary Wollstonecraft. Although the Princess seemed to be reasonably well afterwards, shortly before midnight she was sick and complained of noises in her head. She was given camphorated mixture and was sick again. After a cup of tea she slept for half an hour, then woke irritable and restless. She was given twenty drops of laudanum in wine and water and she told Baron Stockmar, her husband's secretary, that the doctors had made her tipsy. At 12:45 A.M. on November 6 she complained of uneasiness in the chest and difficulty in breathing. Her pulse was rapid, feeble and irregular. She became increasingly restless and at 2:30 A.M. she died. At the post-mortem "about a pound of blood" was found in the uterus. This probably contributed to her death but Croft had ignored or not bothered to find it. Denman's book advised *against* releasing accumulated blood from the uterus after delivery.

Baron Stockmar, himself a trained physician, who was in the next room during the labour commented, "It is impossible to resist the conviction that the Princess was sacrificed to professional theories." The public thought so too. There was widespread hostility to Croft until he killed himself, and a change in the customary practice of midwifery to a greater willingness to interfere when things do not go well.

Princess Charlotte's labour was better documented than most but probably was not in other ways atypical of complicated labours at the time. But many of the mothers who died were different in one respect. Charlotte had no children. Since childbirth becomes more dangerous with each birth after the third, many of these mothers left large numbers of children behind them.

No accurate figures are available for deaths in childbirth in England and Wales before 1838. We do know, however, that from that date, in spite of improvements in knowledge during the nineteenth and early twentieth century, and in spite of improvements in general health [and decreases] in overall mortality and in infant mortality, the maternal death rate remained almost stationery for nearly a hundred years (1838–1935). Some of the causes of this are to be found in the attitudes of men to women and the lack of time, energy and technology devoted to the health of expectant mothers. Only when special attention was paid to the problem of death in childbirth did the situation improve. After women won the vote pioneer suffragettes together with men and women of strong social conscience turned their attention to such problems and one of these problems was maternal mortality. As a result institutions were founded, including the Royal College of Obstetrics and Gynaecologists and the National Birthday Trust Fund, which aimed to increase knowledge by research and to raise standards of practice. The maternal death rate has been falling ever since. In England and Wales in 1855–64 the maternal mortality rate was 4.7 per thousand live births. In 1925–34 it was 4.3. In 1945–50 it was 1.2 and in 1979 it was down to .12, now expressed as 1.2 per 10,000 live births. When we give birth today, provided we look after ourselves and follow expert advice, we can be confident of survival.

Today almost no woman who follows the advice of her doctors is in danger of dying during childbirth. Women who, in spite of modern medicine, are still in genuine danger usually suffer from severe disease, perhaps of the heart or kidneys, but they are so rare that when one of them survives a hazardous birth, she is liable to make headlines in the newspapers. The essence of safe childbirth for all women is good health and food, good antenatal care and good obstetric care during delivery. This is one of the great scientific truths of our time. The aids are careful observation and record-keeping, frequent monitoring and preventive action, antibiotics and other drugs, blood or its derivatives for transfusion, and the skilful performance of Caesarian sections and other obstetric procedures when necessary. Only recently have we discovered that, even though many healthy babies can be born "naturally," without medical care, huge numbers of babies and many mothers die if all is left to Nature. Antenatal care did not exist at the beginning of the twentieth century, apart from general advice about such matters as diet and exercise. In Boston in 1901 the Instructive Nursing Association began to pay antenatal visits to some of the women in the out-patient department of the Boston Lying-In Hospital. In 1909 Mrs. William Lowell Putnam of the Infant Social Service Department of the Women's Municipal League of Boston organized intensive prenatal care of patients registered for confinement at the Boston Lying-In Hospital. In May 1911 the pregnancy clinic of the hospital was opened for out-patients. A similar clinic had already been started the year before in Adelaide, Australia, followed in 1912 by one in Sydney, Australia, and, in 1915, in Edinburgh, Scotland. In 1919 the Maternity and Child Welfare Act provided for advice, treatment and social assistance [for] pregnant women in Great Britain. Nowadays all western countries and many others provide comprehensive antenatal care and it is known that the mortality among the babies of those who attend early in pregnancy is only half that of those who do not attend before the sixteenth week.

The wheel has turned again. No sooner has the lesson been learned than there are pressures to forget it. This time it is the women who clamour that childbirth is natural and should be left to Nature. In the generation that followed the first mothers whose childbirth was safe there is disquiet concerning "inhuman" obstetrics and "patriarchal" obstetricians. Childbirth has been made so safe that we tend to forget that it is potentially dangerous. We are also aware that this safety has been achieved at considerable emotional cost. Childbirth is now a highly technological process and many mothers experience the "factory belt" system and the clinical and scientific atmosphere that accompanies it as dehumanizing. For some years there have been movements for "natural" childbirth and for home deliveries. This has created one of the new dilemmas of motherhood. It is virtually impossible to be or to feel "natural" as a patient in a modern obstetric ward, and although some wards make efforts to satisfy their patients' feelings, these efforts must, by the very nature of the situation, be rudimentary and unsatisfactory. There can be enormous emotional satisfaction in giving birth in one's own home with just a midwife in attendance. I can testify to this personally as two of my own babies were born in this manner. But the scientific evidence is strong. Nature tends to be wasteful of life and however healthy the mother and however normal the pregnancy, things are liable to go wrong, often very fast. If things go wrong, the safest place for both mother and child to be in is a well-equipped obstetric unit. A delivery can only be described as normal when it is finished and the baby is alive. My own homeborn babies were perfect, but one of the changes that has taken place in my own adult life is the realization of these dangers. Given the opportunity I would not again risk my children's lives in this way. However, I can sympathize with the current argument that modern obstetric methods also create complications that would not occur in the patient's home.

So much death as existed until recent times meant that large numbers of children grew up motherless, and often fatherless too. The word *orphan* has almost gone out of our language but was all too common until recent times. Lawrence Stone has told the story:

> In pre-modern times only a minority of adolescent children had two living parents. Of those marrying for the first time in Brittany and Anjou in the late eighteenth century, on the average in their middle twenties, one

in five were orphans and two in three had lost one parent. Among the sixteenth and seventeenth century English aristocracy, one in three children had lost one parent by the age of fourteen, and the proportion of English apprentices (who normally entered service at fourteen) who were fatherless was thirty-four percent at Bristol, twenty per cent in the London Stationers' Company and twenty-five per cent in the London Fishmongers' and Bakers' Companies. These figures are on the high side, since apprenticeship was a common way of looking after orphans, but they are nonetheless very striking. More typical are the records of first marriages in Manchester in the 1650s, where over half the brides and almost half of the grooms had lost their fathers. In 1696 one-third of all the children in Bristol were orphans.[24]

One only has to look at biographies of famous people to see that this state of affairs was common in all sections of society. Illingworth has collected some of them. Descartes, Rousseau, Froebel, Paderewski and Mary Shelley all lost their mothers in their first year of life. Those who lost their mothers at the age of two included Nero, Tolstoy and Anne Brontë, at three, Isaac Newton, Pascal and Ronald Knox; at five, Dante, Lavoisier and Charlotte Brontë; at six, Michelangelo, Mahommed and William Cowper; at seven, Robespierre and Hume; and at eight, Wordsworth, Voltaire, Charles Darwin, Joseph Conrad, Ivan the Terrible and Ernest Bevin. Today it is rare for a child to have no living mother. If he is separated from her it is more likely to be because she has abandoned or deserted him or cannot cope with him, or is physically or, more often, mentally ill. We have few orphans but there are large numbers of children in care, and their numbers are tending to increase.

We hear a great deal today about "broken homes," by which we usually mean a family in which the parents are divorced or separated. Since there was virtually no divorce between the middle ages and the late nineteenth century and very little until the middle of the present century, it is sometimes assumed that, before our more permissive age, families were more intact than in our time. This was not the case. They were broken by death, probably at least as often as they are now broken by divorce. It was rare for a couple to marry and raise all their children together, and even if they managed this they probably did not have long to live after they were grown. Aging grandparents were rare. Of course, the deaths of so many young adults meant that there were large numbers of remarriages, just as there are today, though for different reasons. Not only orphans but also wicked stepmothers feature largely in Victorian children's books and fairy tales. Cinderella, Hansel and Gretel, and the Babes in the Wood are just a few of those who suffered from their fathers' second wives. It is interesting to note that in these stories it is nearly always the children's mother who has died, sometimes both parents, but rarely the father alone. In real life it was common for a man to have several wives in succession, each of them dying, often in childbirth, and each leaving behind a family of small children. But of course it was not always the mother who died. Sir Ralph Verney died in 1543 leaving nine young children. Their mother subsequently remarried four times and, we are told, "had others matters on her hands than the care of her first husband's children." A later member of the same family, Sir Francis Verney, lost his own mother when he was five years old and was brought up by his father, who had frequently to be away attending to his business. The children were left in the care of their father's third wife, Mary. We are told that Francis "seems never to have been under any control either from affection or education."[25] Thus widespread loss of parents, their remarriages, and difficult relationships with step-parents are not new in our time though the causes differ.

Death at home was accompanied by rituals and patterns of behaviour in which the children participated and had a special role to play. They were accustomed to losing playmates and brothers and sisters. Sometimes they were aware that they or their parents were not long for this world. When his wife Emily was seriously ill with consumption in 1861, the poet Coventry Patmore wrote to his schoolboy son: "Remember that you are not likely to have your poor Mama long so you should make the best of the time you have left to please her. . . . Although your learning well is important, there are other things much more important . . . to be *pure* (you know what I mean). If you are not pure . . . you will not see your dear Mama any more when she is gone."[26] Another child, the seven year old son of Benjamin Haydon the painter, was not unusual when, on the death of his sister, he remarked that his turn would come next. He duly died the following year.[27] Nearly all modern western children grow to adult life without thinking of the possibility that they might die young, and often also without losing a single friend or close relative. Some even think that death is something that happens by violence on the television screen. The taboo about death which has developed in our society often creates a powerful and sinister "conspiracy of silence" between parents and children.

Along with control of survival has come control of conception. In the past, no matter at which period or place one looks, and still in parts of the world, there was no sure method, apart from total abstinence, of preventing the arrival of children. True, fertility has varied from time to time and from place to place according to such influences as nutrition and social customs—for example, variations in age at marriage. There have always been women who have attempted to prevent pregnancy by various means, some of them surer than others but all of them uncertain. There have also been periods when whole groups of people have produced small families as a result of deliberate choice. An example is the Victorian middle classes from the 1870s onwards.[28] But only in our own time have the Pill, other contraceptive devices, and abortion made it possible for an individual woman to choose with certainty whether or not to have a baby as and when she pleases. Choice is now absent only in those whose religion forbids contraception and those who wish to become mothers but turn out to be infertile. There are of course those who do not exercise their choice for any of a number of reasons including ignorance, personal motives, medical advice and fecklessness. There are also those who cannot choose because they have been brought up and trained not to choose.

The fact that any woman can choose, at least in theory, whether or not she becomes a mother has profound effect on women, on men, on families and on parenthood itself. First, there is the common idea that one should only have children if one is able to care for them properly, physically, economically and emotionally, according to today's high standards. For most people this means getting married, acquiring what is regarded as adequate material possessions, and, at the time chosen, producing a small family, usually two children, and devoting to them a tremendous amount of time, emotion and money over many years in order to give them what one believes is the best chance of a good life. The wherewithal to organize things like this has had a profound effect on family life. Without it many of our ideas about families, children and motherhood would inevitably be different. It also raises new questions and creates new dilemmas. For instance, questions are now being asked about whether motherhood is any longer a woman's chief *raison d'être*. The belief that woman's chief role in life is motherhood has existed through the ages and persists today but is now seriously questioned, probably for the first time. Many women resent the years they would have to give to motherhood or regret that they had children before they felt they had a choice. Many reject conventional family patterns and choose either to have children without marriage or not to have them at all. Today if a woman is unmarried with a family, or if she decides never to have children, she will find communities and social circles where such attitudes are wholly acceptable. Moreover, fertility is now regarded as a world problem, and, for the first time in history, having babies is, in some circles, regarded as antisocial and irresponsible. At the same time the belief that one should only have children if one can provide them with the love, care and material needs that are needed for optimum development also creates dilemmas.

Notes

1. The various reasons why figures are unreliable are discussed in Hewitt, *Wives and Mothers in Victorian Industry,* Chapter Eight.
2. It is interesting to note that it was in studies such as this that the deleterious influence of a mother's employment on the life of her baby was first discussed and became the concern of philanthropists. See Hewitt: Chapter Eight.
3. Quoted by Stone, *The Family, Sex and Marriage in England 1500–1800,* p. 68.
4. Quoted by Hewitt, p. 89.
5. Quoted by Stone, p. 68.
6. Quoted in de Mause (Ed.), *The History of Childhood,* p. 325.
7. Clifford, J. L., *Hester Lynch Piozzi,* pp. 83–94.
8. Ariès, *Centuries of Childhood,* p. 39.
9. Quoted by Shorter, *The Making of the Modern Family,* p. 174.
10. Quoted by ibid, p. 174.
11. Stone, p. 409.
12. Quoted by ibid., p. 409.
13. Pinchbeck and Hewitt, *Children in English Society,* p. 7.
14. Stone, p. 101.
15. *Encyclopaedia Britannica,* 11th Edition.
16. *Chambers Encyclopaedia,* 1959 Edition.
17. Shorter, p. 9.
18. The details of Mary Wollstonecraft's confinement have been taken from Claire Tomalin, *The Life and Death of Mary Wollstonecraft,* 1974. London: Weidenfield and Nicolson.
19. This has been noticed by many doctors who have read Mrs. Gaskell. It was discussed by Philip Rhodes, a professor of obstetrics, in the Brontë Society Transactions, 1970.

20. Gaskell, *The Life of Charlotte Brontë,* vol II, p. 321–2.
21. Ibid., p. 322.
22. Gaskell, E. C., *The Life of Charlotte Brontë.* Second Edition in two volumes. 1857. Cornhill: Smith, Elder & Co. 65. Peters, Margaret., *Unquiet Soul. A Biography of Charlotte Brontë.* 1978. London: Hodder & Stoughton.
23. Sir Eardley Holland, *F. Obst. Gynae. Brit. Emp.* 1951. 58.905ff.
24. Stone, p. 58.
25. Quoted by Pinchbeck and Hewitt from *The Memoirs of the Verney Family,* Ed. F. P. Verney, 1892. Vol. 1, p. 52.
26. Quoted in de Mause, p. 12.
27. Haydon, B. R., *Diary.* 1808–1846. Ed. W. B. Pope, 1960 and 1963. Cambridge: Harvard University Press.
28. Banks, *Prosperity and Parenthood.*

References

Ariès, Philippe. *Centuries of Childhood.* 1962. London: Cape. Translated from the French *L'Enfant et la vie familiale sous l'ancien regime.*1960.

Banks, J. A. *Prosperity and Parenthood.* 1954. London: Routledge & Kegan Paul.

Chambers Encyclopaedia. 1959.

Clifford, J. L. *Hester Lynch Piozzi.* 1968. Oxford: Oxford University Press.

de Mause, Lloyd (Ed.). *The History of Childhood.* 1974. London: Souvenir Press.

Encyclopaedia Brittanica. 11th Edition.

Hewitt, Margaret. *Wives and Mothers in Victorian Industry.* 1958. London: Rockcliff.

Pinchbeck, Ivy & Hewitt, Margaret. *Children in English Society.* Vol I. 'From Tudor Times to the Eighteenth Century'. 1969. London: Routledge & Kegan Paul. Vol II. 1973. London: Routledge & Kegan Paul.

Shorter, Edward. *The Making of the Modern Family.* 1977. London: Fontana Books.

Stone, Lawrence. *The Family, Sex and Marriage in England 1500–1800.* 1977. London: Weidenfeld & Nicholson.

Working-Class Women, Middle-Class Women, and Models of Childbirth

Margaret K. Nelson

This paper began as an attempt to describe the class differences in childbirth procedures in a teaching hospital in New England. I assumed that I could show, as have others, that middle-class women received better medical services than working-class women, and that although the hospital had a long way to go before it provided all women with an optimum birth experience, one's chances of reaching that goal were greatly enhanced if one entered as a middle-class client. This paper, then, began as a critique of birth practices in a modern hospital and the class biases implicit among medical personnel.

Responses to my questionnaires and interviews suggested that women could be divided along certain significant social dimensions which corresponded to kinds of birth experiences. One group of women experienced birth in a relatively active and involved way. Another group had more passive births, involving more monitoring, medication, transfers to the delivery room, and use of forceps.

I then went one step further: were the women within each of these groups having the kind of birth experience for which they had indicated preferences during the prenatal period? I hypothesized that middle-class women would be more likely to have their choices respected in the hospital than working-class women. I suspected that doctors would use low social status as a justification for disregarding client preferences, and select the procedures *they* deemed necessary for working-class women.

I was wrong on two counts. First, neither of the two groups of women that I studied received the precise treatment they wanted. Second, there were few differences between the two groups in the extent to which the women got what they wanted. What I found instead was that the middle-class women generally wanted active, involved births free from medical interventions; some of their requests were respected in the hospital. The working-class women wanted more passive birth experiences with more medical intervention; some of their requests also were met within the hospital.

An earlier version of this paper was presented at the annual meetings of the Society for the Study of Social Problems, Toronto, August 22–24, 1981. The author thanks the Department of Obstetrics and Gynecology of the Medical Center Hospital of Vermont for supporting the collection of data, Middlebury College for leave, and Helen McGough for her criticism and encouragement.

The data thus suggested that within the hospital at least three different models of an appropriate childbirth were operating: two different client models and a medical model. My initial approach to this topic had overlooked the existence of more than one client model distinct from . . . the doctors' model.

The literature on women's control over childbirth has highlighted the importance of this life event for women. It has also used a set of implicit assumptions: (1) women share a set of common desires and make choices about childbirth independent of their social backgrounds; and (2) women's desires are different from those of doctors. In short, the literature assumes that women all want (or will come to want) conscious control over a basically "natural" childbirth experience and that doctors have resisted these demands. However, my data suggest that these assumptions are not entirely accurate. There is clearly more than just one client model of childbirth: not all women want the same kind of birth experience. And doctors, in fact, appear to resist and reject aspects of *each* client model in favor of their own approach.

Social Class in Childbirth Research

Three traditions of research and theory on childbirth have, each for its own reason, ignored social class differences. These are: (1) the feminist literature; (2) the general medical sociology treatment; and (3) studies which focus on the effects of preparation for childbirth.

Middle-class feminists, eager to take childbirth out of the hands of male obstetricians, seem more intent on describing how childbirth has become distorted over the years than in examining whether the "warping" (Haire, 1978) has affected all groups in the same way. Numerous historical studies document how male physicians wrested control of childbirth from female midwives, and class biases in the way new technologies were distributed (Ehrenreich and English, 1973; Kobrin, 1966; Wertz and Wertz, 1977). They do not tell us whether women of different social classes felt the same way about the changes—or whether there are class differences in attitudes towards childbirth today. (For an exception see Hubert [1974], who explicitly notes the lack of homogeneity in attitudes about childbirth.)

Shaw (1974) found class differences in treatment during the prenatal and hospital periods: the medical staff were aware of the class origins of their clients and treated them according to preconceived notions of what was most appropriate for each group of women. However, the solutions Shaw offers at the end of her book suffer from the opposite type of discrimination and totally ignore social class differences. She assumed her solutions would be equally acceptable to all clients, but never asked how they—as individuals or as representatives of social categories—would like childbirth to proceed.

The heavy emphasis on personal experience in much of the childbirth literature has resulted in the emergence of a single critique which presumes to speak for all women (e.g., Comaroff, 1977; Hart, 1977; Oakley [1979:627] makes a similar point). Most of those who write about childbirth are middle-class women. They are motivated by a feminist consciousness and possess the verbal ability which is part of class privilege. Thus, those who are most interested in women defining for themselves the nature and meaning of childbirth are, perhaps, guilty of prescribing a perfect birth for all women, regardless of individual needs or motivations.

The non-feminist literature has also ignored social class, albeit for different reasons. First, the ahistorical bias in much social science has inhibited attention to the social history of childbirth movements, a history which is important for understanding different class attitudes towards childbirth. Second, the use of some of the major sociological concepts might also inhibit a consideration of social class. For instance, although Stewart and Erickson (1977) attack mainstream sociology for failing to seriously consider childbirth, their own emphasis on "roles" as the best possible approach to understanding pregnancy and childbirth leads them to ignore social class. They note, for example, that "the manner in which women describe their labor and delivery varies by many factors including the setting, the difficulty of the labor, their definitions of themselves as sick or healthy, their expectations and how well these were met" (1977:41).

The view of childbirth expounded by middle-class feminists has been the best articulated and, therefore, frequently adopted by academic writers as the only view. Thus, as feminist critiques of contemporary obstetric care became more frequent and solidified, they were adopted by academic writers as representative of a single model or paradigm of childbirth which conflicted with that offered by the medical establishment. For example, Nash and Nash (1979:493) argue that "in American society at the present time there exist two primary interpretations of the meaning and practice of childbirth: the medical and the 'natural' view."

Oakley (1979) offers by far the most sophisticated exploration of competing childbirth paradigms. She notes the paucity of client-oriented studies and emphasizes the different models at work in medical science, clinical psychiatry and psychology, and academic psychology and sociology. Until recently the sociologist's contribution had not been "to investigate the women's experience but to extend the limits of the medical model and propose a more elastic conception of the variables which can be seen to influence the biological outcome of maternity" (1979:624). However, Oakley emphasizes the "natural" model of childbirth as the principal one in conflict with the various medical models. Danziger (1978), in a paper on prenatal encounters between physicians and clients, also assumes that there is only one *client* paradigm.[1]

Some research on childbirth has ignored social class by matching or controlling independent variables too rigorously. Studies on preparation for birth clearly fall within this category. Most research shows the preparation for childbirth has both physiological and psychological effects on the birth process (Doering *et al.*, 1980; Norr *et al.*, 1977), though some studies indicate little or no effect (Zax *et al.*, 1975). Motivation to learn about birth does not appear to be the key factor at work here: studies which compared women who wanted to take classes in childbirth preparation but could not with women who did take classes (or were randomly assigned to classes) found that preparation was the critical variable (Enkin *et al.*, 1972; Huttel *et al.*, 1972). To test whether preparation is a significant factor in the birth process, researchers have been careful to control for socio-economic status and education in experimental and control groups. For example, Doering and Entwisle's (1975) work on the effects of preparation on the ability to cope with labor and delivery dismisses social class after noting that there were no significant social differences between trained and untrained subjects, even though only 18 percent of the total number of subjects were working-class women. Gaziano's work (Gaziano *et al.*, 1979) only looked at working-class women who used a clinic, and therefore could not compare clients at different levels of income or education. Other researchers who compared the effects of different kinds of preparation for childbirth also controlled for the class origins of the client groups (e.g. Zimmerman-Tansella *et al.*, 1979). Researchers have given only cursory attention to the issue of who chooses to attend childbirth classes and why.

Much of this research assumes that the outcomes of preparation—knowledge, control, cooperation, and an avoidance of medication—are definite, clearcut, and desirable. That is, the studies assume that everyone wants an identical birth. Yet not all women, and particularly working-class women, may perceive the outcome of preparation as a "benefit." In fact, the data I collected for this paper suggest otherwise, and I am no longer willing to assume that all women want the same kind of birth.

Method

Background

In response to the declining U.S. birth rate, the movement for home birth, and the criticisms of women committed to hospital birth without extensive intervention, the Department of Gynecology and Obstetrics of the Medical Center Hospital of Vermont (MCHV) in Burlington, Vermont, decided in 1979 to revamp its maternity services. It hired certified nurse-midwives to work with clients (both alone, for low-risk clients, and in conjunction with obstetricians for all other clients), opened a labor lounge, altered labor rooms to do double duty as delivery rooms, and stated that clients could choose their own birth style. It immediately hired two social scientists to evaluate whether these changes were satisfying the demands of knowledgeable, consumer-conscious, low-risk clients. I was one of those hired.[2] We thus collected the data on which this paper is based within the context of a specific mandate. The sponsors of the project were not interested in the particular issues underlying my present concern.

The Data

We collected data in three stages from all clients who were served by a private group of obstetricians in MCHV; this group accounted for 80 percent of all births in the hospital during a six-month period in the winter of 1979–80. During the ninth month of their pregnancy we gave the women questionnaires about their previous birth experiences, their feelings about pregnancy and childbirth, and their choices for childbirth procedures. Three or four days after the women gave birth we interviewed them in the hospital, asking them about the birth itself. When the women returned to the doctor for a post-partum check-up (generally six weeks after birth) we gave them a second questionnaire, which asked for their feelings about the birth. A total of 322 women completed the first questionnaire (94 percent of those asked to participate in the evaluation study); 273 were interviewed in the hospital; and 226 completed the second questionnaire. The attrition rate of 30 percent was the result of a number of factors, including early hospital discharges and client failure to keep scheduled appointments. Equal numbers of working-class and middle-class women were lost in this process.

Independent Variables

There are three independent variables in this study: social class, preparation, and parity. The first of these is the most important.

1. *Social class:* Since I suspected that social class affected choices about childbirth, I sought a way to distinguish class position among the clients. I chose education as the best indicator: women with no more than a high school diploma were categorized as working class; those with at least four years of college were categorized as middle class. Women with some college education or vocational training beyond high school were assigned to a category on the basis of the type of job they held at the time of participation in the evaluation study, or their prior work experience.[3] These procedures resulted in a total of 127 working-class women and 124 middle-class women included in the analysis.

Information on client income was not available. In any case, the fact that my sample includes a small proportion of "voluntary poor"—highly educated women who chose subsistence farming or craft work as a way of life—made income a poor indicator. Nor could occupation alone be used. I found that differences in education made a significant difference in the kind of occupations the women held, either at the time of the study or prior to it, and the pattern of their work involvement. However, not all the women were working or reported ever holding jobs. Occupations of the husbands was also inappropriate, because I wanted a variable which would reflect the background experiences of the women themselves. Furthermore, whether a woman had a college education made a difference along a range of other experiences, such as whether she was a native of Vermont, her religion, and her age at the birth of her first child. I wanted to investigate whether education also made a difference in women's attitudes towards, and experiences during, childbirth. If it did, I could at least argue that childbirth, for these women, was experienced through a set of social mechanisms. I use the notions of middle class and working class to denote the two groups in my sample, although I am aware of the weakness of my indicator for examining social class.

2. *Preparation for childbirth:* There is a strong relationship between social class and formal preparation for childbirth. Seventy-nine percent of the middle-class women in my sample took childbirth classes, compared with 50 percent of the working-class women. The middle-class women also read an average of three

books about pregnancy and childbirth, compared with an average of one for working-class women. These two kinds of preparation were themselves related: women who took childbirth classes were more likely to read about pregnancy and childbirth than women who didn't. This naturally raises the question of whether I'm not, in fact, examining differences in knowledge rather than social class differences. My data do not support this conclusion. Among middle-class women, preparation for childbirth made little difference in the kinds of attitudes I am studying in this paper. Among working-class women, however, preparation for childbirth was extremely important: the attitudes of working-class women who were prepared for childbirth—whether through classes, reading, or a combination of both—were closer to those I defined as "middle-class" than the attitudes of their unprepared peers. Had I examined the unprepared women in each social class I would have found even greater differences between the two groups than I did when I combined the prepared and unprepared women. Therefore, preparation is not relevant to the issue of attitude, except insofar as the findings about class differences in preparation reinforce my fundamental conclusions. When preparation is relevant to my analysis, I mention it below.[4]

3. *Parity:* One would expect women who have given birth before (multiparas) to have different attitudes about childbirth compared to women who have never given birth (primiparas). Surprisingly, this was not the case. There were relatively few instances where multiparas and primiparas had different attitudes during the prenatal period about what they wanted, although parity was an important determinant of what actually happened once a woman entered the hospital: multiparous women were less likely to have births marked by extensive medical intervention. In those cases where parity was important, it had the same effects among middle-class women as it did among working-class women. Therefore, since parity—like preparation—is not crucial to most of the issues under consideration, I will discuss it only when it can help clarify my findings.

Attitudes toward Childbirth

The middle-class and working-class women I studied had different attitudes towards childbirth during pregnancy, different experiences during childbirth, and different post-partum evaluations of their experiences.

Attitudes during Pregnancy

Working-class women were more likely than middle-class women to have negative feelings about pregnancy [Table 1]. They were less likely to say they felt good about the way they looked or felt and they did not feel they received sufficient consideration from others. Pregnancy was not an unambivalently positive state for working-class women. There were obvious material causes for this attitude: working-class women were more likely to become pregnant by accident (39 percent) than middle-class women (22 percent) and less likely to have the resources with which to find space to rest and relax. Ideological issues may also have been at the root of these differences. Middle-class women felt that pregnancy, labor, delivery and the post-partum presence of a baby were

Table 1.   Client Attitudes towards Pregnancy, Labor, and Delivery during the Ninth Month of Pregnancy

Statements	Percentage of Working Class (N = 127)	Percentage of Middle Class (N = 124)
A. *Attitudes towards Pregnancy:*[a]		
When I'm pregnant people don't take my feelings seriously.	25	14
I like the way I look when I'm pregnant.	27	40
When I'm pregnant I feel well most of the time.	67	77
When I'm pregnant I feel depressed a lot of the time.	35	17
B. *Concerns about Labor and Delivery:*[b]		
I worry that I won't know when I'm in real labor.	50	30
I worry that I won't be able to bear the discomfort.	43	33
I worry that I don't know what is going to happen to me in the hospital.	36	25
I worry that I don't know enough about the process of childbirth.	32	17
I worry that my doctor won't be there for the birth of my baby.	49	31
I worry that the birth of my baby won't be the way I want it to be.	52	58
I worry that there will be something wrong with my baby.	49	31
I worry that I won't love the baby.	7	6
C. *General Attitudes towards Childbirth:*[a]		
I feel that the birth experience can affect the quality of the parent's relationship with the baby.	48	78
I feel that a natural childbirth will be best for my baby.	54	69

Notes:

a. Five response options were offered for these statements: "Strongly Agree," "Agree," "Neither Agree nor Disagree," "Disagree," and "Strongly Disagree." Percentages include those who gave either the "Agree" or "Strongly Agree' responses.

b. Four response options to indicate the importance of each of these concerns were offered for these statements: "Very Important," "Pretty Important," "Not Too Important," and "Not Important at All." Percentages include those who gave either the "Very Important" or the "Pretty Important" responses.

interrelated pleasures, and this was true regardless of either their preparation for childbirth or parity. Working-class women made a greater distinction between the stages that led to birth and the presence of the baby itself: the former was not necessarily desirable, though the latter was. As with middle-class women, these attitudes were unaffected by parity and preparation.

Furthermore, during pregnancy working-class women were more apprehensive than middle-class women about labor and delivery. They worried about their own knowledge and competence; they worried that they wouldn't know when they were actually in labor; they worried that they didn't know what would happen in the hospital. Clearly, the context in which birth occurred was somewhat threatening. In addition, working-class women were more worried than middle-class women about the discomfort of labor and delivery, and whether or not their personal physician would be present for the birth.[5] On the other hand, working-class and middle-class women had almost identical attitudes toward one birth issue and one issue pertaining to the baby itself: they all expressed strong concern about whether the birth would proceed according to personal desire, and they all felt certain that they would love the baby once it was born.

Among both groups, parity was relevant for all issues except concern about whether the baby would be healthy, and whether the mother would love it; those who had given birth before were less anxious. Yet among the primiparas within each social class the differences between the two social groups remain. Moreover, preparation for childbirth was related to concern about two issues: bearing the discomfort and having the birth as planned. However, in both groups those with more preparation were *more* concerned about these issues than were those with less preparation. Different levels of preparation do not account for the differences between the two groups.

Two additional questions in the questionnaire I gave to women in their ninth month of pregnancy were designed to elicit their *general* attitudes towards childbirth. The first of these asked clients whether they agreed with the statement: "I feel that the birth experience can affect the quality of the parent's relationship with the baby." Seventy-eight percent of middle-class women agreed with this statement, compared with 48 percent of working-class women. This indicates that middle-class women place more emphasis on the birth experience itself as a critical stage in becoming a parent. In response to a second question, 69 percent of middle-class women and 54 percent of working-class women agreed with the statement: "I feel that a natural childbirth will be best for my baby." This suggests that, not only do middle-class women think that the birth experience is significant in and of itself, but they have a *specific* idea about what kind of experience will be most appropriate.

Parity was not relevant to either of these attitudes. Among working-class women, preparation altered both attitudes; among middle-class women, only the feeling about a natural childbirth was affected by preparation. The class differences remained when I compared prepared women in each group (Nelson, 1982).

Similar differences between the middle-class and working-class women emerged when the multiparas within each group commented during pregnancy about how they would like the impending birth to differ from past ones.

Middle-class women and working-class women shared a desire to have a spouse or partner present during the birth if he was not present before. Women in both groups complained about the treatment they received, but the content of their complaints was not the same. Middle-class women complained in detail about personality conflicts with their doctors, mismanagement (by the staff) of various aspects of labor, and the fact that medication was offered too frequently. Working-class women complained mostly about the lack of information offered to them during labor and delivery.

There were other differences as well. Working-class women often mentioned medical complications and the discomfort of labor and delivery. They expressed a wish that the next birth be faster and easier—if necessary, through the use of more intensive medication. Two comments were typical: "I would have liked to have been put to sleep—it was a long and painful labor"; and "Next time I want a quicker labor—my first was only eight hours but the pains were hard and came every two minutes." Middle-class women rarely mentioned either the intensity of pain or the length of labor. They stressed instead obstacles to a pleasurable experience: "I did not see my baby being born"; and "I would have wanted a more creative delivery."

Both working-class and middle-class clients felt they had a right to evaluate the past performance of medical personnel: if any of the women felt constrained by the professionalism of the staff, the constraint did not totally inhibit subsequent evaluation. Women in both groups felt the medical structure could be modified. However, there were significant differences between the groups. Working-class women felt that the responsibility for providing information rested with the doctor. In addition, they wanted to reduce the length of labor and avoid medical complications. They wanted a birth marked by less pain. In contrast, middle-class women were looking for a pleasurable, and often "natural," experience, and a more cooperative—rather than instructional—relationship with the doctor.

Two issues must be considered in evaluating the women's responses to concrete questions about what they had wanted to happen when they entered the hospital to give birth: (1) whether the women even thought about the birth experience in detail during their ninth month of pregnancy; and (2) if so, what they wanted to have happen to them [Table 2].

1. With respect to the first issue, we can clearly divide the women into two groups: those who knew about and had already considered the different aspects of the birth process and those who had not. In fact, more middle-class women than working-class women considered the procedures surrounding birth: with the exception of the delivery site, less than 90 percent of the working-class women considered any of the procedures; over 95 percent of the middle-class women considered each of the procedures except artificial rupture of membranes, fetal monitoring, and position at birth. However, these differences between the groups were not found for those procedures directly related to family formation: having the husband present, watching the birth, and holding the baby after it is born. Over 90 percent of the women in *both* groups considered each of these procedures. Middle-class women as a group thus considered each step of the birth

Table 2 Prenatal Planning for Childbirth: Choices about Procedures and Hospital Events

Procedures	Percentage of Clients Who Had Thought about the Procedures		Percentage Who Wanted Each Procedure[a]		Hospital Events: Percentages of Clients Who Had Each Procedure		
	Working Class (N = 127)	Middle Class (N = 124)	Working Class	Middle Class	All Clients (N = 203)	Working Class (N = 105)	Middle Class (N = 98)
Shave	85	97	20 (47)	20 (67)	65	61	67
Enema	85	98	42 (55)	46 (68)	49	54	47
Labor Medication	81	98	57 (51)	11 (55)	44	50	35
Delivery Medication	84	96	58 (55)	17 (64)	41	52	30
Artificial Rupture of Membranes	44	68	59 (17)	4 (25)	70	69	75
Episiotomy	64	95	64 (14)	62 (37)	85	83	88
Fetal Monitoring	53	86	90 (31)	55 (44)	85	87	80
Lithotomy Position	64	77	—	—	75	84	67
Delivery Room Birth	90	95	80 (89)	45 (76)	87	96	82
IV Attached during Labor	—b	—	—	—	85	91	74
Forceps or Vacuum Suction	—	—	—	—	20	24	13
Support Person Present during Labor	96	100	88 (116)	98 (107)	94	96	98
Support Person Present during Delivery	93	100	83 (112)	96 (108)	87	83	94
Watch the Birth	91	92	89 (112)	93 (99)	45	44	46
Hold Baby at Birth	94	99	92 (106)	97 (111)	85	81	88

Notes:
a. Based on the number of clients, in parentheses, who made a choice—positive or negative—with respect to the procedure.
b. Items for which there are no data, as indicated by a dash, were not asked on the pregnancy questionnaire or, in the case of the lithotomy position, did not have simple response options.

331

process; a substantial minority of working-class women focused only on the final stage—the creation of a new family.

Parity was not relevant here, with the exception that those who had given birth before (in both groups) were less likely to say that they wanted medication during labor than those who had never before given birth. Preparation for childbirth was important here but, as indicated above, preparation changed the attitudes of working-class women but not the attitudes of middle-class women. Most of the unprepared working-class women had not thought about the issues; those who had wanted medical intervention (Nelson, 1982).

2. Among the women who actually thought about what they wanted to happen, there were differences in the content of their choices—differences which again corresponded to class. Working-class women selected medication during labor and delivery, artificial rupture of membranes, delivery room births, and fetal monitoring more often than middle-class women. The differences between the two groups on these issues ranged from 35 percent for delivery room births and fetal monitoring to 55 percent for the artificial rupture of membranes. Differences between the two groups with respect to the "social" aspects of birth were never more than 7 percent. Over 90 percent of both the middle-class and the working-class women chose to have the birth become an event in which they could participate by having a partner present during labor and delivery, watching the birth, and holding the baby as soon as it was born.

The working-class women seemed to be striving for speed (enema, episiotomy, artificial rupture of membranes), less pain (medication) and technological safety (delivery room birth, monitoring). They favored intervention because they thought it could bring the product easily, quickly, and safely. The middle-class women favored a process which entailed safety (as they defined it) and personal participation, but excluded medical intervention in a "natural" process.

In sum, the content of middle-class choices was "non-intervention." When middle-class women did not make choices, it was often because they wanted to leave control in the hands of the physicians or were unwilling to commit themselves in advance—not because they had not thought about the issues. "I'll let the doctor decide" was often how they responded to questions about their attitudes to specific procedures. Middle-class women selected this option more frequently than working-class women. In contrast, when working-class women made choices they favored intervention; when they didn't make choices it was more often because they had not thought about the issues.

Among working-class women there was a tension between not thinking about the impending event and preparing for it by making decisions, between avoidance and self-determinatioin. For the middle-class women the tension was between self-determination and reliance on professional expertise. Moreover, the goals of self-determination were also different for the two groups. Among middle-class women the goal was a . . . childbirth free from the prevailing medical and technological model embodied in the authority of the male physician. Working-class women sought freedom from the birth process itself through the use of strategies which would reduce pain and effort. Working-class women were not trying to give the experience a unique definition. They were trying to survive it with a minimum of embarrassment, discomfort, and isolation. There were exceptions to all of these generalizations. We can begin to speak about models only in the most general terms.

Experiences during Childbirth

Not only did working-class and middle-class women have different ideas about what they wanted to happen during childbirth, they also had different experiences during the actual birth. Working-class clients had births marked by more medical intervention and less client participation than middle-class women. To a certain extent these features are interrelated: the use of medication during labor and delivery makes it more likely that the delivery will take place in the delivery room and that forceps (or vacuum suction) will be required; the use of forceps ensures that an episiotomy will be necessary and that the client will have to be in a prone rather than sitting or semi-sitting position. And the more intervention, the less likely the woman is to be able to respond to the baby immediately.

Many middle-class women also had a great deal of intervention during labor and delivery: over 70 percent of them experienced an artificial rupture of membranes, an episiotomy, fetal monitoring, a delivery room birth, and forceps or vacuum suction. The proportion of middle-class women who had such intervention was less than for working-class women by more than 10 percent for the issues of labor and delivery medication, lithotomy position, delivery room birth, IV attached during labor, and forceps or vacuum suction. The middle-class women were more able to be active participants in the birth: they controlled the contractions with breathing techniques, pushed the baby out themselves, and held the baby as soon as it was born. Ninety-eight percent of them had a partner during labor and 94 percent had a partner present at the birth.

Parity was relevant to the birth experience in the same way within each group: primipara women had births which involved more extensive medical intervention. Preparation for childbirth influenced only the use of medication and the presence of a support person—and these only among working-class women. Therefore, preparation cannot explain the class differences (Nelson, 1982).

The difference between the births of middle-class and working-class clients corresponded roughly to what the women actually selected during pregnancy [Table 3]—although not, perhaps, to the motives behind the choices, in the case of working-class women. Working-class women wanted speedy access to the product. They didn't necessarily get speed, nor did they get the baby immediately. The middle-class concern with the entire process might have ensured a speedier labor and delivery and more immediate access to the baby (Doering *et al.*, 1980; Huttel *et al.* 1972; Zax *et al.*, 1975).

Neither working-class nor middle-class women had all their choices met during labor and delivery. The extent to which client choices about shaves, labor medication, episiotomies, watching the birth, and holding the baby were respected was about the same for both groups. But the two groups differed in the extent to which other choices were respected. More middle-class women than

Table 3   Discrepancy Between Choice and Event: Percentage of Clients Who Got
What They Wanted

Procedure	Working Class		Middle Class		Percentage Difference: Working Class v. Middle Class
	Percentage	*Number*	*Percentage*	*Number*	
Shave	65	(34)	56	(52)	9
Enema	50	(38)	65	(51)	-15
Labor Medication	59	(37)	59	(37)	0
Delivery Medication	53	(51)	78	(60)	-15
Artificial Rupture of Membranes	50	(20)	38	(13)	12
Episiotomy	67	(9)	61	(28)	6
Fetal Monitoring	87	(23)	58	(31)	29
Delivery Site	86	(66)	70	(60)	16
Support Person Present During Labor	86	(85)	98	(87)	-12
Support Person Present During Delivery	79	(84)	95	(87)	-16
Watch the Birth	48	(84)	44	(73)	4
Hold the Baby at Birth	83	(76)	84	(81)	-1

working-class women had their wishes met with respect to enemas, delivery
medications, and the presence of a support person during labor and delivery.
More working-class women had their way with respect to fetal monitoring,
artificial rupture of membranes, and the delivery site. The data do not indicate
that doctors impose their will on working-class clients more frequently than they
do on middle-class clients; nor do the data indicate that working-class clients are
less effective in stating what they want than are middle-class clients. Both
working-class and middle-class models of birth conflict with hospital protocol.
Women in neither group were entirely successful in getting their way.

Post-Partum Evaluations

In the second questionnaire after birth, I asked a final question about their
impressions of the experience: "If you were to tell a woman who had never given
birth what it was like, what would you say?" Both working-class and middle-
class women indicated that birth was worthwhile. But working-class women said
that it was worthwhile in spite of the pain because you have a baby at the end: "I
think it's worth it, a day of pain for all this." At the same time, many
working-class women said that they forgot about the pain quickly. They said
they wouldn't frighten other women, the way they had been frightened, with
predictions of pain, and that women shouldn't believe all the terrible things they
heard about giving birth.

Middle-class women had a very different set of ideas about what it was appropriate to tell a women who had never before given birth. First, they would focus on the process as an experience itself: "a high and painful experience"; "a fantastic experience." Second, they would talk about the work involved: "It's hard work; preparation is important"; and "Now I know why it is called labor. You really have to work." Third, they would be more likely to give details. Indirectly, they suggested that they had been told positive things about birth by their peers: "It's as good an experience as I had been told it was"; "It was even better than my friends said it would be."

These responses reveal a further basic difference between the two groups of women. The working-class women did not value the process of birth itself. They almost never used the word "experience." They focused, instead, on the product—the baby. Labor and delivery were something to be endured to get the product. Middle-class women valued the process as well as the product. They felt fortunate to be able to enjoy the experience of birth en route to motherhood.

Discussion

There are at least two possible explanations for the different attitudes of middle-class and working-class women towards birth, and for their different experiences during the birth process.

One possibility is that working-class women are simply more inhibited by the context in which birth occurs. They don't become interested in the birth process because they don't think that they can determine what is going to happen to them. Caught between medical experts and nature, they see little room for individual initiative. This is clearly an element of working-class disaffection with birth. But working-class feelings of impotence cannot entirely explain the particular nature of the choices that some working-class women make, particularly since these choices are *not* congruent with those of the professionals who manage their care.

A second possibility is that the greater interest of middle-class women in childbirth issues derives from greater knowledge. Not only are middle-class women more likely to prepare themselves for childbirth through reading and attending classes, but they draw on different kinds of information.[6] But these facts cannot entirely explain different attitudes either: the middle-class women hold their attitudes regardless of whether they have educated themselves about childbirth; the same is not true among working-class women: those who are prepared frequently hold different attitudes from those who are not. In any case, the search for information is probably the result—not the cause—of interest in childbirth.

Why, then, do working-class women remain uninterested in learning about childbirth? Why do they reject the middle-class ideology which not only stresses the value of information but holds as its goal a client-structured, "natural" childbirth? The answer lies in the contexts in which each group of women gives birth and in the fact that the movements that have created the middle-class model of the birth experience do not speak to both contexts equally.

The working-class women in our study started their families at a younger age, and at every subsequent age level had more children living in the home than did the middle-class women. The working-class women were more likely to have accidental pregnancies. Furthermore, when they chose to become pregnant, a small number of factors were taken into account, and these factors concerned only the family structure. Middle-class women were more likely to plan their pregnancies and the total number of children they wanted to have. As with working-class women, the ideal family structure was central to their thinking, but this factor was diluted by self concerns (work and career, child care facilities) and world concerns (overpopulation). Working-class women, then, had their children earlier, had more of them, and frequently had them without planning. They also had fewer material resources with which to raise these children.

The movements that created the "middle-class" model of birth experience do not clearly address the working-class context of childbirth. In the early 1960s, middle-class women were not very interested in childbirth; in the early 1970s only elite portions of the middle-class took childbirth classes or attempted to define birth independently of the prevailing, high-technology, medical model. The change came with the convergence of (and occasional tension among) four social movements: (1) the natural childbirth movement; (2) feminism; (3) consumerism; and (4) "back to nature" romanticism.

Advocates of natural childbirth initially glorified it as a step toward motherhood. The movement appealed largely to middle-class women who were eager to be more active participants in this important event but who continued to accept professional (as distinct from technological) control over it. The feminist movement, on the other hand, told many of these same women that it was time to reject the authority of men in specifically female experiences, in order to gain personal control of their lives and their bodies. Feminists also rejected the notion that childbirth was primarily important as a step towards motherhood. Consumerism advocated questioning attitudes towards any and all prevalent medical practices. And the "back to nature" movement advocated rejecting modern technology and returning to great-grandmother's way. None of these movements speaks to working-class women.

Natural childbirth preparation requires time, money, and a willing alliance with professionals. Within the feminist movement, the focus on middle-class concerns of access to professional jobs and consciousness-raising has alienated many working-class women who face employment problems of a very different cast and who are less able to live independent of their husbands' paychecks. Moreover, an "educated" contempt for professionals is easier for those who live among them than it is for those who may have to submit to experts in a wider range of life experiences. The failure of middle-class feminists to make contact with working-class concerns has been noted frequently: this analysis merely points to an additional consequence of this failure.

Consumerism depends on a steady income, mobility, and time. Middle-class women can afford to shop around for goods and services. But working-class women pay more out of necessity, not out of choice (Caplovitz, 1967); clinic clients see the doctor assigned to them. And a rejection of technology is the luxury of those who have already benefitted from it. That class of women who have always had access to the most sophisticated medical technology may make the decision to reject some aspects of that class privilege; those who have not yet consistently received these benefits may not be ready to abandon them.

In sum, I argue that the middle-class model of childbirth has its roots in social movements which do not have immediate relevance for working-class women. The model is also predicated of the idea of choice, the idea that one can take control of one's life and one's body (e.g., Boston Women's Health Book Collective, 1976). Working-class women have fewer opportunities for making choices; even pregnancy often appears to be outside their control.

The emerging model of hospital birth is, in fact, closer to the middle-class model than it is to the working-class model. Doctors have been greatly influenced by the criticisms of their most vocal clients and, in "progressive" hospitals, are making a conscious effort to "humanize" birth. Some of these changes may converge with working-class goals. But reducing the frequency with which medication is administered is foreign to working-class concerns and may seem like a threat to a woman (of any social class) who is unprepared to do without medication. In fact, doctors may use the middle-class model to force working-class compliance: one woman we interviewed said she was told by a doctor that if she "didn't stop yelling he would make [her] go natural."

Each of the two models of childbirth makes sense within the context of the lives its adopters lead. Each model confers benefits on the women who adhere to it. Each model may also have drawbacks. The middle-class model mystifies childbirth. Accepting it produces a sense of guilt and personal failure in women whose births fail to conform to its high standards. The working-class model engenders a dependence on a potentially harmful medication and creates an anxiety which can prolong and complicate labor.

This kind of evaluation brings me back onto thin ice. My reading and research suggest that a single model of childbirth has too often been held up for all women. Initially, doctors defined the experience for all women. Then one group of women began speaking for all women. But women are not a single, undifferentiated category. Childbirth is a biological experience mediated by class position. We have to learn more about what women at different locations in the social structure want for themselves rather than pass judgment on what they do. If changes are to come in either working-class or middle-class birth styles, they must come from the women themselves—not from one group of women speaking for another, or from doctors dictating to all of them.

Notes

1. Comaroff (1977) offers an alternative approach. She notes that within the medical world, the midwives and the physiotherapists have different paradigms of pregnancy, and that clients adopt one or the other of them (though sometimes sequentially). The clients are assumed not to bring with them their own paradigms of pregnancy but to be *tabula rasa* upon which competing health personnel write a script. Comaroff does not see social background determining which script is adopted, although she does acknowledge the influence of psychological factors.

2. The other was Helen McGough, who became director of the Mary Johnson Day Care Center in Middlebury, Vermont. Our evaluation of the maternity services (McGough and Nelson, 1981) showed that although most clients were pleased with the treatment they received, those clients who did not have the treatment they anticipated were less satisfied than those who got what they wanted. We also found that the medical staff was not giving full support to the innovations and that there remained a high level of medical intervention in childbirth.

3. I excluded all nurses and allied health workers from the study on the grounds that their perspective on birth would reflect their training and level of knowledge rather than their class position. In fact, most of the women with some college education or vocational training were nurses.

4. When I did include childbirth preparation as a variable, I measured it by attendance at a series of childbirth classes for the latest, or an earlier, pregnancy. For a more complete discussion of these issues, see Nelson (1982).

5. This is not related to the fact that more working-class women than middle-class women see doctors in a clinic rather than in a private office, since clinic patients, like private patients, are assigned a regular doctor whom they see at each prenatal visit. In fact, no client in the group practice was promised that her personal doctor would be present at the birth.

6. Working-class women were far more likely than middle-class women to say that they relied on mothers and other relatives to provide them with information about childbirth. The middle-class rejection of their mothers as a source of information about childbirth suggests that they were aware that the ideology about childbirth has changed since they themselves were born and that their mothers' retelling of a painful—but ultimately anesthetized—birth offered nothing to them. Working-class women felt that more information could be obtained from their mothers, indicating that they had not recognized the changes that have occurred since the time when they were born.

References

Boston Women's Health Book Collective. 1976. *Our Bodies, Ourselves*. New York: Simon and Schuster.

Caplovitz, David. 1967. *The Poor Pay More*. New York: The Free Press.

Comaroff, Jean. 1977. "Conflicting paradigms of pregnancy: Managing ambiguity in antenatal encounters." Pp. 115–134 in Alan Davis and Gordon Horobin (eds.), *Medical Encounters: The Experience of Illness and Treatment*. London: Croom, Helm Ltd.

Danziger, Sandra Klein. 1978. "The uses of expertise in doctor-patient encounters during pregnancy." *Social Science and Medicine* 12(5A):359–367.

Doering, Susan G., and Doris R. Entwisle. 1975. "Preparation during pregnancy and ability to cope with labor and delivery." *American Journal of Orthopsychiatry* 45(5):825–837.

Doering, Susan G., Doris R. Entwisle, and Daniel Quinlan. 1980. "Modeling the quality of women's birth experience." *Journal of Health and Social Behavior* 21(1):12–21.

Ehrenreich, Barbara, and Deidre English. 1973. *Witches, Midwives and Nurses*. Old Westbury, N.Y.: Feminist Press.

Enkin, N. W., S. L. Smith, S. W. Dermer, and J. D. Emmett. 1972. "An adequately controlled study of the effectiveness of PPM training." Pp. 62–67 in Norman Morris (ed.), *Psychosomatic Medicine in Obstetrics and Gynecology*. New York: S. Karger.

Gaziano, Emanuel P., Marlene Garvis, and Elaine Levine. 1979. "An evaluation of childbirth education for the clinic patient." Birth and the Family Journal 6 (Summer):89–94.

Haire, Doris. 1978. "The cultural warping of childbirth." Pp. 185–201 in John Ehrenreich (ed.), The Cultural Crisis of Modern Medicine. New York: The Monthly Review Press.

Hart, Nicky. 1977. "Parenthood and patienthood." Pp. 98–114 in Alan Davis and Gordon Horobin (eds.), Medical Encounters: The Experience of Illness and Treatment. London: Croom, Helm Ltd.

Hubert, Jane. 1974. "Beliefs and reality: Social factors in pregnancy and childbirth." Pp. 37–51 in Martin Richards (ed.), The Integration of a Child into a Social World. New York: Cambridge University Press.

Huttel, F. A., I. Mitchell, W. M. Fischer, and A. E. Meyer. 1972. "A quantitative evaluation of psychoprophylaxis in childbirth." Journal of Psychosomatic Research 16(2):81–92.

Ilsley, Raymond. 1967. "The sociological study of reproduction and its outcome." Pp. 45–141 in Stephen A. Richardson and Alan F. Guttmacher (eds.), Childbearing—Its Social and Psychological Aspects. Baltimore: Williams and Wilkins.

Kobrin, Frances E. 1966. "The American midwife controversy: A crisis of professionalization." Bulletin of the History of Medicine 40 (July–August):350–363.

McGough, Helen, and Margaret K. Nelson. 1981. "An evaluation of obstetric services at Medical Center Hospital of Vermont." Unpublished report, Department of Obstetrics and Gynecology, Medical Center Hospital of Vermont, Burlington.

Nash, Anedith, and Jeffrey E. Nash. 1979. "Conflicting interpretations of childbirth: The medical and natural perspectives." Urban Life 7(4):493–511.

Nelson, Margaret K. 1982. "The impact of childbirth classes on women of different social classes." Journal of Health and Social Behavior 23(4):339–352.

Norr, Kathleen L., Carolyn R. Block, Allan Charles, Suzanne Meyering, and Ellen Meyers. 1977. "Explaining pain and enjoyment in childbirth." Journal of Health and Social Behavior 18 (September):260–275.

Oakley, Ann. 1979. "A case of maternity: Paradigms of women as maternity cases." Signs: A Journal of Women in Culture and Society 4(4):607–631.

Shaw, Nancy Stoller. 1974. Forced Labor. New York: Pergamon Press.

Stewart, Mary, and Pat Erickson. 1977. "The sociology of birth: A critical assessment of theory and research." Social Sciences Journal 14 (April):33–47.

Wertz, Richard W., and Dorothy C. Wertz. 1977. Lying-In: A History of Childbirth in America. New York: Schocken Books.

Zax, Melvin, Arnold J. Sameroff, and Janet E. Farnum. 1975. "Childbirth education, maternal attitudes, and delivery." American Journal of Obstetrics and Gynecology 123(2):185–190.

Zimmerman-Tansella, C., G. Dolcetta, V. Assini, G. Zacche, P. Bertagni, R. Siani, and M. Tansella. 1979. "Preparation courses for childbirth in primipara: A comparison." Journal of Psychosomatic Research 23(4):227–233.

Technology and Motherhood:
Reproductive Choice Reconsidered

Robyn Rowland

All human life on the planet is born of woman. The one unifying, incontrovertible experience shared by all women and men is that months-long period we spent unfolding inside a woman's body. . . . Most of us first know both love and disappointment, power and tenderness, in the person of a woman. . . . We carry the imprint of this experience for life, even into our dying.[1]

Women, Men, and Procreation

In the last ten years, medical research has led to the creation of children through laboratory methods and without sexual intercourse. These technologies are creating a challenge to our understanding of the relationship between women and reproduction. The "test-tube baby" technique seems now to be a simple process compared to those currently being developed. For feminists, these new techniques mean rethinking our attitudes toward motherhood, pregnancy, and, most important, the relationship between an individual woman's right to exercise choice with respect to motherhood and the necessity for women to ensure that those individual choices do not disadvantage women as a social group.

Though we can develop positions on each technology, we must realize that they all form an interlocking chain leading us from the test-tube baby to eugenics and genetic engineering. In reality most of these new technologies are being developed in Western countries for use by white, middle-class, heterosexual women. Third World women struggle to feed their children, while Western women seek out expensive medical techniques to create more children. The new reproductive technologies discussed here will include only some of the techniques developed to assist an infertile woman (or in some cases a woman with an infertile husband) to conceive. It should be noted, however, that these technologies can be used by women who are not infertile or by those who may be infertile due to sterilization.

The women's movement of the 1960s characteristically rejected biological determinism and the nuclear family because these were seen to entrap women. Many women made the choice to be childfree. In this context motherhood

This article is based on papers written for the Fourth Women and Labour Conference, Brisbane, Australia, July 1984, and "Women's Worlds: 'Strategies for Empowerment,' " Interdisciplinary Congress, Groningen, The Netherlands, April 1984. From Robyn Rowland, *Signs* Vol. 12, No. 3 (Spring 1987): 512–528. Copyright© 1987 by The Univeristy of Chicago. All rights reserved. Reprinted by permission of The University of Chicago Press and the author.

became conflated with "the family" and with its rejection. Women were understood to have a variety of motivations for motherhood. They had children because they were socialized or conditioned to do so; because they were convinced of the rewards of mothering; in order to gain a self-identity in a world that continually denied this to them; to prove their worth and attain the status of a "mature adult"; or to consolidate a relationship. For many, motherhood represented a power base from which to negotiate the terms of their existence and survival. For many this is still the case.

In more recent years, however, another reevaluation of motherhood has begun that attempts to re-create the experience of motherhood and family in a nonexploitive way. A major text within this new perspective has been Adrienne Rich's *Of Woman Born: Motherhood as Experience and Institution.* Rich explores the *institution* of motherhood as a distorted and controlled experience at the expense of women for the benefit of men. She argues that it is the institutionalization of motherhood that is the problem, not the experience itself. Men, through their dominance within culture, have worked to divorce women from this experience because of the fear men have of the procreative power of women.[2]

In *The Politics of Reproduction,* Mary O'Brien maintains that some feminists have been too ready to leave reproduction out of their lives because of its history of entrapment. She advocates that we should in fact be using motherhood as a starting point for a new political theory: to redefine an understanding of gender relations beginning with reproduction. O'Brien claims that men have rituals and ritualistic meetings that reinforce their sex-based identity, but women do not. To celebrate being "female," O'Brien claims we need our own rituals, and the birth experience is a primary one that in the past was shared with other women. This tradition has been broken by the intervention of medical technologies in the birthing process.[3] As men became more involved in birthing and the general medical control of women's bodies, the emphasis in delivery moved away from the mother toward the newborn—away from women's ritual presence and toward the relationship between father and child. Reducing the isolation of women now in maternity hospitals is represented by the presence of the father, *not* by a reassembling of women's ritual presence.

O'Brien goes on to discuss what she calls "reproductive consciousness." In her terms, the first significant historical change was the discovery of physiological paternity, which transformed male reproductive consciousness: men discovered that they delivered the seed. The second and more recent change in reproductive consciousness was triggered by technology in the form of contraception: women gained the freedom to choose or reject parenthood. Women could thus control the role of the seed.

Because women labor at birth to bear children, women can be certain of their essential participation in genetic continuity, but men do not have this assurance. O'Brien includes all women in the female reproductive consciousness, since the experiences of menstruation, menopause, and pregnancy all indicate, in their own specific ways, the universal relationship of women to new life. Men have annulled male "alienation" from the reproductive process by their "appropriation of the child." Thus, by law or by force, men can control children *and* women.[4] Barbara Wishart, an Australian lesbian mother who conceived her daughter through artificial insemination by an unknown donor, reinforces the arguments of Rich and O'Brien. She writes that the experience of motherhood "has given me a deep bond with other mothers I know, and a sense of continuity, not only with the women in my own family, but also with the continuous line of women from antiquity to the present day who have borne children."[5] Wishart stresses that the experience of motherhood itself still has "something *positive* or *worthwhile* or even *wonderful* about it."[6]

Nancy Chodorow, in her book *The Reproduction of Mothering,* traces the way mothering is passed on from mother to daughter. She writes that women, by and large, want to mother, that they find mothering gratifying, and, finally, that with all the conflicts and contradictions, women have succeeded at mothering.[7] In her article on "maternal thinking," Sara Ruddick analyzes the qualities of thinking and caring that enforced mothering has developed in women. Thus, though the practice of enforced motherhood is oppressive, the best qualities of mothering or maternal thinking embody the kinds of caring we wish men, too, could express to others. These qualities stand in opposition to the destructive, violent, and self-aggrandizing characteristics of "masculinity." Ruddick insists that the only way of introducing these values into the political domain is to assimilate men into the private domain of child care. This would break down the separation of the two spheres, take the pressure off women to live vicariously through their children, and give men an investment in making the public domain more committed to reforming child-care practices. However, she warns, "in our eagerness we mustn't forget that so long as a mother is not effective publicly and self-respecting privately, male presence can be harmful as well as beneficial."[8]

Some are wary of this increased role for men in parenting.[9] One anxiety is that if men do get involved they will in fact take over, leaving many women with *no* sphere of influence: "He creeps in like another mother, between the mother and child."[10] A second anxiety stems from the fact that not all men are "good" fathers, as the rates of incest indicate.[11] Finally, with the intensification of male power inside the home comes the greater demand for a father's *rights* but not necessarily a parallel increase in his *responsibilities.* Jo Sutton and Sara Friedman outline this third anxiety by describing changes proposed in British law that specifically stress fathers' rights without an accompanying stress on their economic responsibilities to their children. Sutton and Friedman conclude, "What has resulted is a minimal change in caring and a significant move by men to increase their *rights* and, hence, control."[12] They comment that women in the 150 refuges for battered women will argue that "when a man has access to a child, he is able to use the child to further his own interests and to control that child's mother."[13]

In an ideological context where childbearing is claimed to be necessary for women to fulfill themselves, whether this is reinforced by patriarchal structures or by feminist values, discovering that you are infertile is a devastating experience.[14] The knowledge of one's infertility is a dramatic shock because we all assume our fertility and guard ourselves against its consequences. The testing process to detect infertility is extremely intrusive and exhausting. It can take from six months to six years for a woman finally to be diagnosed as infertile. In many instances, when the woman is in a heterosexual relationship, she is assumed to be the infertile partner, and tests are carried out on her before the man is tested.[15] Miriam Mazor has described the testing process as "assaultive": women are required to "expose their bodies for tests and procedures" and to "expose the intimate details of their sexual lives and their motivations for pregnancy."[16]

The experience of infertility has been called a life crisis. Part of that crisis comes from the knowledge that something over which a woman thought she had control was in fact not within her control. A woman may feel particularly frustrated and resentful if she has been using, for example, the pill or an intrauterine device for years only to find that birth control was unnecessary. The experience of infertility has been likened to the grief experienced after the death of a loved one. Barbara Eck-Menning discusses the experience of being isolated through infertility and of suddenly seeing fertility everywhere in the world except within yourself.[17] Naomi Pfeffer and Anne Woollett have stressed that the right of infertile women to have children is as imperative a right as that of being childfree.[18] Although the plight of infertile women clearly demands attention, the technologies supposedly developed to address their need for biological offspring affect us all. My concerns have gradually developed into one that focuses on the impact of these technologies on women as a social group.

Feminist arguments that have stressed the need for liberation from child-bearing are beginning to appear in some medical and ethical literature as a justification for developing those technologies. Shulamith Firestone maintained that women could be liberated from maternity through use of a test-tube baby-creating system. In 1972, she wrote, "Pregnancy is barbaric . . . the temporary deformation of the body of the individual for the sake of the species." Women, she said, should be freed from "the tyranny of reproduction by every means possible."[19] Some reproductive techno-patriarchs[20] claim this as feminist support for the artificial womb, conveniently ignoring Firestone's demands that power structures would need to change with the developing technology. Peter Singer and Deane Wells used Firestone's analysis to argue that feminists would support ectogenesis because it would "make a fundamental contribution toward sexual equality. Feminists who accept this argument will wish to see research into the development of complete ectogenesis pushed ahead with all due speed."[21]

In the past, when the new artificial means of conception have been discussed, some feminists may well have been receptive. But Firestone's discussion of the potential of artificial means of conception, for example, took place when asexual reproduction was not a reality. The techniques currently being developed are clearly not moving women toward greater freedom and liberation. In practice, mainly women who are white, middle class, and in a relationship with a man can have access to these technologies in Australia and Britain. In addition, techniques like in vitro fertilization (IVF) carry with them a false promise of success.

There are currently a number of feminist arguments against the new reproductive technologies.[22] Ruth Hubbard, for example, has argued against IVF on the grounds that it ties women's reproduction to marriage alone; that its complicated and closed training program for professionals excludes women from administering and controlling it, locking us all into a male-controlled high-technology model of birth; and that the enormous expense of it means offering minimal health care to other women.[23]

My own concerns have been developing around the issue of male control of reproductive technology; its inevitable route to eugenics and genetic engineering; and the issues of choice and control.[24] Barabara Ehrenreich and Deirdre English have clearly outlined the history of the gradual usurpation of the birth process by a male-dominated medical profession.[25] I would add that medical research is now expanding into the area of early pregnancy and conception, and that these moves represent the interests off masculine science in controlling women's bodies.

For feminists the issue then becomes one of choice versus control. Within the area of abortion, we claimed the "right to choose," but I argue that we mean the "right to control" our own bodies. We have then to ask whether the new reproductive technologies give women greater control over our lives. The evidence to date shows that they patently do not.[26] As Jalna Hanmer has pointed out, women lack input into the development of science and technology, but adding more women will not be a solution.[27] According to Rebecca Albury, "male domination doesn't necessarily require a majority of men. Some women have been socialised by the profession. 'Male control' doesn't essentially mean control by individual men, it means control which benefits men more than women most of the time. Far from each man exercising personal authority, things are much more complex. We live in a network of power relations that both defines 'masculinity' and ensures the success of individuals and activities that reinforce that definition."[28] The ethic of control in science, supported by the promise of professional and economic gain, has encouraged research on reproductive technologies. The unwillingness of scientists to consider the social implications of their work has allowed them to expand research in this area without community debate. However, the argument that they are addressing the needs of women is beginning to look less altruistic as their efforts to generate profits intensify.[29]

New Reproductive Technologies

In Vitro Fertilization

As with all of these developments, IVF began with animal experimentation. According to Gena Corea, the experiment progressed from mice to rats to sheep to cows to women. It was not tested in higher primates.[30] For humans the process involves taking an egg from a woman and sperm from her husband or partner, then putting the two together within fluid in a petri dish. This led to the phrase "test-tube baby." The resulting embryo is then placed back inside a woman's uterus for implantation and, it is hoped, pregnancy. It was originally designed for women who were infertile for reasons such as blocked or diseased fallopian tubes. Variations on this technique include surgical extraction of sperm for in vitro fertilization; the use of sperm from an unknown donor; the use of donor eggs; and, finally, the use of a donor embryo—an embryo that is not the genetic material of either the woman into whom it is transplanted or the social father.

The woman who is involved in IVF usually has undergone a series of exhaustive and intrusive tests over a period of many years. The IVF cycle lasts for about two weeks, with the monitoring of the woman for her daily plasma levels, cervical mucus, and ultrasound examinations to determine ovarian progress. The woman is then involved in inpatient care with hormonal assays, the laparoscopic collection of eggs, and, if egg collection is successful, fertilization and embryo transfer. The laparoscopy to collect eggs is not without the normal risks of general anaesthesia and surgery. In addition, most of the women are superovulated. This means they are given doses of hormones or fertility drugs to increase the number of eggs that their bodies will produce per cycle, usually five or six eggs, but instances have occurred where women have been superovulated to produce up to eleven eggs.[31] The major risk here is that the ovaries will be hyperstimulated, but there are a number of other possible side effects as well.[32]

The promises by the "technodocs" of a solution to infertility have been misleading at best.[33] What they have sometimes produced is a technological product—the baby. But a baby is not a cure for infertility, and even this promise of a child has been a false promise for most couples. The success rates of in vitro fertilization are extremely low and vary greatly across clinics. Australian national figures from the Perinatal Statistics Unit, 1979—84, indicate that 909 pregnancies took place in eleven centers. Only 54 percent resulted in *live* births. There were 5 percent ectopic pregnancies and 25 percent spontaneous abortions. In addition, 34 percent—or four times that of the normal population— of the babies born had a low birth weight, with all the encumbent dangers to the child.

The perinatal mortality rate is also four times that of the normal population. In addition, 43 percent of births were by cesarean section. Of those who became pregnant, 53 percent had had previous pregnancies. Some probably lost children through abortion or miscarriage and then became infertile. Some were sterilized in a previous marriage and now wanted a child with a second husband.[34]

The figures indicate that, on the average, for every 100 women who go into an IVF program in Australia and Britain, at least eighty-six of them will never become pregnant.[35] Internationally, however, clinics continuously announce more encouraging (20–25 percent) but less accurate rates. A recent survey in the United States found that, of fifty-four clinics questioned, half had never sent a patient home with a baby. Yet, as Gena Corea and Susan Ince indicate, these clinics still claim success rates of 25 percent.[36] Doctors questioned in this survey indicate that the highest rate for IVF births in Australia is 10 percent. "Success rates" should more accurately be called "failure figures."

The medical profession itself is very concerned about the misleading information given to the public. In a recent editorial in *Fertility and Sterility,* doctor Michael Soules writes that the truth about IVF procedures has been widely abused, "primarily by IVF practitioners." He details the way in which medical researchers have manipulated the statistics and places the blame unquestionably on IVF practitioners.[37]

The financial cost has been found in one Australian study by Ken Mao and Carl Wood to be the main reason for withdrawal from programs. It costs patients in Australia up to $3,000 Australian per attempt, and about two-thirds of this is refundable through medical insurance. Other costs are involved too; taking time off from work, traveling, and staying in hotels. This study reported that couples also withdrew because of the emotional costs: anxiety, depression, disruption of a normal life and of work and career, and the strain placed on the marriage. Mao and Wood estimate a 43 percent dropout rate, which they consider to be high.[38] These costs are only a portion of the overall expense, including the costs to society in terms of the diversion and commitment of medical expertise, staff, research funding, hospital facilities, and now, in Australia, extensive counseling services—all for a basically *unsuccessful* technology.

The cost to participating women is more difficult to quantify. Their bodies are used as living laboratories. One recent study carried out by Barbara Burton, herself a patient on an IVF program, suggests that the kind of issues arising in this area are identical to those women confront constantly in their relationship with a male-dominated medical profession. The women speak of the lack of dignity of the process, the lack of information given to them, the lack of concern from the medicos involved, and the fact that doctors ignore the women's experiences with the various drugs given to them. One woman, discussing the lack of dignity, said, "You feel like a piece of meat in a meat-works. But if you want a baby badly enough you'll do it." The stress women experience when the program fails them and they do not get pregnant is enormous. They experience it as a personal failure rather than a failure of the technology. In reaction to failure, one woman said: "My husband went to pieces, I felt I was dying, I was really crook [ill], but I didn't let any pent-up emotions come out, I had to look after him."[39]

The women in Burton's study report the inability of the doctors to talk to them about this experience: "I would really have liked to have gone back and talked to [my gynecologist] after it didn't work, but as [the IVF scientist] says, 'You're history, we're on to the next one, we haven't time for you now, we want to get on with it.'" This same IVF scientist also commented: "One way the teams cope with failure is to avoid follow-up contact with failed patients." Many of the women were anxious about being used as guinea pigs. One wrote, "The professor tells us that according to the labels and his books they [the drugs] don't have side effects. Once someone comes out and is brave enough to say you get side effects, other women say so too. I think that's what he's worried about, that side effects are catching." And another, "I sometimes get concerned [about] what's going to happen to us in ten to fifteen years time. Our generation were guinea pigs for the Dalkon Shield, and now we're guinea pigs for a new form of modern technology."[40]

Surrogate Embryo Transfer

This is often called lavage. I call it "flushing." This technique uses a fertile woman as an incubator for the first few days of life of the embryo. She is inseminated with the sperm of the husband of an infertile woman, conceives, and the embryo is then flushed from her body and placed in the infertile woman if all goes well. If all does not go well, the incubator woman may become pregnant or miscarry, and if the pregnancy is viable she will have to choose either to abort or to carry the child to full term. She may experience pelvic infection and/or ectopic pregnancy, "either one of which could terminate her physiological reproductive career."[41]

In North America, this procedure has already been used. The results of twenty-nine flushings after artificial insemination of nine donor women (using sperm from the husbands of twelve infertile women) were twelve embryos. These were transferred to the infertile women, yielding two successful pregnancies and one ectopic pregnancy, which had to be surgically removed. One donor woman had a "retained pregnancy" that aborted spontaneously.[42]

If flushing were to become regularly used, the donor would eventually face the same superovulation that IVF patients currently undergo. This would be the next logical step. Leroy Walters, in the *Journal of the American Medical Association,* warns of the "potential risks of uterine lavage—and, in the future, of possible superovulation to the embryo donor."[43] Indeed, the researchers responsible for the application of this technique have indicated that they feel "donor fecundity needs to be improved."[44] In Australia, the ethics committee of the National Health and Medical Research Council, under pressure from feminists, has put a moratorium on surrogate embryo transfer for the time being.[45]

Cloning

Cloning has been successfully carried out with frogs and mice.[46] Basically, the offspring has the genetic constitution identical to that of the "parent" who donated the original cell nucleus. Chilling statements have emerged in the medical and ethical literature, such as that by American Nobel laureate Joseph Lederberg, who commented that "we would at least enjoy being able to observe the experiment of discovering whether a second Einstein would outdo the first one."[47] Jane Murphy claims that, within the literature on cloning, "women are viewed as passive physical material for the cloning process: ovaries, eggs, uteri. Meanwhile, men are seen as 'parents' of clonal offspring— simply by donating a set of chromosomes."[48]

Sex Predetermination

This can now be attempted at two stages: during pregnancy or before conception itself.[49] During pregnancy, amniocentesis or ultrasound can be used to assess the sex of the fetus, so that the parents can abort the fetus if it is of an unwanted sex. Sex predetermination before conception is being developed as a method to separate out the male-determining from the female-determining sperm.[50] In fact a sperm-washing technique is being used in North America in at least seven clinics by a company called Gametrics Ltd. It is 75 percent successful for selecting boys. The company has patented the method.[51]

Most studies have indicated that most societies are male-preferring.[52] With the introduction of these techniques the sex-ratio balance may be severely disrupted. In India, where amniocentesis followed by the abortion of female fetuses is on the increase, this is already happening. Madhu Kishwar has documented a shift in the sex-ratio balance since 1901. In that year, there were 972 women per 1,000 men, but by 1981 there were only 925 women per 1,000 men. In other words, in 1901 there were 9 million more men than women and, by 1981, there were 22 million more men than women.[53] The result of such practices may be, as Colin Campbell says, "more of everything, in short, that men do, make, suffer, inflict and consume."[54]

Ectogenesis

This is the scientific term for growth of the fetus *outside* the womb. At Stanford University in the United States, scientists have developed an artificial womb or fetal incubator. Oxygen and nutrients are pumped into it, and young human fetuses that are products of spontaneous abortion have been kept alive for up to forty-eight hours.[55]

From the birth end of the continuum of pregnancy, younger and younger premature babies are now kept alive in increasingly sophisticated artificial environments, possible now from twenty-four weeks into the pregnancy. If we consider the process from the other end, that is, from the point where an embryo is created in vitro, we find that it is possible to keep them alive at least until the thirteenth or fourteenth day. Researchers need only find an artificial environment that would bridge the gap of fourteen days to twenty-four weeks. The real problem with ectogenesis is in perfecting the artificial placenta. When this succeeds, an egg could be fertilized and brought to term within an artificial or "glass" womb.[56]

Development of the artificial womb has been promoted as having the following advantages: fetal medicine would be improved; the child could be immunized while still inside the "womb"; the environment would be safer than a woman's womb; geneticists could program in some superior trait on which society would agree; sex preselection would be simple; women would be spared the discomfort of childbirth; women could be permanently sterilized; and, finally, a man would be able to prove beyond a doubt that he is the father of the child. Children may then be created who are neither borne by, nor born of, woman.[57]

Impact on Women

Increased technological intervention into the processes by which women conceive is increasing the male-dominated medical profession's control of procreation and will lead inevitably to greater social control of women by men.[58] Already, the language of reproductive technology vividly illustrates the degree to which women's bodies are dehumanized with discussions of "harvesting" of eggs and "uterine environments." Linked with the emergence of these technologies is the development of a concept of a "surrogate mother." The term itself is a misnomer. The woman is in no way a surrogate and is *in fact* the biological mother of the child. By naming her as a surrogate, commercial enterprises can more easily control and exploit the woman's pregnancy by denying her biological relationship to her child.

The issues within surrogacy are too complex to debate here, but, briefly, surrogacy promotes the economic, physical, and emotional exploitation of women. A woman who contracts her body as a "surrogate" mother agrees to give up control over her pregnant body in return for money. She faces the possible future of grieving similar to that experienced by women who relinquished their children for adoption.[59]

There is also an increasing debate occurring concerning the rights of the fetus to be treated as a "patient," which stems from the way reproductive technologies are splitting women from the embryo/fetus. Discussions of the fetus as "patient" are horrifying in their representation of women as merely the capsules or containers for the fetus.[60] In debates concerning coerced cesarean section, physicians have claimed the right to restrain a woman and do the surgery under a court order if the woman refuses surgery and the fetus is said to be at risk.[61]

Commercialization of the new reproductive technologies and of surrogacy have led to the promotion of research for profit (as opposed to public health services). These technologies also attract huge government funding in Australia, drawing research and funding away from the less glamorous work on the prevention of infertility.

Research on surrogate embryo transfer was not funded by the National Institute of Health but by Fertility and Genetics Research Incorporated, a Chicago-based for-profit company. Three of the researchers working for this company have been offered shares in it. The company has applied for a patent both on the instruments used in the procedure and on the *process* itself.[62] If granted, it would mean that this company owned and controlled both the instruments and the process, thereby restricting evaluation by other researchers and empowering the company to deny information and use of the technique.

In Australia, the Monash University IVF team, headed by Carl Wood, has entered into a commercial enterprise. The details of this company, IVF Australia, nearly two years after negotiations first began, have still not been released to either the university council or the public who funds the institution. The shroud of secrecy around IVF Australia has been seen as a threat to academic freedom, to scientific scrutiny, to public access to tax-supported research information, and, of course, to public control and scrutiny.[63] Such a collaboration between research and commercial interests uses women in essentially experimental programs and asks the participants and the public to underwrite the expense so that the researchers can enter into commercial contracts for profit. In addition, commercializing the processes of reproduction underscores a perception of a child as a product, a product that will eventually be "custom" designed.

The validation of white middle-class definitions of the perfect baby; an inability to accept infertility, mortality, and imperfection; and the impact on human society of the split between sexuality and procreation are just a few of the problematics of this scenario.[64] Because women, even in patriarchal culture, have always retained without question the power and responsibilities of reproduction, the new technologies have disturbing implications for our lives. For many women—past, present, and future—childbearing represents the major power base they have from which to negotiate the terms of their existence. But as Leon Kass, a doctor himself, has said, power "rests only metaphorically with humankind; it rests in fact with particular men, geneticists, embryologists, obstetricians."[65] Men run the governments, train the doctors, make birth-control devices, allocate research grants, decide on the availability of abortion, run the companies that will market the products, and make the money. As Jalna Hanmer and Pat Allen have said, women act as agents of male individual and social power.[66] We continue to collude to our own disadvantage.

The renewed positive attitude toward motherhood explored in the first part of this paper assumes that all women can voluntarily and easily become pregnant through sexual intercourse. It was emerging before the technologies discussed here came into existence. Ironically, this move to value positively women's role in reproduction has given technopatriarchs within medical research a justification for their continuing control of and experimentation with women's bodies, in the name of the power of mothering.

Within the context of biomedical research and its complement, genetic engineering, we need to reassess what "choice" is for women. As Barbara Katz Rothman has commented, in gaining the choice to control the quality of our children, we may lose the choice *not* to control the quality, that is, the choice of simply accepting them as they are. She points out that we also forfeit the right *not* to know some things, like the sex of the unborn child.[67] One of the basic tenets of the women's movement has been to secure and protect a right of choice with respect to sexuality and reproduction. We demanded the right to choose whether to have children or not and gained the double-edged access to contraception and abortion.

In the past, these choices opened up opportunities for women as a social group. But what of a choice that closes opportunities for the majority of women and places our future at risk? Does the desire, the need, the wanting of choice have no limits? If a time comes when the rights of one group of women place the majority of women in a dangerous position, does not the concept and terminology of rights become meaningless? Some would argue that the principle of freedom of choice may be second to that of "fairness" and equal treatment.[68]

It may be that stressing the value of choice gives the medical profession more, and not less, control in terms of reproductive technologies. The right to choose the sex of your child; the right to use donor ova; the right to use or to be a surrogate mother; and the right of the medical profession to service these rights and make money out of them have evolved tacitly as new biomedical developments are made available. And that *is* what we wanted with abortion and contraception: the availability of options.

Kass has commented that "the advent of these new powers for human engineering means that some *men* may be destined to play God, to re-create other *men* in their own image" (emphasis added).[69] Where will women's place be in this new society? Will we be obsolete, permanently unemployed, disposable? Have we learned anything from experiences like those associated with the pill and the Dalkon Shield? As Roberta Steinbacher says, "Who invented it, who manufactured it, who licensed it, who dispenses it? But who dies from it"?[70]

Notes

1. Adrienne Rich, *Of Woman Born: Motherhood as Experience and Institution* (London: Virago, 1977), 11.
2. Ibid.
3. Mary O'Brien, *The Politics of Reproduction* (London: Routledge & Kegan Paul, 1981).
4. Ibid., 33, 36. As O'Brien puts it, "Men are necessarily rooted in their biology, and their physiology is their fate" (ibid., 192).
5. Barbara Wishart, "Motherhood within Patriarchy: A Lesbian Feminist Perspective," *Third Women and Labour Conference Papers* 1 (1982): 23–31.
6. Ibid., 27, Wishart's italics.
7. Nancy Chodorow, *The Reproduction of Mothering: Psychoanalysis and the Sociology of Gender* (Berkeley: University of California Press, 1978).
8. Sara Ruddick, "Maternal Thinking," *Feminist Studies* 6, no. 2 (1980): 432–67, esp. 461.
9. Scarlet Pollock and Jo Sutton, "Fathers' Rights, Woman's Losses," *Women's Studies International Forum* 8, no. 6 (1985): 593–600.
10. Elizabeth Badinter, *The Myth of Motherhood: An Historical View of the Maternal Instinct* (London: Souvenir Press, 1981), 324.
11. See e.g., Elizabeth Ward, "Rape of Girl-Children by Male Family Members," *Australian and New Zealand Journal of Criminology* 15 (1982): 90–99, and *Father-Daughter Rape* (London: Women's Press, 1984).
12. Jo Sutton and Sara Friedman, "Fatherhood: Bringing It All Back Home," in *On the Problem of Men,* ed. Sara Friedman and Elizabeth Sarah (London: Women's Press, 1982), 125. Their emphasis.
13. Ibid., 124.
14. See Robyn Rowland, "Women as Living Laboratories, the New Reproductive Technologies," in *The Trapped Women: Catch-22 in Deviance and Control,* ed. Josefina Figueira-McDonough and Rosemary Sarri (New York: Sage Books, 1987).
15. Barbara Eck-Menning, *Infertility: A Guide for the Childless Couple* (Englewood Cliffs, N.J.: Prentice-Hall, Inc., 1977); and Miriam D. Mazor, "Barren Couples," *Psychology Today* 12 (1979): 101–12.
16. Mazor, 104.
17. Eck-Menning.
18. Naomi Pfeffer and Anne Woollett, *The Experience of Infertility* (London: Virago, 1983).
19. Shulamith Firestone, *The Dialectic of Sex* (London: Paladin, 1971), 188, 193.
20. I am indebted to Renate Duelli Klein for this term.
21. Peter Singer and Deane Wells, *The Reproduction Revolution: New Ways of Making Babies* (Melbourne: Oxford University Press, 1984), 137. See also William Walters, "Cloning, Ectogenesis, and Hybrids; Things to Come?" in *Test-Tube Babies: A Guide to Moral Questions, Present Techniques and Future Possibilities,* ed. William Walters and Peter Singer (Melbourne: Oxford University Press, 1982).
22. See, e.g., Rita Arditti, Renate Duelli Klein, and Shelley Minden, eds., *Test-Tube Women: What Future for Motherhood?* (London: Pandora Press, 1984); Gena Corea et al., eds., *Man-Made Women: How the New Reproductive Technologies Affect Women* (London: Hutchinson, 1985); Gena Corea, *The Mother Machine: From Artificial Insemination to Artificial Wombs* (New York: Harper & Row, 1985).
23. Ruth Hubbard, "The Case against In Vitro Fertilization and Implantation," in *The Custom-Made Child? Women-Centered Perspectives,* ed. Helen Holmes, Betty Hoskins, and Michael Gross (Clifton, N.J.: Humana Press, 1981).

24. See, e.g., Robyn Rowland, "Reproductive Technologies: The Final Solution to the Woman Question?" in Arditti et al., 356–70; "Motherhood, Patriarchal Power, Alienation and the Issue of 'Choice' in Sex Preselection," in Corea et al.; and "A Child at Any Price? An Overview of Issues in the Use of the New Reproductive Technologies and the Threat to Women," *Women's Studies Internatioinal Forum* 8, no. 6 (1985): 539–46.

25. Barbara Ehrenreich and Deirdre English, *For Her Own Good: 150 Years of the Experts' Advice to Women* (New York: Anchor Books, 1978).

26. I am currently expanding this argument. See Robyn Rowland, "Choice or Control? Women and Our Relationship to the New Reproductive Technologies" (paper delivered at the conference "Liberation or Loss? Women Impact on the New Reproductive Technologies," Canberra, Australia, May 1986).

27. Jalna Hanmer, "Transforming Consciousness," in Corea et al., 98–99.

28. Rebecca Albury, "Reproductive Technology and Feminism," *Australian Left Review,* no. 89 (Spring 1984), 46–55, esp. 47.

29. A public outcry followed the establishment of IVF Australia at Monash University. See, e.g., Philip McIntosh, "Community Group Calls on Uni. to Reveal IVF Details," *The Age* (March 29, 1985), and "Secret In Vitro Plan Angers Academics," *The Age* (March 20, 1985). Also, Calvin Miller, "IVF: Who Will Reap the Profits?" *Australian Doctor* (March 6, 1985).

30. Corea (n. 22 above).

31. Carl Wood, "In Vitro Fertilization—the Procedure and Future Development" (paper delivered at the Conference on Bioethics, St. Vincent's Bioethics Centre, Melbourne, Australia, May 1984).

32. Pfeffer and Woollett (n. 18 above); B. Henriet et al., "The Lethal Effect of Super-Ovulation on the Embryos," *Journal of In Vitro Fertilization and Embryo Transfer* 1, no. 2 (1984); Gabor Kovacs et al., "Induction of Ovulation with Human Pituitary Gonadotrophin," *Medical Journal of Australia* (May 12, 1984), 575–79.

33. "Technodocs" indicates doctors involved in technological processes in this field. The word was coined by Renate Duelli Klein.

34. Perinatal Statistics Unit, *In Vitro Fertilization Pregnancies, Australia and New Zealand; IVF Figures, Australia and New Zealand. 1979–1984* (Sydney, Australia: University of Sydney Publication, 1986).

35. There are various ways of presenting IVF statistics, and each method yields a different result. David Davies, a member of the Warnock Committee in Britain, cited success rates there of 10–15 percent (paper delivered at the YWCA conference, "A Child at Any Price?," Exeter, England, November 1984). Michael Soules notes a worldwide average of 13 percent pregnancy rate per cycle ("The In Vitro Fertilization Rate: Let's Be Honest with One Another," *Fertility and Sterility* 43, no. 4 [April 1985]: 511–13).

36. Gena Corea and Susan Ince, "IVF: A Game for Losers at Half of U.S. Clinics," *Medical Tribune* 26, no. 19 (1985): 11–13.

37. Soules. Soules names the commercialization of IVF as the reason for misleading statistics: "Competition appears to be the root of the problem. . . . Many IVF programs in this country are struggling to treat a sufficient patient volume to maintain the program. . . . The widespread practice of exaggerating the IVF pregnancy rate appears to be a marketing ploy" (ibid., 513).

38. Ken Mao and Carl Wood, "Barriers to Treatment of Infertility by In-Vitro Fertilization and Embryo Transfer," *Medical Journal of Australia* (April 28, 1984), 532–33.

39. Barbara Burton, "Contentious Issues of Infertility Therapy—a Consumer's View" (paper delivered at the Australian Family Planning Association Annual Conference, March 1985), 5, 8.

40. Ibid., 9.

41. Howard Jones, "Variations on a Theme," editorial, *Journal of the American Medical Association* 250, no. 16 (1983): 2182–83.

42. Maria Bustillo et al., "Non-Surgical Ovum Transfer as a Treatment in Infertile Women," *Journal of the American Medical Association* 251, no. 9 (1984): 1171–73. See also Robyn Rowland, "A Child at Any Price?" (n. 24 above).

43. Leroy Walters, "Ethical Aspects of Surrogate Embryo Transfer," editorial, *Journal of the American Medical Association* 250, no. 16 (1983): 2183.

44. Bustillo et al., 1173.

45. Philip McIntosh, "Research Council Rejects Surrogate Embryo Transfer," *The Age* (February 22, 1985).

46. See Jane Murphy, "From Mice to Men? Implications of Progress in Cloning Research," in Arditti et al. (n. 22 above).

47. Joseph Lederberg. "Experimental Genetics and Human Evolution," *Bulletin of the Atomic Scientists* 22 (1966): 4–11, esp. 10.

48. Murphy, 87.

49. Betty Hoskins and Helen B. Holmes, "Technology and Prenatal Femicide," in Arditti et al. (n. 22 above).

50. Rowland, "A Child at Any Price?" (n. 24 above).

54. See Richard Lyons, "Ordering Your Baby's Sex: Is It Playing God?" *Sydney Morning Herald* (May 30, 1984); Ferdinand Beernick and Ronald Ericsson, "Male Sex Selection through Sperm Isolation," *Fertility and Sterility* 38, no. 4 (1982): 493–95.

52. Rowland, "Motherhood, Patriarchal Power, Alienation and the Issue of 'Choice' in Sex Preselection" (n. 24 above); Nancy Williamson, *Sons or Daughters? A Cross-Cultural Survey of Parental Preferences* (London: Sage Publications, 1976).

53. Madhu Kishwar, "The Continuing Deficit of Women in India and the Impact of Amniocentesis," in Corea et al. (n. 22 above).

54. Colin Campbell, "The Manchild Pill," *Psychology Today* (August 1976), 86–91, esp. 88. For a negative vision, see also John Postgate, "Bat's Chance in Hell," *New Scientist* 5 (1973):11–16, esp. 16.

55. Rosalind Herlands, "Biological Manipulations for Producing and Nurturing Mammalian Embryos," in Holmes et al. (n. 23 above).

56. John Buuck, "Ethics of Reproductive Engineering," *Perspectives* 3, no. 9 (1977):545–47.

57. Edward Grossman, "The Obsolescent Mother: A Scenario," *Atlantic* 227 (1971):39–50.

58. There is no space to detail here the increasing links between IVF development and genetic engineering. But see, e.g., "DNA Libraries Are Now Being Built for Genetic Studies," *University Bulletin,* 33, no. 17 (January 1985); Christopher Joyce, "Human Genetic Experiment Likely Soon," *New Scientist* 19 (January 1984):7.

59. See Susan Ince, "Inside the Surrogate Industry," in Arditti et al. (n. 22 above), 99–116; and Corea (n. 22 above).

60. Ruth Hubbard, "The Fetus as Patient," *Ms. Magazine* (October, 1982), 31–32; Corea.

61. Sally Koch, "Treatment of Gravida against Her Wishes Debated," *OB Gyn News* 20, no. 9 (January 1985):26–27; "Some Guidance Emerging on Rights of Fetus, Neonate," *OB Gyn News* 20, no. 10 (May 1985):17; Claudine Escoffier-Lambiotte, "The Fetal Medicine Debate: The Controversy over 'Pre-Birth' Intervention," *World Press Review* (September 30, 1983), 34–36.

62. George Annas, "Surrogate Embryo Transfer: The Perils of Patenting," *Hastings Centre Report* (June 1984), 25–26.

63. McIntosh, "Secret In Vitro Plan Angers Academics" (n. 29 above); Nigel Wood, "Monash and IVF—Why the Secrecy?" *Journal of Advanced Education* (July 1985), 5; Rosemary West and Claire Miller, "IVF Investment Questioned," *The Age* (May 12, 1986), 3.

64. Women will also be differentially disadvantaged by reproductive technology depending on race and class with respect to access to programs. However, I point this out *only* in order to show how women are divided into worthy and unworthy mothers, depending on race and class. I do not argue for equal access in this case because that would be tantamount to supporting yet another system by which they would be exploited.

65. Leon Kass, "Making Babies—the New Biology and the 'Old' Morality," *Public Interest* (Winter 1972), 13–56.

66. Jalna Hanmer and Pat Allen, "Reproductive Engineering: The Final Solution?" in *Alice through the Microscope: The Power of Science in Women's Lives,* ed. Brighton Women and Science Group (London: Virago, 1980).

67. Barbara Katz Rothman, "The Meanings of Choice in Reproductive Technology," in Arditti et al. (n. 22 above).
68. Tabitha Powledge, "Toward a Moral Policy for Sex Choice," in *Sex Selection of Children*, ed. Neil Bennett (New York: Academic Press, 1983).
69. Kass, 45.
70. Roberta Steinbacher, "Futuristic Implications of Sex Pre-Selection," in Holmes et al. (n. 23 above), 187–92, esp. 189.

Gender-Role Orientations in Older Child-Free and Expectant Couples

Kristine M. Baber and Albert S. Dreyer

One of the first cohorts of women to delay childbearing in significant numbers is now making the transition to parenthood—or committing themselves to a child-free lifestyle. It is of particular interest that couples who delay having their first child until later in their adult life appear to be very similar demographically to couples committed to a child-free lifestyle. Both groups tend to be better educated, tend to have a higher degree of labor-force participation by women, tend to have a higher income, and tend to be more egalitarian than couples who have their first child early in their adult lives (Bram, 1978; Feldman, 1981; Veevers, 1979; Wilkie, 1981). Both groups appear very similar, and yet some of these couples decide to have a child while others remain child free.

It is proposed that the cohort of women who are now in their 30s, especially those among them who are highly educated, are a unique group for several reasons. Most importantly, perhaps, is the influence of the feminist movement of the 1970s. This is a group of women who were raised and began their adult life with basically traditional values and attitudes but who have moved towards more feminist and egalitarian thinking as the result of philosophical reevaluations and life experiences (Bardwick, 1980; Potts, 1980). What is not clear is how these conflicting sets of values might influence childbearing decisions and related aspects of these women's lives and the lives of those with whom they form intimate relationships.

Another phenomenon that affects the gender-role orientations and fertility decisions of the women in this cohort is the dramatic growth in labor-force

From Kristine M. Baber and Albert S. Dreyer *Sex Roles* Vol. 14, Nos. 9/10 (October/November 1986): 501–12. Reprinted by permission of Plenum Publishing Corporation and the authors.

participation by females. Most young women now work after completing their education. In 1979, for example, 69% of women 20–24 years of age were employed, and it is expected that more than 85% of this age group will be workers by the end of this decade (Maymi, 1982). Women's labor-force participation is clearly related to delayed childbearing, though the direction of causation is not, and may never be, clear.

Women's Commitment to Work

Because women continue to carry primary responsibility for child care in the vast majority of families, a woman's commitment to work and the significance of her work to herself should be expected to be important considerations in fertility decisions. It would be expected that women who are more highly educated, who are in higher status professions, and who have been in the work force for a longer period of time would be more committed to their work than other women. Such findings are consistently reported in the research on child-free women. Daniels and Weingarten's (1978, 1982) findings suggest that this also may be the case for women who have their first child later in their adult life. They found it was predominantly the college-educated, late-timing women who pursued simultaneous work/parenting patterns, rather than the sequential pattern of leaving work for parenting. These women were found to have very high expectations for themselves and tended to define themselves both in terms of "work in the world" and in terms of reproductive generativity.

Wilkie (1981), on the other hand, maintained that for those who postpone their first birth, it is financial considerations rather than career aspirations that lead women to dedicate themselves to a career before motherhood. She further contended that postponers differ little from early childbearing women in regard to their attitudes and values about traditional roles and parenthood.

Type of Relationship

Child-free relationships have consistently been described as egalitarian in nature (Bram, 1978; Cumber, 1977; Feldman, 1981; Veevers, 1976, 1979, 1980). However, what is not clear is whether they tend to be more egalitarian because they are free of the responsiblities of child care, or if individuals who choose to be part of a child-free couple are different in values and attitudes than couples in general. Previous research provides little guidance in regard to this question because the samples usually used have consisted only of child-free couples or have compared child-free couples with couples who are already parents. This confounds the findings because longitudinal research, such as that of Cowan, Cowan, Coie, and Coie (1978), Entwisle and Doering (1980) and LaRossa and LaRossa (1981), has indicated that traditional role behaviors increase after the birth of the first child.

Assuming traditionalization is related to the transition to parenthood rather than traditionalism itself being characteristic of the individuals who choose parenthood, no significant difference on the modern/traditional dimension would be expected between older child-free individuals and individuals who have only postponed their childbearing. This would be particularly true since both groups generally exhibit characteristics that reinforce a tendency toward egalitarian relationships—both partners employed outside the home in relatively high-status positions; little discrepancy in hours worked, income, or earning capacities; and both partners having histories of stable and consistent employment (Veevers, 1980).

However, Bram's (1978) intriguing study that included couples who planned to have a child, as well as voluntary child-free couples and couples who already had their first child found that childless couples were more egalitarian than the parental couples or the postponers, even when the childless women did not work. This suggests that there may be differences in orientation prior to the birth of the child.

Since no combination of social demographic variables seems to account for the differences between couples who decide to remain child free and those who choose parenthood in their 30s, the current study was a first step towards clarifying the relationships between various psychosocial factors and childbearing decisions. Gender-role orientation, egalitarianism, and career commitment were chosen for investigation because previous research has indicated their importance, but systematic testing of their relationship to variant childbearing patterns is yet to be done.

Methods

Sample

The sample consists of 40 women, 20 voluntarily child free and 20 expectant, and 34 of their husbands. Three women in each group chose to participate even though their partners were not available due to geographical separation or lack of interest. To participate in the study, the woman in each couple had to be at least 30 years of age. No participant, male or female, could have been a parent by this or a previous relationship. Individuals with a history of fertility problems were not included in the study.

Nine couples, five child-free and four expectant, volunteered to participate in response to a one-page information sheet distributed to doctors' offices and Lamaze instructors. The other 31 couples were identified by colleagues of the researchers, other participants in the study, or from a waiting list at a university day care center, and agreed to participate when contacted and informed of the study. Nine other couples, three expectant and six child free, declined to participate when contacted.

There were no significant demographic differences between the child-free and expectant groups. The average age of the child-free women was 33.16 years and the expectant, 33.20 years. Ages ranged from 30 to 38 years. The ages of the men had a somewhat greater range, 26 to 41 years. The mean age for the child-free men was 35.18 and for the expectant, 33.77 years. There was no significant difference between the groups in regard to the length of their relationship or years married. Child-free couples had known each other an average of 10.72 years, the expectant 9.31 years. Many of these couples had lived together before their marriages. The mean years married for the child free was 7.76 and for the expectant, 5.84 years.

Eighty-nine percent of the participants had at least an undergraduate degree. Sixty-five percent of the females and 70% of the males had advanced degrees of some type. All but five subjects, four of whom were students, were employed at the time of the study, mainly in professional, managerial, or executive positions. Sixty-five percent of the child-free and 60% of the expectant participants said that religion plays little or no role in their lives.

Procedure

Data were collected through in-depth semistructured interviews and two self-administered questionnaires. An attempt was made to interview all expectant participants in the last trimester of their pregnancy, generally in the seventh month. No couple was interviewed prior to quickening, and in cases where the woman was to have amniocentesis, the interview was scheduled after the results were received and a normal pregnancy confirmed. Whenever possible, interviews with the child-free couples were scheduled alternately with those of the expectant couples so that there was a somewhat equal distribution of the interviews over time.

Interviews were generally conducted in the participants' homes by two trained female interviewers. Interviewers alternated between interviewing males and females and, whenever possible, between child-free and expectant individuals. Each partner was interviewed individually because of the interest in sex differences as well as to allow each individual to express his/her own thinking on the subject, whether it was in agreement or disagreement with the partner's. All interviews were tape-recorded.

The semistructured interviews were used to gather core information on certain topics from all subjects regardless of sex or group. Questions focusing on the decision-making process regarding childbearing, the marital relationship, career importance, and division of labor regarding financial, domestic, and other maintenance tasks were content analyzed and coded. Percent agreement between the coders ranged from 74 to 100% for the variables used in this study.

Other Instruments

Each participant completed a one-page demographic questionnaire that provided basic information on age, sex, education, occupation, income, marital history, family of origin, and religiosity.

An instrument developed by Miller (1980), the Feminine Interest Questionnaire, was used to investigate participants' orientations to female roles because it had been used previously in research on fertility decisions. It measures modern vs traditional preferences regarding roles for women. The instrument was called the Role Questionnaire in this study because it was administered to both males and females. The Modern–Traditional Scale and two subscales—child and home orientation, and spousal role equality—were used to provide additional information about gender-role orientations of the participants. The reported Cronbach's alpha for the overall scale is .90; the four-week test-retest correlation is .93.

The Role Questionnaire uses a Likert format with four levels of agreement. The Modern–Traditional Scale consisted of 25 items focusing on various aspects of women's roles. Thirteen of the items reflect a modern orientation and are scored positively. The other 12 reflect a traditional orientation and are negatively scored. An example of a "modern" item would be:

> Having a challenging job or career is as important as being a wife or mother.

An example of traditional item would be:

> A woman must get married to feel completely fulfilled.

The scores could conceivably range from 40, for someone who completely agreed with all modern items and completely disagreed with all traditional items, to -35 for someone with the reverse orientation.

Scores on the six-item child and home orientation subscale could range from 1, for a very modern response, to 19 for a traditional response. Items from this scale include:

> Raising a family is a small part of being a woman.

> A woman's most important role is in the home.

Scores on the six-item spousal role equality subscale could range from 6 to 24. Items from this scale include:

> It can be quite natural for a woman to work and the man to stay home with the children.

> Women should not compete with men in many of the things that they do.

Results

Career Importance

The importance of career in relationship to other life goals and activities was coded from the tapes. Each individual had rated him- or herself on a scale from 1 (*least important*) to 7 (*most important*). A significant group difference was found, $F(1, 70) = 4.91$, $p = .03$, with both expectant males ($M = 6.06$) and females (M

Table 1. Means and Standard Deviations for Role Questionnaire Scales

	Child free		Expectant	
	Males	*Females*	*Males*	*Females*
Modern–traditional orientation[a]	25.29	26.90	21.41	23.37
	(11.48)	(5.48)	(8.09)	(7.60)
Home and child orientation[b]	6.41	5.53	8.81	6.84
	(2.65)	(1.87)	(4.26)	(2.89)
Spouse role equality[c]	20.24	21.21	20.35	19.70
	(2.41)	(5.18)	(2.29)	(5.17)

[a]Higher means indicate a more modern orientation.
[b]Higher means indicate a greater preference for women to be home and family oriented.
[c]Higher means indicate a greater endorsement of equal roles for men and women.

= 5.40) indicating that their career was more important to them than [it was to] the child free (M = 5.18, males; M = 5.05 females). There were no significant sex-related differences regarding career importance.

Reasons for career importance were also content analyzed and coded. There were no significant differences between groups regarding intrinsic reasons for working, such as self-improvement. Seventy-seven percent of the sample gave this as the main reason for the importance of their career. The child free were significantly more likely to spontaneously mention financial reasons than were the expectant, χ^2 = 10.24, df = 1, p = .001. There were no statistically significant differences between men and women regarding why their careers were important to them.

Gender-Role Orientation

Table 1 presents the mean scores for each group on the subscales of the Role Questionnaire, Two-by-two ANOVAs were done to test for significant sex and group differences on these variables.

Expectant individuals were significantly more likely to prefer women to be child and home oriented than the child free, F (1, 68) = 4.64, p = .03. They were also more traditional in regard to role orientations than were the child–free couples, F (1, 68) = 3.53, p = .06. No significant differences were found in regard to attitudes about spousal role equality. However, the child–free women had the highest mean score and the expectant, the lowest of the four groups.

Egalitarianism

There were no statistically significant differences between groups or between sexes on the spousal role equality subscale. The means for all four groups fell near the upper end of the range of possible scores on this scale. This suggests that there is general agreement that men and women are equal, and that they should have equal rights and responsibilities.

Coding of participants' taped discussions of who takes responsibility for various financial, domestic, and other maintenance tasks indicated that their behavior was not necessarily consistent with their beliefs. Although there is no difference between groups regarding egalitarian attitudes, there are significant differences in the day-to-day division of labor. Child-free couples were twice as likely to have egalitarian relationships as were the expectant couples, $\chi^2 = 6.78$, $df = 2$, $p = .03$. Independent coders categorized a relationship as egalitarian if there was equal sharing of responsibilities with no indication of a breakdown by sex. If subjects indicated that they tried to share responsibilities, but the distribution tended to be by sex, the relationship was coded as modified traditional. Included in this category were cases where the male "helped" the female with a task, indicating an assumption that it was primarily her responsibility. If the distribution of responsibilities followed the classic gender-role patterns, it was classified as traditional.

Discussion

Traditional Orientation

Gender-role orientation is a variable that does differentiate delayed childbearers from their child-free counterparts. However, the relationship between gender-role orientation and variant childbearing decisions appears to be fairly complex. The expectant individuals, particularly the males, are more traditional than are the child free. This traditionalism manifests itself differently, however, in various aspects of these individuals' lives. It is seen most clearly in their preference for women to be home and child oriented. Because men generally have more traditional and stereotyped views of women than women have for their own sex (McBroom, 1984), it is important to look at differences between the two groups of females on this issue. Interview data suggest that the critical factor may be child orientation. Many of the child-free females have nontraditional views of themselves in relationship to the mothering role. They do not necessarily see having children and being mothers as part of who they are as women.

> *Child-free woman, age 31:* I can't remember even as a child strongly wanting to have a child. I just can't picture myself having children. I just can't envision myself, and usually I can picture myself doing something, but I don't envision myself having children.

> *Child-free woman, age 33:* I can't even get that close. I can't picture me being a mother. I picture it in kind of a storybook picture of someone else who looks like me. But I can't picture it.

> *Child-free woman, age 31:* I had this dream the night before last that I had a kid and went home and forgot it at the hospital and they called me up and said you have to come and pick up your child.

On the other hand, the expectant women could easily see themselves as mothers. For them it was the timing that was at issue.

Expectant mother, age 33: I always knew I would have children, but [prior to now] there was never a time when I thought they would fit in my life.

Expectant mother, age 33: I think, in a sense, I've always foresaw myself with children. The question was when.

When the focus moves from the individual women to the couple relationship, the findings are somewhat equivocal. While there are no statistically significant differences between the child free and expectant in regard to their beliefs about spousal role equality, there are differences in the way these beliefs are played out in the relationship. The child free are more likely to show consistency between their judgments and their actions. the expectant tend to be more traditional in negotiating and assuming role responsibilities than their stated values would suggest.

It is important to note that when we speak of traditionalism in these couples and their relationships, it is a relative traditionalism. Though the expectant have more traditional scores than the child free on the Role Questionnaire, for example, both groups' scores are skewed toward the modern end of the range of possible scores. Likewise, in categorizing relationships based on a day-to-day breakdown of responsibilities, the expectant were more likely to have modified traditional relationships than they were to have classically traditional ones. The difference between an egalitarian and a modified traditional relationship is illustrated by excerpts from the interviews. In some cases, the relationship would seem to be egalitarian, but closer examination would reveal that the woman would have the responsibility for seeing that it functioned that way. The following excerpts are from separate husband and wife interviews in which they were speaking about sharing domestic chores. The husband has described the relationship as egalitarian:

Expectant husband: I do the cleaning of the bathtub, the toilet bowl, the tub . . . . I feel like I want to help.

However, when his wife is interviewed about the distribution of tasks, a somewhat different picture of the relationship emerges:

Expectant wife: I give him the responsibility of the bathroom . . . It wasn't cleaned for three weeks, so I cleaned it. This weekend, I will remind him again.

Interviewer: How do you work out who does what around the house?

Expectant wife: We have no set pattern. [She takes out a list.] For [husband] . . . these are all the things that have to be done in the house, things that don't get done by themselves. But it's there and we are somehow going to have to split these.

The child free speak of their egalitarian relationship in a subtly different way:

Interviewer: With both of you working, how do you handle the responsibilities around the house?

Child-free wife: Either shared or neglected. We shop together. We cook or we don't cook . . . .

Interviewer: Is this something you've negotiated?

Child-free wife: No. Every once in a while one of us will say, "Hey, how come I've been doing the towels all the time?" or "How come it's me who always empties the dishwasher?" But it's not always me that says it or it's not always him.

There is also an indication in the interviews of the child-free couples that the expectation of an egalitarian relationship preceded in marriage. A child-free woman, asked whether her egalitarian relationship with her husband had just evolved or had been negotiated, explained:

> I guess it has just evolved. We've discussed it at times, but . . . I knew when we were dating he was that kind of person. Of course, I was looking for someone who would not see me as a traditional wife. I would not have married the person. I knew I was not going to be a traditional wife.

Although expectant individuals may be more traditional in their marital roles and in their attitudes regarding women's domestic roles, the findings of this study indicate that there is no reason to believe delayed childbearers are any less career oriented than their child-free counterparts. Contrary to Wilkie's assertion, it was not financial considerations that led the delayed childbearing women to commit themselves to a career before motherhood. Rather, these women, like the child-free women and the men in the sample, report that their work identity is an important part of who they are as individuals. In this sense, both groups of women are untraditional in their attitudes about normative female roles.

The Rapoports' (1976) concept of "identity tension line" helps integrate the results of this study and helps clarify why traditionalism might manifest itself differently in particular aspects of an individual's life. Identity tension line refers to the point at which discomfort arises as one modifies behavior and values in the direction of being more egalitarian and less traditional. Individuals may accommodate different degrees of change in different aspects of their lives. Being committed to a career seems comfortable for all of the women in the sample and does not seem to strain their identity tension line. It may be that for the delayed childbearing women in this sample it is at the point of relinquishing the traditional childbearing role that the accommodation required would be too incongruous with their sense of identity as women. Personality and individual developmental differences may explain why some women, such as the child free in this sample, have pushed back this boundary further and do not see motherhood as integral to their sense of self.

Likewise, it may be that the expectant men, while accepting an egalitarian relationship with their spouse in the sphere of work and espousing a belief in role equality in general, have more difficulty with the assumption of day-to-day domestic responsibilities. While they may have modified their values about equality between males and females, their behaviors suggest they have not yet become comfortable with a sense of self that includes traditionally female domestic responsibilities.

Because expectant couples were interviewed during their pregnancy, it might be argued that the differences in the traditional-modern orientations are a function rather than an antecedent of the pregnancy. However, there is evidence from a number of sources that supports the contention that the difference exists prior to the pregnancy. Our findings are consistent with those of related research. Bram (1978), who interviewed postponers prior to conception, found them to be more similar to the parental couples than to the child free in gender-role orientation and egalitarianism, indicating that a difference existed that was not related to pregnancy itself. Bram suggested that the "blurring of the traditional sex-role distinctions" (p. 383) seemed to derive more from a value orientation than from structural factors.

This relationship between fertility decisions and sex role orientation has been found in women even before marriage. Greenglass and Borovilos (1984) studied three groups of unmarried undergraduate women: women planning not to delay having children, women planning to delay having children until education and career goals were met, and those planning to remain childless. Although they found there were no significant differences in career commitment, women who planned to remain child free deviated from the traditional female sex role in regard to their beliefs and expectations regarding marriage and children. Their personality profiles suggested they were psychologically different from the two groups of women planning to have children. While the voluntarily child free appeared to be aggressive, independent, domineering, and analytical—more culturally defined masculine traits—those who planned to delay having children did not seem to have less traditionally feminine personality traits than women who planned no delay in having children.

Additional support comes from our own follow-up done approximately two years after the first interviews. Two women, originally in the child-free group, were found to be pregnant. During the original interview, both women had indicated that they wanted children, although their husbands did not. At the follow-up, one woman was pregnant by the man to whom she'd been married at the time of the original interview. The other had divorced, had remarried, and had become pregnant. In examining the women's scores on the role Questionnaire, it was found that one had scored 23 and the other 16 on the Traditional-Modern Scale. Both scores are lower (more traditional) than the mean score of the women in the original expectant group (23.37).

To conclusively determine whether differences such as those found in this study are truly antecedents of childbearing decisions, it is necessary to do prospective studies. The next step in our investigation of variant childbearing decisions is to do such a study focusing on key identity and personality variables, as well as on the decision-making process.

References

Bardwick, J. M. The seasons of a woman's life. In D. G. Mccguigan (Ed.), *Women's lives: New theory, research and policy.* Ann Arbor: The University of Michigan, Center for Continuing Education for Women, 1980.

Bram, S. Through the looking glass: Voluntary childlessness as a mirror for contemporary changes in the meaning of parenthood. In W. B. Miller & L. F. Newman (Eds.), *The first child and family formation.* Chapel Hill, N.C.: Carolina Population Center, 1978.

Cowan, C. P., Cowan, P. A., Coie, L., & Coie, J. D. Becoming a family: The impact of a first child on the couple's relationship. In W. B. Miller & L. F. Newman (Eds.), *The first child and family formation.* Chapel Hill, N.C.: Carolina Population Center, 1978.

Cumber, B. *To have or not to have: Married couples' decision to be childfree.* Unpublished master's thesis, University of Connecticut, Stors, 1977.

Daniels, P., & Weingarten, K. *Late first-time parenthood: The two sides of the coin.* Wellesley, Mass.: Center for Research on Women, Wellesley College, 1978.

_____ . *Sooner or later: The timing of parenthood in adult lives.* New York: Norton, 1982.

Entwisle, D. R., & Doering, S. C. *The first birth: A family turning point.* Baltimore, Md.: Johns Hopkins University Press, 1981.

Feldman, H. A comparison of intentional parents and intentionally childless couples. *Journal of Marriage and the Family,* 1981, *43*(3), 593–600.

Greenglass, E. R., & Borovilos, R. *Psychological correlates of fertility plans in unmarried women.* Unpublished manuscript, 1984.

LaRossa, R., & LaRossa, M. *Transition to parenthood: How infants change families.* Beverly Hills, Calif.: Sage, 1981.

Maymi, C. R. Women in the labor force. In P. W. Berman & E. R. Ramey (Eds.), *Women: A developmental perspective.* Bethesda, Md.: National Institute of Health, 1982. (NIH #82-2298.)

McBroom, W. H. Changes in sex-role orientations: A five-year longitudinal comparison. *Sex Roles,* 1984, 11 (7/8), 583–592.

Miller, W. B. *The psychology of reproduction* (Appendices 3–4). Unpublished manuscript, 1980.

Potts, L. Considering Parenthood: Group support for a critical life decision. *American Journal of Orthopsychiatry,* 1980, *50* (4), 629–638.

Rapoport, R., & Rapoport, R. *Dual-career families re-examined.* New York: Harper & Row, 1978.

Veevers, J. E. Voluntary childless wives: An exploratory study. *Sociology and Social Research,* 1976, *57*(3), 356–366.

_____ . Voluntary childlessness: A review of issues and evidence. *Marriage and Family Review,* 1979, *2*(2), 1–26.

_____ . *Childless by choice.* Toronto, Canada: Butterworths, 1980.

Wilkie, J. R. The trend toward delayed parenthood. *The Journal of Marriage and the Family,* 1981. *43*(3), 583–591.

7

Child Rearing and Parenthood

> Childrearing in the United States today stands out as an activity that is conducted despite, rather than because of, economic self-interest. The decision to raise a child imposes truly phenomenal costs upon parents and provides virtually no economic benefits. The fact that these costs continue to be incurred bears testimony to the intrinsic benefits of parenthood. These rewards may be misperceived or misunderstood, and women may pay more than an equal share of the price for them. But parenting constitutes one of the few truly craftlike activities of modern life, where process is as important as productivity and where happiness of individuals overrides most other concerns   [*Nancy Folbre, 1984:279*].

Although voluntary childlessness has been increasing in recent years, most couples do have children. In addition, a growing number of unmarried women are becoming parents. In 1986, 29 percent of never-married women between the ages of thirty and forty-nine had given birth to at least one child, up from 24 percent in 1980 and 17 percent in 1970 (U.S. Bureau of the Census, 1985:62; U.S. Bureau of the Census, 1987:66). In all, nearly 90 percent of American women now have children at some point in their lives. Therefore, in this chapter we turn our attention to parenthood and child rearing.

Unlike other animals, the human infant is almost completely helpless at birth and subsequently requires extended care before being capable of independence from adults. This prolonged dependence is the product of an evolutionary process that equipped human beings with large brains and the adaptive capacities of culture. All other animals are born with reflexes and instincts that minimize the role of adults in their upbringing. In contrast, adult caretakers must teach human children virtually everything they need to know to function autonomously.

Women and men who embark on this long and sometimes arduous journey of child rearing often do so with little idea of what to expect. Despite prevalent images of children as fun, lovable, cute, and carefree, children are often none of these (Skolnick, 1987:329). Further, the time and resources consumed by children can often severely test the strength of relationships between husbands and wives and create great hardships for single parents. In order to get a clear picture of the impact of the decision to have children, we first examine childhood in historical perspective, then some of the rewards and costs of making the transition to parenthood.

The Discovery of Childhood

All societies make distinctions between people on the basis of age. Further, ideas about the appropriate behavior and characteristics of individuals in different age categories vary from one society to another and over time. For example, it is often observed that the aged are no longer regarded with the same veneration or accorded the same high status as they were in preindustrial societies. It is less well known that contemporary ideas about children and their place in the family differ dramatically from ideas that were prevalent in the past.

In his groundbreaking work, *Centuries of Childhood* (1962), the French historian Phillipe Aries argues that childhood did not exist as a separate stage of life in medieval Europe. In sharp contrast to the present situation, children became a part of adult society as soon as they no longer needed the constant care of their parents or other adult caretakers. By the age of six or seven, children participated in work, play, and even war alongside adults. Further, children were considered to possess mental and emotional capabilities similar to those of adults. In Aries's view, the lack of importance attached to childhood as a distinct stage of life did not mean that children were "neglected, foresaken, or despised." Instead, he suggests that an awareness of a "particular nature" that distinguished children from adults simply did not exist (Aries, p. 128).

Aries relies on a variety of historical sources to demonstrate the lack of importance attached to childhood in the past. Particularly interesting is his use of paintings. Aries notes, for example, that artists portrayed children as little men and women, differing from adults in their height but not in their other physical features. He concludes that the absence of a concept of childhood as a distinct stage of life did not allow painters to "see" the physical differences between children and adults (p. 33). Aries (p. 37) also observes that while portraits of children were rare prior to the seventeenth century, collective scenes often depicted children alongside adults, suggesting that "children mingled with adults in everyday life, and any gathering for the purposes of work, relaxation or sport brought together children and adults." As further evidence of the lack of importance attached to childhood, Aries notes that children and adults dressed alike. Infants and very small children were dressed in swaddling bands, strips of cloth wound around the body to restrict movement. However, when swaddling clothes were finally removed, children dressed like all others of their gender and social class.

John Demos's (1970) study of family life in Plymouth Colony shows that in most respects the lives of children in seventeenth-century New England differed little from those of the children in medieval Europe whom Aries described. Demos found that by the age of six or seven children had begun to take on the roles of small adults. They participated with their parents in work, relaxation, and religious worship and often served as apprentices or servants in the households of others. Demos did find that between infancy and the age of six or seven both boys and girls dressed in gowns similar to those worn by women, indicating that the residents of Plymouth Colony believed that the early years of childhood required some special treatment (Demos, pp. 139–40). In fact, child-rearing practices of the time emphasized the importance of these early years for establishing a pattern of submissiveness in children so that, in the words of one Puritan minister, the foundation of their later education would be "laid in humility and tractableness" (in Demos, p. 135). Nevertheless, this special treatment occurred early in the child's life, and once its result was accomplished, the child was prepared to join in the daily round of adult activities.

However, children were not the equals of adults in the past, nor did they engage in exactly the same tasks. The preindustrial world was hierarchical, with authority following lines of both gender and age. Children worked under the direction of their parents or other adults. In addition, some preindustrial labor was extremely arduous and some required a high degree of skill. Since six- and seven-year-olds were less skilled and less developed physically than their elders, they were no doubt excluded from these activities. It is likely that other, less demanding, tasks were the responsibility primarily of the very young. However, the critical point emphasized by both Ariès and Demos is that children were not segregated from the adult world in the past and were not considered to require special treatment or to possess qualitatively different characteristics. Instead, they were considered to be temporarily less competent, and smaller, members of adult communities.

New ideas about children began to appear in the mid-1700s and became widespread during the nineteenth century. Specifically, children began to be perceived as possessing distinctive mental and emotional qualities which required that they be treated with special solicitude. The Swiss philosopher Jean Jacques Rousseau was among the first to present these new ideas about childhood. In the influential book *Emile* (1762), Rousseau assumed the role of a tutor describing the ideal education of a young pupil. Significantly, Rousseau believed that children should be protected from the corrupting influences of the adult world for which they were unprepared, and he educated his imaginary pupil in an isolated setting in the country. In *Emile* Rousseau distinguished several stages in a child's development, each with its own special characteristics and requirements. For example, Rousseau thought that between the ages of two and twelve a child's education should be devoted to developing the powers of the senses and that learning should take place primarily through experience and observation. Only later would the capacity for intellectual and moral reasoning develop, which would require different modes of learning. Rousseau anticipated some of the insights concerning child development of nineteenth- and twentieth-century psychology. However, from our perspective, his important contribution was the idea that children were different and required special treatment. In an often-quoted passage Rousseau (1901:54) stated:

> Nature wants children to be children before they are men. If we deliberately pervert this order, we shall get premature fruits which are neither ripe nor well-flavored, and which will soon decay. . . . Childhood has its own way of seeing, thinking, and feeling, and nothing is more foolish than to try to substitute our own for them. I would as soon require a child to be five feet in height as to have judgement at the age of ten.

In short, Rousseau espoused the belief that children were unprepared to participate in adult activities and that their special qualities needed to be appreciated and nourished.

Indicative of these new ideas was the appearance of books written especially for children. Literature aimed at instructing children and instilling morals existed prior to the eighteenth century. However, a genre designed to appeal to the newly perceived characteristics of children became widespread in the nineteenth century. By the beginning of the Civil War, over 300 new books for children appeared in the United States each year, and more than twice that number were published in England (Degler, 1980:69). These new books sought to entertain as well as to instruct, and they presented a separate and distinctive world for children. Some books featured fantasy characters, others related children's adventures, and still others depicted children experiencing true-to-life problems (Greenleaf, 1978:68).

Also appearing in the nineteenth century were advice books for parents. These books popularized the emerging views of children and created new standards of child rearing. No longer could enlightened parents simply follow the traditional practices of previous generations. Instead, they consulted one of a long string of bestselling child-rearing manuals of which Dr. Benjamin Spock's *Baby and Child Care* is only a fairly recent example. Fashions in child care have varied from one generation to the next since the nineteenth century. For example, early child-care manuals advocated rigid scheduling and the importance of establishing submissiveness in children. Later manuals advocated flexibility in responding to children's needs and permissiveness toward children's transgressions. However, a common thread runs through the advice books of the nineteenth and twentieth centuries—children have special needs, and it is parents' responsibility to recognize these needs and provide the care that their children require.

Although the audience for early child-care manuals was probably limited to the affluent, the huge circulations of child-rearing manuals in this century suggest that they are read by working- and middle-class parents alike. *Infant Care,* first published by the Children's Bureau of the Department of Labor in 1914, had gone through twelve editions and nearly sixty million copies by the 1970s. As late as 1976 it was still the most requested publication of the federal government. Dr. Spock's book, first published in 1946, had sold over twenty-eight million copies by the mid-1970s (Weiss, 1977:520).

Until recently, many historians believed that changes in ideas about childhood were partly the result of a decline in the death rate among children.

According to this argument, the high mortality rates of the past prevented parents from developing strong emotional attachments to their children simply because they had little confidence that their children would survive the first years of life. Consequently, parents did not pay enough attention to their children to gain insights into their unique characteristics or special needs. As death rates fell, parents developed deep bonds of affection with their children and began to pay increased attention to their needs. The problem with this line of reasoning is that the demographic evidence now available shows that changes in ideas about childhood preceded declines in the death rate by more than a century. In fact, Edward Shorter (1975) suggests that changes in attitudes toward children resulted in improvements in their care, which, in turn, increased their chances of survival.

An explanation more promising than a decline in the childhood death rate for the development of new ideas about children and their proper treatment lies in the changes in the organization of work and the family that we examined in Chapter 2. When work and family life were intertwined, the integration of children into the daily round of activities was unavoidable. The variety of work performed in preindustrial households allowed children to participate in many tasks with their parents, and the labor of children was a necessary contribution to the total productive effort of the family. Even if parents had wished to separate their children from these activities, limitations of physical space would have made it difficult for any but the very wealthy to do so. However, the gradual separation of production in factories, shops, and offices isolated children in the home and restricted the sphere of their activities, just as it had done for women. Further, changes in work itself operated to alter the position of children in the family. The technical skills and the education required by many of the jobs created in a commercial, industrialized economy prolonged the training necessary to enter the occupational world.

Industrialization probably increased the opportunities for the employment of working-class children initially. In fact, children were not excluded from the paid labor force until well into the twentieth century. The first workers in a spinning mill set up in Rhode Island in 1790 were children between seven and nine, and in 1820 over half of all workers in Rhode Island textile mills were children. The percentage of all children aged ten to fifteen employed for wages remained fairly constant in the nineteenth century, although the percentage of very young children who were employed probably decreased as the century progressed. Opposition to child labor began to grow after the Civil War. The proponents of restrictions on child labor denounced employers who hired children as greedy and accused parents who sent children out to work of selfishly sacrificing their offsprings' health and safety. They maintained that children should be completely separated from the marketplace. By 1900 over twenty-eight states had some form of child-labor law. Although effective federal legislation did not pass until 1938, only 5 percent of children ten to fifteen were in the paid labor force in 1930. At that time, the transformation of children from "useful to useless" was virtually complete (Zelizer, 1985:56–72).

The relegation of children to the home and the increasing length of time required to prepare them for occupations created childhood as a distinct stage of life. These new arrangements isolated children in the family and called attention to the mental and emotional differences between children and adults. As this separation occurred, psychologists developed elaborate theories of child development describing specific maturational changes and the special requirements of children at each stage. The declining usefulness of children contributed to the redefinition of the child's place in the family. Instead of being contributing members of a productive group, children became dependents requiring the prolonged care and protection of their parents. Although some argue that the segregation of children in schools and the home accentuates and prolongs the differences between children and adults, most people now consider the separation of children from adult activities as not only necessary but natural. However, we may now be witnessing a further change in the role of children, spurred by the increasing prevalence of two-job and single-parent families. As more parents find the time for household chores limited by the demands of work, children may take on increasing responsibilities in the home. As Viviana Zelizer (1985:223) points out, "the demise of the full-time housewife may create a part-time 'househusband' and 'housechild.' "

The Transition to Parenthood

The discovery of childhood redefined the role of parents. As the amount of care that children required increased and the economic contribution they made to the family declined, the responsibilities of parents correspondingly expanded. In fact, the investments in time and money that children represent are now so great, it is important to ask why people choose to become parents at all. What rewards make these "phenomenal costs" worthwhile?

Two studies from the late 1970s provide some answers to this question. Lois Hoffman and Jean Manis (1979) investigated the psychological satisfactions that children provide for parents. They report the results of a survey of approximately 2,000 married men and women, some with and some without children. The survey asked each participant to describe the "advantages and good things about having children compared with not having children at all." Although the question elicited a variety of responses, the answers fell into several broad categories. Among the respondents who were parents, nearly two-thirds mentioned that children provided opportunities for love and companionship, and over half stated that having children was stimulating and fun. About one-third of the responses of individuals with children fell into the category that Hoffman and Manis call "expansion of self." Included in this category were statements that children provided parents with a learning experience or the opportunity to re-create themselves. Less frequent were responses stating that having children allowed parents to achieve adult status or to feel a sense of accomplishment. Economic utility was the most infrequent response, mentioned by under 10 percent of those surveyed. Although nonparents were less likely than parents to mention all these advantages, the differences were not large.

Hoffman and Manis also found that various groups differed in their opinions of the satisfactions provided by children. For example, women were more likely than men to cite children as sources of love and companionship, and women working in the home were more likely than women in the paid labor force to state that raising children gave them something "worthwhile" to do. Nevertheless, this study identifies some of the rewards that children provide for parents and that children promise for prospective parents. Hoffman and Manis conclude that although economic considerations may set the upper limit on the number of children people desire, these rewards set the lower limit. In other words, people are willing to shoulder the high costs of having children to obtain the perceived benefits.

In a slightly different approach, Judith Blake (1979) investigated opinions about childlessness. She reports the results of a survey of approximately 1,600 adults who were asked to state their agreement or disagreement with statements about the advantages and disadvantages of childlessness. Blake found that few of the respondents regarded childlessness as advantageous. Only 15 percent agreed that couples without children have the "best times" or have closer, more intimate relationships. However, perceptions of the disadvantages of childlessness were widespread. More than half the respondents agreed that childless couples were more likely to be lonely, get divorced, and lead unfulfilled and empty lives than couples with children. Significantly, only 15 percent of the respondents thought childless couples were more likely to have financial difficulties in old age. Blake concludes that while few view children as an economic investment, a majority see children as "socially instrumental." Like Hoffman and Manis, she concludes that the perceived social rewards are great enough to motivate people to have children in spite of the financial burden they impose.

Although having children can provide many rewards, the addition of a child to the family requires adjustment to a new set of responsibilities and relationships. In the late 1950s, Edgar LeMasters (1957) argued that the transition to parenthood precipitated such severe difficulties that it deserved to be labeled a crisis. Although many students of the family have questioned the appropriateness of such a dramatic designation, agreement exists that becoming a parent presents many problems.

Alice Rossi (1968) suggested that some of these problems are the result of the unique features of the parental role. Rossi compared parenthood with the marital and occupational roles and concluded that becoming a parent involves some special difficulties. For example, individuals have little preparation for parenthood in contrast to the other two adult roles. The assumption of occupational roles often follows a lengthy period of specialized training and practice. As Rossi points out, a doctor seeing his or her first patient not only has completed many years of schooling but has also treated many patients under supervision as an intern. Even the less skilled have opportunities to obtain rudimentary job skills at home and school, as well as in part-time work. Similarly, people rarely marry without some experience in relationships with members of the opposite sex. Dating, engagement, and, increasingly, cohabitation allow individuals to develop interpersonal skills that facilitate the adjustment to marriage. However, individuals rarely receive any preparation for parenthood. An occasional high school class, babysitting, and observation are often the extent of the training individuals receive. When families were larger, young people sometimes cared for younger siblings or even the children of an older sibling. Today, when families typically include few children, young people have these responsibilities less frequently.

Rossi discusses several other factors that contribute to the difficulties of the parental role. First, the transition to parenthood is abrupt. While the assumption of marital and occupational roles often follows a period of gradually increasing responsibilities, new parents immediately assume round-the-clock responsibilities. Parents may greet their second child with considerable aplomb, but the responsibilities of the first child often seem overwhelming. Second, guidelines for successful parenting are lacking. Although most can agree that children need a loving and secure environment as well as certain standards of physical care, fool-proof methods for raising a competent adult are not known. Further, the criteria for judging one's success as a parent are unclear. Guidelines for achieving a successful marriage may be equally elusive, but occupational roles are often governed by specific procedures and explicit evaluation criteria. Finally, entry into parenthood is irrevocable. Although one can quit a job or end a marriage, it is difficult to quit being a parent. In Rossi's words, "we can have ex-spouses and ex-jobs but not ex-children" (p. 32).

Rossi's analysis provides some insight into the unique difficulties of the transition to parenthood. However, when new parents are actually asked to explain how the births of their babies have changed their lives, they mention the lack of time most frequently. According to Ralph LaRossa (1983:579), new parents complain that their lives have become more hectic than before the baby, and they "report that sleep time, television time, communication time, sex time, and even bathroom time are in short supply, thanks to their newborns." Although feelings of lack of time are pervasive, LaRossa suggests that parents probably differ in their reactions to the time demands made by their children. For example, people who have been married for several years before having their first child may have developed routines and relationships that are severely disrupted by their new responsibilities. Their reactions to the time consumed by the care of an infant may be quite different from the reactions of those who have their first child shortly after marriage. Similarly, men and women may respond differently to the time demands of newborns. Because women typically have greater responsibilities than men for the care of children, their lives change more as the result of the birth of a child. Some women may welcome this dramatic change in their lives, while others may resent the disruption of activities to which they have developed commitments. Some men may resent even the small amount of time they contribute to child care, while others may welcome it as a pleasant diversion.

A study by Renee Steffensmeir (1982) of the problems experienced by fifty-four new parents illustrates the variation in responses to the demands of new parenthood. Steffensmeir found that women were more likely than men to express dissatisfaction about the added responsibilities and restrictions of parenthood. However, women with high education were more likely to express dissatisfaction than were women with low education. In contrast, men with high education expressed less dissatisfaction than men with low education. A possible explanation of these results is that women with high education are more committed to nonfamily roles than are other women. Men with high education may be more committed to their family roles, however limited those may be, than are other men.

Although the work of Rossi, LaRossa, Steffensmeir, and many others has demonstrated that the transition to parenthood is often not an easy one, most individuals make the initial adjustment without experiencing severe problems. Once this adjustment is made, however, the tasks of parents have just begun. Next, parents must guide their children on the complicated journey to adulthood. The articles in this chapter examine some patterns of child rearing and their consequences.

Readings

The development of new ideas about children corresponded to changes in women's role in the family in the nineteenth century. As we learned in Chapter 2, the doctrine of separate spheres assigned women primary responsibility for the home and invested their domestic duties with special importance. Although women had always cared for children, the new ideas about the special treatment required by children were consistent with the new definition of women's proper place. Increasingly, nineteenth-century Americans saw child rearing as the central and natural activity of women. In the twentieth century, these beliefs were reinforced by psychological theories emphasizing the importance of the mother/child bond. Structurally, the family wage made it possible for many women to remain in the home as full-time mothers.

In the first article in this section, "American Fathering in Historical Perspective," Joseph Pleck examines the distant and peripheral role of fathers in child rearing—a role that developed along with the new views of women and children. As Pleck explains, the lack of involvement of fathers in child rearing was criticized in the mid-twentieth century by psychologists who held overprotective mothers and absent fathers responsible for everything from juvenile delinquency to homosexuality. Although links between these "problems" and the relative involvement of mothers and fathers in child rearing are the subject of debate, the critique did provide support for an increased role for fathers with their children. In more recent years, feminist scholars have criticized the lack of involvement of men in child rearing, suggesting, among other things, that women's continuing responsibility for child care contributes to gender inequality.

Pleck points out that although cultural support for increased participation of fathers in child rearing is growing, change has been slow in coming. Typically, the failure of men to become more involved than they now are in child care is explained by suggesting that they have not been socialized to value "mothering." According to this line of reasoning, men who do "mother" have somehow been able to rise above their socialization. However, Barbara Risman (1987) argues that the slow pace of change in child-rearing patterns must also be attributed to structural factors that make it difficult for men to participate in "mothering" even if they desire to do so. For example, continuing wage differentials between men and women rarely make it practical for men to leave the labor force to care for small children while their wives remain at work. Similarly, if maternal leaves are available while paternal leaves are not, it is understandable that women spend more time with infants than men. Risman (p. 27) suggests that change in child-care patterns "depends upon restructuring the social environment rather than simply resocializing individuals." Like Pleck, she suggests the development of policies that reduce work/family conflicts for fathers.

In the next article, "The Effects of Social Class on Parental Values and Practices," Melvin Kohn examines the impact of another aspect of the social environment on child rearing. Kohn (1959) conducted his first study of the relationship between social class and the values parents hold for their children in the late 1950s. He asked parents to select from a list of seventeen values the three they considered to be most important for their children. He then compared the relative importance that middle- and working-class parents attached to these seventeen values. Kohn discovered clear differences between parents in different social classes. In this article, Kohn summarizes the results of nearly two decades of research on the relationship between social class and parental values. The results of this research have been remarkably consistent, both over time and between countries. Briefly, Kohn and others have found that middle- and working-class parents agree on the overall importance of several basic values for their children but differ in the relative importance they assign to these values. Middle-class parents emphasize values supporting self-direction, and working-class parents emphasize values supporting conformity to external authority.

Kohn locates the source of parental values in the conditions of life associated with class position, specifically with a factor he calls occupational self-direction. In this connection it is important to note that the subjects of most of the research on parental values and social class have been men. When women have been the subjects, their social class has been determined using their husbands' occupations. In these studies, women's values have been shown to reflect their husbands' occupations. However, Kohn states that preliminary evidence indicates that occupational experiences affect women's values in the same way they affect mens' values. Therefore, as women increase their participation in and commitment to the paid labor force, their values may reflect their occupational experiences and not their husbands'. In studying child-rearing values in the future, it will be important to compare the values and occupational conditions of individual husbands and wives. Particularly interesting will be cases in which the occupational experiences of husbands and wives do not coincide.

In "Development of Androgyny: Parental Influences," Mary Ann Sedney examines the impact of parental behavior on sex-role development. (Most sociologists would now use the term *gender role*.) All societies make some distinction between the behavior and traits believed to be appropriate for men and women. However, as Margaret Mead (1935) demonstrated in her classic study of sex roles in three tribes in New Guinea, societies differ quite dramatically in the degree of differentiation between men and women and in definitions of masculinity and femininity. Mead characterized one tribe, the Arapesh, as gentle and cooperative with few differences in their expectations of the traits appropriate for men and women. Among the Mundugumor, both men and women were aggressive and hostile. In the third tribe, the Tchambuli, men possessed traits stereotypically associated with femininity in our society, and women possessed traits associated with masculinity. Mead's findings, along with the results of many other cross-cultural studies, have led social scientists to conclude that differences in traits and behaviors between men and women are the result largely of learning rather than of underlying biological predispositions. Although biological sex is certainly not without influence on the roles of men and women, masculinity and femininity are social constructions.

Social scientists have developed several theories to account for the acquisition of sex-typed behavior. As Sedney points out, these theories propose different processes of sex-role development, but they all focus primarily on the interaction of young children with adults. For example, social learning theory suggests that children acquire sex-typed behavior just as they learn other kinds of behavior. Through a process of reinforcement they are rewarded for sex-appropriate behavior and punished for inappropriate behavior. According to social learning theory, individuals do not necessarily need to be directly rewarded or punished in order for learning to occur. Individuals can also learn by generalizing from one situation to another and by observing others receiving rewards (Stockard and Johnson, 1980:179). This theory suggests that sex-typed behavior results from differences in the ways boys and girls are treated. Specifically, this theory predicts that parents will reward and punish their sons and daughters differently to produce masculine and feminine behavior at early ages. Cognitive development and psychoanalytic theory also predict that sex-role learning will occur early. In fact, studies show that children's behavior is clearly sex-typed in some ways by the age of three or four.

Sedney does not attempt to evaluate the validity of these theories; all have received some empirical support. Instead, she moves beyond the question of how sex-typed behavior develops to consider how parents influence the development of behavior that is not sex-typed. To do so, she focuses on two questions. First, what explains the persistence of sex-typed behavior in young children whose parents actively attempt to discourage it? Second, what explains the development of androgynous behavior in adults? In answering these two questions, Sedney's article raises another question that again draws our attention to the social conditions influencing child rearing: How can parents raise androgynous children in a sex-typed society?

In the final selection, "Child Care 2000: Policy Options for the Future," Sally Lubeck and Patricia Garrett address the problem of reconciling the demands of work and child rearing—a problem parents face increasingly as more and more married women with children enter the paid labor force. As the authors point out, the United States lags far behind many other nations in developing policies to help parents balance their economic and child-care responsibilities. Ambitious federal child-care legislation was actually proposed on several occasions in the 1970s in this country. In 1971, both houses of Congress passed the Comprehensive Child Development Bill, which would have provided funds for the construction and operation of day-care centers. However, President Richard

Nixon vetoed the bill, claiming that it would diminish parental authority, weaken the family, and commit the moral authority of the federal government to communal child rearing. Nixon's veto set the tone of public debate for the remainder of the decade, and opposition to similar child-care bills introduced in 1975 and 1979 was strong.

However, the development of child-care policies will continue to be the subject of public attention and debate in the 1990s for several reasons. First, the need for child care will grow because the percentage of married women in the labor force is increasing. Second, as more and more young children spend time away from home, concern over the quality of the care they receive will continue to rise. A third reason why child care will remain a critical issue is its cost, particularly for young families, whose earning power is often lowest when their child-care expenses are highest. Lubeck and Garrett are among the supporters of a comprehensive family policy, and their article presents a model for considering alternative approaches to meeting the need of parents for more, higher quality, and affordable child care than is now available.

References

Aries, Phillipe. 1962. *Centuries of Childhood: A Social History of Family Life*. New York: Vintage Books.

Blake, Judith. 1979. "Is Zero Preferred? American Attitudes toward Childlessness in the 1970s." *Journal of Marriage and the Family* 41:245–57.

Degler, Carl N. 1980. *At Odds: Women and the Family in America from the Revolution to the Present*. New York: Oxford University Press.

Demos, John. 1970. *A Little Commonwealth: Family Life in Plymouth Colony*. New York: Oxford University Press.

Folbre, Nancy. 1984. "Of Patriarchy Born: The Political Economy of Fertility Decisions." *Feminist Studies* 9:261–84.

Greenleaf, Barbara Kaye. 1978. *Children through the Ages: A History of Childhood*. New York: Barnes & Noble.

Hoffman, Lois Waldis, and Jean Denby Manis. 1979. "The Value of Children in the United States: A New Approach to the Study of Fertility." *Journal of Marriage and the Family* 41:583–96.

Kohn, Melvin L. 1959. "Social Class and Parental Values." *The American Journal of Sociology* 64:337–51.

LaRossa, Ralph. 1983. "The Transition to Parenthood and the Social Reality of Time." *Journal of Marriage and the Family* 45:579–89.

LeMasters, Edgar. 1957. "Parenthood as Crisis." *Marriage and Family Living* 19:325–55.

Mead, Margaret. 1935. *Sex and Temperament in Three Primitive Societies*. New York: Morrow.

Risman, Barbara J. 1987. "Intimate Relationships from a Microstructural Perspective: Men Who Mother." *Gender and Society* 1:6–32.

Rossi, Alice. 1968. "Transition to Parenthood." *Journal of Marriage and the Family* 30:26–39.

Rousseau, Jean Jacques. 1901. *Rousseau's Emile*. Translated by William H. Payne. New York: Appleton. (Original work published 1762.)

Shorter, Edward. 1975. *The Making of the Modern Family.* New York: Basic Books.

Skolnick, Arlene. 1987. *The Intimate Environment: Exploring Marriage and the Family.* 4th ed. Boston: Little, Brown.

Steffensmeir, Renee Hoffman. 1982. "A Role Model of the Transition to Parenthood." *Journal of Marriage and the Family* 44:319–34.

Stockard, Jean, and Miriam M. Johnson. 1980. *Sex Roles: Sex Inequality and Sex Role Development.* Englewood Cliffs, N.J.: Prentice-Hall.

U.S. Bureau of the Census. 1985. *Statistical Abstract of the United States: 1986.* 106th ed. Washington, D.C.: U.S. Government Printing Office.

_____. 1987. *Statistical Abstract of the United States: 1988.* 108th ed. Washington, D.C.: U.S. Government Printing Office.

Weiss, Nancy Pottishman. 1977. "Mother, the Invention of Necessity: Dr. Benjamin Spock's *Baby and Child Care.*" *American Quarterly* 29:519–46.

Zelizer, Viviana. 1985. *Pricing the Priceless Child: The Changing Social Value of Children.* New York: Basic Books.

American Fathering in Historical Perspective

Joseph H. Pleck

In American society, there has been an explosion of interest in fathers and fatherhood today. One can hardly watch television, open a national magazine, or go to a movie without seeing themes of father-child relationships, fatherhood, or fatherlessness—from *Star Wars*'s Luke Skywalker's search for his true father, to a recent cover story in the Sunday supplement *Parade* about the actor James Caan as a father, tellingly titled "The Only Role That Matters." In the last decade and a half, calls for greater father involvement have become increasingly insistent.

Yet, in spite of this contemporary interest, and signs of widespread support for an enlarged father role, the pace of change has been slow. While men are doing more child care and housework than they used to, women still perform the bulk of these activities (Pleck, 1985). Beneath the apparent contemporary support for

Research reported in this article was conducted as part of the Fatherhood Project, supported by the Ford, Levi Strauss, Ittelson, and Rockefeller Family Foundations. Earlier versions have benefited from comments by Harris Dienstfrey, Michael Kimmel, Michael Lamb, James Levine, and Elizabeth H. Pleck.

greater father involvement lies a deep-seated ambivalence about what the role of the father really should be, rooted in the complex historical legacy of American culture's perceptions of fathering. Contradictory images of fatherhood from the past have left their mark on contemporary attitudes. This chapter analyzes the dominant images of fatherhood in earlier periods of U.S. history,[1] and considers their impact today.

Eighteenth and Early Nineteenth Centuries: Father as Moral Overseer

There is no question that colonial mothers, like their counterparts today, provided most of the caretaking that infants and young children received. But fathers were nonetheless thought to have far greater responsibility for, and influence on, their children. Prescriptions for parents were addressed almost entirely to fathers; the responsibilities of mothers were rarely mentioned (Degler, 1980).

Fathers were viewed as the family's ultimate source of moral teaching and worldly judgments. The father was viewed as a moral pedagogue who must instruct children of both sexes what God as well as the world required of them. A diary entry by Cotton Mather when he was still young and in good health provides a perhaps extreme illustration:

> I took my little daughter Katy into my study and there I told my child that I am to die shortly, and she must, when I am dead remember everything that I said unto her. I set before her the sinful and woeful condition of her nature, and I charged her to pray in secret places every day without ceasing that God for the sake of Jesus Christ would give her a new heart. . . . I gave her to understand that when I am taken from her she must look to meet with more humbling afflictions than she does now [when] she has a careful and tender father to provide for her   [*in Demos, 1982:426*].

When ministers and others wrote about fatherhood, they emphasized a variety of responsibilities. Fathers ought to concern themselves with the moral and religious education of the young. If literate himself, he should teach reading and writing. He was responsible for guiding his sons into an occupational "calling." He played a key role in the courtship and marriage making of both his sons and daughters, by approving a proposed match and alloting family property to the couple.

Notions of the "duty" of fathers to their children, and of children to their fathers, were central to father-child relationships (Rotundo, 1982). One expression of the family hierarchy, viewed as ideal during this period, appears in *The Token of Friendship, or Home, The Center of Affections* (1844):

> The father gives his kind command,
> The mother joins, approves;
> The children all attentive stand,
> Then each obedient moves   [*in Ewen, 1976:152*].

This emphasis on the paternal role was rooted in this period's conception of the differences between the sexes, and the nature of children. Men were thought to have superior reason, which made them less likely than women to be misled by the "passions" and "affections" to which both sexes were subject. Children were viewed as inherently sinful, ruled by powerful impulses as yet ungoverned by intellect. Because of women's weakness of reason and inherent vulnerability to inordinate affections, only men could provide the vigorous supervision needed by children. Fathers had to restrain their children's sinful urges and encourage the development of sound reason. Mothers were less able to provide these needed influences because of their own tendency to "indulge" or be excessively "fond" of their children. Consistent with these conceptions, common law assigned the right and obligation of child custody to the father in cases of marital separation.

Some descriptions of actual father-child interactions appear in diaries, letters, and other personal accounts: a father and his 10-year-old son carting grain to the mill; a father counseling his adult daughter on her impending marriage; a father and son "discoursing" on witchcraft; a son and daughter joining their father in an argument with neighbors. From such records emerges a "picture, above all, of active, encompassing fatherhood, woven into the whole fabric of domestic and productive life. . . . Fathers were a visible presence, year after year, day after day. . . . Fathering was thus an extension, if not a part, of much routine activity" (Demos, 1982:429). This integration of fatherhood in daily life derived in large part from the location of work, whether farming or artisanship and trade, in the family context. It was natural and even necessary for children to be involved.

Relationships between fathers and children, especially sons, often had strong emotional components. Sons were often regarded as extensions of their fathers; young or newly born sons were commonly described by their fathers as "my hope" or "my consolation" (Demos, 1982:428). However, since fathers believed they could and should restrain their emotions, fathers "tended to express approval and disapproval in place of affection and anger" (Rotundo, 1985:9).

Another indicator of the strength of father-son relationships is that boys serving apprenticeships, and young men on their own, maintained contact with their family primarily through letters to and from their fathers. In contrast to the large volume of letters from children to their fathers that have survived, there are few letters written directly to mothers. Sons would often ask to be "remembered" to their mothers, but in terms that seem formal or even perfunctory. For example, a man whose father had just died . . . included the following message for their mother when he wrote home to a brother: "I sincerely condole with her on the loss of her husband; please tender my duty to her" (Demos, 1982:428).

Early Nineteenth to Mid-Twentieth Centuries: Father as Distant Breadwinner

New conceptions of parent-child relationships began to appear during the nineteenth century. A gradual and steady shift toward a greater role for the mother, and a decreased and more indirect role for the father is clear and unmistakable. Whereas in the earlier period fathers were the chief correspondents of their adolescent and adult children, mothers played that role at least as often in the nineteenth century. To the extent that either parent was involved in the marital choices of their children, it was now usually the mother. In contrast to the earlier period, when mothers showed little concern with any aspect of their sons' lives after childhood, letters and diaries now indicated they were emotionally entangled with sons well into adulthood. Where it had been common earlier to give blame or credit for how children turned out as adults entirely to their fathers, now the same judgment was made about mothers (Demos, 1982).

This shift paralleled a new ideology about gender. While social historians do not agree on its ultimate structural sources, they have documented its centrality to social thought during the nineteenth century. This gender ideology emphasized the purity of the female "sphere" (i.e., the home) and feminine character as unselfish and nurturant. Women's "purity" elevated her above men, making her particularly suited for "rearing" the young. At the same time, infancy and early childhood (as opposed to middle childhood and adolescence) received greater emphasis; mothers were thought to have a special influence in these earlier periods. The belief in maternal influence extended even to the period before birth: the mother's experience during pregnancy, it was thought, might literally shape the destiny of her child (Demos, 1982).

This period saw the development of the contemporary presumption of maternal custody following divorce. It is difficult to define with precision when all vestiges of the earlier practice of awarding custody to fathers disappeared. Increasingly, the interests of the child were interpreted as justifying if not requiring maternal custody. In the latter part of the nineteenth century, court decisions more often promulgated the notion that women have a unique right and obligation to take custody (Grossberg, 1983).

Consistent with these trends, educators during the nineteenth century came to view children as needing a "feminine" influence in their schooling (Suggs, 1978). It is little remembered today that among the foremost "reforms" of nineteenth century educational innovators such as Horace Mann and Ichabod Crane was their introduction of female teachers in the elementary schools.

It took some time for this shift in parental patterns to become fully reflected in all areas of American social thought. Until well into the twentieth century, psychology continued to be dominated by European theorists, grounded in quite different conceptions of family life. To both Jung and the early Freud, the father was unquestionably the towering figure in the life of the child. Freud, it is true, gave a role to the mother, but primarily as the object of the male child's libidinous drives, not as the molder of his character. To the early Freud at least, the mother was psychologically important primarily because the male child's love for her brought him into competition with his father, in an Oedipal drama whose outcome (identification with the father and consolidation of the superego) creates adult male character structure.

Freudian and other psychodynamic theories began to change in the early twentieth century, reflecting an increasing emphasis on the child's primary affectional tie to the mother. Led by Freud himself, psychoanalysis in the 1920's began to focus on pre–Oedipal issues (the psychoanalytic code word for the mother). Central to the many variant formulations was a clear theme: the Oedipal conflict is the key to the clinically less serious neurotic disorders, but the more severe and less treatable forms of psychopathology (the psychoses and personality disorders) result from earlier, more fundamental problems with the mother.

Harry Stack Sullivan, one of the most influential figures in modern clinical psychiatry, also gave almost exclusive attention to the mother: She transmits anxiety and irrational societal expectations to the child, potentially leading to personality "warps" of varying severity. Sullivan's writings hardly ever mention the father. The same is true for John Watson, the founder of "behaviorism," whose advice to parents not to give too much affection to the child was addressed almost entirely to mothers.

While the elevation of the maternal role was the dominant theme from the mid–nineteenth to mid–twentieth centuries, some observers expressed reservations about it. Bronson Alcott wrote in 1845 that "I cannot believe that God established the relation of father without giving the father something to do" (in Demos, 1982:432). At the turn of the century, cultural critics attacked rising maternal influence, along with urbanization and immigration, as having a feminizing effect on American political, cultural, and religious institutions (Kimmel, 1986). In the first decade of the twentieth century, J. McKeen Cattell, an early founder of American psychology, criticized the "vast horde of female teachers" to whom children were exposed (in O'Neill, 1967:81).

A major structural source of the decline in the father's role and increased maternal influence was the emergence of new paternal work patterns away from the family, brought about by industrialization.[2] "For the first time, the central activity of fatherhood was sited outside one's immediate household. Now being fully a father meant being separated from one's children for a considerable part of each working day" (Demos, 1982:434). As geographical distance between the workplace and the home increased, so too did the father's direct involvement with his children. "The suburban husband and father is almost entirely a Sunday institution," noted a writer in *Harper's Bazaar* in 1900 (in Demos, 1982:442).

This new kind of father focused entirely on breadwinning was depicted in early twentieth century advertisements. Mothers were shown as the general purchasing managers of the household, while fathers were portrayed primarily as breadwinners whose wages made family consumption and security possible. Life insurance promotions reminded fathers of their primary function as breadwinners. A 1925 Prudential ad showed a widowed mother visiting her children in an orphan asylum. The child in the ad says the asylum authorities told him "father didn't keep his life insurance paid up" (Ewen, 1976:153–54). The mark of a good father had become a good insurance policy.

In his new role, father's authority was reduced. In a well-known passage, Alexis de Tocqueville described how weak paternal authority seemed when he visited the United States in the 1830s:

> A species of equality prevails around the domestic hearth. . . . I think that
> in proportion as manners and laws become more democratic, the relation

of father and son becomes more intimate and more affectionate; rules and authority are less talked of, confidence and tenderness are often increased. . . . The father foresees the limits of this authority . . . and surrenders it without a struggle   [*in Degler, 1980:75*].

The father continued to set the official standard of morality and to be the final arbiter of family discipline, but he did so at more of a remove than before: He stepped in only when the mother's delegated authority failed. "The father . . . was kicked upstairs, as they say in industry, and was made chairman of the board. As such, he did not lose all his power—he still had to be consulted on important decisions—but his wife emerged as the executive director or manager of the enterprise which is called the family" (LeMasters, in Sebald, 1976:19).

A potential consequence of this indirect authority was that fathers lost touch with what was actually going on in the family. Clarence Day's portrayal of a turn-of-the-century middle-class family, *Life with Father* (1935), was a popular comic expression of this hazard: In spite of his high-status job and the elaborate deference he appears to receive from his wife and children, he is in fact easily manipulated by them. Contemporary concerns about "declining" paternal authority find many of their roots in this period.

Lynd and Lynd's (1929/1956) study of Middletown in the 1920s documents the results of these trends. One resident says: "It is much more important for children to have a good mother than it is for them to have a good father because the mother not only establishes their social position, but because her influence is the prepotent one." A business-class mother says: "My husband has to spend time in civic work that my father used to give to us children." Lynd and Lynd observed little difference in the amount of fathers' involvement between the working-class and business-class fathers; however, business-class wives more often accepted the low involvement, while the working-class wives more often expressed resentment about it.

Middletown notes a "busy, wistful uneasiness" about not being a better parent among many elite fathers: "I'm a rotten dad. If our children amount to anything it's their mother who'll get all the credit. I'm so busy I don't see much of them and I don't know how to chum up with them when I do." Another remarked: "You know, I don't know that I spend any time having a good time with my children. . . . And the worst of it is, I don't know how to. I take my children to school in the car each morning; there is some time we could spend together, but I just spend it thinking about my own affairs and never make an effort to do anything with them." This emotional gap led children to long for greater father involvement. Middletown high school students chose "spending time with his children" among a list of 10 possible desirable qualities in a father far more often than any of the others (Lynd & Lynd, 1929/1956:148–149).

1940–1965: Father as Sex Role Model

During and following World War II, the criticisms that had accompanied the rise of maternal influence in the earlier period became increasingly powerful. At the turn of the century, excessive mothering had been one of a cluster of social transformations creating concern. Now, while other discomfiting trends such as urbanization and immigration had either been accepted or brought under control, mothers stood more alone as objects of social unease (Kimmel, 1986). During the postwar years, this heightened critique of mothering helped usher in a new perception of the father's direct importance in child rearing as a sex role model. This new view derived from negative perceptions of mothers, and encouraged paternal participation of only a limited sort. The new conception did not become dominant; the distant father-breadwinner still prevailed. Nonetheless, the sex role model interpretation of fathering is historically important as the first positive image of involved fatherhood to have a significant impact on the culture since the moral overseer model of the colonial period.

The intensified critique of mothers' influence is particularly evident in Philip Wylie's (1942) popular *A Generation of Vipers*:

> Megaloid momworship has got completely out of hand. Our land, subjectively mapped, would have more silver cords and apron strings criss-crossing it than railroads and telephone wires. Mom is everywhere and everything and damned near everybody, and from her depends all the rest of the U.S. Disguised as good old mom, dear old mom, sweet old mom, your loving mom, and so on, she is the bride at every funeral and the corpse at every wedding   [*p. 185*].

In academic psychology, David Levy's *Maternal Overprotection* argued that contemporary mothers took too dominant a role in the lives of their children because they were not fully satisfied in their relationships with their husbands. "The child must bear the brunt of the unsatisfied love life of the mother" (Levy, 1943:121). Following the war, military psychiatrists blamed the battle breakdowns and other problems of the American fighting man on the American mother (Strecker, 1946). Even the early feminist critiques of the traditional housewife role, written during the early 1960s, sounded a similar theme. Betty Friedan's *The Feminine Mystique* prominently features the argument that the housewife-mother has too close a relationship with her sons, resulting in the "rampant homosexuality" which she described as "spreading a murky smog throughout every area of American life, especially the arts" (1963:265).

New attention to the father's direct role was first manifested not in research on normal father-child relationships, but rather in studies of what happened when the father was absent. The post-war father was seen as a towering figure in the life of his child not so much by his presence as by his absence. Many of the social factors contributing to this enormous post-war interest in father absence directly or indirectly derived from the events of the war. Most obviously, fathers had gone away to the war en masse, and many had not returned. The first studies of the effects of paternal separation were in fact conducted with children of wartime-absent fathers (e.g., Bach, 1946). In addition, wartime induced changes in women's roles. Wives entered paid employment on a large scale, and learned greater independence from men through having to live without their husbands for the duration. Partly as a result, the divorce rate immediately following demobilization was high. Further, the war's economic boom stimulated an enormous and historically unprecedented migration of rural dwellers, especially blacks, to the older cities of the Northeast and Midwest and the newer cities of the West. Traditional family structure broke down, at least among many of these new urban migrants. Rates of father absence rose.

Parallel to the cultural concern about father absence was a more general concern about fathers' weakness and passivity even when they were technically "present." Mass culture expressed it in parody. "The domesticated Dad, who was most entertaining when he tried to be manly and enterprising, was the butt of all the situation comedies. Danny Thomas, Ozzie Nelson, Robert Young, and (though not a father in the role) Jackie Gleason in 'The Honeymooners,' were funny as pint-sized caricatures of the patriarchs, frontiersmen, and adventurers who once defined American manhood" (Ehrenreich and English, 1979:240).

Father absence and father passivity became linked in the public mind with a perceived epidemic of juvenile delinquency in the 1950s. A dramatic expression of this connection occurs in the film *Rebel Without a Cause*. In one of the film's most powerful scenes, the delinquent son finally seeks out his father for advice during a crisis. But when he finds his father wearing an apron while washing dishes in the kitchen, the son recoils in disgust.

A new theory about gender came to dominate developmental psychology which theoretically articulated an extremely significant role for the father, particularly with sons. This theory held that boys face a terrible problem in developing male identity: Developing masculinity is absolutely essential to psychological health, but contemporary child rearing practices make it difficult for boys to do it. Male identity is thwarted by boys' initial identification with their mothers, and by high rates of father absence and the relative unavailability of fathers even when "present." According to the theory, the combination of too much mothering and inadequate fathering leads to insecurity in male identity. This insecure masculinity is manifested directly in homosexuality, as well as more indirectly in delinquency and violence, viewed as "overcompensations" or "defenses" against it (Pleck, 1981, 1983). As this theory evolved, fathers came to be seen as essential for the sex role development of their daughters as well. This conception of father as sex role model served as the equivalent of the much earlier view of the father as moral pedagogue. Healthy sex role identification replaced salvation as the moral imperative.

This new view of the father's role encouraged paternal involvement with children, but also drew a clear distinction between paternal and maternal roles. "The mother has a primarily expressive relationship with both boys and girls; in contrast, the father rewards his male and female children differently, encouraging instrumental behavior in his son and expressive behavior in his daughter. The father is supposed to be the principal transmitter of culturally based conceptions of masculinity and femininity" (Biller, 1971:107).

This new interpretation of the role of the father gave the father a direct but limited role with his children. Some academic authorities expressed great concern about the father being over-involved, or having a role too similar to the mother, particularly if combined with the mother taking a "masculine" role. A standard anthology on the family states that "severe personality problems in one spouse may require the wife to become the wage-earner, or may lead the husband to perform most maternal activities." It further suggests that "a child whose father performs the mothering functions both tangibly and emotionally while the mother is preoccupied with her career can easily gain a distorted image of masculinity and femininity" (Bell and Vogel, 1968:32, 586).

Nor was it thought that fathers should be directly involved in the birth of their children. An obstetrician asserted in 1964 that whether he is "short, thin or fat, of any race, color, or creed," an expectant father "tends to pace, chain smoke, and talk to himself out loud." The doctor went on to observe that "a prospective father behind the wheel is more dangerous than a drunk on the Fourth of July." A guide for the expectant father of the same era suggested that all fathers-to-be learn from the model of an accountant who passed the time in the hospital waiting room by "determining how much tax money would be saved over the years as a result of the new dependency claim that was on the way" (in Gerzon, 1982:203).

Some Implications for the Present

There is no question that the father-breadwinner model established in the nineteenth and early twentieth centuries remains culturally dominant today, both in fathers' actual behavior and its media representation. It is important to recognize that this model has a specific history. To become dominant, it had to supplant an earlier view in which fathers had the ultimate responsibility for, and influence on, their children. The conception of father as moral overseer was promulgated and reinforced by the paramount colonial social institution, the church. It is perhaps difficult for us today to appreciate the power and depth of this past cultural mentality in which fathers' role was considered so important.

As the influence of the church declined, the changing nature and increasing importance of the economy promoted a new model of father as distant breadwinner, paired with a new view of mother's role. Even as this model arose and became dominant, some criticized it or promoted other views. At the turn of the century, their objections appeared to focus at least as much on mothers' influence being too strong as fathers' being too weak. In the 1950s and 1960s, such reservations attained a new level of cultural influence. In particular, academic psychology absorbed and systematized these criticisms in its sex role theory, and then used its own growing influence to disseminate it throughout the culture. Thus the sex role model of fatherhood became a strong though still secondary counterpoint to the dominant father-breadwinner image.

Today, the critique of the distant father-breadwinner is intensifying further. A new image, summed up in the term "the new father," is clearly on the rise in print and broadcast media. This new father differs from older images of involved fatherhood in several key respects: he is present at the birth; he is involved with his children as infants, not just when they are older; he participates in the actual day-to-day work of child care, and not just play; he is involved with his daughters as much as his sons.

The new father represents the further extension of the sex role model and other counter-images challenging the dominant breadwinner model over the last century. Several other phenomena parallel or contribute to the new father image. The increase in postwar wives' employment, and the postwar feminism associated with it, have been its greatest impetus. These led mothers to demand that fathers become more involved. Further, feminist scholars generated new developmental theories of gender (Chodorow, 1978; Dinnerstein, 1976) which support a much broader father role than the older sex-role-model theory. Some feminist analyses imply or directly hold that men are impoverished by not being more active as fathers. This argument has been adopted and highly elaborated as one of the central ideas of the contemporary men's movement, and diffused through the culture more broadly.

It is important to recognize that alongside the "new father," the older alternatives to the father-breadwinner model still have considerable cultural force. The theory of paternal sex role modeling remains the most widely expressed formal argument (that is, the one expressed in most college courses, newspaper articles, popular psychology literature) for greater father involvement. (In recent years, I have been asked repeatedly to testify in support of the Boy Scouts' argument to exclude women as scoutmasters because "boys need male models.")

The moral overseer model of fatherhood also continues to influence a large and probably growing number of fathers today. Its earlier decline coincided with the waning of organized religion as a paramount social institution. One component of the fundamentalist Christian resurgence of recent decades is a revival of Christian fatherhood as an ideal. Today's Christian-father movement is accompanied by its own literature of books (see Benson, 1977; MacDonald, 1977) and periodicals.[3]

The fathers' rights movement is also a significant force on the cultural scene. This movement reflects a complex amalgam of fathers driven by antifeminist backlash (echoing the critics of maternal influence earlier in this century) with other fathers motivated by an actual denial of their genuine desire to remain involved as fathers after divorce. The "new father" coexists somewhat uneasily with this as well as the other profathering ideologies having an impact today. Seifert (1974), for example, describes the problems for men working in child-care centers when some staff and parents want greater male involvement to help break down traditional sex roles, but others want it to help reinforce them.

The discrepancy between the actual pace of change in men and the profusion of profathering imagery has led some to dismiss the image of the new, involved father as only media "hype." While this element clearly exists, it is also important to recognize that the new father is not *all* hype. This image, like the dominant images of earlier periods, is ultimately rooted in structural forces and structural change. Wives *are* more often employed, and do less in the family when they are; men *are* spending more time in the family, both absolutely and relative to women (husbands' proportion of the total housework and child care rose from 20% to 30% between 1965 and 1981; see Pleck, 1985). If the distant father-breadwinner has a social-structural base, so too does the new father.

The historical legacy of American culture's images of fatherhood includes both the distant father-breadwinner model and a variety of alternatives to it. While the father-breadwinner model is under increasing attack, it is still unquestionably dominant. The tensions among these competing models will continue to be expressed in both American social institutions and in the lives of American fathers. In the future, tension between the breadwinner model and more involved conceptions of fatherhood will continue, if not increase.

Such tensions are reflected directly in the current debate about improving parental leave policies in the workplace, including broadening them to apply to fathers (Pleck, 1986). Although the actual cost of offering paternity leave is minimal compared to the cost of parental leave for mothers (simply because fathers use it much less), paternity leave receives a highly disproportionate share of attention as a frivolous and exorbitantly expensive consequence of gender-neutral parental leave policies. (A 1986 national conference on work and family issues [co-sponsored by the U.S. Department of Labor, the AFL-CIO, and the National Association of Manufacturers] at which I was scheduled to speak on paternity leave had to be canceled because labor contract negotiations between the conference vendor and one of its unions had come to an impasse over the issue of paternity leave, and the union threatened to picket the conference!) Paternity leave and other policies to reduce work-family conflict for fathers evoke negative responses not so much because of their actual cost, but because they so directly challenge the father-breadwinner model.

Notes

1. My analysis is especially indebted to Demos (1982) and Rotundo (1985). Both of these rely heavily on Rotundo (1982).
2. There was, of course, considerable diversity in the ways in which industrialization affected patterns of work and family life in the United States and Europe, and diversity in work and family patterns both before and after whatever benchmarks are used to date industrialization (Pleck, 1976).
3. For example, *For Dads Only: A New and Creative Ideas Resource for Christian Dads and Husbands,* PO Box 340, Julian, CA 92036.

References

Bach, G. (1946). Father-fantasies and father typing in father-separated children. *Child Development, 17,* 63–80.

Bell, N., & Vogel, E. (Eds.). (1968). *A modern introduction to the family* (rev. ed.). New York: Free Press.

Benson, D. (1977). *The total man.* Wheaton, IL: Tyndale House.

Bernard, J. (1981). The good-provider role: Its rise and fall. *American Psychologist, 36,* 1–12.

Biller, H. (1971). *Father, child, and sex role.* Lexington, MA: Heath.

Bloom-Feshbach, J. (1981). Historical perceptions of the father's role. In M. E. Lamb (Ed.), *The role of the father in child development* (2nd ed., pp. 71–112). New York: Wiley-Interscience.

Chodorow, N. (1978). *The reproduction of mothering: Psychoanalysis and the sociology of gender.* Berkeley: University of California Press.

Day, C. (1935). *Life with father.* New York: Knopf.

Degler, C. (1980). *At odds: Women and the family in America from the Revolution to the present.* New York: Oxford University Press.

Demos, J. (1982). The changing faces of fatherhood: A new exploration in American family history. In S. Cath, A. Gurwitt, & J. Ross (Eds.), *Father and child: Developmental and clinical perspectives* (pp. 425–450). Boston: Little, Brown.

Dinnerstein, D. (1976). *The mermaid and the minotaur: Sexual arrangements and the human malaise.* New York: Harper & Row.

Ehrenreich, B., & English, D. (1979). *For her own good: 150 years of the experts' advice to women.* Garden City, NY: Anchor/Doubleday.

Ewen, S. (1976). *Captains of consciousness: Advertising and the social roots of the consumer culture.* New York: McGraw-Hill.

Friedan, B. (1963). *The feminine mystique.* New York: Norton (pagination in citations from 1970 Dell paperback edition).

Gerzon, M. (1982). *A choice of heroes.* Boston: Houghton Mifflin.

Grossberg, M. (1983). Who gets the child? Custody, guardianship, and the rise of judicial patriarchy in nineteenth-century America. *Feminist Studies, 9,* 235–260.

Kimmel, M. (1986). *From separate spheres to sexual equity: Men's responses to feminism at the turn of the century.* Working paper #2, Rutgers University, Department of Sociology.

Levy, D. (1943). *Maternal overprotection.* New York: Norton.

Lynd, R., & Lynd, H. (1956). *Middletown: A study in modern American culture.* New York: Harcourt, Brace. (Original work published 1929.)

MacDonald, G. (1977). *The effective father.* Wheaton, IL: Tyndale House.

O'Neill, W. (1967). *Divorce in the progressive era.* New Haven, CT: Yale University Press.

Pleck, E. (1976). Two worlds in one: Work and family. *Journal of Social History, 10,* 178–195.

Pleck, J. (1981). *The myth of masculinity.* Cambridge: MIT Press.

———. (1983). The theory of male sex role identity: Its rise and fall, 1936–present. In M. Lewin (Ed.), *In the shadow of the past: Psychology views the sexes* (pp. 205–225). New York: Columbia University Press.

———. (1985). *Working wives, working husbands.* Newbury Park, CA: Sage.

———. (1986). Employment and fatherhood: Issues and innovative policies. In M. E. Lamb (Ed.), *The father's role: Applied perspectives* (pp. 385–412). Boston: Little, Brown.

Rotundo, A. (1982). *Manhood in America: The northern middle class, 1770–1920* (Doctoral dissertation, Brandeis University). (University Microfilms No. 82-20, 111.)

Rotundo, A. (1985). American fatherhood: A historical perspective. *American Behavioral Scientist, 29* (1), 7–23.

Sebald, H. (1976). *Momism: The silent disease of America.* Chicago: Nelson-Hall.

Seifert, K. (1974). Some problems of men in child care center work. In J. Pleck & J. Sawyer (Eds.), *Men and masculinity* (pp. 69–73). Englewood Cliffs, NJ: Prentice-Hall.

Strecker, E. (1946). *Their mothers' sons*. Philadelphia: Lippincott.

Suggs, R. (1978). *Motherteacher: The feminization of American education*. Charlottesville: University of Virginia Press.

Wylie, P. (1942). *A generation of vipers*. New York: Rinehart.

The Effects of Social Class on Parental Values and Practices

Melvin L. Kohn

My thesis is straightforward and relatively simple: that there are substantial differences in how parents of differing social-class position raise their children; that these differences in parental practices result chiefly from class differences in parents' values for their children; and that such class differences in parental values result in large measure from differences in the conditions of life experienced by parents at different social-class levels. This essay attempts to spell out this thesis more concretely and explicitly.[1] Without getting into technical aspects of methodology, it also attempts to give some idea of the type of empirical evidence on which the generalizations are based.

Social Class

Since the heart of the thesis is that parents' social-class positions profoundly affect their values and child-rearing practices, it is well to begin by defining *social class*. I conceive of social class as aggregates of individuals who occupy broadly similar positions in a hierarchy of power, privilege, and prestige.[2] The two principal components of social class, according to most empirical evidence, are education and occupational position. Contrary to the impression of most laymen, income is of distinctly secondary importance, and subjective class identification is virtually irrelevant. The stratificational system of the contemporary United States is probably most accurately portrayed as a continuum of social class positions—a hierarchy, with no sharp demarcations anywhere along the line.[3] For convenience, though, most research on social class and parent-child relationships employs a somewhat over-simplified model, which conceives of American society as divided into four relatively discrete classes: a small "lower class" of unskilled manual workers, a much larger "working class" of manual workers in semiskilled and skilled occupations, a large "middle class" of white-collar workers and professionals, and a small "elite," differentiated from the middle class not so much in terms of occupation as of wealth and lineage. The middle class can be thought of as comprising two distinguishable segments: an upper-middle class of professionals, proprietors, and managers, who generally have at least some college training; and a lower-middle class of small shopkeepers, clerks, and salespersons, generally with less education.

It is probably unnecessary to underline education's importance for placing people in the social order, and it is self-evident that level of educational attainment can be treated as a quantitative variable: a college graduate unequivocally has higher educational credentials than does a high school dropout. But it may be less apparent that occupational position is also a major criterion of ranking in this—and in all other—industrial societies. One of the most important and general findings in social science research is the relative invariance of people's ratings of occupational prestige, regardless of which country is studied. This finding is of great theoretical importance in its implication that the stratification system is much the same across all industrialized societies.

As a methodological aside, I want to note that our knowledge of the stability of occupational prestige rankings is the result of a long series of studies by many investigators. The first major work in this area was a 1946 cross-sectional survey of the U.S. population by the National Opinion Research Center.[4] At that time, the American population agreed to a remarkably high degree on the relative prestige of various occupations: regardless of which segment of the population was examined, and regardless of people's own occupational levels, most Americans ranked occupations similarly, in a regular and nearly invariant hierarchy from bootblack to physician. Later studies showed that this pattern remained stable over the next quarter-century and that it applied to various specific subpopulations, even to children as young as nine years of age.[5] Another major step in the process of discovery was a 1956 reanalysis of studies of occupational prestige in six industrial societies: the United States, Great Britain, Japan, New Zealand, the Union of Soviet Socialist Republics, and the German Federal Republic.[6] Extremely high intercorrelations (mainly in the .90s) were discovered among these countries despite their cultural differences and despite the inclusion in the analysis of a major noncapitalist state. The stratification system thus appears to be much the same in all industrialized societies. More recent studies have extended this finding to many other countries, several of them non-Western, several of them noncapitalist, and some of them nonindustrialized or only partially so.[7] The evidence for the universality or near universality of occupationally based stratification systems is considerable.

These facts are impressive in themselves, and they become even more impressive when we recognize that people's positions in the class system are related to virtually every aspect of their lives: their political party preferences, their sexual behavior, their church membership, even their rates of ill health and death.[8] Among these various phenomena, none, certainly, is more important than the relationship of social class to parental values and child-rearing practices. But it is well for us to be aware, when we focus on this relationship, that it is one instance of a much larger phenomenon: the wide ramifications of social stratification for people's lives. Any interpretation we develop of the relationship between social class and parental values and behavior must be applicable, at least in principle, to the larger phenomenon as well.

Social class has proved to be so useful a concept in social science because it refers to more than simply educational level, or occupation, or any of the large number of correlated variables. It is useful because it captures the reality that the intricate interplay of all these variables creates different basic conditions of life at different levels of the social order. Members of different social classes, by virtue of enjoying (or suffering) different conditions of life, come to see the world differently—to develop different conceptions of social reality, different aspirations and hopes and fears, different conceptions of the desirable.

The last is particularly important for our purposes, because conceptions of the desirable—that is, values—are a key bridge between position in the larger social structure and behavior. Of particular pertinence to our present interests are people's values for their children.

Parental Values

By values, I mean standards of desirability—criteria of preference.[9] By parental values, I mean those standards that parents would most like to see embodied in their children's behavior. Since values are hierarchically organized, a central manifestation of value is to be found in choice. For this reason, most studies of parental values require parents to choose, from among a list of generally desirable characteristics, those few that they consider most desirable of all, and, in some studies, those that they consider the least important, even if desirable.[10] Such a procedure makes it possible to place parents' valuations of each characteristic on a quantitative scale. We must recognize that parents are likely to accord high priority to those values that are not only important, in that failing to achieve them would affect the children's futures adversely, but also problematic, in that they are difficult of achievement. Thus, the indices of parental values used in most of the pertinent inquiries measure conceptions of the "important, but problematic."[11]

There have been two central findings from these studies. One is that parents at all social-class levels value their children's being honest, happy, considerate, obedient, and dependable.[12] Middle- and working-class parents share values that emphasize, in addition to children's happiness, their acting in a way that shows respect for the rights of others. All class differences in parental values are variations on this common theme.

Nevertheless, there are distinct differences in emphasis between middle- and working-class parents' values. The higher a parent's social-class position, the more likely he is to value characteristics indicative of self-direction and the less likely he is to value characteristics indicative of conformity to external authority.[13] That is, the higher a parent's social-class position, the greater the likelihood that he will value for his children such characteristics as consideration, an interest in how and why things happen, responsibility, and self-control, and the less the likelihood that he will value such characteristics as manners, neatness and cleanliness, being a good student, honesty, and obedience. More detailed analyses show that the differential evaluation of self-direction and conformity to external authority by parents of varying social-class position obtains whatever the age and sex of the child, in families of varying size, composition, and functional pattern.[14]

This essential finding has been repeatedly confirmed, both for fathers and for mothers. The original finding came from a small study in Washington, D.C., in the late 1950s, but it has since been confirmed in several other U.S. studies, including three nationwide studies, one as recent as 1975. It has also been confirmed in studies in Italy, Germany, Great Britain, France, Ireland, and Taiwan. There are no known exceptions.[15]

The correlations of class with parental valuation of the individual characteristics (e.g., self-control and obedience) are not very large: none is larger than .20. The correlation of class with an overall index of valuation of self-direction or conformity, based on factor analysis, is a more substantial .34. But even a correlation of .34 is, by absolute standards, only moderate. What makes the class differences in parental values impressive is their consistency. It has repeatedly been confirmed that social class continues to be nearly as strongly correlated with parents' valuation of self-direction when all other major lines of social demarcation—national background, religious background, urbanicity, region of the country, and even race—are statistically controlled.[16] Social class, in fact, is as strongly correlated with parental valuation of self-direction as are all these other major lines of social demarcation combined.[17] Thus, social class, even though only moderately correlated with parental values, stands out as the single most important social influence on parents' values for their children.

Parenthetically, it is pertinent to ask whether there have been changes in parental values, especially in parental valuation of self-direction or conformity to external authority, over the few years for which data are available. The evidence, unfortunately, is equivocal. There is no substantial evidence that there have been changes, but also no conclusive evidence that there have not. In any case, the magnitude of the correlation between social class and parental valuation of self-direction is as strong in the latest available data, a national survey conducted in 1975, as in earlier studies.[18] The class-values relationship is as important for understanding parental values in the mid-1970s as it was in the mid-1950s.

Parental Values and Parental Practices

We would have little interest in parental values but for our belief that parents' values affect their child-rearing practices. The evidence here is much less definitive than on the relationship of class to parental values, but what evidence we do have is altogether consistent. Parents do behave in accord with their values in the two important realms where the question has been studied: in their disciplinary practices and in the allocation of parental responsibilities for imposing constraints on, and providing emotional support for, their children.

Disciplinary Practices

Most early research on class differences in disciplinary practices was directed toward learning whether working-class parents typically employ techniques of punishment different from those used by the middle class. In his definitive review of the research literature on social class and family relationships through the mid-1950s, Bronfenbrenner (1958, p. 424) summarized the results of the several relevant studies as indicating that "working-class parents are consistently more likely to employ physical punishment, while middle-class families rely more on reasoning, isolation, appeals to guilt, and other methods involving the threat of loss of love." This conclusion has been challenged in later research.[19] Whether or not it is still true, the difference in middle- and working-class parents' propensity to resort to physical punishment certainly never has been great.

For our purposes, in any case, the crucial question is not which disciplinary method parents prefer but when and why they use one or another method of discipline. The early research tells us little about the when and why of discipline; most investigators had relied on parents' generalized statements about their usual or their preferred methods of dealing with disciplinary problems, irrespective of what the particular problem might be. But surely not all disciplinary problems evoke the same kind of parental response. In some sense, after all, the punishment fits the crime. Under what conditions do parents of a given social class punish their children physically, reason with them, isolate them—or ignore their actions altogether?

Recent studies have shown that neither middle- nor working-class parents resort to punishment as a first recourse when their children misbehave.[20] It seems instead that parents of both social classes initially post limits for their children. But when children persist in misbehavior, parents are likely to resort to one or another form of coercion. This is true of all social-class levels. The principal difference between the classes is in the specific conditions under which parents— particularly mothers—punish children's misbehavior. Working-class parents are more likely to punish or refrain from punishing on the same basis of the direct and immediate consequences of children's actions, middle-class parents on the basis of their interpretation of children's intent in acting as they do.[21] Thus, for example, working-class parents are more likely to punish children for fighting than for arguing with their brothers and sisters and are also more likely to punish for aggressively wild play than for boisterousness—the transgression in both instances being measured in terms of how far the overt action transgresses the rules. Middle-class parents make no such distinction. But they do distinguish, for example, between wild play and a loss of temper, tolerating even excessive manifestations of the former as a childish form of emotional expression, but punishing the latter because it signifies a loss of mastery over self.

To say that working-class parents respond more to the consequences of children's misbehavior and middle-class parents more to their own interpretation of the children's intent gets dangerously close to implying that while middle-class parents act on the basis of long-range goals for children, working-class parents do not. On the contrary, the evidence suggests that parents of both social classes act on the basis of long-range goals—but that the goals are different. The interpretive key is provided by our knowledge of class differences in parental values. Because middle- and working-class parents differ in their values, they view children's misbehavior differently; what is intolerable to parents in one social class can be taken in stride by parents in the other. In both social classes, parents punish children for transgressing important values, but since the values are different, the transgressions are differently defined. If self-direction is valued, transgressions must be judged in terms of the reasons why the children misbehave. If conformity to external authority is valued, transgressions must be judged in terms of whether or not the actions violate externally imposed proscriptions.

The Allocation of Parental Responsibilities for Support and Constraint

The connection between values and punishment of disvalued behavior is direct: punishment is invoked when values are transgressed. There are also less direct but broader behavioral consequences of class differences in parental values. In particular, class differences in parental values have important consequences for the overall patterning of parent-child interaction.

In common with most investigators, I conceive of parent-child relationships as structured along two principal axes: support and constraint. This conception is derived in part from Parsons and Bales's (1955) theoretical analysis of family structure and in part from Schaefer's (1959) empirical demonstration that the findings of several past studies of parent-child relationships could be greatly clarified by arraying them along these two dimensions.

Because their values are different, middle- and working-class parents evaluate differently the relative importance of support and constraint in child rearing. One would expect middle-class parents to feel a greater obligation to be supportive, if only because of their concern about children's internal dynamics. Working-class parents, because of their higher valuation of conformity to external rules, should put greater emphasis upon the obligation to impose constraints. We should therefore expect the ratio of support to constraint in parents' handling of their children to be higher in middle-class than in working-class families. And this, according to Bronfenbrenner (1958, p. 425), is precisely what has been shown in those studies that have dealt with the overall relationship of parents to child:

> Parent-child relationships in the middle class are consistently reported as more acceptant and equalitarian, while those in the working class are oriented toward maintaining order and obedience. Within this context, the middle class has shown a shift away from emotional control toward freer expression of affection and greater tolerance of the child's impulses and desires.

Whatever relative weight parents give to support and constraint, the process of child rearing requires both. These responsibilities can, however, be apportioned between mother and father in any of several ways. Mothers can specialize in providing support, fathers in imposing constraints; both parents can play both roles more-or-less equally; mothers can monopolize both roles, with fathers playing little part in child rearing; and there are other possible, but less likely, arrangements. Given their high valuation of self-direction, middle-class parents—mothers and fathers both—should want fathers to play an important part in providing support to the children. It would seem more appropriate to working-class parents' high valuation of conformity to external authority that fathers' obligations should center on the imposition of constraints.

The pertinent studies show that in both the middle class and the working class, mothers would prefer to have their husbands play a role that facilitates children's development of a valued characteristic.[22] To middle-class mothers, it is important that children be able to decide for themselves how to act and that they have the personal resources to act on these decisions. In this conception, fathers' responsibility for imposing constraints is secondary to their responsibility for being supportive; in the minds of some middle-class mothers, for fathers to take a major part in imposing constraints interferes with their ability to be supportive. To working-class mothers, on the other hand, it is more important that children conform to externally imposed rules. In this conception, the fathers' primary responsibility is to guide and direct the children. Constraint is accorded far greater value than it has for the middle class.

Most middle-class fathers seem to share their wives' views of fathers' responsibilities toward sons and act accordingly.[23] They accept less responsibility for being supportive of daughters—apparently feeling that this is more properly the mothers' role. But many working-class fathers do not accept the obligations their wives would have them assume, either toward sons or toward daughters.[24] These men do not see the constraining role as any less important than their wives do, but many of them see no reason why fathers should have to shoulder this responsibility. From their point of view, the important thing is that children be taught what limits they must not transgress. It does not particularly matter who does the teaching, and since mothers have primary responsibility for child care, the job should be theirs. Of course, there will be occasions when fathers have to backstop their wives. But there is no ideological imperative that makes it the fathers' responsibility to assume an important part in child rearing. As a consequence, many working-class fathers play little role in child rearing, considering it to be their wives' proper responsibility.[25]

Theories of personality development, including Parsons and Bales's (1955) sociological reinterpretation of the classical Freudian developmental sequence, have generally been based on the model of a family in which the mothers' and fathers' intrafamily roles are necessarily differentiated, with mothers specializing in support and fathers in constraint.[26] However useful a first approximation this may be, both middle- and working-class variations on this general theme are sufficiently great to compel a more precise formulation.

The empirical evidence is partly consistent with the mother-supportive, father-constraining formulation, for even in middle-class families, almost no one reports that fathers are more supportive than mothers. Yet, in a sizable proportion of middle-class families, mothers take primary responsibility for imposing constraints on sons, and fathers are at least as supportive as mothers. And although middle-class fathers are not likely to be as supportive of daughters as their wives are, it cannot be said that fathers typically specialize in constraint, even with daughters.

It would be a gross exaggeration to say that middle-class fathers have abandoned the prerogatives and responsibilities of authority in favor of being friends and confidants to their sons. Yet the historical drift is probably from primary emphasis on imposing constraints to primary emphasis on support.[27] In any event, mothers' and fathers' roles are not sharply differentiated in most middle-class families; both parents tend to be supportive. Such division of functions as exists is chiefly a matter of each parent's taking special responsibility for being supportive of the children of the parent's own sex.

Mothers' and fathers' roles are more sharply differentiated in working-class families, with mothers almost always being the more supportive. Yet, despite the high valuation put on the constraining function, fathers do not necessarily specialize in setting limits, even for sons. In some working-class families, mothers specialize in support, fathers in constraint; in many others, the division of responsibilities is for the mothers to raise the children, the fathers to provide the wherewithal. This pattern of role allocation probably is and has been far more prevalent in American society than the formal theories of personality development have recognized.

Social Class, Values, and Conditions of Life

There are, then, remarkably consistent relationships between social class and parental values and behavior. But we have not yet touched on the question: Why do these relationships exist? In analytic terms, the task is to discover which of the many conditions of life associated with class position are most pertinent for explaining why class is related to parental values. Since many of the relevant conditions are implicated in people's occupational lives, our further discussion is focused on one crucial set of occupational conditions: those that determine how much opportunity people have to exercise self-direction in their work.

The principal hypothesis that has guided this line of research is that class-correlated differences in people's opportunities to exercise occupational self-direction—that is, to use initiative, thought, and independent judgment in work—are basic to class differences in parental values. Few other conditions of life are so closely bound up with social class position as are those that determine how much opportunity, even necessity, people have for exercising self-direction in their work. Moreover, there is an appealing simplicity to the supposition that the experience of self-direction in so central a realm of life as work is conducive to valuing self-direction, off as well as on the job, and to seeing the possibilities for self-direction not only in work but also in other realms of life.

Although many conditions of work are either conducive to or deterrent of the exercise of occupational self-direction, three in particular are critical.

First, a limiting condition: people cannot exercise occupational self-direction if they are closely supervised. Not being closely supervised, however, does not necessarily mean that people are required—or even free—to use initiative, thought, and independent judgment; it depends on how complex and demanding is their work.

A second condition for occupational self-direction is that work allow a variety of approaches; otherwise the possibilities for exercising initiative, thought, and judgment are seriously limited. The organization of work must not be routinized; it must involve a variety of tasks that are in themselves complexly structured.

The third and most important determinant of occupational self-direction is that work be substantively complex. By the *substantive complexity* of work I mean, essentially, the degree to which performance of that work requires thought and independent judgment. All work involves dealing with things, with data, or with people; some jobs involve all three, others only one or two of these activities. Work with things can vary in complexity from ditch-digging to sculpturing; similarly, work with people can vary in complexity from receiving simple instructions to giving legal advice; and work with data can vary from reading instructions to synthesizing abstract conceptual systems. Although, in general, work with data or with people is likely to be more complex than work with things, this is not always the case, and an index of the overall complexity of work should reflect its degree of complexity in each of these three types of activity. What is important about work is not whether it deals with things, with data, or with people, but its complexity.

No one of these occupational conditions—freedom from close supervision, nonroutinization, and substantive complexity—is definitional of occupational self-direction. Nevertheless, each of these three conditions tends to be conducive to the exercise of occupational self-direction, and the combination of the three both enables and requires it. Insofar as people are free of close supervision, work at nonroutinized tasks, and do substantively complex work, their work is necessarily self-directed. And insofar as they are subject to close supervision, work at routinized tasks, and do work of little substantive complexity, their work does not permit self-direction.

The Relationship of Occupational Self-Direction to Parental Values

Since most of the research on the relationship between occupational self-direction and parental values deals only with men's occupational conditions and men's values, I shall first discuss father's values, then broaden the discussion to include mothers' values as well. All three occupational conditions that are determinative of occupational self-direction prove to be empirically related to fathers' values.[28] Men who are free from close supervision, who work at nonroutinized tasks, and who do substantively complex work tend to value self-direction rather than conformity to external authority for their children. This being the case, it becomes pertinent to ask whether the relationship between social class and fathers' values can be explained as resulting from class differences in the conditions that make for occupational self-direction.

It must be emphasized that in dealing with these occupational conditions, we are concerned not with distinctions that cut across social class but with experiences constitutive of class. The objective is to learn whether these constitutive experiences are pertinent for explaining the class relationship. To achieve this objective, we statistically control occupational dimensions that have proved to be related to values and orientation, to determine whether this reduces the correlation between class and fathers' valuation of self-direction or conformity for their children. This procedure is altogether hypothetical, for it imagines an unreal social situation: social classes that did not differ from one another in the occupational conditions experienced by their members. But it is analytically appropriate to use such hypothetical procedures, for it helps us differentiate those occupational conditions that are pertinent for explaining the relationship of class to parental values from those occupational conditions that are not pertinent. In fact, statistically controlling the conditions that make for occupational self-direction reduces the correlation of class to fathers' valuation of self-direction or conformity by nearly two-thirds.[29] The lion's share of the reduction is attributable to the substantive complexity of the work, but closeness of supervision and routinization are relevant too. By contrast, though, statistically controlling numerous other occupational conditions has a much weaker effect—reducing the class correlation by only one-third.[30] And controlling both sets of occupational conditions reduces the correlation of class to fathers' values by no more than does controlling occupational self-direction alone. Thus, other occupational conditions add little to the explanatory power of the three that are determinative of occupational self-direction.

These findings come mainly from a cross-national study in the United States.[31] They are confirmed by a smaller-scale study in Turin, Italy.[32] A study in Taiwan failed to confirm these findings, but it is impossible to say whether this is because occupational conditions have different consequences in that partially industrialized, non-Western society, or because methodological problems of the Taiwanese study may have obscured the phenomenon.[33] A number of other pertinent but not entirely comparable studies—in Peru, West Germany, Ireland, and the United States—tend to confirm the original U.S. and Italian findings.[34] But definitive confirmation awaits the completion of studies now in progress in Ireland, Poland, and West Berlin.

Much less is known about the relationship between occupational conditions and mothers' values. My colleagues and I are currently analyzing data on the relationship between employed mothers' occupational conditions and their values for their children.[35] Preliminary results indicate that women's occupational conditions affect their values in much the same way as do men's occupational conditions. We are also investigating the relationship between housework, conceptualized in essentially the same way as any other work, and parental values, but on this issue we do not yet have findings. There is information from a study in Turin, Italy, that men's occupational conditions affect their wives' values; this appears to be particularly the case in the middle class.[36] But these data say nothing about the mechanisms by which men's occupational conditions affect their wives' values—it may be that men's occupational conditions affect their own values and that men influence their wives; it may be that men communicate something of their occupational experience to their wives and that this knowledge affects the wives' value choices; or it may be any of several other possibilities. These questions, too, are currently being studied in research that attempts to unravel the processes by which each spouse's occupational conditions affect the other's values. Clearly, much remains to be learned. But even now, there is every reason to believe that women's values are affected by class-associated conditions of life through processes similar to those operating for men.

Because the relationship between exercising self-direction on the job and valuing self-direction for children is so direct, one might conclude that parents are simply preparing their children for the occupational life to come. I believe, rather, that parents come to value self-direction or conformity as virtues in their own right, not simply as means to occupational goals. One important piece of evidence buttresses this impression: studies in both the United States and Italy show that the relationship between men's occupational experiences and their values is the same for daughters as for sons, yet it is hardly likely (especially in Italy) that most fathers think their daughters will have occupational careers comparable to those of their sons. It would thus seem that occupational experience helps structure parents' views not only of the occupational world but of social reality in general.

The Direction of Causal Effects

It could be argued that the empirical interrelationships of social class, occupational self-direction, and parental values reflect the propensity of people who value self-direction to seek out jobs that offer them an opportunity to be self-directed in their work and, once in a job, to maximize whatever opportunities the job allows for exercising self-direction. But we know that occupational choice is limited by educational qualifications, which in turn are greatly affected by the accidents of family background, economic circumstances, and available social resources. Moreover, the opportunity to exercise self-direction in one's work is circumscribed by job requirements. Thus, an executive must do complex work with data or with people; he cannot be closely supervised; and his tasks are too diverse to be routinized—to be an executive requires some substantial self-direction. Correspondingly, to be a semi-skilled factory worker precludes much self-direction. The substance of one's work cannot be especially complex; one cannot escape some measure of supervision; and if one's job is to fit into the flow of other people's work, it must necessarily be routinized. The relationship between being self-directed in one's work and holding self-directed values would thus seem to result not just from self-directed people's acting according to their values but also from job experiences affecting these very values.

This, of course, is an *a priori* argument. But we also have empirical evidence that the most important of the three occupational conditions determinative of occupational self-direction—the substantive complexity of the work—actually does have a causal impact on parental values.[37] This evidence is based on a statistical technique called *two-stage least-squares,* which was developed by econometricians for analyzing reciprocal effects. With this technique, it has been shown that the substantive complexity of work has a causal effect not only on parental values but on people's values and orientation generally, even on their intellectual functioning. These effects are independent of the selection processes that draw men into particular fields of work and independent of men's efforts to mold their jobs to fit their needs and values. Admittedly, cross-sectional data cannot provide definitive evidence of causality—only analyses of longitudinal data measuring real change in real people can be definitive. Nevertheless, these findings do establish a strong *prima facie* case that the substantive complexity of work has a real and meaningful effect on parental values and also on a very wide range of psychological processes.

More definitive, albeit less extensive, evidence comes from longitudinal analyses currently in process.[38] Analyses of longitudinal data are immensely difficult because they require the development of "measurement models" that separate unreliability of measurement from real change in the phenomena studied. Such measurement models have thus far been constructed for substantive complexity and for one facet of psychological functioning: intellectual flexibility. The latter was chosen precisely because it appeared to offer the toughest test: intellectual flexibility is obviously pertinent to job placement, and it might be expected to be one of the most stable psychological phenomena.

Stable it certainly is. The correlation between the men's intellectual flexibility 10 years later, shorn of measurement error, is .93. Nevertheless, the effect of the substantive complexity of work on intellectual flexibility is striking—on the order of one-fourth as great as the effect of the men's earlier levels of intellectual flexibility. Since this analysis is based on men no younger than 26 years of age, who are at least 10 years into their occupational careers, the effect of the substantive complexity of the job on intellectual flexibility is indeed impressive.

The longitudinal analysis demonstrates also something that no cross-sectional analysis could show—that, over time, the relationship between substantive complexity and intellectual flexibility is truly reciprocal. Substantive complexity has a more immediate effect on intellectual flexibility: today's job demands affect today's thinking processes. Intellectual flexibility, by contrast, has a delayed effect on substantive complexity: today's intellectual flexibility has scant effect on today's job demands, but it will have a sizable effect on the further course of one's career. Cross-sectional analyses portray only part of this process, making it seem as if the relationship between the substantive complexity of work and psychological functioning were mainly unidirectional, with work affecting psychological functioning but not the reverse. Longitudinal analysis portrays a more intricate and more interesting, truly reciprocal, process.

Granted, the research has not yet demonstrated that substantive complexity directly affects parental values. Still, because of its remarkable stability, intellectual flexibility offers the crucial test of the hypothesis that the substantive complexity of work actually has a causal effect on psychological functioning. Moreover, intellectual flexibility is intimately related to valuation of self-direction. It is, in fact, an important link between social class and parents' valuation of self-direction or conformity to external authority.[39] Thus, demonstrating the causal impact of substantive complexity on intellectual flexibility gives us every reason to expect substantive complexity to have a causal impact on parental values too. Further analyses will assess this hypothesized causal impact of substantive complexity—and of other determinants of occupational self-direction—on parental values and also on self-conception and social orientation.

The Role of Education in the Relationship between Social Class and Parental Values

Education matters for parental values in part because it is an important determinant of occupational conditions. A major reason for looking to such occupational conditions as substantive complexity, closeness of supervision, and routinization as possible keys to understanding the relationship between social class and parental values is that few other conditions of life are so closely related to educational attainment. This explanation has been confirmed in further analyses that have assessed the effects of education on occupational conditions at each stage of career. Education is a prime determinant, for example, of the substantive complexity of the job; and the substantive complexity of the job, in turn, has an appreciable effect on parental values. It is precisely because education is crucial for the very occupational conditions that most strongly affect parental values that education is so powerfully related to parental values.[40]

Education also has important direct effects on parental values, quite apart from its indirect effects mediated through occupational conditions. Education matters, aside from its impact on job conditions, insofar as education provides the intellectual flexibility and breadth of perspective that are essential for self-directed values.[41] Thus education has both direct and indirect effects upon parental values, both types of effect contributing importantly to the overall relationship between social class and parental values.

Conclusion

The facts and interpretations reviewed in this paper have many implications for medicine. One set of implications that I have dwelt on at length elsewhere is that these findings may help us interpret the consistent statistical relationship between social class and rates of schizophrenia.[42] They may also help us understand the role of the family in the etiology of schizophrenia. Most generally, these findings are pertinent to our conception of what is normal and what is not in family functioning. I have tried in this paper to show that there are considerable variations in normal family functioning and that these variations are to be understood in terms of the actual conditions of life that families encounter. The values and child-rearing practices of American families must be seen in terms of the realities parents face.

Notes

1. This essay does not purport to be a systematic review of the entire research literature on social class and parent-child relationships. Instead, it focuses on my own research and that

of my NIMH colleagues, as well as that of other investigators who have dealt with the same research issues. For a definitive review of the literature on social class and parent-child relationships through the mid-1950s, see Bronfenbrenner (1958). Research of the next decade or so is summarized in Kohn (1969). A seminal essay that reviews and assesses more recent work in the field, and also appraises the major interpretations of social class and parent-child relationships, is that by Gecas (1979).

2. See Williams (1960, p. 98). See also Barber (1968, p. 292).

3. See Kohn (1969, pp. 129–131). See also Kohn (1977).

4. See Hatt (1950), North and Hatt (1953), and Reiss, Duncan, Hatt, and North (1961).

5. See Gusfield and Schwartz (1963), Hodge, Siegel, and Rossi (1964), and Simmons and Rosenberg (1971).

6. See Inkeles and Rossi (1956).

7. See Tiryakian (1958), Svalastoga (1959), Thomas (1962), Hodge, Treiman, and Rossi (1966), and Haller and Lewis (1966).

8. See Berelson and Steiner (1964). See also the references in Kohn (1969, p. 3, note 2).

9. See Williams (1968, p. 283).

10. See Kohn (1969, pp. 18–19, 47–48).

11. See Kohn (1969, pp. 23–24).

12. See Kohn (1969, pp. 20–21, 42–43, 50–51).

13. See Kohn (1969, Chapters 2, 3, 4; 1977).

14. See Kohn (1969, pp. 48–59, 68–69).

15. See Kohn (1969, Chapters 2, 3, 4), Olsen (1971), Perron (1971), Platt (n.d.), Hynes (1977), Hoff and Grueneisen (1977a, b), Bertram (1976, 1977), Franklin and Scott (1970), Clausen (1974), Campbell (1978), Wright and Wright (1976), and Kohn (1976d). See also LeMasters (1975) and Sennett and Cobb (1973).

16. See Kohn (1969, pp. 59–72), Wright and Wright (1976), Kohn (1976d), Kohn (1977).

17. This is not to say that other major lines of social demarcation are unimportant for parental values. Race, for example, has a consistent effect on parental values at all social-class levels. But the effect of race on parental values is only about one-fourth as great as that of social class.

18. This statement is based on my unpublished analysis of the data of the 1975 National Opinion Research Center's General Social Survey as compared to earlier studies cited above.

19. See Erlanger (1974). Erlanger found that subsequent studies failed to confirm the pattern Bronfenbrenner had discovered in the earlier studies, particularly as regards working-class parents' allegedly greater propensity to use physical punishment.

20. See Kohn (1969, pp. 92–95, 102–103).

21. See Kohn (1969, Chapter 6) and Gecas and Nye (1974). Class differences in the conditions under which parents punish their children's misbehavior probably do not begin until the children are about 6 years old, but they seem to apply regardless of age thereafter, at least until the mid-teens.

22. See Kohn (1969, pp. 120–122).

23. See Kohn (1969, pp. 113–114).

24. See Kohn (1969, pp. 120–122).

25. The general picture of class differences in parental role-allocation sketched above appears to apply regardless of the age of the child, beginning at least as young as age 10 or 11 and probably earlier.

26. See also Bronfenbrenner (1960) and Kohn (1969, p. 124, note 11).

27. See Bronson, Katten, and Livson (1959) and Bronfenbrenner (1961).

28. See Kohn (1969, Chapter 9), based on data from the United States and Italy. The generalization is also supported by Hoff and Grueneisen (1977a,b), using West German data; by Hynes (1977), using data from Ireland; by St. Peter (1975) using U.S. data; and by Scurrah and Montalvo (1975), using data from Peru; but not by Olsen (1971), using data from Taiwan.

29. See Kohn (1969, pp. 161–163).

30. See Kohn (1969, pp. 182–183 and Table 10–7).
31. See Kohn (1969, pp. 152–164, 182–183).
32. See Kohn (1969, pp. 143–152).
33. See Olsen (1971) and Kohn (1977).
34. See Scurrah and Montalvo (1975), Hoff and Grueneisen (1977a,b), Hynes (1977), and St. Peter (1975).
35. In 1974, we conducted a 10-year follow-up to the 1964 study of employed men that is the basis of many of the findings presented in Kohn (1969). In the follow-up study, we not only reinterviewed the men, but this time we also interviewed their wives and children (see Kohn, 1977).
36. See Kohn (1969, Chapter 9).
37. See Kohn and Schooler (1973).
38. Kohn and Schooler (1978).
39. See Kohn (1969, p. 186).
40. See Kohn and Schooler (1973).
41. Kohn (1969, pp. 186–187).
42. See Kohn (1973). Pertinent, too, are Kohn (1976a,b).

References

Barber, B. "Social stratification." In D. L. Sills (Ed.), *International encyclopedia of the social sciences* (Vol. 15). New York: Macmillan Company and Free Press, 1968.

Berelson, B., & Steiner, G. A. *Human behavior: An inventory of scientific findings*. New York: Harcourt Brace Jovanovich, 1964.

Bertram, H. *Gesellschaftliche and familiäir Bedingungen moralischen Urteilens*. Unpublished doctoral dissertation, Universität Dusseldorf, 1976.

———, Personal Communication, 1977.

Bronfenbrenner, U. "Socialization and social class through time and space." In E. E. Maccoby, T. M. Newcomb, and E. L. Hartley (Eds.), *Readings in social psychology*. New York: Holt, Rinehart & Winston, 1958.

———, "Freudian theories of identification and their derivatives." *Child Development*, 1960, *31*, 15–40.

———, "The changing American child—a speculative analysis." *Journal of Social Issues*, 1961, *17*, 6–18.

Bronson, W. C., Katten, E. S., and Livson, N. "Patterns of authority and affection in two generations." *Journal of Abnormal and Social Psychology*, 1959, *58*, 143–152.

Campbell, J. D. "The child in the sick role: Contributions of age, sex, parental status and parental values." *Journal of Health and Social Behavior*, 1978, *19*, 35–51.

Clausen, J. A. *Value transmission and personality resemblance in two generations*. Paper presented to the annual meeting of the American Sociological Association, Montreal, August 27, 1974.

Erlanger, H. S. "Social class and corporal punishment in childrearing: A reassessment." *American Sociological Review*, 1974, *39*, 68–85.

Franklin, J. I., and Scott, J. E. "Parental values: An inquiry into occupational setting." *Journal of Marriage and the Family*, 1970, *32*, 406–409.

Gecas, V. "The influence of social class on socialization." In W. R. Burr, R. Hill, F. Ivan Nye, and I. Reiss (Eds.), *Contemporary theories about the family*. Vol. 1: Research-based theories. New York: Free Press, 1979.

Gecas, V., and Nye, F. I. "Sex and class differences in parent-child interactions: A test of Kohn's hypothesis." *Journal of Marriage and the Family*, 1974, *36*, 742–749.

Gusfield, J. R., and Schwartz, M. "The meanings of occupational prestige: Reconsideration of the NORC scale." *American Sociological Review*, 1963, *28*, 265–271.

Haller, A. O., and Lewis, D. M. "The hypothesis of intersocietal similarity in occupational prestige hierarchies." *American Journal of Sociology*, 1966, *72*, 210–216.

Hatt, P. K. "Occupation and social stratification." *American Journal of Sociology*, 1950, *55*, 533–543.

Hodge, R. W., Siegel, P. M., and Rossi, P. H. "Occupational prestige in the United States: 1925–1963." *American Journal of Sociology*, 1964, *70*, 286–302.

Hodge, R. W., Treiman, D. J., and Rossi, P. H. "A comparative study of occupational prestige." In R. Bendix and S. M. Lipset (Eds.), *Class, status, and power* (2nd ed.). New York: Free Press. 1966.

Hoff, E. H., and Grueneisen, V. "Arbeitserfahrungen, Erziehungseinstellungen, und Erziehungsverhalten von Eltern." In H. Lukesch and K. Schneewind (Eds.), *Familiär Sozialisation: Probleme, Ergebnisse, Perspektiven*. Stuttgart: Klett, 1977(a).

———, Personal communication, 1977(b).

Hynes, E. Personal communication, 1977.

Inkeles, A., and Rossi, P. H. "National comparisons of occupational prestige." *American Journal of Sociology*, 1956, *61*, 329–339.

Kohn, M. L. *Class and conformity: A study in values*. Homewood, Ill.: Dorsey Press, 1969. (2nd ed. published 1977, by University of Chicago Press.)

———, "Social class and schizophrenia: A critical review and a reformulation." *Schizophrenia Bulletin*, 1973, *7*, 60–79.

———, "The interaction of social class and other factors in the etiology of schizophrenia." *American Journal of Psychiatry*, 1976(a), *133*, 177–180.

———, "Looking back—A 25 year review and appraisal of social problems research." *Social Problems*, 1976(b), *24*, 94–112.

———, "Social class and parental values. Another confirmation of the relationship." *American Sociological Review*, 1976(c), *41*, 538–545.

———, "Occupational structure and alienation." *American Journal of Sociology*, 1976(d), *82*, 111–130.

Kohn, M. L., and Schooler, C. "Occupational experience and psychological functioning: An assessment of reciprocal effects." *American Sociological Review*, 1973, *38*, 97–118.

———, "The reciprocal effects of the substantive complexity of work and intellectual flexibility: A longitudinal assessment." *American Journal of Sociology*, 1978, *84*, 24–52.

LeMasters, E. E. *Blue-collar aristocrats: Life styles at a working-class tavern*. Madison: University of Wisconsin Press, 1975.

North, C. C. and Hatt, P. K. "Jobs and occupations: A popular evaluation." In R. Bendix & S. M. Lipset (Eds.), *Class, Status, and Power*. New York: Free Press, 1953.

Olsen, S. M. *Family occupation, and values in a Chinese urban community*. Unpublished doctoral dissertation, Cornell University, 1971.

Perron, R., *Modèles d'enfants, enfants modèles*. Paris: Presses Universitaires de France, 1971.

Platt, J. *Social class and childrearing norms in Britain and the U.S.* Unpublished manuscript, University of Sussexs, n.d.

Reiss, A. J., Duncan, O. D., Hatt, P. K., and North, C. C. *Occupations and social status.* New York: Free Press, 1961.

Scurrah, M. J., and Montalvo, A. *Close social y valores sociales en Peru.* Peru: Escuela de Administracion de Negocios Para Graduados (Series: Documento de Trabaio No. 8), 1975.

Sennett, R., and Cobb, J. *The hidden injuries of class.* New York: Vintage Books, 1972.

Simmons, R. G., and Rosenberg, M. "Functions of children's perceptions of the stratification system." *American Sociological Review,* 1971, *36,* 235–249.

St. Peter, L. G. *Fate conceptions: A look at the effects of occupational tasks on human values.* Unpublished doctoral dissertation, University of Nebraska, 1975.

Svalastoga, K. *Prestige, class and mobility.* Copenhagen: Glydendal, 1959.

Thomas, R. M. "Reinspecting a structural position on occupational prestige." *American Journal of Sociology,* 1962, pp. 561–565.

Tiryakian, E. A. "The prestige evaluation of occupations in an underdeveloped country: The Philippines." *American Journal of Sociology,* 1958, *63,* 390–399.

Williams, R. M., Jr. *American society: A sociological interpretation* (2nd ed.), New York, Knopf, 1960.

_____, "The concept of values." In D. L. Sills (Ed.), *International Encyclopedia of the Social Sciences* (Vol. 16). New York: Macmillan and Free Press, 1968.

Wright, J. D., and Wright, S. R. "Social class and parental values for children: A partial replication and extension of the Kohn thesis." *American Sociological Review.* 1976, *41,* 527–537.

Development of Androgyny: Parental Influences

Mary Anne Sedney

Traditionally theories of sex-role development within the family have focused on the ways stereotyped sex-role characteristics—femininity for girls and masculinity for boys—develop. The present paper represents an attempt to move beyond those questions to a consideration of the impact parents have on the development of nonstereotyped sex-role behavior, here conceptualized as androgyny.

Introduction of the concept of androgyny to the psychology literature by Bem (1974), and Spence and her colleagues (Spence, Helmreich, & Stapp, 1975) generated an explosion of interest. Controversies about measurement, conceptualization, correlates, and consequences fueled more than a decade of research and writing (cf. Jones, Chernovetz, & Hansson, 1978; Kaplan & Sedney, 1980; Kelly & Worell, 1977; Locksley & Colten, 1979; Pedhazur & Tetenbaum, 1979; Taylor & Hall, 1982). Recent writings by Bem and Spence suggest that both originators are moving toward examination of more specific processes in understanding gender-related behavior (Bem, 1985, toward study of gender schemas; and Spence, 1985, toward study of gender identity).

Some researchers and reviewers may think it is time to leave the concept of androgyny for dead, buried as it is in a morass of words and controversies. Some of the controversies in the field can be traced to variations among researchers both in definitions of androgyny and ways of conceptualizing personality processes in general (Sedney, in press). Nevertheless, when viewed as a general construct, androgyny remains a useful term to conceptualize an alternative to traditionally sex-typed behaviors and traits. It is in that spirit in which the term is used in the present paper. As used here, androgyny refers to the combination in an individual of traits and behaviors that traditionally have been stereotypically and differentially assigned to females and males. This definition is consistent with Bem's (1974, 1976) original conceptualization and scale development; the emphasis is on how people describe themselves vis à vis culturally held schemas of "femininity" and "masculinity."[1]

The author would like to thank Alexandra G. Kaplan, Lila Ghent Braine, and several anonymous reviewers for their comments on earlier drafts of this manuscript. Parts of this paper appeared in a talk prepared by Mary Anne Sedney and Alexandra G. Kaplan, and presented to a meeting of the Alberta State Psychological Association.

Work in the years since Constantinople (1973) pointed out conceptual and empirical problems with the "masculinity—femininity" concept has revealed that sex is most appropriately conceptualized as a multidimensional term. "Sex" refers to biological, psychological, social, and political processes. Among the dimensions encompassed in the concept of sex are: biological sex, gender identity, sexual orientation, social sex role, and psychological sex role (Kaplan & Sedney, 1980). "Biological sex" refers to one's physical status as female or male, usually decided at birth on the basis of genitals. "Gender identity" refers to an awareness of and comfort with one's biological sex. "Sexual orientation" refers to one's choice of a sexual partner, while "social sex role" refers to the social role one chooses to adopt such as wife, mother and/or paid worker. "Psychological sex role" includes the personality traits and behaviors that, although not involved in actual sexual behavior, are included in people's stereotyped notions about how females and males differ; a person's expression of these traits and behaviors represents [his or her] psychological sex role.

These dimensions of sex are potentially independent. Thus, a person may be biologically female, have a secure feminine gender identity, prefer males as sexual partners, adopt a social role as mother and paid worker, and be androgynous. The use of the terms "feminine," "masculine," and "androgynous" in the present paper is limited to the psychological sex role dimension.

Traditional theories of sex-role development do not consider the multidimensional nature of sex and gender. As noted by Constantinople (1973), they are based on an assumption that "masculinity–femininity" is a unidimensional concept encompassing biological, sexual, social, and psychological components that correspond. Some theories, such as psychoanalytic ones, embrace this assumption to a greater extent than others, such as social learning theories. Nevertheless, when traditional theorists write about sex-role development, at the very least they include the development of the psychological sex-role dimension.

Theories of Psychological Sex-Role Development

Although psychoanalytic (Freud, 1925), social learning (Mischel, 1966, 1970), and cognitive developmental (Kohlberg, 1966) theories of sex-role development diverge in their ideas of the processes involved in the development of psychological sex roles, they converge in a number of ways. All three of these traditional theories suggest a process through which children incorporate characteristics of another person, usually a parent and usually the parent of their own biological sex, into their personality. It is in this way that children are said to learn the distinction not just between being female or male, but between being feminine and masculine in [a] psychological sex role, that is, in personality and behavior.

Further, all three traditional theories emphasize the ways that stereotyped traits and behaviors develop. They concentrate on childhood, particularly the preschool years, and seem to lose interest once girls have learned to be feminine and boys to be masculine. To these theorists, development of a psychological sex role apparently is complete at that point. Thus, one cannot look to these theories for assistance in understanding development of a psychological sex role that may occur after early childhood. Nor can one look to these theories for discussion of developmental stages beyond stereotypic behaviors to androgyny.

However, two more recent conceptualizations include development beyond stereotypic to androgynous psychological sex roles. Block[2] (1973, 1984) provided one such alternative to the traditional theories. Block's work is based on Loevinger's stages of ego development (Loevinger, 1966; Loevinger & Wessler, 1970), which are conceived as an invariable sequence of stages, each more complex than the earlier ones, and each representing the person's ability to cope with increasingly deeper problems. Block conceptualized psychological sex-role development proceeding in a parallel fashion, as the result of the individual's efforts to attain an identity that permits her or him to deal with life's increasing complexity. Thus, the goal of development of a psychological sex role becomes the balancing of femininity and masculinity, rather than the attainment of a fixed, sex-typed identity.

Block described a five-stage process of sex-role development. Stage one (parallel to Loevinger's Impulse Ridden stage) includes development of gender identity (beginning awareness that "I am a girl [or boy]"), self-assertion, self-expression, and self-interest. Stage two (parallel to Loevinger's Conformity stage) involves conformity to external roles, development of sex-role stereotypes, and the splitting of sex roles. Stage three (parallel to Loevinger's Conscientious stage) includes an examination of one's self as an instance of sex role in relationship to internalized values. Stage four (parallel to Loevinger's Autonomous stage) involves a differentiation of sex role, and coping with conflicting feminine and masculine aspects of the self. Finally, stage five (parallel to Loevinger's Integrated stage) involves the achievement of an individually defined sex role, integration of both masculine and feminine aspects of the self, and the achievement of an androgynous sex-role definition.

Thus, throughout these stages there is a movement toward an increasingly individualized notion of one's genderness. In the early stages this notion is derived directly from socially defined stereotyped roles that prescribe that one must be either "feminine" or "masculine." However, at later stages it matures into self-defined concepts that can bridge the rigid stereotypes characteristic of more youthful thinking.

The second, but less well-developed, alternative theory of psychological sex-role development is that offered by Hefner, Rebecca, and Oleshansky (1975). As they conceptualize the process, the individual first goes through an *undifferentiated* conception of sex roles, at an early period of life, characterized by global thinking: She or he is not aware of a female-male distinction. With maturation and the development of logical thought, the child moves to a *polarized* notion of sex roles. This shift includes an active acceptance of one's own psychological sex role, together with an active rejection of what is then conceptualized as the "opposite" sex. Thinking at this stage is in terms of polarities: One is either female or male and, hence, either feminine or masculine. Some people remain at this point, while others are able to make the transition to a third stage of sex-role development, the stage of *sex-role transcendence*. This is a dynamic stage in which one can transcend polarities in order to adopt more adaptive and personally relevant strategies.

There are two major distinctions between these newer theories and the traditional ones of Freud, Mischel, and Kohlberg. First, unlike the traditional theories, the new ones suggest a developmental process that goes beyond the awareness of self as masculine or feminine to one that can incorporate the presence of both feminine and masculine elements within the self. That is, development is seen as going beyond that which is socially sanctioned to that which is humanly possible. Second, it is only the newer theories that see the process of psychological sex-role development extending past childhood and into the adult years. In both of these theories an androgynous stage is one that is achieved, if it is achieved at all, in adulthood, and only after the individual has proceeded through the more traditional stage of psychological sex-role polarization.

In addition to the evidence presented by Block (1973, 1984) in support of her theory, other evidence consistent with her thinking has accumulated. In a cross-sectional study of people ranging in age from late adolescence to middle-adulthood, Fischer and Narus (1981) found that, while the endorsement of self-described characteristics stereotypically ascribed to one's own sex was uncorrelated with age, endorsement of self-described characteristics stereotypically ascribed to the other sex tended to be greater among older than younger people. On average, androgynous people were older than sex-typed women and men. Additional support for the notion of psychological sex-role development as a life-span process has been provided by Cunningham and Antill (1984), Katz (1979), Leahy and Eiter (1980), and Sedney (1986).

While Block's thinking and research won her a great deal of recognition and her work continues to be widely cited, its implications for the role parents play in psychological sex-role development are often overlooked. Unlike traditional theories that suggest that parents play a major and immediate role in psychological sex-role development, both Block's and Hefner et al.'s theories imply that internal, developmental factors play a major role in children's psychological sex-role development.

This distinction is not apparent as long as one studies only the development of stereotypic behavior, for the stereotypes of parents seem to match the stereotypes of children. However, differential predictions emerge with the newer theories when one considers the case of androgynous parents. Theoretically a truly androgynous integration of masculinity and femininity is not possible in childhood. Thus, one would predict that there are limits to the extent that parents can be influential in developing androgyny in their children. Parental influences on the development of androgyny would be more likely to be apparent as long-term rather than short-term effects.

Evidence Regarding Parental Influence on Psychological Sex-Role Development

There is increasing evidence that, although average parents treat their children in a manner consistent with traditionally sex-typed behavior, and although average children do behave in sex-typed ways, the relationship between these parent and child behaviors in specific parent–child pairs is not as often apparent as one might expect.

One consistent finding in the research literature is that average children are aware of and engage in sex-stereotypic behaviors from early ages. Comprehensive reviews of these data can be found in Katz (1979) and Huston (1983); the following examples are presented as representative of findings in this area. Children reliably choose same-sex-stereotypic toys as early as the second year (O'Brien & Huston, 1985). By two years, children can identify the different sexes and show rudimentary knowledge of sex-typing of certain objects; by three years, they display good awareness of cultural sex typing (Thompson, 1975). Gender labeling, gender identity, sex-typed toy preferences, and awareness of adult sex-role differences can be observed in a significant percentage of two-year-olds (Weinraub, Clemens, Sockloff, Ethridge, Gracely, & Myers, 1984). Seven-year-old girls demonstrate stereotyped attitudes in terms of their opinions about sex-stereotypic activities, female competence, own preference for work, and expected activities as an adult (Meyer, 1980). In general, differences in girls' and boys' behavior increase from infancy to the preschool years, and then increase again in middle childhood (Katz, 1979).

A second consistent finding in the research literature on sex-role development is that parents typically think about and behave differently with daughters and sons. Parents' efforts at sex-role socialization are apparent both in their attitudes and expectations about their children, and in their actual interactions with their children. Comprehensive reviews of this area can be found in Block (1973, 1984) and Katz (1979). For example, parents have differential expectations of sons and daughters as early as 24 hours after birth (Rubin, Provenzano, & Luria, 1974). Both the decorative motif and toys provided in the rooms of girls and boys vary systematically with the child's gender (Rheingold & Cook, 1975). Many parents provide same-sex-typed toys for their children and make sex-typed predictions of their children's toy choices (O'Brien & Huston, 1985). Parental encouragement of sex-typed activities has been well documented (Maccoby & Jacklin, 1974). Parents' responses to their toddler children have been shown to be contingent on the sex-role appropriateness of the child's behavior (Fagot, 1978). Significant differences in reported childrearing emphases are found in parents of daughters and sons at a variety of ages: Parents of boys place greater emphasis on achievement, competition, control of feelings, and conformity to rules, while parents of girls report a greater stress on close interpersonal relationships, encouragement to talk about troubles, and more frequent expression of physical affection, comfort and reassurance (Block, 1973).

Although it is often assumed that sex-stereotypic behavior in children is linked to the sex-related socialization practices of their parents, this relationship is surprisingly difficult to detect, at least by the methods commonly used by psychologists. Two- and three-year-olds' uses and preferences for sex-role labels bear no relationship to mothers' sex-role attitudes or other family factors (social class, parents' work time outside the home, parental education), despite the fact that there are clear differences among the parents (Thompson, 1975). Observation of the play behavior of four- and five-year-olds reveals strongly sex-stereotypic play, regardless of sex-role behavior or attitudes in the parents (Sutton-Simon & Menig-Peterson, 1977). In naturalistic observations over a period of 14 months, O'Brien and Huston (1985) did not find clear and consistent relationships between children's (ages 14 to 35 months) sex-typed play and their parents' expectations and provisions of toys. In a study of one- and two-year-olds and their parents, there was no evidence of a relationship of parental stereotyping and the degree of sex-typed behavior in their children (Smith & Daglish, 1977).

Some findings in this area are mixed. Although children (ages 60 to 80 months) of working mothers were less likely to misidentify a depicted female physician than children of nonemployed mothers, there was no evidence that maternal employment was related to misperceptions of a depicted male nurse (Cordura, McGraw, & Drabman, 1979).

However, at times, interpretations of relatively small differences that coincide with the assumption of a link between parent and child sex-typing can be overemphasized, while a failure to find evidence for such a link is ignored. For example, discussion of a study of the relationship of sex stereotyping in parents and their children in the third year emphasized the "pivotal role" that fathers play in "sex-role acquisition" (Weinraub et al., 1984, p. 1502). The data showed that none of the 60 correlations of mother-child sex-typing variables were significant, and 9 of the 60 correlations of father-child sex-typing variables were significant. Understanding the 111/120 relationships that did not reach statistical significance would seem to be at least as interesting a topic for discussion.

Huston's (1983) review found little evidence of relationship between parents' attitudes about sex-role stereotypes and the thinking and behavior of their children. Regarding the more general range of traits and behaviors traditionally stereotyped as "feminine" or "masculine," Huston found more evidence of parental influences. However, the relevant parental variables tended to be those associated with qualitative factors in the parent-child relationship, rather than specific, direct attempts at sex-role socialization. Thus, while the evidence for a direct link between parent-child sex-role stereotypes is weak, there is the suggestion of a less deliberate parental influence via subtle interactional factors that need not be mediated by conscious attitudes about gender. These factors will be discussed following an examination of the role children may play in helping to orchestrate their own psychological sex-role development.

Children's Resistance to Nonstereotyped Behavior

Research on children's reactions to socialization pressures contrary to sex-role stereotypes suggests that it may be particularly difficult to direct children toward androgyny. At least in the context of a society that is stereotypic in its pressures, young children frequently opt for stereotypes even in the face of isolated pushes toward androgyny. This may be a function of the combined influence of the child's cognitive level and the strength of the prevailing cultural pressures. Huston (1983) noted that children use gender as an organizing principle very early, with little direct teaching from socialization agents; children's concepts of gender develop in most known societies.

If social pressure alone is responsible for children's stereotyped behavior, one would expect that social pressure would induce children away from stereotyped behavior. That such is often not the case suggests that children's sex-stereotypic behaviors represent the result of processes more complex than social pressures. Findings regarding interactions with both important adults and peers suggest that young children often resist efforts to mold their behavior away from stereotypes. Katz (1986) reviewed research in this field and concluded that results are mixed, with effectiveness of interventions interacting with a number of factors. She suggested that one of these factors is children's developmental level.

In United States society, boys are particularly strong in their resistance to what they consider "sex-inappropriate" behavior when it is advocated or modeled. A highly regarded female teacher tried to persuade four- and five-year-olds to give up a sex-appropriate toy. Most boys and girls resisted the teacher's advice and kept the toy, although boys resisted more strongly and displayed more anxiety than girls did (Ross & Ross, 1972). Some even tried to discredit the usually admired teacher ("Poor teacher, she must have a real bad throat," p. 345) or explain her position ("Teacher has too much to do today. You shouldn't ask her to do more things. Let's pretend we never asked her," p. 345).

An intensive home-based program (80 minutes/day for 10 days) using nonstereotypic play materials (toys, songs, books) was not associated with evidence of changes in children's (ages 48 to 77 months) sex-role identity, knowledge of sex-role identity, or knowledge of sex roles (Roddy, Klein, Stericker, & Kurdek, 1981). Mothers were trained to serve as the "teacher" in this study.

Children also resist the messages of a peer model when the peer deviates from the stereotype. Six-year-olds watched a videotape of a child playing with a sex-inappropriate toy (doll for boys, fire engine for girls). When given a chance to play with the toys, boys in particular were unlikely to follow the model's behavior. An adult was even less effective as a model in this case (Wolf, 1975). There is some suggestion that this resistance to violating sex-stereotypic rules increases in middle childhood, for Vieira and Miller (1978) found that ten-year-olds avoided sex-atypical toys more than five-year-olds did and boys avoided the sex-atypical objects more than girls did.

The effects of behavioral consequences seem to interact with a selective attention in many children that emphasizes stereotypic behaviors. While positive reinforcement for male-typed activities affected boys more than girls, positive reinforcement for female-typed activities affected girls more than boys in a study of four-year-olds (Lamb & Roopnarine, 1979). In other words, attempts to reinforce a child for counterstereotypic activities would meet with more difficulty than reinforcing the child for stereotypic activities. Similarly, Fagot (1985a) found that there seemed to be more than a simple reinforcement principle operating in the maintenance of sex-typed behaviors among two-year-olds. She found that some behaviors were maintained even under conditions of no response, and that positive responses were most effective when processed in terms of gender.

When there has been evidence of success in modifying children's sex-typed behaviors, this success seems to be quite situation-specific, even with long-term programs. Carpenter, Huston, and Holt (1986) randomly assigned preschoolers to different types of activities in their classroom over the course of a semester. While they demonstrated that the experimental manipulation did affect the children's behavior within the 15-minute activity that was the focus of the intervention, they also found that the effects did not extend even into the next play period; as soon as the 15-minute intervention period was over, children returned to their usual behaviors. Working with fourth and fifth graders over the course of an academic year, Lockheed (1986) also found no evidence that the effects of a classroom-based intervention program generalized to more global preferences. Although children in classrooms with teachers trained to encourage cross-sex interaction did engage in more cross-sex interaction than did students in control classrooms, there was no evidence that their actual sociometric ratings of cross-sex classmates differentiated less on the basis of sex than did those of children in control classrooms.

Thus it appears that children are not passive recipients of intervention efforts; attempts to influence children's psychological sex role interact with the child's existing preferences, developmental level, and influences from other sources. It is notable that in both those intervention studies that did demonstrate some effect, albeit circumscribed, the interventions did not focus directly on children's sex-typed behavior (e.g., by offering non-sex-typed toys or reinforcing cross-sex behavior). Rather, they tried to influence children's sex-typing in more subtle, indirect ways such as the degree of adult direction provided for activities and the degree of interaction with other-sex peers.

Long-Term Consequences of Non-Sex-Typed Parenting

Although the research discussed to this point suggests some limits to the influences parents can have on the development of androgyny in their offspring, this is not equivalent to concluding that parents have no influence. The newer theories of sex-role development discussed above suggest that androgyny may be a phenomenon of adulthood rather than childhood. Young children's conceptions of themselves and the world may be too simplistic to deal with anything other than dichotomous ways of thinking: "I'm either feminine or masculine and cannot be both." Since androgyny may not be fully developed until after childhood, it is necessary to look to adulthood for a view of the full consequences of non-sex-typed parenting.

Longitudinal studies of sex-role development are rare, but one exception is the work of Block, von der Lippe, and Block (1973). They obtained information from interviews and observations of parents and their children, then compared these data with information collected from the "children" when they were in their 30s. The 66 men and 68 women in the study were originally recruited into the Oakland Growth and Berkeley Guidance Studies in the first few years of their lives. Early data included ratings of mothers, family ratings, and environmental descriptions; adult data included psychological test scores and ratings based on extensive interview protocols. Thus, data for the children, their parents, and the grownup "children" included both self-reports and reports by trained observers.

Two parental factors emerged as strongly related to the development of androgynous offspring. First, it was necessary that the family atmosphere be warm and supportive with psychologically healthy parents who were emotionally available to their children. Parents of androgynous offspring were stable and financially secure members of their communities, they generally were satisfied with their lives and their marriages, they agreed about discipline, and they emphasized values of fairness and responsibility to others. Parents in this group were judged to have good marital adjustment. In those families marked by emotional tension and conflictual parent–child relationships, the children adopted extremes of stereotypic sex-role behavior as adults, regardless of other aspects of the children's upbringing. Thus, a positive family atmosphere appears to be one significant contribution to the development of androgynous children.

In addition, the androgynous adults came from families in which the parents themselves exemplified androgynous personality styles and flexibility in their social-role definitions. Personally, both parents demonstrated both nurturance and support for achievement in their relationships with their children. Also, the parents' relationship was characterized by some form of unconventional sharing of responsibility (at a time when there was little social support for such a stance). Those children who came from loving families in which the parents held to clear and conventional social-role definitions, as adults, were emotionally stable and psychologically similar to the same-sex parent.

On the basis of these data it seems that parents who are themselves both loving and androgynous are the ones most likely to raise androgynous offspring. Additional evidence on the importance of exposure to androgynous or non-sex-typed parents for the development of androgynous adults comes from retrospective studies that compare sex-typed and androgynous adults' accounts of their childhoods. Several aspects of parents' nontraditional behaviors seem to be most salient. One of these is the ways that power and dominance are handled within the family. Lipman–Blumen (1972), for example, found that women with a contemporary sex-role ideology tended to come from families in which most of the time neither parent was dominant or from families in which the mother was dominant. The traditional pattern of a dominant father seemed to foster more traditional development in daughters. No information was available in this study on the development of sons.

Another salient factor in the development of androgyny concerns the ways in which parents communicate interest in aspects of their children's development. Kelly and Worell (1976) found that androgynous women had mothers who were involved and interested in their cognitive development, and who in particular stressed intellectual curiosity. For androgynous men, in contrast, cognitive stimulation was of little importance, while parental warmth and caring was much more at issue. It is as if some positive parental support of the nonstereotypic aspect of personality—intellectual interests for daughters and warmth for sons— was important for the development of androgyny.

Yet another pertinent factor is parents' allocation of work and family roles. DeFronzo and Boudreau (1979) found that non-sex-stereotypic women tended to be those whose mothers were active participants in the paid labor force, while non-sex-stereotypic men had strong recollections of their fathers' active involvement in household tasks. Hansson, Chernovetz, and Jones (1977) found that mothers of androgynous college women were more likely to be employed outside the home than mothers of feminine women. Huston (1983) concluded that children of mothers employed outside the home had less stereotyped ideas about sex-typing than did other children. Maternal employment has long been known to be correlated with career orientation and choice of nontraditional careers in college women (Almquist & Angrist, 1970; Birnbaum, 1975; Ginzberg, 1971; Tangri, 1972).[3]

Even if androgyny does not fully develop until adulthood, one can find hints of these interactional and role influences in data on child development. For example, Stein and Bailey (1973) found that girls are more likely to develop achievement behavior and independence when parents are moderately warm and moderately to highly permissive, and when they encourage achievement efforts. In her more recent review, Huston (1983) presented evidence suggestive of the importance of maternal warmth for the development of communal-type behavior in boys; agentic patterns of behavior tend to be linked with high demands, control and encouragement of independence in a context of moderate warmth. Children raised in such a context should seem to be well on the way to the development of a range of behaviors, even though they may temporarily reject activities that conflict with their notions of gender-appropriate behaviors.

It may be that behavior that is inconsistent with cultural sex-role stereotypes takes longer to develop than stereotypic behavior; thus, androgyny would take longer to develop than traditional psychological sex roles. Behavior and activities differentiated on the basis of gender fit nicely with the young child's structured cognitive and ego-developmental levels. In addition, development of counterstereotypic behaviors requires not only learning but then deciding to counter cultural stereotypes. For example, Meyer (1980) found less stereotyping in the sex-role attitudes of eleven- than seven-year-old girls. Further, the correlations of mother-daughter scores were higher for the older than the younger girls. Yet, even among the older girls, those with homemaker mothers were more similar to their mothers than those with working mothers. It is as if, while the influence of the more stereotyped mothers could be perceived at eleven years, the influence of the less stereotyped mothers might not yet be fully apparent at that age.

Discussion

Once psychological sex-role development is conceptualized as a process that potentially continues across the lifespan, it becomes important for researchers interested in parental influences to look at the relationship of parent-adult as well as parent-child variables. The assumption of a strong, immediate, and direct effect of parental sex-typing on children's sex-typing is not always supported, particularly when androgyny is the outcome considered. Understanding of psychological sex-role development is enhanced by examination of the developmental path taken by nonstereotyped people. Consideration of the cases in which parental influences attempt to diverge from other societal influences opens the way for teasing out the relative influences of various internal and external factors in psychological sex-role development.

There is evidence that the effects of non-sex-typed parenting are more likely to be apparent in adulthood than childhood. There is also evidence that non-sex-typed parenting goes beyond attitudes toward sex roles and specific ways of relating to children's gender. More subtle forces seem to be at work. Central to non-sex-typed parenting is the example set by parents of personality styles that are not stereotypically feminine or masculine, and a flexible, egalitarian approach to power relationships between the parents and the allocation of work and family roles. In other words, it is not sufficient for parents to suggest to children that they "do as I say, not as I do." What parents do in their own lives may be the most important lesson they hand down to their children in their psychological sex-role development.

Both theories and research presented here suggest that, despite the propensity of many children for stereotyped behavior and attitudes, stereotyped children may become androgynous adults. A parent's task may be conceptualized as similar to that of a gardener who feeds, waters, and nurtures a tomato plant. The gardener does not despair when no tomatoes appear after a month of care. Rather, the gardener is patient, knowing these efforts will bear fruit eventually. The fruitfulness of the plant is partly a result of the gardener's ongoing contributions to its growth and development, partly a result of external factors, and partly a result of its own maturation and readiness.

The recognition that there are limits to environmental influences on development is reflected in an increased interest in more complex models of development within psychology in general. Scarr and her colleagues' (Scarr & McCartney, 1983; Scarr, Webber, Weinberg, & Wittig, 1981; Scarr & Weinberg, 1983) work with biologically related and adoptive families serves as evidence for genetic and maturational influences. These data "challenge the belief that children acquire attitudes and beliefs by modeling themselves after their families" (Scarr & Weinberg, 1983, p. 265).

While researchers in the area of sex-role development may be reluctant to accept such a strong statement, Fagot (1985b) has suggested that there is a need to move beyond simple social learning explanations of sex-role development to views that include the interaction of the social information children receive and the cognitive development of their understanding of gender. A view of only internal or only external influences is likely to be incomplete.

It would be inappropriate to suggest that limits on parental influences on development of androgyny in children are attributable entirely to maturational limits in the child. Not only internal developmental but also other external influences, such as schools, peers, and the media, affect children's psychological sex roles. As Huston (1983) has pointed out, while children in most societies form concepts of gender, the rigidity of those concepts varies across societies. It may well be that parents in a society less rigidly sex-typed than our own would have an easier time turning out androgynous children. To return to the tomato plant analogy, even the most dedicated gardener may not be able to compensate for a severe environment. But truly dedicated gardeners cannot know unless they try.

Notes

1. Although androgyny researchers may be accused of perpetuating these schemas in their very use of the concept of androgyny (cf. Lott, 1981), a long tradition of research in developmental and personality psychology suggests that many people do think differently about females and males. Although the research literature certainly does not support as broad an array of psychological sex differences as people perceive, these ideas remain a central part of the way many research participants think about themselves and their children. It would seem to be inappropriate to discard the terms "masculinity" and "femininity," in deference to our colleagues' politics, at the expense of the subjective reality of many of the research participants we are trying to understand.
2. On a personal note, it was Jeanne Block's pioneering work suggesting sex-role development as a process extending beyond stereotypes and across the life span that initially raised questions for me about alternative views of sex-role development. Her untimely death was a loss not only for her family and friends, but for psychology as well. Her voice and her vision already are missed.
3. We must be cautious in generalizing this past research to present families. Increases in percentages of mothers who work for pay may be associated with increased variability in the motives and meaning of women's work. Further, the context, and hence the meaning to the child, of maternal employment might be different as this status becomes the majority rather than the minority.

References

Almquist, E. M., & Angrist, S. S. (1970). Career salience and atypicality of occupational choice among college women. *Journal of Marriage and the Family, 32,* 242–249.

Bem, S. L. (1974). The measurement of psychological androgyny. *Journal of Consulting and Clinical Psychology, 42,* 155–162.

_____. (1976) Probing the promise of androgyny. In A. G. Kaplan & J. P. Bean (Eds.), *Beyond sex-role stereotypes: Readings toward a psychology of androgyny* (pp. 47–62). Boston: Little, Brown.

_____. (1985). Androgyny and gender schema theory: A conceptual and empirical integration. In T. B. Sonderegger (Ed.), *Nebraska Symposium on Motivation* (Vol. 32, pp. 179–226). Lincoln: University of Nebraska Press.

Birnbaum, J. A. (1975). Life patterns and self-esteem in gifted family oriented and career oriented women. In M. T. S. Mednick, S. S. Tangri, & L. W. Hoffman (Eds.), *Women and achievement: Social and motivational analyses* (pp. 396–419). Washington, DC: Hemisphere.

Block, J., von der Lippe, A., & Block, J. H. (1973). Sex-role and socialization patterns: Some personality concomitants and environmental antecedents. *Journal of Consulting and Clinical Psychology, 41,* 321–341.

Block, J. H. (1973). Conceptions of sex role. Some cross-cultural and longitudinal perspectives. *American Psychologist, 28,* 512–526.

_____. (1984). *Sex-role identity and ego development*. San Francisco: Jossey-Bass.

Carpenter, C. J., Huston, A. C., & Holt, W. (1986). Modification of preschool sex-typed behaviors by participation in adult-structured activities. *Sex Roles, 14,* 603–615.

Constantinople, A. (1973). Masculinity–femininity: An exception to a famous dictum? *Psychological Bulletin, 80,* 389–407.

Cordura, G. D., McGraw, K. O., & Drabman, R. S. (1979). Doctor or nurse: Children's perceptions of sex-typed occupations. *Child Development, 50,* 590–593.

Cunningham, J. D., & Antill, J. K. (1984). Changes in masculinity and femininity across the family life cycle: A reexamination. *Developmental Psychology, 20,* 1135--1141.

DeFronzo, J., & Boudreau, F. (1979). Further research into antecedents and correlates of androgyny. *Psychological Reports, 44,* 23–29.

Fagot, B. I. (1978). The influence of sex of child on parental reactions to toddler children. *Child Development, 49,* 459–465.

_____. (1985a). Beyond the reinforcement principle: Another step toward understanding sex-role development. *Developmental Psychology, 21,* 1097–1104.

_____. (1985b). Changes in thinking about early sex-role development. *Developmental Review, 5,* 83–98.

Fischer, J. L., & Narus, L. R. (1981). Sex-role development in late adolescence and adulthood. *Sex Roles, 7,* 97–106.

Freud, S. (1925). Some psychical consequences of the anatomical distinction between the sexes. In J. Strachey (Ed. and Trans.), *Standard edition of the complete psychological works of Sigmund Freud* (Vol. 19, pp. 248–258). London: Hogarth Press.

Ginzberg, E. (1971). *Educated American women: Life styles and self-portraits*. New York: Columbia University Press.

Hansson, R. O., Chernovetz, M. E., & Jones, W. H. (1977). Maternal employment and androgyny. *Psychology of Women Quarterly, 2,* 76–78.

Hefner, R., Rebecca, M., & Oleshansky, B. (1975). Development of sex-role transcendence. *Human Development, 18,* 143–158.

Huston, A. C. (1983). Sex typing. In P. H. Mussen (Ed.), *Handbook of child psychology* (4th ed., Vol. 4, pp. 387–467). New York: Wiley.

Jones, W. H., Chernovetz, M. E. O'C., & Hansson, R. O. (1978). The enigma of androgyny: Differential implications for males and females? *Journal of Consulting and Clinical Psychology, 46,* 298–313.

Kaplan, A. G., & Sedney, M. A. (1980). *Psychology and sex roles: An androgynous perspective*. Boston: Little, Brown.

Katz, P. A. (1979). The development of female identity. *Sex Roles, 5,* 155–178.

_____. (1986). Modification of children's gender-stereotyped behavior: General issues and research considerations. *Sex Roles, 14,* 591–602.

Kelly, J. A., & Worell, J. (1977). New formulations of sex roles and androgyny: A critical review. *Journal of Consulting and Clinical Psychology, 45,* 1101–1115.

Kelly, J. A., & Worell, L. (1976). Parent behaviors related to masculine, feminine, and androgynous sex-role orientations. *Journal of Consulting and Clinical Psychology, 44,* 843–851.

Kohlberg, L. (1966). A cognitive-developmental analysis of children's sex-role concepts and attitudes. In E. E. Maccoby (Ed.), *The development of sex differences* (pp. 82–173). Stanford: Stanford University Press.

Lamb, M. E., & Roopnarine, J. L. (1979). Peer influences on sex-role development in preschoolers. *Child Development, 50,* 1219–1222.

Leahy, R. L., & Eiter, M. (1980). Moral judgment and the development of real and ideal androgynyous self-image during adolescence and young adulthood. *Developmental Psychology, 16,* 362–370.

Lipman-Blumen, J. (1972). How ideology shapes women's lives. *Scientific American, 226,* 34–42.

Lockheed, M. E. (1986). Reshaping the social order: The case of gender segregation. *Sex Roles, 14,* 617–628.

Locksley, A., & Colten, M. E. (1979). Psychological androgyny: A case of mistaken identity. *Journal of Personality and Social Psychology, 37,* 1017–1031.

Loevinger, J. (1966). The meaning and measurement of ego development. *American Psychologist, 21,* 195–206.

Loevinger, J., & Wessler, R. (1970). *Measuring ego development* (Vol. 1). San Francisco: Jossey-Bass.

Lott, B. (1981). A feminist critique of androgyny: Toward the elimination of gender attributions for learned behavior. In C. Mayo & N. M. Henley (Eds.), *Gender and nonverbal behavior* (pp. 171–180). New York: Springer-Verlag.

Maccoby, E. E., & Jacklin, C. N. (1974). *The psychology of sex differences.* Stanford: Stanford University Press.

Meyer, B. (1980). The development of girls' sex-role attitudes. *Child Development, 51,* 508–514.

Mischel, W. (1966). A social-learning view of sex differences in behavior. In E. E. Maccoby (Ed.), *The development of sex differences* (pp. 56–81). Stanford: Stanford University Press.

————. (1970). Sex-typing and socialization. In P. H. Mussen (Ed.), *Carmichael's manual of child psychology* (Vol. 2, pp. 3–72). New York: Wiley.

O'Brien, M., & Huston, A. C. (1985). Development of sex-typed play behavior in toddlers. *Developmental Psychology, 21,* 866–871.

Pedhazur, E. J., & Tetenbaum, T. J. (1979). Bem Sex Role Inventory: A theoretical and methodological critique. *Journal of Personality and Social Psychology, 37,* 996–1016.

Rheingold, H. L., & Cook, K. V. (1975). The contents of boys' and girls' rooms as an index of parents' behavior. *Child Development, 46,* 459–463.

Roddy, J. M., Klein, H. A., Stericker, A. B., & Kurdek, L. A. (1981). Modification of stereotypic sex-typing in young children. *Journal of Genetic Psychology, 139,* 109–118.

Ross, D. M., & Ross, S. A. (1972). Resistance by preschool boys to sex-inappropriate behavior. *Journal of Educational Psychology, 63,* 342–346.

Rubin, J. Z., Provenzano, F. J., & Luria, Z. (1974). The eye of the beholder: Parents' views on sex of newborns. *American Journal of Orthopsychiatry, 44,* 512–519.

Scarr, S., & McCartney, K. (1983). How people make their own environments: A theory of genotype-environment effects. *Child Development, 54,* 424–435.

Scarr, S., Webber, P. L., Weinberg, R. A., & Wittig, M. A. (1981). Personality resemblance among adolescents and their parents in biologically related and adoptive families. *Journal of Personality and Social Psychology, 40,* 885–898.

Scarr, S., & Weinberg, R. A. (1983). The Minnesota adoption studies: Genetic differences and malleability. *Child Development, 54,* 260–267.

Sedney, M. A. (1986). Growing more complex: Conceptions of sex roles across adulthood. *International Journal of Aging and Human Development, 22,* 15–29.

————. (In press). Conceptual and methodological sources of controversies about androgyny. In R. K. Unger (Ed.), *Images of Gender.* Farmingdale, NY: Baywood Press.

Smith, P. K., & Daglish, L. (1977). Sex differences in parent and infant behavior in the home. *Child Development, 48,* 1250–1254.

Spence, J. T. (1985). Gender identity and its implications for the concepts of masculinity and femininity. In T. B. Sonderegger (Ed.), *Nebraska Symposium on Motivation* (Vol. 32, pp. 59–95). Lincoln: University of Nebraska Press.

Spence, J. T., Helmreich, R., & Stapp, J. (1975). Ratings of self and peers on sex-role attributes and their relation to self-esteem and conceptions of masculinity and femininity. *Journal of Personality and Social Psychology, 32,* 29–39.

Stein, A. H., & Bailey, M. M. (1973). The socialization of achievement orientation in females. *Psychological Bulletin, 80,* 345–366.

Sutton-Simon, K., & Menig-Peterson, C. (1977, February). *The effects of parents' sex-role behavior upon children's sex-typing.* Paper presented at the meeting of the Association for Women in Psychology, St. Louis, MO.

Tangri, S. S. (1972). Determinants of occupational role innovation among college women. *Journal of Social Issues, 28,* 177–199.

Taylor, M. C., & Hall, J. A. (1982). Psychological androgyny: A review and reformulation of theories, methods, and conclusions. *Psychological Bulletin, 92,* 347–366.

Thompson, S. K. (1975). Gender labels and early sex-role development. *Child Development, 46,* 339–347.

Vieira, K. G., & Miller, W. H. (1978). Avoidance of sex-atypical toys by five- and ten-year-old children. *Psychological Reports, 43,* 543–546.

Weinraub, M., Clemens, L. P., Sockloff, A., Ethridge, T., Gracely, E., & Myers, B. (1984). The development of sex-role stereotypes in the third year: Relationships to gender labeling, gender identity, sex-typed toy preference, and family characteristics. *Child Development, 55,* 1493–1503.

Wolf, T. M. (1975). Response consequences to televised modeled sex-inappropriate play behavior. *Journal of Genetic Psychology, 127,* 35–44.

Child Care 2000: Policy Options for the Future

Sally Lubeck and Patricia Garrett

In recent years social change has been rapid and profound, and there is a general awareness that social policy has not been attuned to the emerging realities of family life and child rearing in the United States. Many families have transformed the ways in which they organize their lives at work and at home. Since 1948, the number of working women with children under the age of six has increased approximately 10 percent per decade. In 1986, 54 percent of women with children under six were working (U.S. Bureau of the Census, 1987, p. 383), with the greatest increment evident in the labor force participation of married women with infants—from 31 percent in 1975 to nearly 50 percent in 1985 (Hayghe, 1986, p. 43). High divorce rates, decreasing rates of fertility, declining real wages, the impetus of the women's movement—all have contributed to the rise in the number of women in the workforce. Recent estimates suggest that fully three-fourths of all school-age children and two-thirds of preschool children will have working mothers by 1995 (Hofferth and Phillips, 1987, p. 561).

Though the direction of change is similar throughout the industrialized world, the demographic shift in the composition of the U.S. workforce is occurring in a unique social and political milieu. For decades, other countries have recognized that children are valuable societal resources, and they have provided families with a broad base of support. Sixty-seven countries, including all developed nations except the United States, provide family or child allowances in the form of cash benefits to supplement the incomes of those raising children. In addition, most European countries guarantee jobs, seniority, and pension entitlements to parents who leave work for an average of six months to one year at the time of childbirth. Most also provide some cash benefit through the social security system as wage replacement during the leave period (Kamerman, 1980, pp. 24–25). All now provide additional unpaid leave from six months to three years.

The United States is thus the only industrialized nation that fails to provide workers with comprehensive health-care services, maternity benefits, paid or unpaid leaves, or job guarantees. Although the infrastructure to support a vastly expanded child-care industry is now emerging (O'Connell and Bloom, 1987), no national child-care policy currently exists to guide its formation. Of all the

From Sally Lubeck and Patricia Garrett, *Social Policy,* Vol. 18 (Spring 1988):31–37, published by Social Policy Corporation, New York, N.Y. 10036. Copyright © 1988 by Social Policy Corporation. Reprinted by permission of the publisher.

nations in the world, only five lack a family policy: South Africa, New Guinea, South Korea, the Sudan, and the United States.

In this context, concern is mounting that American policymakers will need to address issues related to work and child care in a more comprehensive way. How these issues come to be addressed, however, will do more than meet the immediate needs of young families. Policies that are put in place now have the potential to restructure work, family, and schooling in the future. The purpose of this article, therefore, is to explore the current situation as a basis for delineating alternative strategies for the future care and education of young children.

The family in our society traditionally has been the unit most likely to create the conditions necessary for the growth and development of children (Clark-Stewart, 1977, p. 93). As Morgan (1985) writes: "Kith and kin will have an irrational attachment to children and their parents that money cannot buy and states cannot regulate" (p. 2). Yet today American families at all levels are experiencing conflict between the two major roles the family traditionally has fulfilled: the economic responsibility to maintain households and the social responsibility to meet children's physical and psychological needs (Morgan, 1983).

Family policy is becoming an issue in the United States because responsibilities for work and child care are increasingly difficult to reconcile. Current reform efforts bypass or de-emphasize the role that families have played in rearing the young. By placing the major emphasis on the improvement and expansion of extrafamilial child care, policy advocates are now seeking: (1) to provide financial assistance to homes and centers and to ensure that such settings are licensed or regulated; (2) to provide tax incentives to business; or (3) to lay the foundation for a school-based child-care system. Though increasing numbers of parents need these options, many would prefer to find a more effective balance between their work and child-care responsibilities.

Social policies can enhance the abilities of families to protect and nurture their members, but to do so policy options must be considered in the broadest possible light. National data provide important information about the child-care arrangements of working mothers.

Present Child-Care Arrangements

Despite the attention currently directed at group-based alternatives, analysis of Census Bureau data indicates that family-based care (by parents, grandparents, older children, or other relatives) remains important. Although 54 percent of the mothers with children under six years of age are in the workforce, fully 46 percent are not, and these children continue to be reared primarily at home.

For families in which the mother is employed, child-care arrangements vary by both employment and marital status. Over 62 percent of the mothers of preschool children who work part time depend on family-based child care, while a smaller, but still substantial, percentage (39.4 percent) of those who work full time rely on family-based arrangements.[1] Similarly, mothers who are currently married and living with spouse are somewhat more likely to use family-based arrangements than are mothers who are not currently married (U.S. Bureau of the Census, 1987, Table 3).

Nearly one child in four under the age of five (1.9 million) is in some form of organized facility, either a preschool or day-care center; about 15 percent are in a day-care center as their primary arrangement (U.S. Bureau of the Census, 1987, Table 3). Between 1965 and 1980, enrollment of three- and four-year-olds in preschool programs more than tripled (U.S. Bureau of the Census, 1986). The increase in the numbers of children cared for in organized facilities is mainly attributable to the decline in care provided by nonrelatives in children's homes. As sitters, maids, and nannies became less prevalent, outside placements in day-care homes and centers have become increasingly important.

Change in the recent past has been marked. Reliance on group-based facilities coincides with increases in the labor force participation of women with young children and indicates that individual providers and institutional centers are responding to meet the needs of mothers working full-time. Far fewer children, however, are enrolled in full-day, full-year group-based care. Nearly half (47.9 percent) of the preschoolers whose mothers work are cared for primarily by a parent or family member; another 22 percent are in a family day-care home (U.S. Bureau of the Census, 1987, Table D).

Child-care arrangements tend to vary according to the age of the child. Working parents who seek extrafamilial care traditionally have opted to place infants and toddlers in homes that emulate a family setting, and widespread use of centers for infants and toddlers is a recent phenomenon. There also has been an 8 percent increase in the number of three- and four-year-olds in center-based care in only two years (1982–1984).

There is some evidence that center-based care is used primarily by those most and least well-off. Families that have a high income, with the mother well-educated, are the principal users of centers (U.S. Bureau of the Census, 1983, p. 11). Some poor families also use centers either because care is subsidized through the Social Services Block Grants to states under Title XX or because they qualify for Project Head Start. Only 16 percent of eligible children are currently enrolled in the latter program, however. Greater proportions of black mothers and those who are single, divorced, or widowed use organized child-care facilities, though family-based care is also prevalent in these groups (U.S. Bureau of the Census, 1987, Figure 3). Family-based care is used more by working-class mothers, particularly by parents who work different shifts and alternate care (Presser, 1986).

American women are expected to increase their labor force participation rates and to approximate higher European levels (O'Connell and Bloom, 1987; Kamerman, 1980; McMahon, 1986). It is safe to assume, therefore, that mothers will continue to work in large numbers and that needs for child care will continue and even increase.

Policies for the Future

All policies have implicit goals and potential consequences. The extent to which policies that address the crisis in child care will support continued parental and

Figure 1   Models of Child–Care Arrangements.

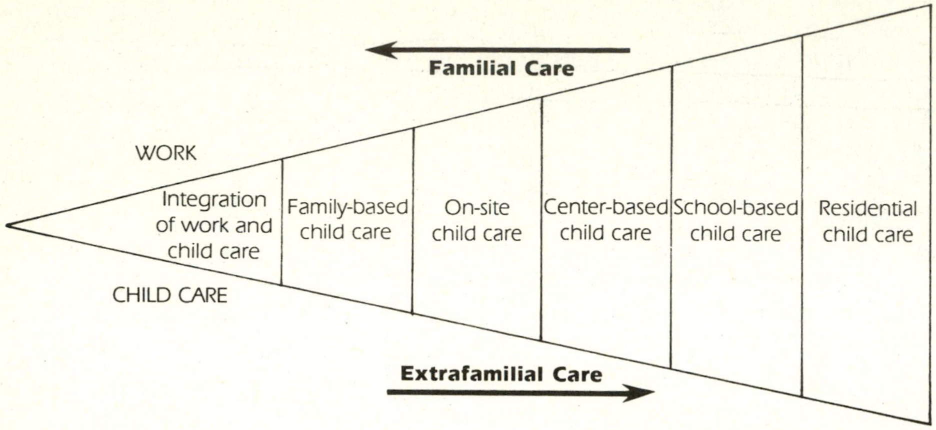

familial child rearing and/or encourage other institutions (day-care centers, public schools, and so forth) to assume child-rearing responsibilities is a critical and as yet unanswered question. As a basis for delineating alternatives, we propose a model for conceptualizing policy choices for the future.

Family-based child care continues to be the most common arrangement chosen by parents. In recent years, however, it has been declining as more women enter the workforce and are, therefore, not available to care for young relatives. For each cohort of children (infants and toddlers, threes and fours), policy initiatives will move in one of two directions: either toward increased support for and integration of work and child-care responsibilities or toward the support of extrafamilial child rearing in homes, centers, or schools [Figure 1].

Support of Child Rearing by Working Parents

Integration of work and child care   Throughout most of human history, work and child care have been closely integrated. In agrarian societies, children participated in the life of the farm or village, working and playing beside parents and kin. Parents provided for and nurtured children, who reciprocated through obligatory work and filial loyalty (LeVine and White, 1986, p. 33).

In a modern context, however, a variant of an integrated model seems unlikely. The nature of work has changed, and the image of infants crawling around a boardroom or playing along an assembly line suggests that such integration is not realistic. Nonetheless, social policies could be designed to increase the integration between work and family life.

Several policies have the potential to make it easier for parents to both work and care for their children. To varying degrees, they have been implemented in Europe and in some large American corporations. Flexible benefit plans directed at the changing needs of families include maternity benefits, paid job-protected leaves, and supplementary unpaid leaves (Kamerman, 1983b). Innovative scheduling has also been suggested: flexitime, compressed work weeks, flexiyear contracts, permanent part-time work, and job splitting (Best, 1982).

Flexible Benefits: Despite the changes that have occurred in the composition of the workforce, most fringe-benefit packages have changed little since the 1940s and 50s (Kamerman, 1983b). With the increasing heterogeneity of the labor force, however, has come pressure to meet the needs of specific subgroups (Bloom and Martin, 1983). Bloom and Trahan (1986) have noted:

> Health insurance does not benefit a working wife who is covered by her husband's health insurance policy; child health insurance coverage does not benefit a worker who has no children; life insurance is of little benefit to a single wage earner who does not plan to have a family [p. 3].

As the numbers of women in the workforce rise, plans that include options for maternity benefits, parental leave, and child care are increasingly desirable.

Today, women (and men) having children are unlikely to leave their jobs. Maternity benefits in the United States are granted through disability payments that some employers provide or through the temporary disability insurance benefits available in California, Hawaii, New York, New Jersey, and Rhode Island (Kamerman, Kahn, and Kingston, 1983). Though the government requires that pregnant women be treated the same as any employee with a disability, only those women whose employers provide disability benefits or who live in states with such benefits actually are eligible for coverage.

It has been estimated that no more than 40 percent of American women are eligible for employer-provided disability insurance, sick leave, or paid leave, and most of the employers who do provide it limit eligibility to six to eight weeks (Kamerman et al., 1983). The Family and Medical Leave Bill (HR 925), introduced by William Clay (D-Mo.) and Patricia Schroeder (D-Colo.) and under consideration in the House of Representatives, would provide job guarantees in the event of childbirth, adoption, and illness. Employees would be guaranteed up to 18 weeks *unpaid* leave.[2] American women now return to the workplace shortly after the birth of a child because they must, yet every developed nation except the United States provides *paid* parental leave in some form.

Regardless of theoretical predilection, child-development researchers have shown the early months of life to be extremely important for both young children and their parents. Drawing on this evidence, Gamble and Zigler (1986) argue that paid infant-care leave is the most attractive alternative to infant day care.

Innovative Scheduling: A 1980 Gallup Poll asked employees to select the types of programs that would help them to deal with the conflicting demands of job and family. More than half indicated the need for more flexible schedules (Rothman and Marks, 1987, p. 471). Flexitime allows employees to decide within a two-hour span, morning and evening, when they will arrive and depart. Most plans retain a "core time" from 9:30 a.m. to 3:00 p.m. when all employees must be present. The principal advantage of this arrangement is that it increases employees' ability to handle conflicts between personal/family obligations and job requirements (Kuhne and Blair, 1978).

Other plans now provide flexiweek and flexiyear options. These include compressed time (e.g., four 10-hour days; three-and-a-half 11–12 hour days) and plans whereby employees can buy more vacation time with a percentage cut in pay (e.g., 5 percent for 10.5 days). When the latter plan was implemented in Santa Clara, Calif., 17 percent of all county employees asked to participate in the first year (Best, 1982, p. 310). Free time was especially desirable during the summer months when children were home from school. Some flexiyear plans are built on full-time work during the academic year and part-time during the summer, so that parents can more easily care for out-of-school children. This option is available in some European countries, but it is virtually untried in the United States.

Another set of innovations involves part-time work. The principal alternatives are permanent part-time positions that provide fringe benefits and career advancement and jobsharing (job splitting) that enables two or more workers to share one job.

A survey conducted by the Bureau of Labor Statistics during the summer of 1987 showed that a surprising 60 percent of all work establishments with 10 employees or more have instituted some practices to aid employees in caring for their children. These included provisions for flexitime, voluntary part-time work, jobsharing, work at home, and flexible leave (U.S. Department of Labor, 1988, Table 1).

Each of these policies has the potential to decrease the disjuncture between work and family life. However, it may well be that widespread changes in work will have to prove beneficial to both employers and employees—enhancing productivity and improving the quality of life.

Characteristic of the tension between families and work are the recommendations made by two national commissions. The 1980 White House Conference on Families stated as their first priority that employers become more responsive to employees who have children. The White House Conference on Small Business held in 1986 came out in opposition to many of the reforms discussed here.

Family-based child care   Child care among kith and kin comes in a variety of forms, including arrangements that can be made with family members and close neighbors or friends:

> staggering the parents' work hours so that a parent is always at home
>
> leaving children in the care of relatives either in the children's home or the relative's home
>
> using older siblings to provide care
>
> leaving children with very close friends of the family (Morgan, 1985, p. 1).

The percentage of preschool children of working mothers currently cared for by family members as their primary arrangement is 46.5 (U.S. Bureau of the Census, 1987, Table 3). From a policy standpoint, however, family-based care has several characteristics that make it different from other options. It is unlikely to be licensed or, in some form, regulated by the government, and it has frequently been nonmonetized and unsupported through public funds (Morgan, 1985).

Government support of extrafamilial options may well have the effect of accelerating the decline in the amount of care provided by families. However, a precedent for government support of family-based care has been set at the federal level in legislation that allows family members to be paid to care for handicapped children.

If an important objective of child-care policy is to support families, it should be legitimate, under defined circumstances, to subsidize payments to relatives. It is not known whether many parents currently using family-based care prefer it or select it because they cannot afford group-based alternatives. Only a system that assists parents with child-care costs according to need, while allowing them choice, will be capable of preserving family-based child care for those who value and prefer it.

Employer-supported child care   The Bureau of Labor Statistics recently found employer-supported provisions for child care to vary depending upon public or private ownership and the size of the firm. Government agencies and large companies were among those most likely to provide child-care benefits and services to their employees (U.S. Department of Labor, 1988, Table 3).

There are numerous ways in which business can assist employees in obtaining quality child care. Glasser (1981) divides assistance into two categories: child day care owned, operated, or subsidized by the company and services, benefits and policies. Several options exist whereby a company directly can assist employees with child care. The company can establish a day-care center at the worksite (on-site model) or join with other businesses in the area to establish a joint center (consortium model). It can contract with existing centers to reserve places for employees' children (vendor program) or provide vouchers that can be used in the setting of a parent's choice (voucher program). Less directly, the company can offer a referral service, arrange for sick-child care, or establish some of the policies (paid leave, flexitime, flexiweek) discussed above.

Of these alternatives, the arrangements that most significantly integrate work and child care are those which enable a parent to balance responsibilities (flexitime, jobsharing, permanent part-time work) and which provide on-site child care. In the latter arrangement, a child is cared for by others at the workplace but remains near one or both parents. Only about 2 percent of American work establishments with 10 employees or more sponsor child-care centers for employees' children (U.S. Department of Labor, 1988, p. 1).

Policies currently in place have served to encourage some firms to assist working parents with their child-care needs. The Economic Tax Recovery Act of 1981 (ERTA) enables companies to treat child-care costs as business expenses when the purpose is to improve employee retention rates. Employers who establish child-care centers receive several benefits. Start-up and operating costs are deductible, and capital costs (building, renovation, and equipment) can be depreciated over five years. Finally, if the center has an open admissions policy, it is exempt from federal income tax (O'Brien, 1987, p. 10).

Under the Dependent Care Assistance Plan (DCAP), several benefits accrue to employees. Costs for child care can be deducted as business expenses and, therefore, excluded from taxable gross income. Parents can also claim tax credits for one or two children on a sliding scale, based on their gross income.

Support for Extrafamilial Child Rearing

Group-based child care   Group-based child care currently takes two principal forms: family day-care homes and day-care centers. A hybrid of these is the large day-care home or "mini-center."

Family day-care homes constitute regulated, if informal, care in most states (Morgan, 1985), although many homes operate outside the system. Generally, a caregiver is responsible for no more than six children. The largest study of family day-care homes ever undertaken, the National Day Care Home Study (1976–1980), found that 5.2 million children were cared for 10 or more hours a week in family day-care homes. Most (94 percent) were in informal arrangements with families, neighbors, and friends. Despite the informality of the arrangements, most parents paid for care (Divine-Hawkins, 1981). There appear to be more parents now who contract with providers they do not know well. The most recent Census Bureau report, based on data collected in 1984–85, found 22.3 percent of the preschool children of working mothers in family day-care homes (U.S. Bureau of the Census, 1987, Table D).

Child-care centers can be categorized as: for-profit centers, not-for-profit, and public (government sponsored). For-profit centers are locally owned and operated ("mom and pop") operations or national franchises such as Kinder Care or La Petite. About 15 percent of preschool children are in a day-care/group-care center as their primary arrangement (U.S. Bureau of the Census, 1987, Figure 1).

Despite the fact that formal child care is plagued by low wages, it continues to be expensive. The cost in median dollars for care in organized facilities was $43.50 per week; for family day-care homes $41.10, and for relative care $28.40 (U.S. Bureau of the Census, 1987, Table G). In some urban areas such as Boston and New York, however, costs are much greater.

Family day-care homes and day-care centers share certain commonalities. The success of each is predicated on the low wages of the women who care for children (Nelson, 1987; Zinsser, 1986). Inadequate pay and benefits, frequent staff turnover, limited ability of clients to pay, funding cutbacks, expensive liability insurance, and the scarcity of trained teachers have created problems for those who both work in and rely on homes and centers.

Currently, there is federal funding for child care for low-income families, principally through Head Start and block grants under Title XX, while middle- and upper-income families benefit from the Dependent Care Tax Credit. Title XX funds for children from low-income families have declined in the 1980s, and there are long waiting lists for services. At the same time, there has been an increase in the benefits accruing to families that are better off, from $956 million in 1980 to $3.4 billion in 1986 (Kahn and Kamerman, 1987, Table 1.8). Families are able to deduct a portion of their child-care expenses from their income taxes. Currently, even those in the highest income brackets are able to take the deduction, while those with incomes too low to pay taxes receive no benefit.

Much of the recent activity at the federal level is focused on securing funds to improve care in homes and centers. Two bills are currently under consideration. Democrats are focusing their efforts on the Act for Better Child-Care Services, a $2.5 billion bill supported by the Alliance for Better Child Care. The act aims to provide child care for low- and moderate-income families through entitlements to states as an incentive for matching funds. It also sets federal standards for licensed and registered programs and provides means by which those out of compliance can meet standards. The $375 million Child-Care Services Improvement Act, with Republican sponsorship, provides more modest funds to establish a block grant program, assists states in setting up liability insurance pools and revolving loan funds, and provides tax credits for employer-supported on-site care. This bill has now been retargeted for the working poor.

School-based child care   Public schools are the principal providers of child-care services to school-age children. Approximately 75 percent (13.8 million) of the children of working mothers are in school during the hours their mothers work (U.S. Bureau of the Census, 1987, p. 2).

Since public schools already provide child-care services to a large segment of the population, it is not surprising that many of the reforms proposed to address child-care needs are extensions of this universally available institution (Lubeck, 1987). Before- and after-school programs (Seligson, 1986), programs for special populations of children (Morado, 1985, 1986), and programs for prekindergarten children are now being offered or proposed in public schools throughout the nation.

Public schools have already witnessed a downward extension of services. More five-year-olds are attending kindergarten and for longer periods of time (Robinson, 1987), and public school-based programs for threes and fours appear to be increasing (Mitchell, 1987). Recent suggestions have been made to further extend school-based prekindergarten programs with supplementary child care provided either at school or in neighboring day-care centers (Blank, 1985; Zigler, 1987; Schweinhart, Koshel, and Bridgman, 1987).

Since schools are universally available, safe, and convenient, the utilization of school facilities has had appeal. Zigler (1987), after making the case that public schools should only provide services to special populations of three- and four-year-old children and, under no circumstances, serve infants and toddlers, recently has advocated that public schools should provide universal child-care services (Trotter, 1987). Other prominent figures have made similar or complementary claims (Heath, 1987; Coleman, 1987).

The prospect of universal public school-based child care, however, is not welcome in many child-care circles. Some specialists have registered fears that the young may be regimented too soon or that scarce funds will be spread too thin (Elkind, 1986; Winn, 1983; Zigler, 1987).

Senator Christopher Dodd (D-Conn.) has introduced a bill, the New School Child-Care Demonstration Projects Act of 1987, to fund 60 model programs in public schools that would provide before- and after-school care for school-age children and full-day child care for preschool children. Another bill, recently introduced by Senator Edward Kennedy (D-Mass.), would provide $4.25 billion in federal matching grants to state and local governments to establish full-day, full-year programs for four-year-olds. Half of the available spaces would be for children from low-income families.

Currently, school-based programs for preschoolers continue to be for special populations of three- and four-year-olds: those considered to be at-risk, handicapped, or bilingual (Morado, 1985, 1986, 1988; Mitchell, 1987). No state offers universal preschool education for children of any age.

Conclusion

This article has presented a conceptual model for considering policy alternatives based on whether and to what extent an option supports child rearing by the nuclear/extended family or by others. Traditionally, children have been raised by relatives, and recent data indicate that working parents continue to select family-based arrangements. Family-based care is decreasing, however, and current policy initiatives at both the state and national levels foster group-based alternatives. Since societal forces militate against the support of children by parents and family members, policies aimed at addressing the child-care dilemma need to be more comprehensive and supportive of both familial and extrafamilial arrangements.

It may be that a particular type of care is more appropriate for very young children, while another may be best for "older" three- and four-year-olds. Preschool programs have been more extensive in Europe for two- to five-year-olds, while out-of-home care for infants and young toddlers has been less available (Kamerman, 1980, p. 26; Tietze, in press, Table 1). Nonetheless, many countries have implemented policies that both encourage and enable parents to care for very young children.

American family policy has been a policy by default, characterized both by a reluctance to interfere in family life and also by a resistance to change the structured inequities that affect families in profound ways. Grubb and Lazerson (1982) contend: "When the welfare of children conflicts with economic constraints, children lose" (p. 187). A comprehensive U.S. family policy would represent a qualitative break with the past, placing the needs of people above the need for profit. Though some American businesses have worked with their employees to relieve the tensions between work and family life, others, through lobbying by the national Chamber of Commerce, have organized to forestall efforts as minimal as the Family and Medical Leave Act. Parents and workers are not organized to influence these matters, and although child-care professionals are, their efforts have largely been directed toward policy initiatives that foster extrafamilial child care. Such funding, when other options are not equally supported, encourages public responsibility for what has traditionally been a private concern.

As the year 2000 approaches, there will be an increasing need for women in the workforce, and child care promises to be the major employment issue of the

1990s (Hofferth, 1988; Quinn, 1988). The extent to which policies support parental and familial care and/or extrafamilial care will shape the future.

Notes

1. The Census Bureau reports who provided care and its location. We suggest that the relation of the caregiver to the child is the significant distinction and thus analyze the data in terms of "familial/family-based" and "extrafamilial/group-based" arrangements.
2. The national Chamber of Commerce opposes this bill. Originally written to affect all firms with 15 employees or more, the bill was modified to pertain only to companies with 50 employees or more. After three years, the legislation will affect companies with 35+ employees. Although an important piece of legislation, the Family and Medical Leave Act will provide neither job guarantees nor unpaid leave to the vast majority of American workers.

References

Best, F., "Flexible Life Scheduling," in J. O'Toole, J. L. Schuber, and L. C. Wood (eds.), *Working, Changes and Choices* (New York: Human Sciences Press, 1982).

Blank, H., "Early Childhood and the Public Schools," *Young Children* (May, 1985), pp. 52–55.

Bloom, D., and Martin, M., "Fringe Benefits à la Carte," *American Demographics* (February, 1983), pp. 22–25.

Bloom, D., and Trahan, J., "Flexible Benefits and Employee Choice," *Work in America Institute Studies in Productivity* (New York: Pergamon Press, 1986).

Clark-Stewart, A., *Child Care in the Family: A Review of Research and Some Propositions for Policy* (New York: Academic Press, 1977).

Coleman, J., "Families and Schools," *Educational Researcher* (August/September, 1987), pp. 32–38.

Divine-Hawkins, P., *National Day Care Home Study: Family Day Care in the United States* (Washington, D.C.: U.S. Government Printing Office, 1981).

Elkind, D., "Formal Education and Early Childhood Education: An Essential Difference," *Phi Delta Kappan* (May, 1986), pp. 631–36.

Gamble, T., and Zigler, E., "Effects of Infant Day Care: Another Look at the Evidence," *American Journal of Orthopsychiatry* (January, 1986), pp. 26–42.

Glasser, F., *Helping Working Parents: Child Care Options for Business* (Raleigh, N.C: Office of the Governor, 1981).

Grubb, W., and Lazerson, M., *Broken Promises: How Americans Fail Their Children* (New York: Basic Books, 1982).

Hayghe, H., "Rise in Mothers' Labor Force Activity Includes Those with Infants," *Monthly Labor Review* (February, 1986), pp. 43–45.

Heath, S., "A Child Resource Policy: Moving beyond Dependence on School and Family," *Phi Delta Kappan* (April, 1987), pp. 576–80.

Hofferth, S., "The Child Care Debate in Context." Paper presented at the annual meeting of the American Sociological Association, Chicago (January, 1988).

Hofferth, S., and Phillips, D., "Child Care in the United States, 1970 to 1995," *Journal of Marriage and the Family* (August, 1987), pp. 559–71.

Kahn, A., and Kamerman, S., *Child Care: Facing the Hard Choices* (Dover, Mass.: Auburn House Publishing, 1987).

Kamerman, S., "Child Care and Family Benefits: Policies of Six Industrialized Countries," *Monthly Labor Review* (November, 1980), pp. 23–28.

_____, "Child-care Services: A National Picture," *Monthly Labor Review* (December, 1983a), pp. 35–39.

_____, *Meeting Family Needs: The Corporate Response* (New York: Pergamon Press, 1983b).

Kamerman, S., and Kahn, A., *Child Care, Family Benefits, and Working Parents* (New York: Columbia University Press, 1981).

Kamerman, S., Kahn, A., and Kingston, P., *Maternity Policies and Working Women* (New York: Columbia University Press, 1983).

Kuhne, R., and Blair, C., "Flexitime," *Business Horizons* (April, 1978), pp. 39–44.

LeVine, R., and White, M., *Human Conditions: The Cultural Basis of Educational Developments* (New York: Routledge and Kegan Paul, 1986).

Lubeck, S., "Child Care in Public Schools: Before, After, Especially, As Soon As Possible . . . ," *Tennessee's Children* (Fall, 1987), pp. 15–18.

McMahon, P., "An International Comparison of Labor Force Participation, 1977–84," *Monthly Labor Review* (May, 1986), pp. 3–12.

Mitchell, A., "Public Schools and Young Children: A Report of the First National Survey of Public School Districts Regarding Their Early Childhood Programs." Paper presented at the annual meeting of the American Educational Research Association, Washington, D.C. (April, 1987).

Morado, C., "Prekindergarten Programs for Four-Year-Olds: State Education Agency Initiatives." Paper prepared for the National Association for the Education of Young Children, Washington, D.C. (October, 1985).

_____, "Prekindergarten Programs for Four-Year-Olds: Some Key Issues," *Young Children* (July, 1986), pp. 61–63.

_____, "A Report from the States: Current State-Level Policy Initiatives." Paper presented at the annual meeting of the American Educational Research Association, New Orleans (April, 1988).

Morgan, G., "Child Day Care Policy in Chaos," in E. Zigler, S. Kagan, and E. Klugman (eds.), *Children, Families, and Government: Perspectives on American Social Policy* (New York: Cambridge University Press, 1983).

_____, "Child Care and Early Education: What Legislators Can Do." Paper presented at the Advanced Legislative Program Services in Education meeting, Austin, Tex. (February, 1985).

Nelson, M., "Providing Family Day Care: An Analysis of Home-Based Work." Paper presented at the annual meeting of the American Sociological Association, Chicago (September, 1987).

O'Brien, P., *How to Select the Best Child-Care Option for Your Employees* (Binghamton, N.Y.: Almar Press, 1987).

O'Connell, M., and Bloom, D., *Juggling Jobs and Babies: America's Child Care Challenge* (Washington, D.C.: Population Reference Bureau, February, 1987).

Presser, H., "Shift Work among American Women and Child Care," *Journal of Marriage and the Family* (August, 1986), pp. 551–63.

Quinn, J., "Child Care in Crisis," *Newsweek* (February 15, 1988), p. 57.

Robinson, S., "Kindergarten in America: Five Major Trends," *Phi Delta Kappan* (March, 1987), pp. 529–30.

Rothman, S., and Marks, E., "Adjusting Work and Family Life: Flexible Work Schedules and Family Policy," in N. Gerstel and H. Gross (eds.), *Families and Work* (Philadelphia: Temple University Press, 1987), pp. 469–77.

Schweinhart, L., Koshel, J., and Bridgman, A., "Policy Options for Preschool Programs," *Phi Delta Kappan* (March, 1987), pp. 524–29.

Seligson, M., "Child Care for the School-Age Child," *Phi Delta Kappan* (May, 1986), pp. 637–40.

Tietze, W., "An International Perspective on (Pre) Schooling for Fours," *Theory into Practice* (in press).

Trotter, R., "Project Day-Care," *Psychology Today* (December, 1987), pp. 32–38.

U.S. Bureau of the Census, "Child Care Arrangements of Working Mothers: June 1982," *Current Population Reports,* Series P-23, No. 129 (Washington, D.C.: U.S. Government Printing Office, 1983).

_____, "School Enrollment—Social and Economic Characteristics of Students: October, 1985," *Current Population Reports,* Series P-20, No. 409 (Washington, D.C.: U.S. Government Printing Office, 1986).

_____, "Who's Minding the Kids? Child Care Arrangements: Winter 1984–85," *Current Population Reports,* Series P-70, No. 9 (Washington, D.C.: U.S. Government Printing Office, 1987).

U.S. Department of Labor, Bureau of Labor Statistics, "Half of Mothers with Children under Three Now in the Labor Force," *News* (August 20, 1986).

_____, "Reports on Employer Child Care Practices," *News* (January 15, 1988).

Winn, M., *Children without Childhood* (New York: Penguin, 1983).

Zigler, E., "Formal Schooling for Four-Year-Olds? No," *American Psychologist* (March, 1987), pp. 254–60.

Zinsser, C., *Day Care's Unfair Burden: How Low Wages Subsidize a Public Service* (New York: Center for Public Advocacy Research, 1986).

8

Divorce

Divorce from the bonds of matrimony shall not be allowed in this state   [*South Carolina divorce statute, circa 1900*].

In 1887 the Congress of the United States directed the Bureau of Labor to collect national statistics on marriage and divorce, as well as information on the laws governing marital dissolution in the various states. This directive reflected a growing concern in the United States about the increase in the number of divorces in the decades following the Civil War. Because most states in the nineteenth century did not keep vital statistics for their populations, collection of data on the incidence of divorce was a formidable task. The Bureau of Labor eventually assembled information from approximately 2,600 courts having jurisdiction over divorce and published the results in *A Report on Marriage and Divorce, 1867–1886* (1889). The report confirmed the fears of many, showing an increase in the number of divorces in the United States from 9,937 to 27,919 over the twenty-year period. This increase represented a rise in the divorce rate per 1,000 existing marriages from approximately 1.6 to 2.6 (Gordon, 1978:294).

At the turn of the century, concern over the rising divorce rate had not abated. In 1905 President Theodore Roosevelt urged the Congress to authorize another investigation of divorce. According to Roosevelt:

> The institution of marriage is, of course, at the very foundation of our social organization and all influences that affect that institution are of vital concern to the people of the whole country. There is a widespread conviction that the divorce laws are dangerously lax and indifferently administered in some States, resulting in a diminishing regard for the sanctity of the marriage relation   [*U.S. Bureau of the Census, 1909:4*].

Shortly thereafter Congress passed a joint resolution directing the Bureau of the Census to conduct a further study of divorce rates and divorce laws. The subsequent report, *Marriage and Divorce, 1867–1906* (1909), showed that the number of divorces had more than doubled between 1886 and 1906 to 72,062, reflecting a rate of 4.2 divorces per 1,000 existing marriages.

Although these rates of divorce now seem comparatively low, they demonstrate a pattern of steady increase beginning in the mid-nineteenth century. The increase continued, with some notable exceptions, in the twentieth century. In 1920, the divorce rate reached 8 per 1,000 married women. The rate remained fairly steady throughout the 1920s but dropped to 6.1 during the early years of the Depression. The rate rose again in the late 1930s and during World War II to a peak of 17.9 in 1946. The rate then declined in the 1950s, although it never fell below prewar rates. After a modest increase in the early 1960s, the divorce rate began to increase dramatically. Between 1965 and 1970, the rate rose from 10.6 to 14.9 per 1,000 married women, and by 1980 the rate had reached 22.

One way to comprehend the significance of this long-term increase in the divorce rate is to examine the experiences of successive birth cohorts. A birth cohort is composed of all people born during a specific interval—for example, all people born between 1900 and 1904. The experiences of individuals in a particular birth cohort who marry reflect the divorce rates over the duration of their marriages. Andrew Cherlin has assembled data on three cohorts of women in the twentieth century. He reports that about 15 percent of women born between 1910 and 1914 eventually married and divorced, while about 25 percent of women born between 1930 and 1934 did so. It is predicted that 45 percent of women born between 1950 and 1954 (most of whom married in the 1970s) will marry and subsequently divorce (Cherlin, 1981:71). If one restricts consideration to only those women who do marry, the percentage divorcing rises. For example, Norton and Moorman (1987:12) predict that approximately 55 percent of women of the 1946–1950 cohort who do marry have ended or eventually will end their first marriages in divorce.

Since 1980 the divorce rate has stabilized, leading some to speculate that it has reached a plateau and may even decline slightly in the years to come (Kemper, 1983). Nevertheless, divorce has clearly become a relatively common experience in the United States. This chapter considers some developments associated with the rise in divorce rates and the impact of divorce on those who experience it.

Divorce Laws and Changing Expectations of Marriage

At the time of the settlement of the American colonies, church authorities controlled marriage in England. Divorces were prohibited, although annulments and separations could be obtained. American colonists rebelled against ecclesiastical control and placed marriage under the jurisdiction of civil authorities (Halem, 1980:10–15). Some colonies, particularly in the South, continued to prohibit divorce. However, others granted divorces, usually by action of colonial assemblies or an executive body.

Nancy Cott's (1976) study of divorce records in Massachusetts between 1692 and 1787 demonstrates the infrequency with which divorces were sought and granted in early America. In Massachusetts, the governor and his council considered petitions for dissolution and could grant annulments, separations, or divorces. Cott discovered only 229 petitions for dissolution in this ninety-five year period, 128 filed by women and 101 by men. Massachusetts law did not list specific causes for which divorces could be granted. However, the most frequent cause included in the 229 petitions was adultery, followed by desertion and cruelty. Men were more likely than women to petition for divorces because of adultery. When women did cite infidelity in their petitions, they usually combined it with other grievances. No men petitioned for divorce on the basis of cruelty. (Charges of sexual incapacity and bigamy were included in many of the petitions, but these grievances were grounds for annulment, not divorce.)

Without doubt, these 229 petitions represent only a small fraction of marriages in which spouses had been unfaithful or cruel or had deserted. Further, these petitions reveal simply that individuals sought to dissolve their unions by claiming that their spouses had failed to live up to major marital obligations. They do not reveal the other reasons these individuals may have had for seeking divorces, only the grounds available to them.

Perhaps as revealing as the petitions themselves were the actions on them of the governors' councils. Only 143 of the 229 petitions resulted in divorce, and men were more likely to be granted divorces than women. The greater success of men in obtaining divorces was the result primarily of a double standard regarding infidelity. Men who petitioned for divorce on the grounds of adultery were likely to be successful. Seventy percent of men's petitions claiming adultery as a sole grievance and 80 percent of petitions including adultery with other causes resulted in divorces. Women, however, were much less successful in their attempts to gain divorces for the infidelity of their husbands, and they rarely attempted to or did obtain divorces with adultery as the sole grievance. Women were also less likely to receive divorces for desertion than men, and none of twenty-three female petitioners were granted divorces for the sole grievance of cruelty. Cott did discover a trend toward more equal treatment of women's petitions and a more liberal stance toward divorce at the end of the period of her study. However, these trends only presaged far-reaching changes in divorce and divorce legislation.

In the nineteenth century, divorce statutes become less restrictive than they had been. When Massachusetts codified the grounds for divorce in 1786, its statute included only consanguinity, bigamy, impotency, and adultery (Cott, 1976:612). The 1785 Pennsylvania statute allowed the courts to grant divorces for physical incompetence, bigamy, adultery, and willful desertion for a period of four years. In New Jersey in 1794, the grounds for divorce were limited to adultery and desertion (Gordon, 1978:285). Gradually, various states added other grounds to their divorce statutes. In 1815 Pennsylvania added cruel and barbarous treatment by the husband as cause for divorce and reduced the required period of willful desertion to two years (Halem, 1980:19). In 1811 Massachusetts liberalized its law to include a husband's neglect, cruelty, or desertion of his wife, and in 1843 Connecticut added habitual intemperance and intolerable cruelty to its law. Jurisdiction over divorce had passed to the courts in most states by the end of the Civil War.

By the opening of the twentieth century, a typical divorce statute included desertion, extreme cruelty, adultery, intemperance, conviction of a serious crime, and impotence as causes for divorce. Eighteen states had also added neglect of marital responsibilities as a ground for divorce, usually a husband's neglect to provide support for his wife. Not all states changed their laws to the same degree; the divorce laws in some states remained restrictive. At the turn of the century, New York, for example, allowed divorce only on the grounds of adultery, and South Carolina did not allow divorces at all (U.S. Bureau of the Census, 1909:268–69).

The variation in divorce laws in the nineteenth century contributed to the phenomenon of migratory divorce. As some states loosened the requirements for divorce and reduced the residency requirements for obtaining a divorce, residents of states with more restrictive laws sometimes traveled elsewhere to end their marriages. Indiana obtained an early reputation as a "divorce colony" because it had no residency requirements and a so-called omnibus clause in its divorce statute. An *omnibus clause* allowed courts to grant divorces for any causes they deemed sufficient, in addition to the specific grounds listed in the statutes. Indiana eventually added a two-year residency requirement, but other states simply took its place for those willing to travel to escape unhappy marriages. For the first part of the twentieth century, Nevada was the migratory divorce capital, at one point reducing its residency requirement to six weeks (Gordon, 1978:288–91). Although migratory divorce drew much public attention and was the object of a great deal of teeth gnashing by opponents of divorce, most couples obtained their divorces in their states of residence in the nineteenth and early twentieth century, as they still do today (Degler, 1980:167).

Despite the liberalization of divorce laws, a double standard continued to exist with regard to marital fidelity. The laws of most states made no distinction between husband and wife when it came to adultery. Nevertheless, in the late nineteenth and early twentieth centuries about one-third of all divorces granted to men were for adultery, while only about 10 percent of divorces granted to women were for this cause. It is probable, if contemporary patterns are an indication, that infidelity was more common among husbands in the past than among wives and, consequently, that more women than men continued to live with adulterous spouses. The 1909 census report offered a possible explanation for this double standard:

> The difference may be attributed to the probability that the offense when committed by the wife is less likely to be condoned and perhaps more likely to be discovered. . . . Public sentiment doubtless condemns the offense more strongly than in the husband, and possibly the courts are in some degree influenced thereby [*U.S. Bureau of the Census, 1909:28*].

Thus, the gender inequities in patterns of divorce that Cott discovered in the eighteenth century continued to exist. As we will see, divorce laws and practice contained other double standards as well.

Nevertheless, the liberalization of divorce laws did make it easier for both men and women to end their marriages. At the turn of the century, discontented spouses could obtain divorces on grounds that were not recognized one hundred years earlier. Changes in the courts' interpretations of these grounds also increased the possibilities of obtaining a divorce. For example, the courts determined that extreme cruelty meant not only physical abuse but mental cruelty as well. Sometimes the courts considered cruelty as simply the failure to live up to "reasonable" expectations of marital behavior, such as a wife's refusal to cook her husband's meals or a husband's failure to speak civilly to his wife (Degler, 1980:170–71).

What accounts for these changes in divorce legislation in the nineteenth century? Because divorce laws define the circumstances that allow individuals to dissolve their marriages, they reveal the beliefs held by members of a society about appropriate marital behavior (Weitzman and Dixon, 1980:355). In Chapter 4, we saw that industrialization led to changes in the expectations individuals held for marriage. Kirk Jeffrey suggested that nineteenth-century Americans nourished utopian hopes for their families and marriages. Sociologists Ernest Burgess and Harvey Locke (1945) held the view that marriage was evolving from an institutional form based on economic rights and duties to a companionate form based on love and mutual interests. The gradual liberalization of divorce laws reflects these changing views of marriage. Individuals began to expect more of their marriages than adherence to major obligations such as fidelity and cohabitation. They also sought companionship and emotional fulfillment and were willing to end marriages that did not meet these expectations.

Two important studies of divorce records in California illustrate the changing expectations of marriage held by nineteenth- and twentieth-century Americans. Robert Griswold (1982) examined 401 divorce cases in the years between 1850 and 1889 in San Mateo and Santa Clara counties. The residents of these counties lived in small towns and on farms, as did the majority of Americans at this time. Roughly one-third of those seeking divorces were from farm families, and the rest were fairly evenly distributed among families in which the husbands were merchants, shopkeepers, or laborers. According to Griswold, when these Californians sought divorces they often stressed lack of affection, companionship, or mutual respect in their marriages. He found that women especially were demanding emotional intimacy as well as the fulfillment of traditional obligations.

Elaine May's (1980) study focuses on the early twentieth century. She examined the records of 500 divorce cases filed in the city of Los Angeles in 1920 (as well as 500 filed in 1880 for comparative purposes) and concludes that twentieth-century urban Americans were beginning to hold high hopes for their marriages. According to May, the grievances of the men and women seeking divorces in Los Angeles indicate the emergence of a new definition of marital happiness that stressed the pursuit of "fun and excitement" in marriage. This pursuit included an emphasis on joint participation in leisure activities, sexual gratification in marriage, and consumer spending. May suggests that while Hollywood films played a role in spreading new hopes for marriage, these views reflected the underlying changes in the family accompanying industrialization.

Like Griswold, May emphasizes the crucial role of women in expressing these new views of marriage.

The No-Fault Revolution

In 1970 California passed the nation's first no-fault divorce law. The new law allowed a divorce when either husband or wife claimed that "irreconcilable differences" had caused the "irremediable breakdown" of their marriage. By 1985, seventeen states had adopted no-fault laws similar to the California statute, and all states, with the exception of South Dakota, had added no-fault provisions to their divorce laws (Weitzman, 1985:41). No-fault statutes dramatically alter divorce proceedings and institutionalize new ideas about the obligations of husbands and wives to one another (Weitzman and Dixon, 1980:354).

As we have seen, traditional divorce laws required grounds for divorce, such as cruelty or adultery. In essence, these grounds defined the minimal standards of conduct that husbands and wives had the right to expect from one another. According to Lenore Weitzman and Ruth Dixon (1980:358–61), traditional divorce law contained three additional elements. First, divorce proceedings were adversarial. One spouse brought suit against the other and was required to prove marital misconduct in order to be granted a divorce. If the accused spouse wished to contest the divorce, he or she could mount a defense or file a countersuit charging the other party with misconduct. Second, the guilty party was punished by the financial terms of the divorce. For example, a husband found guilty of adultery would sometimes be required to pay alimony to his ex-wife, but a husband would not be required to do so if his wife were the guilty party. The courts also divided property based on the determination of fault, the innocent party getting a larger share.

Finally, traditional divorce law reinforced a gender-based division of labor in marriage in several ways. Provisions for the payment of alimony reflected the belief that the husband was responsible for the support of his wife in return for her domestic labor. Child-custody statutes contained a "maternal preference" based on the assumption that mothers were the appropriate caretakers of children, and child-support awards routinely assigned economic responsibility for children to the father. The interpretation of the grounds for divorce also reinforced traditional gender roles. For example, the courts granted divorces to women on the grounds of cruelty if their husbands had been physically abusive. However, men sometimes obtained divorces on the grounds of cruelty if their wives failed to keep the house clean or cook dinner. In another example, wives who refused to move when their husbands wished to change their place of residence were considered to be guilty of desertion, while husbands who refused to move with their wives were not.

No-fault laws change each of the four elements of traditional divorce. No-fault laws do not require grounds for divorce. One spouse need only assert that irreconcilable differences make the continuation of the marriage undesirable, and the individual initiating the divorce can determine the definition of irreconcilable differences. The elimination of grounds also makes adversary proceedings unnecessary because proof of marital misconduct is no longer required.

Some states have not gone as far as have California and other "true no-fault" states in abandoning the determination of legal responsibility for marital break-downs. These states have added no-fault provisions to traditional fault-based statutes. Divorces for irreconcilable differences are allowed only if both husband and wife agree that their marriage should end. In the absence of mutual consent, one party must sue the other and establish legal grounds for divorce.

No-fault laws also eliminate those aspects of traditional divorce law that reinforced gender-typed marital roles. The single standard of irreconcilable differences for dissolution applies equally to men and women. Further, no-fault laws require that financial settlements be based on economic need and the ability to pay rather than on gender-typed roles and the determination of blame (Weitzman and Dixon, 1980:362). In alimony and child-support orders, the courts in no-fault states consider the economic situation of both husband and wife and assume that both are capable of economic self-sufficiency. Alimony, when ordered, is only a temporary award to allow a spouse who has worked in the home or made career sacrifices in other ways the opportunity to establish the means of economic support. When children are involved, the noncustodial parent is often ordered to pay child support, but both parents have responsibility for the economic support of their children.

In one respect no-fault laws represent a continuation of the trend toward permissive divorce legislation that began in the nineteenth century. By requiring only the assertion of irreconcilable differences to end a marriage, no-fault laws reflect the expectation that marriage be a mutually satisfying personal relationship. However, in other respects, no-fault laws represent a radical departure from previous divorce law. First, by eliminating provisions that reinforced traditional gender roles, no-fault laws attempt to initiate new standards of equality between men and women. Second, by eliminating adversarial proceedings, no-fault laws attempt to reduce the hostility and trauma created for divorcing couples by the legal process itself (Weitzman, 1985:16).

Advocates of no-fault laws believed that these changes would make divorce laws both more fair and more realistic than they had been. However, the changes create problems of their own. For example, the assumption that men and women are equally capable of self-sufficiency after divorce does not reflect labor-market conditions for most women. As we will see, the economic consequences of divorce are much different for women than they are for men. Also, by abandoning attempts to assign blame for marital breakdown, no-fault laws fail to penalize individuals who violate widely accepted standards of marital conduct, such as fidelity. It may be true that some couples are now able to end their marriages quickly and with a minimum of bitterness. However, for individuals who feel they have been treated unfairly by their spouses and made to endure hardships that were no fault of their own, the law now offers no recourse. For these individuals the brevity of legal proceedings may offer only small comfort (Weitzman, 1985:22–26).

Who Divorces?

Although divorce rates have increased generally in the last several decades, people with certain social and demographic characteristics are more likely to divorce than others. Numerous factors have been found to be associated with the likelihood of divorce, but age at marriage, religious affiliation, socioeconomic status, and race and ethnicity are among the most important.

For example, those who marry as teenagers are much more likely to divorce than individuals who marry in their twenties. Norton and Moorman (1987:9) found that 32 percent of women who had married before twenty years of age reported being divorced in a survey by the Census Bureau. Only 18 percent of those marrying between the ages of twenty and twenty-four said they were divorced. Spanier and Glick (1981:333) found that women marrying between fourteen and seventeen were twice as likely to divorce as those marrying in their twenties. There are many possible explanations for the high rates of divorce among those who marry as teenagers. First, some teenagers marry because of premarital pregnancies. These young people may have chosen different partners under other circumstances. Second, some teenagers may be emotionally unprepared for marriage, perhaps choosing to marry as a way to escape an unhappy home life. Third, people who marry early are at risk for divorce for a longer time than people who marry later in their lives. Without doubt, a combination of these and other factors explains the high divorce rate for teenagers.

Not surprisingly, those who have no religious affiliation have higher rates of dissolution than those affiliated with some faith. Among the faiths, Catholics are less likely to divorce than Protestants, and Jews have lower divorce rates than either group. These differences may be the result, in part, of religious prohibitions against divorce. However, this explanation fails to account for the lower rate of Jews or the fact that conservative Protestants (Nazarene, Pentecostal, Baptist) have higher divorce rates than other religious groups.

Glenn and Supanic (1984:572–73) suggest that an explanation of these anomalies lies in the relationship of religious affiliation to "social integration." Social integration refers to participation in groups "characterized by solidarity, value consensus, and effective social controls." Glenn and Supanic suggest that individuals who are highly involved in such groups may be dissuaded from engaging in conduct that would lead to divorce and may find help in reaching solutions to their marital problems in these groups. Further, cohesive groups may exercise some control over mate choice, which may prevent marriages that are at high risk for divorce. Glenn and Supanic hypothesize (1) that individuals with no religious affiliation are less likely to be members of integrated groups, (2) that Jews are a very cohesive group, and (3) that many conservative Protestants are recent converts who come from segments of society with low levels of social integration—for example, the highly mobile and economically disadvantaged.

Generally, the lower the socioeconomic status, whether measured by income, education, or occupation, the higher the divorce rate. One explanation for this negative association is that individuals in lower socioeconomic groups are more likely than those in higher groups to experience stressful life events or circumstances that can cause marital strain—for example, unemployment, inadequate housing, alcoholism, and mental illness.

However, there are some important exceptions to the association of low socioeconomic status with high divorce rates. First, wives' earnings are positively associated with divorce rates (Price-Bonham and Balswick, 1980:960). In other words, when women have independent sources of income, their probability of divorce rises. Second, while the divorce rate for men falls consistently with level of education, this relationship does not hold for women. The divorce rate of women with postgraduate educations is surpassed only by the rate of women with less than a high school education (Houseknecht, Vaughan, and Macke, 1984:273). Together, these two exceptions suggest that the relationship between socioeconomic status and divorce is a complex one. When the husband is the primary source of economic support, his success leads to increased family stability, in part because his wife is unlikely to have satisfactory alternatives if she is discontented with her marriage. As a result the relationship between family income and divorce is generally a negative one. However, women who are employed and particularly women with postgraduate educations have higher divorce rates because for them outside opportunities compare more favorably with marriage than they do for their unemployed or less educated sisters. Among the lower class, stressful life events and men's lack of success in the occupational world probably combine to produce a high rate of divorce.

Finally, race and ethnicity are related to divorce. For example, black Americans have higher rates of divorce than white Americans. This difference appears to be related to the economically disadvantaged position of many blacks in the United States (Cherlin, 1981:100–109). However, Mexican Americans have much lower rates of divorce than white Americans even though their economic position differs little from that of black Americans. Researchers have stressed both a strong familistic orientation and the high percentage of Mexican Americans who are Catholic to explain these differences (Frisbie, Opitz, and Kelly, 1985).

Readings

The increase in the divorce rate and the trend toward liberal divorce laws in the nineteenth century were not without their critics. In the first article in this chapter, "Divorce in the Progressive Era," William O'Neill examines the opposition to divorce in the United States around the turn of the century. As the article makes clear, the opponents of divorce were many and vocal. Although these critics made both moral and social arguments against divorce, they attempted to stem the tide of divorce primarily through legal reforms. They were able to temporarily reverse the trend toward less restrictive divorce statutes in some states. However, as the article explains, they encountered opposition from individuals espousing the novel idea, for the time, that increasing divorce rates were the result of the emergence of a new kind of marriage based on love and companionship.

This account of the attempts of opponents of divorce to pass restrictive legislation raises a question about the relationship between divorce laws and divorce rates that is relevant today: Do liberal divorce laws encourage individuals to end their marriages and, therefore, increase the divorce rate? George Wright and Dorothy Stetson (1978) addressed this question in a study of the impact of no-fault divorce laws. They found that states enacting no-fault laws in the 1970s did not experience greater increases in divorce rates than did states failing to reform their laws. They concluded that no-fault laws were a response to increases in divorce rates rather than the cause of increased rates. In fact, Lenore Weitzman's (1985:16–20) examination of the legislative history of California's no-fault law shows that many advocates of reform did see no-fault laws as the appropriate legal response to a preexisting social phenomenon.

Divorce has now become a relatively common experience, and legislative reforms have simplified the legal phases of the divorce process. In the next article, "Divorce and Stigma," Naomi Gerstel focuses attention on the psychological and social aspects of divorce. Despite the frequency of divorce, research shows that it is traumatic for most people. Robert Weiss (1975) discovered that separated and divorced individuals experienced several common reactions. For example, he found that many experienced "separation anxiety," a feeling of discomfort, anxiety, and sadness because of the inaccessibility of the absent spouse. Weiss speculated that individuals who had initiated the divorce would suffer less than those who were left. His speculation has been borne out by subsequent research (Kelly, 1982).

Gerstel's study contributes to our understanding of the difficulties of divorce. She begins by noting that public tolerance of divorce has increased dramatically in the last few decades. One study she cites as evidence of this change is Arland Thornton's (1985) examination of the attitudes toward divorce of approximately 1,000 women in the Detroit area. The women were interviewed five times between 1962 and 1980. In each interview they were asked whether they agreed or disagreed with the following statement: "When there are children in the family, parents should stay together even if they don't get along." Fifty percent of the women disagreed with this statement in 1962 (indicating a tolerance of divorce). The percentage disagreeing increased in each subsequent year, with 80 percent of the respondents disagreeing by 1980. However, Gerstel's research shows that the growing public acceptance of divorce is not always reflected in the personal experience of divorced individuals. Many people she interviewed reported encountering negative attitudes following divorce. Further, she found that the divorced often share these negative attitudes toward other divorced people. Gerstel points out that although the courts may no longer assign blame to one party in a divorce, other people frequently do. Therefore, the divorced must learn to manage the stigma of being divorced in addition to the distress of ending a relationship that most expected to endure for a lifetime.

The breakup of a relationship as intimate as marriage, no matter how commonplace, will probably always involve some degree of emotional distress. Nevertheless, studies show that the psychological trauma of divorce usually passes and that most divorced people conclude that they are better off after the breakup, all things considered. For example, Stan Albrecht (1980) studied the reactions and adjustments to divorce of approximately 800 individuals. He found that although two-thirds of the people he questioned said that the divorce was stressful or traumatic, over 90 percent said that their present situation was better than the predivorce situation. Similarly, Helen Weingarten found few differences between the married and divorced on several dimensions of psychological well-being. According to Weingarten (1985:659):

> The finding that experiencing divorce . . . has, at most, limited impact on current adjustment is also consistent with trends in the life crisis literature. Social scientists interested in crisis intervention have long emphasized not only that individuals confronted with overwhelming life events require a period of time to recover but also that life crises that initially lead to maladaptive coping responses can, over time, also foster considerable personal growth.

However, the characterization of divorce as an emotionally wrenching but eventually positive experience requires substantial modification, particularly for women.

In the third article, "Divorce: A Women's Issue," Terry Arendell shows that the emotional distress experienced by women who divorce is accompanied by an additional and often permanent source of trauma, a dramatic decline in economic well-being. This drop in class position is most pronounced for women with children, and the rise in the divorce rate is partly responsible for the increasing numbers of women and children living below the poverty line. At present nearly two-thirds of all adults in poverty are female, and approximately one-quarter of all children live in poverty (Sidel, 1986:3). In addition, many more women and children live only marginally above the official poverty line. Arendell discusses the factors responsible for the downward mobility of women after divorce and raises the important issue of how women who have devoted themselves to home and child rearing should be compensated after divorce. On the basis of sixty in-depth interviews, Arendell also describes how women attempt to cope with their severe and continuing financial difficulties after divorce.

One factor contributing to the decline in women's economic status after divorce is their continuing responsibility for children. As Arendell points out, over half of all divorces involve minor children, and the courts assign custody of over 90 percent of these children to their mothers. For most of this century, a maternal preference governed custody decisions. Often referred to as the "tender years doctrine," this preference derived from the widespread belief that women were the natural caretakers of children. The 1960s and 1970s witnessed the gradual erosion of the tender years doctrine in favor of the "best interest of the child" standard, under which the courts must consider a variety of factors in determining custody awards. For example, the Uniform Marriage and Divorce Act includes five criteria: the wishes of the child's parents; the wishes of the child; the interaction of the child with his or her parents; the child's adjustment to home, school, and community; and the mental and physical health of all individuals involved. Although the best interest standard does not give preference to either parent, fathers rarely attempt to gain custody of their children after divorce. However, studies show that when men do seek custody in court, they are successful 50 percent of the time or more (Weitzman, 1985:233, Chesler, 1986:66).

Whether mothers or fathers retain custody of the children, divorce radically alters relationships between parents and children. In the final article in this chapter, "Parenting Apart: Patterns of Childrearing after Marital Disruption," Frank Furstenberg and Christine Nord consider how the rapid rise in the divorce rate has changed both parenting practices and conceptions of parenthood. The authors draw their information from interviews with a national sample of children whose parents had divorced or separated. The children were questioned about their relationships with custodial and noncustodial parents. Because about three-quarters of the divorced remarry, the children were also asked about relationships with stepparents. The findings presented in this article help explain why single parenting is so difficult, but the results also attest to the ability of children to adapt to changed and often complicated family situations.

References

Albrecht, Stan L. 1980. "Reactions and Adjustments to Divorce: Differences in Experiences of Males and Females." *Family Relations* 29:59–68.

Burgess, Ernest W., and Harvey J. Locke. 1945. *The Family: From Institution to Companionship*. New York: The American Book Company.

Cherlin, Andrew J. 1981. *Marriage, Divorce, Remarriage*. Cambridge: Harvard University Press.

Chesler, Phyllis. 1986. *Mothers on Trial: The Battle for Children and Custody*. New York: McGraw-Hill.

Cott, Nancy. 1976. "Divorce and the Changing Status of Women in Eighteenth-Century Massachusetts." *William and Mary Quarterly,* Third Series, 33:586–614.

Degler, Carl N. 1980. *At Odds: Women and the Family in America from the Revolution to the Present*. New York: Oxford University Press.

Frisbie, W. Parker, Wolfgang Opitz, and William R. Kelly. 1985. "Marital Instability Trends among Mexican Americans as Compared to Blacks and Anglos: New Evidence." *Social Science Quarterly* 66:587–601.

Glenn, Norval D., and Michael Supanic. 1984. "The Social and Demographic Correlates of Divorce and Separation in the United States: An Update and Reconsideration." *Journal of Marriage and the Family* 46:563–75.

Gordon, Michael. 1978. *The American Family: Past, Present, and Future*. New York: Random House.

Griswold, Robert L. 1982. *Family and Divorce in California, 1850–1890: Victorian Illusions and Everyday Realities*. Albany: State University of New York Press.

Halem, Lynne Carol. 1980. *Divorce Reform: Changing Legal and Social Perspectives*. New York: Free Press.

Houseknecht, Sharon K., Suzanne Vaughan, and Anne S. Macke. 1984. "Marital Disruption among Professional Women: The Timing of Career and Family Events." *Social Problems* 31:273–84.

Kelly, Joan B. 1982. "Divorce: The Adult Perspective." In *Handbook of Developmental Psychology,* edited by Benjamin B. Wolman, 734–50. Englewood Cliffs, N.J.: Prentice-Hall.

Kemper, Theodore D. 1983. "Predicting the Divorce Rate Down?" *Journal of Family Issues* 4:507–24.

May, Elaine. 1980. *Great Expectations: Marriage and Divorce in Post-Victorian America.* Chicago: University of Chicago Press.

Norton, Arthur J., and Jeanne E. Moorman. 1987. "Current Trends in Marriage and Divorce among American Women." *Journal of Marriage and the Family* 49:3–14.

Price-Bonham, Sharon, and Jack O. Balswick. 1980. "The Non-Institutions: Divorce, Desertion, and Remarriage." *Journal of Marriage and the Family* 42:959–72.

Sidel, Ruth. 1986. *Women and Children Last: The Plight of Poor Women in Affluent America.* Baltimore: Penguin.

Spanier, Graham B., and Paul C. Glick. 1981. "Marital Instability in the United States: Some Correlates and Recent Changes." *Family Relations* 30:329–38.

Thornton, Arland. 1985. "Changing Attitudes toward Separation and Divorce: Causes and Consequences." *American Journal of Sociology* 90:856–72.

U.S. Bureau of Labor. 1889. *A Report on Marriage and Divorce, 1867–1886.* Washington, D.C.: U.S. Government Printing Office.

U.S. Bureau of the Census. 1909. *Marriage and Divorce, 1867–1906.* Special Report, Part I. Washington, D.C.: U.S. Government Printing Office.

Weingarten, Helen R. 1985. "Marital Status and Well-Being: A National Study Comparing First-Married, Currently Divorced, and Remarried Adults." *Journal of Marriage and the Family* 47: 653–62.

Weiss, Robert S. 1975. *Marital Separation.* New York: Basic Books.

Weitzman, Lenore J. 1985. *The Divorce Revolution: The Unexpected Social and Economic Consequences of Divorce for Women and Children in America.* New York: Free Press.

Weitzman, Lenore J., and Ruth B. Dixon. 1980. "The Transformation of Legal Marriage through No-Fault Divorce." In *Family in Transition,* 3d ed., edited by Arlene Skolnick and Jerome Skolnick, 354–67. Boston: Little, Brown.

Wright, George C., and Dorothy N. Stetson. 1978. "The Impact of No-Fault Divorce Law Reform in the American States." *Journal of Marriage and the Family* 40:575–80.

Divorce in the Progressive Era

William L. O'Neill

During the Progressive years the divorce rate, which had been rising steadily since the Civil War, attained critical dimensions. Consequently, Americans of this period took a graver view of the problem than any subsequent generation. Their varied responses proved to be decisive as far as the future of divorce itself was concerned, and they illuminate aspects of the Progressive Era which have received little attention from historians.

The precipitate growth of the divorce rate can be easily demonstrated. In 1880 there was one divorce for every twenty-one marriages; in 1900 there was one divorce for every twelve marriages; in 1909 the ratio dropped to one in ten, and by 1916 it stood at one in nine.[1] Naturally this dramatic increase in the divorce rate stimulated public alarm.

In 1881 the New England Divorce Reform League was established to conduct research on family problems, educate the public and lobby for more effective legislative curbs on divorce.[2] Under the leadership of Samuel Dike, a Congregational minister, the league enjoyed a long and useful life, but Dike's reluctance to advance legislative solutions to the divorce problem failed to deter others from resorting to politics.

Efforts to arrest the spread of divorce by legal means took two forms. State campaigns were waged to amend local divorce laws, and repeated attempts were made to achieve uniform marriage and divorce laws either through a constitutional amendment or through the voluntary enactment of uniform codes by the several states.[3] Typical of the many local fights to alter state divorce laws was the successful battle in 1893 to end South Dakota's status as a divorce colony. After their admission to the Union in 1889 North and South Dakota retained Dakota Territory's generous ninety-day residence requirement. Sioux City, largest and most accessible town in the two states, soon developed a substantial divorce trade and gained national fame as a divorce colony. The resulting notoriety provoked local resentment which was mobilized by the return from Japan of the popular Episcopal Bishop William Hobart Hare, who in 1893 led Protestants, Catholics, and Populists in an attack on the ninety-day residence requirement. The state legislature was successfully petitioned to extend the residence requirement to six months and the migratory divorce trade was diverted to North Dakota.[4]

The South Dakota campaign conformed to what was already an established pattern. It was led by conservative clergymen, supported by women's groups,

From William L. O'Neill, *American Quarterly,* Vol. 17, No. 2 (Summer 1965):203–17. Published by the American Studies Association. Copyright ©1965. Reprinted by permission of American Quarterly and the author.

and met little apparent opposition. Although these local campaigns did not succeed anywhere in abolishing divorce, they were part of a widespread tendency toward stricter divorce legislation.[5] When such local crusades failed, it was usually because of public apathy, sometimes coupled with undercover resistance from commercial and legal interests which profited from the divorce trade.

Serious attempts to secure uniform marriage and divorce legislation through a constitutional amendment began in 1892, when James Kyle, the Populist Senator from South Dakota, introduced a joint resolution which read in full: "The Congress shall have the exclusive power to regulate marriage and divorce in the several states, Territories, and the District of Columbia."[6] Senator Kyle's resolution died in committee as did all later resolutions, presumably because of a disinclination on the part of Congress to increase the power of the Federal government at the expense of the states.[7]

More popular, if equally unsuccessful, was the movement to secure voluntary uniformity through the drafting of model statutes which were to be enacted by the states. The most persistent of the organizations dedicated to this goal was the National Conference of Commissioners on Uniform State Laws, which met annually in connection with the American Bar Association. It was established by the Bar Association in 1889 to frame model codes on a wide range of subjects. The Commissioners were usually appointed by their state governors and over the years drafted seven model statues concerning marriage and divorce.[8] However, few of the states demonstrated an interest in these models, and by 1916 the Commissioners were forced to admit that their approach had been a failure.

If the experience of the National Conference of Commissioners on Uniform State Laws to 1906 had not been conclusive, the fate of the National Divorce Congress in that year was. A national meeting to draft uniform legislation had been talked about for years on the grounds that it would attract sufficient attention to succeed where the more diffident Commissioners had failed. In 1906 President Roosevelt was persuaded to request a new census study of marriage and divorce, and the interest aroused by this led Governor Pennypacker of Pennsylvania to call a national conference to draft model uniform legislation on these subjects. The congress met twice, once in Washington to appoint committees and again in Philadelphia to ratify the proposed statutes. The first meeting was attended by delegates from forty-two of the forty-five states and consisted largely of clergymen and lawyers, many of the latter having also been members of the NCCUSL. Despite the widespread approval which met their efforts, few states adopted their model statutes.[9]

The antidivorce forces were also active within the established Protestant churches. During the Progressive Era repeated efforts were made in almost all the great Protestant denominations to stiffen their positions on divorce. The Episcopal church, traditionally more hostile to divorce than most Protestant bodies, was in the van of this movement, thanks principally to William Croswell Doane, Bishop of Albany, New York. Doane was perhaps the most vocal and consistent enemy of divorce in the whole country. He favored prohibiting divorce altogether, and his activities within the Episcopal church were directed at the canon which allowed the innocent party in an adultery suit to remarry. This canon was only slightly less severe than the refusal of the Roman Catholic church to allow any divorced person to remarry, but it seemed dangerously lax to Doane and he regularly introduced an amendment which would have denied the sacraments to all divorced persons without exception.

In 1898 the House of Bishops, usually more conservative than the lower House, which included laymen, at the policy-making Triennial Convention, rejected Doane's amendment thirty-one to twenty-four.[10] In 1901 his amendment was defeated by a narrower margin, but in 1904 it passed the House of Bishops only to fail in the House of Deputies, whose members felt that it was too far removed from the spirit of the country.[11] Thereafter enthusiasm within the Episcopal church for the Doane amendment declined, and while it was reintroduced at later conventions, it failed to pass even in the House of Bishops. Similar efforts were made in the other Protestant denominations with what proved to be an equal lack of success.[12]

American attitudes toward marriage and divorce during the Progressive years must be seen in terms of the widespread fear of divorce demonstrated by these examples. It is not too much to say that there was a national crisis generated by divorce. It was a crisis to begin with because people believed it was. As Daniel Bell has demonstrated in his *The End of Ideology,* it is not necessary for activities seen to be antisocial actually to increase in order to create a crisis atmosphere—it is enough if people simply believe that such activities are increasing.[13]

An even better example perhaps was the white slave panic of 1912–1913. If anything, prostitution was declining, but irrespective of the facts, widespread public alarm over this presumed social evil was triggered by local investigations and newspaper publicity.[14]

However, divorce actually was increasing by leaps and bounds. When one marriage in twelve ended in divorce, there were legitimate grounds for concern. These were crucial years for divorce, finally, because the Progressive period was the last time when public opinion could reasonably have been expected to support genuinely repressive action. With the 1920s and the advent of the revolution in morals, the opportunity to abolish or seriously restrict divorce was lost forever. Some of the antidivorce leaders sensed that time was running out for them, and this awareness gave their strictures an urgent tone which became more shrill with the years.

Although divorce had political, psychological, and other dimensions, the increase of divorce was usually seen as a moral and social problem.[15] It is difficult, if indeed not actually pointless, to try to determine which of these two aspects alarmed critics of divorce the most. The enemies of divorce invariably regarded it as both immoral and antisocial. Since most opponents of divorce were either clergymen or strongly religious people, it seems fair to assume that the moral side of the divorce question was what first engaged their attention, but having once declared divorce to be immoral, there is little more one can say in that direction, and most of the serious attacks on divorce emphasized its antisocial character.[16]

The attack on divorce hinged on the common belief that divorce destroyed the family, which was the foundation of society and civilization. Theodore

Schmauk, editor of the *Lutheran Church Review,* President of the Lutheran General Council and a leading theologian, characterized the family as "the great and fundamental institution in social life."[17] The *Catholic World* in an attack on H. G. Wells' view of divorce felt that it had demolished his position when it observed that Wells failed to see that the family "was the cradle of civil society."[18] Lyman Abbott, an influential Progressive editor and associate of Theodore Roosevelt, once charged a prominent divorcee with being "the worst type of anarchist" because divorce, like anarchy, threatened to destroy society altogether.[19] President Roosevelt, in addressing Congress on the need for uniform legislation, described marriage as being "at the very foundation of our social organization. . . ."[20] Marriage and the family are, of course, quite different institutions, but the critics of divorce did not usually distinguish between them.

Felix Adler took this contention a step further when he insisted that divorce menaced "the physical and spiritual existence of the human race. . . ."[21] Adler was in some ways a surprising figure to find on this side of the divorce question. The founder of Ethical Culture and a leading advocate of liberal religion, he consistently attacked dogma and orthodoxy and supported a wide variety of social reforms.[22] He had earlier supported divorce but by 1915 had changed his mind and accepted the point, usually advanced by the theologically orthodox, that divorce had to be suppressed as a matter of social survival. His conversion showed how this argument operated independently of its conservative religious base and helps to explain why some enemies of divorce attached such importance to their campaign. One could hardly play for higher stakes.

A related theme which engaged the attention of divorce critics was the role of woman. It was generally believed that the family was woman's special responsibility and its protection her primary concern. Moreover women were thought to be more active than men in securing divorces (and they probably were since about two-thirds of all divorces were awarded to women). The *North American Review* reflected this point of view when it entitled one of its divorce symposiums, "Are Women to Blame?"[23] The *Review's* female panelists charged women with responsibility for the divorce rate and accused them of being spoiled, romantic, impatient, jealous of men, and usurpers of the male's time-honored functions. Many of these women were successful writers, as was Anna B. Rogers, a popular essayist, who repeated the same charges in her book, *Why American Marriages Fail,* [twenty] years later.[24]

While the critics of divorce, especially the men, were inclined to argue that women were really happier when they stayed at home and held the family together, the more tough-minded accepted the fact that the woman's traditional role was often painful and difficult.[25] Few had a clearer picture of what was involved than the respected novelist Margaret Deland. Mrs. Deland was a warm supporter of many Progressive causes and a woman with courage enough to defend the rights of unwed mothers in Victorian Boston. But she believed that civilization "rests on the permanence of marriage."[26] For this reason women dared not turn to divorce, for it would mean the end of everything. "If we let the flame of idealism be quenched in the darkness of the senses," she cried, "our civilization must go upon the rocks."[27] Even adultery was no excuse for giving up the fight, she continued, because men were instinctively promiscuous, and their lapses from grace had to be tolerated for the sake of the greater good.

Implicit in these arguments was the belief that the individual was less important than the group. Most opponents of divorce agreed that divorce was part of an unwholesome tendency toward a "dangerous individualism." Margaret Deland bewailed the absence of team play among women and Professor Lawton called frankly for the "suppression of the individual in favor of the community."[28] Samuel Dike in his Cook Lecture attributed divorce to the rising tide of individualism menacing all progressive societies, while Felix Adler as early as 1890 was tracing the whole ugly business back to Rousseau's "false democratic ideals."[29] Although, as we shall see, most leading sociologists believed in divorce, Charles A. Ellwood did not. This future president of the American Sociological Society, despite his Progressive sympathies, also attributed divorce to excessive individualism.[30] Francis Peabody, an eminent theologian and student of the Higher Criticism, believed that the family's major enemies were scientific socialism and "the reactionary force of self-interested individualism. . . ."[31]

The opponents of divorce were more varied and had much more to say than I have been able to indicate, but the foregoing gives at least some idea of who they were and what they thought. The defenders of divorce, by way of contrast, were fewer in number and easier to locate. Opinion against divorce was so widespread and diffuse that it cannot be attributed to a handful of groups, but the sentiment favoring divorce was largely confined to sociologists, liberal clergymen, and feminists. The defenders of divorce, like its enemies, viewed the problem primarily in moral and social terms. But unlike the critics of divorce, its supporters, who were with few exceptions liberals, were much more interested in the morality of divorce and more inclined to see its moral and social dimensions as too interrelated for separate discussion and analysis.

The case for divorce gained initial momentum in the 1880s and 1890s, when a trickle of protest against Victorian marriage began to make itself heard. The plays of Henrik Ibsen, especially *A Doll's House* (1879) and *Ghosts* (1881), were affecting English audiences in the late 1880s and American opinion somewhat later. By the 1890s a number of Englishmen were attacking marriage and the views of Mona Caird and Grant Allen became well known in the United States through their own writings and through the publicity given their ideas by the American press. Mona Caird was a feminist whose essays appeared for the most part in high-quality limited circulation periodicals. Her most controversial proposal was an attempt to substitute for divorce short-term marriage contracts whose expiration would leave both parties free to separate or to negotiate a new contract.[32]

Grant Allen's best-known statement on the question was a sensational novel boosting feminism and free love entitled *The Woman Who Did*.[33] Allen was really calling for an end to marriage altogether, but his polemics against the institution supported divorce as much as free love. Within a few years the radical attack on marriage enlisted such big guns as H. G. Wells, who in a characteristically exuberant preview of the future in 1901 announced that monogamy was dissolving and sexual standards relaxing to the point where in a hundred years the present moral code "would remain nominally operative in sentiment and practice, while being practically disregarded. . . ."[34] Marriage was also under fire from the new moralists like the mystical Edward Carpenter, Havelock Ellis and his wife Edith, and the South African feminist Olive Schreiner, among others.[35]

The effect of this stream of marriage propaganda was to invigorate and inspire those Americans who believed in the right to divorce. Few respectable Americans were prepared to go as far as new moralists like Wells and Carpenter, but a substantial number of liberals were beginning to feel that traditional marriage was needlessly tyrannical and repressive, that it discriminated against women, and that divorce was not only an escape hatch for abused women but offered real opportunities for a reform of the whole marriage system. At the bottom of most, if not all, of this sentiment was the feminist impulse, for most divorce liberals were acutely conscious of the usefulness of divorce as an instrument for the emancipation of women.

Unlike the new moralists, whose feminism was concerned with freeing women for a fuller sex life, the American feminist was inclined to defend divorce because it freed women from sex. Benjamin O. Flower, who edited the populistic *Arena,* called for easier divorce laws as a way of protecting women from the excessive sexual appetites of their husbands. He argued that the common prostitute was "far freer than the wife who is nightly the victim of the unholy passion of her master. . . ."[36] By 1914 this argument had become so familiar that it was thought fit for the respectable readers of the cautious *Good Housekeeping* magazine. In that year Jesse Lynch Williams, feminist and playwright, asked rhetorically, "Is allowing herself to be owned body and soul by a man she loathes doing right?" before going on to delicately suggest "that seems rather like a dishonorable institution more ancient than marriage."[37]

Many feminists contended that not only did traditional marriage make women the sexual victims of their husbands, but it also exaggerated the importance of sex by denying women the chance to develop their other traits of character through work and education, and by forcing them to compete in the marriage market largely on the basis of their sexual attractions. The most desirable women had the best marital opportunities and so, through a kind of natural selection, sexuality prospered at the expense of other attributes. Divorce, along with expanded opportunities for education and employment, was a way of combatting this pernicious tendency.[38]

If the impulse to defend divorce came first from feminists who agreed with Elizabeth Cady Stanton on the need for a "larger freedom in the marriage relation," social scientists performed a crucial service in coping with the public's fear of the social consequences of divorce.[39] The first man of stature to defend divorce was Carrol Wright, U.S. Commissioner of Labor Statistics and a self-trained social scientist, who at the national Unitarian convention in 1891 boldly declared himself for liberal divorce laws. A few years later he wrote:

> The pressure for divorce finds its impetus outside of laws, outside of our institutions, outside of our theology; it springs from the rebellion of the human heart against that slavery which binds in the cruelest bonds human

beings who have by their haste, their want of wisdom, or the intervention of friends missed the divine purpose as well as the civil purpose of marriage.[40]

But it was not until 1904 that a leading professionally trained social scientist joined the fight. In his massive *A History of Matrimonial Institutions* and subsequent writings George E. Howard, an eminent historian and sociologist, tried to show how the divorce rate was the product of forces which were dramatically improving American society.[41] He argued that industrialization, urbanization, and the other pressures which were breaking up the old patriarchal family produced not only more divorces but a new kind of marriage marked by higher spiritual standards and greater freedom. Closing with the problem of individualism, which so alarmed the enemies of divorce, he declared that the growing power of the state was tending to make the individual and not the family the functional unit of society and that this process not only freed the individual from familial authoritarianism but elevated the family by abolishing its coercive power and transforming it into a "spiritual and psychic association of parent and child based on persuasion."[42]

Within a few years Wright and Howard were joined by a host of social scientists including most of the leading men in the field.[43] The weight of sociological opinion was solidly on the side of divorce by 1908, when the American Sociological Society devoted its third annual meeting to the family.[44] President William G. Sumner, the crusty, aging president of the society who had done so much to establish sociology as an academic discipline, opened the proceedings by observing gloomily that "the family has to a great extent lost its position as a conservative institution and has become a field for social change."[45] The program of the convention confirmed Sumner's fears, for virtually every paper described the changes affecting the family, called for more changes, or did both. Charlotte P. Gilman read a paper summarizing her *Women and Economics,* and a group of papers dealt with the damage inflicted on the family by urban, industrial life.[46]

The high point of the meeting was George Howard's "Is the Freer Granting of Divorce an Evil?" Howard repeated his now familiar views and touched off a controversy which showed the drift of professional opinion.[47] He was attacked by Samuel Dike, who insisted that divorce was produced by a dangerous individualism and the decline of ideals, and by Walter George Smith. Smith was prominent Catholic lawyer who had advocated stricter divorce laws for many years and was a leader in the campaign for uniform divorce legislation. His criticisms stressed divorce's incompatibility with orthodox religion and he accused Howard of condoning a social revolution that destroyed the divinely constituted order of things. Nothing, he declared, could alter the fact of feminine inferiority. Howard replied that marriage was a purely social institution "to be freely dealt with by men according to human needs."[48]

Despite this unusually spirited clash, Smith and his friends were making an illusory show of strength. The moralistic flavor of their language, so different in tone from Howard's, revealed their professional isolation. Theirs was the faintly anachronistic rhetoric of a discredited tradition of social criticism. The opponents of Howard's position were, moreover, all laymen with the exception of President Sumner and Albion Small, while on his side were ranged most of the speakers, including E. A. Ross, James Lichtenberger, and other leading scientists. As a profession then, sociology was committed to a positive view of divorce at a time when virtually every other organized group in the country was opposed to it. But although heavily outnumbered, the sociologists were the only people who could claim to speak on the problem with expert authority, and in the Progressive Era expertise was coming to be highly valued. As experts, the social scientists conferred respectability on the cause of free divorce at the same time as they did much to allay public anxiety over its effects.

A final problem that remained for the divorce liberals was finding some way to weaken the general conviction that divorce was forbidden by the Bible and to diminish the impact of the clergy's opposition to divorce. It was here that the handful of liberal ministers who supported divorce performed a signal, and indeed indispensable, service. Simply by saying that divorce was a morally acceptable device, the liberal ministers endowed it with a certain degree of legitimacy. If supporting divorce with their moral prestige was the more important function performed by the liberal ministers, some went beyond this and effectively disputed the traditional charge that the Bible specifically prohibited divorce.

One of the most impressive statements of the liberal position was delivered by William G. Ballentine, classicist, Bible scholar, one-time president of Oberlin College, and for twenty years editor of the *Bibliotheca Sacra*. Ballentine argued that "even if all thoughtful Christian men were today united in a resolute purpose of conformity to the letter of Scripture the path of duty would be far from plain."[49] He pointed out that a Biblical injunction against divorce cited by Bishop Doane in a recent magazine article appeared in the same passage as the admonition to resist evil. How, he asked, were Christians to know which commandment to obey and which to ignore? Ballentine described the life of Jesus as a struggle against Talmudic literalism:

> During His whole life, He fought against the tyranny of mere words, and for the lordship of the present living spiritual man. In his discourse He suggested great truths by parables, by questions, by metaphors, by paradoxes, by hyperboles, by every device that could elude the semblance of fixed judicial formulas. It is the irony of history that such language should be seized upon for statute law.[50]

Other scholars, theologians, and Higher Critics attacked the presumed Biblical sanctions against divorce in different ways, but the effect of their work was to undercut the general belief that the Bible clearly forbade divorce.[51]

On a more popular level the Rev. Minot J. Savage declared that as love was the essence of marriage, two people who no longer loved each other had every reason to get divorced.[52] This same conviction informed the writings of John H. Holmes, a great civil libertarian and advocate of liberal Christianity, who believed that the passing of love destroyed marriage in fact if not in name.[53]

Gradually the climate of opinion began to change. As noted earlier there was a substantial organized opposition to divorce during the Progressive period but, despite local victories, the movement to retard divorce by legal and political means was resoundingly unsuccessful. There were other signs which demonstrated that attitudes were being modified. Samuel Dike died in 1913 and his League expired shortly thereafter. It was essentially a one-man operation, but it was supported by the enemies of divorce, whose financial contributions had declined sharply even before his death, to the point where receipts after 1910 were about half of what they had been in the 1890s.[54] The Committee on the Family, which was routinely formed by the Federal Council of Churches, in 1911 was singularly inactive, and in 1919 it was dropped altogether.[55]

At the same time the solid wall of opposition to divorce maintained by the nation's press was repeatedly breached. Before 1900 no important American magazine defended the right to divorce except the radical *Arena*. Articles favorable to divorce were very rare in the general press. After about 1900, however, a few bold magazines like the *Independent* endorsed the right of divorce editorially, and many more began to print occasional articles defending divorce. The *North American Review,* which was more interested in the problem than any other major periodical, began the new century with a rousing attack on the opponents of divorce by the aging but still magnificent Elizabeth Cady Stanton.[56] Other magazines, too numerous to mention, also began to print articles favoring divorce. Even the uncompromisingly hostile *Outlook* unbent to this extent, and in 1910 it conceded editorially that there were times when divorce was permissible.[57] This shift influenced popular as well as serious magazines. In 1910 the slick monthly *World's Work* announced that "The True View of Increasing Divorce" was that the divorce rate was not alarming, and that divorces should not be subject to excessive restrictions.[58]

Obviously the changes in public opinion which these articles represented did not constitute a general recognition of the desirability of divorce. Although a few journals accepted the liberal argument that divorce was a therapeutic social mechanism, most did not. In many cases nothing more was involved than the admission that there were probably two sides to the question. This of itself, however, was a form of moral relativism on the issue which would have been unthinkable in the 1890s. This new tolerance of divorce coincided with the eruption of a number of curious phenomena like the dance craze and the white slave panic which marked the onset of the revolution in morals.[59]

Divorce was a part of the complex transformation of moral values and sexual customs which was to help give the 1920s their bizarre flavor. It was not only the most visible result of this vast social upheaval, but in many ways it was the most compatible with traditional modes of thought. It was, on the whole, an orderly, public, and institutionalized process which took due account of the formal difference between right and wrong, guilt and innocence. It had the blessings of the highest sociological authorities, and it was recommended by many feminists as a cure for the brutalizing sexual indignities known to occur in some marriages. Conservatives could, therefore, more easily resign themselves to divorce than to other, more extravagant, demonstrations of the changing moral order.

Although divorce has today assumed proportions undreamed of in the Progressive Era, the nature of the American response to mass divorce was determined at that time. Between 1905, when the magnitude of divorce as a social problem had become fully apparent, and 1917, when the movement to limit or direct the spread of divorce had clearly failed, something of importance for American social history had occurred. This was the recognition by moral conservatives that they could not prevent the revolution in morals represented by mass divorce. Their failure of morale in the immediate prewar period paved the way for spectacular changes which took place after the war.

Notes

1. The definitive statistical study is Paul H. Jacobson, *American Marriage and Divorce* (New York, 1959). Two great government reports contain the raw materials—they are U.S. Bureau of Labor, *A Report on Marriage and Divorce, 1867—1886* (1889), and the later, more comprehensive U.S. Bureau of the Census, *Marriage and Divorce, 1867–1906* (1909). Interesting contemporary analyses are contained in E. A. Ross, *Changing America* (New York, 1912), and William B. Bailey, *Modern Social Conditions* (New York, 1906).
2. Its origins are described in an untitled autobiographical manuscript by Samuel Warren Dike in the Dike Papers, Library of Congress.
3. The legal and political history of divorce is described very fully in Nelson Manfred Blake, *The Road to Reno* (New York, 1962).
4. See M. A. DeWolfe Howe, *The Life and Labors of Bishop Hare* (New York, 1912), *passim;* Blake, "Divorce in South Dakota," *Nation,* IX (January 26, 1893), 61.
5. National League for the Preservation of the Family, *Some Fundamentals of the Divorce Question* (Boston, 1909). A pamphlet written by Samuel Dike and published by his organization, which had undergone two changes of name since its founding, deals with these changes at some length. They involved extending the time required to obtain divorces and limiting the causes for which they could be granted.
6. U.S. Congressional Record, 52 Cong., 1st Sess. (February 3, 1892), 791.
7. See Senator Shortridge's candid remarks to this effect during hearings on a similar resolution years later. Senate Judiciary Committee, "Hearings on S. J. Res. 31" (November 1, 1921), *passim.*
8. "Secretary's Memorandum," *Proceedings of the 26th Annual Meeting of the NCCUSL (1916).*
9. See Blake, 140–145, and *Proceedings of the Adjourned Meeting of the National Congress on Uniform Divorce Laws* (Harrisburg, Pa., 1907).
10. "The Canon on Marriage and Divorce," *Public Opinion,* October 27, 1898.
11. "Remarriage after Divorce," *Outlook,* October 22, 1904.
12. The positions of the principal denominations on divorce and the efforts to change them are summarized in James P. Lichtenberger, *Divorce: A Study in Social Causation* (New York, 1909), chap. vii.
13. Daniel Bell, *The Myth of Crime Waves* (New York, 1961), 151–174.
14. Roy Lubove, "The Progressives and the Prostitute," *The Historian,* XXIV (May 1962), 308–329.
15. Generalizations of this sort which depend upon a close acquaintance with the popular literature are notoriously hard to document. My own conclusions are derived from an examination of almost everything dealing with marriage and divorce published either in book form or in more than thirty leading periodicals from 1889 through 1919. For details see my unpublished "The Divorce Crisis of the Progressive Era" (Doctor's dissertation, Berkeley, Calif., 1963).
16. By dismissing the moral side of the opposition to divorce so casually I do not mean to imply that it was not important but only that it was unremarkable and required no detailed

analysis. Divorce was considered immoral because it was forbidden by the New Testament and because it encouraged lust. Naturally the clergymen who opposed divorce supported themselves with Scriptural citations. One of the most elaborate efforts to relate divorce to licentiousness was Samuel Dike's first major address on the subject, reprinted in *Christ and Modern Thought: The Boston Monday Lectures 1880–1881,* ed. Joseph Cook (Boston, 1882).

17. "The Right to Be Divorced," *Lutheran Church Review,* XXVIII (October 1909), 661.
18. W. E. Campbell, "Wells, the Family, and the Church," *Catholic World,* XCI (July 1910), 483.
19. "The Worst Anarchism," *Outlook,* August 11, 1906, 826.
20. U.S. Bureau of the Census, *Marriage and Divorce,* 1867–1906, 4.
21. *Marriage and Divorce* (New York, 1915), 15.
22. Henry Neumann, *Spokesmen for Ethical Religion* (Boston, 1951), deals with Adler's career at some length.
23. Rebecca Harding Davis, Rose Terry Cooke, Marion Harland, Catherine Owen, Amelia E. Barr. *North American Review,* CXLVIII (May 1889).
24. Boston, 1909.
25. Among the frequent male efforts to sentimentalize over the role and nature of woman were Lyman Abbott, *Christianity and Social Problems* (Boston, 1896), and Robert Lawton, *The Making of a Home* (Boston, 1914).
26. "The Change in the Feminine Ideal," *Atlantic Monthly,* CV (March 1910), 295; see also her interesting autobiography: *Golden Yesterdays* (New York, 1940).
27. Ibid., 297.
28. *The Making of a Home,* 594.
29. "The Ethics of Divorce," *Ethical Record,* II (April 1890), 207.
30. *Sociology and Modern Social Problems* (New York, 1913).
31. *Jesus Christ and the Social Question* (New York, 1903), 145.
32. *The Morality of Marriage and Other Essays on the Status and Destiny of Women* (London, 1897), a collection of articles which had previously appeared in the *North American Review,* the *Fortnightly Review,* the *Westminster Review* and the *Nineteenth Century.* Typical of the American press's treatment of her ideas are "The Millenium of Marriage—Mona Caird's Views," *Current Literature,* XVI (July 1894), reprinted from the *Boston Herald,* "The Practice of Marriage," *Current Literature,* XVIII (October 1895), reprinted from the *Saturday Review.*
33. Boston, 1895.
34. "Anticipations: An Experiment in Prophecy—II," *North American Review,* CLXXIII (July 1901), 73–74.
35. Carpenter, *Love's Coming of Age* (New York, 1911). *Little Essays of Love and Virtue* (New York, 1921) summarized the ideas Havelock Ellis had been advocating for years, and the *New Horizon in Love and Life* (London, 1921) contains the thoughts of his wife, who died in 1916. Schreiner, *Woman and Labor* (New York, 1911).
36. "Prostitution within the Marriage Bond," *Arena,* XIII (June 1895), 68.
37. "The New Marriage," *Good Housekeeping,* LII (February 1914), 184.
38. Charlotte Perkins Gilman, *Women and Economics* (Boston, 1898), was an especially influential exposition of this point of view. For other information on this remarkable woman's life and work see Carl N. Degler's appreciative article, "Charlotte Perkins Gilman on the Theory and Practice of Feminism," *American Quarterly,* VIII (Spring 1956). See also Rheta Childe Dorr, *What Eight Million Women Want* (Boston, 1910), and C. Gasquoine Hartley, *The Truth about Women* (London, 1914).
39. "Divorce vs. Domestic Warfare," *Arena,* I (April 1890), 568. Alone of the great feminist leaders, Mrs. Stanton was a lifelong supporter of divorce, and in her later years it became one of her major interests. In this respect she was hardly a typical feminist, for while most divorce liberals were also feminists, they remained very much a minority within the women's movement.
40. *Outline of Practical Sociology* (New York, 1900), 176.
41. Chicago, 1904.

42. "Social Control and the Function of the Family," Congress of Arts and Sciences, *Proceedings,* VII (St. Louis, 1904), 701. This abbreviated summary may not bring out the markedly utopian flavor which permeated discussions on the family by liberal sociologists and feminists during the Progressive period. Indeed, they entertained hopes for the future of the family which seem fantastically imaginative by the standards of our own more somberly clinical age. This visionary strain in Progressive social thought has been underestimated by historians in recent years, especially by Richard Hofstadter, whose influential *The Age of Reform* (New York, 1955) ignores the role played by feminism and the new morality in shaping the Progressive mood.

43. So many statements were made on marriage and divorce by sociologists during these years that I can list only a few of them here. Walter F. Willcox, *The Divorce Problem* (New York, 1891), was a seminal monograph that laid the statistical base for most later studies of divorce but . . . was not well known outside of the profession and did not have the impact of other works which were more widely publicized. Elsie Clews Parsons, *The Family* (New York, 1906), caused a minor sensation by calling for trial marriages. Mrs. Parsons was a student of Franz Boas and the most radical of the academicians who dealt with the problem. Arthur W. Calhoun, *A Social History of the American Family, From the Civil War* (Cleveland, 1919), Vol. III, was written from an avowedly socialist point of view and is still the only comprehensive work on the history of the American family.

44. *Papers and Proceedings of the American Sociological Society,* III (Chicago, 1909).

45. Ibid., 15.

46. "How Home Conditions React upon the Family," *Papers . . . of the American Sociological Society,* 16–29; Margaret F. Byington, "The Family in a Typical Mill Town," 73–84; Edward T. Devine, "Results of the Pittsburgh Survey," 85–92; Charles R. Henderson, "Are Modern Industry and City Life Unfavorable to the Family?" 93–105, among others.

47. *Papers . . . of the American Sociological Society,* 150–160.

48. Ibid., 180.

49. "The Hyperbolic Teachings of Jesus," *North American Review,* CLXXIX (September 1904), 403.

50. Ibid., 447.

51. E.g., Ernest D. Burton, "The Biblical Teachings Concerning Divorce," *Biblical World,* XXIX (February and March 1907); Norman Jones, "Marriage and Divorce: The Letter of the Law," *North American Review,* CLXXXI (October 1905); Thomas S. Potwin, "Should Marriage Be Indissoluble?" *New Englander and Yale Review,* LVI (January 1892).

52. *Men and Women* (Boston, 1902).

53. *Marriage and Divorce* (New York, 1913).

54. Annual Reports of the National League for the Protection of the Family.

55. *Annual Reports* of the Executive Committee of the Federal Council of Churches of Christ in America.

56. "Are Homogenous Divorce Laws in All the States Desirable?" *North American Review,* CLXX (March 1900).

57. E. R. Stevens, "Divorce in America: The Problem," *Outlook,* June 1, 1907; "Just Grounds for Divorce," November 23, 1910.

58. *World's Work,* XIX (January 1910).

59. Henry F. May, *The End of American Innocence* (New York, 1959), II, Part IV, 333, 343–344.

Divorce and Stigma

Naomi Gerstel

By most accounts, tolerance of variation in family life has increased dramatically in the United States. Public opinion polls over the last two decades reveal declining disapproval of extended singlehood (Veroff et al., 1981), premarital sex and pregnancy (Gerstel, 1982), employment of mothers with young children (Cherlin, 1981), and voluntary childlessness (Huber and Spitze, 1983). Divorce resembles these other situations; in fact public tolerance of divorce appears to have increased especially dramatically over the last few decades (Veroff et al., 1981).

In the mid-1950's, Goode (1956:10) could still observe: "We know that, in our own society, divorce has been a possible, but disapproved, solution for marital conflict." However, comparing attitudes in 1958 and 1971, McRae (1978) found an increasing proportion of adults believing that divorce was only "sometimes wrong" while a decreasing proportion felt that it was "always wrong." These data, he claimed, indicated attitudes toward divorce had shifted "from moral absolutism to situational ethics" (1978:228). In an analysis of panel data collected between 1962 and 1980, Thornton (1985) found that changes in attitudes toward divorce were not only large but pervasive: all subgroups— whether defined by age, class, or even religion—showed substantial declines in disapproval of marital separation.

What are the implications of declining disapproval of divorce? In historical perspective, it is clear that the divorced are no longer subject to the moral outrage they encountered centuries, or even decades, ago. Certainly, divorce is no longer treated as a sin calling for repressive punishment, as it was in theological doctrine and practice (be it Catholic or Protestant) until the beginning of the twentieth century (Halem, 1980; O'Neill, 1967). In electing a divorced president and many divorced senators and governors, U.S. citizens seem to have repudiated the idea that divorce is grounds for exclusion from public life. With the recent passage of no-fault divorce laws in every state, U.S. courts no longer insist on attributing wrongdoing to one party to a divorce (Weitzman, 1985).

An earlier version of this paper was presented at the annual meeting of the American Sociological Association, August, 1986. For helpful comments and criticisms, I would like to thank Robert Zussman, Toby Ditz, Allan Horwitz, Mary Claire Lennon, Jack Pressman, and Sarah Rosenfield. In addition, I would like to express appreciation to three anonymous reviewers for providing valuable suggestions. I would also like to thank Catherine Kohler Riessman, with whom I collaborated on this study.

Most recent commentators on a divorce even argue that it is no longer stigmatized. For example, Spanier and Thompson (1984:15) claim that "the social stigma associated with divorce has disappeared" and Weitzman (1981:146) suggests that "the decline in the social stigma traditionally attached to divorce is one of the most striking changes in the social climate surrounding divorce."

However, I argue in this paper that the stigma attached to divorce has disappeared in only two very limited senses. First, although other studies have shown a clear decline in disapproval of divorce as a general category, disapproval of divorced individuals persists contingent on the specific conditions of their divorce. Thus, as I show below, some divorced people experience disapproval and at least one party to a divorce often feels blamed.

Second, while many of the formal, institutional controls on divorce—imposed in the public realm of church or state—have weakened, the individual who divorces suffers informal, relational sanctions. These are the interpersonal controls that emerge more or less spontaneously in social life. I will present evidence indicating that the divorced believe the married often exclude them and that the divorced themselves frequently pull toward, yet devalue, others who divorce.

In these two senses, I argue that the divorced are still subject to the same social processes and evaluations associated with stigmatization more generally. As in Goffman's (1963:3) classic formulation—which stresses both the conditional and relational aspects of stigma—my findings suggest that the divorced come to be seen (and to see themselves) as "of a less desired kind . . . reduced in our minds from a whole and usual person to a tainted, discounted one."

Methods

My data come from interviews with 104 separated and divorced respondents: 52 women and 52 men. Based on a conception of marital dissolution as a process rather than a static life event, the research team sampled respondents in different stages of divorce: one-third of the respondents were separated less than one year; one-third separated one to two years; one-third separated two or more years. To obtain respondents, we could not rely on court records alone, for most couples who have filed for a divorce have already been living apart for at least a year. Thus, 61 percent of the respondents were selected from probate court records in two counties in the Northeast; the others came from referrals.[1] Comparisons between the court cases and referred respondents show no statistically significant differences on demographic characteristics.

A team of three interviewers conducted household interviews, using a schedule composed of both open- and closed-ended items. Each interview, lasting from two to seven hours (an average of three hours), was taped and transcribed in full. My analysis is based primarily on the extensive information collected on social ties. Using measures adapted from Fischer (1982), interviewers asked each respondent to name all those individuals with whom, in the last month, they had a series of common exchanges: engaged in social activities, discussed personal worries, re-

ceived advice in decisions, etc. Respondents were also asked to name those individuals with whom interaction had become difficult since the separation. To
complete the network list, the interviewer compiled a list of those named, gave
it to the respondent, and asked: "Is there anyone important to you who doesn't
show up on this list?" Any new names were then added to the network list.
Respondents (both women and men) named a mean of 18 people (with a minimum
of 8 and a maximum of 35). Using the list, the interviewers asked the respondents
a series of questions about each person named including, for example, the person's
marital status, how long [he or she] had known the person, and whether or not
he or she disapproved of the divorce. Respondents were also asked to expand on
these close-ended items, to answer a number of open-ended questions about how
their relationships had changed since the divorce, and to discuss their participation
in organized groups (including sports, cultural, religious, and service groups as
well as those "singles groups" set up by and for the divorced—e.g., Parents
Without Partners). In addition, two measures of mental health status were included: the Center for Epidemiological Studies Depression Scale (CES-D) and a
generalized emotional distress or demoralization scale (PERI).[2]

Sample Characteristics

In contrast to the samples in most previous research on separation and divorce,
the respondents are a heterogeneous group. They include people in the working
class as well as in the middle class whose household incomes ranged from under
$4,000 to over $50,000, with a median of $18,000 (with women's significantly
lower than men's).[3] Levels of education varied widely: about one-fourth had less
than a high school degree, and slightly less than one-fourth had four or more
years of college. The sample also includes significant numbers whose primary
source of income came from public assistance and from manual, clerical, and
professional jobs. Only 11 percent were not currently employed while another 9
percent were working part-time. The median age of the respondents was 33
years, and the mean number of years married was nine. Finally, 30 percent of the
sample had no children, 19 percent had one child, and 51 percent had more than
one child.

Findings

Disapproval of Divorce

When asked whether people they knew disapproved of their divorce, 34 percent
of the respondents named no one and another 21 percent named only one person
(out of a total of eight to thirty-five people in their networks), although the
number named as disapproving did range from zero to nine. If we consider just
respondents' perceptions of friends (or non-kin), only 18 percent (of the total)
said more than one friend disapproved while fully 60 percent said no friend
disapproved. The respondents were somewhat more likely to suggest that

Table 1   Correlations between Percentage of Kin or Non-Kin
Who Disapprove of Divorce and Other Variables
by Sex of Respondent

| | Male Respondents | | Female Respondents | |
| | Disapproval | | Disapproval | |
Variable	Kin	Non-Kin	Kin	Non-Kin
Education	.14	.13	−.05	.04
Income	.23	.07	.07	−.02
Age	.17	−.04	.05	.12
Affair[a]	.16	.38**	.10	−.18
Child[b]	.15	.11	.36**	.07
Yngch[c]	.02	.10	.41***	.18

Notes:
[a]Respondent had an affair before marriage ended: no = 0; yes = 1.
[b]Respondent has any children: no = 0; yes = 1.
[c]Respondent has any children less than 12 years old: no = 0; yes = 1
* $p < .05$ ** $p < .01$ *** $p < .001$.

relatives disapproved. However, only 23 percent named more than one relative who disapproved while just over half (51 percent) named none. Moreover, although the respondents perceived more criticism from relatives than friends— perhaps because one of the privileges accorded kin in our society is to remark on things friends might think better left unsaid—the divorced nonetheless often dismissed their few critical relatives as "outdated," "old farts," or "living in the past."

Of course, these data are based only on the perceptions by the divorced of others' reactions to them. It is possible the divorced misperceive the true feelings of friends and relatives. But, as noted earlier, large scale surveys find that relatively few Americans say they disapprove of divorce. More importantly, a person's perceptions of the disapproval of others is central to the production of a lessened sense of self-worth (e.g., see Rosenberg, 1979). Conversely, the very belief that people do not disapprove of one's divorce may diminish the negative consequences of any disapproval that might exist. As one indicator of this, I found that the higher the proportion of those, especially non-kin, in their network whom the divorced believed disapproved, the greater the depression they experienced: the correlation of the CES-D scale and proportion of non-kin who disapprove is .23 (significant at .05 level).[4]

However, other evidence suggests that a mere count of those who disapprove gives an incomplete view of the stigma attached to divorce. As Table 1 shows, the respondents' experience of disapproval varied to some extent with the circumstances surrounding divorce.[5] For example, men—though not women—who had begun affairs during marriage that continued after separation were more likely than other men to say they encountered disapproval of the divorce. In particular, men who had such affairs were significantly more likely to experience the disapproval of non-kin. For women, what mattered most was children. Women with children believed a larger proportion of their kin network disapproved than did women without children. Such disapproval mounted when women's children were young. In contrast, the presence—or age—of children did not significantly affect the amount of disapproval men believed they encountered.

In sum, the circumstances of divorce, rather than the mere fact, are now the subject of disapproval. The conditions associated with the experience of disapproval vary for women and men, reflecting a gender-based ideology of divorce—and marriage. If a "bad" man is a cavalier home-wrecker, a "bad" woman is one who does not (or cannot) sacrifice for her children. While McRae's (1978) longitudinal data suggest divorce has been removed from the realm of absolute moral condemnation or categorical blame, these findings indicate that the specific conditions of the divorce may nonetheless generate disapproval.

The Experience of Blame

Even though categorical disapproval of divorce has declined, individuals may still feel they are held accountable and blamed for their divorce. Evidence for this can be seen in the "splitting of friends." Numerous studies show that ex-spouses often split friends they shared while married (e.g., see Spanier and Thompson, 1984; Weiss, 1975). Among those interviewed in this study, over half of the men (55 percent) and close to half (43 percent) of the women spoke spontaneously[6]and sadly of dividing friends—e.g., finding "our friends polarized" (C007, male), "our social group split down the middle" (C035, female). Many divorced people lose friends who feel loyal to their ex-spouse and, *consequently,* are estranged from them as well.

To be sure, the respondents reported that this process of splitting friends is complicated: one spouse keeps particular friends because she or he brought those friends to the marriage—from childhood, from work, or from independent leisure activities. That spouse then "owns" those friends and receives them almost as if they were property when the marriage ends. But this pattern of splitting also indicates ways the divorced individual comes to experience social devaluation. In the splitting of friends, we discover processes that provoke others to at least act as if they blame one party to a divorce.

Feeling hurt or angry, the divorced themselves may put pressure on friends to take sides. One woman said it quite emphatically:

> I am furious at Ted [her ex-spouse]. I can't stand him being with my friends. I don't want him to have anything   [*N004, female*].

To be supportive to one ex-spouse, [friends] may have to agree to attribute blame (or at least act as if they do) to the other. As one young mother of two put it:

> Things have become difficult with friends. He [her ex-husband] has tried to put friends in the middle   [*N013, female*].

When asked, "What do you mean?", she replied:

He tries to get them to choose sides or to, I think, feel sorry for him. To turn them against me.

Her response suggests that friends and kin are pushed to define one ex-spouse as "guilty," the other as "innocent." They may feel pressured to blame at least one spouse in order to justify their detachment from that one and attachment to the other. One 37-year-old nurse felt she had been unfairly assessed:

I find that some of our friends avoid me; they're not as friendly. It's the old double standard, I think. It's funny; I was saying to my father last night that it doesn't make any difference that he was the one who left, that some people will just feel that it's the woman's fault   [*N010, female*].

Like many others, she feels that most of the divorced split friends and that the split implies "fault," the assumption that somebody acted badly. But she incorrectly assumes her entire experience is typical, or that when other ex-spouses split friends, they become the husband's. In fact, friends were reported to be somewhat more likely to "leave" husbands than wives. One 35-year-old CPA, feeling he had been unfairly blamed, put it this way:

I guess I wasn't very happy or thrilled with the people that put blame on one person or another. Obviously those were the people who thought my wife was correct   [*C005, male*].

Such responses suggest that blame is attached to the individual rather than the institution: while both ex-spouses got a divorce, wrongdoing is attached to only one.

To forestall such blame, many of the respondents "told the story" of their divorce to those they had known when married. Some dreaded that telling:

Telling other people, that is the greatest difficulty. I'd just rather people didn't know. I would almost go out of my way to avoid them rather than face them and tell them   [*C023, male*].

When asked what the greatest difficulty with separation was, one man even replied:

Facing your friends. I thought I was doing something wrong all the time. It was all my fault. I started thinking what if, what if this or what if that. That is a hard thing to do. Telling my friends was the hardest. It tore me up to tell my friends. Eventually I had to tell them   [*C011, male*].

Many worried, in particular, about acquaintances: if they "knew" (N019, female), "will I have to tell them, will they find out?" (N014, female) or whether "I could just keep it to myself for a while" (N024, female). The divorced, then, come to believe they have a potentially discreditable attribute. As Goffman (1963:42) suggests, the issue becomes not simple "managing tension generated during social contacts" but "managing information" about their "failing."

But "managing information" also may mean giving it out: some of the divorced clearly also wanted to get their side across—"to win people over" (C041, male)—because they anticipated friends' "side-choosing" (C027, male). One woman spoke of "gathering her colleagues to announce" her divorce because she "wanted to rally the troops around" (C008, female). To give their own story or "account" would, they hoped, ease and legitimate their divorce.

Many divorced individuals want to provide such accounts and, as Weiss (1975) found, people often call upon the divorced to explain why their relationships did not work out. So, too, we have recent public declarations—novels written and stories told—which seek to provide "accounts."[7] For example, in her recent book *Heartburn,* Nora Ephron makes one such plea with the public not just to accept but to understand who (not what) went wrong. Such accounts allocate blame in divorce.

In his study of the divorced, Weiss (1975:15) argues that "developing the story" or the "account" of the divorce is a "device of major psychological importance not only because it settles the issue of who was responsible but because . . . it organizes the events into a conceptual, manageable unity." I would argue that the development of accounts is not simply a psychological mechanism but a social device. As Scott and Lyman (1968:46) observe, "accounts" are "statements made by a social actor to explain unanticipated or untoward behavior."[8] The development of accounts is a means by which the divorced justify their actions not only to themselves but to others as well. That the divorced feel the need to develop such accounts suggests that divorce is neither experienced nor greeted neutrally. Rather, it is an aspect of biography that must be managed and negotiated socially. In the splitting of friends, then, others often are pressured to "blame" one ex-spouse. And, by offering "accounts" for their actions, the divorced not only share but sustain the notion that blame should and will be allocated.

Social Exclusion: Rejection by the Married

Partners to a divorce not only split friends; they are often excluded from social interaction with the married more generally.[9] Many ex-husbands and ex-wives found they could not maintain friendships with married couples: about one-half of both men (43 percent) and women (58 percent) agreed with the statement: "Married couples don't want to see me now." Moreover, less than one-fourth (23 percent) of the women and men agreed: "I am as close to my married friends as when I was married."[10] By getting a divorce, then, they became marginal to at least part of the community on which they had previously relied.

One man summed up the views of many when he spoke of the "normal life" of the married.

> One of the things I recognized not long after I was separated is that this is a couple's world. People do things in couples, normally   [C043, *male*].

Remembering his own marriage, he now recognized its impact:

> We mostly went out with couples. I now have little or no contact with
> them.

Discovering "they don't invite me anymore" or "they never call," many of the
divorced felt rejected:

> The couples we shared our life with, uh, I'm an outsider now. They stay
> away. Not being invited to a lot of parties that we was always invited to.
> It's with males and females. It sucks   [*C030, male*].

The divorced developed explanations for their exclusion. Finding themselves outsiders, some simply thought that their very presence destabilized the
social life of couples: "I guess I threaten the balance" (N004, female). They found
themselves social misfits in that world, using terms like "a third wheel" (N010,
female; N027, male) and "odd person out" (N006, male) to describe their newly
precarious relationship with the married.

Some went further, suggesting that those still in couples felt threatened by
the divorce or were afraid it would harm their own marriages. "They say, 'My
God, it's happening all over.' It scares them" (N027, male). Men and women
expressed this form of rejection in terms of "contagion" (C027, male) and "a fear
it's going to rub off on them" (N010, female).[11] Because the difficulties of
marriage are often concealed, others found their divorce came as a surprise to
married friends. That surprise reinforced the idea "it can happen to anyone" and
"so they tend to stay away" (C027, male).

A few turned the explanation around, suspecting that married couples
rejected them out of jealousy rather than fear. One woman, speaking of a friend
who no longer called, explained: "It was like me living out her fantasies" (N008,
female). A salesman in his mid 40s who had an affair before getting a divorce
believed:

> I get a kick out of it because . . . I am the envy of both men and women
> because, some of it is courage, others look upon it as freedom. Both
> words have been used a number of times. People become very envious,
> and a spouse of the envious person will feel extremely threatened   [*N043,
> male*].

These few could turn an unpleasant experience into an enviable one. For a small
minority, then, the experience of exclusion did not produce a sense of devaluation.

But more of the divorced, men as well as women, were troubled by the
thought that old friends now defined them in terms of their sexual availability
and, as a result, avoided them. One woman, a teacher's aide with a very young
daughter and son at home, felt insulted that friends misconstrued her situation:

> Well, I now have no married friends. It's as if I all of a sudden became
> single and I'm going to chase after their husbands   [*N011, female*].

And a plumbing contractor, unusual because he had custody of his five children,
was particularly hurt by the image of sexual availability because he had resisted

any sexual entanglements. Describing one woman who "couldn't understand why I didn't want to hop into bed with her," he noted, "she told me there must be something wrong with me" (C047, male). He went on:

> I would say couples in general, there seems to be a, well, they are nice to me, but distant. I think the men don't want a single man around their wives.

And when asked, "Can you tell me about that?", he associated his seeming sexual availability with a threat to the cohesion of the community:

> [They] don't really want to involve me in things that are going on . . . neighborhood picnics . . . couples' things. . . . I have had men say that they figure that I'm out casing women all over. So I'm considered somewhat of an unstable person.

He added that he was not the only person who had reached this conclusion:

> And this is quite common with divorced people. In group discussions, everyone seems to experience the same thing.

As his final comment indicates, the divorced talk to each other about this experience and generate a shared explanation for it—that they are viewed as somewhat "unstable." Thus, some divorced people come to believe that married acquaintances [see] them as "misfits"—unstable individuals who could not maintain a stable marriage, a threat to the routines of a community made up of the "normal" married.[12]

The exclusion of the divorced from the social life they had enjoyed while married constitutes a negative sanction on divorce. This is not simply a functional process of friendship formation based on homogamy (cf. Lazarsfeld and Merton, 1964): it involves conflict, producing a sense of devaluation on the part of one group (the divorced) who feel rejected by another group still considered normal (the married).[13]

The divorced try to come to terms with their experience by talking to others who share it. Together they develop a shared understanding similar to what Goffman (1963:5) calls a "stigma theory": the married feel uncomfortable, even threatened by them, and act as if divorce, as a "social disease," is contagious. Or divorce poses a threat because of the desired freedom and sexuality it (perhaps falsely) represents. Finally, divorced people mutually develop a broader explanation for the modern response to them: they are avoided because the dissolution of marriage is so common, so possible, that it becomes a real threat both to any given couple and to the social world built on, and routinized by, groups consisting of couples.

Colleagues and Demoralization

The separation of the divorced from the married is even more clearly apparent in the social life developed by the divorced themselves. The divorced pull away from the married and into the lives of others like them. Goffman (1963:18) argues that the stigmatized turn to others like them in anticipation that "mixed social contact will make for anxious, unanchored interaction." Accordingly, many of the divorced said they felt "uncomfortable" (C042, female), "strained" (C003, male; N014 and C029, females), "strange" (C034, female), and "awkward" (C019, male) in a world composed of couples. And some abandoned the married: "I've been pulling way from my coupled friends" (C026, female).

Drawing together with other divorced, they can develop as well as share their "sad tales" (Goffman, 1963:19) and learn how to behave. In fact, over half of the people with whom these divorced men (52 percent) and women (62 percent) socialized were other divorced individuals, a far higher proportion than is found in the general population (U.S. Bureau of the Census, 1983). The divorced used many well-worn phrases to talk about others who shared their marital status: "birds of a feather flock together" (N021, male) and "likes attract likes" (N025, female).

Many discovered their interests and concerns, at least for a time, were based on their new-found marital status. When asked to respond to the statement, "I have more in common with singles now," over half of the men (55 percent) and women (58 percent) agreed. One 28-year-old working-class man sought out divorced people for the same reason many respondents avoided the married. He said of others who shared his marital status:

> We have something in common. We have almost right off the bat something to talk about. It makes it easier to talk because you have gone through it   [C018, male].

Equally important, respondents often felt they could turn to other divorced people as experienced "veterans" (Caplan, 1974) and "colleagues" (Best and Luckenbill, 1980) for their new-found marital state. These others served as role models, showing them ways to cope as spouseless adults and, in doing so, bolstered their new identities. A man referred to other divorced as providing an "experience bank" and elaborated by saying:

> I solicited assistance, guidance from people who had gone through or who were going through similar experiences. So I might get a better understanding of how they reacted to it   [C043, male].

So, too, other divorced people could help them do what Hochschild (1983:254) has called "feeling work" or "the shaping, modulating, or inducing of feelings." That is, colleagues encouraged them to manage and change their feelings, and to realize how their marriage or many marriages were not as good as they had thought. That helped them disengage from their ex-spouses.

But these colleagues could do something more. They showed them that the life of a divorced adult was not all anguish and pain. One 30-year-old middle-class woman found she felt closest to her old friends who had been through divorce because:

> I could talk to them and they helped me to talk about my problems. What went wrong. I felt they could understand. And it was interesting to hear what they had been through, you know   [C016, female].

Importantly, she added:

> I wanted to hear what it was like. It sorta helped me to think that they had made a go of their life again. They were happy afterwards.

The divorced needed reassurance that divorce did not imply a serious character flaw. They needed to find those who, after getting a divorce, had made a successful transition. A 32-year-old man, who in the first month "isolated" himself "for fear that people might think I'm doing something wrong," found a few months later that:

> It's nice to hear people who have gone through the same experience, talking to me about it. It's nice to hear a lot of these things because you realize: "Hey, I'm not so bad. I'm not the only one this happens to." And looking at the person and seeing that they made it okay. And that I will, too   [N009, male].

What Goffman (1963:20) wrote more generally about the stigmatized, then, characterizes the modern divorced: "They can provide instruction for tricks of the trade and a circle of lament to which he can withdraw for moral support and comfort of feeling at home, at ease, accepted as a person who is really like any normal person." The divorced turn to others like themselves to get reassurance, advice, and encouragement, and to make sense of their often dislocated lives. Telling their story to those like themselves is therapeutic (Conrad and Schneider, 1980).

Yet, there are also pitfalls in this attraction to others like them. As time passes, the divorced may find themselves bored by constant discussion of divorce, that "the whole matter of focusing on atrocity tales . . . on the 'problem' is one of the largest penalties for having one" (Goffman, 1963:21). As a man divorced close to two years put it:

> You see, I've been locked in too much with divorced people. You're relating to them relative to the separation. And what happened to you, when you did it, you know   [N019, male].

The divorced, especially those who had been separated more than a year, spoke of how they were getting tired of "problems dominating the conversation" (C042, female, divorced three years) as they felt "dissipated" (C009, male, divorced two years) and "wanted to talk to people about something different" (N016, female, divorced a year-and-a-half) because "the less you talk about the problems, the less you think about them, and the less you feel about them" (N028, female, divorced a year-and-a-half). One man described how, in the first months of divorce, he had "learned a lot about divorce" from others who had the same experience because "they understood me." But then he went on to complain about the problems with this association: "You feel up and then someone drags you down with their problems" (C021, male).

In fact, additional quantitative evidence indicates that association with others who are divorced becomes, over time, demoralizing. Among those separated less than one year, demoralization (PERI) is negatively correlated with the proportion of divorced in their networks ($r = -.27$, $p< .05$). In contrast, for those separated one to two years, the correlation between demoralization and proportion of divorced in networks becomes positive ($r = .26$, $p< .05$). And, for those separated more than two years, this positive correlation becomes even stronger ($r = .37$, $p< .01$).[14] Thus, while the divorced may initially seek out others like them, association with others who are divorced eventually may come to produce a lowered sense of self-esteem.[15]

The Devaluation of Self

Perhaps the most striking evidence that the divorced devalue their own condition is found in their assessment of organizations established for the divorced. Only 10 percent of the respondents were in such groups.[16] In fact, most of the divorced— male as well as female—explicitly rejected such formal mechanisms of integration set up by and for others like them.

For the relatively small number of people who did join, such groups provided both a source of entertainment for their children as well as an opportunity to meet other adults. However, in explaining why they joined, the divorced typically stressed child care. Thus, children were not simply a reason for joining; they provided legitimation for membership. By explaining membership in instrumental rather than expressive terms, and in terms of children rather than themselves, the divorced distanced themselves from the potentially damaging implications of membership for their own identity. In this sense, children provide a "face saving device," much like those inventoried by Berk (1977) among people who attended singles dances.

The notion that groups for the divorced—and therefore those who join them—are stigmatized is substantiated still further by the comments of those who did not join. They gave a number of reasons for their reluctance. Some attributed their lack of participation to a lack of knowledge. Others simply felt they did not have the time or energy. When asked why she had not joined any divorce group, one 25-year-old saleswoman said:

> I've thought about it, but I have just never done anything about it. I know it is not getting me anywhere by not doing anything. Basically I am a lazy person   [*C024, female*].

But while she first blamed herself for non-participation in these groups, she then went on to add a more critical note: "I think I would feel funny walking into a place like that." Her second thought reiterated a common theme—an attitude toward divorce and membership in organizations for them—which came through with compelling force. Many imagined that people who joined such groups were unacceptable in a variety of ways, or even that to join them was somehow a sign of weakness. For example:

> These people really don't have somebody to turn to. I guess that's the main reason for them belonging and I do have someone to turn to, matter

of fact, more than one. They're really not sure of themselves, they're insecure   [*N013, female*].

Such comments reveal that respondents saw divorce as a discredit, at least insofar as it became the axis of one's social life. Consequently, to join such groups was to reinforce the very devaluation they hoped to avoid. One welfare mother with a young child had been told by her social worker that joining a singles' group might alleviate the enormous loneliness she experienced. But she resisted:

It's kind of degrading to me or something. Not that I'm putting these other people down. I could join something but I couldn't join something that was actually called a singles' group   [*N016, female*].

Others reiterated the same theme. To them, groups of the divorced were "rejects looking, you know, going after rejects. They need a crutch" (N011, female). Or they asked rhetorically, "Is that for the very, very lonely?" (C016, female). These to them were "people with as many, if not worse, problems than I have" (C040, male) or "weirdos" (N029, female). As these comments show, the divorced were quick to put a pejorative label on groups consisting of other divorced.

Or, the divorced we spoke to felt that such groups were unacceptable because they were sexual marketplaces. In the words of a 28-year-old plant supervisor, who (like most others) had never actually been to any organization for the divorced:

I refuse to go to a place where I'm looked at as a side of beef and women are looked at as sides of beef. It disgusts me   [*C040, male*].

Association with such groups would reinforce the very view that so many of the divorced work so hard to dispel. While their rejection of such groups is a way to separate themselves from a stigmatized status (Berk, 1977:542), the very character and strength of the rejection confirms that the status is stigmatized. Thus, in distancing themselves, the divorced reveal that they share the belief that individuals who divorce, especially if they use that divorce to organize their social worlds, continue to be somehow tainted.

Despite their negative reaction to divorce groups, respondents did not reject all organized routes to friendship formation. The majority (82 percent) were members of at least one group—including, for example, sports, cultural, religious and service groups. Women participated in a median of 2.24 groups; men, a median of 3.56. In fact, many spoke of joining these other groups as a way to "make friends" and to cope with the loneliness they felt. Such groups may provide access to others who are divorced, but only coincidentally. These organizational memberships—and the relationships they allow—are legitimized by their *dissociation* from marital status. It is in this context that respondents' resistance to joining divorce groups becomes especially compelling as evidence for their devaluation of the status of divorce.

Conclusion

To argue that the divorced are no longer stigmatized is to misunderstand their experience. To be sure, divorce is now less deviant in a statistical sense than it was a decade ago. As a group, the divorced are not categorized as sinful, criminal, or even wrong. Moreover, even though the divorced lose married friends and have smaller networks than the married, they do not become completely ghettoized into subcultures of the divorced (Gerstel et al., 1985; Weiss, 1979). Finally, as I have shown here, the divorced themselves do not think that most of their kin and friends disapprove.

However, a decrease in statistical deviance, a relaxation of institutional controls by church or state, or a decline in categorical disapproval is not the same as the absence of stigmatization. Although a majority of Americans claim they are indifferent in principle to those who make a "personal decision" to leave a "bad" marriage, this indifference does not carry over into the social construction of private lives. The divorced believe they are the targets of informal relational sanctions—exclusion, blame, and devaluation. If we understand stigma as referring not simply to the realm of public sanctions but rather see it as emerging out of everyday experience, then we can see that the divorced continue to be stigmatized.

I have shown that divorced individuals believe they are subject to censure for what others see as their misdeeds. Such disapproval is, however, not categorical; it is contingent on the particular conditions of the divorce. The experience of devaluation attaches to the cause or circumstances surrounding the divorce rather than to divorce *per se*.

The conditional response to divorce, and the blame attached to one party, is still embodied in the law. Critics of the fault grounds in divorce law argued they were too restrictive and invaded privacy (Krause, 1986). But most states have *added* no-fault bases to laws concerning marital dissolution; they have not completely replaced the traditional (or modernized) set of fault grounds. As legal scholar Harry Krause (1986:337) explains:

> Many legislators remained persuaded that fault grounds should continue
> to provide immediate relief in severe cases. And, at least in the popular
> mind, there *does* remain a "right" and "wrong" in marriage and divorce.

Thus, as I have argued, the decline of categorical disapproval of the institution of divorce is not the same thing as the absence of notions of wrongdoing concerning individuals who divorce. And we should not be surprised that the divorced still think of themselves as "failures" even when they live in an era of "no-fault divorce."

Moreover, we might expect that the very disjunction between public tolerance and private, interpersonal sanctions would itself chagrin and distress the divorced. Feeling shame or guilt, they carefully manage information about their divorce. As one strategy of information control, they engage in "preventive disclosure"—a kind of "instrumental telling" used by the stigmatized to "influence others' actions and ideas toward the self" (Schneider and Conrad, 1980:40).

Thus, the divorced create "accounts" to pressure old friends to take sides. While it may remove blame from the self, such preventive disclosure attaches blame to the ex-spouse. In fact, it is intended to do so. Here, we see that much of the censure they experience is created out of the interaction between the divorced and those in the networks surrounding them. The assumption, then, still lingers (or is socially reaffirmed) that divorce is linked to or results from defects in at least one partner.

The divorced also seek out others "like them" from whom they can learn how to behave and present themselves. With these other divorced, their "sad tales" have a different purpose: they are meant to be "therapeutic" (Schneider and Conrad, 1980:40). However, the cathartic effects of such disclosures are temporary; over time, interaction with other divorced men and women produces demoralization. Thus, either type of information management—preventive disclosure or therapeutic telling—may reinforce the very stigmatization it is intended to dispel.

The divorced are not merely victims. In both their talk and action, the divorced sustain the idea that to be married is to be "normal." Similar to other "outsiders," they "subscribe to the very rules they have broken" (Becker, 1963:3). In so doing, the divorced reinforce rather than criticize the social order. Rather than attacking marriage, they uphold it. Given these processes, it is not surprising that most of the divorced hope to and do remarry rather quickly (Furstenberg, 1982).

My findings suggest a methodological weakness of previous research. Studies of the divorced, and the stigmatized more generally, often look only at those who join self-help groups. However, as I have shown, many do not join. More importantly, they label those who do as somehow tainted. While many self-help groups have developed to counter the view of the disabled as pathetic or as victims (Zola, 1983), the need for such groups implies—rather than denies— that these groups experience stigma. In particular, the very development of singles' groups is further evidence that the divorced (like other disabled) are stigmatized and that such groups are "stigmatic situations" (Berk, 1977). Only by comparing those who join with those who do not can we establish whether participation in such groups promotes the favorable sense of self many claim for it (see Best and Luckenbill, 1980).

Future research might fruitfully look at the issues explored here— conditional disapproval and relational sanctions—from the perspective of those who compose the networks of the divorced. A full understanding of the processes of stigmatization must include an analysis of the interaction between self-labeling and the actual response of the "normals."

Finally, my findings may be generalizable beyond the divorced. Those discussed at the beginning of this paper—the unwed mother, the childless adult, and even the employed mother with an infant—may encounter some of the same relational sanctions and conditional disapproval as do the divorced. Thus, for example, Miall (1986) found that involuntarily childless women view their infertility as discreditable and experience isolation and conflict. But she also found conditions under which childlessness is less personally stigmatizing; if involuntary rather than voluntary, the "fault" of the husband rather than the wife. While some observers suggest that we can transform deviance to diversity by relabeling these arrangements as "alternative lifestyles," the consequent decline in public disapproval towards them may be as limited, and conditional, as is the case with divorce.

Notes

1. A small number of these referrals were located through a "snowball" strategy: various people who heard about our study told us about individuals who had just separated. But the majority of referrals were located through respondents. At the end of each interview, we asked for the names of other people who had been separated less than a year and interviewed a maximum of one person named by each respondent.

2. A shortened 27-item version of PERI was chosen because of its reliability and validity as a measure of nonspecific emotional distress or demoralization. The shortened version was chosen in consultation with Bruce Dohrenwend, the creator of the scale. The self-report CES-D scale was included to measure the more specific items of depression experienced during the week previous to the interview. Developed for studies of the general population, the CES-D scale consists of 20 items selected from previously existing scales which represent the major factors in the clinical syndrome of depression. Items measure depressed mood, including feelings of guilt, worthlessness, helplessness, and hopelessness as well as psychophysiological manifestations such as psychomotor retardation, loss of appetite, and sleep disturbance.

3. Women's mean household income was $14,000 while the men's mean income was $22,000.

4. Controlling for income and the presence of children (two characteristics often found to be associated with depression, e.g., Gove and Geerkin, 1977; Kessler, 1982), I found the correlation between the CES-D scale and disapproval of non-kin was .21 (still significant at the .05 level). Depression was not significantly associated with proportion of kin who disapproved. Of course, the causal order of the relationship between depression and disapproval is difficult to determine: those who are more depressed may, as a result of their depression, believe more people disapprove of them. Alternatively, those who believe they encounter more disapproval may, as a result, become more depressed. These two explanations are not necessarily mutually exclusive but instead probably interact in complex ways.

5. In Table 1, I have presented correlations between *percent* of kin and non-kin who disapproved and other variables. I do not present the data on correlations between *number* of kin and non-kin who disapproved and other variables because of the range in number of network members named. However, it should be noted that the correlations for *number* are almost identical with those for *percent*.

6. We did not directly ask a question about the splitting of friends; these figures are based on the number of people who brought up the topic spontaneously in the open-ended questions. Thus, these figures are probably conservative.

7. For further discussion of the "accounts" of the divorced, see Riessman and Gerstel (1986).

8. Given the social import of accounts for divorce, it is likely that they have varied historically—as have the legal rationales for divorce. The work of Kitson and Sussman (1982) provides some support for this expectation. They compared the reasons respondents offered for separation to those Goode (1956) received several decades earlier. The more recent explanations emphasized affectional and sexual incompatibilities as opposed to the instrumental ones offered in earlier decades. While such listings of complaints to an interviewer are clearly different from the accounts of which I write, they do reinforce my argument that accounts offered to interviewers and probably others will vary over time.

9. Using a variety of methods and samples, a number of other studies also find that the divorced lose married friends (e.g., Spanier and Thompson, 1984; Wallerstein and Kelly, 1980; Weiss, 1979).

10. In contrast to my finding that divorced men and women were equally likely to experience a certain distance from the married, Hetherington et al. (1976:422) found "dissociation from married friends was greater for women than for men." However, they studied only divorced parents of children in nursery school. Fischer's (1982) findings would lead us to believe that, of any group, mothers—married or divorced—of young children are most isolated. In fact, my data suggest that the gender differences may well characterize only this very special group. Among male respondents, the presence of children is not significantly associated with their belief that "married couples don't want to see them" or their feeling they "are not as close to those couples." In contrast, for women, the presence of any children, especially young children, increases disassociation from the married. Among female respondents, the correlation between "married couples don't want to see me now" and the presence of any children is .25 (p < .05) and with having children less than 12-years-old is .39 (p < .01). This difference between women and men may well be a result of the fact that women obtain custody of the children far more often than do men. While Hetherington's findings are often cited as evidence for general gender differences in the social life of the divorced, this implication probably should be limited to this special group—the parents of young children.

11. This belief that others see their "condition" as "contagious" is similar to the experience of others who are stigmatized, like the mentally ill. See Foucault (1967) for a discussion of the development of the belief that "unreason" is contagious, that anyone could "catch it," and the consequent movement to isolate the insane.

12. Wallerstein and Kelly (1980:33) hypothesize that still another factor may explain why the married move away from the divorced: the married "feel uncomfortable and inadequate in providing solace." While this is certainly a possible (and generous) explanation, the divorced nonetheless experience the loss of friendship as rejection and exclusion.

13. To be sure, research on "single individuals" —be they widows (Lopata, 1979), never married (Stein, 1981), or divorced—suggests there is a general pattern of friendship based on homogeneity of marital status. Indeed, as Simmel (1950) points out in his classic work, the triad is a more unstable group than the dyad. Hence, a "third party" is likely to be excluded. Here, I am suggesting that such third parties, especially the divorced, are likely to interpret the separation of marital groups as exclusion and hence as devaluation.

14. This relationship—a different effect of proportion of divorced in networks on depression across stages of the divorce process—is maintained after controls for income and the presence of children are introduced in a multiple regression procedure; the interaction term of length of time separated and proportion divorced is [statistically] significant at the .05 level.

15. Of course, the direction of causation between homogeneity and depression is unclear: I am suggesting that association with other divorced produces depression over time. However, it is possible that in the later stages of divorce, those who are especially demoralized are more likely to seek out other divorced while in the earlier stages those less demoralized are most likely to seek out other divorced.

16. These findings suggest, of course, that those studies which draw entirely on members of singles' groups are seriously flawed; they represent a small and atypical population of the divorced.

References

Becker, Howard S. 1963. Outsiders: Studies in the Sociology of Deviance. New York: Free Press.

Berk, Bernard. 1977. "Face saving at the singles dance." Social Problems 24:530–44.

Best, Joel, and David Luckenbill. 1980. "The social organization of deviants." Social Problems 28:14–31.

Caplan, Gerald. 1974. Social Supports and Community Mental Health. New York: Behavioral Publications.

Cherlin, Andrew J. 1981. Marriage, Divorce, Remarriage. Cambridge, MA: Harvard University Press.

Conrad, Peter, and Joseph W. Schneider. 1980. Deviance and Medicalization: From Badness to Sickness. St. Louis: C. V. Mosby.

Ephron, Nora. 1983. Heartburn. New York: Pocket Books.

Fischer, Claude. 1982. To Dwell among Friends. Chicago: University of Chicago Press.

Foucault, Michel. 1967. Madness and Civilization. London: Tavistock.

Furstenberg, Frank P. 1982. "Conjugal succession: reentering marriage after divorce." Pp. 107–46 in Paul B. Bates and Orville G. Brim (eds.), Life-Span Development and Behavior. Volume 4, New York: Academic Press.

Gerstel, Naomi. 1982. "The new right and the family." Pp. 6–20 in Barbara Haber (ed.), The Woman's Annual. New York: G. K. Hall.

Gerstel, Naomi, Catherine Kohler Riessman, and Sarah Rosenfield. 1985. "Explaining the symptomatology of separated and divorced women and men: the role of material resources and social networks." Social Forces 64:84–101.

Goffman, Erving. 1963. Stigma. Englewood Cliffs, NJ: Prentice-Hall.

Goode, William. 1956. Women in Divorce. New York: Free Press.

Gove, Walter R., and Michael Geerkin. 1977. "The effect of children and employment on the mental health of married men and women." Social Forces 56:66–76.

Halem, Lynne Carol. 1980. Divorce Reform: Changing Legal and Social Perspectives. New York: Free Press.

Hetherington, E. M., M. Cox, and R. Cox. 1976. "Divorced fathers." The Family Coordinator 25:417–28.

Hochschild, Arlie Russell. 1983. "Attending to, codifying and managing feelings: sex differences in love." Pp. 250–62 in Laurel Richardson and Verta Taylor (eds.), Feminist Frontiers. Reading, MA: Addison-Wesley.

Huber, Joan, and Glenna Spitze. 1983. Stratification: Children, Housework, and Jobs. New York: Academic Press.

Kessler, Ronald D. 1982. "A disaggregation of the relationship between socioeconomic status and psychological distress." American Sociological Review 47:752–64.

Kitson, Gay, and Marvin Sussman. 1982. "Marital complaints, demographic characteristics and symptoms of mental distress in marriage." Journal of Marriage and the Family 44:87–101.

Krause, Harry D. 1986. Family Law. Second Edition. St. Paul, MN: West.

Lazarsfeld, Paul, and Robert K. Merton. 1964. "Friendship as a social process: a substantive and methodological analysis." Pp. 18–66 in Monroe Berger, Theodore Abel and Charles Page (eds.), Freedom and Control in Modern Society. New York: Van Nostrand.

Lopata, Helena. 1979. Women as Widows. New York: Elsevier.

McRae, James A. 1978. "The secularization of divorce." Pp. 227–42 in Beverly Duncan and Otis Dudley Duncan (eds.), Sex Typing and Sex Roles. New York: Academic Press.

Miall, Charlene E. 1986. "The stigma of involuntary childlessness." Social Problems 33:268–82.

O'Neill, William L. 1967. Divorce in the Progressive Era. New Haven: Yale University Press.

Riessman, Catherine, and Naomi Gerstel. 1986. "It's a long story: women and men account for marital failure." Paper presented at the World Congress of Sociologists, New Delhi, India.

Rosenberg, Morris. 1979. Conceiving the Self. New York: Basic Books.

Schneider, Joseph W., and Peter Conrad. 1980. "In the closet with illness: epilepsy, stigma potential and information control." Social Problems 28:32–44.

Scott, Marvin B., and Stanford M. Lyman. 1968. "Accounts." American Sociological Review 33:46–62.

Simmel, Georg. 1950. The Sociology of Georg Simmel. Kurt H. Wolff, Translator. New York: Free Press.

Spanier, Graham B., and Linda Thompson. 1984. Parting. Beverly Hills, CA: Sage.

Stein, Peter (ed.). 1981. Single Life. Englewood Cliffs, NJ: Prentice-Hall.

Thornton, Arland. 1985. "Changing attitudes toward separation and divorce: causes and consequences." American Journal of Sociology 90:856–72.

U.S. Bureau of the Census. 1983. "Marital status and living arrangements: March, 1983." Current Population Reports. Series P-20, #389. Washington, DC: U.S. Government Printing Office.

Veroff, Joseph, Elizabeth Douvan, and Richard A. Kulka. 1981. The Inner American: A Self-Portrait from 1957–1976. New York: Basic Books.

Wallerstein, Judith S., and Joan B. Kelly. 1980. Surviving the Breakup. New York: Basic Books.

Weiss, Robert S. 1975. Marital Separation. New York: Basic Books.

_____. 1979. Going It Alone. New York: Basic Books.

Weitzman, Lenore J. 1981. The Marriage Contract. New York: Free Press.

_____. 1985. The Divorce Revolution: The Unexpected Social and Economic Consequences for Women and Children in America. New York: Free Press.

Zola, Irving. 1983. Sociomedical Inquiries: Recollections, Reflections and Reconsiderations. Philadelphia, PA: Temple University Press.

Divorce: A Women's Issue

Terry Arendell

Divorce is a women's issue. Men just can't understand—they don't have the foggiest understanding of what we're going through.[1]

Divorce is undermining status and economic gains made by women in recent decades. The link between women's economic well-being and dependency on men is shown dramatically when the effects of divorce on women are examined.[2] Over two-thirds of all women who divorce experience a significant reduction in family income because in most families the husband is the primary income earner. Despite their efforts, most women are not able to recover financially from divorce. Women today are caught between two traditions: first, economic dependency on men, and, second, limited access to independent means of economic self-sufficiency.

Economic decline following divorce is unique to women. Men not only recover economically from divorce, but by the end of the first year after divorce their standard of living increases. For example, Weitzman's 1981 California study showed that women experience a 73 percent loss in standard of living and men experience a 42 percent improvement the first year after divorce.[3] Longitudinal studies done at the University of Michigan show a similar pattern.[4] Socioeconomic decline shapes women's, not men's, divorce experience.

Divorce does more than mirror society's gender inequities: it widens them. Women's socioeconomic status declines and men's rises after divorce; divorce then widens the economic gap between men and women. Social and economic gains made by women in recent decades are eroding because of divorce.

The divorce rate is at an all-time high. Annually there are over one million divorces in the United States. For every two marriages, there is one divorce. Approximately 65 percent of divorcing couples have minor children. Over 90 percent of children of divorce go into their mother's custody. There are about thirteen million children living with mothers only, mostly as a result of divorce. One in five minor children lives with a single parent.[5] Because children remain with mothers, the economic effects of divorce on mothers are felt by children also.

Mother-headed families are characterized by disproportionately high rates of poverty. Over one-half of all poor families are female-headed and over a third of female-headed families are below the poverty level.[6] Many more live marginally close to poverty.[7]

Four factors contribute to women's economic hardships after divorce. The first is that women remain responsible for the emotional support and care of children. It is mothers who are the primary parent in most two-parent families still today; women remain in the home to parent and it is women who interrupt their employment or career development to provide emotional maintenance in families. Upon divorce this pattern of mothers being primary parent is continued. Child-care and parenting responsibilities limit women's employment options both within and after marriage.

Financial responsibility for children is the second element in women's economic decline after divorce. Despite the law, which states that parents share financial responsibility for children, it is mothers who carry the economic burden of child rearing after divorce.

Child-support orders are made in the majority of divorce cases. But noncompliance is the most common response to child-support orders. Some 65 percent of absent fathers pay no child support. Only about one-fifth of fathers are in compliance with support orders; the other 15 percent pay irregularly.[8] Further, child-support orders are generally low in amount and do not meet one-half the costs of child care. Few support orders include provisions for automatic cost-of-living increases; even fewer recognize that child-rearing costs rise as children get older. There is no legal obligation for the noncustodial parent to provide for a child once he/she reaches age eighteen.

Continued gender inequities in divorce-related laws is the third major factor in the harsh economic effects of divorce on women. Community-property statutes generally provide women more protection than is available in common-law states. (Forty-two states remain common-law states.) However, community-property statutes continue to reflect patriarchal traditions, discriminating against women. Material assets and debts, tangible items, are defined as community property. A wife's contribution to her husband's earning level or potential, her contributions to his education, career development and earning ability do not get valued. The husband leaves the marriage with his earning ability intact, viewed as private property and not part of the marital property. To date, recognition of a wife's legal interest in these family assets has been determined only on a case-by-case basis. No legal precedent exists recognizing the exchange of resources and services made within the marriage which contributed to the level of or potential for family economic well-being.

Spousal support is awarded in less than 14 percent of all divorces and is received in less than 7 percent.[9] Women are expected to become self-supporting after divorce regardless of the extent of their economic dependency within marriage. No careful consideration is given to their earning possibilities or the inevitable drop in standard of living which follows divorce for women. Their roles as child and family caretakers are not valued. Nor are their contributions to family life and its socioeconomic status given their due within the law.

Community-property statutes do not recognize that mothers represent their children's as well as their own interests. Children's interests in family assets are not considered. For example, in order for children to remain in the family home after divorce, the wife must generally buy out her spouse by paying him a full one-half of the equity. The home is viewed as community property, owned jointly by husband and wife. Regardless of her financial circumstances or the value of the children remaining in their home, the husband must be paid one-half of the home's value.

The fourth factor in the economic distress following divorce is the continued wage discrimination based on gender. Because women are not able to earn wages comparable to men's, they are not able to adequately provide for their families through their own efforts. Women workers who work full time, year round earn only 63 percent of what men do.[10] Lodged in the secondary employment sector, most women have jobs which offer little training, few opportunities for advancement, and few flexible work options enabling work and family lives to be more easily coordinated. Women who reenter the job sector after having spent time in the home caring for children and families are at a particular disadvantage; such necessary work is devalued on the labor market.

Over three-quarters of divorced mothers are employed, most of them full time. But the median family income of families headed by women in 1981 was 49 percent that of families headed by men.[11] The continued disparity in wages for women and men, the lack of comparable-pay statutes, costly and inadequate child care, and the devaluing of women's work create formidable barriers to women seeking to secure adequate family incomes.

Welfare is not a viable option for the majority of divorced women and their families. Welfare neither significantly improves their standard of living nor provides a route out of poverty. Recent changes in welfare regulations have had only negative impacts on women with children. Supplemental grants for women who are employed but have inadequate family incomes have been cut. Families have lost food stamp assistance. The options facing many women today are to be poor and on welfare or to be poor and employed. The present welfare program contributes to women's inabilities to recover from the economic decline experienced with divorce. This is particularly significant in this society, which constrains most women's earning abilities.

A Study of Sixty Women

Despite its high incidence, there are relatively few studies of divorce. Particularly lacking are studies which explore the social and economic situations of middle class, divorced mothers. Little probing of their perceptions, situations, or responses has been systematically undertaken. Statistical data provide a base for speculation but do not give a picture of the situations as experienced by divorced mothers. Inadequate attention has been given the various adaptations made in response to changed situations.

I conducted a study in 1983 in northern California in which I interviewed sixty divorced women. The in-depth interview was chosen as the research methodology because the objective was to discover and examine parts of the empirical social world: namely, postdivorce situations as perceived and responded to by divorced mothers.

Divorce significantly alters social situations. It requires a redefining and interpreting of social events and circumstances. Action has to be directed along terrain not previously explored by the divorced mothers. Analysis of survey and statistical data does not reveal these processes or sufficiently lift the curtain to reveal what is taking place within the social worlds of divorced women. In-depth interviews allow investigation of participants' experiences, perceptions, and responses to postdivorce situations. The interviews in this study lasted three or more hours.

Each of the sixty women had custody of at least one minor child. The women ranged in age from twenty-five to fifty-six. While all had been divorced at least two years, the median postdivorce time was between four and five years. The number of children in these families varied from one to five. Most mothers had only one or two children although some mothers had three or more children. Children ranged in age from toddlers and preschoolers up through older teenagers. One woman was pregnant and several women had grown children as well as dependent ones.

All of these women viewed themselves as being middle class during marriage. They viewed their families of origin as middle class, with some range evident between lower and upper middle class. None had experienced poverty as a child.

Family social status was determined by the husband's status. His education, occupation, and earnings established the family class membership. The majority of these husbands had some college education; many had degrees. More than a quarter of them had specialized training, graduate educations, or professional degrees. Only two of the husbands were manual laborers, and because of their unusually high earnings and levels of education, they too viewed themselves as middle class.

Husbands' occupations were diverse. Among others they included: physician, accountant, pastor, pilot, civil servant, teacher, professor, social worker, senior manager, computer programmer, and self-employed businessmen.

Family incomes varied for the families before divorce. The range covered a span from incomes approximating the national median income to ones exceeding a hundred thousand dollars annually. Most family incomes were slightly higher than the national median income. Despite the income variations, the families had similar lifestyles. Class membership shaped family lives along common patterns.

Most families lived in single-family dwellings they were purchasing. Husbands were viewed as heads of household. Both spouses put efforts toward the husband's career development. Wives, particularly, participated in church, school, and community activities. They were frequently volunteer workers.

Nursery or preschool experiences for children were common for children whether or not mothers had any employment. Most children attended neighborhood public schools although some went to private schools. Children's educations were enhanced by a diverse combination of additional activities, such as sports, music, and academic lessons.

Most women married during their early or mid-twenties, after some employment or college education. A few women married later. Only three had a child before age twenty-one. Women had been socialized for marriage: none had had thoughts of a life for themselves other than marriage and family.

These women's experiences of marriage were greatly similar. The division of labor within the marriage fell along traditional gender-role lines. Women were family caretakers and primary parents. Fathers were preoccupied with building careers and supporting families. They tended to have somewhat minimal involvement with their children; according to the wives, only two of these fathers were active coparents.

Analysis of Postdivorce Situations

The postdivorce experiences and situations of these sixty women were greatly similar. A significant reduction in family income was the most commonly shared experience. This aspect of their lives tended to shape nearly all others. Parenting, providing, and creating different social and personal lives were areas of common experiences. Responses and adaptations to the similar situations and experiences varied to some extent as each woman individually interpreted her situation and worked out strategies within it.

Upon divorce husbands left their families. They took with them their income and earning potential. Consequently, women and children experienced an immediate, usually drastic, reduction in family income. Only two of the sixty women did not encounter a sudden and dramatic decline in income, even after including any monies received as child, family, or spousal support. Since the family had only one less residential member, expenses were not significantly reduced. As is the case for most married mothers in our society, marriage had obscured these women's economic dependency. Divorce dramatically unveiled this dependency.

The financial crises which followed divorce for these women exceeded even their worst fears. For most, the crises continue to occur. Economic hardship is, for the great majority, the worst single component of the divorce experience. It outweighs even the emotional and identity chaos connected to the marital breakup. Many women noted that the emotional traumas of divorce have been greatly worsened by the continuing economic uncertainties.

Financial hardship remains the fundamental problem in their lives. Few have attained adequate "family incomes" despite their full-time employment and assorted efforts to enhance their positions in the labor force. None has reestablished economic security comparable to that [which] she had when married. Few have any savings and most live literally from paycheck to paycheck.

Even women receiving child support regularly experience economic hardships. Generally, however, those families most destitute are those who receive no child-support payments. Just over one-half of these families do receive child support. This payment rate is higher than the national average, probably because most of the absent fathers remain connected occupationally to their communities. Only three women receive spousal support; only one woman has an indefinite award, the others have only short-term support. Several women who had been married more than twenty years received support for only two years.

All but three of these mothers are employed, most full time. They simply do not earn incomes sufficient to support their children. The majority of women take home between 800 and 1,200 dollars a month. Only two earn more than 1,500 a month.

The low earnings of these divorced mothers, as for most women, are the result of limited job training and experience due to their life-cycle patterns of marriage and childbearing, major child-care responsibilities, and, most importantly, the continued discrimination against women in the employment sector. Even women with extensive employment experience or college educations remain largely relegated, with the others, to the secondary sector of the wage-labor market. Some of the women have had to find employment after more than twenty years out of the wage-labor market. Most do clerical kinds of work. Child care is available at none of their places of work.

Strategies employed to handle the decline in family income varied. In addition to obtaining employment (if not already employed), mother's responses to the changed circumstances included various combinations of the following: moving, changing jobs, changing dietary patterns and reducing amounts spent on food, stopping private lessons of various sorts for both themselves and their children, selling off personal items such as jewelry and silver, stopping insurance coverages, locating public and private assistance to meet child-care expenses for younger children, stalling creditors, moving children from private to public schools and having college-age children transfer from private to public universities, borrowing money, turning to parents for assistance, and taking second jobs. Often decisions regarding finances had to be made quickly and during times of emotional stress, so the women wondered in retrospect if they had acted wisely. Further, they were not only unfamiliar with having to cope with such financial distress but . . . also inexperienced in making critical decisions alone.

The issue of the family residence, when owned, is a major one. Typically mothers were offered the option of remaining in the home since the children were with them. But if they chose to stay, they had to buy out their husbands' interest as part of the property settlement. Property in California is viewed as being jointly owned by the community, but the community consists of the husband and wife, not the children also. So the mother must buy out the children's father by paying him a full one-half of the equity value if she wants to remain in the home. Most of these women, however, can barely maintain house payments let alone pay half the equity, whatever it is. So family homes were frequently sold forcing the mother and children to move. Moving only further worsened the economic situation and further unsettled children who were still caught in the throes of confusion surrounding the family changes. Resentment and bitterness are especially keen around this issue.

Several women were granted postponements in buying out their former spouse to the time when the youngest child would turn eighteen. In each of these cases the youngest child was in the mid-teen years at the time of divorce and is now approaching the age of eighteen. So the time is near for the final property settlement. But these mothers must now find even greater amounts than they would have had to at the time of the dissolution because house values have risen. Their own financial situations, however, are little changed from that time. And while the homes have been maintained at the occupants' expense, there is no compensation for the women for these costs in the buy-out clauses.

A hidden danger exists for all of these women in regard to the family home situation. When the residence is sold in order to divide the community property, the women's share of the equity is not sufficient to buy another home with comparable payments. They cannot afford higher payments nor can they afford to lose any profits to capital gains taxes if they rent rather than buy. They feel they are in a no-win situation.

Over a third of these women depend to some extent on their parents for direct financial help, and another one-third find their parents giving more gifts and things to their grandchildren than they did before the divorce. The parents have, according to these mothers, varying amounts of knowledge about the financial hardships being lived through by their daughters and grandchildren. Often their information is obtained through conversations with their grandchildren.

Children's school clothing and shoes, dental or medical expenses not covered by insurance, and recreational and educational activities are often obtained or sponsored by maternal grandparents. Two mothers had their family homes saved from pending foreclosure; another was able to stop her court-ordered eviction when her father provided the months' backdue rent and the landlord's court costs. Many turn to parents for help when the monthly expenses exceed income.

Numerous women discussed at length their renewed, and unexpected, dependency on parents. They have gone as a result of divorce from economic dependency on husbands to a form of dependency on parents. The former was largely obscured and, when it was recognized, seemed logical; the latter seems blatant and is demoralizing. This dependency has complex meanings for these women: they work, even struggle, to support themselves and their children. But, for reasons generally beyond their control, they cannot meet all of their expenses or maintain a reasonable standard of living for their children by their own efforts. They know, too, that the older generation's ability to support another family, even in limited ways, is restricted.

The need to turn to parents for financial assistance is particularly poignant for many of these women in view of their feelings about their own upbringing. Most believe they were channeled because they were female into marriage by messages, both explicit and implicit, begun during their early years. Even those who had college educations paid for by their parents were expected to marry and raise children; none believe they were raised to be aware there might be other alternatives. Occupational and career development were of secondary, if that, importance in their socialization. The women most outspoken about this facet of gender socialization are those who have brothers. Brothers were brought up with expectations to be career oriented and self-supporting regardless of their personal decisions about marriage. The women see their need to accept parental assistance as reinforcing their parents' assumptions that they as female offspring are unable to take care of themselves.

Public assistance, in the form of Aid [to Families with] Dependent Children, is used presently by three of the sixty women. Three others depended on welfare for between two and three years while they completed their educations or advanced training immediately after divorce. These women are now fully employed as a lawyer, teacher, and personal counselor. One mother depended on welfare for two years while her children were babies. Other women depended on welfare for temporary assistance directly following separation from their husbands and until employment was found. Three others turned to welfare during periods of temporary unemployment.[12]

Each of the three women currently receiving public aid [has] children under age six. All three are attending school in pursuit of specific career goals. Attending school allows them more time with their young children than would full-time work.

Other women in this group received supplemental support to their earned but inadequate incomes before the 1981 Budget Reconciliation Act, which altered welfare policies. The changes forced the women to choose between welfare and work. Neither source of income alone is adequate, but there are no longer any sources of public support for these women who economically are among the working poor.

Total income—earnings combined with child or other support—does not exceed the amount available from welfare for over a quarter of these mothers. For various reasons they struggle on with their employment even though it means, at least immediately, greater demands on time and energy with no economic returns. Employment does bring some benefits to these women, particularly the contacts with other adults and the satisfaction of being free of dependency on the government.

All of the women who have used public assistance found it to be a demeaning and demoralizing experience. Some complained of being "hassled by welfare workers," accosted verbally in stores by strangers for using food stamps, or turned away from medical facilities with a sick child because payment was to be in the form of Medi-Cal. According to these mothers, the injury of substandard incomes is hard enough to live with, insults given in addition are unbearable. They resent being stereotyped as "free-loaders" or "welfare chiselers."

Being faced continuously with financial uncertainty and hardship because they are now divorced confounds these mothers. They have gone from relatively comfortable and established lifestyles in marriage to living with economic uncertainty. They had never even considered the possibility of living with such hardships. They and their children observe and know that these hardships are not being experienced by the absent fathers or by friends and relatives who have retained the two-parent family. The irony is made all the more profound by the women's knowledge that the surest and quickest way to reverse the situation they are experiencing is to remarry. However, a large majority of these women do not expect to remarry. They are reluctant to risk losing their newly gained sense of independence. Over two-thirds of the women noted that the best part about being divorced is the new appreciation they have of themselves as individual persons. How to be self-supporting and able to secure for themselves and their children a reasonable standard of living without depending on a man is the question asked by many.

While the majority of the mothers are working toward improving their income-earning levels through education, technical training, establishing businesses, or advancing in their present occupations, significantly few have plans or predictions about their futures. They are aware that plans and expectations held when married are no longer relevant. Some note how surprised they were to realize the extent to which they previously took for granted their futures and their security. Even those who had desperately wanted divorce were unprepared for the extent of disruption in their lives and images of the future.

Enhanced self-awareness and flexibility are possible outcomes of the divorce experience and are viewed by the women as being well earned. However, neither extends into optimism about the future. Immediate needs and demands require most of their thoughts and energies; the economic uncertainties of their futures are too threatening to consider carefully. Some women hold as a comforting thought the fact that their children will eventually grow up and become self-supporting. Others worry because they know that any legal obligation to pay child support by absent fathers ends in California when a child reaches eighteen regardless of schooling or continued dependency on the family. Several women confessed that the thought crosses their minds occasionally that they may one day be among the "shopping-bag ladies on the streets." None of these women expressed any confidence that social reforms will enable them to make wages comparable to men even though most commented on the personally felt effects of wage discrimination. And none of the women, not even those from exceptionally affluent marriages, was granted as part of the divorce settlement funds for a retirement account.

Additional Tasks and Adjustments

The process of living involves coping with a series of situations. Family life, for example, encompasses not only providing income, but also parenting, maintaining a home and family, and creating social and personal lives. Many tasks face these mothers besides that of dealing with economic circumstances. All of these mothers juggle time and energy between assorted tasks. Unexpected but not completely unusual family crises such as illness, accidents, and death demand attention also, regardless of family circumstances, and deplete emotional resources. The weight of these tasks is compounded by the fact that the mother alone must accomplish them in the single-parent family whereas during marriage they were shared by two adults.

Additional tasks have emerged as a result of the divorce itself. Ongoing aspects of these women's lives include: coping with the legal system; dissolving the marriage union, which is not accomplished solely by divorcing; redefining relationships to extended family and family friends; coming to terms with a changed identity—single rather than married—and building a personal life beyond that of mother. None of these tasks is easy. They entail altered situations and identities which are open to varied definitions and interpretations. There are few social supports or guidelines giving direction as to how to proceed. And not only do these tasks and roles compete for limited time and energy but they often conflict.

Involvement with lawyers and the courts, necessary to secure a divorce, does not end with acquisition of the final dissolution decree. Rather, for many women, it is an ongoing process because of the need to seek enforcement of child-support and, in a few instances, spousal-support orders. Repeated challenges by former husbands to custody awards have kept two women even more deeply enmeshed in the legal system. The intimidation felt by nearly all of these women early in their dealings with the legal system has given way to distrust, dismay, and anger. High costs of legal representation, the perceived indifference to their situations, legal "double-talk," and substantial time delays render them powerless and frustrated. Some mothers have simply given up in their efforts to obtain help legally either through private legal aid or the District Attorneys' offices.

It is the custodial mother, in this study as well as in the nation at large, who carries the burden of child rearing and parenting after divorce. While most of these women become custodial parents by default—children's fathers did not entertain the possibility of having custody in the majority of cases—all these women are firm in their desire to remain the primary parent. The two instances in which the mothers have repeatedly been challenged in the courts for custody by their former husbands are defined by these women as forms of harassment; neither has reason to believe the children's father is serious about having full-time custody.

There are several exceptions in this group of women to the general pattern of full-time custody and care of children by mothers. Two mothers share custody with their former spouses. According to the mothers, this arrangement is working well but both they and their former husbands view the mothers as the primary parent because they are expected to assume full parenting and child care whenever the fathers have a conflict between work or social obligations and parenting. This expectation is not reciprocal.

Two mothers have made alternative arrangements for care of some of their children. Both have done so out of economic necessity and as a last resort. One parent of four has recently sent her oldest two children to live with their father who, while he has never paid child support, has agreed to have these children rather than for all four of them to continue living in poverty. (This mother is employed by the state government as a clerical worker; her earnings simply do not support her family.) The other mother, in a similar situation, has the oldest of her three children living temporarily with her parents.

Demands and satisfactions of parenting vary, especially according to ages and numbers of children. The most overworked and stressed mothers are those with young children. Balancing employment with child rearing, arranging and maintaining child care, and meeting medical or financial emergencies consume the energies of divorced mothers with young children. Older children require fewer arrangements for child care and can assist in domestic tasks; mothers of older children invest more time and energies in activities and conversations with their children. However, the lack of money is often felt more acutely with older children and mothers have strong regrets about their inabilities to provide more.

Relationships with their children are better than before the divorce, according to these mothers, despite the economic circumstances. They, with their children, have had to work to redefine their relationships and shared situations. The drastic changes in their lives and the intensity of the changes have fostered changes in the established communication systems and the mothers see themselves now as more open and democratic parents.

But being a single parent is not all rewarding and certainly is not easy. While the absence of the father means the mother can alone make and implement decisions without the need to negotiate or compromise with another parent, it also means no other parent is available to support her in or relieve her from parenting. This aloneness is complicated for many of the single mothers by their fatigue and task overload.

Parenting often conflicts with income-providing, especially since both are done alone. Mothers, particularly of preschool children, worry about their extensive absences from children because of employment. A forty-hour workweek with additional time for travel and lunch brings the time away from children's waking hours to fifty or more hours. A crisis, such as the need to find other child care or to free herself to attend to an ill child, can throw the working single mother into a state of alarm and chaos. These untimely, but not unlikely, events are worsened in their effects because most workplaces remain inflexible to family needs.

Two mothers have changed the uneasy balance between parenting and providing attained by the majority of mothers who work typical workweeks, primarily as clerical workers. These two have found ways to secure greater incomes, but it requires sacrificing time spent in parenting. Through these efforts their earnings are comparable to the median incomes of families headed by males. But their average workweeks far exceed even the average for employed persons who are not parents. Each of these women works more than sixty-five hours a week. One woman, with a college degree, works as a skilled laborer in a power plant. She works split shifts and extensive overtime. The other mother sells insurance on a commission-only basis, working evening and weekend hours also. Their sense of success for having moved their families out of poverty is combined with ambivalence and sorrow about their inability to be more available to their children. These mothers lament that the schools and babysitters are raising their children.

Others of the women also note their nearly constant exhaustion even though they work a forty-hour week. Mothers of preschool and early elementary-school children especially experience chronic fatigue. They are rushed much of the time. Getting themselves and their children off in the mornings requires early rising, hurried children, and, all too often, emotional chaos. Evening hours cannot be spent just in child contacts: meals, laundry, shopping, cleaning, and other family maintenance tasks must be accomplished, and there is no surplus money with which to obtain help. Mothers who try to supplement their incomes with second jobs do such things as bookkeeping and typing in their homes, and these must be done during evening or weekend hours also. Few of the working divorced mothers get more than an average of six hours of sleep. Illness—theirs or a child's—only adds twists to their already tightly scheduled and stressful lives.

The conflicts between parenting and providing are for the majority of these women direct and continuous. There are no easy answers available to them. There are few social supports available. The American family continues to be viewed in policies, programs, and articulation with the workplace as the traditional, two-parent, nuclear family, supposedly self-sufficient and autonomous. The exhaustion, task-overload, worries about effects of absence from children, and the realities of inadequate incomes continue to be seen as primarily personal problems. According to these divorced mothers, the larger society is unaware, unconcerned, or indifferent—or all three—to their situations, as is evidenced by the lack of social action to bring about change.

Nevertheless, divorce is, for the majority, an emotionally painful experience. Legal dissolution of marriage does not undo a shared history, shared but often thwarted and unrealized dreams, or joint parenthood. And divorce does not completely separate most of these parents; they remain tied to each other in varying ways because of shared parenthood. These mothers feel this connection acutely.

There is the ongoing matter of dealing with children about the absent father. Visitations require planning and scheduling. More importantly though, visitations often keep the custodial parent and children continually in the process of redefining their relationship around divorce; family-system continuity is disrupted as children move between parents. Especially during the first years following divorce, visitations prompt a sense that the postdivorce family is deformed and in need of structural repair. Conflicts over child rearing and lifestyles occur and require additional contacts between former spouses. Few parents have transcended the emotional hurts surrounding the divorce sufficiently to deal with each other easily regarding their children.

Children whose fathers have little or no contacts with them create and live with fantasies of their absent fathers. The created images generally represent saintly angels, occasionally a fallen one. Having to cope with romantic images of fathers carried by children who in reality are ignored is a major emotional task for these mothers. Mothers are not confident about their ability to help their children deal with paternal neglect. Mothers worry about these children and carry lively resentments about their former husbands.

Many mothers note their realization that they may remain feeling married until the youngest child is grown, perhaps even longer. Joint parenthood and shared years do not dissolve upon divorce. The present and future remain juxtaposed with the past. These interpretations are personal ones; none of the women has discussed with a former spouse the awareness of these links.

Divorce is not just a single event involving only a husband and wife who legally dissolve their union—it is a process which separates family and social lives as well. Not only children but extended family and family friends remain, in varying ways, attached to both spouses and children. The relationships must be maintained, redefined, or ended. Significantly few opt for the latter, so these attachments demand attention.

During marriage most of these women were the primary liaison to both his and her families. After divorce the relationship to relatives must be assessed and acted upon; children remain members of two extended families. But how to proceed is not as clear as the commitment to maintain family contacts. Because divorce is a crisis for the larger as well as the nuclear family unit, there is seldom a consensus of perspectives and understandings about divorce itself or the appropriate postdivorce behavior. Mothers usually find themselves continuing in the role of family liaison after the divorce for both his and her families and so work to redefine relationships.

Most close friendships are altered as a result of divorce. According to the divorced women, many of their close friends, especially those in couples, maintain their ties to their former husbands but neglect or reject continued ties with them. Explanations given by the women for this common experience are: the husband continues to be included because he shares common career endeavors; contacts with her are threatening because divorce is too real a possibility for others; and the continuance of old but persistent stereotypes about the behavior of "divorcees" toward other women's husbands. Also, the women report being difficult to be around during the initial phases of the divorce because of their great emotional instability and self-preoccupation. And friends seem to have realized, accurately, that now as a divorced mother she can no longer afford to engage in the activities they all once took for granted. Her realities are different. Her primary concerns have become how to meet immediate needs and maintain her family. She can no longer seriously entertain plans for shared cultural events or travels.

New friendships are gradually formed but the pain remains of being thrust out of the fabric of former social worlds as well as out of marriage (whether by choice or not there is some pain in the divorce process). Divorce and its companion downward mobility affect every aspect of women's lives. Lives are different as well as disrupted. Friendships are changed. There is decreased participation in social, as well as civic, activities.

Having a social life outside family activities is problematic for single mothers. Time spent with other adults is taken from the already limited time with children. Yet these adult women have personal needs which children cannot fulfill. There is no easy balance found between being a single mother and an adult single woman. Perhaps because these women had been primary parents even while married, the shift to single parenting was adapted to with relative ease. The shift to being a single woman is far more difficult. Mothers are familiar with parenting; they are inexperienced in relating to others, especially men, as single women.

The continuum of behaviors as a single person among these women ranges between two extremes. The first is to have no sexual involvements and no social activities outside the family. The other is to give priority to developing adult relationships, especially sexual ones. The great majority of these women shift between positions of lesser extremes as they seek a resolution to the conflicts between single mothering and being single. The lack of an easy solution is complicated because the situation is dynamic and requires ongoing evaluation and choices as experiences are had, people are met, confidence is heightened, or decisions altered. The perceived lack of social guidelines around adult sexual behavior is particularly confounding to these mothers who have, for the most part, come out of marriages which had defined and stabilized sexual components.

Only five of the mothers have some sense of ease and control about the issue of being both mother and single woman. Two of these women share child custody with their ex-husbands, and the children of the others have regularly scheduled overnight (usually every other weekend) visitation with their fathers. Mothers whose children have regular times away with fathers have some time they can feel comfortable in calling their own. They have some privacy as well.

In summary, life is hard in many ways for these women. They are newly poor or perilously close to being poor but remain largely middle class in expectations, hopes, and values. Most had no knowledge about how to cope with poverty or continuing economic hardships. They are lodged in social and economic realities which conflict with their world views. Although increasing numbers of women and children are in this predicament, significantly few scholars, politicians, social commentators, or even mothers recognize the complexity or potential long-term implications of the problem.

Life without father is complex: doing alone as a single parent what two parents formerly did requires resourcefulness, commitment, and energy. Feeling competent, strong, and in control of their lives is possible for single mothers as it is for anyone. And these divorced mothers are confident they are doing well as parents, considering their situations. In addition, they share a satisfaction and some degree of amazement at their newly acquired sense of self as an independent and separate person. They see themselves as being "whole persons" and are surprised at the extent of relief felt in being free of the role of wife as they had experienced it. Few question any longer whether they can survive. They have regained confidence and are determined to maintain their families as best they can. But economic hardships continue to constrain their abilities to manage successfully.

Access to decent wages, part-time employment options for mothers of young children, enforcement of child-support awards and awards of reasonable amounts, increased availability of quality and affordable child care, some form of supplemental support to assure all families a decent minimal standard of living are not, any of them, new or radical proposals. The plight of the mother-headed family demands more serious consideration and implementation of these family supports. Disruption of lives through divorce is likely to continue, affecting men, women, and children. Adaptations to changed situations will continue to require and take varying forms. But for women and children to have as the overriding experience of divorce significant economic decline and financial hardship goes beyond personal actions and choices. The feminization of poverty following divorce is a social process. It is indicative of continued gender discrimination.

The freedom to be not married—the option to leave an undesirable or unwanted marriage—is a hollow gain in personal liberties for women who must face continuing economic hardship following divorce unless they remarry. The lack of economic protections for women who divorce, continued gender inequities in the wage-labor market and in family and divorce laws, an employment sector geared for the male wage earner who has a wife parenting and maintaining the home life, and an inadequate welfare system which perpetuates poverty—all these make women, and their children, the victims of divorce. Without legal and social changes enabling women to recover economically from divorce, marital dissolution will continue to undermine the status of women.

A Theoretical Consideration

Although the divorced mother's situation constitutes a social problem sociologically and empirically, it does not appear to have been defined yet as one. There has been no collective recognition of the phenomenon as a problem.[13] The feminization of poverty following divorce has been steadily increasing for more than a decade yet little public attention has been given it. Why the divorced mother's situation has not been defined as a social problem is particularly curious given the climate around women's issues and the increased awareness about gender discrimination and female subordination.

Only recently has this phenomenon been receiving media attention. And to date attention has been essentially limited to recitation of the quantitative scope of the problem. Little attention has been directed at the economic and social effects of divorce. The issue has not actively been picked up as a major agenda item by politicians or social activists. Even less has occurred in the way of actions geared to changing the situation or process of downward mobility. There simply has been no "mobilization for action."

There has been little active debate as to what is happening, what or who is responsible, or ways to remedy the situation. It would appear that social processes and institutions which perpetuate gender discrimination and divorced fathers who do not contribute to the support of their children are indicted as major contributing factors to the feminization of poverty following divorce. But in fact there has not been a serious challenge to these vested interests. If there had been we would be witnessing more avid attention, discussion, and controversy around the situation of divorced mothers and their children. This lack of attention and active debate further indicates that this has not yet been collectively defined as a social problem. Yet millions of women and children continue to be adversely affected by divorce; what occurs to them and how they respond in some way affect the larger society whether the matter is recognized or not.

How some situations come to be collectively defined as social problems and others do not remains unclear. The social and economic situations of divorced mothers and their children may provide a case study for observing how a social process or phenomenon comes to be collectively defined as a social problem. The recent media attention and publication of government data showing the feminization of poverty affecting middle-class women as well as others may promote collective definition of this as a social problem and incite widespread discussion. Mobilization for action and official lines of action can only emerge from such collective definition. And it is unlikely that divorced women themselves will soon become sufficiently organized and powerful to draw attention to their situations or to demand corrective action.

Women's roles are changing, dramatically and profoundly. These changes are not met, however, with comparable changes in social institutions. Women are kept in a highly vulnerable and precarious position because social changes have not kept even pace.

Institutions remain geared for traditional family arrangements and roles. They are organized for wage-earning men with economically dependent wives responsible for children. The wage and political systems, particularly, remain oriented to male household heads. Despite the dramatic increase in female-headed families, few changes have occurred to ease the way for these families. Changes in family life organization are not met by other institutional changes.

Social institutions have been able to resist change because they remain enmeshed in a patriarchal tradition. Women have relatively little political power and their issues remain inadequately represented. Female heads of household, particularly, have no strong representation in the political process. Families remain, as they have traditionally been, represented in the public sphere by male household heads. The myth of the self-sufficient, autonomous, private nuclear family persists, maintained by biased representation.

Gender politics continue to shape society, marriage, family, and divorce. Pervasive gender inequities and discrimination limit women's functioning in every sphere. As women assume new roles in addition to traditional ones through divorce, they encounter systematized patriarchal traditions. Women's work, lives, and situations go largely unnoticed and devalued. Their hardships following divorce are regarded as personal, not yet recognized as social, institutional, and political.

Whether or not this issue becomes collectively defined as a social problem, it is likely to continue because divorce is likely to continue. Without social change, divorce will continue to have drastic social and economic effects on women and their children.

Notes

1. Statement by a forty-one-year-old divorced mother of three teenagers who receives no child support. The four of them live on her $14,000 annual earnings from full-time work.
2. "For American women, the correlation between marital status and economic well-being has become an increasingly harsh reality in the latter half of the 20th century" (U.S., Commission on Civil Rights, *A Growing Crisis: Disadvantaged Women and Their Children,* Clearinghouse Publication 78 [May 1983]: 5).
3. Lenore Weitzman, "Economics of Divorce: Social and Economic Consequences of Property, Alimony, and Child Support Awards," *U.C.L.A. Law Review* 28 (August 1981):1181–268.
4. S. Hoffman and J. Holmes, "Husbands, Wives, and Divorce," in *Five Thousand American Families,* ed. G. Duncan and J. Morgan, vol. 4 (Ann Arbor: Institute for Social Research, 1976).
5. "In 1981, of the children who lived with only their mothers, 43 percent had a mother who was divorced, 27 percent had a separated mother and 16 percent had a mother who had never married." (U.S., Department of Commerce, Bureau of the Census, *Marital Status and Living Arrangements: March 1981,* series P-20, no. 372:5). "Since 1970 female-headed families have increased by 2.8 million. Of all families with children under 18 years of age, female-headed families now comprise 18.8 percent" (U.S., Department of Commerce, Bureau of the Census, *Household and Family Characteristics: March 1981,* series P-20, no. 371:7).
6. "In overall terms, the poverty rate for female householders in 1981 was more than three times that for male householders (34.6 percent compared to 10.3 percent) and more than five times that for husband-wife families (6.8 percent)" (U.S., Department of Commerce, Bureau of the Census, *Money Income and Poverty Status of Families and Persons in the United States,* series P-60, no. 132 [1981]: 21). "About one-half of all families below the poverty level in 1981 were maintained by women with no husband present" (ibid., p. 4).

According to Coe, even after adding income from alimony, child support, money from friends or relatives, and welfare payments, 28.7 percent of female householders remain in poverty (R. Coe, "Dependency and Poverty in the Short and Long-Run," in *Five Thousand American Families,* ed. G. Duncan and J. Morgan, vol. 6 [Ann Arbor: Institute for Social Research, 1978]).

7. "The poverty level is a severe measure of hardship and does not give a complete indication of how many families are really under stress trying to make ends meet" (U.S., Department of Commerce, Bureau of the Census, *Statistical Abstract* [1983]: 441).

   Nearly 60 percent of children under eighteen living in female-headed families fall below the 1.25 percent of poverty level. By increasing the hardship standard to 1.25 times the official poverty threshold, 44.6 percent of families headed by females are poor *(A Growing Crisis,* p. 17).

8. U.S., Department of Commerce, Bureau of the Census, *Child Support and Alimony: 1978* (Washington, D.C.: 1981).

9. Ibid.

10. U.S., Department of Commerce, Bureau of the Census, *Statistical Abstract of the United States: National Data Book and Guide to Sources, 1982–83* (Washington, D.C.: 1983).

11. Ibid.

12. Eighty percent of the 3.4 million families with 7.2 million children who were AFDC recipients in 1979 were headed by women. Forty-three percent of AFDC families were black, 40 percent white, and 14 percent Hispanic. Fifty-five percent of families receiving AFDC had a child under six years of age (U.S., Department of Health and Human Services, Social Security Administration, *1979 Recipient Characteristics Study* [Washington D.C.: 1982]:1).

    Father absence due to divorce or separation is the basis of eligibility for about half of the families receiving public assistance. Of women receiving no child support, nearly 90 percent have received some assistance in the form of AFDC *(Bureau of the Census, Statistical Abstract . . . 1982–83).*

13. This approach to defining social problems is taken from H. Blumer, "Social Problems as Collective Behavior," *Social Problems* 18 (Winter 1971):298–306.

Parenting Apart: Patterns of Childrearing after Marital Disruption

Frank F. Furstenberg, Jr., and Christine Winquist Nord

Historians of the 20th century family may look back on the period from 1965 to 1980 as no less remarkable than the baby boom era that preceded it. Any illusions that the shaping of the modern family was completed by the middle of the 20th century were utterly shattered by the experience of the recent past. The institution of marriage was changing long before the last decade, but the rapid rise in divorce seems to have accelerated the transformation and ushered into place a new set of marriage practices.

If current rates are maintained, half of those who have married recently will eventually divorce. Most of these individuals, however, will ultimately remarry. Approximately three out of four divorced women and five out of six divorced men make the transition to second marriages (Glick, 1984). Thus, the expectation of conjugal permanency has given way to a pattern of conjugal succession (Furstenberg, 1982a).

Divorce has only minor implications when a couple is childless. In about three out of five divorces, however, children are involved (Glick, 1979). A sociological proposition, derived from Malinowski's observations, holds that marriage provides a social contract for assigning parental—particularly paternal—rights and obligations. Unless provisions are made for dealing with the dissolution of that contract, parents and children are placed in an anomalous situation.

Remarriage further complicates that predicament. It restores the integrity of the family, but it also can add to the complexity of family life. Parents are not supplanted as in previous times when death preceded remarriage. Conjugal succession permits parents to be added onto the existing roster of caretakers. Consequently, a large number of families today are facing circumstances that are culturally uncharted (Bohannon, 1970; Cherlin, 1978; Furstenberg, 1979; Weiss, 1975). Parents must divide their attention and resources between two or more families; and children, in turn, frequently grow up with multiple parents. Our kinship system provides little guidance for adjudicating the conflicting claims of

An earlier draft of this paper was presented at the meetings of the American Sociological Association, San Francisco, 1982. The research was funded by grants from the Foundation for Child Development and the National Institute of Mental Health (5 R07 MH 34707-02). The National Survey of Children—Wave 2 was carried out jointly by Frank F. Furstenberg, Jr., at the University of Pennsylvania and James L. Peterson and Nicholas Zill of Child Trends, Inc.

coparents and stepparents or for assigning priorities to children who may have to deal with many parent figures (Duberman, 1975; Ahrons, 1980; Walker et al., 1977).

An intriguing question, not fully addressed in previous research, is how parents and children respond when their families are restructured by divorce and remarriage. Drawing on data from a nationally representative household sample of children, this paper describes relations among parents, stepparents, and children after separation and divorce, with particular attention to how divorce and remarriage may be altering conceptions of parenthood and parenting practices.

The Data

In 1976 the Foundation for Child Development funded a study on the well-being of children (Zill, in press). Data were collected from a nationally representative sample of households containing children between the ages of 7 and 11. Up to two children between these ages in each household were interviewed, yielding a total of 2,279 children from 1,747 households, or 80% of the identified households. In 1981, in collaboration with Nicholas Zill and James L. Peterson, who carried out the initial survey, a follow-up to the original National Survey of Children (NSC) was designed to examine the effects of marital disruption on the development and well-being of children and on the operation of single and multiparent families. Because we wanted to concentrate on the households that had experienced a change in the marital situation of the parents, all children whose parents were known (from the earlier survey) to have experienced marital disruption or who were at risk of separating because they had reported a high-conflict marriage were included in the follow-up. In addition, we drew from the initial sample a randomly selected subsample of children living in stable, low-conflict families as a comparison group; these were later weighted back to represent their true proportion in the original sample.

Nearly 90% of the children identified to be reinterviewed were located. Interviews were obtained in over 90% of those found, yielding an overall response rate of 79.3%. . . . The interview procedure and content [are] fully described in an earlier paper (Furstenberg et al., 1983).

Although occasional reference is made here to the larger group of children living with both biological parents or with adopted parents in intact marriages, this paper concentrates on the experiences of children in single-parent and stepparent families. Children whose parents have formally divorced dominate the group (75%), but children whose parents have only separated (16%) and children whose parents have never married (8%) also are included in the discussion that follows. Because we are interested in patterns of parenting by both the resident and nonresident parent, only children whose nonresident parents are alive are included in the analysis.

In previous analyses of the NSC, we estimated that close to half of all children would not live with both of their biological parents continuously during childhood. Moreover, most children whose parents separated or divorced would not maintain regular contact with the parent living outside the home. In fact, a near majority of children in our sample (49%) had not seen their nonresident parent in the preceding year, and only one child in six averaged weekly contact or better.

A sharp attenuation of contact occurred over time, partly owing to geographical mobility; regular visits were much more likely if the nonresident parent lived nearby. Attrition of contact was higher in families of low socioeconomic status, where the noncustodial parent also was less likely to pay child support. Although the payment of child support was an important correlate of continued contact, we did not find that the current marital status of the parents (either the custodial or noncustodial) had much effect on the amount of contact between nonresident parents and their children or the amount of support that they provided. (For further details see Furstenberg et al., 1983; Furstenberg, 1982b.)

This paper picks up where the previous analyses have left off, exploring in greater detail the quality of family relations after divorce and particular consequences of continued contact for family functioning. We begin by characterizing the nature of contact, when there is any, between children and their outside parent, taking into account the interval of time that has elapsed since separation. This leads us to a discussion of the extent of childrearing responsibilities assumed by outside parents, relations between former spouses and, finally, a brief examination of the implications of continued contact for the children's adjustment to life in single-parent or stepfamily households.

Results

The Nature of Contact between Outside Parents and Their Children

Each child's interview contained a series of questions about the nature of contact with the outside parent and the respondent's subjective impression of the quality of that contact. The data presented in Table 1 point to the limited role that outside parents play in the day-to-day lives of their children. According to the adult informants, three out of five children had not seen their outside biological fathers in the past month. Children were much more likely to have had contact, however, if their parents had separated recently. The parents' accounts square rather well with the children's reports of the amount of contact occurring in a typical month. Except for the period immediately after separation, children typically report infrequent contact with their parents, averaging only about two visits per month.

Visits only rarely involved sleeping over at the outside parent's house. Four out of five children said that they never slept over at the nonresidential fathers' houses in a typical month, and half of those who did sleep over at least occasionally did so only once or twice a month. Again, there are clear differences by length of time since separation. Conceivably these figures understate the

Table 1 Children's Relations with Their Outside Biological Parents by Duration since Separation and Gender of Parent (Percentages, U.S. Children Aged 11–16, 1981)

Relation Items	Duration since Separation (in Years)			Total of Outside Fathers	Total of Outside Mothers
	< 2	2–9	10+		
When child last saw outside parent					
1–30 days ago	74	53	28	40	64
31–365 days ago	24	15	19	18	29
1–4 years ago	2	12	5	7	4
5+ years ago	—	20	49	35	3
		$p < .01^a$		$p < .01^b$	
In a Typical Month:					
Number of times child sees outside parent					
Never	31	55	74	64	42
1–3 days	20	21	13	16	39
4+ days	49	25	13	20	18
Mean number of days	7.4	2.0	2.2	2.5	4.5
		$p < .01$		$p < .05$	
Number of times child sleeps over at outside parent's					
Never	60	71	89	80	42
1–3 days	22	19	7	12	40
4+ days	18	10	5	8	18
Mean number of days	1.6	0.8	0.5	0.7	2.9
		$p < .01$		$p < .01$	
Child talks with outside parent on telephone					
Never	6	41	70	55	18
1–3 times	48	28	17	23	39
4+ times	46	31	13	22	43
Mean number of times	8.1	4.3	1.8	3.1	4.1
		$p < .01$		$p < .01$	

(Table continues)

Table 1 *continued*

Relation Items	Duration since Separation (in Years)			Total of Outside Fathers	Total of Outside Mothers
	< 2	2–9	10+		
Child receives a letter from the outside parent					
Never	92	92	93	93	65
1+ times	8	8	7	8	35
Mean number of times	0.1	0.2	0.1	0.1	0.8
		$p < .1$		$p < .01$	
Child spends a week or more at a time at the outside parent's	28	31	16	22	57
		$p < .01$		$p < .01$	
Child thinks outside parent's home is					
Like own home	35	27	18	22	74
Like someone else's home	23	28	13	19	16
Child was never in it	42	44	69	58	10
		$p < .01$		$p < .01$	
Child has a place to keep things at the outside parent's	14	25	14	18	56
		$p < .01$		$p < .01$	
Unweighted N^c	(25)	(131)	(239)	(395)	(28)

Note: Restricted to children living with one biological parent and whose other biological parent is presumed alive. Length-of-separation figures are calculated only when outside parent is the biological father.
[a]Represents significant chi-squares comparing outside biological parents with varying degress of duration since separation.
[b]Represents significant chi-squares comparing outside father and outside mother.
[c]Ns vary slightly by question because of nonresponses.

amount of intimate, intensive contact because some families cluster their over-night stays during vacations or in the summer months. About one out of five children reported staying at their outside fathers' houses for a week or more, indicating that in the course of a year some children manage more contact than is reflected by the typical pattern. Although there are still differences by length of time since separation, they are not as sharply delineated. This could mean that there is a transitional stage for some outside parents between a period of intense involvement and a greater degree of disengagement, perhaps occasioned by a geographical move or a remarriage. Thus, child-care practices are something like patterns of interacton with extended kin. Fewer than one out of five children stated that they had space in their nonresidential fathers' homes to keep clothing or personal effects, and the majority of children reported that their outside fathers' homes were like "visiting in someone else's home" (19%) or that they never visited their outside parents at all (58%).

Furthermore, outside fathers tended to have little contact with their children by telephone. Overall, children averaged fewer than one conversation per week with their noncustodial fathers. Phoning, too, declines sharply as duration since separation increases. Letter writing was even more uncommon. Thus, it would seem that indirect forms of communication do not make up for the lack of direct contact that characterizes relations between outside fathers and their children.

As for mothers living outside the home, Table 1 reveals that they tend to maintain a much more active role in childrearing. Although few in number, nonresident mothers are distinctly more likely to visit with their child on a regular basis, have overnight visits, and have more indirect contact by phone and letter. Accordingly, children living apart from their mothers are more likely to say that they have places to store their things at the mothers' houses and that they feel like their own homes. There are not enough cases to examine the pattern of contact between children and their noncustodial mothers by duration since separation, but our impression is that the level of contact does not drop off so sharply for mothers over time. Nonetheless, even most mothers living outside the home do not have frequent and continuous contact with their children.

Extent of Childrearing Responsibility Taken by the Outside Parent

Contact with the outside parent, if it occurs at all, is usually social or recreational (Table 2). Among the minority of children who had seen their parents during the past week, only a tenth had been given assistance with schoolwork; slightly more than a fifth had worked on projects together, such as making something, cooking, or sewing; about a fourth had played some game or sport. These figures are overstated owing to the exclusion of children who have not seen their outside parents in the past year. Were we to include these cases, it would turn out that only a minuscule percentage of the sample had received help with homework; and a small fraction of the sample—less than one child in ten—had worked on projects together or played some game or sport with their outside parents. While this list of behavior hardly represents a complete inventory of childrearing activities, it is clear that the outside parent normally plays a very limited role.

We get a clearer impression of the extent of childrearing by outside parents when their behavior is contrasted to parental practices of parents living inside the home. Table 2 displays the activities and family practices of resident and nonresident parents in single-parent and stepfamilies as reported by the children. For purposes of comparison, the reports of children living with two biological parents also are included. Thus, the relative influence of family structure and of the parent's residential status can be assessed on patterns of family interaction.

Table 2 Child–Care Activities and Expectations by Family Form (Percentage of Children Answering in the Affirmative—U.S. Children Aged 11–16, 1981)

Activities and Expectations	Intact (Biological Parents)	Reconstituted (Resident Parent)	(Outside Parent)	Single-Parent (Resident Parent)	(Outside Parent)	p^b	Total (Outside Parent)	p^c
Parent-Child Interaction								
Activities with parents in past month								
Gone to the movies	23	22	5	27	20		15	*
Gone out to dinner	66	56	49	50	44	**	45	**
Gone shopping for you	70	60	37	68	41		41	**
Taken trip to museum or sports event	41	29	22	26	18	**	19	**
Activities with parents in past week								
Did a project together	49	52	15	42	24		21	**
Worked on schoolwork together	34	22	9	23	12	**	11	**
Played game or sport	42	41	34	27	27	**	29	**
Family Rules and Expectations								
Household expectations								
Clean your room	96	96	73	97	60		65	**
Clean rest of house	82	80	55	91	48	**	51	**
Do dishes	61	69	46	72	45	**	46	**
Cook	32	43	22	41	22	**	22	**
Household rules								
Watching TV	33	37	22	25	4	*	11	**
Telling your whereabouts	95	93	78	93	78		78	**
Doing homework	77	76	37	76	39		38	**
Dating	70	65	59	61	52	*	54	**
Rule making								
Report parents discuss decisions	39	28	49	38	31		37	**
Report parents listen to their arguments	42	34	59	39	44		49	**
Unweighted N^d	(785)	(136)	(55)	(298)	(110)		(165)	

Note: Restricted to children who are living with at least one biological parent. All of the above information about outside parents was collected from children who had at least 14 days of contact with their outside biological parents in the past year.
[a]Family type refers to living situation of the resident parent.
[b]Represents significant chi-squares comparing resident parents in intact, reconstituted, and single-parent families: * $p < .05$; ** $p < .01$.
[c]Represents significant chi-squares comparing all resident and outside parents regardless of family type: * $p < .05$; ** $p < .01$.
[d]Ns vary slightly by question because of nonresponses.

Keep in mind that most of the data on the outside parent were collected only if the child reported at least 14 days of contact during the preceding year.

Children generally have significantly lower levels of contact with outside parents than with parents living inside the home, even when comparisons are confined to the more active group of outside parents. Differences in patterns of parenting are generally much greater between resident and nonresident parents than between any of the family forms. The disparity in social and recreational activities is not quite as large as task-oriented activities such as homework. Again, this would seem to suggest that the role of the outside parent is generally confined to entertainment and excludes most of routine caretaking responsibilities of household management. Partly because their contact frequently occurs outside the home, nonresident parents are less likely to expect their children to straighten up around the house or help prepare meals or to have definite rules about their children's day-to-day routines. Although the relative differences are quite sizable, a minority of outside parents who see their children at least 14 days a year do manage to exercise parental responsibilities.

As an interesting aside, Table 2 also shows that instrumental exchanges between parents and children do not vary greatly by family type. Children in reconstituted and single-parent families are as likely as children in unbroken families to say that their parents make demands on them for helping out. Indeed, if anything, more seems to be expected of children in single-parent households. Rules are not more lax for children of disrupted marriages, with the possible exception of dating restrictions. Family structure also appears not to affect significantly the degree to which children are included in the process of rule making.

The Quality of Children's Relations with Their Outside Parents

A clearer picture of how children in different family circumstances feel about the time spent with parents is gained from their own reports on the quality of relations with parents living inside and outside the home. Because each biological parent was assessed separately, we can learn from Table 3 whether the quality of the parent-child relationships varies more by family structure or by residential arrangement. Unfortunately, there are too few single fathers to appear as a separate subgroup in the table. Remember also that most entries in Table 3 exclude children who had little or no contact with their outside parents.

In general, children in all family situations are disinclined to report serious disturbances in their relationships with their outside parents. A majority say that they do not often argue with their outside parents; that they feel loved, appreciated and trusted; and that they spend enough time with their outside parents. Close to half say that they want to be like their outside parents when they grow up.

In comparing children's perceptions of residential and nonresidential parents, however, some interesting differences emerge. A strong similarity exists in children's feelings towards their mothers regardless of the latter's marital or

Table 3 Children's Reports of the Quality of Parent-Child Relations by Family Type (Percentage Answering in Affirmative—U.S. Children Aged 11–16, 1981)

Children's Reports	Intact		Family Type Reconstituted				Single-Parent	
	Child Living with Mother	Father	Child Living with Mother	Outside Parent Father	Child Living with Father	Outside Parent Mother	Child Living with Mother	Outside Parent Father
Often argue with parent[a]	6	6	11	2	7	4	12	3
Spends enough time with you[b]	80	75	71	75	60	76	77	73
Gives enough affection to you[b]	78	71	76	44	74	81	72	48
Frequently do things together[c]	34	43	37	40	35	47	32	45
Feel very/extremely close to parent[b]	87	81	86	54	82	97	82	45
Would be like when grown[b]	72	73	67	49	84	59	59	40
Parent:[a]								
Makes clear, consistent rules	45	61	53	45	79	53	53	36
Trusts you	77	80	78	84	94	97	76	73
Is firm with you	49	59	48	58	52	58	48	47
Wants to know your whereabouts	80	70	78	63	90	79	86	73
Encourages you to do your best	87	80	82	85	79	86	85	76
Appreciates your accomplishments	76	70	71	74	63	77	79	67
Loves and is interested in you	87	83	87	93	86	91	88	76
Changes expectations	19	20	27	13	12	19	25	20
Unweighted N	(785)	(785)	(118)	(70)[d]	(20)	(17)	(287)	(160)[d]

Note: Restricted to children living with at least one biological parent.
[a]Questions were asked only if children had 14 or more days of contact with outside parents in past year.
[b]Questions were asked of all children with outside parents, regardless of their amount of contact.
[c]Question was asked only of children who saw their outside parents three or more days in past year.
[d]The unweighted Ns for outside fathers are the Ns for the largest category—i.e., children with outside parents regardless of amount of contact. No N falls below 40.

residential situation. Children from nonintact families are somewhat less likely to say that they want to be like their mothers when they grow up, but they are otherwise similar in their relations with their mothers. By contrast, children with fathers living outside the home are decidedly more discontent with their paternal relationship than those residing with their father. More than half say that they do not get all the affection they need, and nearly as many say they are only fairly close or not close at all to their fathers. Outside fathers are also faulted for not making clear and consistent rules and for not being firm enough.

A possible reason for the differences in the way that children regard mothers and fathers living outside the home was suggested in the findings presented earlier, namely that children have more contact with outside mothers than with outside fathers. Conceivably, the lesser degree of contact—rather than parent's gender—explains children's lower assessment of their fathers. While the number of cases precludes a definitive test of this hypothesis, greater paternal contact does have some effect on the children's assessment of the quality of relations with their fathers (not shown). However, the effect is not as large as might be expected. Only at the extreme, when contact had not taken place in the past year, were children noticeably more critical of their fathers. It appears, then, that children who see more of their fathers do not generally enjoy much closer relations than those with occasional contact.

Mothers with infrequent contact were accorded even more importance. These rather extravagant evaluations may be nothing more than poignant reminders of the symbolic importance to the child of maintaining links to the biological parent, but it also appears that children are prepared to adopt something like a sliding scale when they judge their relations with nonresident parents. Less is expected and, therefore, whatever attentions are given are gratefully received. These findings closely parallel the results of previous research among low-income blacks, focusing on relations between unmarried fathers and their children: what seem like tenuous or nonexistent ties to outside observers are experienced by participants as important and meaningful relations (Furstenberg and Talvitie, 1979).

A mark of the significance of the outside parent is indicated by children's responses to the question, "When you think about your family, who specifically do you include?" Virtually all children included the biological parents with whom they were residing, and more than two out of three (72%) mentioned stepfathers, if their biological mothers were remarried. By contrast, only half of the children with outside fathers included them in their family list. Nonetheless, this latter proportion is impressive in view of what little contact many have with these individuals. Children who saw their parents only occasionally, 3 to 13 days a year, were only slightly less likely to regard their outside parents as members of their families, compared with children who saw their parents on a weekly basis. When visits occurred less often than three days a year, the outside father was only rarely regarded as a "family member" by the child.

Are children more likely to omit their outside parents from their lists of family members if they are living with stepparents? The data for children living apart from their fathers clearly show that having a stepparent has no effect on the likelihood of the child listing the father as a family member. Children appear to accumulate rather than replace fathers, particularly when the father outside the home maintains an active presence in the child's life. The fact that many children expand the boundaries of their family to include both their biological and stepfathers does not mean, of course, that parents do the same. Indeed, when asked to list the people they considered to be family members, about 1 in 20 adult respondents included their former mates. While hardly surprising, this finding alerts us to the potential complications in the socialization process when parents and children define themselves in family systems that only partially overlap.

Relations among Resident and Nonresident Parents

This brings us to a pair of critical questions about which previous research has had little to say: How do resident and nonresident parents share the responsibilities of child care, and how are these arrangements altered when stepparents become involved as well? A few previous studies have addressed these questions in small-scale research (Keshet, 1980; Goldsmith, 1980; Goetting, 1979; Spanier and Thompson, 1984). The data presented in the remainder of this paper provide only an introduction to these topics.

Table 4 includes only families—about half of the disrupted ones—in which the outside parents have remained involved at least to some degree in the past five

Table 4 Level and Quality of Adult Respondents' Interaction with Outside Parent (Percentages—U.S. Children Aged 11-16, 1981)

Interaction Reports	Amount of Contact with Outside Father					Outside Parents		
	Last Contact 1–5 Years Ago	Number of Days of Contact in Last Year			p^a	Total for Outside Father	Total for Outside Mother	p^b
		1–13	14–51	52+				
	Residential Parent Responses							
Rarely or never discuss matters concerning child with the outside parent	81	77	57	44	**	67	59	
Rarely or never agree with outside parent in rearing child	22	26	32	48	**	32	20	
Outside parent takes too little responsibility in rearing child	87	73	74	61		75	71	
Outside parent has very little or no influence on decisions about child	91	87	68	45	**	73	77	

Table 4 *continued*

Interaction	Amount of Contact with Outside Father					Outside Parents		
	Last Contact 1–5 Years Ago	Number of Days of Contact in Last Year			p^a	Total for Outside Father	Total for Outside Mother	p^b
		1–13	14–51	52+				
Outside parent often breaks plans to see child	12	15	4	5	**	9	12	
Outside parent often meddles in the way you bring up child	3	3	6	10		5	0	
Outside parent often tries to undermine your rules for child	0	4	8	16		8	0	
Child sometimes or often takes advantage of differences between you and outside parent	2	9	31	43	**	23	17	
Sometimes or often use child to communicate with outside parent	30	28	40	53	**	38	31	
Hardly ever or never talk with child about your relationship with outside parent	98	91	69	57	**	46	38	
Child Responses								
Outside parent and resident parent sometimes or often fight over child's time	3	7	10	14	**	9	20	
In matters concerning child, outside and resident parents do not get along	7	13	16	14	*	14	13	
Unweighted N^c	(45)	(65)	(65)	(55)		(238)	(28)	

[a]Represents significant chi-squares comparing outside fathers with varying degrees of contact with their children, including those with no contact in the past year, as long as outside parent is presumed alive: * $p < .05$; ** $p < .01$.

[b]There are no significant chi-squares when comparing outside fathers and outside mothers who had some contact with their children in the last year.

[c]Ns vary slightly by question because of nonresponses.

years. Key indicators of the relationship of the outside parent to the parent in the household are cross-tabulated by the gender of the outside parent and, for outside fathers, the amount of contact with the child. Because the number of children who are not living with their mothers is small, caution should be used in generalizing the results for outside mothers.

Looking first at the total figures for outside mothers and fathers, it is striking how little communication about the child there is between formerly married couples. These responses are in part a reflection of the limited contact that outside parents have with their children. Still, this lack of communication indicates that the pattern of cooperative coparenting, so widely portrayed in popular media, is, in fact, rather rare. Close to half of the resident mothers and nearly two out of five (38%) of the resident fathers say they hardly ever or never talk with their children about their relationship to the outside parents, and a substantial minority (38% of the mothers and 31% of the fathers) report that they sometimes or often communicate with the outside parents through their children. It would appear that children often provide a key communication link between the biological parents, who are reluctant partners in the childrearing process.

Given the low level of communication, it is not surprising that, when asked how much input the nonresident parents have in the decision-making process, about three-fourths of the respondents replied that they had little or no influence and two-fifths stated that the biological parents never made decisions together. This low level of collaboration led most parents to complain about the level of childrearing responsibility assumed by the nonresident parent.

As involvement by the outside parent increases, the proportion of residential mothers who state that they rarely or never discuss childrearing matters with the outside father, that he has little influence on their decisions, and that he takes too little child-care responsibility drops. The proportion of residential mothers who use the child to communicate with the outside father, however, increases significantly. The increase in indirect communication with the outside parent indicates a strategy for reducing potential strain—minimize personal contact.

This explanation seems plausible for two reasons. First, as the level of contact increases, so does the proportion of residential mothers who report that they rarely or never agree with the outside parent in raising the child. Second, even when contact averages once a week, many residential mothers do not discuss child-care matters with the outside fathers or admit their influence on child-care decisions. This suggests that parents often contrive to stay away from one another in order to minimize the potential for open hostility. Even in families where the couple is presumably coparenting, child-care decisions often are made without the benefit of direct consultation and deliberation.

Incidentally, the negative feelings expressed are in sharp contrast to reports by remarried respondents about their current spouses. An overwhelming majority of remarried parents express a high degree of contentment with the level of the child-care support provided by spouses living inside the home, indicating that the negative reports about the outside parents are not merely the inevitable expressions that the other parent is not doing enough (not shown).

The above interpretation gains more support when we examine a set of questions, asked of the resident parents, about tensions that could arise through direct dealings between the outside parents and the children. The resident parents were asked if the outside parent broke plans to see the child, meddled in the raising of the child, or tried to undermine rules for the child. Very few parents complained of any of these problems. Although the amount of strain evidenced by two of these questions (meddling and undermining rules) increased with increasing levels of contact between the outside parent and the child, the proportion who complained about interference was remarkably low even at high levels of contact. It appears that formerly married couples try to minimize the effect of any tension between themselves for their children. Indeed, even though resident parents indicate that they rarely or never agree with the outside parents, very few children report that their biological parents often fight or do not get along well.

From the above discussion, it is apparent that resident fathers are about as likely as resident mothers to report that the parent living outside the home does not assume a fair share of child care. Gender appears to be of less importance than custodial position in shaping perspectives on childrearing and evaluations of coparenting arrangements (cf. Furstenberg and Spanier, 1984).

Contact with the Outside Parent and Family Relations

Remarriage can either alleviate or complicate tensions between parents. Virtually no differences turned up when the patterns of communication, the assessments of involvement, and the problems of relating to the outside parent were cross-tabulated by the current marital status of each parent. Remarried respondents also were asked directly whether their contact with the outside parent put a strain on their marriage. Only 3% said this happened often, and another 9% said that it sometimes occurred. The respondents who were in more active coparenting relationships were actually less likely to report that dealings with the outside parents introduced tensions into their marriages (not shown).

Similarly, stepfamily relations were not adversely affected by contact with the outside parent. Only 8% of the sample said that the nonresident parent sometimes interfered with the relationship of the child and stepparent, and 3% said such instances of interference occurred often. Again, no relationship existed between the amount of contact by the outside parent and complaints of intrusion.

In addition to these subjective appraisals by the adults, the children's interview provided further confirmation that the outside parent was not complicating parent-child relations inside the household or making family life more difficult. This conclusion was reached after examining the impact of contact with the outside parent using a wide range of indicators of family functioning drawn from the children's interview. The measures included reports of the quality of relations with custodial parents and stepparents, when present in the household, as well as children's descriptions of their family life during the months immediately preceding the survey.

The consistency of the results is impressive. Children in regular contact with the parents outside the home were no more likely than those whose contact was sporadic or nonexistent to report relational problems with either their custodial parents or their stepparents. This is not to say that family disruption had no consequences for relations with parents or views of family life. Children from broken marriages were not as happy with the quality of family relationships and were more critical of how their families functioned (Furstenberg and Seltzer, 1983). However, the displeasure of children living in single-parent households or in stepfamilies cannot be traced to the level of involvement by the biological parents living outside the home.

Before completely dismissing the possibility that contact with the outside parent disturbs relations in the child's household, a separate analysis was undertaken of children living in three different family types: stepfamilies with biological mothers, stepfamilies with biological fathers, and children living only with mothers. Not enough cases exist to permit a separate examination of children living with fathers only. Even in the three subgroups mentioned above, the number of cases is small—particularly in households where the children are living with stepmothers—requiring that caution be exercised in interpreting the results.

Contact with the outside father clearly does not impair relations with resident parents. In fact, the data hint that satisfaction with family relations may be ever greater when children maintain regular contact with fathers living outside the home. Moreover, relations with stepfathers show no evidence of disturbance when biological fathers outside the home play an active role. Our data suggest that children are usually able to expand their families to include more than one father and perhaps even benefit from doing so in the event of divorce.

The situation looks somewhat different for children living with stepmothers. These children are generally less content with the quality of family life, and they specifically experience difficulties with their stepmothers. Although the number of cases are few, the results imply that regular contact with the outside mother may complicate relations with the stepmother. Children seem to find it harder to incorporate new mothers than new fathers.

Before drawing any policy implications about the advisability of different custody practices from this particular result, several possible interpretations must be considered. Children living with their biological fathers and stepmothers may be different to begin with, because they represent exceptions to the ordinary practice of assigning custody of the children to the biological mothers. Therefore, it seems likely that children living with their fathers may have been exposed to a difficult custody negotiation or may have a special history of troubled family relations. Furthermore, the children in our study are in late childhood and early adolescence; they were all born in the period when divorce rates were just beginning to accelerate. Many, therefore, experienced family disruption a decade ago, when divorce was less common and custody practices more uniformly prescribed. How children would respond to particular custody arrangements today requires a comparable study of children whose parents have divorced more recently.

Conclusion

Despite inevitable qualifications about the limitations of the data, the National Survey of Children yields some surprising results on the way that marital disruption is altering parenting practices. Our major findings can be summarized as follows.

1. Marital disruption effectively destroys the ongoing relationship between children and the biological parents living outside the home in a majority of families. Nearly half of all children have not seen their nonresident fathers in the past year. Only a minority have ever slept over at the father's house; among those who have, overnight visits are a special treat (or perhaps in some cases a special obligation) rather than a regular routine. Children of divorce rarely have two homes as is commonly suggested in the mass media. Many—probably a majority—have never set foot inside the houses of their nonresident fathers, which undoubtedly are less familiar to them than the homes of many relatives or friends.

2. Contact with the outside parent, when there is any, normally takes the form of a social rather than an instrumental exchange. Parents occasionally go out to dinner with their children, take them on trips, or play with them; but they rarely help them with schoolwork or carry out some project together. Outside fathers who socialize their children at all usually do so from a distance and with a great deal of laxity. There seems to be more than a grain of truth to the stereotype that parents outside the home behave more like pals than parents.

3. Most children who see their outside parents on a more or less regular basis do not complain about the amount of love or attention they receive. Children with fathers living outside the home are not as content with their relationship as children with mothers living outside the home; but regardless of who is the custodial parent, children seem to apply a sliding scale in assessing relations with the outside parents, a scale that is far more generous than objective standards might permit.

4. Residential parents disproportionately assume the responsibility of child care. Accordingly, they commonly complain about low level of involvement of outside parents in childrearing tasks. They credit them with little decision-making authority and indicate that direct discussions about the child rarely if ever take place. Over half report that they rarely or never discuss childrearing matters with the outside parents, even when they are in fairly regular contact with the children; the absence of communication dampens the possibility of conflict between the parents. "Parallel parenting" might be a better way of characterizing the pattern of childrearing between formerly married couples, compared with "coparenting," a term that is widely used but rarely practiced.

5. Our data do not seem to support the speculations of a number of researchers and clinicians that stepfamily life is frequently afflicted with problems created by the presence of a multitude of parents. Typically, as we have seen, no more than two parents, if that many, are actively involved after a marriage breaks up. When the residential parent remarries and the outside parent remains on the scene, we find little evidence from either parent or child of difficulties that can be directly traced to the participation of multiple parents. At least in stepfamilies consisting of the children's mothers and stepfathers, which are the majority of cases, active participation by the outside parents does not generally elevate level of tension in the family or complicate the relationship of children and stepfathers.

In the rarer cases of families with stepmothers, there was some evidence that regular contact with the outside mothers created tensions in the families and complicated the children's relations with their stepmothers. Children seem to find it more difficult to replace mothers than fathers, though the circumstances in families with stepmothers are so different and the number of cases so small that this interpretation must be considered only conjecture.

In general, the ability of children to deal with complexity was impressive. Children seemed to be doing as well if not better in expanded family situations than in arrangements that involve the loss or replacement of a parent. Partly, this may reflect the fact that outside parents who are committed to maintaining a relationship are a special breed and their children recognize it. They also may have experienced a less traumatic divorce, a fact that contributes to the well-being of their children and the relatively low level of conflict with their former spouse.

Finally, we must reiterate that the data presented in this paper do not address the critical question of how divorce and remarriage affect the adjustment of children and their level of functioning with peers, in school, or in the larger society. This is the subject of a separate analysis (Furstenberg and Allison, 1984). All that we have shown here is that the ability of children to manage the trauma of separation and divorce seems to be reasonably high when we consider their relations with their biological parents. Those who encounter family disruption usually retain reasonably close ties to their resident parents and continue to make what they can of their relations with their nonresident parents. In most instances, they are obviously making do with very little.

Stepping back from the data, what do these particular findings tell us about how the growing pattern of conjugal succession is likely to affect the socialization process and the operation of the American kinship system? It is clear that at the present time coparenting among formerly married couples is more of a myth than a reality in all but a tiny fraction of families. Even among the highly educated, the extent to which parental responsibilities are shared after separation or divorce is minimal. As a rule divorce implies not only the dissolution of marital bonds but a partial if not total withdrawal from parenting as well. When noncustodial parents move out, parenting—if it continues at all—usually is reduced to a ritual relationship. Parents outside the home retain certain symbolic rights, but they relinquish most of their actual responsibilities. Thus, while they continue to be their children's "real parents" and are generally accorded a place in the immediate family even when they have little contact with their offspring, they typically give up decision-making authority and exercise little direct influence over their children's upbringing.

How and why outside parents withdraw from their children is a question of vital importance to understanding the impact of divorce on parenting. Clearly, part of the explanation stems from an unwillingness to provide child support, part from the difficulty of maintaining relations with the former spouse who retains custody of the child. The withdrawal from parenting also may be traced to the pattern of conjugal succession itself. Over time, many fathers assume caretaking responsibilities in second families (Furstenberg and Spanier, 1984). One way of portraying our system, then, is to visualize it as a form of child swapping. Parents, fathers in particular, exchange one set of children for another as they move from one household to the next. They are at least as conscientious in the role of resident surrogate parent as they are in their role as nonresident biological parent. On the basis of behavior alone, it might seem that sociological parenthood is more salient than biological parenthood.

There are several grounds for objecting to this conclusion. In the first place, it does not accurately describe all cases. Some outside parents maintain a high degree of involvement in childrearing. Second, our system is currently in a state of flux as custody practices are being reconsidered in response to the changing roles of fathers and the growing involvement of women in the marketplace. Admittedly, the picture we have provided is a static one that does not take account of changes that may be under way. Current practices as described in this paper are not inevitable, and they may indeed be changing. Finally, it is important to recognize that the perspective presented here not only is historically cross-sectional but also focuses on the family at a single point in its development. Noncustodial parents sometimes become more involved in late adolescence or early adulthood, when the child is emancipated from the household.

These objections notwithstanding, our data suggest that the significance of biological parenthood may be waning in response to the emerging pattern of conjugal succession. Biological ties to the child seem to count for less, sociological ties for more. This observation is consistent with another more general trend that may be taking place in family relations. Like marriage, childbearing and childrearing are processes that have become dictated less by constraint and obligation and determined more by voluntary participation. Increasingly it seems that parenthood is no less impermanent than marriage.

References

Ahrons, C. R. 1980. "Joint custody arrangements in the postdivorce family." Journal of Divorce 3 (Spring):189–205.

Bohannon, P. (Ed.). 1970. Divorce and After: An Analysis of the Emotional and Social Problems of Divorce. Garden City, NY: Anchor Books (Doubleday).

Cherlin, A. J. 1978. "Remarriage as an incomplete institution." American Journal of Sociology 84:634–650.

Duberman, L. 1975. The Reconstituted Family: A Study of Remarried Couples and Their Children. Chicago:Nelson-Hall.

Furstenberg, F. F., Jr. 1979. "Recycling the family: perspectives for researching a neglected family form." Marriage and Family Review 2(3):1,12–22.

_____1982a. "Conjugal succession: reentering marriage after divorce." Pp. 107–146 in P. B. Baltes and O. G. Brim (Eds.), Life-Span Development and Behavior (Vol. 4). New York: Academic Press.

_____1982b. "Child care after divorce and remarriage." Paper presented at the MacArthur Foundation Conference on Child Care: Growth Fostering Environments, Chicago.

Furstenberg, F. F., Jr., and Allison, P. D. 1984. "How marital disruption affects children: variations by age and sex." Unpublished manuscript, Department of Sociology, University of Pennsylvania, Philadelphia.

Furstenberg, F. F., Jr., Nord, C. W., Peterson, J. L., and Zill, N. 1983. "The life course of children of divorce: marital disruption and parental contact." American Sociological Review 8(5):656–668.

Furstenberg, F. F., Jr., and Seltzer, J. A. 1983. "Divorce and child development." Paper presented at Orthopsychiatric Association, Boston.

Furstenberg, F. F., Jr., and Spanier, G. B. 1984. Recycling the Family: Remarriage after Divorce. Beverly Hills, CA: Sage Publications.

Furstenberg, F. F., Jr., and Talvitie, K. 1979. "Children's names and paternal claims: bonds between unmarried fathers and their children." Journal of Family Issues 1(1):31–57.

Glick, P. C. 1979, "Children of divorced parents in demographic perspective." Journal of Social Issues 35(4):170–182.

_____1984. "Marriage, divorce, and living arrangements: prospective changes." Journal of Family Issues 5(1):7–26.

Goetting, A. 1979. "The normative integration of the former spouse relationship." Journal of Divorce 2:395–414.

Goldsmith, J. 1980. "Relationships between former spouses: descriptive findings." Journal of Divorce 4:1–20.

Keshet, J. K. 1980. "From separation to stepfamily: a subsystem analysis." Journal of Family Issues 1(4):517–532.

Spanier, G. B., and Thompson, L. 1984. Parting: The Aftermath of Separation and Divorce. Beverly Hills, CA: Sage Publications.

Walker, K. N., Rogers, J., and Messinger, L. 1977. "Remarriage after divorce: a review." Social Casework 58:276–285.

Weiss, R. S. 1975. Marital Separation. New York: Basic Books.

Zill, N. In press. Happy, Healthy, and Insecure: A Portrait of Middle Childhood in America. Garden City, NY: Doubleday.